Mural in Cayuga

Mural in Newport at VFW

Mural in Dana across from Ernie Pyle State Memorial

Mural in Cayuga at Railroadman's Bar

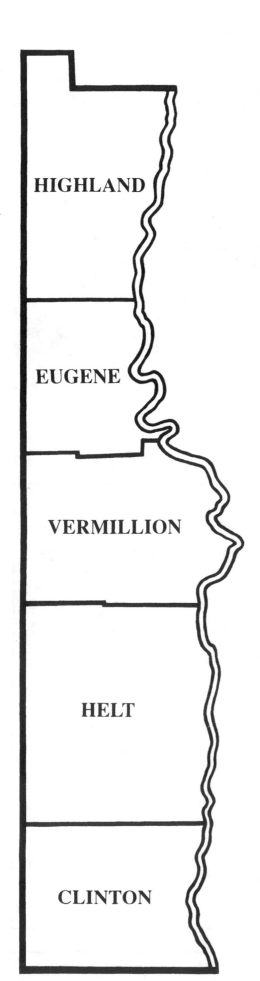

HIGHLAND

EUGENE

VERMILLION

HELT

CLINTON

VERMILLION
COUNTY
INDIANA

History &Families

Vermillion County Court House in Newport

Turner Publishing Company
Publishers of America's History

Author: Vermillion County
Historical Society

Copyright ©1990 by Vermillion
County Indiana Historical Society

This book or any part thereof may not be
reproduced without the written consent of
the Author and Publisher

The materials were compiled and produced using
available information; Turner Publishing Company
regrets they cannot assume liability for errors
or omissions.

Created by: Mark A. Thompson,
Independent Publishing Consultant
for Turner Publishing Company

Book Design: Elizabeth Dennis

Library of Congress Catalog
Card No.: 88-51841

ISBN: 978-1-68162-532-4

Limited Edition of 600 copies of which
this book is number _____.

TABLE OF CONTENTS

Martha Helt first president of Vermillion County Historical Society

FOREWORD

In bringing to you, the citizens of Vermillion County, some of the past events over the past one-hundred years, we wish to dedicate this book in its entirety to all who have made this endeavor possible.

Your response has been wonderful and the contributions in Customs, Traditions and Religions are now recorded in print to be read and enjoyed through the years to come!

The Vermillion County Historical Society was organized in 1958, with the purpose-"to seek to collect and preserve articles and facts of historical interest and facts connected with the development of our county, and the State and the Territory of Indiana."

VERMILLION COUNTY HISTORICAL
SOCIETY 1988 OFFICERS

Patti (Patricia) Crum, President
Bill (William) Walthall, Vice-President
Bill Pearman-Secretary
Evelyn Hixon-Treasurer

Board of Directors:

Clinton Twp.-Dot Lindsey
Leo Reposh, Jr.

Helt Twp.-Lucille Jones
Martha Helt
Vermillion Twp.Donna Hollingsworth
Jim Johnson

Eugene Twp.-Anna Beth Lallish
Bill Heidbreder

Highland Twp.-Norman Skinner
Rodney Prather

History Book Representatives:

Clinton Twp.-Jim Graham
Helt Twp.-Helena Bishop
Highland Twp.-Donna Prather
Clinton Twp.-Leo Reposh, Jr.
Mrs. Kenneth Foltz
Vermillion Twp.-Jim Johnson
Eugene Twp.-Anna Beth Lallish

PROOF READERS
Pauline Guyer
Rachel Milligan
Margaret Umland

Vermillion County Historical Society

Founded in 1958

CHARTER MEMBERS

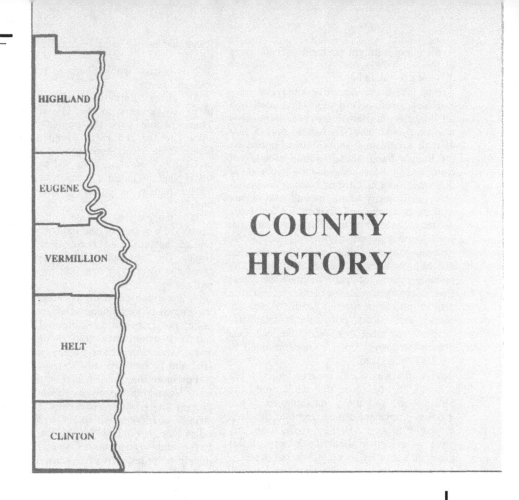

COUNTY HISTORY

HIGHLAND

EUGENE

VERMILLION

HELT

CLINTON

William Volkel and
his Franklin Car

Rays of sunlight peak through the trees as the sun slowly rises over this small area of west central Indiana.

But, before this land was known as Indiana, and even before the white man had settled here, this fertile area was home to a race of people who left behind only a hint of their civilization and culture. Formed by the human hand, these strange mounds of earth, one 300 feet long and 86 feet wide at the base, remain clustered along the landscape. A majority of the mounds are twenty to forty feet long and four to six feet high. As many as eighty or as few as ten have been found grouped together.

When the white man moved into the area and brought with him a world of roads and buildings, some of these mounds were leveled. Clues about the life of this ancient race were found beneath the earth. Skeletons, copper beads, axes, pots, crocks, stone implements and other items were removed. One excavation turned up a coin determined to be 2,000 years old.

The area was once home to Indian tribes such as the Miamis, the Kickapoos, the Mosquitans, and the Pottawatomies. When the first permanent settlers came to this land in the 19th century they found one tiny piece of evidence about the history of this place in a scar in an old white oak tree.

When the tree was cut down in the early 19th century. the rings of growth showed a scar made by the axe of a white man no later than 1720. During these years, it is believed that French missionaries traveled through the area and converted a number of the Indians to Christianity.

Stories about the French involvement here have been documented and stories passed down from generation to generation. Perhaps the most interesting of all these stories occurred near the city of Clinton.

A creek in this area that empties into the Wabash was once the site of trading activity between the French and the Indians. Two brothers, Michael and Pierre Brouillet, took part in the trading and became allies to the Indians. During the early 1800s, Michael's occupation was not only that of a trader, but also as a "traitor" of sorts. He became a spy for Indiana Governor William Henry Harrison and reported frequently on Indian activities. As careful as he was, the Indians learned of his secret activities and captured him.

Before he was to be burned at the stake, an Indian squaw whose son had been killed in battle, asked that he be spared. She wanted to adopt him. Usually a request such as this was granted. This time it was denied.

Perhaps out of anger, or maybe disappointment, the squaw secretly freed Brouillet and helped him to escape in a canoe along the creek and out of reach of the Indian's arrows.

Today, the creek that once carried Brouillet to safety still bears his name.

The land, with its rich history of varied cultures and races, is now bounded on the east by the waters of the historic Wabash

River and on the west by the Illinois State line.

This narrow strip of land is called Vermillion County.

The name "Vermillion" has its own history, dating back to the Miami Indians. These people gave the name "pe-auk-e-shaw" to the red earth found along the banks of the rivers known today as the Big and Little Vermillion. This red earth, in its native state, is called cinnabar and was used by the Indians as a paint to decorate their bodies.

It is thought that this red earth was accidentally discovered by the Indians when they burned the brush and weeds along the river banks. The fires burned the shale that surfaced the outcrop of coal and produced the red color.

A literal translation of "pe-auk-e-shaw" by the French is Vermillion, which means a red color, not as bright as scarlet.1 This word, but spelled with two "l's," hung on until 1824, when Vermillion County was organized and become Indian's 51st county.

For more than a year after it was organized, Vermillion County extended up to the present city of Chicago. Today, the "shoe-string" county, seven miles wide and 37 miles long, is bordered by Warren, Fountain, Parke and Vigo counties and is approximately 65 miles west of Indianapolis.

Fertile soil, surrounded by numerous springs, originally covered one-fourth of the land between the county's boundaries. Timber land occupied the rest.

A fine grade of clay was abundant in the county and provided a profitable business from as early as 1840 until 1890. Many other businesses flourished at one time or another over the years.

Today, Vermillion County's major businesses and industries include Eli Lilly and Co., Public Service Indiana, Peabody Coal Company, Inland Container Corporation and the Newport Army Ammunition Plant.

Despite the success of this and other industries during the 18th and 19th centuries, Vermillion County remains primarily an agricultural community.

A government report issued in 1910 showed 45,000 acres dedicated to growing corn, producing 1,739,000 bushels. Sixty-eight years later in 1978, with the aide of advanced farming technologies, 42,701 acres of corn produced 4,853,004 bushels by more than 270 farms.

Major money-making products in 1910 included oats, wheat, rye, clover seed, hay and forage, timothy, cattle, horses, mules, swine, sheep, poultry and bees.

Today's principle county crops include corn and soybeans.

The farms and businesses that support Vermillion County call home such towns as Clinton, Newport, Perrysville, Cayuga and Eugene.

The Parke and Vermillion Counties History written in 1913 lists the original "village plats." The following condensed version notes the name of each village and the year it was platted.

Cayuga, (formerly Eugene Junction) September 1827
Springfield, October 1828
Clinton, January 1829
Perrysville, May 1832
Highland, September 1835
Solon, April 1836
Sheperdstown, August 1836
Newport, March 1837
Transylvania, May 1837
Jones, February 1862
Alta, May 1871
Summit Grove, November 1871
Gessie, March 1872
Hillsdale, November 1872
Dana, August 1874
Geneva, December 1900
Fairview Park, August 1902
Rhodes, December 1903
Rileysburg, June 1904
Needmore, September 1904
St. Bernice, August 1905
Centenary, October 1910
Chum's Ford, December 1910
Universal, March 1911
West Clinton Junction, May 1911
Rangeville, September 1911

By 1988, several of the original village plots had disappeared from maps and Bono, Sandytown, Easytown, Jonestown, Randall, Quaker, Blanford, Eugene, had been added.

In addition to television, radio, letters and word-of-mouth, local information comes in the form of The Daily Clintonian newspaper and the Herald News (weekly). The latter is published in Cayuga and is a (recent) consolidation of the former Highland Herald, Dana News and the Cayuga Herald newspapers.

The first edition of the Clinton Exponent began in 1873. The paper changed hands and the presses were moved to Perrysville in 1877 as the Perrysville Exponent. Soon the paper was returned to Clinton where it became the Western Indianian.

The first paper in the county was the Newsletter which started in 1837. The Banner, Vermillion Register and the Perrysville Republican were names under The Newsletter.

Numerous other papers have rolled off the presses, been sold, consolidated or called by a different name since the late 1800s, including the Tomahawk and the Scalping Knife (the name was quickly changed to the Democrat), The Clinton Times, the Dana News, the Vermillion Democrat, the Record, the Vermillion County News, the Olive Branch, The Hoosier State, the Vermillion Transcript, the Cayuga Journal, the Cayuga Herald, the Cayuga Times, the Tribune and the Blue Pencil.

Most likely, headlines in 1843 carried the news of Indiana's newly elected governor James Whitcomb, a Vermillion County resident.

This Windsor, Vermont native purchased a house and surrounding farm land in Clinton.

As the first democratic governor of Indiana, Whitcomb played an important part in getting Indiana out of debt, establishing

GOVERNOR/SENATOR JAMES WHITCOMB

James Whitcomb, eighth Governor of Indiana, was born December 1, 1795, near Windsor, Vermont. He spent his early life on a farm near Cincinnati, Ohio. His family was poor and although he attended some school, he did a lot of reading and studying on his own prior to entering Transylvania University at Lexington, Kentucky. He helped pay his way through college by teaching during vacations. After earning his degree, he studied law and was admitted to the bar in Fayette County, Kentucky in 1822.

In 1824 he settled in Bloomington, Indiana where he served successfully as prosecutor from 1826 to 1829. In 1830 he was elected State Senator representing Greene, Monroe, and Owen Counties, and was re-elected to a second term. He also served on the judiciary committee where he vehemently opposed excessive state spending.

In 1836 when his second senate term was over he was appointed Commissioner of the Federal Land Office in Washington, D.C. As commissioner, he had the important job of administering the land grant system. In 1841 he came back to Indiana and set up a law office in Terre Haute.

He received the Democratic nomination for Governor of Indiana in 1843 and was elected by 2,013 votes over incumbent Governor Samuel Bigger. Three years later he was re-elected by 3,958 votes over Joseph C. Marshall, a Whig. Whitcomb was Indiana's first Democratic governor.

When Whitcomb took office the state was heavily in debt. By selling the Wabash and Erie Canal he restored Indiana's credit and was able to issue state bonds for a low rate of interest. During his governorship the Mexican War broke out and Whitcomb organized and mustered five regiments of infantry.

No public man in the state had more to do with the establishment of our public schools and creation of the school fund than did Whitcomb.

In 1849 James Whitcomb was elected United States Senator and resigned the governorship to serve in Washington. He died during his senate term on October 4, 1852, in New York and is buried in Indianapolis.

On March 24, 1846, he had married Mrs. Martha Ann (Renick) Hurst in Pickaway, Ohio. On July 1, 1847, their daughter, Martha, was born and a short while later, on July 17, 1847, Mrs. Whitcomb died.

James Whitcomb purchased the Hazel Bluff house and farm in rural Clinton, Vermillion County, from George Wright. The house was originally built by Dr. William Kile who once served as a state representative.

James Whitcomb had numerous relatives living in and holding prominent positions in Vermillion County. His daughter grew up to be the wife of Governor Claude Matthews who lived many years in the house on the Hazel Bluff Farm.

public schools and organizing five regiments of infantry to serve in the Mexican War.

Whitcomb resigned as Indiana's governor in 1849 to become a United States Senator and died in 1852 during his stint in the Senate.

And, 50 years later the election of Indiana's 22nd governor, Claude Matthews, also most likely made headline news.

Although born in Kentucky, Matthews and his wife Martha moved to Vermillion County in 1868. Martha Whitcomb Matthews was the daughter of former Indiana Governor James Whitcomb.

Matthews' 2,000-acre farm included crops, and a stock breeding operation that produced trotting horses, Jersey and Shorthorn Cattle, South Down Sheep, Berkshire Hogs and Shetland Ponies. Matthews was also involved in forming the Indiana and American Shorthorn Breeders Association.

He served as a State Representative in the 1877 General Assembly. In 1880, Matthews became a candidate for Indiana Lieutenant Governor in the Democratic State Convention but lost to Isaac Gray. Matthews lost another political battle in 1882 when the Republican candidate won as State Senator for Parke and Vermillion Counties.

But, his luck changed in 1890 when Matthews was elected Indiana Secretary of State. At the close of this term, he was elected Governor and served from 1893 until 1897.

Besides boasting a fine political history, Vermillion County can also boast a rich military history. A few soldiers from the county fought in the war with Mexico from 1846 to 1848, but the county had no formal organization for recruiting men. The same occurred during the Spanish-American war in 1898—a few Vermillion County men fought, but not through a county-established organization.

The county's most significant involvement was in the Civil War. Vermillion County men were involved in the following companies regiments: the Fourteenth Infantry, the Sixteenth Infantry, the Eighteenth Infantry, the Thirty-first Infantry, the Forty-third Infantry, the Seventy-first infantry (later the Sixth Calvary), the Eight-fifth Infantry and the One Hundred and Twenty-ninth Infantry.

Within its slim boundaries, Vermillion County holds a rich history—its Indian heritage to modern-day pride of place.

This pride was tested in the summer heat of 1988. Temperatures rose throughout the summer, with almost no rain to quench the land's thirst and produce a successful crop.

So extensive was the drought that residents in Vermillion County and throughout the state were asked to conserve water. Even lawn sprinkling was banned until the drought eased. In the capital city, Governor Robert Orr declared Indiana a fire hazard due to the dry conditions.

Although firework displays were cinched, the spirit of the holiday was patriotically carried out. During July, a light rainfall raised the hopes of some county farmers, but county extension agent Merrill Jacks likened

GOVERNOR CLAUDE MATTHEWS

Governor Claude Matthews Marker.

Claude Matthews is described by the 1888 History of Vermillion County as one of the leading agriculturists of Vermillion County. But, his fame reached farther than the county lines. In 1893 he became Indiana's 22nd governor.

Matthews was born in Bethal, Bath County, Kentucky, on December 14, 1845, the only child of Thomas A. and Eliza Fletcher Matthews. His mother's family had come from Virginia and his father's from Maryland. His mother died at home in March 1846 at age twenty. He attended school at Bethal and became interested in farming and stock raising.

When Confederate John Morgan raided Kentucky, Claude's father sent him to Ohio with 500 mules to avoid having them stolen. It was there he met Martha, James Whitcomb's daughter. Later Claude attended Centre College in Danville, Kentucky, and Martha attended a girls school there. He graduated in 1867 and in 1868 he and Martha were married and settled on the Hazel Bluff Farm in rural Clinton, Vermillion County, Indiana.

The Hazel Bluff Farm was then comprised of 600 acres. Matthews added 1400 acres for a total of 2,000, of which 1300 were under cultivation. This added land became more than a farm. Matthews cultivated a high classed stock breeding operation that produced trotting horses, Jersey and Shorthorn Cattle, South Down Sheep, Berkshire Hogs, and Shetland Ponies. He played a prominent roll in forming the Indiana and American Shorthorn Breeders Association.

Democrat Claude Matthews was nominated and elected to represent Vermillion County as the State Representative serving in the 1877 General Assembly. He played a major roll in passing the Free Gravel Road Bill which benefited the county greatly.

In 1880 he was a candidate for Indiana Lieutenant Governor in the Democratic State Convention. However, the conclusion of a close contest for the gubernatorial nomination the winner, Franklin Landers, recommended that his nearest competitor, Isaac Gray, be nominated for lieutenant governor. Isaac Gray had been elected lieutenant governor in the previous election, and had become acting Governor when the incumbent died. In the 1880 General Election, Landers lost, and Gray was elected lieutenant governor. Again the governor died and Gray succeeded to the governorship.

In 1882 Matthews was a candidate for state senator to represent Parke and Vermillion Counties, but he lost to the Republican. The 1888 Vermillion County History book says he quietly returned to farming. However, in 1890 he was back, and was nominated and elected Indiana Secretary of State and served from 1891 - 1893. In 1892 at the conclusion of his term he was elected Governor of Indiana.

Claude Matthews was elected Governor of Indiana by the largest plurality in Indiana History. As governor, from 1893 to 1894, he found it necessary to send the National Guard to re-establish peace during a coal mine strike and again during a railroad strike. He had to face bitter opposition when he suppressed an organization promoting racing and prize fighting.

After the completion of his term as governor Matthews returned to Clinton, but preferred to live on 4th Street rather than return to the farm. He suffered a stroke in Veedersburg while addressing an old settler's meeting and died three days later, August 28, 1898.

Claude and Martha Whitcomb Matthews had a son, Renick Seymour (called Seymour) born Jan. 4, 1872, died Nov. 14, 1895, and three daughters, Mary Fletcher born Nov. 5, 1869 died —, Margaret born May 15, 1875, died Aug. 12, 1876, and Helen born Feb. 21, 1878, died June 20, 1953. Helen was married to a Mr. Somerville and had a daughter, Martha Webster born Apr. 22, 1901, died Sept. 7, 1983. Martha's son, Charles Webster, is a career military man. Helen was later married to a Mr. Krekler and had a daughter, Mary Stinz, and a son, Albert Krekler who taught at Clinton High.

the half inch total to "spitting on a hot griddle."

When it was over, there was hardly a farmer in Vermillion County or the state that didn't suffer from what Purdue University agronomists predicted would be the worse corn and soybean drought loss ever recorded.

These farmers, and the statesmen and business who helped shape the development of this varied community will continue to make their mark into the 21st century, leaving behind their own traces of the past for future generations to study.

[1]*The Merriam-Webster Dictionary.* New York: Simon & Schuster, Inc., 1974.

COUNTY POST OFFICES

Receiving letters and packages from loved ones and friends back east in a reasonable amount of time was a necessity to Indiana's newest pioneers.

Almost four years before Vermillion County's borders were officially set, a post office was established at Newport just before the Christmas of 1820. The post office opened and closed regularly for the next seven years under postmasters Solomn Thomas, John Collett and James T. Pendleton.

Then, for some undocumented reason, the office was discontinued May 10, 1827 but, was re-established just six days later on May 16, 1827.

Soon after the establishment of the post office at Newport, other offices sprung up across the area. In 1823, doors opened to the Clinton post office. 1826 and 1827 saw the establishment of offices at Eugene and Perrysville, respectively.

More than 45 years after the first post began its operation, Vermillion County boasted its first female postmaster, Sarah Grimes. She was appointed in 1866 at the town of Jones (later known as St. Bernice). Other early postmistresses included Flora Sanders in Newport, Mary H. Hall and Jervine Banks in Gessie, Margaret McCarty in Hillsdale, Ella Dickson and Ellen Hunsicker in Perrysville, Marietta Blythe in Clinton, Susan Haworth in Quaker Hill and Lucy Kinderman in Eugene.

Today's Vermillion County post offices include Blanford, 47831; Cayuga, 47928; Clinton, 47842; Dana, 47847; Hillsdale, 47854; Newport, 47966; Perrysville, 47974; St. Bernice, 47875; and Universal, 47884.

1847 marked a special date in the history of the United States postal service — the use of prepaid adhesive postage stamps.

These new stamps, issued on account to postmasters and sold to the public, provided an accurate and automatic check on revenues. In the past, methods used often proved quite inaccurate.

However accurate the new stamps were, they were not always used. It wasn't until January 1, 1856 that the government made the use of pre-paid adhesive stamps the only legal means to send mail through the postage system.

The printing of the adhesive stamps was bid out awarded to private manufacturers from 1847 until 1894 when all stamps were printed by the Bureau of Engraving and Printing, Treasury Department.

From 1885 until 1917 the nationwide postage rate was set at two cents. It was raised to three cents from 1917 until 1919 when it was lowered again to two cents. This marked the only postage reduction in the nation's history.

For thirteen years, Americans paid two cents to mail a letter. Then in 1932 the rate changed to three cents. This one cent increase remained unchanged for 26 years until 1958, when it went up again by one cent.

The following years saw these increases: 1963, five cents; 1968, six cents; 1971, eight cents; 1974, 10 cents; 1975, 13 cents; and in 1978, an eagle stamp was issued worth 15 cents. By 1979 an 18 cent stamp was required to mail a letter, in 1980, 20 cents were required, 1986, 22 cents and in 1988 the first 25 cent stamp went into circulation.

HENRY DANA WASHBURN

Henry Dana Washburn was born in 1832 in Vermont and came to Vermillion County in the early 1850s. He taught school in Helt Township and Newport schools and during that time he studied law with Thomas C.W. Sale in Newport.

In 1853, he was admitted to the bar and entered partnership with M.P. Lowry. By 1854, he was elected Vermillion County Auditor and served one term. His career and interests turned next to the military.

Washburn entered the U.S. Army as captain of Company C. Eighteenth Indiana Infantry and was promoted to lieutenant colonel and colonel and breveted to brigadier general and major general. His first four years were spent in Missouri and Arkansas where he fought at Black Water and Pea Ridge. He was then transferred to Grant's Army and fought at Grand Gulf, Port Gibson, Champion's Hill, Black River Bridge, and the siege of Vicksburg in July 4, 1863. Grant's Army was later active in Louisiana and Texas and then joined Sheridan's Army at Shenendoah and participated in the Battles of Opequon, of Early, and of Cedar Creek. After these expeditions, they worked on fortifications of Savannah and were the first to raise the Stars and Stripes at Augusta, Georgia.

In 1864, Washburn was elected to the United States Congress from the old 6th District defeating well-known and well-liked Daniel Voorhees of Terre Haute. After his first term, he was re-elected, defeating Mr. Claypool. Washburn served in Congress from March, 1865, to March, 1896. It was during this time that he opposed the impeachment of President Andrew Johnson. Because the *Hoosier State Newspaper* of Newport called for the impeachment, Washburn bought the paper and sold it to a supporter of his own views, Samuel B. Davis, the county treasurer.

President U.S. Grant appointed Henry Washburn in 1869 to be Surveyor General of the Territory of Montana. He also made the first explorations of Yellowstone National Park in 1870. Today, Mt. Washburn in Yellowstone, still bears his name. It was during these expeditions that he suffered a severe illness. He returned to Clinton and died there in 1871.

Henry Dana Washburn is one of the most heroic leaders in Vermillion County's recorded history. Henry Washburn was a teacher, a lawyer, a general, a Republican, a congressman, and finally an explorer. *Article submitted by Leo Reposh, Jr. A librarian assisting Mr. Reposh discovered on March 19, 1989, that Washburn's pictures had been stolen from the archives of the Indiana State Library in Indianapolis. The picture accompanying this article was taken from a 1921 Indianapolis News article.*

Henry D. Washburn Monument

North Vermillion Jr.-Sr. High School

North Vermillion Community School Corp.

South Vermillion High School

South Vermillion Middle School

HIGHLAND TOWNSHIP

Highland is the extreme northern sub-division of Vermillion county. Its northern boundary is the line between Vermillion and Warren county. To the east is the Wabash river, marking the line between Vermillion and Parke counties. This, like the other four townships of this county, extends from the eastern to the western side of Vermillion county. It contains sixty square miles. In 1880 this township had a population of 2,433, and an assessed valuation of personal property amounting to $1,400,000. The United States census for 1910 gives the township a population of 1,845. In 1911 the county records show that there was an assessed valuation of $2,465,000 in this township.

Perrysville, Rileysburg and Gessie are small towns and villages within this civil township. The "Big Four" railroad passes through the northwestern corner of Highland township.

The date of arrival of the pioneers to this part of Vermillion county is indicated by the years at the head of the following paragraphs:

1822–G.S. Hansicker, born in Virginia in 1792, died here about 1885. His son, H.C. Hansicker, was born in this county in 1832. George Hicks, a soldier of the Revolutionary war, was (some say) a pioneer in this township, but possibly this is an error; he may have served in the war of 1812, for there is an account of George W. Hicks, a native Massachusettsborn 1795, and who died here in 1878. Another settler of about 1822 was Jacob Hain, of Pennsylvania, born in 1799, and died in this county.

1823–David Goff, born in Connecticut in 1799, remained a resident here until his death, September 7, 1881. His brother Almond died here about 1867, and another brother, Brainard, moved to Laporte, Indiana, where he died. His son Philander, born in 1834 in this township, was still a resident here in the eighties. Another settler that year was Lemon Chenowith, who for many years resided at Perrysville, this township.

1824–John Chenowith settled on the Wabash, died in 1857. He was the father of Lemon, just mentioned, and also of Hiram, an older son. Thomas Chenowith was a member of the constitutional convention in 1850, and Isaac Chenowith was state senator in 1844-45. Isaac was born in Kentucky in 1794, arrived here in March, 1825, and died in April, 1856. William Chenowith, born in Ohio in 1823, was brought here in 1832 and always resided in this county. Solomon M. Jones, born in Tennessee in April, 1812, died March 15, 1887, leaving a family of ten children. He was a soldier in the Black Hawk war. John N. Jones, Sr., was born in September, 1809, came here at a very early date, was a partner of J.F. Smith in milling and merchandising business for many years, and died here in June, 1874. William Skinner, from Ohio, came in 1824, and died a few years later. His son Norman was born in Ohio in 1816, and died here about 1880. Thomas Wright, who it is said brought the first hogs into Vermillion county, was a settler that year, also. One of his oxen dying, he cultivated his first crop of corn with a single ox. Milton Wright was born here in 1832. Both he and his brother Stephen were the sons of Thomas Wright.

1825–John Fultz, above Perrysville, settled here and died many years later. His sons were John, Andrew and William V., all long since deceased. Also Allen Rodgers, from New Hampshire, died in Iowa or Wisconsin many years ago. J.M. Rodgers, his son, born in New Hampshire in 1815, died here in the spring of 1887.

1826–James Blair, who had first settled in Eugene township, died at Perrysville, May 11, 1861, aged seventy-nine years. Robert D. Moffatt, born in New Jersey in 1812, for many years a merchant at Perrysville, at which place he retired in 1874. David Beauchamp, in range 10, had a large family and died about 1873. John W. Beauchamp was born in Ohio in 1821; Andrew, his brother, born in 1828 in this county, removed to Illinois. Hiram Shaw, born in Ohio in 1805; E.G. Shaw, born in this county in 1830, was still living in 1887.

1827–Benjamin Whittenmyer, born in Pennsylvania in 1799, died in 1879. The parents of Harvey Hunt, who was born in Indiana in 1820, was an old pioneer and a most excellent citizen. William Fleshman also was a settler of 1827. His son Amos, still living in 1888, was born in Indiana in 1822.

1828–Jonas Metzger, a soldier of the war of 1812, from Ohio, died here February 9, 1872, aged seventy-eight years. He first located in Eugene township, and in Highland in 1833. Constantine Hughes, from Virginia. His son Ehud, born in Virginia in 1817, was still living here in 1888. Israel, William and John Hughes were pioneers of Coal Branch country.

1829–William Nichols, born in Virginia in 1809, was still residing here in 1887. Moses, Charles and Daniel Bowman, from Virginia.

Daniel remained here until his death and Charles died in the West. J.S. Stutler, born in Ohio, settled here and died in this township. Ezekiel Sanders, born in Virginia in 1827, died July 10, 1875. He first settled in Eugene township, and later moved to Highland.

1830–Richard Shute, father of Daniel, John and Ephraim, settled this year in Highland township. Elisha N. Reynolds, born in Maryland in 1804, died in this township in the eighties. G.H. Reynolds, born in 1835, was an old and honored resident of this township in 1887. John Tate, born in Ohio in 1807, survived until the nineties. Thomas J. Mitchell, born in Ohio in 1808, resided many years at Perrysville. James A. Prather, born in Kentucky in 1814, died here in 1886. Another settler of 1830 was Joseph Briner, of Perrysville.

1831–Herbert Ferguson, born in Virginia in September, 1799, died here January 26, 1877. Ephraim Betzer, from Ohio, came in previous to 1831. Jacob Betzer was born in 1805 in Ohio, died about 1883. Aaron Betzer moved to the far West.

1832–Captain Andrew Dennis, a boatman, born in New Jersey in 1801, died in Danville, Illinois, in the early eighties. John Hoobler, a United Brethren minister, born in Pennsylvania in 1801, died in Illinois. William Trosper, born in Kentucky in 1808, died in this township in December, 1886. Nehemiah Cossey, from Maryland, came first to Parke county and in 1832 to this county; died long ago. His son Peter, born in that state in 1812, is also deceased. Fielding Rabourn, born in Kentucky in 1815, died here in the eighties. William H. Carithers from Ohio, long since died in this township; he was the father of Jonathan, Frank and Henry, all living in the county in 1887. William Callihan, a potter by trade, moved from Ohio, settled here and later removed to Danville. M.B. Carter, who was county recorder in 1887 in this county, was born in 1832.

1833–J.F. Will, William P., Thomas H., G.H. and David Smith, from Virginia, all became settlers this year. Thomas Gouty came 1832 or 1833, died June 10, 1863, aged sixty-one years. His son Elias was born in this township in 1833. Henry Gouty may have settled in the township two or three years later; he died in 1864. David Gouty was the son of Henry and Rebecca Gouty. John S. Kilpatrick, a miller, born in Kentucky in 1812, lived at Gessie for a time, and moved to Danville, where he died. Norman Cade died soon after his arrival in the township. His son David later removed from this county. Jacob Givens, born in Virginia in 1815, died in this township. The same year came James Hansen, father of Smith Hansen.

1834–Jacob Rudy, born in Switzerland in 1818, died here in the early eighties. Martin Rudy, his father, died here several years afterward. Others who came in that year were Peter Switzer; his son Wesley, born in Ohio in 1821, was still an honored resident in 1888.

1835–Thomas Moore, who died in 1843, was the father of Joseph and Washington.

T.H. Harrison, born in Virginia in 1810, was still a resident of this township in the late eighties.

1836–John R. and George H. McNeill, from Maryland, the former born in 1811 and the latter in 1818. Lewis and John Butler, from Ohio, the former born in 1813, and the latter in 1816; Lewis was deceased in 1886, when John was still living in Vermillion township. Elijah Roseberry, who died in 1857, aged fifty-one years. Thomas Cushman, born in New York in 1814, was living at Newport in 1887; he had served as county auditor.

1837–James J. Lewis, born in Maryland in 1805, still residing in this township in the late eighties. He was the father of J.A. Lewis and Joshua Lewis; the latter lived at Cayuga many years. Robert J. Gessie, born in Cumberland county, Pennsylvania, in 1809, was residing here in 1887. Another old citizen was Charles Chezem, born in Indiana in 1827.

1838–Walter B. Moffatt, a native of Indiana, born in 1822, died August 14, 1882. Horatio Talbert, long since deceased, was the father of Henry, born in Pennsylvania in 1816 and died in this township in the middle of the eighties. Samuel Harris, born in Virginia in 1819, moved to another section of the country.

1839–John Dunlap, deceased, born in Ireland in 1809. Others who settled that year were Samuel Swingley and Samuel Watt, from Ohio.

Other pioneers in this township were J.F. Smith, John N. Jones, merchants and millers; Joseph Cheadle, father of Joseph B., who served in Congress from this district, was born May 9, 1789, in one of the Eastern states, and died in this township June 19, 1863; William B. Palmer, who died about 1876.

It was stated in 1887 that there were but three keeping house in Highland township who were in that relation in 1833, when Thomas H. Smith settled, he being the man who made this statement. These three were Mrs. Chestie Hain, Adaline V. Jones and Mrs. Glover.

Taken from Parke-Vermillion Counties History, 1913.

PERRYSVILLE

Perrysville was laid out in 1826, by James Blair, on a pleasing situation on the banks of the gently winding Wabash, and named by him in honor of the commander of the Lake Erie fleet in 1812, Commodore O.H. Perry. For many years this was the largest town within the limits of Vermillion county. For a time it was ahead of Danville, Illinois–really until the present railroad system was projected. Since then it has lacked thrift, enterprise and growth. It was said thirty years ago that "the passing days are like one eternal Sabbath. Grass and weeds have overgrown the streets and the lovely shade trees continue to do their sweetest duty." There is a station a little to the west of the old town. Among the enterprising men who were engaged in

Perrysville Woolen Mill

Perrysville Depot

business here in the more palmy days of the town's history may be recalled J.F. and T.H. Smith, J.N. Jones and Robert Moffatt. The old warehouses and grist-mill were used to some advantage in 1890. They were built and operated many years by Smith & Jones. Jones also built another grist-mill at the wharf, but it was burnt down many years since. March 31, 1884, occurred the largest conflagration ever experienced in the place. It entirely destroyed the three chief business blocks, two story bricks; these were the property of Smith Brothers. The fire originated in the roof of an adjoining building. By this fire the Masonic hall, with all of its valuable records and paraphernalia, was destroyed.

A few years after the close of the Civil war, the Perrysville Woolen Mills were erected in the western portion of the town by Riggs, Head & Company, who furnished the machinery mainly from Covington, Indiana, in which place they had previously operated a factory. The Perrysville factory was oper-

ated until 1881, but with only partial success. It stood idle a year or more and was then purchased by B.O. Carpenter, who converted it into a mill, having two run of stones for wheat grinding. It was an excellent flouring-mill plant, and had a capacity of about eighty barrels per day.

In an historic account of this town, written in 1886, it is learned: "H.S. Comingmore & Son's Perryville Stove Works, in the southern part of town, is a modern, neat establishment. It is in a brick building, erected in June, 1884. Its two wings are for foundry and finishing rooms. The firm started in business in Perrysville, in 1858, in a small frame building."

At the time above named–about 1887–there was then running the Perrysville Creamery, on the bank of the Wabash. It had a capacity of two thousand pounds of butter per week. E.A. Lacey was secretary and superintendent, while J.F. Compton was president of the company.

Perrysville was incorporated in January, 1881, and its first officers were: First ward, William Collins; second ward, John R. McNeill; third ward, Samuel Shaner. W.M. Benfield was elected clerk; Rezin Metzger, assessor; Lewis A. Morgan, treasurer; Peter S. Moundy, marshal. In the fall of 1884 the question of whether the corporation should be continued or not was up to a vote by the citizens of the place, and resulted by a small majority in favor of letting the municipality go down. It is not now an incorporated place, but a quiet, orderly country village, where many of the older inhabitants live on the past glory of former days!

In 1910 the population of Perrysville was six hundred, and there were the usual number of stores and shops for a town of its location and size.

Taken from Parke-Vermillion Counties History, 1913.

Oliver Hazard Perry never fought any battles here, but the hero of naval skirmishes during the War of 1812 impressed enough people with his courage and tenacity as a sailor to have towns named after him far and wide – including this one in northern Vermillion County on the banks of the Wabash River.

James Blair served under Perry during the war, and years later, as he settled in this new Wabash Valley community, named the town after him. "Lots of towns and babies were named after Perry during that era," said Ray Storms, a local historian and former teacher and editor.

Perrysville looked like a promising settlement in its early days, at one time being larger than Chicago and Danville, Ill. "This place was the town of towns around here," Storms said. "It was larger than Chicago for a couple years, 1825 to 1827."

Chicago caught up, of course, and is the second largest city in the U.S. today. Danville is now 10 times its size. Population here is around 500 people.

"We got a head start on Chicago," Storms said, "so that's really the reason we were bigger. Chicago grew fast."

Storms said Perrysville was once known as the last good port on the Wabash River. The old Wabash and Erie Canal once snaked along the river, passing near Perrysville, which was plotted in 1826.

The historian said during its 1840-1860 heyday, Perrysville had a pottery shop, metal shop, grist mill, woolen mill, saw mill and iron foundry. From the 1820s through the 1830s it was the "only town in Vermillion County that was really a town. Clinton didn't even exist as a town."

The glitter of Perrysville's golden age faded quickly. "What did it in was not getting a railroad through here," he said.

Storms and his wife, Maryellen, are late arrivals to Perrysville, lured by a house that is a historical landmark. "We were passing through the area on highway 63 when we stopped to take a picture of this beautiful Victorian house," Mrs. Storms said. But they did more than take a picture of the house.

Standard Opera House now Ping's Store

Perrysville street scene

They bought it – in 1971 – and have been here ever since.

Living in the Chesterton area of northern Indiana, her husband was taking a summer course at Indiana State University. "So you see we came to Perryville because of this house," said Mrs. Storms.

The Stormses weren't the first ones to wheel into the long driveway of this imposing, 18-room near-mansion just west of Indiana 63. "During the summertime people stop all the time to take pictures," said Mrs. Storms of the home completed in 1876. "We've even had people stop and ask to go through it."

The house was built by Thomas Smith. The story goes that the Smith brothers, local merchants, had a contest to see who could build the grandest house. "They say Thomas Smith won," Mrs. Storms said. A picture of Smith hangs in the dining room.

After buying the house, the Stormses got interested in learning more about its history and began studying old newspaper clippings. "We got so interested in it that we decided to write a book about this community," she said. The book is entitled "Highland Township, Vermillion County, 1824-1924."

As former editor and publisher of the nearby Herald-News of Cayuga, Storms learned quite a bit studying the 19th century newspapers. "The minister wasn't the keeper of the town's morals," Storms said. "It was the editor, because he had the final say."

Today, downtown Perrysville has a post office, a couple restaurants, a small county library, gas station, feed mill, school, United Methodist church and Ping's General Store.

With no industry, Postmaster Charles Jackson said most Perrysville people commute to jobs in Danville, Ill., 14 miles to the west. But the life-long resident remembers past days when the town was booming and taverns were a big attraction.

But business has been dying slowly over the years. Just last month, Cedar Lake Lumber Company, which operated here for years, closed down.

Robert Ping is a member of the third generation to work in his family's general store. It's the only place in town to buy groceries and hardware and it stocks everything from meats to animal traps.

If you look high on the front of the building you'll see a white sign that says "The Standard 1884 J.M. McNeill." The sign marks the town's opera house. Opera houses were popular in many Midwestern towns in the days before television, radio and movies. Local and touring groups would put on plays, musicals and other entertainment in the hall.

"It's not in real great shape, but it's still here," Ping said after he climbed the wide wooden staircase leading to the second floor opera house.

Rain seeping down from the roof has stained the 14-foot-high ceiling that supports its ornate glass and brass chandelier. The large room still contains row upon row of fancy folding seats.

On one side of the room stands an old potbellied stove and a rare square piano. Light streams into the room from narrow 10-foot-high windows.

"We've researched the piano and discovered that it's a square baby grand made by the William B. Bradbury Co. of New York," Ping said. "It's supposedly one of the first square baby grands they made."

Probably as unusual as an old opera house for a small community is a Saab car dealership. But Frank Gibson and his relatives have been selling these $12,000 to $25,000 Swedish imports since the late 1950s.

"Our cars are different from Fords and Chevys and this has allowed us to survive here," said Gibson, whose been told by Saab officials that Perrysville is one of the smallest communities in the nation to have such a dealership for imported cars.

Gibson said his customers come from as far as Michigan and Kentucky to buy cars. He doesn't sell many locally.

Quite a few people have heard the story of how thieves broke into the dealership and stole a car in 1971. But before they left, they spray painted it with hopes of a clean escape. It wasn't long before police caught up with them...in their pink Saab.

Rex Crowder has operated the town's Shell gas station for well over half a century.

"If I can hold out till July 19th I'll have been at this same spot selling gas since 1933," said Crowder, an active 80-year-old. He said when he started pumping gas 53 years ago it was 15 cents a gallon. Today a gallon is $1.24.

"This is a nice, quiet little town," said Crowder, a graduate of the defunct Perrysville High School.

As it's been for generations in small Hoosier communities, basketball continues to provide wintertime amusement in Perrysville. Years ago, Crowder wore the colors of PHS

on the basketball court. These days, talented teens from Perrysville play their basketball at nearby North Vermillion High School.

"Mike Newell and Terry Ferrell have given us a lot of nice entertainment with their basketball," said Crowder, whose grandson, Tom Crowder, played on the same ISU team that featured Larry Bird.

Crowder got most recognition, however, for his unique jumping ability.

"He was able to jump up and put his foot on the backboard," Rex said, showing a faded newspaper clipping of his grandson doing just that.

Highland Elementary is where local kids in kindergarten through sixth grade attend classes.

"Our school is the social center of our town," said principal Michael F. Bosc. "There's been talk of consolidating our school," he said.

"There'd be major disapproval by the townspeople if this ever happened."

An article by Dave Delaney, The Terre-Haute Tribune-Star, February 23, 1986, Tribune-Star Publishing Co., Inc.

Wabash River Bridge at Perrysville-Built 1901-Replaced 1985

Perrysville High School 1917-1960

Perrysville School 1861-1960

BUSINESSES - 1988

Beef House Restaurant
Boling Livestock Dealers
Brannin & Sons Implement Co.
Brannin Grain Co.
Crowder Service Station
Foxworthy Appliance Service
Gessie Machine & Tool Co.
Gessie West Central Co-Op. Assn. Inc.
Gibson Motor Co.
Ima Development Co.
J's Beauty Oasis
Jerry's Snack Bar
Johnson Blacksmith Shop
Karen's Beauty Shop

Langley Trucking
Pat's Beauty Shop
Pawley Lumber Co.
Perrysville Cafe
Ping General Store
R. & R. Truck Stop
Sare & Hicks, Auctioneers
Skinner Farm Museum
Skinner Sawmill
Smith Upholstery
State Line Veterinary Clinic
Superior Coach Sales
Wooster Feed Mill
Young's Trucking Co.

This message was printed on envelopes from William Morgan, General Merchandise, Perrysville, Indiana.

An interesting town of 800 inhabitants situated in Vermillion County in Western Indiana on the Chicago & Eastern Railroad and the Wabash River. It is in one of the richest farming sections of the Central States. A new High School, fine churches and neighboring people make Perrysville a good place to live. Perrysville is the second oldest town in the state. It was a PAST, is having a PRESENT—and with the aid of this Booster it will have a FUTURE."

This may have been about 1919.

DAVID & BARBARA WITTENMYER BRICK HOUSE

Built in 1844 one mile west of Perrysville, Indiana, now at northwest corner of the intersection of State roads 63 and 32. Bricks were made near by. The walls are 12" thick. The house is Federal style, being 63' long and 20' wide and is two story. It has three fireplaces and all of the woodwork is walnut.

The Wittenmyer boys had a band of their own and would go out on the big front veranda of the new brick house and play their instruments so loudly that they could be heard over a mile away in Perrysville.

Besides the brick house, David had a slaughter house, a bark mill, a tanyard and brick kiln. He was well-known as an excellent bootmaker. David and the boys hauled by wagon, boots, shoes, and farm products, such as apples, onions and potatoes to Chicago and exchanged them for sugar, coffee and other supplies.

A family tradition story is told that an aristocratic gentleman had a fine pair of boots made but when he couldn't pay David the $75.00 for them, he offered ten acres of land. The land was known to be swampy and of little value so the offer was rejected. That same tract of land today is the Loop of Chicago.

As David's six sons grew up in the Shoe-string County, they had their fun as well as their chores. Sometimes they would put their father's pigs in a barrel and let them roll down a hill, David always wondering what made his pigs so stiff and slightly crippled for a few days. When they needed some new dog-skin gloves, they would knock any stray dog that came around in the head, later skin it to make the gloves.

As the Wittenmyer family of ten children grew and prospered, David and Barbara took in five orphans to rear. They were Hannah Fisher, Cynthia Pinegar, Martha Morningstar, Isabella Paine (a granddaughter) and Louisa Jane Judd.

In 1979 this brick house was moved three miles west by Norman Skinner, a great, great, grandson, and is now being restored as part of his farm museum.

1826 CUNNINGHAM LOG HOUSE

This two story log house originally stood in the northeast corner of Highland Township on a bluff west of the Wabash River. It was built in 1826 by Thomas Cunningham. Thomas was born in Ross County, Ohio on December 16, 1799. He came to this area in 1820. He lived in a small log house until this two story house was built in 1826. One of four children born to Thomas and Eliza, Cyrus was the only one to attain maturity. Thomas was extensively engaged in taking flat boats loaded with produce down the Wabash, Ohio and Mississippi Rivers to New Orleans until 1840. He died on December 24, 1846 at the age of 47.

Cyrus Cunningham was a farmer at the time of his death. He owned over 1,400 acres of improved farm land in Vermillion and Warren Counties. There are several descendants of this pioneer family still living in the area.

This log house was moved in 1971 by Norman Skinner and is restored as part of his farm museum.

POEM BY JACOB WITTENMYER (1839-1921)

"Take me back to the old tanyard
Were in youth we worked so hard."
"Once more I hear the old bark mill
And the tread of old Joe as he pulls with a will."
"I want to hear the old bark mill ring,
As it did when I used to pound and sing.
Six barrows a day, an easy task,
But boys never know how much to ask."
"Let me ride once more in the old ox-cart
That's so plainly engraven on memory's chart."
"I want to swing that kitchen door,
Be quick, let me to that table rush,
For tonight we'll all have milk and mush."

PERRYSVILLE JAIL

Built in 1881 and was used in Perrysville for a jail for several years.

It is 12' by 12', built of 2 x 4 laid flat for walls, making the walls four inches thick. It

Old Wittenmyer Brick House Built 1844-Moved 1979

1826 Cunningham Log House

Perrysville Jail

Justice of the Peace Building

has two small windows with five bars in each and a big sliding latch on the door.

It was later moved south of town and used for a farm grainery for many years.

In 1986 it was moved by Norman Skinner to be a part of his farm museum.

JUSTICE OF THE PEACE BUILDING

Built in 1850 and used by Rev. John Wesley Parrett, a Methodist minister, for his office as Justice of the Peace from 1850 to 1910. Four hundred and forty couples were married here in that 60 year period. The octagon 16' building originally stood southeast of the Court House in Newport, Indiana.

John Wesley Parrett was a very important man helping in the development of this State and County. He was born in 1818 in Lawrenceburg, raised in Evansville, went to Asbury University (now DePauw), which his father helped found. In 1842 he became a Methodist Circuit rider at a Church in Newton in Fountain County. With Newton as his base, he would ride for over 100 miles to serve 20 other congregations on horseback. For all of this he received a salary of $75 a year.

While at Newton he married Elizabeth Mick. They had three sons but only one lived to maturity. Not too long after, his wife died, too.

In 1850 he was assigned to a Church in Newport. From his base in Newport his circuit riding ministry began to slack off with only two other churches to serve, Lebanon and Vermillion Chapel. In 1851 he married the daughter of pioneer settlers of Newport, Lydia Zener. They had one son, Robert, born April 11, 1852.

He continued to preach part time, was Justice of the Peace in Newport, and engaged in farming until his death in 1911.

This building was moved by Norman Skinner in 1986 after efforts to get the octagonal structure moved to uptown Newport proved fruitless. It has been restored as part of his farm museum.

GESSIE

Gessie is a village on the railroad, three miles northwest of Perrysville station. It was laid out in 1872 by Robert J. Gessie and named for him. In 1887 this place had a population of one hundred and forty. The 1910 United States census bulletin gives it as having one hundred and fifty.

Dr. William Isaiah Hall, who purchased the first town lot in the place, also erected the first building. He was still practicing medicine in the place in 1888. His partner was for many years Dr. James Barnes, who afterward practiced alone in the village. Early business men were J.C. Stutler, with a general store; L.A. McKnight, general store and grain dealer; D.M. Hughes, drugs and groceries; John Cade, postmaster, drugs and groceries; A. Van Sickle, blacksmith; Silas Hughes, wagon and repair shop; C.L. Randall, painter and jobber; John Haworth, station agent; H.C. Smith & Company, proprietors of tile factory; this was built in 1884 and the first year's output of the plant was six thousand dollars' worth of tile.

Taken from Parke-Vermillion Counties History, 1913.

ROBERT J. GESSIE

Earl Clingan lives on the old homestead that his father, Dennis Clingan, purchased from William Gessie and Flora Herrick (heirs of Robert J. Gessie) in 1900. This is the farm (a little less than one mile west of Gessie) that Mr. Gessie lived on for many years. Mr. Clingan has a ledger and diary that Mr. Gessie kept and from these and from other sources he has written the following:

Robert J. Gessie, the founder of the village of Gessie, Indiana was born November 5, 1809 in Cumberland County, Pennsylvania.

He was proprietor of a store in Perrysville, Indiana, and I have his Old Ledger. The first accounts were entered with Thomas Wright, April 8, 1843. Some of his other many customers were John Hines, Isaac Switzer, Jacob Rudy, David Wittenmyer, Samuel Smith, George Hicks, Benjamin Beckelhymer, Isreal Hughes, Margaret Rudy, Daniel Dennis, John Hunt, Samuel Mosbarger, Leroy Marshall,

William A. Lawlyes, Widow Rudy, Benjamin Whittimeyer, John A. Kiger, Cornelius Miller, Feilding Rayborn, Jacob Saltsgaver, John LaTourette, John Rayborn, Jacob Stutler, James Cossey, John Dennis, Jonathan Wittemyer, Solomon Jones, James I. Lewis, James A. Prather, Reese Rayborn, John W. Rayborn, Isaac Howard, Robert Brewer, Jacob Ruby, Sidney Cronkite, Egbert Beckett, Henry Gouty, John Hunt, Andrew Beauchamp, William Lacy, Daniel Shute, Samuel Prather, William Cox, Dorman Cade, Joseph Randall, Jeremiah Prather, William V. Fultz, Thomas Wright, Elizabeth Talbert, James Collins, Amos Fleshman, Alexander Dunlap, Nathaniel Jones, Andrew Dennis, Diana Skinner, James Beauchamp, David Metzger, Milton Howard, Isaac Switzer, William Hughes, Andrew Dennis, Peter Cossey, John McNeill, Edward Jones, and many others too numerous to mention and the last entry in the Ledger was October 29, 1846. These are the early pioneers of this area.

In the back of the Old Ledger he kept a daily diary. The first entry was made September 1, 1885 and the last entry made December 26, 1894. On the last entry he said that he had moved part of his furniture to Perrysville.

Robert Gessie was a deeply religious man. In the Diary in his old Ledger he always wrote a lovely prayer on his birthday each year for example – November 5, 1886:

"This is my Birthday, I am this day 77 years old being born in Newville, Cumberland County, Pennsylvania, on the 5th day of November 1809 and I am this day in the enjoyment of good health, remarkably good for one of my age and while nearly all of my contempories, male and female, have gone to try the realities of a future state, I am permitted by my heavenly Father to remain here and enjoy his special Blessings and for which I am truly thankful and hoping that I will still enjoy these heavenly blessings that He in His great mercy and goodness is pleased to confer on me. Oh! How can I express my great thankfulness to Him for these great blessings of health and happiness that most certainly come from Him."

There are many interesting items in the Old Ledger about the people and their way of life at this time. Among his many tenants are listed the names of Bowman, Carithers, and Saltsgaver.

The yield of corn on his farms were from 30 to 44 bushels per acre.

Some people in this Ledger bought as much as $7.00 to $8.00 a year on credit and paid at the end of the year.

Some of his customers settled their bills by so much wheat at around 50 cents per bushel.

In the records of this Ledger is a memorandum where he gave Calvin Marble 104 Hog Heads or barrels to be finished. They packed their pork during the winter months in these and it was shipped down the river.

He accepted from a firm several boxes of pills to be sold on commission. He was to receive 33-1/3% commission on the sale of the pills. He was a real business man and made a note of all of his transactions.

At his death he left a will leaving an estate valued at $100,000 to $120,000, which was considerable in that day.

His son, William Gessie, was a veteran of the Civil War, and never came home after the war, and Robert Gessie only left him a small sum in his will. When William Gessie left for the war he left a young wife and unborn baby which he had never seen even after his return. This baby was Mrs. Flora Herrick of Chicago which is mentioned as a heir.

When Robert Gessie died, William and Mrs. Robert Gessie were the only legal heirs and William Gessie engaged lawyers to contest the will. Also, at his death Mrs. Flora Herrick hired attorneys to contest the will. She had never seen her father (William Gessie) and did not know he was alive until the lawyers of both contestants filed their claims. Then a happy reunion followed when father and daughter met for the first time in their lives.

They won their suit and the widow of Robert Gessie was forced to divide. In legal terms, it is almost impossible to break a will. The law considers the deceased is unable to protect his wishes and has the power by will to disinherit any child but cannot disinherit his widow or husband.

By now Robert Gessie was very eccentric and in his will he stated that the bulk of his estate was to be used to build a school in the area. It also provided that his home was to be closed on the old farm and was to be opened each year and aired out, that his clothing was to be placed in a glass case and every so often the pupils of said school were to be marched by the case to view the clothes of their benefactor.

The law requires that a man must be proved incompetent at the time the will was made by a jury, this will was broken, we are told because of the eccentric wording of the items regarding the school.

Many people who knew Robert Gessie were convinced that although he was eccentric, he knew what he was doing about the will, but the jury decided differently.

Robert Gessie, the founder of Gessie, Indiana, before coming to this area taught school at Columbus, Indiana and at one time was a member of the Legislature for several years.

He had a love for flowers and one of his hobbies was growing many flowers. His flower gardens were enjoyed by all. Even to this day some of the flowers come up each season in my pasture lots that were once formal flower gardens. Also, Mr. Gessie had a board walk built from his home into the town of Gessie. (This is about one mile.)

Robert Gessie's handwriting was a thing of beauty – out of this world – even the headings on his Old Ledger looked like they were engraved. Would you like to match this handwriting using a goose quill pen?

I now live on the Old Homestead of Robert Gessie that my father purchased from William Gessie and Flora Herrick in 1900 – 72 years ago. Also, I have a copy of the original land patent issued to a William Boyles by the United States Government by President Martin Van Buren about 1837 for the 80 acres of the old farm that I now own.

I have added an original poem to this article:

To you hardy pioneers of long ago,
For many years you've laid
Beneath the good soil you gave.
Let's not forget the price you paid.

Four generations of the Clingan Family now live on the former Gessie farm west of the village of Gessie.

D. Earl Clingan

In 1897 Robert J. Gessie died and was buried by the grave of his first wife in the Hicks Cemetery west of Perrysville. According to instructions left in his will a suitable marker was provided by his widow with this inscription that he wanted: **"The Ledger of Life Is Balanced".** His second wife Mary lived for several years in Perrysville and at her death she, too, was buried in the Hicks Cemetery.

GESSIE INDIANA HORSE THIEF DETECTIVE COMPANY

The Gessie Indiana Horse Thief Detective Company was formed on March 1, 1884, for the purpose of mutually protecting against the depredations of horse thieves, counterfeiters, burglars, and all other felons.

When a member was satisfied that a theft had been committed, he was to immediately and personally notify the deputy Captain who in return notified the Captain and the President. Every member on receiving notice of a theft should notify at least one other member.

Every member who pursued a thief by the order of his commander was allowed his actual traveling expenses, and seventy-five cents per day. If he pursued through the night he was allowed one dollar for such service.

Meetings were held quarterly and members were assessed twenty-five cents at each meeting unless the treasury had two hundred dollars in it.

Members were Ephram Shute, George Johnson, Wesley Switzer, V.S. Virgin, Joseph H. Nicholas, Lewis H. Johnson, John R. Currant, George Talbert, David Bennet, John W. Rouse, Joseph Gouty, R.B. Moudy, Dennis Rouse, and Ezra Hartman.

ARTICLES
-OF-
ASSOCIATION
-OF THE-
GESSIE INDIANA HORSE THIEF
DETECTIVE COMPANY.

FRIEND PRINT,
COVINGTON, INDIANA,
1884.

RILEYSBURG

The village of Rileysburg is located in the northwestern part of Highland Township, Vermillion County, Indiana, three-eighths mile east of the Illinois-Indiana line. This section was originally peopled by the Pottawatomies.

In the autumn of 1834, several tracts of land were "entered" from the government. Among those listed were Henry Prather, Jonathan Prather, James A. Prather, Robert Banford and John Russell.

The first home built by Jonathan Prather, Sr. was about one-fourth mile east of the road and Jonathan Prather, Jr. built his homestead one-fourth mile south, where Lawrence Prather now lives.

Jacob Riley, father of Francis M. Riley, for whom Rileysburg was named, purchased 100 acres and moved from Perrysville in 1842. This is the farm where Michael Turner now lives. It is said that Mr. Riley planted maple trees on each side of the road thru Rileysburg.

The railroad, then called the Evansville, Terre Haute and Chicago was completed in 1870. Thru the influence of Francis M. Riley a station was secured at Rileysburg. It was originally called Riley, but there being another station on the road bearing that name, the name of this station was changed to Rileysburg in the spring of 1885. At one time it was a station of some importance where

Rileysburg Tile Plant

considerable shipping was carried on. The first mail came to Rileysburg on the railroad in 1887 and continued until the post office was transferred to Covington. Now residents have a Covington, Route 2 address. The depot building has been removed but it is the beginning of the Brewer Yards for the Louisville and Nashville Railroad and CSX Transportation.

The first house in the village itself was built by Isaac and Hannah Shute Prather a short time after their marriage in March, 1875. In 1903, R.C. and S.E. Peterson laid out a plot of lots on the southwest corner of their farm. Four houses were built on these lots. Isaac Prather built the first store on the east side of the road. It was later sold to Wm. S. Martin and Wm. Isgrieg. They sold it to Edgar Prather.

Frank Riley and Ephrim Shute built a tile factory where, it is said, tile of "superior quality" were manufactured. Mr. Riley later sold his interest in the factory to Wm. Martin, father of Presley Martin. Later Charles and Edgar Prather were owners. The building was torn down in 1920 and a garage built by Oral Prather.

Until about 1889 children from Rileysburg attended a school across the road from the Richardson's home, called the Point. This school house was moved to Rileysburg and served until 1915. It was moved away and the two room brick school house built. Church, Grange meetings, literary societies and debates that enlivened many winter evenings were held there. Some teachers of that period were Wm. Marble, Charles Carithers, Joshua Lewis, Solomon Jones, and Susie Smith.

The elevator was built by Wm. and Presley Martin, then sold to Frank Davis who later sold it to Jacob Marble and on to Martin Current. In September, 1916, a disastrous fire burned the elevator, general store and depot. They were all rebuilt.

It was during the horse and buggy days that Rileysburg enjoyed its time of greatest importance, since it was difficult to drive a greater distance for supplies.

Former businesses included: JUSTICE OF THE PEACE—Jacob Marble. LUMBER YARD—August Knoth. GRAIN ELEVA-TOR—Wm. and Presley Martin, Frank Davis, Jacob Martin, Martin Current, Edgar Prather, Robert Snavely and Paul Snellenbarger, Covington Grain Co., Rileysburg Grain Co., Summerville Grain Co., and Brannin Grain Co. BLACKSMITH—Reuben Ramsey, Lon Sconce, and Joseph Stuckey. BARBER SHOP—Morris Fader. GENERAL STORE—Isaac Prather, Wm. S. Martin and Wm. Isgrieg, Edgar Prather, Austin and Inez Marshall, Phillip and Pearl Kranz, Marvin Dunagan, and Cora and Frank Shannon. HARDWARE AND IMPLEMENTS—Presley Martin and Fred Wolter, Dewey Prather, and Brannin and Sons.

In 1889 an enterprising Court of Honor Lodge built the Hall which has been the center of community life since. It has been the scene of many jolly social events, suppers, plays, bazaars, farmer's institutes, class parties and other community activities. It's primary use through the years has been Church and Sunday School.

The Rileysburg school was closed, students enrolled and the teachers transferred to Highland Elementary at Perrysville, in January, 1961.

The train depot and the General Store buildings have been removed.

At present, in 1989, The Brannin and Sons Implement store and Brannin Grain co. elevator are the remaining business. The store is the gathering spot for local farmers to visit, purchase Massey-Ferguson equipment, parts, fertilizer and repair service.

SMITH CEMETERY

In Highland Township, about two miles southwest of Perrysville, there is an old cemetery that lies totally encompassed by the 1980s. Smith Cemetery it is called. On one side cars and trucks speed by on four lanes of modern highway, en route to somewhere. On the other three sides, rows of crops groomed by big machines and pampered with all the proper chemicals, soak up sunshine during the summer months. Nearby, folks live in comfortable houses surrounded by all sorts of modern gadgets.

Vermillion County has come a long way since the first pioneer put down roots here, and things are bound to keep changing as we head toward the 21st Century. In our usual fashion, the past will be discarded along the way and relegated to museums, history books and cemeteries. Like all cemeteries, Smith Cemetery links us to the past.

Many of the county's earliest settlers are buried there, and gravestone memorials tell a tale of names and dates. Unlike most cemeteries, though, Smith Cemetery boasts another link to the past – prairie plants.

At the time of settlement, most of Indiana was covered by extensive forests. However, a landscape feature known as "prairie" covered much of northwestern Indiana and reached westward through Illinois and beyond. Prairie covered nearly one-fourth of Vermillion County. What was this prairie anyway? It was land without trees; a sea of tall, luxuriant grass. It was Big Bluestem, Indian Grass and Compass Plants all taller than a man. It was open sky everywhere. It was beautiful sun-loving wildflowers from May to October. It was Baptisia, Bison and Bobolinks, Puccoons and Prairie Chickens. Gayfeathers, Upland Sandpipers, Prairie Gentians and so much more. It was a meadowland wilderness just as awesome to the pioneers as the forest primeval.

Just as much a part of those prairies as grass were the fires that swept across the grasslands regularly during spring and fall, consuming the lush vegetation. Unlike forests, prairies thrive on fire. Fire returns nutrients quickly to the soil, bares the ground to encourage early spring warm-up (and thus, early green-up), breaks dormancy and stimulates germination in many plants. Perhaps most importantly, it kills back woody vegetation. Without the fires, the eastern prairies would have begun succeeding into forests. Although many of the fires were started by lightning, most were set probably by the Indians, who were managing the prairie to maintain the unique and abundant game populations that were associated with the prairies and prairie-forest borders.

Early explorers believed generally that prairies were unfertile since they were treeless. They assumed mistakenly that fertility was related to the land's ability to grow trees. In reality, most prairie soils are exceptionally fertile, and the settlers soon realized that. Perhaps the first settlers to Highland Township already knew about the richness of prairie ground when they arrived in 1822.

According to the **Biographical and Historical Record of Vermillion County, Indiana** (1888), Jacob Haine, G.S. Hansicker, and George Hicks were the first settlers in

Horse power baling scene. Notice the scale, every bale was weighed

Threshing scene at Volkel's farm

Highland Township. That historical record is full of names and dates and places, but it really does not tell us much about the natural history of the region. There are very few references to prairies and those that there are simply identify them as a place with a name – Helt's Prairie, Hiddle's Prairie, Eugene Prairie, Coleman's Prairie. Nowhere is there any discussion of their natural features.

The best source of information on the whereabouts of Vermillion County's original prairies can be found in the surveyor's notes from the original Public Land Survey of the area. Most of Highland Township was surveyed in 1820 by a man named William Polke. By analyzing his survey notes, one can reconstruct a reasonable picture of the vegetation cover at the time of the survey. Smith Cemetery lies at the northeast corner of Section 8, Township 18 North, Range 9 West.

That entire section was almost all prairie, and it was at the northern end of a prairie tract that covered nearly seven square miles. The entire line between Sections eight and nine was described as being "rich prairie, level and first rate." However, the corner post for the northeast corner of Section eight was set "in the edge of prairie" with the nearest witness trees being a 6-inch (diameter) red oak about 88 feet away and a 30-inch white oak about 261 feet away.

If Highland Township's first settlers came in 1822, then little time had passed until they attended a burial on the prairie ground at the place now known as Smith Cemetery. In 1823, the name Conger became the first of 53 family names to occupy the face of a stone there. Over the years, nearly 150 other pioneers and several decades of other descendants of pioneers found their final resting place at Smith Cemetery. At some point during those years, the last patch of prairie disappeared from Vermillion County.

Today, untouched remnants of the tall grass prairie are nearly non-existent, not only in Indiana, but in the entire Midwest. Here in Indiana, railroad rights-of-way, which were established through the original prairies, contain some of our only remnants of prairie vegetation. Less often, pioneer cemeteries established on prairie ground still harbor some prairie plants. As prairie remnants, they are little more than scraps. Certainly they are accidental. No one meant to preserve them. It seems a little ironic that these prairie scraps gasp for survival along the steel rails and among the gravestones of the dead pioneers who opened the way to the conquering of the wilderness and the subsequent destruction of the prairies.

Today at Smith Cemetery, the bronzy stalks of Big Bluestem and Indian Grass reach skyward again in late summer. This latest chapter in the history of Smith Cemetery began in 1979 when botanists from the Department of Natural Resources went in search of a rare prairie wildflower called Royal Catchfly that had been collected many years ago at a "cemetery prairie" south of Perrysville. The scarlet blossoms of Royal Catchfly were rediscovered at Smith Ceme-

tery sharing a narrow refuge in the fence row with several other prairie plants. The cemetery itself was well-mowed with no evidence of prairie plants in sight. After having been abandoned for many years, the cemetery was "cleaned up" about 25 years ago.

In other States, prairie preservation enthusiasts have recognized that many of these pioneer cemeteries contain the only prairie remnants around. Prairie enthusiasts in Illinois have been particularly successful in working with cemetery boards, township trustees and other cemetery stewards to allow many cemeteries which harbor prairie plants to revert to prairie. Personnel from Indiana DNR decided to follow Illinois' lead in such endeavors and work toward getting the prairie to reign again over Smith Cemetery.

DNR and The Nature Conservancy cooperate in a program called the Indiana Natural Area Registry. Its purpose is to notify owners of significant natural features that they are the steward of a special feature and to encourage their voluntary protection of it. Since Royal Catchfly is significant, being known from only two sites in Indiana, the Natural Area Registry was chosen as the method of approach to encourage the prairie revival at Smith Cemetery. Township Trustee Delores Hicks was approached with the idea of ceasing mowing there and watching to see what came up. She agreed to give it a try.

1981 was the first season it went without mowing. Already in May of that year, another rare plant was discovered when Prairie Violets were seen popping up here and there throughout the cemetery. As the summer progressed, additional species were noted until the list at season's end totaled nearly 30 species. Some of the most exciting plants included Lead Plant, Prairie Alumroot, Side

Oats Gramma Grass, and Purple Prairie Coneflower.

In the spring of 1982, the prairie was burned to simulate the fires which swept the prairies in the old days. During the growing season, five more good prairie species were found: Culver's Root, New Jersey Tea, White Prairie Clover, Wild Quinine, and Puccoon. Many of the others showed significant increases over the year before. The prairie was coming back!

Even as spectacular as the recovery has been, many characteristic prairie species which surely grew in the prairie there years ago are now missing. They could not withstand the frequent mowing and have disappeared. Some will reappear stimulated by annual fires and the cessation of mowing.

If after several years no additional species appear, some which were known to occur in the region in the old days might be re-introduced by scattering seeds to enrich the prairie.

Already a helping hand has been provided on several occasions by removing weeds such as Wild Parsnip, Mullein, and White Sweet Clover. Once the prairie plants are well established, aggressive weeds will have difficulty competing and will virtually disappear. Prairie plants are not aggressive invaders of disturbed ground like most of the Eurasian weeds. It takes them a few years to really get their roots in the ground, but once established, they do well if left undisturbed except for an occasional fire.

The spring of 1983 begins the third year of the prairie project at Smith Cemetery. With it will come the second spring burn, more pulling of weeds, and hopefully another encouraging season of "new" species and spreading of "old" ones. And although some folks' vision of a proper cemetery is narrowly

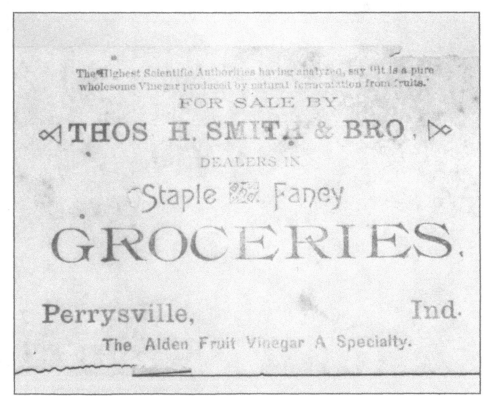

focused on a bluegrass turf, there cannot be a more fitting memorial to the pioneers, so too are the prairie plants to the long-gone prairie wilderness. It is even more fitting that the prairie pioneers and the prairie plants with which they were familiar be allowed to share together a little piece of Highland Township. If the old prairie sod-busters could talk to us now, they would surely approve of the recent change of scenery.

An article by Lee Casebere, Indiana Department of Natural Resources, The Daily Clintonian, May 26, 1983.

SCHOOLS

The following schools were located in Highland Township in Vermillion County, Indiana.

Gessie School
Mound School
Jordan School
Upper Coal Branch School

LOWER COAL BRANCH SCHOOL DISTRICT 11

This school was first known as the Hughes School, then Cromerville, later as Lower Coal Branch. It was built in 1893 after an earlier one burned. It was used until 1925. It was later used as a corncrib. Some of the teachers were E. Helt, William Neal, Pearl Frock, Lizzie Hughes, Ray Rabb, Kate Sanders, Sylvia Nash (Jones), Leah Becklehymer (Morgan), Bob White, Jennie Kibbey, Rachel Lewsader (Smith), Mr. Alward, Mary Patrick, Mrs. Rahm, Fairie Kohm and Tessie Cole.

Often times in the early 1900's, it was used for Church revivals, etc. Some of the ministers were Dan Sollars, Arthur Hayworth, Newt Lawless.

It was moved in 1987 by Norman Skinner and is being restored as part of his farm museum.

HIGHLAND TOWNSHIP TEACHERS 1914

Perrysville - L.J. McClintock, Superintendent; P.A. Etter, Principal; Artie Hartshorn, Assistant Principal; grades—T.M. Pearson, Mary Compton, Mary Lewis, Della Nicholas.

Rileysburg - Anna Jensen, B. Sanders, K. Sanders, Sylvia Nash, Fern Hold, and Ruth Crouse.

Gessie School-Highland Township

Mound School-Highland Township

Upper Coal Branch School-Highland Township

CHURCHES - 1988

Coal Branch Church
Christian Union Church
Gessie United Methodist Church

Perrysville United Methodist Church
Rileysburg Church

HOWARD CHAPEL METHODIST EPISCOPAL CHURCH

Howard Chapel, Methodist Episcopal Church, two miles north of Gessie, is a brick building 30 x 50 feet or more in dimensions, built over thirty years ago. The society has been in existence since pioneer days. There are now about thirty members, with Joseph Nichols as class-leader. Stewards, James J. Lewis, Meredith Lewis, Henry Saltsgaver, David Bennett and Dr. W.I. Hall. Mr. Saltsgaver is also Sunday-school superintendent. Pastor, Rev. Warren, of State Line, where the parsonage is. Among the ministers of the past the most prominent in memory are Revs. Cooley Hall (father of Dr. Hall), Wilson Beckner, Samuel Beck, Whitefield Hall, etc.

The chapel is named after Joseph Howard, who donated the ground and led the enterprise of building the church, and was afterward trustee, etc. He resided there until 1866, and moved West, and finally died in Nebraska. His wife has since died. Mr. Howard was buried in Nebraska, although is monument is in the graveyard here. None of his people reside at present in this county. On coming here from Ohio, about 1825, he settled on the farm now occupied by John Fox; was very poor, a cooper and farmer by occupation, but by economy he at length became wealthy, maintaining all the while an unsettled reputation.

A few years ago a portion of the above society organized a small class in Gessie and began the erection of a small church; but, before it was completed, it was blown down and the little band returned to Howard Chapel.

Taken from 1888 Vermillion County History

PERRYSVILLE METHODIST EPISCOPAL CHURCH

The Methodist Episcopal Church has of course an eventful history, extending back to pioneer times, which is difficult to trace. At present it is a strong and influential society of 133 members, besides probationers. Class-leaders, B.O. Carpenter and J.F. Compton; stewards—David Smith, Mrs. Rebecca K. McNeill, Mrs. Mary C. Moffatt, Mrs. Hannah B. Johnson, Mrs. Sophia S. Rudy, B.O. Carpenter, J.F. Compton and Mrs. Amanda M. Ferguson. Rev. J.H. Mills is a local preacher. Sunday-school all the year, with an average attendance of seventy-five, superintended by B.O. Carpenter. In connection with the church here are several auxiliary societies,—missionary, social, etc. The house of worship, built of brick, was erected in 1843, and its outside measurements are 44 x 52 feet. Value, $3,000, though that money

would not build it now. Locality, southwest-central part of town. A good parsonage exists on the adjoining lot east.

Taken from 1888 Vermillion County History

HOPEWELL BAPTIST CHURCH

Hopewell Baptist Church, a frame building about two miles north of Gessie, is the place of meeting of a society which was organized many years ago by the Rabourns. Among the prominent early members were Wesley and Reese Rabourn, Fielden Rabourn, Mr. Blankenship and others, and of the ministers the most prominently remembered are Revs. James Smith, John Orr, Mr. Whitlock, Mr. Stipp and Samuel Johnson. Mr. Stipp was a Freemason, and some of the members of the church, not believing that freemasonry was consistent with Christianity, seceded, under the leadership of Elder Johnson, so that since that time two small societies are weakly sustained at the same place of meeting, called respectively the "Stippites" and the "Johnsonites." Elder Stipp is now dead. Elder Johnson came from Fountain County in 1871, purchasing the old Joseph Howard residence. Ehud Hughes, Philander Goff, Samuel Johnson and Ephraim Shute are official members.

In 1877 Byron Stevens, a "Christian" residing near Lowe Chapel, about three and a half miles southwest of Gessie, with the assistance of his friends built the church in Gessie which two years afterward they sold to the United Brethren. He was a minister, and he and James Prather were trustees. They organized a small church society at Gessie, which soon ran down. Elder Myers preached regularly for them for a time.

Taken from 1888 Vermillion County History

MOUND CHAPEL UNITED BRETHREN CHURCH

Mound Chapel, United Brethren, 30 x 40 feet, erected ten or eleven years ago, is located three miles and a half north of Perrysville. The class, now comprising about forty members, was organized eleven or twelve years ago: leader, Mrs. Jane Mitchell; steward, Nathan Jacobs. Sunday-school during the summer, of about fifty pupils probably, superintended by the class-leader, Mrs. Mitchell.

Taken from 1888 Vermillion County History

GESSIE UNITED BRETHREN CHURCH

The United Brethren Church at Gessie was organized about 1879, by Rev. F.E. Penny, of Danville, Illinois, who moved to this place

the following year. The trustees were L.A. McKnight, Charles Hay and Harvey Hughes; and Isaiah Thompson the class-leader. There are now seventeen members; class-leader, J.C. Stutler; stewards, J.C. Stutler and Katie Goudy. The Sunday-school is maintained most of the year, with an attendance of forty pupils; superintendent, John Haworth. The pastors have been Revs. J.A. Smith, of Gessie, J. Knowles, of State Line, Kaufman, of Perrysville, S.C. Zook, who lived below Newport, J.R. Horner, who lived here, and Van Allen, who lived a mile south of Cayuga. The church building was erected by the Christians, about 1877, a frame 24 x 40 feet, at a cost of $1,000, and in 1879 they sold it to the United Brethren.

The Union Sunday-school in Gessie is maintained independently of denominational supervision, and its existence of course diminishes the attendance at the United Brethren Sunday-school. It has been running since January, 1887, and L.A. McKnight is superintendent.

Taken from 1888 Vermillion County History

CROSS-ROADS UNITED BRETHREN CHURCH

The Cross-Roads United Brethren Church, two miles west of Perrysville, was organized over forty years ago, and a large frame church built also in early day. The membership there numbers about seventy-five, of whom the leader is Mrs. Sarah Park, and stewards, Jacob Brown and Richard Spandau. Sunday-school throughout the year, with an average attendance of about eighty, superintended by John Park.

Taken from 1888 Vermillion County History

PERRYSVILLE UNITED BRETHREN CHURCH

The United Brethren Church at Perrysville was organized many years ago. The present membership is about eighty. Class-leader, John Patterson; stewards, Mrs. Sarah Smith and Mrs. Rose Hain. Sunday-school is maintained throughout the year, with an attendance of sixty to seventy, superintended by Rev. J.S. Brown, who has also been the pastor of this circuit for the last three years. He is a native of Parke County, this State; at the age of sixteen years he came to this county and worked on a farm two miles southwest of Newport; entered a school in Ohio in the fall of 1881, graduating in the spring of 1884, since which time he has held his present relation, as a member of the Upper Wabash Conference. He occupies the parsonage at Perrysville, in an extremely retired portion of the village, in the northwestern part, and has three or four appointments in his circuit.

The church edifice at Perrysville, a frame, 34 x 48 feet, erected twenty-five or thirty years ago, is a neat building, centrally located.

At Perrysville also resides the presiding elder, Rev. H. Ellwell.

Taken from 1888 Vermillion County History

24

PERRYSVILLE PRESBYTERIAN CHURCH

A Presbyterian Church was once organized at Perrysville, and after struggling along with a precarious existence for a number of years, it became utterly dissolved, when it counted about fifteen or sixteen members. Their house of worship, which they bought of the Universalists, became unsafe, and was sold in 1882, for $150, and afterward torn away. The trustees were D.C. Smith, John E. Robinson and H.S. Collier. Mr. Smith was also ruling elder. Pastors or supplies were Revs. John Hawks, Mr. Steele, R. Wells, William Buffert, etc., and the last one serving was Rev. Tarrance, who was at the time (1872-'73) a resident of Covington, Indiana. There has been no regular preaching since 1873, when there were twenty-one members. There are now probably about half a dozen members.

Taken from 1888 Vermillion County History

PERRYSVILLE UNIVERSALIST CHURCH

The Universalist Church at Perrysville was organized in 1842, and afterward erected a house of worship, a frame about 36 x 50 feet in size, but, being unable to pay for it, they finally, in 1850, sold it to the Presbyterians, and subsequently disbanded. They numbered as high as fifty or sixty members at one time. Among the ministers are prominently remembered Revs. E. Manford, the celebrated editor, a resident of Terre Haute at the time, B.F. Foster, of Indianapolis, George McClure, of Dayton, Ohio, but an itinerant, and Mr. Babcock, of some point east of Indianapolis. The minister organizing the church was Rev. Marble, of Fountain County, who preached once a month for about a year. The leading members were Robert J. Gessie (trustee and mortgagee!), Dr. Thornton S. Davidson, Dr. Porter, Messrs. Lawless, Watt, etc. They had a flourishing Sunday-school.

Taken from 1888 Vermillion County History

PERRYSVILLE CHRISTIAN CHURCH

A "Christian" church, with about a half dozen members, was organized at Perrysville five or six years ago, by Elder Gilbert Lane Harney, of Indianapolis, but they kept up services only a few weeks. The leading members were C.S. Brummett and wife, John Emanuel Sinks, Sarah Bailey, Mrs. Hettie Lacey, and others.

Taken from 1888 Vermillion County History

UNITY CHAPTER, O.E.S.

Unity Chapter, No. 50, O.E.S., at Perrysville, was instituted March 17, 1882, by Willis D. Engle, District Deputy, from Indianapolis, with fifteen members; and the first officers were–Elizabeth Collins, Worshipful Master; James Howard, Worshipful Prelate; Mrs. Sophie Rudy, A.M.; and Mrs. Helen B. Johnson, Secretary. The present officers are–Mrs. Helen B. Johnson, Worshipful Master; Mr. M.J. Rudy, Worshipful Prelate; Mrs.

James Frazee, A.M.; Miss Anna Robinson, Secretary; Mrs. Amanda Henderson, Treasurer; Miss Imo Collins, Conductress; and Mrs. Dora Lyons, Assistant Conductress. The present membership is between thirty-five and forty, and the chapter is in a good financial condition. It meets the first Friday evening after each full moon, in Masonic Hall.

Taken from 1888 Vermillion County History

UNITY LODGE, NO. 344, F. & A.M.

Unity Lodge, No. 344, F. & A.M., was chartered May 29, 1867, with the following officers: W.B. Moffatt, Worshipful Master; James Hemphill, Senior Warden; Jacob S. Stephens, Junior Warden; William Jerrauld, Secretary; Robert E. Townsley, Treasurer; H.M. Townsley, Senior Deacon; John Wolf, Junior Deacon; Thomas Scott, Tyler. The present membership is forty-six, and the officers: Daniel Lyons, Worshipful Master; George R. Hicks, Senior Warden; John B. McNeil, Junior Warden; W.A. Keerns, Secretary; W.A. Collins, Treasurer; John S. Tiley, Senior Deacon; Martin L. Wright, Junior Deacon; D.W. Patterson and M.J. Rudy, Stewards; W.P. Hargrave, Chaplain; and Smith McCormick, Tyler.

Taken from 1888 Vermillion County History

UNITY LODGE, NO. 114, F. & A.M.

Unity Lodge, No. 114, F. & A. M., at Perrysville, was organized about 1850 or before, and increased in time to thirty-four members. The earliest record extant is dated May, 1853, which gives as officers at that time: A. Hill, Worshipful Master; J.S. Baxter, Senior Warden; W.P. Johnson, Junior Warden; R.D. Moffatt, Secretary; G.H. McNeill, Treasurer; W.B. Moffatt, Senior Deacon; James Starr, Junior Deacon; and Andrew Dennis, Treasurer. The other members were E. Brydon, A.C. Blue, John Leech, James Benefiel, John L. Stoll, Harvey Knapp, James Martin and Lewis L. Gebhart. The charter was surrendered to Abel Sexton in May, 1859.

Taken from 1888 Vermillion County History

REBEKAH LODGE

Rebekah Lodge, No. 118, Daughters (or Degree) of Rebekah, was instituted July 24, 1882. First officers: M.B. Carter, Noble Grand; J.T. Chisler, Vice Grand; Sallie E. Carter, Secretary; C.W. Ayres, Treasurer; S. Watt, Guardian. The other charter members

were W.M. Benefiel, W.H. Benefiel, Thomas D. Clarkson, J.H. Benton, W.A. Collins, J.T. Lowe, Anna Benefiel, L. Chisler, M. Benefiel, Susan L. Clarkson and R.E. Watt. The present officers are: Imo Collins, Noble Grand; Cora Chisler, Vice Grand; Mary Ayres, Treasurer; Kittie Chisler, Secretary; W.M. Benefiel, Warden. The membership has about thirty from the first to the present.

Taken from 1888 Vermillion County History

CHARITY LODGE, I.O.O.F.

Charity Lodge, No. 32, I.O.O.F., was chartered April 20, 1846, by D.D.G.M. George Brown. The first officers were Irad Abdill, Noble Grand; Charles Boyles, Vice Grand; T.S. Davidson, Secretary; Thomas Cushman, Treasurer; John Dunlap, Warden; C.N. Gray, Conductor; Samuel Watt, Guardian; John A. Minshall, Recording Secretary. The present officers are–G.W. Dealand, Noble Grand; W.G. Chenowith, Vice Grand; C.W. Ayres, Recording Secretary; J.T. Chisler, Permanent Secretary; W.A. Collins, Treasurer. There are nineteen members, who own the building in which their neat and well equipped lodge room is contained. Total value of all their property, $1,348.60. During the war the lodge was kept alive by five or six faithful members. Of the old members, John Dunlap died about two years ago; Irad Abdill and William Callihan are living in Danville. Of the charter members, Thomas Cushman, of Newport, is the only one living in the county.

Taken from 1888 Vermillion County History

VERMILLION LODGE, K. OF P.

Vermillion Lodge, No. 113, K. of P., was organized December 31, 1884, by District Deputy Talley, of Coal Creek, assisted by members from various lodges. There were sixteen charter members, and the first officers were: Dr. James T. Henderson, Chancellor Commander; F.S. Smith, Vice-Chancellor; L.A. Morgan, Master of Finance; M.J. Rudy, Master of Exchequer; D.H. Cade, Keeper of Records and Seals; W.A. Collins, Prelate; G.R. Hicks, Master at Arms; A.R. Marlat, Inner Guard; E.A. Lacey, Outer Guard. There are now twenty-six members, comprising the best men of the community, who are, in their lodge relations, in perfect harmony. They have a lodge room of their own, and are in fair financial condition.

The present officers are: J.C. Wright, Past Commander; W.M. Collins, Chancellor Commander; Ned Spotswood, Vice-Chancellor; H.F. Royce, Prelate; M.J. Rudy, Master of

Finance; W.T. Ferguson, Master of Exchequer; J.T. Henderson, Keeper of Records and Seals; D. Mossburger, Master at Arms; J.M. Howard, Inner Guard; Smith McCormick, Outer Guard; W.A. Keerns, District Deputy.

Taken from 1888 Vermillion County History

ROBERT E. SPOTSWOOD POST, G.A.R.

Richard E. Spotswood Post, No. 188, G.A.R., was organized in January, 1878, with the following officers: Major J.S. Stevens, Post Commander; B.O. Carpenter, Senior Vice-Commander; M.B. Carter, Junior Vice-Commander; Dr. E.T. Spotswood, Adjutant. The membership has diminished from thirty-two to fifteen. Regular meetings, alternate Saturday evenings. B.O. Carpenter is the present Commander, and George Watt, Senior Vice-Commander.

Taken from 1888 Vermillion County History

HIGHLAND ENCAMPMENT

Highland Encampment, No. 163, was instituted December 7, 1885, by D.D.G.P. David McBeth, of Clinton. First officers–W.M. Benefiel, Chief Priest; J.T. Chisler, High Priest; C.W. Ayres, Senior Warden; Alexander Van Sickle, Junior Warden; D.W. Patterson, Scribe; W.G. Chenowith, Treasurer. Present officers–J.T. Lowe, Chief Priest; William G. Chenowith, High Priest; D.W. Patterson, Senior Warden; W.T. Conner, Junior Warden; W.M. Benefiel, Scribe; W.A. Collins, Treasurer. There were nine members at first, and there are nine or ten at present.

Taken from 1888 Vermillion County History

THE WOMAN'S CHRISTIAN TEMPERANCE UNION

The Woman's Christian Temperance Union of Perrysville was organized in December, 1881, with Mrs. Dr. Spotswood, President; Mrs. H.B. Johnson, Vice-President; Mrs. Sallie Carter, Secretary; Mrs. J.M. Mills, Corresponding Secretary; Mrs. M.J. Rudy, Treasurer. Commencing with a membership of only ten, they soon increased to forty; but now there are only twenty-five. To the present time they have kept up gospel meetings, and have exerted a marked influence in giving the people a temperance education. For a time they edited a column in the *Hoosier State.* The present official board is the same as the first, except that Mrs. Lydia Hepburn is Recording Secretary, *vice* Mrs. Sallie Carter, deceased.

Taken from 1888 Vermillion County History

EQUAL SUFFRAGE CLUB

An *Equal Suffrage Club* was organized at Perrysville July 21, 1882, by the election of Mrs. Sarah S. Spotswood, President; Rev. J.S. White, Vice-President; Lillie Kirkpatrick, Recording Secretary; Icabenda Hain, Treasurer; Executive Committee–Anna McClintick, Honorable J.F. Compton, D.C. Smith, Mrs. Lucy Maynard and Mrs. Sarah Smith. The club "immediately went down."

Taken from 1888 Vermillion County History

Robert J. Gessie

Threshing scene. Early Holsman car in the back. This was the first car in Highland Township. The other car is a Franklin.

This township is the second from the north line of the county, and is bounded on the east by Parke county, the Wabash river being the dividing line; on the south is Vermillion township, on the west is the state of Illinois, and on the north is Highland township. In this portion of Vermillion county, more than at any other point, were the Indian villages, battlefields and first trading posts, as well as the first settlements by white men. While it is true that John Vannest settled the county first in Clinton township, the settlement in Eugene was much more rapid than in other parts of the county. Eugene township contains thirty-three square miles, and in 1880 had a population of 1,340, with personal property valued at $681,000. In 1910 the population was, including Cayuga, 2,112. In 1911 the assessed valuation of both personal and real property in this township was $1,376,085, exclusive of Newport, which had $402,720.

In 1869 Prof. John Collett discovered, in a mound near Eugene, a small coin upon which was an untranslatable inscription, in characters closely resembling Arabic. This mound was covered with full-grown forest trees.

Early settlers near Eugene village found an ax imbedded in the heart of an oak tree, with one hundred and twenty-five rings about it, thus indicating that the implement had been left there as early as 1712, or more than two hundred years ago. It was probably left there by the French people, possibly a missionary. It is true that different kinds of timber, growing in different soils, may vary in the years noted by the "timber rings," but this ax was evidently placed there long before the Revolutionary struggle.

EARLY SETTLEMENT

It was in Eugene township that the Groenendykes, Thompsons, Porters, Armours, Colletts, Hepburns, Colemans, Malones, Naylors, Shelbys and other effected a settlement. Many of these worthy pioneers left numerous descendants who became and are still residents and influential citizens of Vermillion county.

The first mill in this county was that erected in Clinton township by John Beard, either in 1819 or 1820. However, that was a small affair compared to the one built in this township by John Groenendyke, about the same date, on Big Vermillion river, at the point in the northern portion of Eugene township where the village of Eugene was laid out. This was for many years the best and largest mill in Vermillion county.

The following is an incomplete chronological list of pioneers who made their way to Eugene township between 1816 and 1840:

1816—Noah Hubbard, with a wife and a large family of children. After residing here many years he became a Mormon and went to Missouri, to join his people, then to Nauvoo, Illinois, remaining with them until they were driven away by the Gentiles, about 1847, when he returned to this county and began preaching that peculiar doctrine. Rejoining the Mormons in the colony at Council Bluffs, Iowa, he died there.

1818—Isaac Coleman settled three miles south of Eugene, on the prairie since known as Coleman's prairie. Judge J.M. Coleman came to the township a year later, from Virginia, settling on section 16, township 17, range 9 west, and was long and intimately associated with the Collett families. He had aided in laying out the city of Indianapolis, and also Terre Haute, where he also built the old court house. In this county he was one of the first grand jurymen, and an associate judge. Subsequently, he removed to Iowa City, Iowa, where he built the State House, died and was buried there. The same year (1818) came Major James Blair, who settled on the northeast quarter of section 16, township 17, range 9 west, and at his cabin on this place was held the first term of court in Vermillion county. He had been a sharpshooter on Lake Erie, under Commodore Perry, in the war of 1812, when he was detailed to shoot at the Indians in the rigging of the British war vessels; but at the very first fire of Perry's artillery the Indians were so frightened that they hastily "scuttled" down into the hold, and there were no Indians for Blair to do his duty upon. As his vessel sailed past the British man-of-war he could see the glittering tin canisters down through the muzzles of their guns. For his faithful services Mr. Blair received a medal from the American government. On one occasion, after he became a resident of Vermillion county, he was a candidate for the Legislature. He attended a shooting match, in which he participated, and aimed so well that every man present voted for him at the ensuing election! On still another occasion he played an amusing trick upon the simpleminded pioneers and Indians, in the settlement of a controversy between them. Blair married a daughter of Judge Coleman, resided for a time on Coleman's prairie, then moved up the river and founded Perrysville, which place he named in honor of his brave commander, Commodore Oliver H. Perry, remaining there until his death. Both Blair and Coleman had an intimate acquaintance with the Indians and lived in friendship with them for a number of years. It frequently fell to their lot to act as peacemaker between the Indians and what were termed "border ruffians," who were much the worse of the two. These two pioneers always spoke in the highest terms of Se-Seep, the last chief who lived in the vicinity, who it is said was one hundred and ten years of age, when he was foully murdered by a renegade Indian of his own tribe. Like the fading autumn leaves, the Indians of these forests of Vermillion county

died away. The guns and dogs of the white man frightened away the game from their hunting grounds, or destroyed it, and the virtue of a dire necessity called upon them to emigrate, to make room for the ax and the plow, the cabin and the log school house of the incoming white race.

1819—John Groenendyke came in from near Cayuga county, New York, first to Terre Haute in 1818 and the next year to this county, settling on the Big Vermillion river where Eugene now stands. He was the father of James—who built the "Big Vermillion," the first large grist-mill in the county already referred to—and Samuel, and the grandfather of Hon. John Groenendyke and his cousin Samuel, and also the grandfather of the later generations of Colletts. The name was originally Van Groenendyke, a word of two syllables, the first being pronounced "groan." The first family of this line came to America from Holland with the Knickerbockers in 1617, settling in New Amsterdam (New York).

1821—James Armour settled here soon after Mr. Groenendyke, and assisted in building the pioneer mill; he removed to Illinois about 1877. Alexander Arrasmith, born in Kentucky in 1795, emigrated to Sullivan county, Indiana, in 1818, and in either 1821 or 1824 came to Vermillion county. He died at his home, two and a half miles south of Eugene, January 15, 1875, having been a member of the Methodist Episcopal church for forty-odd years. He was the father of Richard Arrasmith, born in Sullivan county, 1818, and of Thomas Arrasmith, a wagonmaker at Newport at an early day.

1822—William Thompson, father of James, John and Andrew, and of Mrs. Jane Shelby, from Pennsylvania, settled near the big spring a mile south from Eugene. Their descendants were frugal, industrious people and hence accumulated a large amount of property. The same year came in Benjamin Shaw, from Vigo county, but originally from Kentucky, and settled near Eugene, and afterward on the Little Vermillion, five miles west from Newport, where he died over three-quarters of a century ago. He was the father of ten children, three of whom survived their mother. Andrew Tipton came to this township in 1822 from Kentucky, where he was born in 1800. He remained here until his death. J.W. Tipton, of Ohio, settled on the Wabash river.

1823—Lewis Jones located here about 1823, and died after the Civil War. J.A. Jones, born in 1821, was brought to this township in 1823.

1824–Jones Lindsey, born in Ohio, in 1818, came here in 1824. The next year there arrived Oliver Lindsley, born in Ohio in 1807. Judge Rezin Shelby, who became very wealthy, died here many years since.

1825–The parents of James Sheward, who was born this year. Ezekiel Sheward about 1870 in the township.

1826–William Fultz, Sr., born in Pennsylvania in 1805, with his wife Nancy, came to Eugene township this year, locating on Sand Prairie. They had thirteen children. The parents of Joseph Holtz, who was born in Ohio in 1822, came to the county in this year. John Holtz, who was born in Ohio, the same year, settled here in 1834.

1827–Samuel W. Malone, born in Ohio in 1810, came to Helt township, this county, in 1824, and to Eugene township in 1827; he conducted a hotel for a number of years. M.W. Newman, born in Virginia in 1811, was still a resident of the township in 1887. Martin Patrick came some time before 1827. Hiram Patrick was born here in 1829, and William Patrick, in 1831, lived here many years, then moved to Missouri. About this date came also John Ross, born in Ohio in 1829, and brought here the same year.

1828–Ignatius Sollars, who died in June, 1833. Nancy, wife of Truman Sollars, died September 15, 1869, aged fifty-seven and a half years. Matthew Cole, born in Ohio in 1824, was brought to this county in 1828, as was also Jesse Smith, from Tennessee, the year of his birth. The same year came also W.L. Naylor, and the next year Lewis T. Naylor, who still resided here in the latter eighties. Both were born in Ohio, W.L. in 1821 and Lewis T. in 1826. Benjamin Naylor, another old resident, was born in 1826. Jacob Iles, who died forty years or more ago, was the father of James B. Iles, born in 1829, and Jacob H., born in 1833, both natives of this county.

1829–John Hepburn, Sr., who was born in Virginia, died here about 1880. John Hepburn, Jr., was a native of Vermillion county, this state. William Hepburn was born in Ohio in 1823, and was brought here in 1829. Enoch W. Lane, born in Ohio in 1798, died here before 1850.

1830–John Sims, born in Virginia in 1808, lived a mile and a half south of Eugene many years. "Crate" Sims, his son, was born in Virginia the same year. Charles S. Little, from Virginia, located near Eugene in 1830, and died in 1852, aged sixty-three years. His wife, whose maiden name was Rachel Moore, died, aged eighty years, southwest of Newport, in 1881. Rev. Enoch Kingsbury came from Massachusetts to Eugene about 1830, and organized the Presbyterian church. His wife, Fanny G., taught school there for a number of terms. Their eldest son, James G. Kingsbury, one of the editors and publishers of the *Indiana Farmer* at Indianapolis, was born at the residence of Dr. Asa R. Palmer, two miles north of Eugene village, in 1832. The same year the family removed to Danville, Illinois, where Mr. Kingsbury organized a church and preached there many years. He also acted in the capacity of a

home missionary, preaching in neighboring counties both in Indiana and Illinois, till the close of his life in 1868.

1831–Harrison Alderson, who died at a very early day here, came that year to this township.

1832–Philo and Milo Hosford, twins, born in New York in 1811. Milo died in January, 1880, after having spent a most useful and excellent life in this county. He was many years in the employ of Samuel Gronendyke. Joseph Wigley, this year, came to Eugene township.

1833–Isaac A. Brown, Sr., born in Tennessee in 1816, settled "Brown Town," and was still living in the latter part of the eighties. He had at one time in his life weighed three hundred pounds.

1834–John Rheuby, about this year, came in from Illinois and settled; he was a pioneer in Illinois in 1826. William Reuby was born in this county in 1834. J.W. Boyd was born in Pennsylvania in 1828, died here in the eighties.

1837–The parents of Edward B. and Joseph Johnson; father died many years since. Edward B. was born in Indiana in 1830, and Joseph in this county in 1834. Goldman M. Hart, born in Tennessee in 1809, died in 1886. James C. Tutt, born in Virginia in 1816, removed from Eugene to the south part of Vermillion county.

1839–Barney Vandevander, born in Illinois in 1827, was a resident of Eugene in 1888.

Other pioneers, whose years of arrival are not given, are Zeno Worth and Shubael Gardner, from North Carolina, who settled in Walnut Grove. Mr. Worth selected lands which were held by his family many years and still largely within the names of his descendants, the generation now numbering five in this county. Alexander Richardson came that year also, and died in Indianapolis in 1864, or possibly a little later. Lewis Hollingsworth was born in this county in 1835. On Coleman's prairie settled families named Wilson, Dicken, Hopkins, etc.

John R. Porter, A.M., circuit judge for many years, and an advanced farmer between Eugene and Newport, was born in Pittsfield, Massachusetts, February 22, 1796, of an "old English family;" graduated at Union College, Schenectady, New York, in 1815, taking the first honors of his class. He studied law, and in 1818 became a partner of his preceptor. About 1820 he came to Paoli, Orange county, Indiana, where he was county clerk, postmaster and circuit judge. While there he married Mary Worth. Receiving while there the appointment of president judge of western Indiana, he moved to this county, settling in Eugene township. His circuit extended from the Ohio river to Lake Michigan. His term expired in 1837. Here he was elected judge of the court of common pleas for the counties of Parke and Vermillion, which office he held until his death, about 1850. He was a prominent statesman in early days, in laying the foundation of Indiana jurisprudence. Was a close reader of Eastern agricultural papers, and also of ancient classics, as well as foreign magazine literature. His con-

versational powers were consequently great, and his letters to the press were gems of eloquence. He was in correspondence, more o[r] less, with such men as General Harrison, Henry Clay, Daniel Webster, etc., besides many Georgia "colonels." Prominent Indiana men were frequently his guests. He was the leading spirit in all the public meetings in his neighborhood assembled for the deliberation of measures of public welfare. He was president of the Logansport convention, which gave initial direction to the construction of the Wabash Valley Railroad. As an agriculturist he was scientific and in advance of all his neighbors–so far indeed as often to excite their ridicule. He led in the rearing of fine wooled sheep, and in the cultivation of Switzer lucerne, ruta-bagas, sugar beets, moris, multicaulis, Baden corn and hemp. These paid him well in pleasure derived therefrom, if not in money receipts. The Judge was a broad, many-sided man, the likes of whom are seldom met with in any generation.

Taken from Parke and Vermillion Counties History, 1913.

COLLETT HOME

This institution is situated near the Vermillion and Eugene township line, about three and one-half miles from Newport, the county seat. It was opened in June, 1902, and was founded by Prof. John Collett and Josephus Collett, both deceased, but whose property had been divided so that it was possible to endow this home. It stands on a beautiful four-hundred-acre tract of farm land. It is a handsome building, costing originally twenty thousand dollars. The home was first opened by a superintendent who had been elected by the trustees of the Collett estate, named Charles W. Ward, and Mr. and Mrs. A.R. Campbell, of Danville, Illinois, as overseer and matron. The conditions upon which this orphans' home was founded were such that any bright orphan who had lived in Vermillion county six months might be received and cared for, but no idiots or feeble-minded children find a home here, save in special cases. At first, before the place became too much crowded, old ladies of good character were allowed a home here, but after a few years it was found that childhood and old age did not seem to agree one with the other, and the ladies had to leave the home. The board reserves the right to reject any they see fit, but the worthy and unfortunate orphan here is ever welcome and well cared for. One thing was stipulated in the endowment, and that was that the place should forever be for orphan children and that the name should never be changed. The building is thirty-seven by ninety feet, and the rooms include library, reading rooms, matron's and superintendent's offices and rooms, an overseer's room, etc. Toilet rooms and bath rooms are provided on both floors. An excellent kitchen and butler's room, a nursery department, for boys and girls, a sick room, a basement, with laundry, dry room, vegetable cellar and coal room with a large attic, where is a play house and room

Collett Home, built in Cayuga in 1902, was founded and endowed by John and Josephus Collett to provide a good home for orphans. John S. Grondyke was member of the board for 51 years.

for ten extra beds, completes the rooms of the home. The floors are hard maple and the rooms are finished in hard pine. A large porch extends over the entire frontage of the building, and attractive columns, two feet in diameter, extend from the ground up in front of both stories, which are of the Southern colonial style of architecture. A heating plant and lighting plant provide many conveniences. This institution is a credit to the designers and the kind-hearted men of philanthropy, who made it possible to provide such an excellent home for orphans in Vermillion county. The board of trustees, with the secretary and treasurer, annually provide for the management of the home, which has accomplished much good already. As the years go by the people more and more appreciate this generous gift from two highly honored men who sought the happiness of the weak and parentless children. The orphan, above all others, will ever exclaim "Peace be to the ashes of the two Colletts."

The present secretary of the home is G.W. Wait, of Newport. The author is indebted largely to the editor of the *Hoosier State*, published at Newport, for the above facts concerning this humane institution.

Taken from Parke-Vermillion Counties History, 1913.

TEMPERANCE

The "red-ribbon" movement was introduced here by Tyler Mason, and the "blue-ribbon" organization by George McDonald. Samuel Chambers, known as "Silvertop," a famous temperance organizer, reorganized the blue-ribbon society, and James Dunn, an old-time rouser, reorganized it again.

In February, 1886, a total abstinence society, composed mainly of reformed drunkards, was organized, with Captain W.S. Jewell as President; L.R. Whipple, Vice-President; J.E. Whipple, Secretary; Ben Lang, Treasurer, and David Higgins, Sergeant-at-Arms. From some cause, but no reason, the society was dubbed the "Reformed Roosters."

The "woman's crusade" never struck Eugene, but a Woman's Christian Temperance Union was established here, of which Mrs. Whitlock was president. The organization was effected by Mrs. Dr. Spotswood and Mrs. Johnson, of Perrysville, but it was suffered to go down.

There is no living temperance organization now in Eugene.

Taken from 1888 Vermillion County History

Shelby Cemetery near Big Vermillion River

SHELBY CEMETERY

On a beautiful day, April 5, 1989, I visited the Shelby Cemetery in Eugene Township at the suggestion of Norman Skinner of Perrysville. The cemetery is along the Big Vermillion River. The large marker there says, "Rezin Shelby, born Dec. 22, 1791, died Jan. 24, 1856". Many of the markers in the cemetery bear the last name of Head. Near the cemetery is a fire place still standing and a great deal of rotten wood suggesting that this is the ruins of a structure, possibly a home.

In this vicinity is located the, so called, Shelby Battle Ground where Hamtramck and his men attacked the Indian Village of Osanamon. This is also an area where many Indian Mounds have been located, including the one in which a chief was found buried in a sitting position with five slaves buried in a radiating circle around him. *Photos and info by Leo Reposh Jr., R. 3, Clinton, Ind.*

CAYUGA

Cayuga (or Eugene Station, as it was called many years ago) is at the railroad crossing of the north and south and the east and west lines of railroads in Eugene township (the "Clover Leaf" and the Chicago & Eastern Illinois). The census books for 1910 gave it a population of almost one thousand people. It was at first named Osonimon, after an Indian chief of that name. The place is alive to every worthy business enterprise and its people are a whole-souled class, who seem to live "for the heaven that smiles above them and the good that they can do."

The Cayuga mills were built in 1885 by a company consisting of Samuel K. Todd, Monroe G. Hosford and Eli H. McDaniel. It was a full roller process with a daily capacity of one hundred barrels. It was run by a seventy-horse-power engine. This mill was built in the midst of a wheat field, and was a success from the start.

A Grand Army of the Republic post was organized at Cayuga in 1876, with about twenty-two charter members and later had as high as thirty-five enrolled. The first post commander was William C. Eichelberger.

A Good Templar society was formed here in 1873 and continued until 1884. It had seventy members. The Red Ribbon movement was introduced here by Tyler Mason and the Blue Ribbon movement by George McDonald. In 1886 a total abstinence society was formed, made up largely of reformed drunkards. It was sometimes referred to as the "Reformed Roosters."

The churches of today in Cayuga are the Christian, United Brethren. In Union, the Presbyterian. The lodges are the Masonic, Odd Fellows, Knights of Pythias, Woodmen of the World and Moose.

The town is lighted by an electric plant owned by a Chicago capitalist, while the telephone service is of home capital. The town has great need of water works. The electric light plant here supplies the county

BUSINESS INTERESTS IN 1912

At Cayuga in the winter of 1912-13 the business interests consisted of the following:

Banking–The First National.

General Dealers–Richardson Bros., Burton Dry Goods Company, Dale & Darrow, Van Houtin (E.E. & Son).

Groceries–Galbreath & Schriner, C.M. Guy.

Hardware–Fable & Son, G.L. Watson & Co. (also undertaking and furniture).

Furniture–Thomas A. Sprouts.

Clothing–L.L. Haughn.

Five and Ten Cent Store–John S. Grondyke.

Drugs–Booe & Booe, Daniel Conway.

Farm Implements–J.O. Higgins.

Lumber–James Morgan & Company.

Grain and Coal–Cayuga Milling Company.

Photographs–A.D. Conelly.

Mills–Cayuga Milling Company.

Jewelry–George T. Ritter.

Harness Shop and Shoes–Whittington Bros. (N.T. and W.W.).

Restaurants–Charles P. Miller, A.N. Mendenhall, Charles Gillis.

Hotels–The Higgins and the Cayuga House.

Newspaper–*The Herald.*

Blacksmith Shops–Claire Van Duyn, William P. Brown.

Barber Shops–T.T. Sollers, Daniel Sollers, Milt Laughlin.

Opera House–Frank Lindsley, manager.

Meat Market–Ed. T. McMillen.

Livery–A.L. Clark.

Bakery–Cayuga Baker, James A. Barr, proprietor.

Canning Factory–C.P. Miller, president.

Telephone and Light Companies.

Physicians–Drs. E.A. Flaugher, W.P. & S.C. Darroch, M.R. Pollom.

Dentist—George E. Wier.

There are several small "farmers" coal mines in the neighborhood. There are two brick plants, the Acme and the Cayuga Brick Company.

The canning factory, a home industry, packs corn, peas and tomatoes.

Taken from Parke and Vermillion Counties History, 1913.

Cayuga Merchants-Frank Darroch, Bert Millikin and John Dale in 1914 photograph. Dale and Darroch operated this grocery store in the Masonic Building in Cayuga. In 1920 Darroch bought Dale's part of the store and Dale started his own grocery store and soda fountain next to the Princess Theater in Cayuga. Mr. Darroch and Mr. Dale both died on May 9, 1936.

seat, Newport, with lights, under a ten-year contract.

The postoffice safe was blown up by dynamite at one-thirty o'clock on the morning of April 12, 1890. So heavy was the charge that the safe was blown to fragments. Window glass was broken in the front of residences and business houses. No money was obtained, however, neither any stamps; but the midnight thieves carried away many valuable papers belonging to the postmaster, and also those of Conway & M.W. Coffin, lawyers. No clue was ever had to the parties who blew up the office.

Cayuga–Living in this northern Vermillion County town is done at a slow pace. But many here will tell you there's still enough going on to keep things interesting.

"I worried about the school system when we moved here 10 years ago," said Town Clerk Linda Butts, who gave up teaching high school in Indianapolis to move to Cayuga. "But I'm really favorably impressed with the school system here."

Her children are now seven, nine and 14 years of age. "This town is all they've ever known," she said. "There really is a slower pace in small towns."

C.W. (Will) Engelland, an ISU political science professor, has also taken a liking to Cayuga. In fact, three years ago he bought the *Cayuga News-Herald.*

"As a political scientist I'm interested in government," said Engelland, who plans on retiring from teaching this spring. "The newspaper will be something for me to do."

The college professor plans on beefing up the paper's coverage of local and county government news. He has the qualifications to carry out this task. For years he's headed up ISU's prestigious Taft Institute of government, an organization existing to help teachers teach the processes of government.

Over the years, Engelland has had everyone from township officials to Sen. Birch Bayh talk to his students on government.

His upgraded news coverage won't stop with government. He also plans to devote more news columns to the area's 4-H program. "There are approximately 400 youngsters in 4-H from this county of 12,000 people," said Engelland.

As a teen-ager growing up in Kansas, his dad considered buying their hometown weekly newspaper if one of his sons would run it. Neither of the brothers jumped at the opportunity.

"Now 50 years later I'm in the newspaper business," he said with a chuckle. Engelland dislikes newspapers such as *USA Today* which attempt to cover too much. "There's no way they can serve the smaller communities."

His editor on the newspaper is Martha Mott. "You'd have to call this a farming town," said Mott, who's been writing for the weekly four years. "The people here are real friendly."

R.F. Thompson has owned the local grain elevator since 1944. Built in 1884, the main part of the elevator is the 101-year-old town's oldest downtown business.

"The Cayuga Mikes" Singing Group around the year 1910. L. to R.: Front Row: Leslie Haughn, George Johnson. Second Row: John Dale, unknown, Oscar Aliee, Frank Darroch. Back Row: Milt Laughlin, Otto Jewel and Eli Shelby.

Cayuga Fable Hotel

Thompson Elevator

"The weather has been good for farming this year," said Thompson, "but the farming economy has been terrible." Thompson describes the prevailing economy in gloomy terms. "It's coming to a time almost like the 1930s," said the local businessman whose elevator handles one million bushels of grain annually.

While farming is the town's number one business, a number of local families derive their incomes from the Colonial Brick Company.

"The plant has been here since 1904 but under different names," said Charles Beck, office manager at Colonial, which employs 50 people and distributes bricks in a five-state area.

The bricks are made from gray shale found in the Cayuga area, said Beck. Last year about 500 ceremonial bricks were made for Cayuga's centennial, stamped with information indicating the community's 100th year.

Thirty-year-old Tim Wilson recently took over as president of the town board. Councilmen are Dennis Naylor, Joe Danile, Margolita Rouse and Les Dowers.

Three years ago the town was hit by problems stemming from breakage of water pipes after work on Indiana 63 was started. "It was a disaster," said Butts. The problem was solved by 1.7 miles of new water lines.

Cayuga is known throughout the area for its Pioneer Days festival the first weekend in June. Highlights of the event in recent years has been a historical pageant staged by local talent. Because of the large crowd, it has been moved to North Vermillion High School a mile north of town.

Local youngsters attended Cayuga High School until consolidation closed it in 1964. However the local grade school is still in business with 263 students enrolled kindergarten through sixth grade. Douglas K. Brown has been principal of the school for about a decade.

Otto Albright and his wife Marguerite have been part of the local scene since they came to town in the late 1920s. He taught from 1926 to his 1971 retirement and was principal for many of those years. Mrs. Albright taught for several years during World War II.

Albright started up six-man football at Cayuga in 1940 and recalls the school's best basketball year when they won the sectional. That was in 1929.

Unlike other small communities in the Wabash Valley, Cayuga has managed to maintain its population. The most recent census shows 1,258 people in town. The 1910 population was right around 1,000.

"There are more people here today than years ago," said the retired principal. His wife speaks highly of this community which has been their home for over half a century.

"You can't find friendlier people than what we have here," said Mrs. Albright. "When tragedy strikes, people help each other out. I've never been in a town where people are as kind and friendly."

There are eight churches in town and a

Cayuga's third high school, (built in 1924) now serves as an elementary school

Cayuga's second school built in 1890 was torn down in 1933. Material was used to build Cayuga Town Hall (as a WPA project).

very active Boy Scout troop run by James Beima. There are eight Eagle Scouts in the troop and two more boys will soon go for scouting's highest honor.

The Cayuga Lions Club was revived about a year ago with 24 members, thanks in part to the efforts of Ned Wright. One of the major Lions programs is a Halloween festival which entertained 700 kids last fall.

Wright operates the family ice cream business which employs seven people and puts out about 40 flavors of ice cream and novelties.

Local barber Roger Hazelwood said the downtown business district is a busy area. "There are no empty businesses in the downtown area," he said. And two new businesses have opened within the past six

months – Eric Vandevender's print shop and Chris C's Fashions, run by Mike and Nancy Crowder.

"It's paying the bills," said the 24-year-old Vandevender of his new business.

Purdue University graduate Tim Bell operates the town's drug store located next to Cayuga's only restaurant, the Cracker Barrel. "We like it here," said Bell, who's been here since 1976. "It seems we know about everybody in town now."

Local teacher Barb Erwin said the school plays a vital role in the town's social life. "We have a big fall carnival every year and make close to $2,000 on it," she said.

An article by Dave Delaney, Terre Haute Tribune-Star, August 11, 1985, The Tribune-Star Publishing Co., Inc.

EUGENE

The towns and villages of this township are chiefly Eugene and Cayuga. Of Eugene, it may be stated that it was laid out by S.S. Collett, in 1827, about the "Big Vermillion" mills of James Groenendyke. Samuel W. Malone, who later became a noted hotel keeper there, located at that point in 1827. He was still hale and hearty in 1887. James P. Naylor, father of William L. Naylor, came in the next year. Eugene is but another example of how a railroad may kill or make a town. The Toledo, Chicago & Eastern railroad built its line a little to the south of this village and then started up Cayuga. In 1887 Eugene had a population of about five hundred people. Its present population is placed at four hundred. The following was written of this village nearly thirty years ago: "Two or three conspicuous features strike the stranger who visits the place. One is a most magnificent row of shade trees for a distance of two squares on the west side of the main business street–these are sugar maple. Each tree, with a perfectly symmetrical head, covers an area of forty feet in diameter. In the western part of the village is the most beautiful, perfect large white elm the writer ever saw.

"The ground on which Eugene is situated is just sandy enough to be good for gardening and at the same time prevent mud in rainy season. Wells are sunk only eighteen or twenty feet to find the purest water in a bed of gravel. Several large springs are in the vicinity. The river, especially below the mill dam, affords the best fishing of all points probably within a fifty mile radius. Fish weighing sixty pounds or more are sometimes caught, and German carp, one of the planted fish, weighing eight pounds are occasionally captured.

"The country here is all underlaid with coal. There is one vein of nine feet with only a seam of ten or twelve inches dividing it."

On the bank of the river here was erected by James Groenendyke some time previous to 1824 a water saw and grist-mill, which, with its successors, enjoyed the greatest notoriety of all in Vermillion county. While Mr. Coleman owned it, more than forty years ago, the dam went out, and in 1885 a new mill was erected, it being the third building on the same mill site, two having burned. The 1885 mill was a large roller-process plant, managed by Samuel Bowers.

The first newspaper in this county had its birth and death at Eugene. It was the *News Letter*, by Dr. R.M. Waterman, and it was established in 1837, and breathed its last six months later!

The business interests of this village are not large, in fact the railroads and building up of other towns has cast a settled gloom over all former hopes of greatness. But around this quiet, quaint old country village rests many a fond, almost sacred memory, to the mind of the pioneers' children and grandchildren.

A notice announcing a public auction at the late residence of John Vansant.

Taken from Parke and Vermillion Counties History, 1913.

Eugene–Citizens in this tiny hamlet in northern Vermillion County are proud of their heritage and are willing to work to ensure that future generations appreciate it as well.

This town on the Big Vermillion River was established long before Vermillion County was carved out in 1824. Today, the Methodist Church is the focal point of the community.

In 1859, local people began construction of the huge church. But while the building was being built, most of the citizens working on it were called to fight in the Civil War.

Men left their ladders leaning on the side of the half-built church and joined the Union Army. Their tools and ladders remained untouched for two years. Then other citizens began the task of completing the work.

Joan Axtell, 51, was only 13 years old when she first began taking care of the church. Then she was the janitor. She vividly remembers the two pot-belly stoves used to heat the building.

Three generations of her family still live here. Her father, Joseph Gebhart, was one of the shakers and movers who donated a lot of time and labor for nearly any community service. Gebhart died in December, but the solid cherry communion rail he built in the church sanctuary serves as his memorial.

Every furnishing in the church is a reminder of its people's love for the church. The communion table, an organ, a piano, chimes that are programmed to play at noon and 6 p.m. are all gifts from former church members or their families.

Those who couldn't afford to buy an item made it. The furniture on the alter was made by a former minister's father.

Each item has its own story and every piece is cherished by today's 74 members.

"Just about every one who goes here is related to me one way or another," Axtell said. "If we're not relatives, they're just like family."

Axtell's daughter, Cary, is the nursery

Eugene Covered Bridge built 1873

class Sunday school teacher. Her aunt, Francis Axtell Weir, is another strong supporter of her town. She's employed by two newspapers as a part-time reporter, but spends the majority of her time in community service.

"This town's history is bigger than it is," Weir quipped while looking at the huge pillars outside the church.

During the annual fall Harvest Days Festival, she's inside the community building across from the church serving chicken and noodles to those who attend. It's the only time you'll see a traffic jam in Eugene," she added.

When church funds are low, members get together to raise money. They all pitch in and serve a meal or canvas the area until the money is raised or their needs are met. Last year they raised money for work done on the heating and cooling systems. They set a goal of $5,000 and raised it in a short time, Weir said.

Axtell agreed that people never refuse to help one another or their community. "When we need to, everybody can dig in and really pull together."

Sam Haun and his wife, Elsie, are active church members. He's familiar with every board in the old building. He said the floor support beams are hand hewn white oak beams. The ceiling was once 20 feet tall, but

to conserve energy it was lowered to 15 feet, he said.

Sam was the church custodian for 15 years. When the bell slid off hangers in the belfry, he climbed up into the structure atop the building and made the repairs. Today that bell rings loud and clear.

Numerous repairs have been made over the years to the church. "If it hadn't been for the people who loved the church it would have fallen apart years ago," Weir said. Members donated labor and money for extensive remodeling in 1960, and a basement was added in 1967.

June Grondyke Heidbreder and her husband, Bill, are active in keeping the town's early history alive. June's ancestors were Eugene's founding fathers.

Her great-great-grandfather, John Groenendyke, came here from Terre Haute in 1819. He was a soldier in the Revolutionary War and his wife, Lucretia Rappleye Groenendyke, was the daughter of another soldier.

In the 1830s, June's great-grandfather, James Groenendyke, John's son, started a sawmill and grist mill at the north edge of town on the south bank of the Big Vermillion river. Their name began to change when he dropped a syllable. Later it became Grondyke.

James' sawmill and grist mill started the

town, but pork packing and shipping made it grow.

The town flourished from 1830 through the 1870s. Then it was known as the pork producing capital of the United States. The Big Vermillion river provided the waterway for transporting salted and smoked pork from Eugene to New Orleans, La. From that southern port the preserved pig parts were shipped to Europe.

The pork industry made it necessary for barrel plants and coopers to develop nearby businesses. There were seven coopers shops working at one time to provide the oak barrels used to pack and transport pork, wheat, corn and other items.

The pork was shipped by flatboat from the river to the Wabash and on to New Orleans, La. The boats varied in length from 40 to 120 feet. The pork shipping season was confined to the spring when the river was at its deepest because flatboats set low in the water.

As the town grew, it boasted a woolen mill, brick yard, mercantile, general store, opera house and many saloons. Farmers from 100 miles away drove their hogs to the Eugene Market and purchased a year's worth of supplies and food.

A huge covered bridge constructed in 1873 still spans the Big Vermillion River. Although no longer used, citizens here hope

Grondyke House in Eugene

to raise funds to repair and preserve the bridge because there are only three covered bridges still standing in the county.

On May 2, 1892, citizens voted to incorporate. The incorporated town survived until 1896 when citizens voted to dissolve it. Local legend says that a murder was committed in 1894 and the cost of providing the killer with housing and a trial proved too much for the citizens. Tired of the legal headaches and prisoner expenses, citizens dissolved the corporation.

One of the community's famous landmarks is the Groenendyke Home located on Main Street. It's a stately structure built to resemble a southern mansion. John Samuel Grondyke, a brother of June Heidbreder, owns the home built in 1856. His sister has been the caretaker since World War II when he moved from the area. He now lives in Indianapolis but makes frequent visits to the home where he and June were born.

The Groenendyke family cemetery is about a quarter mile away in a remote wooded field behind a trailer court. Surrounded by huge poplar and black walnut trees, the remains of the town's founder and nearly all of his descendents are buried. John Groenendyke died in 1824 and was the first family member buried there. June and John Samuel's sister, Altheda May Grondyke, is the last family member. She rests near her

mother and father. She died in August 1985.

June and her husband keep the family graveyard mowed. Both enjoy the quiet moments they spend here. "There's a lot of history and reminders of happy moments here," she said while standing near her great-grandfather's monument. This will be her final resting place, too. Tradition and heritage are sacred to her.

Today the streets are quiet. There are only a few businesses in town. The thriving industries moved in the late 1880s when the mode of transportation changed. A railroad was constructed between Terre Haute and Danville, Ill., and the railroad could transport anything year round.

Local merchants, including Groenendyke's, relocated their businesses near the railways.

The town's only restaurant and ice cream parlor is located in the old Eugene Mercantile Building. It's open from April to October.

Dan and Chris Ridgon own the shop, but Helen Maxfield is the chief cook and waitress. Her friendly chatter and winning smile make visitors feel welcome.

South on the main road is J-Mart, a business that appears to be a junk yard. "The J stands for junk," manager Steve Axtell said.

A smile crept slowly over Axtell's face when he explained how his grandfather, Joe Gebhart, started the business. He said it

began as a hobby and then developed into a full-time job.

The huge building and land surrounding it are filled with used tools, farming equipment, bicycles, dishes, and other collectibles. Antique furniture brings citizens from miles around.

"If we don't have it, you don't need it," Steve said. Business is brisk and an Illinois man standing nearby asked Steve if he could make him a black walnut tabletop. "Yeah, I sure can," he said.

Repairing and reproducing wooden furniture parts are Steve's specialties. He enjoys working with fine woods – oak, walnut and cherry. He said his grandpa knew a lot about antiques and nearly everything he sold. "They say every time an old man dies an encyclopedia is buried," he said sadly, "and that's the way it was with grandpa."

Near the edge of town, Otto and Marguerite Albright built their retirement home. She's known as the Eugene Township historian who writes yearly pageants portraying community history. She and Otto have been sweethearts for 58 years.

Both taught school in the county. They came to the community in 1926 after graduating from college in Indianapolis.

Otto attributed their lengthy marriage to good living and the ability of each partner to "give and take." His wife's eyes glimmered and her smile broadened. "That' right," she interjected, "He gives and I take."

Otto soon will be 86 and Marguerite is 81. They are religious people who agree that their upbringing has had a great impact on their lives.

An article by Patricia Pastore, Terre Haute Tribune-Star, July 5, 1987, The Tribune-Star Publishing Co., Inc.

SCHOOLS

CAYUGA SCHOOL
TEACHERS

1887-1895

P.J. Millikin, Elizabeth Lacey, Gould Rheuby, William T. Coffin, R.E. Whitlock, Maggie Hopkins, E.E. Neel, Cora Lacey, R.E. Newland, Blanche Collett, and Olivia Paul.

1895-1910

R.E. Newland, Lewis Stutsman, Lewis Webster, Anna Ford, Elizabeth Lacey, O.B. Zell, Edwin Dodson, Wendell Hall, Thomas Harlan, Mary Conley, Nellie Lewis, Colfax Martin, Charles Marley, John Patrick, John Butler, Mabel Stark, Mrs. E.C. Dodson, A.W. Nolan, Catherine Smeltzey, Emma Buntin, Mrs. Nolan Margery Crabb, Ada Carpenter, Alice Earl, J.H. Colwell, C.A. Wright, Joseph McClellan, Ella Hudson, Delores Brown, Daisy Merriman, Caroline Bell, Georgia Fable, Gertrude Ogg, Elsie Andrews, Pearl Fultz, Ada Clifton, Mary Compton, Vira Stephens, James Day, Edna Kirk, Jessie Harris, Viola Harvey, S.H. Hall, Rose Wood, Norma Pavey, Alice Patterson, A.R. Parker, O.M. Kyle, Carolyn Stuart, Lewis Samuels, Gladys Coffin, and Wilma Shirk.

1910-1924

A.R. Parker, Carl Watson, Lilian Seybold, Allie Heidbreder, Georgia Fable, Gladys Coffin, Wilma Shirk, Viola Harvey, B.E. Goff, Elsa Green, Bertha Grosswege, Nicy Booe, Emma Johnson, W.L. Bass, Mildred Croft, Lola Wilson, Florence Cardiff, H.E. Stahl, R.H. Schoonover, Beatrice Glenn, Oca Underwood, Daisy Dale, Rose Foster, Edna Brown, Ruth Perkins, Lela Mendenhall, Bessie Sanders, Della DePue, E.A. Birden, Zoe Richardson, Minnie Pace, Blanche Chance, Marie Gross, Blanche Williams, P.R. Cromwell, Minnie Skelton, Mrs. H.B. Spencer, H.L. Risley, Mrs. Stahl, Madeline Cromwell, Ethel Wood, R.J. Reece, Clifford Hadley, F.M. Pierson, Marie Hawkins, Gladys Riggs, Helen Ederle, Edith Rock, Ethel Worland, Doyne Fultz, Doris Wilkerson, George Benham, Agnes Hultz, Bertha Baldwin, Eunice Jones, Mary Helen Smith, Mary Chenoweth, Earl Rouch, Lester Laughlin, H. Hendrix, Ethel Haas, Helen Chew, Bartlette Harvey, Carl Betson, John Albright, John Ewbank, H. Hazelrigg, Fay Richardson, and Ada Hathaway.

EUGENE TOWNSHIP TEACHERS
1914

Cayuga - H.E. Stahl, Superintendent, R.H.

Schoonover, Principal, Allie Heidbreder, Assistant Principal, Beatrice Glenn, grades, Oca Underwood, second intermediate, Daisy Dale, first intermediate, Rose Foster and Nicy Booe, second primary, Edna Brown, first primary.

Eugene - P.R. Cromwell, Principal, Paul Weaver, grades five and six, Magdalene Bailey, grades three and four, Lacey Morris, primary.

Portertown - Lela Mendenhall, Doyne Fultz, Beech Flats, Ruth Philpott, ? Whipple, Edgar Johnson, Belva Cuzzort.

MOUNT OLIVE CUMBERLAND PRESBYTERIAN CHURCH

The Mount Olivet Cumberland Presbyterian Church is three and a half miles southwest of Eugene.

Taken from 1888 Vermillion County History

EUGENE PRESBYTERIAN CHURCH

The Eugene Presbyterian Church was first organized in 1826, when the first meetings were held at the house of William Thompson, a log cabin a little west of the depot, on the Big Vermillion. The name at first was the "River and County Vermillion Church," and comprised, April 29, 1826, Asa Palmer, William Thompson, William Wilson, Ann Wilson, William Armour, Ruhama Armour, Eliza Rodman, Hannah Laughlin, Margaret Caldwell, Mary West, Mary Thompson, Lucy Thompson (who afterward became the wife of Samuel Grondyke, Sr.), and Susan Wilson.

The first minister was Rev. James Hummer, and other ministers who have since served have been Revs. Baldridge, Kingsberry, Cozad, Conklin, C.K. Thompson Venable, Crosby, Henry M. Bacon and W.Y. Allen, of Rockville. During Rev. Bacon's time, 1856-'59, the church grew to the number of forty communicants, but from that time to 1866 they were without a regular supply. In 1867 Rev. Allen began preaching for them once a month, and the church has

sustained services until the present date. The present pastor is Rev. T.I. Fyffe, of Roseville, who preaches here every four weeks. The ruling elders have been Asa Palmer, William T. Kelly, David Wills, James Steele, Robert Kelly, A.J. Richardson, R.H. Ellis and Anthony Fable. M. Fable is the only incumbent of that office at present.

The present membership is about fifty. Sunday-school is maintained all the year, with George L. Watson as superintendent.

The second place of meeting was a brick dwelling, and the third is the present neat frame church, 36 x 60 feet, erected in 1859, in partnership with the Methodists, at a cost of $3,000, and economically built. It is located centrally in the village of Eugene.

Taken from 1888 Vermillion County History

I.O.G.T.
EUGENE LODGE

Eugene Lodge, No. 351, I.O.G.T., was organized January 24, 1873, and ran until about 1884, since which time meetings have been suspended. At one time it had as many as seventy members. W.H. Hood was the last elected chief, and H.H. Hosford, lodge deputy. The Good Templars had organized once or twice previously, and "ran down."

Taken from 1888 Vermillion County History

EUGENE POST, G.A.R.

Eugene Post, No. 22, G.A.R., was organized in 1876, with about twenty-two members, afterward increased to thirty-five, but now there are only ten. The first officers were: William C. Eichelberger, Post Commander; E.B. Johnson, Senior Vice-Commander; Thomas Thompson, Junior Vice-Commander; William Johnson, Adjutant; L.R. Whipple, Officer of the Day; John C. Pierce, Chaplain, and Van Buren Armour. Present officers: R.M. Sturms, Post Commander; E.B. Johnson, Vice-Commander; L.R. Whipple, Adjutant; William J. Ladd, Officer of the Day; William Morris, Officer of the Guard; Homer Lunger, Chaplain; Thomas Patrick, Quartermaster; David Cummins, Surgeon.

CHURCHES - 1988

Cayuga Christian Church
Cayuga Church of the Nazarene
Cayuga First Assembly of God Church
Cayuga United Presbyterian Church

Community Holiness Church
Eugene United Methodist Church
Lindsey Chapel

ORGANIZATIONS - 1988

American Legion
Cayuga Boy Scouts
Cayuga Lions Club

Delta Theta Tau
Eastern Star
Masonic Lodge

The Sons of Veterans once organized here and held a few meetings.

Taken from 1888 Vermillion County History

F. & A. M.
EUGENE

A *Masonic* lodge was organized at Eugene in 1847, with forty-six or forty-seven members. Among the first officers were C.M. Comages, Worshipful Master; Harvey Skelton, Senior Warden; Dr. R.M. Waterman, Junior Deacon; George Sears, Secretary; Anthony Fable, Treasurer; Mr. Elsley, Tyler. Mr. Fable is the only one of the original official board who is now living. The membership in the course of time reached sixty in number, comprising men from almost all parts of the county. The lodge, however, ran down about thirty years ago, as other lodges were organized at neighboring points and drew away the membership. Newport, Lodi and Perrysville obtained their nuclei from the Eugene lodge. Harvey Skelton was the last master.

Taken from 1888 Vermillion County History

SOVEREIGNS OF INDUSTRY

Eugene Council, No. 4, Sovereigns of Industry, was organized in August, 1874, but surrendered its charter a few months afterward. It had some thirty-five members. John Grondyke was President, Joseph McClellan, Vice-President, and Jesse Wallace, Secretary. The work of the society was mainly of an intellectual and social nature.

Taken from 1888 Vermillion County History

Eugene Calaboose

SETTING SUN LODGE, I.O.O.F.

Setting Sun Lodge, No. 583, I.O.O.F., was organized April 27, 1881, with seventeen members, and the following officers: William H. Hood, Noble Grand; E.B. Johnson, Vice Grand; H.O. Peters, Treasurer; D.W. Bell, Secretary. The present membership is twenty-seven, and the officers are: D.L. Peters, Noble Grand; James Thomas, Vice Grand; J.T. Higgins, Secretary; D.W. Bell, Treasurer.

Taken from 1888 Vermillion County History

Cayuga Depot built 1894

VERMILLION TOWNSHIP

Vermillion is the central civil township within Vermillion county, both taking their name from the Vermillion river. The county seat, Newport, is within this sub-division of the county, also the little station hamlet of Opedee. The township contains forty-five square miles. In 1880 its population was 2,215; its personal property was then valued at $1,086,000. The census of 1910 gives the population of the township as 1,974, including the town of Newport, which was listed at 748. The total personal and realty assessed valuation of property in the township in 1911 was $1,940,000, that in Newport being $486,395.

PIONEER SETTLEMENT

It is not certain who constituted the first settlers in the township now known as Vermillion. Illy kept records, the lapse of many years, and the little attention paid by former generations to making note of such things, makes it very difficult to establish beyond a doubt just who was really the first to establish a home and residence in the township. But it will suffice, for all practical purposes, to state that the first settlers included these whose names follow:

Richard and Susan (Henderson) Haworth, who, some claim, were the first couple to locate in the township, came in from Tennessee in the autumn of 1820. Mr. Haworth died in 1850, aged fifty-seven years, and his wife died in 1854, also aged fifty-seven years.

In 1821 came Joel Dicken, from Prairie Creek, Kentucky, settling where Newport now stands. His son, Benjamin K., long a resident in the vicinity, was born in 1818 and died about 1886 in either Michigan or Wisconsin.

In 1821 Joseph Eggleston, father of Attorney William Eggleston, came to this township and died after many years residence. John L. Eggleston was born in 1827 and resided in Newport.

In 1822, it is supposed that John Wimsett, of Virginia, located here. Jacob Wimsett, born January 8, 1827, was still a highly respected citizen there in 1887. The same year came in Jacob Custar and located about one mile and a half above Newport. Philemon Thomas came that year and remained until his death in 1860. Nathan Thomas was five years old when brought to this township in 1827.

In 1823 Carter and Catherine Hollingsworth, of North Carolina, came into the township. Mrs. Hollingsworth died in 1880, aged eighty-eight years. Eber Hollingsworth, born in Union county, Indiana, in 1822, was brought to this county the next year. In 1887 he was a well-known, well-to-do farmer and stock trader, two miles west of Newport. Henry Hollingsworth, born in this state in 1830, died in the latter eighties at Newport.

In 1824 Anna, widow of William Henderson, became a resident of this county.

Adam Zener, born in Kentucky in 1803, came to Clark county, Indiana, in 1812, and in 1826 to Vermillion county, where he remained until his death, March 14, 1877; was a member of the Methodist Episcopal church. Either in 1826 or the following year, came Philip W. Osmon, born in Kentucky in 1803. His son Archibald W., born 1829, became a well-known farmer ten miles southwest of Newport. Jabez B., another son, born in 1836 at Newport, was a well-known man in his day.

In 1827 came Richard Potts, who served as sheriff of this county two terms, died in 1875.

Robert Wallace, a native of Virginia, became a resident of Vermillion county and located in this township in 1828, and died at Newport May 27, 1881, aged ninety-one years. He was a man of fine physical appearance and was never sick to exceed a week during his manhood's days. William Wallace, who was born in Ohio in 1817, was about eleven years of age when he was brought to this county. He died in the eighties.

Joshua Nixon, born in Ohio in 1813, came to Newport this year and resided until his death, May 23, 1875, a faithful member of the Methodist Episcopal church.

James Asbury, born in Virginia in 1815, was another settler of about that day; also came about that time, Aaron Jones, from New Jersey, and William Jones, from Union county, Indiana. Samuel Jones, a native of Ohio, came in 1830 to this township, and died in 1881. George Brindley, a native of Kentucky, born in 1800, died in 1878, came here in 1828.

In 1829 came Robert Stokes; also Samuel Davis, of Ohio, born in 1811, was still an active citizen of Newport in 1888.

Among the settlers of this township in 1830 was Jacob Sears, who emigrated from North Carolina, and died in 1859, aged eighty-five years. Thomas J. Brown, a native of Kentucky, born 1801, died in this township. Ross Clark, another settler in 1830, was born in Ohio in 1797, and died here in 1878. William L. Tincher, a settler of 1830, was born in Kentucky in 1814, was living in Montezuma in the eighties. About the same date came in William W. Doss, born in Kentucky in 1817. He moved over to Montezuma. Another 1830 immigrant to the township was Robert S. Norris, from South Carolina, who died in 1877, aged seventy-three years. Other lifelong residents of this township who came in 1830, when children, were Richard and John W. Clearwater, John L. White, James H. Hutson and George Weller.

In 1831 came William Nichols, born in Virginia in 1804, died October 11, 1876. Isaac and Henry Nichols, sons of William, were brought here in an early day, lived here many years, and both died before 1887. Isaac and Mary Carmack, from Tennessee, settled in the Lebanon neighborhood. He died in 1863. Alfred, a son, born in Tennes-

Bill Myers-rural mail carrier-1910 the post office was in rear of Nixon building.

Shaw's Mill 1824-1886 Little Vermillion River

see, January 8, 1814, died May, 1817; and Andrew, another son, settled at Dana, this county. Henry Wiltermood, born in Indiana in 1821. Charles Herbert, from Kentucky; his son, William J., born in 1819, settled and was living in 1886 on section 27 of this township. John Henderson, who came the same year last named for settlement, located on section 7.

The settlement of 1832 included these: H.F. Jackson, born in Ohio in 1798, died in Missouri. John Jackson and wife Lydia, from Ohio; the latter died in December, 1880, aged seventy-four years. Joseph Jackson, from England, died here before 1886. Ezra Clark, born in Ohio, 1811, in his later years resided in Highland. John G. Gibson, born in Ohio in 1819, lived in this township until his death. Julius Bogart, born in Tennessee in 1811, was still residing in the township in 1886. William B. Hall, who died in 1863, aged forty-two years. James A. Elder, born in Brown county, Ohio, died prior to 1886. James Remley, born in Ohio, 1823, committed suicide.

1834–John C. Johnson, born May 16, 1807, in Belmont county, Ohio, married February 24, 1833, Miss Elizabeth Shaver, a lady of superior education, and the next year located in this vicinity, arriving at the mouth of the Little Vermillion river April 8th. Here he entered a small tract of land, built a cabin and began life on what was later known as the "first bottom." In 1854 he built a new house, which he occupied until 1880, when he removed to Newport, where he died in February, 1883, after having reared an exemplary family of sons and daughters. In 1834 came also Benjamin Davis, who died in 1854, at the age of sixty-four years. His wife, whose maiden name was Rusha Sears, died in 1869, aged sixty-two years.

In 1835–John S. Bush, born in this state in 1828, was still living here in 1887, and was totally blind. William Huff, born in Kentucky in 1812, and James Duzan, born in the same state six years later, both resided at Newport in the latter part of the eighties.

1836–David Albridge, born in North Carolina in 1790, and died September 11, 1877, being at the time about the oldest citizen of Vermillion county. He served as a soldier in the war of 1812-14.

1837–Isaac Tropts, long a resident of the township, was nine years old when he came to the county in 1837.

1838–Hiram Hastey, born in Indiana in 1818, was a harness-maker at Newport, where he died. J.F. Weller, merchant at Newport, was born in Kentucky in 1818; finally moved to Petersburg, Indiana.

1839–T.W. Jackson, born in Ohio in 1816, was still residing here in 1887.

1840–Hugh Dallas came into the township some time prior to 1840, from Virginia.

Abel Sexton, who in 1887 was still a prominent citizen of Newport, was a native of New York, born in 1820, and settled in this county in 1843. Other prominent factors in the settlement and development of this township may be recalled the names of Alvah Arrasmith, Thomas G. Arrasmith, wagon maker at Newport, and G.W. Clark; also David Fry, James Kaufman, Leonard Sanders, Daniel E. Jones, who became a wealthy citizen of Chicago and died there; also Major John Gardner and Henry Betson.

Col. William Craig, born in Newport in 1831, graduated at West Point Military School in 1853, having for his class-mates Generals McPherson, Sheridan and Schofield; crossed the western plains in 1854 as lieutenant and aid-de-camp on General Garland's staff; served in the regular army ten years, being one of the best Indian fighters, and greatly admired by Kit Carson and other scouts. He finally died in the Southwest in 1886.

Taken from Parke-Vermillion Counties History, 1913.

POWDER MILL EXPLOSION

May 4, 1904, at noon, the powder mill at Dorner, two miles southeast of Newport, was

Vermillion County Jail—In June, 1828, the Board of Commissioners of Vermillion County let the contract for the erection of the first jail which was to be "16x28 feet ground area, two stories high of hewed timbers with a partition of twelve feet for a debtor's and criminal's room" Samuel Hedges was the contractor and was to receive $369.00 for his work. There has only been one capital punishment in Vermillion County. On April 3rd, 1879 Walter Watson was hung for the murder of Ezra Compton. The present jail built 1870 is located one block east of the Courthouse on East Market and George Street.

blown up, four men being killed and many more injured. The scene of the disaster was in a little hollow leading off from the main hollow which runs east and west. There were at the time four hundred kegs of powder, of twenty-five pounds weight each, amounting to ten thousand pounds of damp blasting powder. Henry Griffin and DeSoto Biggs, two of the unlucky workmen, were blown literally to atoms. The combined weight of the two men was about three hundred pounds and only sixty pounds of scattered fragments of human remains could ever be gathered together. The other two killed were George and Berkley Mayhew, brothers. The woods caught fire from the terrible explosion and it took much hard fighting upon the part of the men present to extinguish the flames before they reached the other side of the hill, where there was stored two hundred and fifty thousand pounds of powder in the magazines of the Dupont powder works. Only two of the fourteen buildings were destroyed. They were never rebuilt. An almost endless litigation ensued for damages upon the part of the deceased men's friends, some of whom compromised and received small amounts from the company. The explosion was heard at Terre Haute and Clinton. John Potts, who was on his father's farm a mile distant, was knocked down by the explosion. Twenty window lights were broken from the county poor asylum; pieces of shafting of six hundred pounds weight were hurled a half mile distant and planted in the earth. A spring never before observed by man was started from out the hill at the glaze; twenty-five copperhead snakes that had not yet come forth

from their winter quarters were stunned and afterward killed by the men who were searching for the bodies of the unfortunate workmen.

Taken from Parke and Vermillion Counties History, 1913.

NEWPORT

Newport, the seat of justice for Vermillion county, Indiana, was platted, or recorded as a "village," July 28, 1828, and re-platted and corrected up for permanent record, March 8, 1837, by S.S. Collett; its location is in section 26, township 17, range 9 west.

The first dry goods store opened here was by Daniel E. Jones, whose entire stock could have easily been carried on a wagon. This business was established in this manner: Jones was shipping hogs, some of which died. These were rendered into soap, which was sold for goods. Later, Mr. Jones became a wealthy man, went to Chicago, where he became a millionaire, and died in that city.

The first good residence in Newport was a building north of where the Methodist Episcopal church was erected. For many years the trees of this town were noted for their beauty and size. A number of locust trees were planted in 1832 and in 1887 had grown to measure over two feet in diameter, while one apple tree had grown to the unusual size of over three feet in diameter.

Newport was incorporated as a town early in the spring of 1870. The records show that the first officers were: William E. Livengood, president of the board; Clark Leavitt, Benjamin K. Dicken and E.Y. Jackson; J.A. Souders, clerk. Other presidents have been:

E.Y. Jackson, James A. Bell, F.M. Bishop, S.H. Dallas, James A. Foland, William P. Henson, Oliver Knight, James Hasty, Robert Landon, Calvin Arrasmith, Robert E. Sears, John W. Cross. Passing down to the present time the officers are: President, I.M. Casebeer; other members of the board, William Ashton, Herbert C. Sawyer and John A. Darby; clerk, Clarence Magers; marshal, Mathew C. Ashcraft; treasurer, Robert A. Wiltermood; William C. Wait, solicitor.

Three attempts have been made to dissolve the incorporation of Newport, but all failed. The last was in 1877, when the question was put to the voters and by a majority of nineteen it was decided to hold the incorporation. The town is still without a system of water works, but is furnished (under a ten-year contract) from Cayuga with a good electric lighting system. The town hall is leased.

Going back many years, the town was noted for its milling interests. An old mill stood on Market street, called the Eureka Mills, run by steam. It was built by James A. Bell, who sold to Curtis & White, who in turn sold to B.J. Abbott, and while in the possession of the latter, January 26, 1882, it was burned, by a careless act of an employee, and was never rebuilt. The loss was estimated at three thousand five hundred dollars.

The chief industry is now the extensive tile works of William Dee, a Chicago capitalist, who has a series of plants for clay-working in this and Parke county. These works run day and night, the year around

On the night of May 5, 1884, the Newport office was robbed of three hundred and fifty dollars, the safe being blown open. The burglars were frightened away by the passing of a young man in the vicinity before they obtained all that they had intended to. These thieves were never captured.

The town is built in a pleasing style, and many good residences are seen here and there. The site is an ideal one, and has a beautiful natural landscape surrounding it. The Chicago & Eastern Illinois railroad runs north and south, through the eastern part of the platting, about one mile from the court house and business section. The business houses are built largely around the four sides of the court house square.

While the saloon business is no longer a great menace to Newport, in times past it was an "eye-sore" to the better element, and many wrangles grew out of the liquor question. The town finally, in 1906, had its last saloon.

The population of Newport in 1912 was 732.

TEMPERANCE MATTERS

Newport has had her own share of trouble over the liquor traffic, and the usual number of crusades and temperance societies and great temperance revivals. This was a vexatious question back before the Civil war period, when whisky was supposed to be better in grade than since Uncle Sam exacted a large revenue. But passing over these early trials, we come down to a time of which many now remember the circumstances and events, in attempting to make Newport a "dry" town. First the then popular Order of Good Templars was set on working basis at the place in 1868, with a traveling Methodist minister, Rev. J.E. Wright, as president, Betsy Griffin, Joseph Hopkins, Benjamin Carter, Ivy A. Astor, Sally Canady, John Wigley, Rebecca Huff and Joseph Cheadle. The lodge has long since been disbanded.

The next movement was the tidal wave of the "Woman's Crusade" in 1874, having its birth in Ohio, and which struck Newport in 1874, with great force. Meetings were held in the churches, speeches made, and a committee appointed to wait upon the two saloon keepers of the county seat, who soon closed their dram shops and signed a pledge not to again open in Newport. The drug firm of William M. and William L. Triplett (father and son) refused to sign the pledge, offering one in its stead allowing them to sell liquor for medicinal, mechanical and sacramental purposes. They were publicly charged, in a set of formal resolutions, with selling liquor at wholesale for drinking purposes, but they denied the charge. The controversy was long and bitter, but they held their ground. Later the father died and the son removed from the community.

In December, 1874, a woman from the country, becoming enraged at her husband's way of spending his time and money in the saloon, made a general scatterment among the inmates of the saloon, which she entered boldly, and as a result her husband was made to walk straight to his home.

In 1877 that great temperance reformer, Francis Murphy, and his blue-ribbon movement came to Newport like a cyclone. More than three hundred men signed the pledge in two nights' time. Again in 1879 came the red-ribbon movement of Tyler Mason, which proved still greater in its effect.

At one time Newport had a very strong Woman's Christian Temperance Union and edited a department in the *Hoosier State*. Leading members were Mrs. Zachariah Thornton, Mrs. Ramsey, Mrs. Ervin Lamb, Mrs. Sears and others whose good work was not in vain. Fifty ladies in all were thus associated at Newport. Perrysville Woman's Christian Temperance Union was also associated with these ladies.

When it comes to county seats, this town of 704 persons is the second smallest in Indiana.

The smallest county seat in the state is Vernon of Jennings County with a population of 329 people, said Brian Long of the Indiana Association of Cities and Towns. But Newport does beat Nashville of Brown County ... but just by one. The official census of Nashville lists 705 residents.

Newport gained Vermillion's county seat distinction – though it is much smaller than the county's largest town, Clinton – because it was founded in 1828. Clinton was founded in 1829, one year too late.

Clinton's population is around 10,000, but it has been unable to wrestle the county seat away from Newport for 157 years.

BUSINESS INTERESTS OF 1912

Attorneys–Hugh H. Conley, W. Bert Conley, Martin G. Rhoads, E.E. Neel, Homer B. Aikman, Charles N. Fultz, William C. Wait, Forest W. Ingram, Herman J. Galloway.
Abstractors–E.E. Neel.
Banks–R.H. Nixon & Co.'s Bank (private), Citizens State Bank.
Barber Shops–John H. Nichols, James W. Thomas.
Blacksmiths–John A. Darby, James C. Garrigus.
Billiards and Pool–White & Nichols.
Clothing and Furnishing Goods–Henry Watson.
Confectionery and Fruits–Louis Coil.
Cement Works–John G. Myers and Searing M. Robbins, of the firm of Robbins & Myers
Coal, Wood and Props–William H. Wiltermood.
Chicago & Eastern Illinois Railway Agent–Ralph B. Hollingsworth.
Citizens Mutual Telephone Company–H.V. Nixon, president; James W. Thomas, secretary; Adva Julian, electrician.
Dry Goods–E.R. Stephens, John T. Simpson, Ordie E. Pritchard.
Dray Line–Ottie White.
Furniture and Undertaking–Sam D. Chipps.
Groceries–E.R. Stephens, Benton Nichols (with bakery), White & Hughes, John T. Simpson.
Grain–William M. Prillaman.
Garage–"Newport Hill Garage," H.T. Payne and Ralph V. Hughes, proprietors; Byron Hamblen, mechanician.
Harness–L.J. Place & Son.
Hotel–"The Hart," by Robert A. Hart.
Hardware and Implements–L.J. Place & Son, Maurice Hegarty.
Jeweler–Levi P. Bever.
Lumber–Greer-Wilkinson Lumber Company.
Livery–L.J. Place.
Music–Zachariah T. Galloway.
Millinery–Alice M. Nichols.
Meat Market–J.S. McCormick.
Newspaper–*The Hoosier State*, S.B. Davis & Son, publishers, Bird H. Davis, editor.
Physicians–Drs. I.M. Casebeer, M.L. Hall.
Restaurants–Elmer Bush, Wiltermood Bros. (R.A. and George).
Shetland Pony Farm–L.J. Place.
Saw-mill–Charles T. Evans.
Shoe Repair and Custom Work–John D. Brown.
The B.A.W. Gasoline Light Manufacturing Company–Benjamin A. Wiltermood.
Transfer Line–Andrew J. Wise.
Tile Works–William E. Dee Clay Works.
Theater–"Idle Hour Moving Pictures"–Elbert S. Nichols.
Taken from Parke and Vermillion Counties History, 1913.

Pony Farm located Northwest of Newport owned by L.J. Place

When lightning destroyed the county courthouse in Newport on May 27, 1923, Clintonians looked at the bolt out of the blue as something of a Godsend – here was their chance to finally draw the courthouse away from the much smaller community to the north.

In what has been referred to as the big tradeoff, the county's first hospital was built in Clinton then. In exchange, Newport retained Vermillion's county seat.

Besides being the county seat, Newport also has a big festival attraction, the annual Newport Hill Climb. The climb takes place the first weekend of every October, drawing maybe 100,000 spectators from about the Midwest.

Generally a big-name entertainer is on hand to entertain the multitude. Stars from the past have been Crystal Gayle, Ernest Tubb and Lee Greenwood. Greenwood – male country singer of the year the past two years – was grand marshal of last year's parade.

Connie Pearman directs the parade committee. Pearman said last year's parade had 13 entries and drew a crowd of approximately 10,000 people.

Sponsored by the Newport Lions Club, the festival includes competition in 23 classes of antique cars built before World War II. Generally about 300 people take part in the competition.

The hill has a place in history. It was used as a proving grounds for the horseless carriages around the turn of the century. The races began in 1909.

Some of the racers have been famous. "The Chevrolet brothers ran the hill in 1914 and in 1915," Pearman said. Fritz Duesenberg was another who drove a car bearing his name up the hill.

Pearman believes the festival has the largest flea market in Indiana. "We had 125 booths last year," she said.

Diann Stewart knows all about the hill climb. Her house is on the top of the famous hill right near the finish line. Her business, the Woodworking Shop, is on the town square by the starting line.

"The town shuts down during hill climb weekend," Stewart said.

The Newport town square is a classic example of a small town concentrating all its businesses on the square. Everyone shops at West's Grocery store and gets their mail at the post office, where Dorothy Rusk is postmaster.

The town's two attorneys are Mark Greenwell and Malcolm Aukerman. Because this is a county seat community, there are two abstract offices. One is run by Olga Hutson, the other by Mary Swayze.

The town's lone eatery is appropriately called the Hill Climb Restaurant. You can wet your whistle at three taverns – the Newport, the Lone Star and the American Legion.

Nick Swayze runs the Marathon filling station, the town's only gas station, and the Citizen's State Bank has branches in both Clinton and Cayuga. You can wash your car at the Speed Wash, and buy flowers and plants at Collins Greenhouse.

There are six beauty shops where local ladies get dolled up. They're run by Nelle Norman, Vicki Rawls, Debbie Axtel, Ramona Trover, Ruth Ann Harrison and Mona Morrison. Morrison runs Mona's Etc. Etc. shop, which has an extra service for customers – a tanning salon.

James Fortner is president of the Newport town board. William Louis is vice president, and other board members are Louis Stein Jr. and Michael Hall. Anabelle Robertson is town clerk-treasurer.

Vermillion County Courthouse 1868-1923

All that remained after courthouse fire in Newport in 1923

Robertson said the town drilled a new well and installed a new water treatment plant in 1978.

Robertson said Newport needs considerable street repair work. Money's the hindrance. She said $10,000 worth of work was done on town streets last year, but that there won't be anywhere near that much money for this year.

Billy Joe Brown is the only full-time municipal employee, Robertson said. "He takes care of the streets and the water works," she said. It was Brown at the wheel of the lone, blade-equipped town truck clearing snow from Newport streets this winter.

The Lions built the only town park, located near the elementary school. It has shelters, picnic tables, basketball courts and playground equipment.

The Lions maintain their club on the town square and are building an attractive wooden community shelter on the square. Their club is headquarters for all hill climb activities.

Robertson said Newport is without industry and that many residents work in either Terre Haute or Danville, Ill.

Cable television has come to Newport, with the first hookups made just before Christmas. "We get 12 stations and Home Box Office," Robertson said.

The town's library is on the first floor of the courthouse. Librarian Elaine Ramsey said the library also has branch locations in Dana, St. Bernice, Hillsdale and Cayuga.

Teen-age students in Newport attended North Vermillion Junior-Senior High School where 480 students are enrolled in grades seven through 12. Roberta Dinsmore is superintendent at the school built in 1964. William Kilgore is high school principal. An extensive addition was made in the mid-70s.

The community has its own school, Newport Elementary School, housing students in kindergarten through sixth grade.

"We're very proud of our school and feel fortunate to have it," said principal John Buck who said there are 118 students enrolled this year.

The building is also used for many community activities each year. "Our gym is used for the Grand Ole Opry during hill climb weekend," Buck said.

And Monday night for supper the school will offer an appreciation bean dinner from 5-6:30. "It's our way of showing appreciation for the cooperation the community has given us during the year," Buck said.

Buck said there's been a rumor that the town may lose its elementary school. "I think the community would really fight that," the principal said.

Pearman is part of a group forming a committee to have a veterans monument erected on the west side of the town square.

"Lee Greenwood has agreed to do a benefit show in this area," said Pearman. The monument would honor the nation's war dead in every war.

She believes Vermillion County has more Vietnam era veterans than any other county in Indiana. She said the Veterans of Foreign

Newport Basketball Team 1909 L. to R. Groves Barker, Benton Nichols, Ernest Dixon, Charles Swayne, Vic Guilliams, Clay Sager and Otis Turner

Newport's third school was built on Market Street in 1899. Torn down 1970

Newport's fourth school was built in 1924 across the street from the third school house. Now used as an elementary school of North Vermillion High School.

Newport Academy 1852-1897-Newport's second school.

Wars, American Legion and Lion Clubs will be some of the groups promoting the monument.

An article by Dave Delaney, The Terre Haute Tribune-Star, March 3, 1985, Tribune-Star Publishing Co., Inc.

This town, the Vermillion County Seat, was a thriving community until two events occurred – a bridge across the Wabash River collapsed on the east side of town and 7,000 acres of prime farm land on its western border was purchased by the government and removed from the Vermillion Township tax rolls.

The three-span iron bridge was constructed in 1906 and an ice gorge caused one span to topple in 1936. The town's grain elevator that serviced many Parke County farmers was devastated by the incident. Every business in the community suffered.

Vermillion County's commissioners refused to have the span rebuilt because Parke County taxpayers didn't help pay for the original structure.

Today the community has no eastern exit route since it's bounded by the Wabash River. Residents may cross into Parke County by driving to Indiana 274 near

Cayuga to the single lane bridge at Lodi or head south to U.S. 36 then east over the Montezuma bridge.

When the Army bought 6,990 acres of prime farm land in the early 1940s and established the Wabash River Ordinance Plan, now the Newport Army Ammunition Plant, it crippled growth in this township by removing a huge chunk of the taxable acreage, numerous houses, barns and outbuildings. The largest tax base in Vermillion Township had been eliminated with a swift stroke of the pen. These two events were paramount to the decline of business and population here. Many natives believe the county courthouse, located here, kept this community from becoming a ghost town.

Mary Bell Ingram Swayze, a life-long resident, enjoys the slower pace of this quiet town. She's been in the abstract business here for more than 50 years. Her expertise concerning the history of the land ownership is unequalled. All 700 current village inhabitants know her.

Swayze quietly goes about her business collecting information for the numerous abstracts she completes monthly. These small booklets contain a short history of a specific plot of land known as the chain of title. If

there's a defect in ownership or a question concerning who holds title to the property, it is revealed to the lawyer who examines the abstract before the property is sold.

The abstractor visits with nearly every county officeholder daily as she makes her rounds gathering information used in her business from offices of the recorder, auditor, treasurer, clerk and assessor. Her establishment is located on the north side of the square in a building that once served as her husband's barber shop.

Farmers who owned land purchased by the government paid taxes and shopped in Newport, Swayze said. When they were gone, businesses began to fail. The plant workers weren't local men and they didn't make roots here. They spent their money elsewhere on weekends, she said.

"They took the major portion of this township out of taxation. The contractors who had equipment at the plant site didn't pay taxes on that equipment because it was on government property."

Roy Ingram, Swayze's father, was a bailiff at the courthouse. She practically grew up in that building. He was born in Newport, as was her grandfather. The town's only gas station and vehicle service shop is owned by her son, Nick Swayze. His mechanical abilities are in constant demand.

Her husband died when Nick was five years old. She was tempted to leave the area but decided the young boy would have a better opportunity in a small town where he wouldn't be confronted with problems found in a big city.

The Hoosier State Newspaper, a Newport publication, was purchased in 1934 by Donald Collings of Parke County. It carried four pages of local news and the county's public notices.

Collings knew practically nothing about typesetting and printing, so he hired Clair VanSant of Cayuga to assist him.

VanSant moved to Newport and still lives in a two-story brick home formerly owned by his wife's grandparents.

The former reporter said he agreed to work for Collings but only if he'd purchase a new Line-o-type machine. Collings editorials were well written and brought responses from citizens who lived more than 100 miles away, he said. "He was a brilliant man."

The paper was successful and the pair worked as a team until Collings became ill in 1941 and sold the business to George L. Carey, publisher and owner of the Daily Clintonian.

A year later, VanSant left the paper and went to work at the ammunition plant.

After VanSant left, the paper was printed in Clinton but a business office was kept in Newport. The last edition of the old paper was printed in July 1960.

VanSant and his wife, Freda Guilliams VanSant, like the small town where they raised four children. Both agree that the loss of the Wabash River Bridge ruined the growth of the town. "It was a Saturday night town and people came from all over. There were a lot of businesses and three banks then."

VanSant's favorite report was a story he wrote after interviewing Dana's famous World War II War correspondent, Ernie Pyle. He said Pyle had just come home from South Africa. "I never saw him again after that. He never got back from the South Pacific."

VanSant's love for the newspaper business carried over to the next generation. His son, Richard VanSant, is the UPI bureau chief in Cincinnati, Ohio, and his son's wife, Janet Walsh, works as a reporter for the Cincinnati Post.

VanSant's wife is the pianist at the Methodist Church.

When Indiana 63, which was Newport's main street, was moved outside of town, it separated the community from the mainstream of traffic. That further isolated the tiny hamlet.

VanSant and Swayze agree that the annual Newport Antique Auto Hill Climb is the focal point of the community. It's sponsored by the local Lions Club, but nearly every citizen contributes.

VanSant, whose left hand and leg were paralyzed by a stroke in 1979, prints advertising posters for the three-day activity each October and donates them to the Lions. During rehabilitation he learned to put a heavy metal brace on his left leg without help and ties his shoes with his right hand.

The famed Newport hill, which is 2,300 feet long and 140 feet high, is still a challenge to old car owners. Both VanSant and Swayze recalled days when the occupants of vehicles pushed the cars up the hill or if the

Tony Hulman (far right in car) at Newport Hill Climb.

L. to R. Sexton Jones, Melvin Bugg, Vernon Craft, Clifford Barr, Lewis Thomas, David Barr.

gravity flow gas tank wasn't full, drivers backed their cars up the hill.

The hill still challenges more than 200 vehicles to race each year. It's not uncommon for a car to blow an engine attempting to dash up the steep grade.

During the festival, piles of sand and gravel are placed along both sides of the hill so drivers can steer their vehicles into them if they encounter a brake or engine problem.

Former Vermillion County Clerk Josephine Hawkins Lewis and her husband, Charles "Sparkie" Lewis, bought two acres of land near the hill climb finish line. There he cares for a matched team of ponies and an Arabian horse. His newest acquisition is a six-month-old, 75-pound pup named Sam.

Lewis is well known in Vermillion county. She worked in the courthouse 33 years, from 1951 to 1984, when she retired. She and her husband lived in town then.

Her first visit to the courthouse was during a high school history class field trip. She said a teacher brought the entire class there to listen to a trial. "It was a big deal to go to the courthouse. I never thought I'd be working there."

Don Stokes, the clerk, needed help in his office. He knew Lewis through an acquaintance with her father. "I was 26 when he asked me to come to work for him."

She worked with his wife, Babe Stokes, as well as Herbert Donald. Those days mostly men held political positions, she said.

Later, when Lewis decided to run for the office, she knew that without help from Clinton politicians she couldn't get elected.

"If you're not well known and aren't from Clinton you have trouble," she said, adding that about 53 percent of the county's population lives in Clinton Township.

James Gallagher, then the circuit judge, helped her in the southern part of the county.

The Lewis's favorite event is the hill climb. During the festivities they put lawn chairs at the edge of the road and watch the races. The drivers stop their vehicles near their property and often visit with them.

Vera Aston, who claims to be the oldest native, recently moved home after a 43 year absence. The 78-year-old former civil service worker began government service here as a selective service clerk. Then she transferred to Internal Revenue Service, Civil Aeronautics, Ft. Benjamin Harrison Finance Center in Indianapolis, the Small Business Administration and transferred to Washington D.C. where she moved into a position at the Bureau of Mines.

Her next move up the ladder was a transfer to the Bureau of Indian Affairs before ending her career with the U.S. Export and Import Bank. "It's an experience I wouldn't have missed." She retired in 1972.

As a youngster, Aston worked in the Vermillion County Library in the courthouse and in one of the three grocery stores located around the square. Each Friday and Saturday she weighed and sacked flour and sugar in 5 and 10 pound quantities. She said all the merchants had to make preparations for the Saturday night business.

Aston said the community has undergone tremendous changes in the past 40 years. "We had hardware stores, groceries, furniture stores, drugs stores, a mill, a doctor's office and a dentist," she said, probing deep in her memory. "I remember when the melon farmers from Parke County would drive their wagons across the bridge. You could hear them calling 'Watermelon, watermelon!' as they drove through the streets."

Through the years, Aston kept in close contact with her local friends. Now she can visit Freda VanSant and even view her friend's home from a front window. "It's good to be home, but I see a lot of people I don't recognize," she said.

An article by Patricia Pastore, Terre Haute Tribune-Star, February 21, 1988, Tribune-Star Publishing Co., Inc.

VERMILLION COUNTY HOME

The Vermillion County Home is no longer in operation. It is in ruins, with the roof gone and the upstairs floor gone. The land was owned by Peter Smith who owed the county money and was unable to pay so the land reverted to the county. The 1913 Parke and Vermillion County History Book does not give dates for these events until 1886. By then it had been the county home for some time and the buildings had deteriorated. In 1887, Vermillion County decided to erect the new building that is now in ruins. They called it an infirmary. It cost almost $16,000, had thirty-two rooms, and was actually completed in 1888. In 1887, the average number of patients at the home was twenty. At one time in 1912, there were twenty-six males and fourteen females at the institution. It was a farm, so agriculture actually was carried on with the patients who were able to work doing some of the farm work. Most of the patients were ill or handicapped and this functioned as a nursing home.

The home was discontinued in the mid-1960's and the patients were moved to private nursing homes.

O.P.D.

The above are the initials of one of the most prominent citizens of Vermillion County; namely, Oliver P. Davis, and have also become the name of the 1,300 acre farm which he owns three to four miles below Newport, and of the railroad station at that point, when it is generally spelled Opedee.

Hon. O.P. Davis was born in New Hampshire in 1814; learned the art of paper making; came to Indiana in 1838, traveling by coach, steamboat, canal and horseback through the States of New York, Ohio, Michigan and the province of Canada. In New York he rode behind the first locomotive built in that State, then running out of Albany. At Toronto, Canada, he was employed in a book bindery and mill, doing the work more rapidly and efficiently than any of the native hands. In Ohio he fell in with a jolly dentist, of whom he began to learn the art of dentistry, afterward practicing his new trade at Fort Wayne. After residing at Logansport and Delphi, this State, for a time he went to Greencastle and commenced the study of law in the office of Edward W. McGoughey, read two years, and then in 1840, moved to this county and began the practice of his profession, continuing for five years. Since then he has been a tradesman and agriculturist. At first he purchased forty acres, to which he has since made additions until he has 1,300 acres of rich Wabash bottom, whereon he sometimes raises immense crops of corn, occasionally 50,000 bushels or more, and sometimes, by flood or frost, he also loses immense crops. The sediment deposited by the Wabash floods keeps the soil very rich. During the year of the famine in Ireland, Mr. Davis took to New Orleans by flat-boat 25,000 bushels of corn, some of which he bought at 18 cents a bushel, and sold it at 45 cents to $1 per bushel. He is said to have sold in one season $18,000 worth of corn raised by his own hands.

Mr. Davis is familiar with legislation, being a member of the Constitutional Convention of 1850, a member of the General Assembly three terms, a delegate to various important conventions, etc. In his politics he has been a Democrat, Republican, National, etc., and in his religion he is a "free-thinker." He is a man of firm principles and a high sense of justice.

Taken from 1888 Vermillion County History

QUAKER

One of the earliest settlements in Vermillion Township was the Quaker community on the western edge of the county in a romantic setting along Jonathan Creek.

Richard and Susanna (Henderson) Haworth and Jonathan Haworth, a cousin of Richard Haworth, emigrated from Clinton County, Ohio, in the fall of 1820 and settled in Vermillion County before the state line was located between Indiana and Illinois. Richard Haworth supposed the Wabash River would be the line and settled in what he thought was Illinois. Later, when the line was run, it passed through his farm, leaving his house and about one-third of the farm on the Indiana side. The nearest neighbors were sixteen miles distant. Two years later Richard Henderson and son Isaac Henderson came from Ohio. Then Mercer Brown from Georgia, Levi Ellis in 1836, and William B. Walthall in 1842. As more and more settlers came it was evident many were Quakers, or members of the Society of Friends, and the settlement came to be known as Quaker Point. Also three trails intersected there and these later became three roads. On September 7, 1888, the post office was established and it was renamed Quaker Hill; and in 1894 renamed simply Quaker. The neighboring community of Dana was platted in 1875 and outgrew Quaker. In February 28, 1914, the Quaker post office was discontinued. But for more than fifty years, this was a thriving community with a post office, two stores, a blacksmith shop, a lodge hall, a barbershop, school, railroad depot and grain elevator, several fine residences and the Hopewell Friends Church just up the hill to the north.

Day schools were held in the church building until township schools were organized. In 1885 the Quaker school pictured here was built by Thomas Walthall and Jeff Nichols with James Chipps as Trustee. Helen Saunders King was the last teacher and the school building was finally dismantled in 1941.

Early physicians of this community included Dr. Joseph C. Cooke of the Willow Brook Farm, father of Bert Cooke. He lived here thirty years, died in 1875 and his funeral was attended by probably a thousand people. Other physicians were John Gilmore, Hiram and Lewis Shephard, P.H. Swaim, who later practiced in Ridgefarm, Illinois. Dr. Brown came from Humrick, Illinois, until 1910, and Dr. Lindsey Saunders had an office in his home in 1911, later moving to Newport.

In 1905 Bertram Kuhn of Terre Haute

Vermillion County Poor Farm ruins.

Vermillion County Poor Farm ruins.

Quaker Store-North side of road known as Brenner's Store

Quaker School #10

leased land where an elevator was built along the Walsh Road. Later the Milwaukee Railroad built that year down the western side of the county. Running on this line was a one-car passenger train called the Doodle Bug that made daily trips from Terre Haute to Quaker. There was also a Telegraph Operator in a building on the west side of the railroad. In 1970 the railroad was abandoned, but the elevator is still in operation and is locally owned.

Although only an elevator and church and a number of homes remain in Quaker today, a "new" log house built recently on Jonathan Creek by James and Helen Ellis Johnson reminds one that for some this is even today a romantic setting in which to live!

STUMPTOWN

If you are traveling north on State Road 71 out of Dana about four and one-half miles you will go around a curve, to the east you will see a red barn on your left bearing the name "Stumptown". Yes, this was and still is Stumptown. It is found near the center of Section 4, Township 16 North, Range 10 West.

The story goes that so many white oak trees were cut for lumber, barrel staves, and other uses off the grove, it left the ground well spotted with stumps. So it got the name of Stumptown.

In 1888 one acre was purchased from Jonas Fortner on the south side of the east-west road by township trustee, Samuel Davis, who was also the publisher of the Hoosier State paper.

A one-room frame school house was built that year. It was named Stumptown School or School No. 15. Another room was added a year or two later.

In 1898 a one-room United Brethren Church was built just east of the school house. The church was later bought and moved down the hill south on the east side of the road, and used for a barn.

In 1900 Annuel Sykes bought two acres on the north side of the east-west road. He built the house that is presently there. He also built a store building 20 by 40 ft. with

an upper story for a Woodman's Lodge Hall just east of the house.

A postoffice was also added in the store. The post office department picked the name "Galatin" for the post office name. In 1903 Annuel Sykes gave up the post office. No one else wanted to take it over as it didn't bring in any revenue so the name Galatin was forgotten.

Also in 1900 Annuel Sykes built a blacksmith shop nearby. In those days there were several blacksmith shops and small grocery stores over the country. No one got very far from home then with their horse and buggy.

In 1904 George and Elias Sykes built a store south of the school house. They also built a house and blacksmith shop near where the Don Beck house now stands. They ran this store until 1913.

In 1906 the frame school house burned. A new cement block, two-room school house was put up in its place.

In 1925 a new high school was built in Newport and opened in the fall.

The children of families living in the Newport district were transferred there in the fall. School continued a few more years at Stumptown, then all were transferred to Newport. The next few years it was used as a community building. A few Farm Bureau meetings were held there, and I recall two or three revival meetings being held there.

From then until 1942, the school sat there alone, forgotten, except for the well in the northwest corner of the school yard. A pump was kept in the well and a cup hanging by a wire was kept there for anyone passing wanting a drink.

In 1905 Annuel Sykes sold all the 42 acres he owned to William Ditto. In 1916 William Ditto sold it to Allen Myers. After about two years, Allen Myers sold it to Henry L. Lindley. In the fall of 1920, Henry L. Lindley sold to Wilbert Downs who kept

Stumptown School-Big Room-1924-1925-Teacher, W.B. Gosnell. Row 1: Claudie Hollingsworth, Vernon Hollingsworth, Lawrence Jones, Owen Downs. Row 2: Blanche Frazier Downs, Coy Jones Martin, Phyllis Brown, Sarah Keen, Wilma Brown, Frances Downs, Lucille Hollingsworth Jones, Lucile Downs, Mary Wilfong. Row 3: Mr. Gosnell, Laura Bell Wilfong, Mildred Wilfong, Louise Keen, Irene Jones.

Greasy Creek School (No. 14) 1894. (Small Creek near school had traces of oil in it) Teacher-B.S. Bothwell. Bonnie and Bess Bothwell (two girls bottom right), Jimmie Caldwell (first boy in back row), Ed Wise (tallest boy in back row), Carrie Nichol (third person in third row), Ralph Carmack (third boy in second row), John Carmack (fourth boy in first row). Photo compliments of Clair VanSant

it his lifetime. In 1971, his widow, Iva Downs, deeded it to her son, Owen Downs. In 1983 Owen Downs deeded the two acres on the southwest corner of the 42 acres to his grandson, Rick Downs. This included the original house built by Annuel Sykes in 1900. The house was remodeled and a garage was added on the east side a short way from the house. Rick, his wife, Rexi, and a son Micheal, live there. Owen Downs deeded a seven acre strip of groveland on the southeast corner of the 42 acres to another grandson, Bob Ellis, in 1984. Bob, his wife, Carol Sue, and daughter Carly, built a new home and live there.

State Road 71 was built coming from the south and curving to the right, going east toward Newport. This isolated the school house in a corner of its own.

In 1942 when the Wabash Ordinance plant was being built, Stumptown was in the area taken over by the government. The school house and remaining buildings on the south side of the east-west road were destroyed.

A new generation now makes up Stumptown and its community. The old Stumptown is only memories.

Submitted by Owen and Blanche Downs and Lucille Jones.

SCHOOLS

Newport has always had a good school. According to the provisions of the State law, a county seminary was established here in pioneer times, and flourished until the later free-school system converted it into a graded school about 1852. The building was of brick. To it additions have been made, and it is still occupied. The location is on the bluff, overlooking the broad and romantic valley of the Little Vermillion River. The new portion, comprising two rooms was added by the town of Newport, at a cost of about $1,000, and, the municipality having bought the township's interest in the institution, all partnership between the two civil divisions was dissolved last year, 1886. The building now has four rooms, and correspondingly a full board of teachers comprises a principal and three assistants. The departments are the high school, grammar, intermediate and primary. The enrollment last year was 156. The principal for the year 1887-'88 is Edward Aikman. The school has

two literally societies,–the Philadelphians and the Sapphonians.

Taken from 1888 Vermillion County History

NEWPORT TEACHERS

Fall of 1948: Twelve teachers are on the faculty of the Newport school this year. They are Grades 5 and 6, Principal Dewitt Corn; grades 4 and 5, Esther Moore; grades 2 and 3, Mrs. Edwin Allen; grades 1 and 2, Leona Pollard; High School principal and commerce, John G. Pickell; Math and Latin, Omar McMasters; English, Rachel Milligan; H.S. Physical Ed. and Science, W.L. Milam; Music and English, Winifred Dempsey; Industrial Arts and P.E., John W. Parks; Vocational Home Ec., Elizabeth H. Simpson, and Social Studies, Oscar I. Kersey.

VERMILLION TOWNSHIP TEACHERS

First Vermillion Township Trustee was in 1860.

Newport Seminary School owned by the county known as Vermillion Academy — John R. Stahl taught there from 1880-1882. Flora Hasty was also a teacher.

Myrtle Bales taught at Premium School #3 from 1892-1894, Harlan School #4 in 1895-1896.

W.B. Gosnell taught many years in Vermillion Township.

Mary Lucy Campbell taught many years at Newport School.

Elsie Spurgeon taught in 1910-1911 at O.P.D. School.

Edgar Stahl taught at Thomas School in 1912-1913.

John R. Stahl taught at Newport Seminary 1880-1882.

Mary Howard taught in 1877-1878 in the Newport Seminary.

C.M. Parks was also a teacher in the Newport Seminary.

Mary Canady also was a teacher in the Newport Seminary 1879-1880.

Ed Aikman taught from 1886-1889 at the Newport Town School.

Lizzy Lowry taught in 1905-1906 at the Newport Seminary. She also taught at Newlin School #13.

United Brethren Church Newport

The United Brethren Church at Newport was organized in 1870, by Rev. Samuel Garrigus, who was then a resident of Bellmore, Parke County, but is now at Crawfordsville, this State. The society at first comprised but twelve or fourteen members, but it has increased to ninety, principally under the labors of the present pastor, Rev. B.F. Dungan, within the last few months. The first class-leader was C.M. Parkes; the present class-leader is Rettie R. Smith; assistant class-leader, Mrs. Belle Thornton. These ladies have a very large field of spiritual work, compared with class-leaders generally. A lively Sunday-school of about seventy pupils is maintained throughout the year, superintended by Mrs. Thornton. The steward of the church at this point is Z.P. Thornton. The society at present worships in the Presbyterian church, on Market street, one block east of the public square, but they contemplate building a house of worship this year. A pleasant house is rented for a parsonage in the west part of the village.

Taken from 1888 Vermillion County History

Presbyterian Church Newport

The Presbyterians organized a church here many years ago, ran down and reorganized in the spring of 1875, by Rev. Mitchell, of Clinton, with only seven members. The ruling elders were M.G. Rhoads and I.B. Fussehman, now of Danville, Illinois. Mr. Rhoads and his wife are the only members now, and there is no regular preaching. The church building, a frame about 40x50 feet, on Market street a little east of the public square, was erected probably about forty years ago, soon after the first organization was effected, and is now occupied by the United Brethren. There has never been a resident pastor at Newport. Among the ear-

lier pastors were Rev. J. Hawks, of Perrysville, some thirty years ago, who died about ten years afterward; Rev. Henry Bacon, now of Toledo, Ohio, then of Covington, Indiana; after a vacancy, Rev. Mitchell preached once a month for a part of a year, 1875-'76.

Taken from 1888 Vermillion County History

Opedee Church United Brethren

Opedee Church, United Brethren, organized about 1880, has increased in membership from eight to sixteen. No class-leader at present. Steward, Miss Ella Wimsett. A good Sunday-school has recently been established, of which E.D. Brown is superintendent. Meetings are held in a school-house.

Ira Mater, of Hillsdale, is a local preacher of this denomination.

A few United Brethren are meeting at the Eggleston school-house, preparatory to organization. They have a Sunday-school, of which Mr. Dixon is superintendent.

Rev. B.F. Dungan, of Newport, is pastor of all the United Brethren churches in Vermillion Township.

Taken from 1888 Vermillion County History

Lebanon Methodist Episcopal Church

The Lebanon Methodist Episcopal Church, east of Quaker Hill, was organized in pioneer days. The present membership is about thirty. Class-leader, Robert Holliday; stewards, R.P. Little, J.L. Thomas, Frank Carmack and Samuel R. White. Pastor, Rev. R.S. Martin, of Newport. The church building, a frame, 30 x 36 feet in dimensions, was built over thirty years ago. Sunday-school is maintained all the year, with an average attendance of fifty pupils and superintended by Miss Ella Little.

Taken from 1888 Vermillion County History

Bethel Church United Brethren

Bethel Church, United Brethren, two miles southwest of Newport, was organized many years ago. Present number of mem-

bers, forty-seven or forty-eight. Class-leader, Levi Brindley; steward, Thomas White. No Sunday-school at present. The house of worship, about 28 x 36 feet in ground area, was built twenty-four or twenty-five years ago.

Taken from 1888 Vermillion County History

Vermillion Chapel Methodist Episcopal Church

Vermillion Chapel, Methodist Episcopal Church, three and a half miles south and a little west of Newport, has a membership of about twenty. Class-leader, W.P. Carmack; steward, Allen Clearwaters; Pastor, Rev. R.S. Martin, of Newport. The Sunday-school was recently organized. The old church building, erected about forty years ago, has recently been sold, to give place to a fine brick church, costing $1,500 or $1,800.

Taken from 1888 Vermillion County History

Vermillion Lodge, I.O.O.F.

Vermillion Lodge, No. 594, I.O.O.F., was organized in the room over the furniture store of David Hopkins, by Past Grand Hiram Shepard, of Dana Lodge, under a charter granted May 18, 1882, on the petition of Robert E. Stephens, Lewis Shepard, Thomas Cushman, F.V. Wade, Julius Groves and J.M. Taylor. The following members were elected officers and duly installed: Lewis Shepard, Noble Grand; Robert E. Stephens, Vice-Grand; Thomas Cushman, Secretary; J.M. Taylor, Treasurer. At the time of this organization there were thirteen members. There are now thirty-seven members, and the present officers are, M.G. Rhoades, Noble Grand; H.A. Conley, Vice-Grand; Matthew Lytle, Recording Secretary; Thomas Cushman, Permanent Secretary; W.P. Henderson, Treasurer. The society is now in a very prosperous condition. The furniture, equipments and regalia cost about $600, and the room is an unusually nice one, 38 x 50 feet in dimensions, exclusive of the vestibules.

Taken from 1888 Vermillion County History

Churches - 1988

Church of God
Friends Church
Hopewell Friends Church

Mission No. 11
Newport United Methodist Church

Organizations - 1988

American Legion
Newport Lions Club

Newport Masonic Lodge
Vermillion Homemaker's Club

SHILOH POST, G.A.R.

Shiloh Post, No. 49, G.A.R., was organized March 22, 1882, with R.J. Hasty, Post Commander; J.H. Kerdolff, Senior Vice-Commander; J.A. Darby, Junior Vice-Commander; R.H. Nixon, Surgeon; Z. Thornton, Chaplain; A.C. Brokaw, Officer of the Day; T.A. McKnight, Officer of the Guard; who were duly installed by Mustering Officer R.B. Sears. The appointed officers were J.W. Harlan, Adjutant; J.C. Bailey, Quartermaster Sergeant; William C. Myers, Sergeant-Major. The officers comprised the whole membership. The post has not been meeting lately, but the present officers are Edward Brown, Post Commander; R.H. White, Junior Vice-Commander; John A. Darby, Officer of the Day; John Richardson, Quartermaster; William Bennett, Surgeon; H.H. Conley, Chaplain; C.S. Davis, Adjutant; W.P. Henson, Sergeant-Major; J.C. Dillow, Quartermaster-Sergeant. There are about thirty members in good standing. The time of meeting is every second and fourth Friday evening of the month, in Place's Hall.

Taken from 1888 Vermillion County History

NEWPORT CORNET BAND

The Newport Cornet Band was organized a number of years ago, went down, and reorganized, or a new organization effected. John A. Darby and J.W. Hartman are the only present members who were members of the original organization. The present members are, John A. Darby and Quincy Myers, E flat; Ernest Darby and Albert Wheeler, B flat; J.W. Hartman, solo alto; William Sharp, second alto; W.C. Arrasmith and Joseph Hopkins, B flat tenor; L.M. Wheeler, B flat baritone; Fred Duzan, E flat tuba; William Brown, snare drum; Henry Garrett, base drum. This accommodating band "discourses sweet music" every Sunday afternoon at the court-house. The players are skillful, and have often rendered satisfactory service on public occasions.

Taken from 1888 Vermillion County History

A.O.U.W.

The A.O.U.W. organized a lodge at Newport March 4, 1879, with a membership of sixteen, and Dr. M.L. Hall as Past Master Workman; R.B. Sears, Master Workman; W.P. Henson, Grand Foreman; Joseph Dillow, Overseer; C.S. Davis, Recorder; George W. Odell, Financier; L.J. Place, Receiver; L.D. Dillow, Guard; Henry Dillow, Inside Warden; Lon Coil, Outside Warden. The charter was surrendered February 24, 1883. At one time they had as many as twenty-five or thirty members.

Taken from 1888 Vermillion County History

NEWPORT LIGHT GUARDS

The Newport Light Guards were organized under the military law of the State, with over forty members, and J.A. Souders, Captain. They obtained from the State an equipment of fifty guns and the necessary

4-H Club-1925

accoutrements. But in a year or two they got to quarreling over the captaincy, some favoring J.A. Souders, but a majority R.H. Nixon, and consequently let their interest in the drill die.

Taken from 1888 Vermillion County History

HOPE LODGE, REBEKAH

Hope Lodge, No. 268, Daughters of Rebekah, was chartered November 18, 1886, and the first officers elected January 22, 1887, with ten members. Thomas Cushman, Noble Grand; Mrs. D.S. Hopkins, Vice-Grand; Mrs. Dessie Johnson, Secretary; Mrs. Mary Henson, Treasurer. The membership is now (June, 1887) thirteen, who are zealous, with a good exchequer. They comprise the best talent in the community.

Taken from 1888 Vermillion County History

SONS OF VETERANS

A company of *Sons of Veterans* was organized March 20, 1884, with Frank Hasty for Captain. Commencing with ten members, they reached sixteen, but they soon lost their zeal, holding their last meeting December 19, 1884. They contemplate reorganizing. Their last Captain was William F. Thornton.

Taken from 1888 Vermillion County History

Oll Potter, Vermillion County Sheriff, on right, and Angelo Tasso, on left.

HELT TOWNSHIP

Helt township is the second from the southern line of Vermillion county and extends from the Wabash river west to the state line of Indiana and Illinois.

It contains seventy-two square miles, twelve square miles more than any other township in Vermillion County. The principal industry throughout its history has been farming, but is now the home of one of the largest industries in the county, that of Eli Lilly!

Three distinct soil regions are located across the township. Alluvial soils, or river bottoms, clay and black loam.

In the forming of the township, many schools dotted the small neighborhoods, but now there is only one modern grade school, that bearing the name of Ernie Pyle, with grades kindergarten through sixth grade.

The township, as well as Helt's Prairie received its name, when the vote was taken among the early settlers. The family of John Helt, being the largest of membership won the vote!

Much of the land was purchased from the government in 40 acre tracts for $1.25 an acre. This meant that a family could settle if they could raise $50.00! Today this doesn't seem like much money, but then it was a large amount, and many of the men enlisted in battle so they could purchase land for their families!

The towns and villages of Helt township are quite numerous, but none, aside from Dana and St. Bernice, are of any considerable size.

The towns and villages are as follows: Toronto (Bono), Jonestown (now St. Bernice), Hillsdale, Highland, Dana and Summit Grove.

WILLIAM HENRY SKIDMORE

Helt's Prairie Cemetery is the final resting place of the first white male child born in Helt township. William Henry Skidmore was born February 19, 1819, to John and Polly Hopper Skidmore. William was born with but one hand, his left hand and one-third of that arm being gone. Yet, in spite of this handicap and being reared amid the wild surroundings of pioneer life, he was able to chop trees, and do other work required in the clearing and making of a farm as well as anyone.

During his early days, he frequently hauled corn to the Wabash River, which he

William Henry Skidmore

sold for ten cents a bushel and had often taken apples to Chicago. He was married twice, taking for his first wife, Elizabeth Pearman. Three children were born to this union, two of which are known; Thomas J. and Sarah J. After Elizabeth's death, he then married a widow, Mrs. Amelia Anderson Helt. To this union six children were born: William, Henry, George F., Mary, Jasper and Caroline. Amelia had two children by her first marriage, Mrs. Serena Depuy and Mrs. Clarinda Garner.

Mr. Skidmore filled many of the official trusts of his township and county and twice represented the county in the state legislature in the years 1866-1870. While holding the office of constable, he was called to assist in arresting a man, and in so doing, he was shot in the right arm below the elbow. He carried the bullet received there in his arm to the grave.

William was a consistent Christian and an active worker in the Methodist Church. As a boy, he would walk over the settlement and tell the people of the near approach of some religious meeting. He died in May, 1881, in the triumphant hope of a blessed immortality! *Submitted by Patricia Heskett Crum*

CATHERINE (KATIE) HELT

The second white child and the first female born in Vermillion County was the third child of seven, born to Michael Helt

and Elizabeth Aye Helt. She was Catherine (Katie) Helt and was born on March 23, 1819, and died as a maiden lady on April 16, 1888. Her brothers and sisters were: John Helt, Celina Helt (who married Henry Mitchell), Catherine, Charles Baker Helt (My great-grandfather and who married Sarah Taylor), Nancy Helt, (who didn't marry), Hiram Helt (who married Mary Langston, a daughter of John Skidmore and her first husband was John Milton Langston), and Irene Ann Helt (who died at less than two years of age). Her father was born on January 22, 1788, in Pennsylvania and died August 6, 1864. On August 31, 1815, he married Elizabeth Aye of Maryland, who was the daughter of Jacob Aye (of German and English descent) and she was born on August 11, 1788, and died September 13, 1867. He was a veteran of the War of 1812. *Submitted by Patricia J. Frist, taken from the "Helt Family Tree" compiled by Frank R. Miller*

HELT'S PRAIRIE CEMETERY

Why the location of Helt's Prairie Cemetery was chosen where it is today, is not certain. The land containing the old part of the cemetery was donated by the James' family, descendants of the Rev. William James. Perhaps because it was a hill not suitable for farming, and then one thinks of the scripture: "I lift up my eyes unto the hills, from whence cometh my help—", and perhaps there wasn't much time to make a decision, as not long after the first settlers arrived, an orphan boy had made his home with John Helt, and helping to erect the log barn, when part of the frame gave way, and killed him, this being just 1817!

As one walks through the cemetery, the huge native rocks, one coming from the bed of Norton Creek, pay honor to the first settlers, who put their trust in God and came to a new home, laying the foundation for our future today, and then to all those who served their country in time of war and peace that our future would stay intact.

Tradition has it that the grave site of Antoinette Stover in Helt's Prairie Cemetery, is that of the grandmother of the 34th. President of the United States, Dwight David Eisenhower.

While in office as President, it is reported that he flew to Indianapolis and came by car to visit the grave site.

Antoinette Stover resided in Carter County, Tenn., and came to Indiana, Vermillion County, to visit her daughter and son-in-law James C. and Margaret Dugger, who shortly after the civil war had come to the Tennessee Valley to live, and at this time had a baby girl, Daisy, who later became Mrs. Daisy Randall.

In caring for the baby, Mrs. Stover and her daughter, Margaret, both came down the the "grippe" (flu), hence both of the women died, and therefore Mrs. Stover was buried here.

Helt's Prairie Cemetery

Daisy was cared for by Miss Flora Houghland, who later married Ulysses M. Helt, the parents of Joe Helt. Mrs. Stover was born August 10, 1810 and died January 7, 1884.

During the early years of the Cemetery, the graves were dug by neighbors. Around the middle of the 1800's, the first board was formed. The first actual caretaker of Helt's Prairie Cemetery was Mr. Abby Frist, who served twenty-two years, buried over 300 people, dug the graves by hand and hauled the dirt in a wheel-barrow! God rest his soul!

The outside stone wall was erected over seventy years ago, by some neighborhood men, some being White and Wright James, Joseph James, Alonza Mack and Sam Houghland and others.

Not every where is there a country cemetery that can take one through the pages of time from the death of a President's grandmother, the first white child born in the county, the lives of early preachers, to the only execution in the county—just Helt's Prairie!

In Christ, there is no Death, just Eternal Life! by Patricia (Patti) Crum

ARCHAEOLOGY

Helt Township has contributed an interesting share to the science of archaeology. In the summer of 1884, a number of workmen, while digging gravel in the mound just east of William Bales' place, brought to light the skeletons of more than half a dozen of the aborigines. Various relics were found, consisting of bone and stone. There was no metallic tool of any sort in the grave. Under the skull of the first skeleton found,—undoubtedly the chief or sachem of the tribe,—was perhaps half a bushel of arrow-heads. A pipe was found, the bowl of which was perfectly hollowed. It was made of a hard species of soapstone. Was it his calumet of peace? Two pieces of what one would suppose to be a fish-spear, made from the antler of a deer, was procured from the heap of arrow-heads, together with the jaw-bones of a dog and several beaver teeth. One spear-

head, six inches long, the middle portion of which was gone, had barbs, about an inch apart, on one side only. The absence of firearms indicates that these remains have been lying here since a period prior to the advent of the white man.

Taken from 1888 Vermillion County History

FOX DRIVE

March 31, 1883, occurred the first "fox drive" ever held in Vermillion County. The citizens placed themselves, according to advertised programme, in a kind of circle around a large section of territory, mostly in Helt Township. They started forward at 9:30 A.M. All the marshals exercised due diligence to keep the men in proper shape, none of whom were allowed to be intoxicated or to have a dog or gun. The east and north divisions, having to travel over a very broken section of the country, and some of the men also disobeying orders, permitted eight foxes to escape. At half past 11 o'clock men and boys could be seen in every direction, about 800 strong, approaching the center; and it was also observed at this moment, that three red foxes were surrounded. Forming into a ring about forty yards in diameter on the meadow near the Conley schoolhouse, three of the most active young men entered the ring to capture the game by their unassisted hands. One fox, which was crippled in trying to pass out, was soon caught; but the other two were chased for some time, when finally one of them broke the line where some women were standing and got away. The remaining one, after being chased for some time by different ones, was finally caught by Fred Ford.

William Darnell was called for, who at auction sold the two foxes to the highest bidder, Richard Wimsett, of Opeedee. Every one present enjoyed the sport.

It could plainly be seen that many important improvements could be made in the plan and execution of the "drive," and accordingly the next spring, March 15, 1884, they tried it again, on a larger scale, without catching a single fox. The conclusion was

that there were no foxes on the ground to be caught; but some say the territory was too large. It comprised a portion of Helt and Vermillion Townships.

Taken from 1888 Vermillion County History

OLD BONO

I was asked by a friend to write a story about Old Bono.

Well in 1875, 66 years ago to be exact, my father, the late Henry Barnhart, moved from Hickory Grove, Illinois to Bono. At that time there were lots of people in and around Bono. There were Daniel Tillotson's family, Reuben Puffers, French Kerns, Dr. Eaton's, Frank Austin's, Elias, Pritchard's, "Uncle" Johnny Jenks, his brother "Uncle" Tilly and son Stephen and family, Marcus Haskell's, John R. Wishard's, Uncle Jimmy Andrews, Mr. Bilsland, Uncle Johnny Mash, stepfather of the late Mont Aikman, and brothers, Uncle Sammy Aikman, father of the late Levi Aikman, and grandfather of our good friends, Burch Aikman and sister, Mrs. Dewey Kerns, and Evan Thompson and family.

At one time Bono, boasted of a church, dry goods store, grocery store, post office, cheese factory, blacksmith shop, one room school house and shoe shop. Now only the old church, one grocery store and a few scattered neighbors remain.

Mr. Austin's grocery store, is the old building by the public well in Bono. The dry goods store was just across the road from the grocery store, in the corner of what is now the Roscoe Martin place, but at that time it was the Elias Pritchard place. The store was owned and operated by the Taylor brothers, John and Wint. When Dana was started they moved to Dana and started the first dry goods store there. Elias Pritchard took over the Bono store for a few years and when he moved to Newport, Elijah Conley operated the store for awhile, then moved to Clinton. Then John Rusmisel bought the store building and moved it to his farm south of Bono and made a dwelling house out of it. The house still stands and is occupied by Merle Wright and wife.

The post office was in the front end of Mr. Austin's grocery store, and was called the Toronto Post Office, there being another Bono in Indiana. The mail was carried from Clinton to Bono then on to Jonestown, once a week, for a time, by a man driving two horses to a spring wagon. Later it came three times a week, until Dana built a post office, then the old Toronto post office was abandoned.

At one time the church was four churches in one. Rev. McMasters being the Baptist minister, Rev. Griffith of Montezuma, was the Presbyterian minister and Uncle Johnny Mast was the United Brethren minister. I can't recall who was the Methodist minister when we first came to Bono. I can remember when Rev. Johnson was minister and such revivals as we had in those days. People came for miles in their sleighs and sleds with sleigh bells jingling. Such crowds of people and such singing, shouting and praying. They didn't need Evangelists, choirs or all kinds of musical instruments. Dr. Eaton would just get up in front with his tuning fork, and get the right pitch then he would lead in singing and everybody sang. They had some wonderful singers in those days. I'll just make mention of a few: Mrs. Levi Aikman, Lute Mack, his brother Will and wife and Dr. Eaton. I always loved to hear the old church bell. My father usually kindled the fires for revivals and how he could ring that old bell, so loud and long. I love to hear the old bell yet, but it doesn't sound like it used to.

There also was a band in Bono. Aaron Hire was the leader, then others in the band were: the Wishard brothers, Sam Malone, Ike Jordan, John Ayres, and Will and Jim Mack, uncles of Carlton Mack. I don't think this is all the band boys, but it has been so long ago, I have forgotten. Some of these would drop out and others take their places, and after a while it disbanded.

Then there was the G.A.R. Post. They held their meetings the last Saturday afternoon of each month, upstairs over Mr. Austin's store. There was a stairway on the outside of the store building leading to the upstairs.

Dr. Keyes was the leading doctor in those early days. The weather was never too bad or a patient too far away, but what he would go anytime, day or night, usually on horseback. On his last trip, returning home, he was taken suddenly ill, near the home of Mr. Austin, and was taken in there where he soon passed away. He was the father of the late Dr. Otis Keyes and grandfather of Miss Dortha Clark of Dana. Dr. Shepherd took over Dr. Keyes practice for a while and later Dr. Eaton was our Bono doctor.

And last but not least was the old one room school building. French Kearns was my first teacher, and I sure thought him a great teacher. There were four rows of seats, two on each side, and the seats were only large enough for one pupil to sit in. There were long benches along the sides of the room, close to the walls and these were where the large pupils sat. Later they discarded all these and got new seats large enough for two pupils to sit in one seat. I don't remember whether they taught beyond the eighth grade or not, but I do know there were quite a few grown pupils. Stewart Wishard and sisters, Clem and Sib, as we called them, Nate Carter, Oscar Gibson, Addie Aikman and brother Lem, Wilbur Eaton, Belle Fringer, Ed, Sam, Mont and Scott Aikman. All these went when they were grown. I remember when I couldn't get my lessons, I would slip over and sit by Addie Aikman and she would help me with my lessons. I thought she was wonderful. My school mates at different times were: Ella Pritchard, Leila Kearns, Mayme Eaton, Jennie Meriwether, her brother Johnny, Dewey Kerns, Bert Thompson, Nora Palmer, Ona Austin, Frank Smith, Burch Aikman and his sister Doll Mollie Mast, Alma Jenks and my brother Lige, not all in my classes,

Bono High School-1906 Row 1: Clec Lewis, Russell Robinson, Walter Eaton, Adrian Foncannon, Heber Helt, Stimson Ruesmisel, Edgar Stahl, Paul Westbrook, Dan Randall, Frank Stratton, Roy Dicken. Row 2: Edith Richards, Verna Igo, Dena Jenks, Hazel Hooker, Avis Ford, Margaret Jones, Edna Staats, Hazel Crane, Lillian Randall, Minerva Payton, Jessie Boren, Julia Ford. Row 3: Teacher Ida E. Steallings, Ruth Boling, Mary Gosnell, Lenora Newton, Elsie Spurgeon, Nettie Boling, Iva Boren, Mabel Porter, Grace McDowell, Cecile Boren, Eunice McDowell, Nettie Spurgeon, Emma Jackson, Leatha Houchin, Bertha Hale, Principal John Stahl. Row 4: Forest Aikman, Dewey Porter, Elsie Hooker, Teacher Jessica James, Esther Westbrook, Opal Brown, Iva Malone, Ruth Westbrook, Paul Thomas, Ordie Hickman. Row 5: Homer Ingram, Paul James, Billy Bales, Harry Hooker.

Bono Teachers-1924 Front: (l. to r.) Paul Connell, Norma Fillenger, E.E. Helt Back: Doris Beaman, Chloe James, unknown, Margaret Beard, Meredith Goforth, Lois Payton.

but we were playmates and some were classmates.

One time we were practicing for a Literary at the old school house, and all at once such a bright light outside, we thought the house was on fire, but when we got out, we found it to be a big meteor down low. The big ball of fire was a large as a big tub. It went south a little ways and fell on the French Kearns farm, and such an explosion. We were all so excited, we couldn't practice any more so went home. Next day many people went to see it. The greater part of it sank in the ground several feet, but there were fragments of the metal scattered around, and people gathered up those for souvenirs.

Well those good old people have passed

on, and most of their children are gone, too. Just a very few of us remain to tell the story of those wonderful times. There are grandchildren, great-grandchildren and great-great-grandchildren, who are left to carry on, but they can never realize how wonderful their ancestors were or what a grand old place Bono used to be.

Friends, if I have made mistakes just remember 66 years is a long time ago to try to think back. *Written by Ollie Barnhart Hickman in 1941.*

TORONTO

This is the name of an old postoffice at the village called Bono in the southwestern part of this township. The village was started in 1848, by Tilly Jenks and a few more, and at a time when the site was covered with a thick growth of timber and underbrush. The first store was established by James Bacon, between 1850 and 1860. In the spring of 1863, Edward English established a grocery store, selling out in August of the same year to Francis M. Austin, who as late as 1887 was running at that point a good-sized general store. John F. Hays was also in trade there at that time. While the place was never laid out or platted, it had most of the elements of a village proper, save the organization formality. In 1885 it had a population of about eighty persons, with one physician, three churches (Presbyterian, Baptist and Methodist), one church building, a school house, blacksmith shop and a post of the Grand Army of the Republic. The present population is only about seventy-five. The postoffice was established here in 1871, with Francis M. Austin as postmaster, and he held the office many years. Bono was a postoffice established before Toronto was, and it was located a mile and a half to the north, and was discontinued on account of there being another by the same name in Indiana.

Taken from Parke and Vermillion Counties History, 1913.

CENTER NEIGHBORHOOD

In the early 1800's several families settled in South Central Helt Township in an area of about 4 square miles. This area became known as Center Neighborhood. Names of some of the families settled there were Botner, Bright, Church, Crane, Farrington, Ford, Heber, Hedges, Helt, Miller, Myers, Stokesbury, White, Wishard, and others the author cannot recall. Descendants of the Botner, Crane, Heber, Helt and Myers families still reside in the area.

As the neighborhood grew, these families found themselves in need of a school for their children. A log school was erected to serve the children of the community by a wide path in the woods near the center of the neighborhood. The school soon became known as Frog College. The legend about how the school became so known goes like this:

A farmer named White lived about a mile East of the school along Norton Creek. One night his cows escaped their pen and wandered off. Mr. White sent his farm hand in search of the missing cattle. The farm hand found the animals in the school yard, which was surrounded by ponds. Many frogs were singing on the ponds that particular night. When the farm hand arrived back at the farm with the cows, Mr. White asked him where he had found them. His reply was "Over by Frog College." The name seemed to fit and the school was thereafter known as Frog College.

The original log school was replaced by a second building which carried on the name Frog College and was located about one

Center Methodist Church

mile North and 1/4 mile West of the first. In 1894 a third Frog College building replaced the second. It was a two-room brick structure and was located about 1/4 mile West of the second building. Frog College provided the children of the neighborhood with an eighth-grade education and served the community until approximately 1928. People from the neighborhood often bragged that they had graduated from college because of their Frog College education.

Center Methodist Church was founded in the neighborhood in 1853. Services were held in a barn while the building was being erected. Center Church was located one mile South of the present Ernie Pyle school on Jonestown Road and 1/2 mile West of the Frog College School of that time. The original building was moved off the site and replaced by a second church building in 1896. Center United Methodist served the community until the late 1960's when it

consolidated with Fairview United Methodist Church and Centenary United Methodist Church to form the present Wayside United Methodist Church. The Center church building was purchased by Ernest E. and Inez Heber Myers of that neighborhood soon after the consolidation and was remodeled into a home, where Ernie and Inez presently reside.

MY GRANDPA

Actually, he wasn't a famous personage but he certainly was well-known for a number of years to the many people for whom he built and repaired day in and day out.

I imagine there are still many homes around the area that he either built new or remodeled, in later years with the help of his two sons, my dad, Eaton Myers, and my uncle Ernest Myers. They too have left their mark on the community, although my dad is

Frog College School front: (l. to r.) Florence Campbell, Kit Crane, Ray Heber, Bob Church, Fred Church, John Lawfland, Milt Crane. Back: Willett Boren, Nolan, Mary Miller, Mitchell, Miss Wellman (teacher), Nora Ford, Eunice Church, Lawrence Heber.

gone, my uncle still has his workshop in which he makes many beautiful things from wood. He is a true craftsman. But, this is really my grandpa's story.

I've often heard it said by modern day psychologists that this one or that one is a victim of circumstances. He really didn't have a chance. He was deprived as a youngster, etc. When Grandpa was about 10 or 11 years old, the oldest of six boys, his mother Laura Crane Myers, and his little brother, Charlie, both died of "lung fever."

The baby of the family, Uncle Frank Myers, was six months old. My great-grandmother Ford, who had a nursing baby herself at the time, took Uncle Frank for awhile and nursed and cared for him. She was not a relative, just a neighbor who cared, for that is the way people survived back then. She was my mother's grandmother. My great-grandfather, Sam Myers, had left my grandpa and his brothers Omer, Fred and Jim, to care for.

The mother and her small son were buried on Christmas Day in the year 1887. It was the first funeral that young "Jap" Frist had as he was just starting his own undertaking business. I've heard it told that it was so muddy that his hearse couldn't make it from Center neighborhood, where the family lived, to Helt's Prairie Cemetery where they were to be buried beside another little boy who had died two years earlier.

My grandpa's uncle, Billy Bright, had a team and a spring wagon for one casket and another neighbor, who later became my grandpa's father-in-law, my great-grandfather Eaton, had a team of matched blacks and a wagon for the other.

My dad always said that that must have a bleak Christmas for the family, for after burying his wife and child, my great-grandfather Sam Myers came back to his sister's home, the Bright home, where their mother lay at the point of death. The four Bright children, Doll, Ethel, Fern, and Dan were later to lose their mother, too, and my grandpa always talked of how the two families of cousins grew up together, all without a mother.

I can't begin to imagine how they managed to all grow up into the solid responsible citizens they all became. Great-grandfather Sam had a bachelor brother, Henry Myers, who was very miserly and hung on to every penny tenaciously and by the time he died, was considered to be well-to-do by the standards of those days. One old gentleman who had known them well once made the remark that he admired Sam much more than Henry for Sam had raised five boys while Henry had lived only for himself and had only money to show for it.!

When Grandpa was grown he married Anna Eaton and they had the two sons I have already mentioned. When my dad was 10 years old and my uncle only six years, their mother died. My grandpa never remarried but he raised his sons. At one time there was a fine lady who, having no children of her own, greatly admired by dad as a little boy and begged to be allowed to adopt him. She would have raised him as her own, educated him, and having some land and means would have made him her heir. Grandpa refused as he had promised my grandma on her death bed to always keep the boys with him and never separate them.

Among several of the major building projects to his credit was the Vermillion County Hospital. It was constructed by his cousin Dan Bright, who, I'm sure will be remembered by many as a building contractor of some repute. My grandpa worked with him and helped to build the hospital. I've heard him say many times that he and Homer Ritchey, my mother's great-uncle by marriage, mixed every bit of the mortar for the First Methodist Church of Clinton.

He helped build the bank of Dana and I can't begin to recall all the houses around the area he built or helped to build. He had his own workshop, first in the barn where we lived with him when I was a child, just a few miles northwest of Clinton where the old strip-mine pits are now.

In my mind's eye, I can see that old "shop" now. What a haven on a rainy or cold blustery day. In the winter an old heating stove kept it warm and cozy. A gasoline engine ran his power tools with a frightening noise. There were piles of sawdust and curls of wood shavings and all sizes and shapes of small blocks and pieces of wood from which a little girl could make doll furniture to her heart's content. Grandpa never complained about the nails I wasted or the tools I misplaced and never, ever, did he fail to have time, no matter how busy, to make some project for me that I just had to have right away.

He always made me something or other for Christmas and my little girl now plays with the doll house and the miniature kitchen cabinet that he made for me as well as the table and chairs, doll cradle, etc. that he made for my oldest daughter. Whatever I wanted, I always knew that Grandpa would find time to make it. From the vanity dresser and the book-case before I was married; to the kitchen cabinet and table he made for our wedding gift. When my husband and I decided to remodel the old house we now live in, that was originally built in 1828, my grandpa was in the height of his glory. He was in his seventies by then but he tore out and built back and enjoyed every minute of the labor he performed on our old house. He made all new windows and doors, for as could be expected, the doors and windows were all odd sizes that did not conform to modern day standards.

For a number of years, I was the only grandchild so naturally he lavished all his affection and attention on me but when my uncle's three children came along in later years, he loved each one them every bit as much. He adored our first three children and played games on his hands and knees with them. He had them down for visits to his home in Fairview, which they thoroughly enjoyed. He would even come to our home to babysit for us and stayed overnight with us occasionally.

He had a workshop in Fairview, too, where he enjoyed the luxury of electricity for the first time to operate his power tools. His tools were mostly of his own design and making and daddy and Uncle Ernie always said that no one else could work in his shop until they learned their way around. He did cabinet making, saw-filing, and he made inumerable storm doors and windows and screen doors and windows. He made showcases and display tables for local businessmen. Anytime someone needed something unusual made or an odd-size specification, or something made out of nothing, my grandpa was their man! He met each new challenge with zest and enthusiasm.

He continued to be active and work at small jobs until his late eighties. Then his eyesight began to go and his hearing was very poor, also. He died November 24, 1971, exactly one month before he would have been 95 years old. Our family had always gotten together on Christmas Eve to celebrate both Christmas and grandpa's birthday. One time, at Center Sunday School, the primary teacher asked my small cousin whose birthday we celebrate at Christmas time. Without hesitation he said, "Grandpa Myers"!

Surely many will remember him for the things he built that have served so long and so well for so many, and I remember him for all the things he did for me. The stories he read to me when no one else had the time, the times he was tired from working all day but swung me in my rope swing on the big old cotton-wood tree in our yard, anyway, and the "just quiet" times when I was little when I would sit on his lap in an old rocking chair and watch the flames dance in the fireplace he had also built. He asked me teasingly many times, "What are you gonna do when you get too big to sit on Grandpa's lap?" I couldn't even contemplate such a catastrophe!

Wouldn't the world be a wonderful place if every child could have a Grandpa Myers like mine was? *Mrs. Leigh (Barbara) Mack*
An article in The Daily Clintonian, June, 1976.

DANA

Dana was founded in 1874 and named for the then editor of the New York Sun, Charles Dana who was a stock holder in the railroad. The town was located on 80 acres donated by Samuel and John Aikman and Samuel Kaufman. A $1500 donation by the above named men was used to build Dana's first depot. Dana was situated on the Indianapolis, Decatur and Springfield Railroad that was completed in 1873. Later this railroad was known as the B. & O. and today it is the C.S.X. Transportation route.

Prior to 1874 a few cabins had been constructed on lots now in the town of Dana. Records are sketchy up until the time Dana became incorporated in 1886, but by that time houses and business places were being erected.

According to the Biographical and Historical Record of 1888 "Dana is the most rapidly growing town in Vermillion County, comprising a shrewd and enterprising class of business men and surrounded by an unusually good agricultural district".

The first newspaper the Dana News was started in 1885 by M.L. Griffiths. The last Dana News was printed on August 29, 1968 ending 83 years of publication under twelve (12) editors and six (6) name changes. Bound copies of old Dana News from the late 1920's through 1968 are at the Dana Branch Library.

Dana has been governed by a Town Board since its incorporation and seems to have been satisfactory to most Dana residents. The 1988 Town Board Members are Wm. Hooper-President, Arthur Bonwell, Harry Fortner, Philip Myers, Ernest Payton, Anita Bishop-Clerk Treasurer, Lawrence Keller-Town Marshall and Robert Umbarger-Street and Water Superintendent.

In the 1890's Lowry Park, located where Hollingsworth Lime Service is now located south of Highway 36 was known for its horse racing, picnics, outings and ball games. One Dana old timer classified those days as "Regular Jubilee Times". In 1906 on the 4th of July five to eight thousand people attended the celebration. The C.H. & D. Railroad added extra trains in and out of Dana for the days festivities which included The Dana Merchants paying for the People's Band of Marshall, Indiana to entertain all day, the reading of the Declaration of Inde-

Train coming into Dana from the South. Dana depot on the right. The train is across the street coming into Dana.

Lang's Grocery Store located on site presently occupied by Dana Fire House.

The first block of town on the West Side in 1896.

pendence, a community dinner, Judge Rhueby speaking in the afternoon with trotting, racing and pony races and that night a band concert. 1915 was probably the last of the many, many programs at the park. Dana not only had Lowry Park but Chautauqua's, debating teams, spelling bees, cyphering contests, barbershop quartets, Dana's Band and Orchestra, a circus now and then and those famous medicine shows plus their many programs at their Opera House. The town now has its Dana Fall Festival, their cooperative Christmas Dinner for all residents of Dana and surrounding community. Much time is spent by the Dana merchants at Christmas time to decorate the Dana downtown into a magic Christmas Land and the churches of Dana present a live Nativity program each year. Throughout the year there are many other programs sponsored by the Dana Merchants.

Dana's first Fire Department was organized in 1893. In 1952 the Fire Department reorganized with new by-laws. Today in 1988 the Fire Department has thirty-four (34) members with Kevin Wickens-President, Terry Jo Hendrix-V.P., Ernie Adams-Fire Chief, Ronald Rumple-Assistant Chief, Robert Doan-Sec.-Treas. The directors are Lee Schroeder, Phil Hess, Robert Richardson and Tim Overpeck. They have a nice three stall brick fire house with modern kitchen, meeting rooms, restrooms all well equipped with the aid of the Women's Auxiliary which was organized in 1970.

Dana's schools were first held in an old building on Main Street with Porter Andrews as the first teacher with a Mr. Stark teaching a subscription school later. In 1870 a brick building was erected. The number of pupils kept increasing and in 1893 a new six room brick building was erected. In 1897 the school became a commissioned High School. The first graduating class was in 1898. The school was enlarged and a gymnasium was added and was used until 1961 when the school was closed by consolidation and became a part of the South Vermillion School Corporation. The school was being razed in 1962 and caught fire and was a total loss. There is now a town park and parking area for the Dana United Methodist Church where the school was located.

In 1904 the first consolidated school in West Central Indiana was opened with seven school districts being incorporated into what was known as the Bono School. It was a brick school with seven (7) rooms, two (2) large halls and two (2) offices and a basement. The school was located at Bono, south of Dana and was closed in 1928, having graduated some two hundred ten (210) students.

The Bono community was the first to establish a House of Worship with the Presbyterians, Baptist and Methodist erecting a structure in 1851, all using the same building, these arrangements existed until the mid 1870's when many of their congregation moved to the new town of Dana. The Bono Methodists celebrated their centennial on June 24, 1951 and today the Bono Method-

Dana engineer Hal Fillinger of the Indiana State Highway Comission on location.

Main Street of Dana looking south-bank. The bank clock is still in use today.

Main Street of Dana looking north

Dana High School Band 1952-53 Front: Kathryn Elder, Neal Guyer. Middle: Marilyn Campbell, Karin Shoof, Carolyn Cook, Clark Hammersley, Bob Ritchardson, Rosemary Knaflich, Kathryn Janes, Eula Mac McGill, Margaret Roe, Wanita Mullins, Linda Joyce Knight, Joe Douglas, Dale Hess. Back: Dorothy Easton, Janice Ford, Sarah Rose Sanders, Janet Jeffery, Henry Ford-Director, Sue Woodard.

ist is a very active church. Their pastor in 1988 is the Rev. Glenn Howell.

The Dana United Methodist was organized in 1878 worshipping in a store building on Main Street in Dana until 1881 when their first church was erected and used until 1906 when a brick building was erected. In 1955 an educational building was added and in 1973 extensive remodeling and decoration was completed. In 1988 the Rev. Glenn Howell is serving a growing church and Sunday School.

The Dana Baptist was organized in 1880 with a church being erected in 1887 with their second church being erected in 1915-16. In 1988 their pastor is Rev. Don Bruin.

The Nazarene Church was organized in 1923 in a building downtown, later moving to the American Legion Building and then to a house in the north part of town. In 1936 they erected their church and in 1971 they entered an extensive building program. Today they have a comfortable, modern church. Their pastor in 1988 is the Rev. Glenn Stover.

The Dana Community Bible Church was founded in 1959. Their church was enlarged and remodeled in 1970. Their pastor in 1988 is the Rev. Gerald Virostko.

Dana at one time had a Christian Church, organized in 1885 closing out in the mid 1930's. A few years later the building was torn down.

The Presbyterian Church in Dana was a continuation of the one established in Bono-Toronto in 1848. In 1886 they built their building in the north east part of Dana, but

in 1926 the church was closed and the building was torn down.

There was at one time a Seventh Day Adventists group and a Holiness Band in Dana. These were listed in the old newspapers but no further information could be found.

Dana at one time had several doctors but today has none. The early doctors were Hiram Shepard, Cuthbert Keyes, O.M. Keyes, Thomas Hood, A. Smith, Granville Newton, D.S. Strong, G.C. Pritchett, Dr. Green. Later doctors were A.E. Sabin, Dorothy Lauer, W.C. Myers and Lawrence Webb. There probably were others that we have missed and there were several dentists and chiropractors.

Dana's attorneys were George D. Sunkel, E.B. James, Albert Aye, F.H. Smith, Gordon Lang, J.P. York, Bruce Nichols and Allen Helt. Today Dana has no attorneys.

Dana's first mail was carried by saddle bags from Montezuma and Highland, Indiana by W.M. Taylor first postmaster until the railroad was completed. Dana has had sixteen (16) postmasters from 1874 to the present time. June Harris is the 1988 postmistress.

Dana in 1988 has something no other town in Vermillion County has, The U.S. Coast Guard.

Oran Station established in 1966 three miles north of Dana. The word "Loran" is an acronym derived from the term "Long Range Aid to Navigation". It is a station which transmits a precisely timed pulsed signal synchronized with other signals trans-

mitted from similar stations on the East Coast. These signals may be used by navigators of aircraft and ships to determine their geographical position. The other is the Ernie Pyle Birth Place which is The Ernie Pyle State Memorial. It is located on the spot that was a hotel in early Dana times and was used by people traveling by rail. The State Museum is an added plus to Dana as it has many visitors through the year.

Today in 1988 Dana has the following business places: Agricare of Indiana-Fertilizer and Chemicals; R. & R. Junction Restaurant; John Phelps Enterprizes; Fred Craft-Marathon Station; Hollingsworth Lime Service; New Mini-Mart being erected by Mick & Marion Uselman; Dana Farm Supply; Haymakers 76 Station; Marathon Distributors—Roy Stewart and Mark Miller; Jack Martin Repair Shop; Cargill Elevator, Inc.; Willway Mfg. Co.; Dana Laundromat & Car Wash; Haga's Garage; Adams Implement Co.; Country Flowers Shop; Barbara Grimes Shop; K of P Lodge; Frankie's Tavern; Thompson Construction Company; Overpeck Funeral Home; Jeff's Barber Shop & Tanning Salon; Lang Helt Insurance Agency; Homsley Hardware; Dana Restaurant-Pizza; Summerville Sundries; Jackie's TLC Shop; Dana's First National Bank; Hamersley's Grocery Store; Wicken's Construction Company; Pawley Lumber Yard; Mickey's Hair Fashions; Maxine's Beauty Shop-closing April 27th after 51 years; Shepards Fertilizer & Chemicals.

Dana is a close knit, caring community and in 1988 as stated in the 1888 Historical

& Biographical Record is still a town comprising a shrewd and enterprising class of business men and women and surrounded by an unusually good agricultural district, making it one of the nicest communities to live in and raise your family.

Some of the information was taken from the Biographical & Historical Record of 1888 and Dana's One Hundred Years-1874-1974.

ERNEST TAYLOR PYLE
(1900-1945)

Dana and Vermillion County can lay claim to one of the most noted figures of World War II, war correspondent Ernie Pyle. No other journalist ever evoked such mass affection as was accorded him during his tenure as a National figure. There was, of course, a reason for this. He bridged a gap in our knowledge of the great war and the men who were waging it. Ernie was as careful to write down the names and hometown addresses of all the sailors and soldiers he met as if he were covering a meeting of the Rotary Club. It was part of his kindness and a proof of his understanding. He knew what the names and addresses meant to the men at the front no less than to their families and friends back home. To him they were local boys making good in their living, their dying and their enduring. He was anxious to get them home again if it was only in print. Ernie's forebears had lived in Helt Township for many years before the first building in Dana went up in 1869. Will C. Pyle, Ernie's father (1867-1951) was one of seven children born to Samuel Pyle (1826-1904) and Nancy Hammond (1843-1880) Ernie's mother Maria Taylor (1870-1941) was born across the Illinois line. Her father Lambert Taylor was Hoosier-born and in 1895 moved his family back to the one-story frame house a couple miles southeast of Dana. In 1899 Ernie's parents were married and started house-keeping as tenant farmers for the Sam Elder family. This home was located a couple miles southwest of Dana where Ernie was born on August 3, 1900, the only child of the couple. At eighteen months his family moved to the farm home of his grandfather Taylor. Ernie's Aunt Mary (later Bales) lived with him and his parents at the Taylor-Pyle homestead until her marriage.

In 1906 he entered school at Dana. Ernie felt suffocatingly self-conscious among the town boys of tiny Dana. The next year the new consolidated school at Bono was completed and Ernie was transferred. When he was nine, Ernie's dad put him to riding a sulky plow behind three horses. From this time on he acquired an early distaste for farming. A year before Ernie graduated from High school the United States declared war on Germany. His parents refused to let him quit school to join the service but after receiving his diploma he took leave of a tearful mother and enrolled in the Naval Re-

Dana Post Office

serve. Soon after, the Armistice was signed; rather than come back to the farm, he enrolled at Indiana University in 1919. Here his rural shyness was soon largely overcome and he made lifelong friendships, particularly with a salty war-veteran classmate, Paige Cavanaugh, whose yarns of the A.E.R. and of travel gave Ernie visions of postcollege wandering. He was appointed editor-in-chief of the college paper THE STUDENT, on which he was working in connection with the journalism course. He became a "big man on campus". Upon leaving the University he worked a few months as a reporter for the La Porte Herald in northern Indiana, but was offered a $2.50 raise in wages by the Scripps-Howard News Alliance in Washington D.C. Here he met a pretty blond-haired girl from Minnesota, Geraldine Siebold, whom he married in 1925. In 1928 he started writing a daily aviation column, the first ever written concerning aviation on a daily basis. This continued for four years when Scripps-Howard made him Managing Editor, which he endured for three years. In 1935 he proposed a new job for himself as

Ernie Pyle marker erected approximately two miles and a half east of Dana on State Road 36 in the Ernie Pyle Rest Park.

a roving human-interest columnist for the newspaper. During the next five years he and his wife covered all the States, Canada, Central and South America.

In the winter months of 1940-41 Ernie went to England to cover the blitz. His experiences were published in his first book "Ernie Pyle In England." When Pearl Harbor was bombed Dec. 7, 1941, Ernie tried to join the military but was told he was too old. So he went to war armed with only a shovel to dig a foxhole and his typewriter from which he cranked out human-interest stories about the G.I.'s whose names would never appear in any newspaper unless they were promoted, decorated, wounded or killed. Before D-Day in 1943, Ernie was awarded the Pulitzer Prize for Distinguished Correspondent. After the liberation of France, Ernie returned home where the movie "The Story of G.I. Joe" which starred Burgess Meredith as Ernie Pyle was being produced. During this time Ernie received the Doctor of Letters from both Indiana University and the University of New Mexico. Ernie's last mission was to the Pacific Theater in 1945. On the morning of April 18, 1945, on the island of Ie Shima, Ernie was killed by a Japanese sniper's bullet and is buried in the National Cemetery in Honolulu, Hawaii. At the time of his death his columns were appearing in seven hundred newspapers.

Quite a number of honors were bestowed posthumously including the Medal of Merit

Boyhood Home of Ernie Pyle

by the War, Navy, and State Departments; the American Legions Distinguished Service Medal; V.F.W. Citizenship Medal; bearing his name are The Ernie Pyle Hall, school of Journalism at I.U.; Ernie Pyle U.S. Army Reserve Center, Fort Totten N.Y.; Ernie Pyle Media Center, Fort Jackson, South Carolina; State Highway #36 is the Ernie Pyle Memorial Highway; Ernie Pyle Rest Park on #36; B-29 Superfortress Bomber; one ship, the U.S.S. Ernie Pyle; a commemorative stamp issued in 1971; he received the Purple Heart

posthumously in ceremonies in New York in 1983.

The American Legion spearheaded a drive to raise funds to move the birthplace home into Dana, and it was dedicated July 3, 1976. The home, operated by the Indiana State Museum and Historic Sites Division houses the Pyle memorabilia and serves as a reminder that the great American story is the story of the ordinary guy like Ernie Pyle. *S*

Submitted by Evelyn Hobson, Curator
Ernie Pyle State Historic Site

Ernie Pyle (center) Lieutenant Jack Bales (directly behind Pyle) at Saipan in the Marianas (1945). Pyle spent a week or so with the men of the B-29's, including his "nephew" Jack Bales. Jack is a step grandson of Ernie's Aunt Mary.

DANA, INDIANA WELCOMES BALTIMORE AND OHIO RAILROAD PRESIDENT ROY B. WHITE BACK TO THE OLD HOME TOWN

Baltimore, Maryland, July 26, 1941—President White had quite a group of officers with him on his inspection of the Western Lines, July 24 to 30, but nary a one knew of the interesting event scheduled for the stop at Dana, Indiana.

Here the "Special," consisting of five business cars and a combine arrived on the hot afternoon of July 26. Everybody was in good spirits, because the last leg of the trip, east from Springfield, Ill., over the C.I. & W. part of the Toledo Division, was unusually pleasant. This line across Indiana was laid straight. Road bed and track are well maintained, and the uniformly fine stands of corn and soy beans that alternated on both sides of the line promised bumper harvests, prosperous farmers and considerable rail tonnage.

It was about 4:45 p.m. when the "Special" slowed down to a smooth stop at Dana, to find waiting at the station several hundred of the town and country folks in their best Saturday afternoon bib and tucker. To the salute of the high school band, Mr. White stepped quickly off the rear end, and was greeted affectionately by his sister, Miss Edna. Then dozens of others gathered around him. Important among these was Charles H. Peters, who was Agent-Telegrapher Dana when the boy White lived there, and who taught him telegraphy. Mr. Peters, who began his railroad service in 1890, retired in 1937. He was quite a center of interest among the officers of the B. & O. sharing the reception, as the man who gave the new B&O boss his start. But he was not the only one who called him "Roy." From old and young came this familiar salutation and in most cases "Roy" was quickly able to respond in kind.

An additional train stop was later made at Hillsdale, where the C. I. & W. officials detrained and joined a motorcade composed of Government, Du Pont, and C. & E. I. Railroad officials who made an inspection of the proposed site of the planned Ordnance Works to be built. The C. I. & W. was to build a spur track from Dana into the Newport area and the C. & E. I. a spur track from Opeedee into the Ordnance site. Following this important meeting the U.S. Government announced that the multi-million dollar plant would be located near Newport, in Vermillion county.

Commencing Sunday, May 6, 1917, a round trip every Sunday to Indianapolis and Decatur, IL, was available for $1.40 either way, via Cincinnati and Western Railroad, with C.H. Peters, Agent.

HIGHLAND

What was known at a very early day as Highland was a hamlet one mile to the north of Hillsdale, and at one time had a population of one hundred and fifty. It was one of the oldest trading points in Vermillion county, having been in pioneer stage-coach days a station on the route from Lafayette to Terre Haute. It had a postoffice for many years, but when Hillsdale sprung into existence, by reason of the railroads, the postal business and office was transferred to the last named place, the name of the postoffice also being then changed.

Taken from Parke-Vermillion Counties History, 1913.

HILLSDALE

In the year of 1898 or 1899 my father moved to Hillsdale. Possom bottom was used as a picnic ground or park for speaking celebrations. I remember going to a Republican rally on a hay ladder when I was about seven years old, all dressed up in a red, white, and blue dress.

John Osborn owned the place west of the brick building by the C. & E. I. railroad tracks that was a saloon. He ran a general store, carrying everything—shoes, dishes, and groceries. Across the street on the corner was a bakery and restaurant where Jimmie Smyth ran his business. North of this was a store where Mr. York and Levi Bonebrake repaired furniture and built new furniture. Mr. Jennings ran a store which now stands there.

There was an old Grand Army Hall where the old soldiers used to meet and where we had Sunday School and church before the Methodist or United Brethern Church was built. Where the post office is, at this writing, was a store run by Mr. Haffley, and on the corner was the old Opera House. It was a two-story building and had traveling shows and dances. Ren Wilson had a poolroom in the room downstairs. Mark Harding lived just north and west of the Opera House.

There was an old house where people by the name of Monahan lived by the road where the railroads crossed on the north lot of Phil McCarty. The old well is there yet. My grandparents lived there when my father was a small boy. *Written by Maude Billings Brown, date unknown*

The stone steps John Self built on the long hillside in 1903 remain, but they don't get the use they once did. "Years ago everybody used them to get from one end of town to the other," said Maxine Ogle, a librarian in this hilly Vermillion County town of 200 people.

The town sits on a high bluff about a mile west of the Wabash River town of Montezuma. A Parke and Vermillion history

Hillsdale steps

book published in 1913 described Hillsdale as "a beautifully situated little hamlet on the west side of the Wabash River...where the view is indeed splendid."

The community is technically in three parts — Hillsdale, Highland further up the hill, and Alta at the bottom of the big hill and just across the railroad tracks.

"You can't really tell where one stops and the other starts," said Ogle. "We're basically one community."

Hillsdale has the post office and only businesses. It was laid out in 1873 by E. Montgomery and named for the hilly terrain. Hart Montgomery had the first home and store to serve the town's 1912 population of 275.

Back then, Hillsdale was prosperous with two restaurants, three general stores, a drug store and a hotel. The hotel is now an apartment building. This is also where the National Tile and Drain Works made one million units of brick or tile each year.

Merchants lost considerable revenue in the late 1970s when Indiana 63 was made a four-lane highway and routed west of town. Librarian Ogle operated the last general store.

"We've got a nice summer reading program for the children," said Ogle, who checked out books herself as a child in the same library 60 years ago. About 20 youngsters read 964 books last summer, she said.

The library has approximately 1,000 books, Ogle said, with 200 books exchanged for new ones every month or so. "Many of the town's people bring in their magazines for us," said Ogle.

She said area kids are bused to school at Ernie Pyle Elementary. Older students go to South Vermillion High School in Clinton.

Hillsdale High School 1957-58 Bottom: Janet Jeffery, Gale Overpeck, Sandra Howell, June Williams. Middle: Don Harness, Jim Weatherly, Bob Weatherly, Kurt Wilkins, Carl Graham. Top: Charles Roccia-Principal, Tom Johnson, Dale Overpeck, Knie Overpeck, Jim Dunn, Garry Conner, Larry Coonce, Kenneth Keller-Coach.

Students here used to go to a local school. It closed its doors more than 20 years ago. Hillsdale Christian School was started six years ago by Robert Sizemore. Today it has 29 students in kindergarten through 12th grade.

"We believe a true education is a Bible-centered education," said Wayne Shotts, school administrator and pastor of the Hillsdale Christian Church.

Shotts said once or twice a year students at Hillsdale Christian School make a project of cleaning debris and weeds from the town's famed stone steps.

The school plays other Christian schools in sports. Students at the school come from Clinton, Montezuma, Rockville, Hillsdale and Newport.

Like other small communities, downtown Hillsdale is a shadow of its former self. The post office and the library with the Odd Fellow-Rebekah rooms above it are the centers of activity.

Joe Jones has been postmaster here since 1962. He said the government has been threatening to close the Hillsdale post office for 20 years, but hasn't done it yet.

"I was born and raised here," said Jones, whose family came here five generations ago from Virginia. "My ancestors helped settle this part of the country."

Jones — named after Joseph Jones who came here in the 1850s — said the Great Depression dealt this town an economic blow. It never recovered. "There were three brick and tile companies here and two went bankrupt," Jones said.

Jones remembered journalist-educator Claude Billings. The Hillsdale native died recently. "I really miss Claude," Jones said. "He was my good friend and quite a guy."

He said as a teen-ager Billings worked for the now-defunct Burns and Hancock Brick-

yard and that Joseph Burns befriended the youngster and helped him get through Wabash College.

Billings later got a master's degree from Indiana University and went on to work as an editor at newspapers in Indianapolis and Terre Haute. He became secretary of the Indiana Republican Central Committee and president of the Indiana Republican Editorial Association. Billings also was the editor and publisher of the Akron, Ind., News.

"I love Hillsdale," said Helen Davis, who

Hillsdale High School

has lived here nearly all her life. "This is a clean and quiet town." She praised the volunteer fire department for its vigilant work and "good spaghetti suppers" it conducts twice a year."

Lucille Bugg is another senior citizen who has long called Hillsdale home. She and her husband Melvin left once in the 1930s to work in Utah.

"I was so happy when we came back a year later," she said. "I said I'm going home to Hillsdale and I'm not leaving no more." She said they missed the green grass of the Midwest more than anything. "As far as I'm concerned, Indiana is the best state."

She said her husband made his living on the river as a fisherman for more than 50 years. "He caught mostly catfish, suckers, sturgeon and carp," she said.

The Odd Fellows and Rebekahs are probably the most active clubs in town. "We have about 45 members," said Ogle, the Noble Grand. Members are from Hillsdale, Rockville, Cayuga, Newport, Montezuma and even Terre Haute.

"We do a good bit of community work," said the blue-eyed, gray-haired grandmother. The Rebekahs also have the Thetarho club for girls ages 10 to 18. Among their activities are caroling for shut-ins and bringing them homemade candy at Christmas.

Pete Lawson is president of the district Odd Fellows. The Odd Fellows and Rebekahs combine on many community projects.

Gordon Pearman has been living in Highland most of his life. "It's much smaller than it used to be," he said. U.S. 36 goes through the northern edge, but the three gas stations and two restaurants that were once here have closed.

That doesn't seem to bother those who live here. "We like the hills and beautiful foilage of Hillsdale," said Bugg. "We think this is a unique town."

An article by Dave Delaney, Terre Haute Tribune-Star, November 17, 1985, Terre Haute Tribune-Star Publishing Co., Inc.

JONESTOWN AND "NEW" ST. BERNICE

SOME EARLY HISTORY OF THE WEST SIDE OF HELT TOWNSHIP

Jacob Reed and family were one of the first settlers in the west side of Helt Township, near the Illinois State line, about one-half mile west of "New" St. Bernice. The Reeds came from Stokes County, North Carolina, in 1831. They were followed by the Jones and Nolan families (born in the same county).

Wiley Jones, living on Section 24, Helt Township, born in Stokes County, North Carolina, March 27, 1824, was a son of Phillip J. Jones, a native of the same county. Philip and his family settled about one-half mile south of where Jonestown was surveyed and laid out 30 years later (1862). Wiley was reared on the pioneer homestead in the log cabin and now has one of the pun-

Hillsdale Main Street. Post office second building from right.

The Wabash River Bridge at Hillsdale Fell in January 28, 1941

cheons, which composed the floor. He has always given his attention to agriculture and now owns 73 1/2 acres of good land, which has a fine vein of coal underlying it. He has leased three mines, which yield a good quality of coal.

When Phillip J. Jones came to Indiana, he had a family of small children and was in debt $45.00. He sold a pony to pay his indebtedness and was left without a cow or a pig. Wiley was married January 29, 1846, to Elizabeth Dawes, daughter of William Dawes of Hillsdale. They had 13 children, seven of whom are living: William F., John N., Ben F., Harrison, Charles A., Ozias, and Sarah A. Mr. and Mrs. Jones were members of the United Brethern Church.

1874 - SOME JONES PIONEERS AND EARLY SETTLERS OF JONESTOWN VICINITY

Matthew Jones (Cleve's grandfather), was a farmer three miles northwest of the St. Bernice post office. Matthew was born March 3, 1818, in North Carolina, and settled in Vermillion County in 1831. He was a Democrat and a member of the United Brethern Church.

Thomas Jones, was a boot and shoemaker in St. Bernice. He was born in North Carolina in 1820, and settled in Vermillion County in 1831. Thomas was a Republican and a member of the Missionary Baptist Church.

Joseph Jones, lived one and one-half mile northwest of Hillsdale. He was born in Kentucky in 1810, and settled in Vermillion County in 1831. He was a Democrat and a member of the Christian Church.

Willice Jones was a blacksmith and lived five miles southwest of the Dana post office. He was born in Ohio in 1827 and settled in Vermillion County in 1862.

G.H. Jones, a farmer, lived one mile north of the Hillsdale post office. He was born in Vermillion County in 1840 and was a Democrat.

Harmon Jones, lived one-fourth mile west of the St. Bernice post office. He was born in Vermillion County in 1847. He was a Democrat and a member of the United Brethern Church.

John N. Jones, lived one-half mile south of the St. Bernice post office. He was born in Vermillion County in 1848 and was a Democrat.

Eri Jones, was a farmer in St. Bernice. He was born in Illinois in 1853 and settled in Vermillion County in 1872. He was a Republican and a member of the United Brethern Church.

William Jones, the postmaster, boot and shoemaker, was born in 1829, in Indiana. He settled in St. Bernice in 1831. He was a Democrat and a member of the United Brethern Church.

William Bales (father of Mrytle), farmer and stock raiser, resided on Section 36, Helt Township, one mile east of Jonestown, where he owned a half interest in 300 acres of valuable land. He was born in Lee County, Virginia, June 22, 1827. He was a son of George Bales, who was born in the valley of the James River in Virginia. In

1830, he brought his family to Indiana and settled on what is now the farm of his son William. At the time of his settlement here in Vermillion County, it was a very timbered tract, infested with deer, wild turkeys, wolves, wildcats, and other animals. William Bales was reared in the midst of this wilderness and in his early life was obliged to undergo many hardships that the young people of today know nothing about. His education was limited, but he has taken an interest in the affairs of his county, and is well posted on all topics of general importance. He learned the carpenter trade as a young man and has built many of the best houses of the neighborhood, including his own. All this he did in connection with his farm.

William Bales was married February 28, 1862, to Anna Anderson, and to them were born ten children: Pharoba, Effie, Esther, Myrtle, George, Ida, Mattie, Wilhelmina, Mary, and Max. Mr. Bales is a member of the Masonic Fraternity. He and his wife are members of the United Brethern Church.

Some more Bales and school history by Miss Myrtle Bales and her mother—George Bales (grandfather of Miss Mrytle Bales) gave an acre of land for a school. It was on the east end of his place and about 40 rods south of the northeast corner of his place. The log school was small and was used mostly in the summer. Mud and snow was so bad oftentimes in the winter they could not have much school, so in the summer, they would have subscription school. The patrons would pay $.50 to $1.00 per pupil, depending on the length of the term. This is called the Bales School. Years later there was a one-room frame school house but one mile east of Jonestown on the north side of the road just west of the small stream and about one-fourth mile north of the Bales home and this was called the Bales School, too.

Miss Anna Anderson (later Mrs. William Bales) was born July 22, 1843, and when she was 16 years old, in 1859, taught her first term of school in the Old Frog College school. This was a log school house three-fourths mile east of Center Church. She later taught at the Bales School where she met Mr. William Bales. Mrs. Bales died July 8, 1936, lacking 14 days being 93 years old.

Robert Bales, brother of William Bales, was a farmer and leasee of the Jonestown flour mill and resided on Section 35, Helt Township. At the homestead where he was born September 22, 1832, he was reared a farmer until 16 years of age. He then began to work at the carpenter trade, which he followed the greater part of the time until he leased the mill in 1887. He owned half interest in 320 acres of valuable land, which was under good cultivation. Mr. Bales enlisted in the Union Army during the Civil War in Co. A 71st Indiana 6th Cavalry. He served two years as 1st Lieutenant of his company. He was married in March of 1865 to Nancy A. McCown, daughter of Coldwell McCown. To them were born six children, three of whom are living: Minnie, Annie,

and Morton C. Mr. Bales was a member of the Grand Old Army of the Republic.

W.D. McFall was once a postmaster in Jonestown in 1885. He ran a general store and also engaged in stock raising and dealing in stock. He was born in Augusta County, Virginia, February 14, 1850. His father, William McFall, was born in Albermarle County, Virginia, and came to Vigo County in 1871, and from there went to Edgar County, Illinois. He came to Vermillion County in 1877, and was a resident of Jonestown and Dana. He had but $20.20 in which to begin business and by his efforts he accumulated a fine property and was classed among the well-to-do citizens of the county. He owned 315 acres of choice land and established a good business in Jonestown, carrying a full line of dry goods: clothing, groceries, boots, shoes, hats, caps, hardware, etc. His capital stock was valued at $5,000. His annual business was around $12,000. Mr. McFall was married June 11, 1874, to Miss Victoria Dyer. Eight children were born to them, six of whom are living: Fredrick, Claude, Lucy, Rose, Helen, and Ruth.

Mr. and Mrs. McFall were members of the Methodist Episcopal Church at the center of the neighborhood, two and one-fourth miles east of Jonestown. Mr. McFall, some of the Jones, and perhaps some others were instrumental in making the brick for the four brick buildings in Jonestown, being: the McFall's store and dwelling, the one-room school at the south edge of town, and the Amerman dwelling. The bricks were made in a field north of the Amerman home and west of the Roy Sturm home (at the present time) or the Andrews home then.

1888 - JONESTOWN, VERMILLION COUNTY HISTORY

Jonestown is located near the southwest corner of Helt Township. Helt Township has an area of 72 square miles—12 square miles more than any other township in Vermillion County. Villages and towns are: Toronto (Bono), Hillsdale, Jonestown, St. Bernice, Highland, Summit Grove, and Dana. The town of Jones, as it was first called was plotted February 25, 1862, by Phillip J. Jones and Noah Wellman. The town was named for Phillip, who owned part of the land upon which it was founded. A log cabin was on the site and also a better dwelling erected by Dr. Grimes. It has been said that Jim Green's house, formerly a two-room log cabin, housed the post office sometime during the Civil War. The postoffice was established in 1863. For a while Cleve Jones hauled the mail between Jonestown and Dana. Population then was approximately 100. John Amerman was owner of the first store.

By 1879 there was a three-story flour mill, (in 1918 it was struck by lightning and burned down), two blacksmith shops, a carpenter shop, cabinet maker, Grand Old Army of the Republic post, United Brethern Church, Justice of the Peace, and a constable—James Perry Lewis (Agnes Knopp Jones' grandfather).

1881

By this time St. Bernice had two doctors: Thomas Nelson Lonsdale, born in 1844, in Petersburg, Indiana, and a graduate of the Cincinnati School of Medicine, and Dr. Henry T. Watkins, physician and surgeon, born in 1850 in Cincinnati, Ohio. His father, John C. Watkins was a native of England and came to the United States as a young man and for 30 years was engaged in construction and building. Dr. H.T. Watkins was a graduate of Hamerman Medical School of Chicago, and also Kentucky School of Medicine in Louisville. He also took special courses in Chicago in diseases of women and children. He came to Jonestown in 1881.

OBITUARY OF DR. LONSDALE - 1917

Dr. T.L. Lonsdale died at his home in Jones, commonly known as St. Bernice, on June 15, 1917. He was a native of Pike County, Indiana, from where he enlisted for service in the War of the Rebellion, in the 14th Indiana Volunteer Infantry and saw three years of service. He first practiced medicine at St. Peters, Illinois, coming to Jones 29 years ago. He was twice married, four children being born to each union. His second wife survives, also the four children by her; Agnes Kendall of Greenfield, Mary Adams, and Hortense Igo of Scotland, Illinois, and a son, Clair, with the U. S. Army in Hawaii. Dr. Lonsdale was a charter member of the G.A.R. and the I.O.O.F. Lodge of his hometown. Services to be held at the church with Rev. Hess of Atwood, Illinois, in charge. Burial at Wesley Chapel west of Dana.

The following doctors came after 1885: Dr. Tweedy (Wakefield Tweedy Hazelit's and Cora Tweedy Dalton's father), Dr. Grimes, Dr. Newton, and Dr. S.I. Green. Dr. Green came in 1911, his first office was the first house north of the present fire station in St. Bernice on the west side of the highway. He also had an office in his house for a period of time which is south of the present Nazarene Church. He later moved the office to a small building between the Baptist Church and the Nazarene Church. Dr. Newton built the big house on the west side of the highway just south of the main street of St. Bernice. It later housed the telephone switchboard and was operated by the O'Briants. *Submitted by Lucille Jones*

JONESTOWN BUSINESSES

1880 - 1885

John Amerman - first store in Jonestown; W.D. McFall with a large stock of goods and housed the post office; Fred and Ira Jones, groceries.

1913 - Cleve Jones, grocery store.

ST. BERNICE BUSINESSES

1913

O.B. Ayres Drug Store; St. Bernice Pri-

Jonestown School Row 1: Paul "Chick" Campbell (third from left), Iva Price (fourth from left), Millie Osborn (sixth from left), and Ray Campbell (seventh from left). Row 3: Grace McDowell-Teacher (fourth from left), Paul Price (eighth from left), Fitsue Wheeler and Don Chapplaer (last two boys in last row). Others unknown.

vate Bank established on main floor of K. of P. Lodge Hall.

1918 - 1957

Cleve Jones Grocery Store

1925 - 1930

American State Bank; J.P. Hartsook's General Merchandise; Philabauns Restaurant; R.C. Wey Drug Company; The Edison Shop; St. Bernice Electric Company - Housewiring and Everything Electric - Youngman and Parsley, Electrologist; McGinnis Service Station; D. Andrews Dry Goods Company; Kimball and Morrison Funeral Directors and Embalming; G.W. O'Briant and Son General Merchandise; C.M. Botner General Merchandise; Ernest Foltz - Insurance, loans, real estate, and wire fencing; A.L. Inman's Variety Store and Millinery; Bert Michler Feed Store; W.G. Pate - Staples and fancy groceries; H.E. Prall General Merchandise; St. Bernice Motor Company - F.C. Sims - Ford trucks and tractors; Youngman's Drug Company - Wallpaper, paints, etc.; Roy Rice Barber Shop; Chelf's - on the corner - Lunch; R.B. Hafley General Merchandise; Campbell's Cafe - Rachel Campbell; Huber Whited Barber Shop; Blue's Restaurant; Hudson and Essex Sales and Service - Stultz and Frazier; Mighty Majestic Radio - Gilbert LaRue.

1947 - 1961

Cleve Jones Quality Grocery and Home Killed Meats; Reed's Barber Shop; S.H. Pawley Lumber Co., Inc.; Rardin Grain Co.; Paul's Shoe Service, "I Can Heel You and Save Your Sole" - Paul Price; Ira Jones - Meats, Groceries, and Notions; Acton's Roller Rink and Lunch Counter; West Clinton Cafe - Virginia Dagley; Carl O'Briant Service Station and Coal Hauling; Pirtle's Variety Store - Medicines, Cosmetics, Gen-

eral Merchandise, Soda Fountain; Sim's Grocery; Johnson's Barber Shop; Inman's Cafe and School Book Depository; The Silver Front (Food You'll Enjoy) - Audrey Burgess Strain; Armstrong's Grocery; Charles E. Brown and Son - Westinghouse Appliances; Newton's Service Station; Campbell's Grocery - Meats and Notions; Ray Acton's Service Station; John Henry Glass' Poolroom; Inman's Restaurant; Cecil Reed's Barber Shop, Blue's Cafe; The Hornet's Nest - Drugs, Sundries, Luncheonette - Ernest and Gladys Skinner; Holden's Tavern; Vermillion County Insurance Agency; Recreation Room - C.H. James; Jones and LaRue Television - Admiral Dealer, Sales and Service; Horseshoe Lake - Swimming, Fishing, and Boating; Cornwell's Garage, State Line Service Station; Larrison's Cafe; Wayne Fortner Barber Shop; Harley Morgan Barber Shop; Straw's TV Service; Helen's Gift Shop - Helen Douglas; Dale York's Stop and Shop - New and Used Furniture; Sims and Hobart Groceries; Juanita's Beauty Shop; Weyhrauch Insurance Agency; Malone's Grocery; Charley's Cafe, Betty's Beauty Shop; Spears' Air Conditioning and Refrigeration Service; Van Sant Grain Company; Miller's Service Station; Marshall Williams Texaco Dealer; Home Supply - Snodgrass and Board - Radio repairs and electrical work; Dorothy's Beauty Shop; West Clinton Garage - Kenneth Cloyd and Roy Rusmisel; Hartsook's - Eats, Ice Cream, Soft Drinks, Fountain Service, and Home Medical Supplies.

ST. BERNICE

There has been a bit of confusion over the years about the naming of the three towns of "Jones", Jonestown, and St. Bernice. The story goes that Jonestown was originally called "Jones" for the man who owned the land it was founded on. It was later called Jonestown, because there was another town in the state by the name of Jones. In 1863, a post office was established as St. Bernice in Jonestown. No one seems to know who or why this name was chosen. Dr. Wilson Grimes was the first postmaster. Other history of Jonestown is in another article.

After the railroad yards came and located in the south part of town, the population increased rapidly to the north and to the south. After 42 years the post office was moved about one mile north and New St. Bernice was platted August 18, 1905, by Alfred M. and Elizabeth J. Reed. The word "new" was finally dropped and Old St. Bernice was put on a Clinton rural route and again is known as Jonestown. There is not another St. Bernice in the U.S.A. says the "Old Times."

J.P. Hartsook built the first store, with living quarters above, located on the southwest corner of Main Street, east of the elevator, which is near the railroad. The next year (1906), the Knights of Pythians built a two-story building across the street north. This building not only served as a lodge hall, but many different happy events took place here on the upper floor. The main event was the annual community Thanksgiving feasts as they were called then. Others were box suppers, spelling bees, dances, class parties and birthday parties.

On the main floor, the first bank was established in 1913. Officers were: Daniel H. Miller, president; Alfred M. Reed, vice-presi-

OUR NEIGHBOR

There's a little town called Scissorville,
A mile or so away;
They have two stores, and a barber shop,
A pool room or two, they say.

They boast a bank with lots of wealth,
A drug store and a hashery, too;
A blacksmith shop and rural route,
All mail direct to you.

This town is really very young.
Sprung from the open plain;
It is so very, very young,
It really has no name.

This town it shelters five hundred "soles,"
Including Sunday shoes,
Its citizens, 'tis sad to say,
Are very fond of booze.

The Doodle Bug goes twice a day,
To the city miles away,
To carry suckers into town,
Who never mean to stay.

This car is run by gasoline,
They charge you by the hour,
Sometimes you sit a half a day,
When it runs out of power.

Their rent is high, their groceries, too,
They have an independent way,
And lots of folks within their town
Would be glad to get away.

If they could find a little nook
Within our sunny town,
In which to rest their weary bones,
Till rent and meat come down.

Now, neighbor town, we've this to say.
We think not hard of you;
But we will have our good old name,
And our postoffice, too.

And no confusion will there be
When mail is brought around,
If you will get yourselves a name,
That hasn't yet been found.

You have a switchboard moved from here;
All our lines to be replaced;
Now we all hang on to a party line,
And can't talk any place.

You like to attend our Sunday School,
Our lodge and meeting, too.
But when it comes to summing up,
It all belongs to you.

We cannot boast of miners black—
Railroaders, they are few.
But when it comes to honest men,
We can show you quite a few.

Written by Agnes Jones in 1913 at old St. Bernice, Indiana, (Jonestown). Published in The Daily Clintonian at that time in answer to some of the attempts to get our post office in Old St. Bernice.

St. Bernice Main Street-1950's

St. Bernice Grade School Rhythm Band-1937 Row 1: unknown, Barbara Campbell, Bill Scot, Charles Ray Miller, unknown, Jeanne Mindeman, Morris Jenkins, unknown, Barbara Hopkins, unknown, Bobby Dagley, unknown, unknown. Row 2: Gilda Clark, David Crane, Woody Gambill, Barbara Scott, unknown, unknown, unknown, unknown, Betty Jane Chambers, unknown, unknown, Bobby Glass Row 3: unknown, unknown, Earl Foltz, Bob Snodgrass, Charles Coonce, unknown, Miss Branson, Miss Myers, Betty Ann Brown, unknown, unknown, unknown, unknown, unknown, unknown.

Elisah McDonald, Cleve Jones, Fred Jones, "Doc" Williams, Clon Green, "Old Ted" (the dog), Elmer Lientz

dent; Oliver O. Laughlin, cashier; Floyd W. Reed, assistant cashier. It was a private bank and went by the name of St. Bernice Farmers Bank. Later in 1915 a new bank was built and named The American State Bank. This was a brick building located on the northeast corner of Main Street and operated until 1933. The depression years were here.

Dr. Newton built the first house in town, a large two story building, located just south of Main Street on the highway (dirt streets then). A few years later Earl and Mable Rice O'Briant lived there and owned and operated the switchboard for many years. Mable was a resident for 48 years, coming here from Vermillion Township in 1918. There was a movie theater here in the 1920's which was managed by Bill Maloney and Mr. Shuey at times. Margaret Inman played the piano for the silent movies, before the "talkies." There was other entertainment held here, some of which were Black Face Minstrels, and a three act comedy by the Boy Scout Troop. Sunday School was held here until a tabernacle was built north of the brick bank building. In 1944 the Baptists bought the bank building. After the theater closed, Floyd Reed had a mouse-trap factory there and later Ben Reed had a chair

repair business in the building. Other businesses about this time were Cecil Reed's Barber Shop, Rairden Grain Co., Vermillion County Insurance Agency—Eleanor Pinson, and Ruth's Lunch. The Royal Neighbor Lodge celebrated their 50th Anniversary in 1972 with only four of their charter members living then. They were Katherine Males, Clara Hiddle Grimes, Helen Douglas, and Rachel Campbell.

West Clinton Junction, three-fourths mile south of the Jonestown Road, near the railroad yards was recorded May 31, 1911, by H.M. Ferguson, Samuel C. Stultz, and Henry C. Dies. Some of the first houses built in this end of town were Cleve Jones store and home in 1918. Electricity came in 1917. Other homes built were Charles Jones', Charles Miller's, west of Four Corners Road, across from the railroad yards, Murray's, east of Four Corners, Dick Bodle's, Homer "Peck" Wallace's, Ira Jones' home and store, Reed McGinnis' home and service station, Dan Miller's, Elmer Lientz's, Dolph Dunkley's, all on the highway to the north, and Orville Miller's home on Miller Park Road. Others were George Wilkins', William Welch's and several company houses. Some of the carpenters in the area were Oakie

Nolan, Jim Hiddle, Frank King, William Welch, William P. Jones, and William Bales, who is listed in the early Jonestown History. Businesses were Marshall "Doc" William's Service Station, Ora Davis made the stone blocks and built the garage on the highway where Stout's Stop-Lite Service is now. Pete Hall operated it later in the depression years. The county highway trucks were kept there. Later the firehouse was located there. The old barn across the road was built for storage purposes and is owned by Bert Coonce.

There were a lot of musicians in the St. Bernice area. Some of them were the Gibbons', the Stultzs', Fern Nolan, Dan Miller, Herman Weaver, Mary Katherine Chelf, Earl Blue, Harold Eydman, Lymon Foncannon, Glen Ferguson, Virginia Grimes Parker, Louise McBride Hutson, and Wilma Ingle Ferguson. There was also a German band with Ezra Overpeck as the leader.

The towns kept growing until it all blended together as one big town. In 1958 the population was one thousand, however, it was never incorporated.

"The Doodle Bug" was a passenger service operated by the railroad company. The regular run was between Bensonville (near Chicago) and Grover. You had to take a jitney from there if you were going on to Terre Haute.

In the late 1920's and early 1930's there was a public bus service between Clinton and St. Bernice for a time, then in 1947 the new Triangle Bus Line was available from Clinton to St. Bernice, Dana, Paris, and Universal, seven days a week.

Present businesses in town are the St. Bernice Grain Co., St. Bernice Fertilizer, St. Bernice Tavern, G. & L. Video and Tanning, Barnyard Dairy, Stop-Lite Service, and Top Automotive. Gambill's Harvest Barn is just south of town and the Thousand Trails Resort is east of town.

Present churches in town are the St. Bernice Baptist Church, the St. Bernice Nazarene Church, and the Community Full Gospel Church.

The town began declining after the railroad left in the 1950's and the school was closed in 1962. There are still several hundred people living here but most have to drive to other towns to work. *Submitted by Lucille Jones*

DR. SILVA I. GREEN

Dr. Green was born in Lexington, Scott County, Ky., in 1880. He graduated from Hanover College in 1904 and went to the Kentucky School of Medicine for his doctor's degree.

As a young doctor starting out, he first located on the Illinois side of the line near St. Bernice in 1911 where he started his practice.

When one of the doctors in St. Bernice retired, it was an opportunity for Dr. Green to move to St. Bernice for his permanent residence. His first residence in St. Bernice was on the west side of the railroad but then he built a new home across from the Church

St. Bernice

I will try to write a little verse
    About the town of St. Bernice.
Seal was going to put it in corn
    But failed to get a lease.

We have a nice large elevator
    Where they buy the farmers' wheat.
Hartsook runs a general store
And sells all kinds of meat.

Then comes Fairgrief's restaurant.
    He has groceries, too, for sale.
Mrs. Inman runs the Post Office
    Where people get their mail.

Next is Obe Ayers' drug store.
    He sells all kinds of pills.
We have with us Dr. Green
    Who cures the peoples' ills.

Nick Ford runs a big garage
    In the building made of blocks,
He will fix your automobile
    And take out all the knocks.

Bill VanHuss runs a barber shop
    When he's not out rambling.
He also has a checker board
    On which Mirandy does his gambling.

Hafley runs a grocery store
    And sells dry goods on the side
He and Skidmore go fishing
    And leave the store with Jake McBride.

Next comes O'Brien's grocery store
    They sell everything I think,
When Goodwin gets his flivver fixed
    Then we can buy a drink.

John Wimsett runs a pool room
    And sells tobacco and cigars.
I tell you it's a business town.
    It surely beats the cars.

Mirandy Reed sells rhubarb,
    And here I'll put you wise.
Go to McGuire's lunch room
    To get your rhubarb pies.

Ernie Hawkins has a bull dog.
    I dare not tell you why.
But some of the folks in St. Bernice
    Would like to see him die.

Then we have the Farmers' Bank
    Where we get money when need.
O'Brien does the pencil work
    The cashier's name is Reed.

Sam Turk runs a shoe shop
    Puts on all kinds of soles.

He sews them up and shines them too,
    And patches all the holes.

Charles Shuey in his Blacksmith Shop with Bud Reed, Daniel Shuey and Charles Clark.

Pawley will sell you lumber
    If you wish to settle down.
Just build a home in St. Bernice
    And help boost the town.

Shuey has a blacksmith shop,
    Although he likes to shirk
He'll ask you for your patronage
    But he lets Hancock do the work.

Smith Bottom runs a furniture store,
    Although it's second hand.
He busy and sells all kinds of junk
    And also farms some land.

The Southeastern Railroad runs through
    town
    It goes "from here to yonder"
The way that "Doodle Bug" does run
    It surely does beat thunder.

The town is strictly up to date;
    That's what everyone desires.
If you happen in at 12 o'clock,
    Get dinner at McGuire's.

                                    J.M. McGuire

of the Nazarene and an office building was built across the street, where it stands now, before demolition.

Dr. Green served in World War I in the U.S. Medical Corps. He came back to St. Bernice and was the first commander of the St. Bernice American Legion Post No. 108.

He was also a politician and served two terms as trustee of Helt Township, 1941-49.

The doctor was quite busy in the area and made his calls by horse and buggy until one day he stopped at the Harris General Store at Kidley, Ill. Mr. Harris was joking with the doctor while his horse was drinking out of the horsetrough and told the doctor he was old-fashioned and needed a new automobile to drive on his calls.

The doctor scoffed at the suggestion, but it was only a short time later that he bought a new 1914 Ford, which was his pride and joy. His shepard dog would accompany the doctor on his rounds and could always be seen riding the front fender of the car.

One of his patients related a favorite remark of the doctor as he made ready to get back to his office. As he was getting into his buggy he would say, "Well, I gotta get back to my office in Scissorville." That was his favorite name for what is now the town of St. Bernice. The doctor was fond of children and they made him their hero.

Dr. Green's father was a practicing physician in Hanover and his brother, Fred, practiced in Bloomingdale. His sister, Mae, was a high school English and Latin teacher. Dr. Green graduated with high honors from Hanover College. He also graduated from medical college with highest honors of his class.

Many of his escapades in college related to food. The stories mentioned that the doctor was fond of eating and when he smelled good things cooking he was noted for getting into the kitchen for a "bite to eat" without being discovered.

He was a great fox hunter of his day and lived life to the utmost in a jovial frame of mind. Dr. Silva I. Green died in 1957 and is buried in Sugar Grove cemetery. Many of the old-timers of that neighborhood remember him with the kindness of memories.

Taken from an article in The Daily Clintonian, April, 1971.

ELEANOR GOOD

Eleanor Good was a prominent St. Bernice businesswoman, owner of Vermillion County Insurance Agency for many years. She was very active in civic affairs. She was instrumental in securing the St. Bernice water system and was the secretary-treasurer of the St. Bernice Water Corporation. She was a member of the Board of Directors of Wabash Valley Chapter of Red Cross, the Rebekah Lodge, and Christian Church. She was also a member of the St. Bernice Conservation Club, L.I.F.T., and American Legion Post #140 Auxiliary.

About 1950 to better serve Vermillion County, Joe Lowe, Executive Director of the Wabash Chapter American Red Cross, an-

Dr. Silva I. Green

nounced the installation of a two-way radio in Mrs. Good's office in St. Bernice. It was manned by volunteer workers. It was an extension of a network of radio stations across the nation. In addition to the base station in the Chapter House in Terre Haute, the Wabash Valley Chapter had four mobile equipped vehicles, three portable base stations, two walkie talkies and a communication trailer with its own power. This was in line with the Chapter's policy of disaster preparedness.

Mrs. Good was born December 1, 1905, and died November 4, 1969. She was the daughter of Mrs. Abba Conover of Chrisman, Illinois. She had three brothers—Samuel, Robert, and Carl.

RAILROADING PLAYED GREAT PART IN COMMUNITY LIFE OF ST. BERNICE

St. Bernice has an interesting history. For one thing it has not always been called "St. Bernice." Before 1912 or 1913, it was known as "Scissorville." John Q. Pritchard's wife still owns a 1916 Centennial Speller in which a grammar school teacher of hers, Caleb Stephen Pickard, refers to the town by that name.

An adjoining town, now called "Jonestown" used to be called St. Bernice.

"They had a post office over there, but we wanted one here," Mr. Pritchard said. After the population here increased the post office was moved over here about 1912 or 1913 and the name of the town changed to New St. Bernice. After a time, the "New" was dropped.

Even now the election precincts cite Jonestown as St. Bernice No. 1 and the present St. Bernice as St. Bernice No. 2.

The early Pritchard connection with the railroad is significant in the light of St. Bernice history because that history is closely

tied to trains and a structure called "The Roundhouse."

The structure to which he was referring no longer stands but it served the engines of the old Southern Indiana Railroad from about 1905 to 1953.

Pritchard remembers the line well because he worked as a fireman on it from 1923 to 1927 and recalls its earlier history as told him by former co-workers. There aren't many of those left, H.L. Inman, who started with the railroad in 1913 and who is now retired in St. Bernice, is perhaps the only still-living engineer in the immediate area. Another ex-engineer who preceded Inman, Henry A. VanBrunt, used to live in Terre Haute, but is reportedly now retired in Florida.

Pritchard doesn't remember when the Roundhouse was first built, but recalls that it was some short time before he and his wife moved to St. Bernice in 1910. He estimated 1905 as the construction date.

John R. Walsh built the Roundhouse and managed the Southern Indiana Railroad, which ran from Terre Haute to Chicago and St. Louis.

"At that time, he owned the Illinois Central and then he got controlling interest in the Southern Indiana," Pritchard said.

Walsh's story is an interesting one. Despite the fact that men working under him knew him as a "straight-shooting sort," the bigger railroads were not happy with Walsh's success and were working to run him out of business.

"There were a lot more railroads then than there are today," Pritchard explained about the competition. "They tried all kinds of things to stop him. He made the deadline to Chicago the first night, however, despite their burning bridges on him."

Welsh eluded his persecutors for a time, but he was finally sent to prison after being arrested for violation of the Federal Banking Act in about March, 1906. Pritchard didn't know the specifics of the charge, but clearly believes Walsh was innocent of any wrongdoing.

"He was a good man. He was another Eugene V. Debs," he insisted.

"Of course, they confiscated all his money, too, so the workers on the line couldn't be paid. They thought the workers would leave, but most stayed and were paid in script. Some of the stores in Terre Haute would take it, others wouldn't."

The name of the line was later changed to "Chicago, Terre Haute and Southeastern," and Pritchard owns a near-50-year-old lantern with the letters "CTHSE" still visible on it.

If the Roundhouse was built around 1905, then it was sold about 1953 because Pritchard has a photograph of the last steam engine serviced there, dated in that year.

"It was built only to service steam engines, so it couldn't work on diesels," he noted.

The building was sold to Ernie Boetto, a junk dealer situated next to the Clintonian then, Pritchard recalled. Most of the yards were torn out and today nothing except a few markings meaningful only to trained eyes remain at the site on the east side of the railroad tracks just out of St. Bernice near a liquid fertilizer plant.

Pritchard remembers that Mike Donahue was Roundhouse foreman and George Passage was master mechanic when he worked there.

"I fired the engines and got $4.42 a hundred miles for it," he said.

Mrs. Pritchard's family has also been intimately involved with the railroad and the Roundhouse. Her dad, O.M. "Monty" Kuhns, was killed in a railroad accident in 1931 which also badly burned the fireman, Walter Scharf. Her sister's husband, Donald Hehman, worked as chief dispatcher for the Terre Haute division of the line and was in fact writing a book about the railroad's early history when he died nearly four years ago.

It is from this unfinished book that Pritchard got much of his information and in it lies another of Pritchard's hopes. He hopes to see it published and the Walsh story come fully to light.

"Of course, everyone then knew that Walsh was a straightshooter, but that's not so evident today. The railroad didn't know that Hehman was compiling his book but someday the story will break."

Many persons have tried to gain possession of that book without success, Pritchard indicated, and it seems likely that such an account would yield many intriguing facts about a bygone era in St. Bernice's history.

Taken from an article by Paul Wagenbreth in The Daily Clintonian dated April 3, 1973.

New St. Bernice was platted August 18, 1905, by Alfred M. and Elizabeth J. Reed, H.M. Ferguson, Samuel C. Stultz, and Henry C. Dies. The owner of the Southern Railway Company had purchased a plot of 40 acres lying west of what is now Highway 71 and owned by A.M. Reed for the railroad yards and company houses to be built upon. This was a boom to the area and was recorded

May 31, 1911, as West Clinton Junction. The railroad built a roundhouse, car shop, yard office, hotel, and restaurant better known as the "Beanery". It was owned by Olympic Food Company and operated by Edith O'Briant and Mary Acton. Bert Coonce recalls washing dishes there at an early age before old enough to work on the railroad. He started there in 1925.

The railroad was owned by three different companies during the forty-seven years it operated from here, first was the Southern Indiana, second was the Terre Haute and Southeastern, and third was the Chicago, Milwaukee, St. Paul, and Pacific.

Some of the oldtimers living today who worked on the road 40 years or more are Bert Coonce (43), Elwood Endicott (43), Paul Ritter (44), and Ray Weyhrauch (40). Others are Vaughn Allen, David Amerman, Cyrus Bodle, Jr., Lee Brown, Emil Chaney, George Clark, Charles A. Corado, Norman Foltz, Tom Gibbons, Tom Gish, Oscar Hunt, Alva Hutson, Hubert Ingram, Elisa McDonald, John Pritchard, and John Uhrin.

Other railroaders were Ed Acton, Dean Allen, Forrest Allen, Hovey Anderson, John Bailey, Emil Bauer, Joe Bedinger, Clyde Blake, Joe Blue, Paul Blue, Jerry Board, Dick Bodle, Mr. Boltz, Bernard Brown, Charles Brown, Freeman Brown, James Brown, Kenneth Brown, Katy Buckner, William Buckner, Fred Burgess, Jr., Fern Bush, Mr. Carmichael, Orville Carne, Courtney Cartwright, Walter Chambers, Sr., John Church, Don Clark, Claude Clendening, Kenny Cloyd, Earl Coleman, Bennie Conner, Earl Cook, Fred Coonce, David Crane, Thomas Dagley, Raymond Daugherty, Jess Davis, Marion Davis, R.T. Davis, Preston Dorfmeyer, Ben Douglas, Adolphus Dunkley, Frank Ernhart, Oliver Eslinger, Reggie Falls, Harry Ferguson, Don Foltz, John Forehand, Charles Fox, George Gerrard, Leo Gibbons, Walter Glass, Irvin Good, Kenneth Gowens, Nelson Green, John Grimes, Ozro Hadden, George Hadley (44), J.W. Hafley, Elza Hale, Pete Hall, Everett Hancock, Lambert Harris, Bobby Hartsook, Wilson W. Hasty, Heber Haun, Donald Hehman, Ted Hehman, Milo Helms, Mark Hewitt, Claude Hiddle, Clyde Hiddle, Shell Hiddle, Frank Hixon, Jim Hixon, Phil Hixon, Sam Hixon, C.E. "Doc" Hollinger, John A. Hollingsworth, Harry Hopkins, Frank Hunnicutt, Fred Hughes, Mr. Hunt, Martin Inman, Glenn Johnson, Charles Jones, Clyde Jones, Kenneth "Cannonball" Jones, Wallace Jordan (47), Guy Kelley, Collett F. Keltz, Bert King, Bob King, Elmer King, Cassell Kuhns, Clarence Kyle, Elizabeth Brown LeBow, Louis Leek, Cecil Lewis, Carl Lientz, Elmer Lientz, Elmer Long, Homer McBride, Kendall McBride, Charles McCauley, Arthur McCown, Homer McCown, Roy McCoy, Joe McDonald, John H. McDonald, Reed McGinnis, Ralph McGuire, Homer McMillan, Clarence H. McPheeters, Sam McReynolds, Les Maloney, Dan Miller, Orville Miller, Forrest Mott, Carl Mueller, Earl Mullen, James Myers, Clint Nash, Lester Newton, Howard Nolan, Ray Nolan, Leslie Osborn, Orville Page,

Melvin Phillips, Walter Powers, Berlin Ray, Ben L. Reed, J.D. Reed, Stanley Reed (27), W.H. Reed, Slim Reynolds, Don Robertson, Jess Rusmisel, William Seaton, Sr., Mr. Seebren, Ed Servell, George Smith, Elgar Snodgrass, Mr. Spaulding, Orville Spears, Elmer Stevens, Earl Stines, John Steffey, Lester Steffey, William G. Southard, Arthur Stout, Frank Stout, Roscoe Striker, John Travis, Carl Van Meter, Max Vicars, Clyde Wagner, Verlin Wagner, Peck Wallace, Bill Webster, Ernest Wellman, Charles S. Weyhrauch, William Sanford Wheeler, Orlen Williams, Brownie Wilson, and Odus Young.

Due to the changeover of steam locomotives to diesel powered engines the yards were moved to Terre Haute in 1952.

WEST CLINTON JUNCTION

Four buildings located along the east side of the Milwaukee railroad tracks on the south side of the Clinton-Helt township line road south of St. Bernice, Indiana, was known as West Clinton Junction.

The buildings housed a pool room, restaurant and hotel, tavern and garage.

The buildings were owned by different individuals prior to the middle 1920's at which time John Gambill had purchased all of them. Gambill operated Gambill's Hotel and Restaurant from 1923 until 1950. The restaurant and hotel were open 7 days a week 24 hours a day serving the railroaders as well as the general public.

Gambill was assisted in his businesses by his sisters Laura Stevenson and Neoma Hughes, his brother Frank Gambill, nieces and nephews and several other employees. Roy Rusmisel operated the garage.

The buildings were all sold by 1950, and are no longer existing. The land is presently owned by Joe Majors.

GAMBILL'S HOUSE

Gambill's house was built in the early 1880's by Madison Nolan. It is not known how long the Nolan family occupied the house, however Nolan's daughter married Mark Martin and they too lived in the house for an unknown time. Around 1912 the house was sold to Dan and Johanna Miller. The Miller family occupied the house and farmed several hundred acres until 1934 at which time the house and 40 acres was purchased by John Gambill. The Gambill family lived in the house until 1940, at that time they moved to another home and used the house for housing Milwaukee Railroad employees.

In 1945 the John Gambill family moved back into the main level of the house and continued to house railroaders on the second floor. After the Milwaukee Railroad left the St. Bernice area, three retired railroaders continued to live with the Gambill family until mid 1950's. John Gambill occupied the house until his death. In 1959 the house and

Gambill home before remodeling

40 acres was then purchased by John Gambill's son, Woodrow.

In 1964 Woodrow and Ida Gambill remodeled the exterior of the house. The wrap around concrete porch was removed and a two story porch was added. The interior of the house was restored however the floor plan remains the same. The home is still occupied by Woodrow and Ida Gambill and their two children, James and Melissa.

The house is located south of St. Bernice, Indiana just west of State Road 71.

MILLER PARK

Folks around St. Bernice are so proud of Miller Park, located near old West Clinton, that they wish more groups and individuals in Vermillion County knew about it, and would use it. They have raised more than one thousand dollars to pay for the improvements in addition to putting in a lot of time and effort.

This project was started in 1936 when attorney, Frank R. Miller, who has lived in Terre Haute for many years but whose heart has always remained in his old home community in Vermillion County gave the 18 acres to establish the park. A number of improvements were made at that time, but it did not receive the use that it should have and gradually deteriorated. Actually the park is county property, but improvements have been largely managed by the trustees, appointed by the county and are, Attorney Miller, Cleve Jones, Ora Reed, and Dr. S.I. Green. About ten years ago, 1945, public-spirited citizens of the community decided to again turn the park into a beauty spot and they have done their work well. There were plenty of fine shade trees, as well as pines, planted when the park was established and now grown to good size. All the underbrush was cleared away. Most of the money spent on the improvements was earned at the annual Homecoming Celebrations staged about September 1st of each year and new features have been added until now (1955) the park boasts of a shelter house as well as two refreshment stands, a fine water supply, four picnic tables, electric lights and toilet facilities. More tables and benches will be added soon.

Horseshoe Lakes, a popular privately owned fishing and boating resort adjoins Miller Park on the east. The St. Bernice folks want everyone to know the park is open to all residents of the county to enjoy. The community is having a benefit supper at the I.O.O.F. Hall, April 26, 1955, in an effort to make more money to be used for more improvements.

From Between the Lines in The Daily Clintonian, 1955.

Thousand Trails Resort purchased the popular Horseshoe Lakes owned by the Dyer Family in 1984.

CROWD ATTENDS HOMECOMING

The annual Homecoming at Miller Park was held in honor of Attorney Frank R. Miller of Terre Haute, formerly of St. Bernice. A basket dinner was enjoyed at noon. Those present were from Chicago, Danville, Indianapolis, Oxford, Terre Haute, Rockville, Clinton, Dana, and surrounding communities. Dr. Dan T. Miller of Oxford, brother of the honored guest, gave an interesting talk and music was enjoyed. Harold Jones was elected president for the coming year.

The first Homecoming honoring Attorney Frank R. Miller was held in September, 1949, at the American Legion Home (formerly Jonestown Grade School).

Frank R. Miller, was born September 21, 1879, in Helt Township. He was the son of Charles F. and Sarah A. Reed Miller. He attended grade school at St. Bernice. He graduated from Clinton High School in 1900. He was a graduate of Indiana University in 1905. He practiced law in Clinton and Terre Haute. He was associated with Miller and Pike Law Firm in Clinton, and Miller and Causey Law Firm in Terre Haute. He helped establish the Vorhees Law School in Terre Haute, and served six years as probate commissioner of Vigo County Circuit Court. His memberships included Masonic Lodge, Scottish Rite in Indianapolis, Zorah Shrine, and honorary life member of Terre Haute Elks Lodge. He attended the Methodist Church.

He died at age 82 years in Union Hospital on January 15, 1962. Survivors are a step-mother, Mrs. Nina Miller, of Clinton; a brother, Dr. Daniel T. Miller, of Fowler, Indiana; and several nieces and nephews. Burial was in Sugar Grove Cemetery west of St. Bernice.

SHARON JONES MISSIONARY IN AFRICA

Voiture 1264, Vermillion County chapter of the Forty and Eight, has followed the lead of other similar American Legion-affiliated organizations by sponsoring its first nurse's training project. Miss Sharon Jones, daughter of Mr. and Mrs. Charles Jones of St. Bernice, has been selected for the training program. A Clinton High School graduate with the Class of 1963, Sharon began her nursing career at St. Anthony's Hospital in Terre Haute. Above, David Dowdy, Chef de Gare, presents check to Miss Jones while looking on are: Bob Morris, Emerson Hoke, Joe Kazekevich, Charles Kazekevich, Austin Reed, and John Holliday.

Sharon has been a missionary in Africa for many years.

JEAN NEWTON

Newton's Service Station ceased to be at closing time, Dec. 31, 1985.

Jean Newton has worked at that station since 1939, when he went to work for Lovell Miller. In 1942, Jean left St. Bernice to enter the United States Air Force. He returned from the Air Force in 1946, and went back to work for Miller until 1950.

In 1950, "Me and Jack Scott together bought him out," said Newton. The only major change that has been made to the building was the addition of the front "control center" in 1955.

Jean says he remembers 1950, 51, and 53 as his most prosperous years. "You see, that was when the railroad was here, and everyone, it seemed like, bought their gas here."

Jean has been married to his wife, Marceda, since Jan. 12, 1966. His first wife was killed in an auto accident.

There are eight children in the Newton family, ranging in age from 17 to 38. And they have all at one time or another worked at the station. Especially since 1978.

In 1978 Jean ceased to work full time, for health reasons. So the family pitched in and helped keep the business in the family.

Marceda says, "He would be rich today if he had all the money he has given away in candy, gum, tires, gas, oil and fixing bicycle tires for kids. He may not be rich in money but he sure is rich in spirit," says his wife.

Over the years, the business has been dubbed as the unofficial headquarters of the Democratic Party in St. Bernice. When asked what the main topic of discussion for the democrats was for 1985, Jean says, "griping about Reagan."

The front of the station is the local hangout for the older crowd. "They sit around and talk about everything in here," says Marceda. In the morning all the kids wait for the school bus inside the station.

Jean has had a 1940 "some-odd" model Chevrolet sitting out behind the shop for more than 20 years. All the car needed was a universal joint. So Jean finally found one for it, but he got busy and laid it up for safe keeping. However, there was one problem; when he put it up, he put it up too good. He lost it. When the family was sorting through the accumulated parts and tools recently in the back they came across the old transmission for the Chevy. When they were checking it out they found the universal joint that Jean had lost those many years ago.

"Boy dad, you ought to fix that car up, it sure would be a nice ride," commented one of Jean's sons.

When asked what he was going to do with all of his free time, Jean responded, "Loaf." His wife added, "Too many guys wait too late to retire and then they don't get to loaf because they're gone."

Jean also added, with tears in his eyes, that he would like to thank "all of my customers that have traded with me in past years, especially Jack Scott and Scott Oil Company, and especially my wife Marceda for her help in the past."

An article in The Daily Clintonian by Mary Miller, January 3, 1986.

SCHOOLS

SCHOOL SURVEY

In Helt Township the schools have followed the same pattern of development as the one followed in the settlement of the land. Soon after a small area was settled a one room school was built. Only a small number could attend each school because the school had to be within walking distance from the homes of the children. The school was the center of most social activities. Often church was held on Sunday in the school building after a dance or box supper had been held there on Saturday night. The school term was usually seven months, because the children were needed on the farm during the other months.

Springhill Scool Reunion-Sam Taylor is the seventh man in second row. Josiah Davis is the last person in the last row.

The teacher, who often had no more than eighth grade education, was a leader in the community. Since he often had students older than himself, he was usually a strict disciplinarian. He had to act as janitor, to be jack-of-all-trades, as well as teach all eight grades. In 1913 the average wage for the five male teachers was $4.00 a day and for the twenty-one female teachers was $3.00 a day.

At least thirty-five schools have been built in Helt Township but now they have just one, Ernie Pyle Elementary School. The first one room school was built on the prairie around 1830. According to one early teacher, this first school was named Frog College. It was a one room log building with split log seats. Two other log schools were built in this district before 1894 when a two room brick school was erected. This building was abandoned in 1927. Some of the other early schools in the southeastern section were the Mack School, and No. 16. Later these two schools were combined into one two-room brick building which stood at a point of about equal difference from each of the older schools. It was located at Summit Grove.

All of the schools had numbers at the time when they were being used and some had names according to some landmark or the donor of the land. Whenever the numbers were available they were put on the map, but weren't used in the paper except when a name wasn't available.

In the northeastern section of the township, Highland and Alta schools were built before 1866. A school was built in Hillsdale in 1893. Four different buildings have been constructed in Hillsdale. One was a two room frame building, then a brick building was erected sometime after 1900. Other additions were added and a two year high school was taught at this location for sometime before 1916. Another addition was

made in 1916 and a four year high school came into being. The first diplomas were presented in 1918.

One of the earliest schools in the west central section was Wisiker. This was a round log building with a ten foot wide fireplace. It was located near the state line on the road west of Bono. After this building burned, the students walked down the road to Liberty, a one room brick building which was built in 1857. The Saxton School was located about four miles north and east of Bono. Mound School sat on the Indian mound across the road from the Ernie Pyle Home. When the Saxton School was abandoned, they walked to the Mound School. Some of the other districts in this area were Independence, St. John, Conley, Statt's, and Bono. All of these schools were consolidated into Helt Township School in 1904.

In 1904, the first consolidated school in western Indiana was built at Bono when the former seven districts were combined into one, forming a grade school and high school. This brick building consisted of seven rooms, two very large halls and a basement. The trustee, Fred Bear, provided free transportation, horse drawn school "hacks". No law by the legislature provided for free transportation, the parents took turns at driving the hacks. Two years later the legislature enacted a law that provided for free transportation.

Mr. Thornton Newsom was the first principal at the Helt Township School. Some of the other principals were John R. Stahl, Ritter, R.A. Valentine, E.E. Helt, Ward Beanblossom and Lee Shirley. Among the many teachers who will long be remembered are Jessica Hunt, Escal Bennett, and Chloe James. Before its closing in 1928 about 200 students in twenty-one classes graduated from the school that was once a model for Western Indiana.

Before the Civil War the Hood School

was erected one mile east of the location that was later chosen for Dana. About two miles west of this was the location of the Kaufman School.

Two miles east of Dana, a large elm tree stood in the middle of the road and divided the two lanes of traffic; therefore the school located on the north side of this landmark was called the Elm Tree College. Later it was called Jackson School. On down the road from this location was Redman School or Bucktown School.

The first Dana grade school was taught in 1875 on main street in part of the building that had been moved from Bono. When the enrollment increased to over fifty children in 1877 a new twenty-seven by sixty-two feet brick building was erected. The cost of the two story building with two rooms downstairs and one room upstairs was $2200. By early 1890's the population had increased in the Dana area; therefore a larger school was needed. A six room brick building was occupied in the year 1893.

In 1895, the principal, I.C. Rheubell, began working toward equipping the school to become a commissioned high school. In 1897, the State Board of Education granted the commission.

This school system was operated by a school board within the incorporated town until 1926 when the town turned it over to the township. More will be told about this transition later.

Sometime after the establishment of the village Jonestown, a one room school was erected. Before 1897 two other frame and one brick building were used and in 1897 a new two-story, two-room school was constructed. The first six grades were in the downstairs rooms and grades seven through ten were upstairs. This was a non-commissioned high school for grades nine and ten. Some men who attended this school were Cleve Jones, Clyde Andrews, Frank Miller and Oliver Houston. In order to finish the other two years, they rode horseback ten miles each way to Clinton. This building was condemned in 1910; therefore another brick building was built. The high school idea had been abandoned some years before; hence only the first eight grades met in this building.

The location of another school, Pleasant Hill, was about one mile west of Jonestown. It operated until 1906 when the population of St. Bernice called for a school. For four years classes were held in buildings in the business district. In 1911 another two room building was constructed, this time just south of the business district in St. Bernice. This building had two additions until in 1924 it had eight rooms. This building was used for grades one through six until 1947 when the grade school was moved to the high school building.

During the early twenties when the school attendance increased and more emphasis was upon a high school education, the people in Helt Township wanted better high schools. Up until that time none of the high schools had gymnasiums, or indoor plumbing. Dana,

which had its own high school, added five classrooms, an assembly and a gymnasium. After this was finished in 1925, the project proved to be too great a financial burden for the town; therefore the school was turned over to the township in 1926. Dana operated a very successful school for the next thirty-four years. The principals who served during those years were Lee Shirley, Clyde Cunningham, Ward Beanblossom, Francis McClure, John Pickell, George McReynolds and Tom Burkett. Some of the teachers who helped to mold the students were Marzelle Kerns, Parke Lewman, Jesse Kerns, Ernest Boatman, Esther Redman, Hazel Reed, Clio Jenks and Ivy Jordan.

Hillsdale already had a high school, but it lacked a gymnasium and modern facilities; therefore after the old Bono High School was abandoned a new section was added to the Hillsdale High School in 1928. It too had some illustrious principals: Ward Beanblossom, Mort Lewis, Carl Kiger, Otho Shaw, William May, Edward Wolpert, Loran Stevens, Charles Smith, Charles Roccia, and Franklin Thompson. A few of the better known teachers at Hillsdale were Chloe James, Ivan Connell, Nellie Beanblossom, Margaret Thompson and Fern Brown.

Since the population was growing in St. Bernice, and their children had to go out of town to Bono to high school, while the other towns had their own township schools, St. Bernice insisted that a new building should be built in their town. If a new building wasn't erected an addition would be needed at Bono. A new building was built south and east of the business district in 1927. The principals through the years were: H.B. Hayes, Karl Kiger, Franklin Thompson, Parke Lewman, Olin Swinney, Harry Hayes, Milton Bailey, and Francis Bogart.

A few of the teachers who made lasting impressions were Ernestine Aikman Humphreys, Eschol Bennett, Gladys Miller, Blanche Stevens, Florence Miller, Norma Connell, Nellie Beanblossom and Frances Meyers.

Before the additions and new building were completed, all of the one room buildings had been closed and the children were transported to the larger schools. In 1927 Frog College, the last of the two-room elementary schools, was closed. This was not only the last to close but it was the first school in the township.

From 1928 until 1960 Helt Township supported three combined grade and high schools. The rural area was divided so that the enrollment would be as evenly divided as possible, and buses transported them to the schools.

During the 1950's many people became alarmed about the cost of operating three small high schools. Since the enrollment was under 100, the curriculum was narrow. Several attempts were made to build one centralized school or to build a consolidated school for both Helt and Vermillion Township which lay to the north.

After the Indiana School Reorganization Act in 1959, Judge Frank Fisher appointed a

county committee for reorganization. An advisory committee of seventy-five persons was appointed by the fourteen county Parent-Teacher Organizations. An extensive survey was made of the existing school systems in the county. Seven different plans of reorganization were drawn up. After intensive study a two unit plan for Vermillion County was brought before the voters in the 1960 election. The two unit plan was adopted. This placed Helt Township, Clinton City and Clinton Township into one corporation. It took the name of South Vermillion Community School Corporation. It was decided to close all of the existing schools in Helt Township, to send the high school students to Clinton High School, and to build a new sixteen classroom elementary school building. This new $1,200,000 building, erected in the south central part of the township, was given the name **Ernie Pyle Elementary School**. South Vermillion High School opened in the fall of 1977.

From a paper on Helt Township by Rachel Milligan

HELT TOWNSHIP TEACHERS

1859 - The oldest record available of teachers in Helt Township at this time is Miss Anna Anderson (later Mrs. William Bales) in 1859. She taught her first term of school at age 16 in the old Frog College school, a log building, three-fourths mile east of Center Church. Later she taught at the Bales School, a one-room frame building located one mile east of Jonestown on the north side of the road, just west of the small stream.

1903 - Agnes Lonsdale taught at Jonestown. The first school in Jonestown was a one-room brick building located southeast of the United Brethren Church.

1904 - John R. Stahl taught 49 years in several schools in Vermillion County.

1906 - Zoe Lamb taught at Jonestown (see photo - "Jonestown Hopefuls").

1910 - St. Bernice Grade School was built. It was a two-room brick building and was enlarged to a four-room building with a basement two years later.

1911 - Two-room brick grade school was built on Highway 71. It was enlarged by digging a basement in 1916 and occupied in 1917.

Price list for school books in 1914: Primer - 15 cents, exchange 7 cents; First reader - 15 cents, exchange 8 cents; Second reader - 20 cents, exchange 10 cents; Fourth reader - 30 cents, exchange 15 cents; Fifth reader - 40 cents, exchange 20 cents; Arithmetic - 30 cents, exchange 15 cents; Advanced arithmetic - 42 cents, 21 cents.

1914 - Helt Township teachers: No. 17 - Principal, Clarence Church; primary, Lillian Randall. No. 1 - May Pickett. Redman - A.S. Goodwin. Alta - Lenora Pearman. Spring Hill - Ruth Clearwaters. Hillsdale - Superintendent, E.E. Davis; Principal, Rose Small; grades, Virginia Foster and Ruth Hunt. Summit Grove - Principal, Chloe James; grades, Mae Elliott. Frog College - Principal, Zoe Lamb; grades, Ruth Campbell.

No. 21 - Principal, Mollie Linebarger; grades, Ruth McFall. No. 13 - Principal, Ruth Sturm; grades, Geraldine Toops. Bono - Superintendent, W.R. Valentine; Principal, Edgar A. Stahl; Assistant, Mae M. Green; Music and Drawing, S. Helen Jewett; grades, Martha Llewellyn, Mabel Clearwaters, Mrs. C.B. Campbell, and Lillie Cooley.

The annual Commencement of eighth grade graduates of Vermillion County will be held at the Air Dome in Clinton June 18, 1914, at 2 P.M. The address will be delivered by Honorable George L. MacKintosh, President of Wabash College on the subject, "Earning a Living and Living the Living". Diplomas will be presented to the graduates by County Superintendent, Roy H. Valentine. A musical program will be by the Clinton Orchestra.

1915 - Helt Township Teachers (partial list): Hillsdale - Superintendent, E.E. Davis; Principal, Luella Napes; Virgie Swayne and Geraldine Toops.

Bono - Superintendent, W.R. Valentine; Principal, Edgar A. Stahl; Latin and English, Mary Kitsmiller; Music and Drawing, Gladys C. Pierce; grades, Myrtle Conklin, Mabel Clearwaters, Mrs. C.B. Campbell, and Lillie Ooley. St. Bernice - Principal, Ruth Clearwaters; primary, Edna Elwell. Frog College - Principal, Zoe Lamb; primary, Lillian Randall. Summit Grove - Principal, Chloe James; primary, Lillian Randall. No. 17 - Principal, Ruth Sturm; primary, Lenora Pearman. Spring Hill - Edna Phillips. Highland - Leatha Houchin. Redman - Clarence Church.

June 24, 1914, Dana, Notice from E.F. McCown, Trustee of Helt Township—I will receive sealed bids on Thursday June 11, 1914, at my office in Dana, Indiana, at 2 P.M. for the erection of a one-room school building at the old Redman location. Plans and specifications are now on file in my office, and the right is reserved to reject any and all bids. SEAL E.F. McCown, Trustee, Helt Township.

County News Briefs - Collett Merriman of Dana was awarded the contract for building the Redman schoolhouse in Helt Township for approximately $2,300. The first Redman School was destroyed by fire February 18 last and the school term was finished by hauling the children to other schools.

1916 - List of Dana common school graduates - Louise Aldrich, Margaret Toops, Russell Bratton, Diamond Tomey, Paul Payton, Genevieve Ingle, Dana DeHaven, Carl Barnhart, Norma Fillinger, Milton Davis, Gladys Crawford, Dorothy Lauer, W.D. Dicken, Marzelle James, Carl Ingram, Floyd Gosnell, Dwight Thompson, E.F. Kaufman, Cale Bales, Virgle C. Larrance, Cecil Satterlee, and Ernest Brooks. From Hoosier State, Newport.

1920's - Jonestown (two-room brick) — Clyde Andrews, Myrtle Bales.

1925-26 - County Superintendent of Schools - J.F. Lewman. Bono - Principal, Ward Beanblossom; Garnet Lloyd, Leonard E. Pittman, Marie Igo, Olive Hadley, Chloe James, Genevieve Ingle, Margaret Beard,

Meredith Goforth, and Nellie Beanblossom. 202 pupils. St. Bernice Grade School - Principal; Franklin H. Thompson; Georgie Thompson, Karl Kiger, Blanche Brown, Florence Kuhns, Violet McClure, and June Wann. 183 pupils. Jonestown - Myrtle Bales (grades 5-8) and Esther E. Ford (grades 1-4). 38 pupils. Summit Grove - Clarence Cooper (grades 5-8) and Louise Blakesley (grades 1-4). 43 pupils. Frog College - Mary Alice Kuhns (grades 1-8). 27 pupils.

Samuel E. Taylor taught at St. Bernice and Hillsdale schools. He also taught in Gary.

John R. Stahl taught 49 years in Vermillion County and was county superintendent of schools in 1895. He was principal of Bono School from 1874-1923.

Dorotha Clark of Dana taught several years at Bono, Hillsdale, and Dana.

Gertie Aikman taught at Bono School.

Ollie Mack taught at Frog College School.

Laura Hood Wimsett taught at Pleasant Hill and Summit Grove schools.

Maud Fable Wright taught at Dana School.

Frances L. Myers taught 44 years (1928-1972) at St. Bernice and Ernie Pyle Elementary School.

Chloe James taught 43 years at Dana, Clinton, St. Bernice, Hillsdale and Bono.

F.H. Thompson taught 39 years at St. Bernice, Bono, and other schools.

Violet McClure Houston Gardner taught six years in Helt Township and 38 years in Richmond, Indiana.

Rose McFall Small taught several years retiring in 1952. She was an English teacher at Indiana State University for many years.

Clio Platz King Jenks taught 40 years.

Lee Shirley taught 47 years. He served 33 years as a principal, "a forceful educator". He taught at Bono.

Agnes Lonsdale Kendall taught at Summit Grove.

Ward Beanblossom was a teacher and school administrator for 47 consecutive years, 15 1/2 years as Vermillion County Superintendent of Schools and 1 1/2 years as Superintendent of North Vermillion School Corporation. He taught at Bono, Hillsdale, and Dana.

Nellie Beanblossom taught 42 years. She taught at Bono, Hillsdale, and St. Bernice. She served as principal at St. Bernice Grade School at one time.

Florence Miller taught at Rockville, Dana, St. Bernice, and Ernie Pyle Elementary School retiring in 1970.

Agnes Lonsdale was a teacher in the township.

Ruby K. Miller was also a teacher in Helt Township.

Grace E. Cripe taught 40 years, part of that time at St. Bernice High School and Hillsdale High School.

Myrtle Bales taught at Jonestown School.

Gladys Ingram Miller taught in Parke County and St. Bernice High School.

Mable Frazier Ray was a teacher at Summit Grove and St. Bernice.

Virginia Martin taught 33 years, the last 24 at Ernie Pyle Elementary School.

John B. Nelson taught 45 years retiring in 1979.

Parke Lewman taught 25 years, some of those years were at Dana High School and St. Bernice High School.

CLIO KING JENKS

Clio Jenks retired from Ernie Pyle Elementary School in 1968. She also taught at St. Bernice Grade School.

Clio was a dedicated Christian woman in the Dana Community, a noted public speaker in the Wabash Valley, especially her "Hat Talks" depicting her philosophy of life, about 75 years as a Sunday School teacher, having started at 13 years of age, a long time news correspondent for Clinton, Terre Haute, and Chrisman newspapers, a retired teacher with 40 years devoted to that profession, a 66-year member of the Order of Eastern Star, and a 75-year member of the Rebekah Lodge.

FLORENCE K. MILLER

Mrs. Florence K. Miller, St. Bernice, receives a colored, autographed picture of President and Mrs. Reagan from Rep. John Myers, along with other awards presented to her during the concluding session of the 64th annual 4-H Roundup at Purdue University, West Lafayette. She was honored for having served 55 years as a volunteer 4-H leader in St. Bernice. The 4-H Foundation awarded her the silver tray she holds, and Gov. Robert Orr recognized her dedication by naming her a "Sagamore of the Wabash." Her mementos from the President also included a card commending her for many years of volunteer service. This was in 1982.

Mrs. Miller retired from teaching in 1970. At that time she was teaching fifth grade at Ernie Pyle Elementary School. She also taught at Rockville, Dana, and St. Bernice schools.

She is a past president of the state Home Economics Club, past president of the Rebekah Assembly of Indiana, past president of Alpha Alpha Chapter of Delta Kappa Gamma, past president of Phi Chapter of Sigma Delta Pi, a member of the St. Bernice Baptist Church, and a charter member of the Vermillion County Chorus.

Mrs. Miller has traveled extensively. She has been around the world four times.

BONO SCHOOL

The Bono School was built in 1904 located just east of the town of Bono under the trusteeship of Mr. Fred Beard. This was the first consolidated school in West-Central Indiana and the second consolidation in the state. A two-story brick structure had seven rooms, two very large halls, two offices, a basement, and an auditorium. It was built by two neighborhood men, Porter Andrews, brick mason, and O.B. Hickman, Sculptor. It was considered a magnificent structure and a "Tower of Education" even though it had very primitive facilities. Students in grades one through twelve were taught reading, history, math, language, and most importantly spelling. In 1908 music instruction was added to the curriculum.

The standard dress code for girls consisted of high-topped shoes, black stockings, homemade cotton dresses with length of more than half-way from knees to the ankle.

At the time of opening in November, 1904, it brought together students from seven of the small country schools including Spring Hill, Saxton, Staats, St. John, Bono, Liberty, and Mound Schools. Conley, Summit Grove, and Frog College were added about ten years later. It graduated about 200 students from high school in the 24 years it existed.

BONO TEACHERS
1925

Delores Brown Morrison, Escal Stuart Bennett, Jessica J. Hunt, Genevieve Ingle, Chloe James, and Marie Igo.

1926

Marie Igo, Garnet Lloyd, Chloe James, Glen Andrews, Genevieve Ingle, Leonard Pittman, Nellie Beanblossom, Meredith Goforth, and Margaret Beard.

1927

Fauneil Scott, Chloe James, Jessie L. Miller, Marie Igo, Lynn Fisher, Genevieve Ingle, Nellie Beanblossom, Meredith Goforth, Margaret Beard.

1928

Principal, Lee Shirley, high school, Ruth Marshall, Lee Otis Rund, Frances Prentice, Charles Hite, and Jessie Kerns, junior high school, Margaret Sturm, grades four, five, and six—Margaret Beard, primary, Tabitha Bell.

ST. BERNICE SCHOOLS

Rented buildings served as school housing until the grade school was built in 1911 (two rooms). The high school students were transported to Bono and went there until 1928 when the high school was built on an eight-acre site near the west end of the Jonestown Road, housing all seventh and eighth grades and high school students from West Clinton Junction, St. Bernice, Jonestown, and Center area.

The high school building was made possible by the united efforts of the people in this community and the trustee, Davis S. Wellman. It has twelve classrooms, an auditorium seating two hundred, and a gymnasium with no equal in this section of the state. A continuous commission 6-6 type, has been granted to this school, and it is our aim to put it in Class A next year. The first class of graduates in 1929 consisted of ten members.

ST. BERNICE TEACHERS
1930

H.B. Hayes, Prin., M.W. Cooper, E.S. Bennett, E.E. Helt, Zelma L. Harwood, L.C. Northcott, and Ruth Marshall.

1947-1961

Grade School Teachers

Frances Myers, Meda Wright, Blanche Stevens, Nellie Beanblossom, Lucille Gilfoy,

Virginia Ford, Jewel Reed, Bertha Martin, Desree Brown, William Dunlap, Adah Schwab, Wanda Vandivier, and Mrs. Meyers.

High School Teachers

Olin Sweeney, Prin., Kathryn LaRoche, Noble Mayes, David Lee, Norma Connell, Gladys Miller, James Watts, Ezra Overpeck, Harry H. Hayes, Prin., John Kowinski, Angeline Bardon, Ed Linderman, Joan Dunlap, Minerva Roeschlein, W. David Koile, Henry Ford, Don Reel, Milton A. Bailey, Prin., Letha Trout, Robert Meyers, Donald Cooper, Clarence "Nick" Day, Dorothy Brown, Wendell Adams, Parke Lewman, Prin., William Dunlap, Joseph A. Benna, Robert E. Simpers, Michael Vass, Ruby Grinstead, Tom Burkett, Evelyn Hixon, Audrey Brammer, Eugene Davies, Don Greenwood, Francis Bogard, Prin., Sharron Timmerman, Joseph Frisz, Anna Mae Meadows, Janice Bradley, James G. Russell, and Kathryn Russell.

BUCKTOWN SCHOOL - 1912

The old Bucktown School used to be very near the U.S. 36 overpass where it crosses Old 36. That location is about three miles west of the present U.S. 36 and S.R. 63 intersection. Also located in that area was a church and a sawmill owned by Sam and Ellie Kaufman.

Those in the picture are Row 1: Charley Saxton, Charley Brown, Horace Kent, Homer Russell, Paul Sexton, George Brown, Therman Farner, Rheuben Kaufman, Kenneth

Brown. Row 2: Bonnie Douglas, Pauline Jackson, Helen Kaufman, Grace Brock, William Brock, Esther Wellman, Mabel Howard, Goldie Farner. Row 3: Madaline Kent, Mildred Dugger, Ruth Russell, Nona Howard, Vivian Saxton, Sherry Kaufman, Sam Saxton, Roy Wellman. Row 4: Goldie Jackson - teacher, Gladys Kent, George Brock, Margaret Howard, Jennie Kaufman, Juanita Saxton, Ray Russell, Ernest Brown, Raymond Kent, Ruby Russell.

CHURCHES

CENTER METHODIST CHURCH

The Center Methodist Episcopal Church was organized about fifty years ago, at the residence of James Wishard, where services were held for many years. In 1853, the present commodious frame structure was erected, 30 x 40 feet in size, at a cost of about $1,400. Present membership, ninety-seven. Class-leaders, George Campbell and Alanson Church. Stewards, H.P. McCown, B.F. Smith, and Henry Shaffer. Class-meeting every two weeks, and public services every two weeks. Prayer meeting every Thursday evening during the winter. Sunday-school all the year, at 9:30 A.M. Rev. J.B. Combs, of Clinton, is the present pastor.

Taken from 1888 Vermillion County History

Center Methodist Church was situated six miles northwest of Clinton, Indiana. It was built in 1893 on the site of the old church which was built in 1853. The founders of the old church were: Peter Stokesberry, James Wishard, Sr., Erastus Crane, Silas Bright, Josiah Church, and Billie Hays. The minister in charge was Reverend Leech. Before the first church was built, meetings were held in Peter Stokesberry's barn which is still standing and is owned by Mildred Botner Wright. One of the ministers of that time was Reverend Warner.

The Center Sunday School was the first in Helt Township and was organized by an Eastern lady named Sarah McComb.

James Wishard named it Center because it was in the center of Helt Township.

Center Church was closed about 1967 and most of the members went into what is now Wayside United Methodist Church.

The church building has since been re-modeled into a home by Ernest and Inez Myers.

THE HILLCREST COMMUNITY CENTER AND PRESBYTERIAN CHURCH

The Hillcrest Presbyterian Church became part of the United Presbyterian Church in 1962, thus lending its unique heritage and vitality to that newly organized church.

By 1910 many hundreds of southern European immigrants were coming to Clinton and surrounding areas to seek work in the expanding coal mining industry. It soon became evident that there was a definite need for action to aid in improving the conditions of these new Clinton residents, both for their own sakes and to satisfy the waking consciousness of social responsibility which was gradually taking hold of the country. Mr. J.W. Robb, a First Presbyterian Church Elder, believed that the answer to such a need was to provide a building in which could be carried on religious training as well as a program for the parents in homemaking, English, Adaptation to the new ways of living, character training for the children, and to serve as a "friend in need". He presented a plan for an "Italian Mission" to the Crawfordsville Presbytery in 1910, with the result that the Synod's Committee on National Missions and the women of the Synodical joined hands to pledge their support for such a building.

In October, 1911, the little red brick corner building was erected at Eighth and Oak Streets at a cost of $3,000. Mr. Robb was the first superintendent of the Sunday School and the Rev. C.A. Papa, an Italian minister from Chicago was the first to expand the work from Sunday School instruction into the adult education field. The activities included regular preaching services, Sunday School, a fraternal society among men, and industrial classes for boys and girls.

When The Rev. Papa left after three years, Miss Della Brown of Indianapolis was appointed to direct the activities of Hill Crest. By 1915 Miss Brown's brother, the Rev. L.O. Brown and his wife were called to assist his sister in the tremendous job of expanding activities and attendance at Hillcrest. The name "Hill Crest Chapel" was suggested by Mrs. L.O. Brown during those early years, and it was also during this period that perhaps the greatest number of people representing over 25 nationalities truly found this institution to be "A Friend In Need", as it endeavored to carry out the motto which had been adopted by the Hill Crest Chapel. In 1917 Miss Brown returned to Indianapolis and for the next two years, Rev. and Mrs. L.O. Brown carried on the work which was enlarged to include English classes, Boy and Girl Scout activities, library facilities and Vacation Bible School.

In 1919 Miss Elizabeth Pfander who had just graduated from the Presbyterian College of Christian Education in Chicago came from there to assist the Rev. and Mrs. L.O. Brown. By this time the activities had quite outgrown the small quarters provided in the chapel; so the new building was erected in 1922 at a cost of $32,000. This was under the control of the Hillcrest Governing Committee, which assumed full financial support and control of Hillcrest. Gifts for this building came from all over the state, as well as many personal subscriptions. The building provided a gymnasium, domestic science room, class and club rooms, bowling alley, office and living quarters. Miss Pfander was followed by Mr. and Mrs. R.M. Stwalley. Mrs. Stwalley became the assistant at Hill Crest after Miss Pfander's return to Chicago to become secretary to the pastor of the Chicago Millard Avenue Presbyterian Church.

Programs of religious training, home-making classes, English classes and the children's activities continued and expanded. By 1924 they felt a need for more emphasis to be given to the spiritual work and encouraged and approved plans for the organization of a church. A petition was presented to the Crawfordsville Presbytery for the organization of a church and further requesting that the name "Hillcrest Community Center Church." The charter members were: Mrs. Vincenzo Masarachia, Josephine M., Frank, Lena and Joseph Masarachia, Mrs. Rudolph Loos, Mrs. Elizabeth Loos, Bert, Hazel, Wayne and Iretta Wallis, and Alex and Julia Bodnar.

After 17 years continuous service, Rev. and Mrs. Brown returned to Indianapolis and Miss Pfander was called back to become Superintendent, a position which she held until 1943. Mr. and Mrs. R.M. Stwalley, Mr. and Mrs. J.C. Jenkins and many volunteer workers assisted in the Hillcrest work during that time. With Miss Pfander's leaving in 1943, it was decided to institute Hillcrest as a full Presbyterian Church and to combine the pastorates of the First Presbyterian Church and Hillcrest Church. Rev. Charles A. Surber served as minister from 1943 until 1944, one of the hectic war-time years.

With the arrival of Rev. and Mrs. Roy C. Linberg in the fall of 1944, Hillcrest continued in its ever-busy cycle. Many community changes had taken place. Mining in Clinton had almost ceased; there were no longer families coming from across the seas; citizenship and domestic science classes had been discontinued. But the activities of Church, Sunday School, Missionary Societies, Girl Scouts, Boy Scouts, Craft classes, gym activities, choirs, summer camps and Daily Vacation Bible School still proclaimed what the words across the lobby door read: "We Are Laborers Together With God". All through the years since its establishment, Hillcrest had been supported by Synod's National Missions Committee, Synodical, individual gifts and a Christmas Fund contributed to by churches and friends of Hillcrest from all parts of the state and Hillcrest members. The affairs of Hillcrest were directed by a governing board made up of leading state Presbyterians and prominent Clinton residents from various churches.

A new chapter for Hillcrest began on January 1, 1957, when the Board of Managers was dissolved, and Hillcrest Presbyterian Church came into being, with the direct responsibilities of Hillcrest turned over to local church officers. Rev. R.C. Linberg's pastoral services were solely available at Hillcrest at that time. Some aid was still received from National Missions for the daily program of the Church. In 1958, with some financial aid from National Missions but with labor donated entirely by the congregation, a new sanctuary was built in the south half of the gym area. With the retirement of Rev. and Mrs. Roy C. Linberg in 1960, Hillcrest Presbyterian Church was served by Rev. J.J. Saalwachter, the pastor of the First Presbyterian Church.

In the previous four years financial aid from National Missions had been reduced until in 1960 there was no aid available. The officers and leaders of the Hillcrest Church tried to make friends and members aware of this change in its position. In 1962, after many joint meetings of the Sessions of both First and Hillcrest Churches, the two were united to become the United Presbyterian Church of Clinton meeting in the building of the former First church. It was a new church with two long and proud traditions, and its congregation carried on Hillcrest's tradition of providing good fellowship and dignified worship of God, firm in its belief that still "We Are Laborers Together With God".

ST. BERNICE CHRISTIAN CHURCH

A Christian Church was organized in St. Bernice in April, 1883, with 19 members. Some of the families were: Elders, Walter Pauley, and James Holston. The pastor was Elder Williams of Parke County. Sunday School was held during the summer.

The church building was built in 1898. The Ingalls, parents of Sally Daugherty, donated the land.

The last service for the Christian Church was held the last Sunday in 1984.

ST. BERNICE UNITED BRETHERN CHURCH

The St. Bernice Church was organized in the spring of 1851 at the home of James M. Payton, one mile north of St. Bernice. The class, up to the time of building the church was called "Pleasant Hill Class". (Pleasant Chapel Church first organized at Sugar Grove in Edgar County, Illinois, in pioneer days and removed to Pleasant Hill School #13 in the year of 1867). The class was organized by the Reverend S.C. Zuck, Pastor of the Clinton Circuit, with the following members: James M. Payton, Elizabeth Payton, Charles G. Eaton, Hannah L. Eaton, David J. Wolf, Rebecah Wolf, William Andrews, Jane Andrews, John O. Wishard, Abbie Wishard, Amanda J. Nolan, Elizah Gerrish Nolan, Thomas J. Skidmore, Sarah Ricker Burgess, Henry M. Nolan, Hattie Gerrish Marshall, Edward Gerrish, and Lucinda Nichols Newton.

The frame church house at St. Bernice was erected in the year of 1875, under the pastorate of the Reverend J.R. Scott, Pastor of Brouiletts Creek Circuit, by the following trustees: Charles G. Eaton, David J. Wolf, and William Andrews at a cost of $2,200. The house was dedicated November 3, 1875, by Reverend J.W. Nye.

The parsonage at Bernice was erected under the pastorate of the Reverend William Vail in the year 1900, by James P. Hartsook, William Light and Vachel T. Houston (see photo) at the cost of $1,250.00.

The United Brethern Church served the community well for over 100 years. Due to changing times, its doors were closed on March 29, 1971. It was vacant until October 15, 1983. The Rebekah Lodge bought it for their meeting place as the old I.O.O.F. Hall was too large and too expensive to maintain.

St. Bernice Man Dead

"Henry M. Nolan was born in Edgar County, Illinois, October 6, 1846. He died March 17, 1916, at his home in Hunter Township in Illinois, aged 69 years 5 months and 11 days. He came from a sturdy line of pioneers, and got his first schooling in a log school house about one mile northwest of Sugar Grove Church. At the age of ten he entered Edgar Academy at Paris. When 18 years of age he taught in his first school near Clinton. On the 17 of September, 1868, he was married to Miss Elizah Gerrish of Vermillion County, Indiana. They were the parents of one child, Mrs. Ivy E. Wilkin of Vermillion, Illinois. Mr. Nolan early united with the Methodist protestant church. On October 6, 1871, he was ordained to the regular ministry. For ten years he was superintendent of the old St. Bernice U.B. Sunday School, never missing a day in that long period of service. For the past two years he had been leader of the Sunday School at the Christian Church in St. Bernice. On the last Sunday he led the Bible school with his usual vigor and efficiency. He taught the public schools of Edgar and Vermillion Counties for more than 15 years, and only his strong love for his home scenes and associates prevented his acceptance of offers of more flattering positions of rank and position." (the remainder of this obituary of Henry M. Nolan is missing)

From the Hoosier State, Newport, Indiana Wednesday, March 29, 1916

SPRING HILL METHODIST EPISCOPAL CHURCH

The Spring Hill Methodist Episcopal Church was located seven miles north of Salem Church. This picture was taken about 1902.

Zachariah D. James, son of Dr. and Mrs. William James, was one of the principal members who helped organize the Church in 1834. The church shown here was built in 1878-79 at a cost of $1,775. It was of frame construction measuring 30 by 40 feet and in 1888 had a membership of about 30.

Rev. W.C. Aye occupied the pulpit every other Sunday, alternating with Rev. John E. Wright, in the summer of 1901. It was his first church and for several months work, he received $1.25 and a chicken dinner at the home of Mrs. Ellen Carter. He said: "I got all the preaching was worth."

ASBURY CHAPEL METHODIST EPISCOPAL CHURCH

The class meeting here was organized as early as 1830. One of the first ministers was Rev. DeLap. Services were held at private residences and in school-houses until 1850, when a frame church, 30 x 40 feet was erected on the southeast quarter of section 36, township 16, range 10. The most successful revival was held in 1852, under the pastorate of Rev. Arthur Badley, who was living in Iowa when last heard from. Among the pastors who have had charge of this church since the building of the present house of worship have been Revs. J.W. Parrett, Shaw, Thomas Bartlett, Salsbury, Clark Skinner, McDaniel, Wood, Barnard, Nebeker, Barnett, Morrison and E.R. Johnson. The class has, of later years, been considerably reduced in number, and they now have no regular preaching.

Taken from 1888 Vermillion County History

SPRING HILL CLASS METHODIST EPISCOPAL CHURCH

Was organized in 1834, in the house of Joel Blakesley, with Samuel Rush and wife, Joel Blakesley and wife, Zachariah D. James and wife, Jane Ford, Sarah Ponton, Stephen Harrington and wife, William Kearns and wife, Lydia Jackson, Enoch White and wife, Martha Ponton, Betsey Ponton, and Nathaniel Barnes and wife. In 1835 they built a hewed-log house, near the center of section 10, township 15, range 9, which they used several years. The class was then known as "Goshen." They next removed to the school-house a half mile north. The present house, of worship, a frame 30 x 40 feet, was built in 1879, at a cost of $1,775. There are now about thirty members. Sunday-school all the year, with A. Harvey Kearns as superintendent. Trustees—William A. James and Moses Thompson. Pastor—Rev. James Smith. The present name of the class, "Spring Hill," was adopted at the time of the building of the present church.

Taken from 1888 Vermillion County History

HILLSDALE METHODIST EPISCOPAL CHURCH

The Methodist Episcopal Church at Hillsdale was organized July 11, 1880, by Rev. Thomas Bartlett, with the following members: J.W. Casebeer, class-leader; S.R. James, Matilda James, Margaret Owens, Dr. E. Mack, Mrs. Mack, Martha Strowbridge, Ella Casebeer, Martha Casebeer, A.B. Casebeer, C.M. Casebeer, E.M. Casebeer, Sarah Wilson, Mary McLaughlin, Jane Williamson, Wallace Thompson, Mrs. Thompson, Elizabeth Newell, R. Wilson, Thomas J. Williamson, Bertie Casebeer, Billy Ponton, Charles Bassett and Mrs. Mary Marvin.

The present church edifice, a fine frame 34 x 40 feet, and costing $1,650, was built in 1883-'84, principally with money bequeathed by a Sister Bricker. The ground was donated by Mrs. Mary Gibson. Trustees—J.W. Casebeer, J.T. Ponton, S.R. James, W.A. James, E. Mack, A.B. Casebeer and Charles Bassett.

Taken from 1888 Vermillion County History

DANA CHRISTIAN CHURCH

Dana Christian Church was organized temporarily about the first of September, 1886. A Sunday-school of about sixty pupils is superintended by Prof. A.J. Wilson. A few zealous Christians, led by Rev. J.W. Jarvis and his business partner, John Morris—although the latter is not a member of the church—have just built a fine house of worship at Dana, in the northwestern part of the town, the first church erected by this people in Vermillion County. It is a brick structure, 32 x 54 feet in ground area, neatly finished and furnished in modern style, and cost $2,335.38. It was dedicated April 17, 1887, by Elder L.L. Carpenter, of Wabash, Indiana. The present membership of the church is about fifty. Elder J.W. Jarvis is the "temporary" pastor.

Taken from 1888 Vermillion County History

LIBERTY CLASS UNITED BRETHREN CHURCH

Liberty Class, United Brethren Church, was organized in 1878, by Rev. Henry Nolan, with about sixteen or eighteen members, in Liberty school-house, on section 15, township 15, range 10. The first pastor was Rev. Thomas O. Baty, who served from the fall of 1878 to the fall of 1880; W.A. Wainscott, 1880-'83; James Smith, 1883-'84; Levi Byrd, 1884-'86; S.S. Sims, 1886 to the present. Membership twenty-six, worshipping still in Liberty school-house. Class-leader, Frank Skidmore. Thomas Skidmore, superintendent of the Sunday-school, which is at present maintained only during the summer, but efforts are made to continue it the year round. Public service every three weeks. A prayer-meeting is also sustained.

Taken from 1888 Vermillion County History

MIDWAY UNITED BRETHREN CHURCH

Midway United Brethren Church was organized in 1857, by Rev. Joel Cowgill, with probably fifteen or twenty members, in the Castle school-house, which is still their place of worship, though it has been purchased by them and converted into a church. Its size is 22 x 30 feet, and is situated on section 13, township 15, range 10. Public services were discontinued August 28, 1887, with no definite plans for the future.

Taken from 1888 Vermillion County History

HIDDLE'S PRAIRIE BAPTIST CHURCH

In 1852 a branch or "mission" of the Bloomfield Baptist Church was established at Toronto, and July 23, 1853, it was organized as a separate body in the Toronto Presbyterian Chapel, by Rev. G.W. Riley. The constituent members were Chandler Tillotson, John Depuy, James Drinen, Reuben Puffer, Daniel G. Tillotson, John Newton, A.H. Depuy, Hannah Martin, Mary Newton, Eliza J. Depuy, Harriet Puffer, Elizabeth Tillotson, Rebecca Tillotson, Rametha Scott, O.Z. Derthic, Harriet Derthic, Adaline Derthic and Mary Derthic.

Taken from 1888 Vermillion County History

UNITED BRETHREN CHURCH NEWPORT

The United Brethren Church at Newport was organized in 1870, by Rev. Samuel Garrigus, who was then a resident of Bellmore, Parke County, but is now at Crawfordsville, this State. The society at first comprised but twelve or fourteen members, but it has increased to ninety, principally under the labors of the present pastor, Rev. B.F. Dungan, within the last few months. The first class-leader was C.M. Parkes; the present class-leader is Rettie R. Smith; assistant class-leader, Mrs. Belle Thornton. These ladies have a very large field of spiritual work, compared with class-leaders generally. A lively Sunday-school of about seventy pupils is maintained throughout the year, superintended by Mrs. Thornton. The steward of the church at this point is Z.P. Thornton. The society at present worships in the Presbyterian church, on Market street, one block east of the public square, but they contemplate building a house of worship this year. A pleasant house is rented for a parsonage in the west part of the village.

Taken from 1888 Vermillion County History

TORONTO METHODIST EPISCOPAL CHURCH

Toronto Methodist Episcopal Church was organized in February, 1853, by Rev. John Lach, who had just conducted a successful series of revival meetings here. He died twenty years ago. Among the first members were John Jenks and family, William Jordan and wife, Mrs. Tiller Jenks, John R. Wishard and wife, Almeda Jenks (now Eaton), and others. In 1875 a great revival was held by Rev. Jacob Musser. There are now about sixty members, with Stephen Jenks as class-

leader. Services every two weeks, by Rev. William Smith, in the Presbyterian church. Sunday-school, union: Peter Aikman, superintendent.

TORONTO PRESBYTERIAN CHURCH

Toronto Presbyterian Church was organized as early as 1850 or '51, by Rev. Gerrish, the house of worship was built during the latter year. It is a frame, 36 x 40 feet in dimensions, and is still in a good state of preservation. Among the early members of the church were James A. Elder and wife, Samuel Elder and wife, etc. Rev. John A. Tiffany was pastor from 1858 to 1866. There are now about twenty communicants; a large proportion are changing their membership to Dana. Rev. Thomas Griffith is the present pastor. A union Sunday-school is kept up throughout the year: Edwin Tiffany, superintendent. A union prayer-meeting is sustained in the church by the Presbyterians, Baptists and Methodists.

The Toronto Presbyterian Church, at Bono, was organized many years ago, but the members are now changing their places of meeting to Dana, where they have just completed one of the most beautiful frame church edifices in the nation. Its size is 32 x 54 feet, besides a "rostrum" 8 x 14 feet; its style is of course modern and of fancy finish, and the cost about $2,800, not counting the pews and other furniture. It was dedicated June 26, 1887, by Rev. T.D. Fyffe, of Roseville, Indiana. The location is in the northern part of the village, in Samuel Aikman's addition. The leading men in building this church were W.M. Taylor, Samuel Aikman and Samuel Hall.

Taken from 1888 Vermillion County History

ORGANIZATIONS
THE INDEPENDENT ORDER OF ODD FELLOWS LODGE ST. BERNICE

The Independent Order of Odd Fellows Lodge was instituted January 9, 1891. The charter members were: Fred Staats, A.J. Wilson, Fred Rush, J.M. Hayes, A.H. Nichols, Sam Malone, J.R. Stahl, C.B. Davis, George Tillottson, H.B. Davis, Robert Stocks, J.F. Peeler, William Burkin, and W.H. Leedy (Grand Master).

The Columbian Rebekah Lodge was instituted on May 28, 1893, and some of the first officers were (1895): Alda McCown, Emma Mahan, Vivian McCown, Lou McCown, Maude Ayres, J.C. Lynn, George McCown, Minnie Bales, J.P. Hartsook, A.K. Mahan, and Alice Lonsdale.

The Odd Fellows moved their membership to the Clinton Lodge and the Rebekahs are still active in Jonestown. The Rebekahs moved to the old United Brethren Church building and the lodge hall is standing empty.

INDEPENDENT ORDER OF ODDFELLOWS

Dana Lodge, No. 581, I. O. O. F., was

instituted February 10, 1881, with eighteen members, and Hiram Shepard, Noble Grand; Julius C. Groves, Vice Grand; and Fred Rush, Secretary. The present membership is forty, and officers, Solon Johnson, Noble Grand; L.H. Reed, Vice Grand; H. Wells, Secretary; G.H. Fisher, Permanent Secretary; J.M. Taylor, Treasurer; Samuel Jackson, Inner Guard; T.J. Hutchinson and H. Herbin, Supporters. The lodge has a very nicely furnished room in the Peer Block. The furnishings and regalia cost about $2,000.

Taken from 1888 Vermillion County History

MAJOR ARRN POST, G.A.R. HILLSDALE

Major Arrn Post, No. 370, G. A. R., was chartered July 13, 1884, with the following members: J.A. Souders, L. Newell, J.F. Whitson, W.A. James, T.S. King, B.G. Souders, W.J. Lake, A.B. Casebeer, J.W. Justice, H. Casebeer, Cooper Jackson, J.W. Middlebrook, Dr. E. Mack, J.A. Luce, E. Short, A. Pearman, F.M. Lake, William Pearman and W.A. Roeback,—nineteen in all. The first officers were—Cooper Jackson, Post Commander; W.A. James, Senior Vice-Commander; J.A. Luce, Junior Vice-Commander; A.B. Casebeer, Adjutant; J.F. Whitson, Quartermaster; J.A. Souders, Officer of the Day. There are now twenty-one members, who meet on the second and fourth Saturday evenings of each month, in the Hillsdale school-house. The present officers are—W.A. James, Post Commander; A.B. Casebeer, Senior Vice-Commander; B.G. Souders, Junior Vice-Commander; J.F. Whitson, Adjutant; Samuel Lane, Quartermaster; Cooper Jackson, Officer of the Day.

Taken from 1888 Vermillion County History

H.D. WASHBURN POST, G.A.R. DANA

H.D. Washburn Post, No. 220, G. A. R., was organized in 1883, with about eighteen members, and the following officers: William B. Hood, Post Commander; G.H. Fisher, Senior Vice-Commander; O.B. Lowry, Quarter master; H. Wells, Adjutant; J.B. Fillinger, Officer of the Day. The present membership is twenty-six, and the officers: J.B. Fillinger, Post Commander; G.W. Saxton, Senior Vice-Commander; James Burnett, Junior Vice-Commander; J.N. McClure, Adjutant; James Knight, Officer of the Day; Henry Thomasmeyer, Quarter-master; G.H. Fisher, Quarter-master-Sergeant; Daniel Riland, Officer of the Guard; J.C. Harrison, Surgeon; W.B. Hood, Chaplain. Financially, the post is in fair condition. This year they are building a hall, being the second story of the brick business block to be erected by Charles Norris, which is to be 22 x 50 feet in dimensions.

Taken from 1888 Vermillion County History

JOHN C. JENKS POST, G.A.R.

John C. Jenks Post, No. 263, G. A. R.,

was chartered with the following officers and members: Francis M. Austin, Post Commander; William L. Kerns, Senior Vice-Commander; Henry Barnhart, Junior Vice-Commander; George W. Campbell, Quartermaster; Edwin Tiffany, Chaplain; Lewis H. Beckman, Adjutant; Henry H. Aye, Officer of the Day; A.J. Pitts, Surgeon; Solomon Carpenter, John Beard, William F. Morrison, Francis C. Combs, William A. Goodwin and John Myers. The post is in good working order, enjoying peace and harmony. Membership, twenty-six, meeting the first Saturday of each month. Present officers—Henry H. Aye, Post-Commander; W.F. Kerns, Senior Vice-Commander; Henry Barnhart, Junior Vice-Commander; Stephen Jenks, Quartermaster; William A. Goodwin, Chaplain; L.L. Goodwin, Adjutant; F.M. Austin, Officer of the Day; Edwin Tiffany, Officer of the Guard.

This is the most appropriate place we can find for the list of deceased soldiers of the last war, from Helt Township, compiled under the auspices of the Grand Army of the Republic.

Aikman, Elijah
Aikman, James
Aikman, William
Amerman, Henry
Bride, James
Brady, James
Burnett, William
Castle, Dirah
Curry, John
Ford, Henry
Foncannon, Joseph
Foncannon, John
Gamell, Charles
Gerrish, Lucien
Hendrixon, Elliott
Harper, Daniel
Homiday, David
Hunter, Solomon
James, Solomon R.
Luck, Edward
Malone, William
Mitchell, Benson
Mack, Reuben
McNamer, John
Martin, Levi
Nebeker, Jasper
Pearman, Sebert
Potteroff, Marion
Paulley, James
Skidmore, Asa
Smith, William
Southard, John P.
Straight, Elmor
Tullis, Samuel
Wellman, Louis
Whitehead, Thomas
Andrews, Edward
Andrews, John
Andrews, James
Anderson, John P.
Blakesley, Albert
Burnett, Samuel
Clark, John
Crane, Benjamin
Dorsham, Christopher
Ford, Josephus, Leander and Perry

Soldier's Monument-Riverside Cemetery

Fisher, James
Gerrish, Charles
Gosnold, Oscar
Harbison, James
Harris, John
Hamilton, Benjamin
James, Joseph L.
Jackson, Ross
Longfellow, William
Malone, William C.
Millikin, Lintott
Miller, H.B.
Martin, William
Morgan, Marion

Osborn, William
Pollard, Absalom
Price, David
Staats, George
Smith, John
Strain, George
Spriggs, Enoch
Taylor, Leroy
Thompson, James
White, Frank
Winesburg, Henry
Taken from 1888 Vermillion County History

Dana-looking North. Notice bank clock on left and small black gas pump on right.

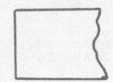
Clinton township, named in honor of De Witt Clinton, a former governor of New York state, is the southern sub-division in Vermillion county. It contains forty-two square miles, and in 1880 had a population of 3,000, with a personal property valued, in 1882, at $643,675. Its population in 1910 was (including the city) 9,341, with an assessed valuation in city and township amounting to $3,842,335.

John Vannest, the first settler in this county, located in section 9, of this township, in 1816. The next to enter Clinton township was John Beard, who located and built the first house in what is now the city of Clinton, and in either 1819 or 1820 built what was later styled Patton's mill, three and a half miles southwest of Clinton, the same being Vermillion county's first mill. Mr. Beard was also an early justice of the peace.

In 1818 came William Hamilton, who had sons, John and William, who lived many years in the county, William dying about 1878. The parents of Nelson Reeder came from Ohio and settled here in 1818.

Judge Porter, of New York state, settled here in 1819. His son Charles was born in 1816, was a good and useful citizen, but finally ended his own life by suicide. John J. Martin, who died in about 1884, was in his second year when his parents moved to Clinton township in 1819. The same year Daniel McCulloch, born in York state in 1797, settled in Clinton township, this county, on a farm five miles southwest of Clinton. His son, W.B. McCulloch, was born here in 1830.

It was in 1820 when the parents of John Wright, Sr., emigrated with him from New York to Clinton township. George Wright came in 1832, and died many years ago.

Major Chunn, a regular army officer, came here from Terre Haute some time previous to 1820, and was an efficient soldier in driving the Indians away from this settlement. He also participated in the battle of Tippecanoe, under General Harrison, on November 7, 1811. He was many years one of the justices of the peace in Clinton township. His son, Thomas, was many years an honored citizen here.

John Clover, from Ohio, located in Clinton township in 1821, with his son, Josepha A. Clover. Joshua Dean, a native of Virginia, born in 1801, settled in this township in 1822, and died about 1877. The Andrews family including several sons, located here in 1822. Henry and Eli Shew, natives of North Carolina, were mere boys when they located as residents of Clinton township. The former was born in 1815 and came here in 1825, and the latter, born in 1819, was brought here in 1823.

Capt. William Swan was born in Pennsylvania in 1802, settled in Clinton township, this county, in 1823, was a member of the first jury in Vermillion county and followed the river, making over sixty trips to New Orleans on both rafts and flat-boats. He was a Universalist in his religious belief, and a Freemason. He died at Clinton, January 29, 1887.

Washington Potter, who was still living in 1887, was eight years old in 1823, when he was brought to this township from Ohio. He was a carpenter by trade.

Silas Davis, a cooper and farmer, was born in 1818, and came to this township in 1823. The parents of William and Israel Wood came here in 1824. The same year came John W. Hedges. His son, Dr. I.B. Hedges, was born October 30, 1819, died February 24, 1883, and was buried in the Clinton cemetery. It was also in 1824 when the father of Walter G. Crabb, born in Fayette county, Ohio, came here to reside. In 1827 came James H. Allen, born in Ohio in 1822.

John Payton, an early merchant in Clinton, born in Ohio in 1818, came here in 1828. The same year came James Clark, Sr., from Ohio, where he was born in 1798. He became a sturdy farmer a mile and a half west of Clinton.

Samuel Davidson, deceased many years since, was born in Ohio in 1817, and settled in this township in 1830. Martin N. Davidson was born in Ohio in 1829, was brought here in 1832, lived here many years and was a resident of Terre Haute for many years later in his life.

George W. Edwards, of Clinton, was born in Indiana in 1827, and became a resident here in 1830. Andrew Reed, a native of North Carolina, settled here in 1830. Thomas Kibby, born in this state in 1810, came to Clinton township in 1830.

Benjamin R. Whitcomb, born in Vermont in 1798, and his cousin and business partner, John Whitcomb, came in 1828, settling in the village of Clinton, where they were among the pioneer merchants, pork packers, etc. John died in August, 1830, aged forty-one years. Benjamin R. died April 23, 1861, and his wife, Anna S., died May 21, 1860.

John R. Whitcomb, another merchant, born in Ohio in 1804, first settled in Edgar county, Illinois, in 1832, and in the village of Clinton in 1834. He died in March, 1873.

Scott Malone, who married Sarah, one of the twin daughters of pioneer John Vannest, came in from Ohio and resided here until his death, in the eighties.

Simeon Taylor, a native of Indiana, born in 1818, settled in this county in 1831, and died in the eighties. John F., his brother, born in Ohio, resided here and survived him.

In 1832 there settled in Clinton township Thomas G. Wilson, born in Virginia in 1804; William J. Noblitt, born in Tennessee in 1825; Benjamin Harrison, born in Virginia in 1805, was a justice of the peace many years and was still living here in 1887.

Robert H. and Adaline (West) Nichols located in Clinton township in 1835. He died here in 1872, aged fifty-five years, and she in 1874, aged sixty-five years.

Hiram B. Cole, John Ferral and John Marks were early Clinton merchants. The latter moved South. Ferral died February 25, 1832, aged thirty-six years.

In 1836 came William Payton and Philo Harkness. Payton was born in Kentucky in 1814, and Harkness in New York in 1816. In 1837 came Reuben Propst, and the next year Isaac Propst, natives of Virginia, but finally removed from this county. Acquilla Nebeker, born in Delaware in 1815, located in Clinton township in 1837. He was a liberal-minded citizen and a very considerate, kind neighbor. He died in 1880. Jesse Spangler, a native of Pennsylvania, born in 1807, settled in 1837, and died here about 1881. D.F. Fawcett came in from Virginia in 1833, settling near Goshen, Vigo county, and then in 1837, in this county, near the southwest corner. He died in 1845 in Jasper county, Illinois.

From the above date on, the settlers came in so rapidly that it is impossible to trace their comings and goings, but they included many of Clinton township's best citizens.

A former history of Vermillion county mentions, in 1887, the fact of there being three or four saw-mills in Clinton township, besides the two located at Clinton. Also that one of the largest agricultural interests in the township, at that date, was the extensive stock farm of Claude Mathews at Hazel Bluff, on Brouillet's creek, some three miles from Clinton.

Taken from Parke and Vermillion Counties History, 1913.

POWDER MILL

As the crow flies the powder mill was a couple of miles south of Wal-Mart, just west of Clinton. As the coal mining industry expanded there was always a need for explosives to bust through the rock and what not to get at the coal so H.M. Ferguson and some other mine owners decided to diversify and get into the business of making explosives. There was also a group of Terre Haute investors involved. Crown Hill Three was nearby so a railroad spur to the mill would not be too difficult, and apparently some explosive was shipped out by rail. Just as expansion of the coal industry meant more business for the powder mill, shrinking of the mining business cut business of the powder mill therefore it was eventually put out of business by lack of demand. The smoke stack of the powder mill was still standing in the 1950's. *Submitted by Leo Reposh Jr. RR 3, Clinton*

INDIANA FURNACE

The opening of the iron mines and building of the "Indiana Furnace," in section 27, township 14, range 10, Clinton Township, commenced in 1837. In 1839 the furnace was in full blast. Stephen R. Uncles was the chief owner and superintendent. Associated with him were Hugh Stuart and Chester Clark, the firm name being, Uncles & Co. Years later, the lands and works passed into the hands of Stuart & Sprague, and still later to E.M. Bruce & Co., the Co. being David Sinton.

In 1859, George B. Sparks, now a resident of Clinton, bought a controlling interest, and under the firm name of G.B. Sparks & Co., the business was continued until 1864. Captain John Lindsey, who still resides near the site of the old Furnace, was many years its superintendent. He relates that of the hundreds of men employed then, all but one, a pattern-maker, voted regularly the Democratic ticket, and jokingly says, no others could get employment. The company's office and large general supply store, and a score or two of cabins of more or less pretensions, made quite a village. Castings of nearly all kinds, largely stoves, were turned out. Pig iron in large quantities were also produced.

The works were among the early enterprises of the Wabash Valley, and distributed a large amount of money among the early settlers as well as furnishing employment to all comers—of the right political faith (according to Captain Lindsey)! The 1,700 acres of land connected with the plant is now owned by George B. Sparks, and devoted to agricultural purposes, and all that remains to indicate the site of the old "Indiana Furnace" is here and there debris of rotting and rusting machinery, and one or two log cabins.

Taken from 1888 Vermillion County History

GOVERNMENT

Township offices are Township Trustee, Township Assessor, and Township Advisory Board. The advisory board advises the trustee. The trustee has a strange hodge podge of duties. Some of his duties apply evenly through the township without regard to whether it is inside or outside Clinton city limits. An example is commodity distribution. Other duties pertain only to things outside the city limits. This was more true in the past than the present, because the trustees used to administer the township schools, but it is still the case, for example, with the trustee administering cemeteries in rural areas.

There is also a township fire department, and the chief is Mark VanBuskirk. The day driver is Philip Kite and the night driver is Larry Hawley.

The present trustee is John Kyle, and his advisory board is Dot Farr Lindsey, Nick Marietta, and Ted Ruffatola. The Township Assessor is Ruby Gallagher. The previous assessor was Elizabeth West who resigned to become county treasurer, and before her it was Ray Pickel who died in office. Previous trustees have been Dominic Natale who resigned to become Clinton City Mayor, Dot Jackson who died in office, her husband Harold Jackson who died in office, Ruth Ballock, Checko Muzarelli, Louis Giovanini. Otha Wright was in office when the school responsibilities were removed from the trustee and given to the South Vermillion School Corporation. Others were Louis Giovanini, Scotty Nesbit who was trustee when Centenary School was discontinued, and Dr. Odell Archer who was trustee when busing was started and many small schools were consolidated in 1936. *Submitted by Leo Reposh Jr.*

GOVERNOR'S MANSION

Same beautiful furniture and woodwork, but a new home and location.

The Governor's Mansion, home of Governors James Whitcomb and Claude Matthews, was purchased by Mr. and Mrs. Doug Thoma of Constatene, Mich. The home's belongings, as well as some of its woodwork, will be moved to northern Indiana and become a museum depicting the era of 1840 - 1850.

The home is presently located in Hazel Bluff, five miles southwest of State Road 163. Thoma purchased the home, but not the land, from Ken Farrington. It had been for sale for five years.

The land on which the house was built was first recorded in 1817 as a grant signed by President James Monroe from the Vincennes Land Office to Solomon Lusk. Lusk sold the land, 1,000 acres, to Dr. William Kile, the first known doctor in the county. Dr. Kile built the mansion in 1840 and sold the property to George Wright. Gov. James Whitcomb purchased it in 1855.

Whitcomb was the governor in 1843, re-elected in 1846 and then elected to the State Senate in 1849. He died during this term of office. Upon his death the home became the property of his daughter, Martha, whose husband, Claude Matthews, became the governor in 1893 until 1897.

Helen Matthews Krekler, daughter of Gov. Matthews, occupied the home until 1946, when it was purchased by Dr. I.D. White, doctor of medicine and a Hazel Bluff farmer. In March of 1958, the mansion was sold to Gerald Farrington, Ken's father.

The New Home

Moving the furniture has been more than a mere task for Thoma. The furniture was hand carved in England, collected in New Orleans and the East, and transported to Hazel Bluff by wagon train and river boat. Even the front pillars of the home traveled up the Wabash River.

"The furniture is some of the finest made in this country," Thoma expressed. All the trim was completed in walnut. The home was described by Thoma to be southern federal with a little Georgian influence. Most of the rooms measure 18 feet by 15 feet.

The full-tester and half-tester beds, in mint condition, stand 10 feet tall and have seven by seven foot mattresses. They are

Hazel Bluff Governor's Mansion

made of rosewood and mahogany. Other furniture pieces include a three-way full length mirror, a built-in-the-wall combination bookcase/fireplace, quezel and tiffany glass shades, a grandfather clock (the oldest piece in the home) and a Chickerring grand piano from the era of 1840-1850.

Thoma, originally from Danville, Ill., was one of over 200 persons to view the home for purchase. The Indiana Historical Society was interested in the furniture, but the price was too high and Farrington was also hoping to sell the entire estate to one person. Actor Ken Kercheval wanted to purchase the grandfather clock, which was probably built in the 1820s according to Thoma, who has been in the antique restoring business for 22 years.

"This area could not support the home," Thoma stressed when questioned why he wasn't restoring the mansion in Clinton. He emphasized that his goal was to basically save the furniture and woodwork of that time. Homes like the governor's mansion are past dreams of hard work and fine craftsmanship.

The actual restoring will be done by Amish workmen. "The Amish are the best craftsmen," Thoma Said. Twenty acres are presently set aside for the new governor's museum. Northern Indiana is basically an agriculture area and the Thomas have applied for permission to build a "business" on the land.

"I wanted enough property to landscape and keep the effect," Thoma commented. The museum will be free to church and school groups.

"This could be one of the finest historical homes in the state," Thoma observed.

An article by Cindi Marietta, The Daily Clintonian, September 29, 1988

THOMPSON HOUSE

The beautiful white house located on State Road 163 west of Clinton is known as the Thompson House. It is presently owned and occupied by Mr. & Mrs. Floyd B. Shannon.

It was built in 1902 by Ben Whitcomb who was a cattle feeder and rancher and had 1000 acres. The walk-in closet upstairs was just for his cowboy suits. He had an elevator installed in the center of the house where the bathrooms are now. He used it to view all his land from the attic. The walls are 18 inches thick on the first floor and 12 inches on the second.

After visiting Natchez, Mississippi, he fell in love with an old antebellum home known as Longwood which was built but not completed by Dr. Haller Nutt. Mr. Thompson designed the Whitcomb home from this house in 1/4 dimensions. Wherever there is a porch in this house, there was an additional room in the original.

TOWNSHIP SCHOOLS

The first school-house in Clinton Township, was a log structure of the most primi-

Thompson House

tive kind, located at the Davidson hill, a mile west of town, when the only school books were the English Reader, Webster's Elementary Spelling Book and the New Testament, and sometimes a copy of Daboll's Arithmetic. Since then a remarkable growth of the present free-school system has taken place. In the meantime, according to the character of the respective periods, two or three attempts have been made toward the establishment of special or select schools of an advanced order. For example, just previous to the war, Myram G. Towsley's Military Institute and the Farmers' College, which went down on account of the war coming on. Part of the building, a large frame, was afterward converted into an opera house, and the wings into dwelling-houses.

The present fine school building, of six rooms, was erected in 1881, at a cost of about $8,000, including seating, furnishing and the ground. The enrollment last year was 368. The school is divided into ten or twelve grades, and prepares its graduates for admission into the State University. The principal is J.H. Tomlin, who has six assistants.

Taken from 1888 Vermillion County History

CLINTON AREA SCHOOLS

The first school in Clinton Township according to limited information was a long structure built of logs. It was located on the Davidson Hill one mile west of Clinton. I believe Davidson Hill was what is now known as Crompton Hill.

As the time of the first consolidation which occurred in 1936-1938 under trustee Odell Archer. There were 16 schools in Clinton Township. During the period of the

twenties a number of small frame buildings (more or less portable) were in use at several of the over crowded schools.

For convenience we shall consider the individual schools in alphabetical order.

Centenary school located in Centenary, where the present Township Fire equipment building is located now, was a brick four room building. During the period of the late twenties to 1936 a one room portable building was also in use.

The Centenary school was one of the last that was closed; it was while Trustee Nesbit was in office. Hazel Twyler was the last principal.

Coon Hollow school was located on second road north after passing Centenary—keep to the left—about one mile from Helt Township line. This was a one room brick building. All eight grades were accommodated when there were pupils in all grades. This school was closed by Trustee Odell Archer. The name came from the school's location in Brouilletts Creek bottoms.

Crompton Hill is a two story school building located at top of Crompton Hill on the north side of Indiana Road 163. It has accommodated eight grades. At one time there were four rooms in the brick building and a one room frame building. During Trustee Archer's period as township trustee, 1937, a W.P.A. project of a brick gymnasium with two large rooms and a small room adequate for an office and a school library above the gym was completed.

In the beginning Alfred Dunkley, trustee, built two rooms one over the other, 1916. He had promised that small children would not have to walk to Hazel Bluff. First, second and third grades started in the two rooms. The south two rooms were built two years later. The building is not used as a school now. The children in this area now attend the Van Duyn School which is located near Centenary and is a part of the South Vermillion School Corporation.

East Union School was a one room frame building and was located 1-1/2 miles west of the Range Line Road, a distance of about four miles from Universal. This one room school accommodated all the grades.

Fairview School was a brick two story building located at the north edge of Clinton in the town of Fairview. The main building had eight rooms with all grades. In the early twenties two portable frame buildings were needed. This was the period of the coal mine prosperity.

Geneva School was a one room frame school, located west and north of Fairview where a small settlement had the name of Geneva.

Hazel Bluff school was a brick two room school located west of Clinton near the corner where the Universal road turns south. This school was a short distance east of the Governor Matthews home. All these schools had eight grades when necessary. This school was in continuous session long before 1878 until in 1930's.

Jacksonville School, a two story brick building, was located just off of Road #71 and at the northeast corner of Jacksonville town. There were eight rooms used in this building at one time. This school was closed in the fall of 1961 as a part of the new South Vermillion Community schools' program. The children are now accommodated at the Van Duyn School.

Klondyke School, a two room brick school, was located in the small community settlement known as Klondyke, which is north of State Road 163 north of the Renatto Inn two miles west of Clinton.

Sandytown School was located just north of the small community known as Sandytown. The small community is about two miles north of Klondyke. It is another of the many small communities which grew up during the mining days. This was a two room school accommodating all eight grades. This school was closed with consolidation.

Scott School, a one room frame school was located south of Jacksonville. The road past Joe Audi's to first road to the right (East) leads to the Scott neighborhood where the school was located. This school a typical early one room school was one only used until better schools were built and buses conveyed students to them.

Smith School, a one room brick school, was located south of Clinton where the road turns south toward Shephardsville. This school was abandoned after Crompton Hill was enlarged. However, after the town of Needmore came into existence another room was added and used until Crompton Hill was enlarged.

Spangler School was located about two miles north of Centenary on the first road north after leaving Centenary going west. Spangler was in the Foltz neighborhood. This was a one room school.

Syndicate School was located on top of Syndicate Hill and served the Valsch Reeder

and Powder Hill area. Traveling south on the Needmore - Shepherdsville road to the foot of Syndicate Hill turn right or travel west up Reeder Hill to the school, a one room school.

Universal School, a brick nine or ten room school located in the town of Universal. This was used by the students of Universal until the 1961 reorganization, then for one year most of the Jacksonville pupils were moved to Universal. Eight grades are housed at Universal. Now all these students go to Van Duyn School and Universal school is closed.

West Union, a one room brick school was located about 2-1/2 miles west of Universal. West and East Union were so named because of their directional relationship to each other.

Wright's School was a one room log building located at the foot of the hill near the coal mine in Universal. This was replaced by the Universal School. *Submitted by Leo Reposh Jr.*

FAIRVIEW SCHOOL

Fairview School was a Clinton Township School. This school was located on the corner of Washington and Fourth Streets in Fairview Park. Raymond Gosnell states that the south portion of the school was built about 1900 and the northern portion in 1918.

There was a brick church just north of the school. After it burned, the schoolground was enlarged to include that area.

The building was split-level with the northern part being higher than the southern part. The first floor had two classrooms on

Coon Hollow School-1928 Row 1: Vernon Botner, Willis Burgess, Roy Ross, Fred Burgess, Jr., Lawrence Stultz, Robert Burgess. Row 2: Helen Botner Moore, Jewel Haun Peer, Ruth Ross, Agnas Stultz, Frances Runyan Amerman, Emma Murray Reed, Evelyn Ross, Mary Elizabeth Botner Clark. Row 3: Harriet Elizabeth Jones Pennington, Blanche Ross, Lola Stultz, Esther Ross. Teacher-Myrtle M. Bales.

Syndicate School 1928

the west side, and the auditorium (later used for the cafeteria) on the east side. A classroom was in the northern portion. The second floor had classrooms and the library. During the 20's two portable buildings were used.

According to Raymond Gosnell, Alva T.M. Hall was Fairview's first mail carrier, but he was also Fairview School principal later.

Some of the teachers at Fairview School were Lucille Gilfoy, Dorothy Ugo, Daisy Buchan, Dorothy Winkler, William Payton, Richard Auer, Melissabelle Ralston, Maxine Prulhiere Ross, Millicent Holt, Ellen Beatty, Glenna Berrisford, Bertha Kennedy Martin, Mrs. Crawl, Mr. Bingham, Bernice Wood, Clio King Jenks, Louise Alderson, Mary Satterlee Wellman, Rosemary Burton, and Donald Kemper (now principal of Central School). Some of the principals were Carlos Watson, Sam Nesbit, Ellen Beatty, Tegwith Heise, William Payton, Dorothy Ugo, Martha Costello, William Keown, and Ray Shew.

The township trustee governed the schools. One of the trustees was Scotty Nesbit. One of the janitors was Horace "Chuck" Little. Dominic Giovanini, brother of trustee Louis Giovanini, also was a janitor. There were two school bus routes coming into the school. Some of the drivers were Leon Woody, Gloyd Earles, Bill Hastings, and Bob Gilman.

This school was closed in 1964.

HAZEL BLUFF SCHOOL

The Hazel Bluff School was discontinued in 1935 when Dr. Odell Archer, the Clinton Township Trustee was in charge of the Clinton Township Schools. The school was located on the north side of the Hazel Bluff Road just west of the intersection with Universal Road in the vicinity of the entrance to the Governor's Mansion property.

Mr. David Dowdy attended the school for a year or two and gives me the following information. The school was a brick structure with two rooms and two teachers. It had outside toilets and an outside water well. At the time Mr. Dowdy attended the school the teachers were Mrs. Curry who was the wife of Clinton City Police Chief Cole Curry, and a lady named Bozarth.

Ethel Reposh recalls an all day P.T.A. meeting being held in the school with people being bussed in to participate and part of the activities included a carry in dinner with fabulous food. This took place in 1938 after the school had been discontinued. The school has since been torn down and a home now stands on the site. *Submitted by Leo Reposh Jr. RR 3, Box 768, Clinton, Indiana*

KLONDYKE SCHOOL

To reach the site of the former Klondyke School take highway 163 and turn north across from Renatto's back parking lot. This road has three names: Klondyke Road, County Road 110, and Reed Street. Pass the Reposh residence and turn west at first intersection. The school was one block west on

the north east corner. It was a brick structure and was torn down in 1946 by employees of Ernie Boetto, a Clinton salvage dealer. Some of the lumber salvaged from the building now comprise the outbuildings on the nearby Reposh property. The official but little used names of the streets at that location are Whitcomb Street east and west and Kennedy Street north and south. The official name of the town is Klondyke Heights. The school was consolidated into Fairview School in 1935 when Dr. Odell Archer, Clinton Township Trustee, was in charge of the Clinton Township Schools.

The first person from whom I obtained additional information was Catherine Mattioda Osella, wife of Frank Osella, of Klondyke. She says originally a wooden building was used but it burned down. She says that the school was brick and had four rooms: two regular class rooms, a furnace room, and a room for home economics and sometimes first grade. It had outside toilets and an outside water well. A wooden structure had previously served as a school but had burned down. At the time Mrs. Osella attended the school the principal was Mr. Goodwin and he drove a Ford Coupe from Dana. It had three teachers including the principal. Other teachers were Hazel Taylor, Helen Newport, and Bertha Newport. The janitor was Mr. Henry Trader who lived approximately two blocks away across from Runyan's junk yard. She says that citizenship school was held there as well as W.P.A. and N.Y.A. recreation programs. She says she remembers the father of another student, Pat Daniels, bringing a Christmas tree to the school with a team of horses and a wagon.

Ivan Clarence "Pat" Daniels of Klondyke confirmed the information provided by Catherine Osella and said that his father who delivered the Christmas tree was James Daniels. James Daniels was the last surviving Civil War veteran in the township. He says that another teacher was a lady named Wright,f the daughter of Bert Wright who lived where Reposh's live. He also added that Mr. Trader had a wife and that their grandson lived with them.

Mr. Daniels, Mrs. Osella, and the senior Reposhs agree that Louis Varda was a student here and later was involved with the W.P.A. recreation program. Another person somehow connected with the program was John Corso who may be remembered by his later occupation as a taxi driver.

Joe Airola known for establishing the Coal Fountain Park commented that when he came from Italy none of the kids at Klondyke School talked English, but that was a half joking exaggeration, because old pioneer Americans like Howes, Daniels's, Runyans, and Gibsons always lived in the area and had kids.

According to Marie Winkler, now deceased, religious revivals were held in the school also. *Submitted by Leo Reposh Jr., RR 3, Box 768, Clinton, Indiana.*

SANDYTOWN SCHOOL

Sandytown School was discontinued in

1935 during the time that Dr. Odell Archer, the Clinton Township Trustee, was in charge of the Clinton Township Schools. To reach the site of the Sandytown School take Range Line Road, turn east on Sandytown Road to the first intersection. It was on the south east corner of that intersection. Coming up from Pike Street (Clinton) or from Klondyke come to Rocky's Corner where it says Sandytown, follow the main road north to the turn, go west and the road turns north again, then one reaches the intersection. The school was consolidated into Fairview School and has been torn down.

Additional information on the Sandytown School was provided by Mr. Kenneth Foltz who attended the school from 1919 to 1926. It was a brick structure and first part of which was built in 1896. It had outside toilets and outside water. It had two rooms and two teachers for grades one through eight. Some of the teachers during Mr. Foltz's attendance were Margaret Beard, Minnie Foltz, Owen Clark, Margaret Gibson, Blanche Malone, Margaret Helms, and Shirely Smothers. Mr. Foltz states that he still has the stone gable from the school which gives the year it was built. *Submitted by Leo Reposh Jr., RR 3, Box 768, Clinton, Indiana 47842.*

SMITH SCHOOL

Smith's No. 5 (or District 6) School was a one-room brick building located about a mile south of Clinton and built in 1900. The windows had shutters which were closed when it stormed during school hours. It was heated by a pot-bellied stove.

Jess Prohaska was one of the oldest living male students (he died in 1987). My mother, Dora May Phipps Riley, is the oldest living female scholar at this writing. Dora was born on August 11, 1891, to Reverend John and Anna Thomas Phipps. She had four sisters and three brothers some of whom also went to Smith School. They were Frances, Luallie, Mary - still living, Whilemine, Roy, Ernest and Arthur.

After the one-room burned in 1921, a two-room school was built. It was heated by a furnace in each room.

I attended Smith's School from 1924-1933 at which time I graduated. Some of the teachers who taught me were Sarah Payton, Lucille James, Rebecca Cooke, Margaret McKinney Bates, and William Payton. Mary Curry and Desera Brown also taught at the school. (Brown and Bates still living.)

Clinton Township schools were consolidated in 1935 and these students were then bussed to Universal School and Crompton Hill School.

By Luella Newkirk Reidelberger

SPANGLER SCHOOL

The information on the Spangler School comes from one of its distinguished alumni, Donald E. Foltz, who served several terms in the Indiana House of Representatives and played a leadership role within that body during his stay. He was also the director of the Indiana Conservation Department which

Spangler School

among other things oversaw the state parks. This department has since been reorganized and renamed the Department of Natural Resources.

Mr. Foltz stated as did his brother Kenneth that the original Spangler school was located where the present Pasco house is now on Spangler road, and that it was wooden structure which has been moved to Range Line Road and is now the home of Kenneth and Esther Foltz. The Spangler School that Donald Foltz attended from the 1st to the 5th grade was a brick structure located on Spangler Road on a corner where Floyd Roscoe and Eva May Runyan now live. This brick structure was torn down. The school closed at the end of the 1935-1936 school year. It had one room and one teacher. It had windows on the south side and those on the north side had been bricked over. It had two outdoor toilets and a coal shed on the south side. It had a well outside. Just inside the entrance it had a closet on each side. It had a flag pole part of which still stands in Runyan's yard. Mr. Foltz states that the teachers during his attendance were LeDonna O'Haver for the 30-31 school year and she now lives in Jasonville, Madeline Metz of Fairview for 31-32 and 32-33, and Alice Wright for 34-35 and 35-36. *Submitted by Leo Reposh Jr., RR 3, Box 768, Clinton, Indiana*

TOWNSHIP SCHOOLS AND TEACHERS

1897 and earlier - Alva Hall taught at Coon Hollow in Clinton Township. It is not known what year the first school which was a frame building was built, but there was a brick two-room building there in 1897.

1914 - Clinton Township teachers (partial list) E.E. Helt, Margaret Kinsley, Ethel M. Brown, Jennie M. James, Enid Frist, Getta James, Margaret Eller, Esther Kruger, Marguerite Kennedy, Hazel Shew, Katherine Crowder, Curtis Hays, Versa Stuthard, Everett Stierwalt, Beatrice Rettich, Lucille Hoover, Edith Pescheck, Ernestine Balfe, Helen Cresser, Mary Owens, Ethel Wright, Mabel Payton, Hazel Chunn, Minnie Hessemer, Olga Semela, Earl Miller, Mary E. Long, Alva T.M. Hall, Helen Hunter, Mary Cooper, and Helen Dick.

1925

Universal - Alva T.M. Hall, principal and grade eight; Sarah Rue Shew, grade seven; Ruth Boyce, grade six; Anselle Davis, grades five and six; Margaret Patch, grades four and five; Gladys Eaton, grade three; Dorothy Shew, grade four; Leone Eaton, grade two; Ann Winstanley, grades one and two; Beatrice Clayton, grade one; Naomi Annakin, grade one.

Fairview - Fred Harve, principal and grade eight; Edmon Goforth, grade seven; Jennie J. Groves, grade six; Alma B. Foltz, grades five and six; Ellen Beatty, grades four and five; Margaret E. Davis, grade four; Desree Bartmess, grade three; Helen L. Hawkins, grade two; Lorraine Walker, grades one and two; Thelma W. Burge, grade one, and Wilhelmine Gosnell, grades one to three.

Jacksonville - C.S. Pickard, principal and grade eight; Margaret I. Gibson, grade seven; Annabel Payton, grade six; Esther M. Gottardi, grade five; Wilma Eller, grade four; Esther Holroyd, grade three; Bernice Cullen, grade two; Helen Newport, grade one.

Centenary - Bertha Foltz, principal and grades seven and eight; Hartley R. Cheek, grades five and six; Virginia Fillinger grades three and four; Clara Goforth, grades two and three; Katherine Dunkley, grade one.

Crompton Hill - Jessie Short, principal and grades seven and eight; Gladys Heaton, grades five and six; Ruth L. Certain, grades three and four; Dorotny Tribble, grades one and two.

Klondyke - A.S. Goodwin, grades seven and eight; Margaret Evans, grades four to six; Eula E. Reid, grades one to three.

East Union - Lula Shew, grades five to eight; and Mary L. Boyce, grades one to four.

Hazel Bluff - Minnie Foltz, grades five to eight; and Glenna Miller, grades one to four.

Sandytown - Margaret Helms, grades five to seven; and Hazel Wilson, grades one to four.

Smith - Owen T. Clark, grades five to eight; and Sara Payton, grades one to four.

Coon Hollow - Marion W. Martin, grades one to eight.

Scott - Hazel Taylor, grades one to seven.

Spangler - Ray Shew, grades one to eight.

Syndicate - Arminta Spencer, grades one to four.

West Union - Eugene Skelley, grades one to seven.

BLANFORD

People here still remember Margaret Gisolo, the girl who made national news in 1928 by making the lineup of the town's American Legion baseball team.

Gisolo was an infield regular on the Blanford team that won the Indiana American Legion championship. Hoosier opponents didn't seem to mind she was a girl playing what was considered a boys' sport.

But when Blanford represented Indiana at the national tournament, the howling began. "I was the only girl playing in that tournament," Gisolo said in a telephone interview from her Arizona home.

A girl playing baseball in 1928 was unheard of, she said. "What happened was that the next year they made a rule to keep girls out of American Legion baseball," she said. Fifty-four years later, the story of her unusual youth activity in her hometown appeared in a book on discrimination against women in athletics. "Sexual Discrimination in Youth Sports: The Case of Margaret Gisolo" was written by Tony Ladd and published as one chapter in the book, "Her Story in Sports," published in 1982 by Leisure Press.

"The writer did lots of research," Gisolo said, "and he felt I was the first to break through (the sexual barrier) in sports. The incident kind of went to sleep until recently."

Gisolo went to college, earned bachelor's and master's degrees, and studied dance at Columbia University and Connecticut College before teaching at Arizona State University from 1954 until her 1980 retirement.

She and others established the department of dance at Arizona State that eventually was ranked one of the five best in the U.S.

Baseball star Reggie Jackson was one of Gisolo's many students at Arizona State. "The thing I remember about him is how he once argued that ballroom dancing didn't take much effort," she said. To prove his point, he grabbed a girl and danced the rest of the period without getting tired.

Blanford was founded in 1912 and named after L.S. Blanford, owner of a large tract of area land. It was always a coal mining town. "The underground mines closed down about 15 or 16 years ago," said Tom Rigsby, a life-long resident. "People moved away as the mines shut down."

Gene Pupilli has lived here 70 years. He ran a local tavern for 30 years, now he's got the town's only laundromat. He said there were seven bars and three restaurants here when he got into the bar business.

"My gosh, this town has really changed," Pupilli said. "Blanford's about all gone now." At one time 600 people lived here. Most worked in the six area deep mines. About 300 people now call this town on Illinois state line their home.

"My parents came here from Italy like a lot of other people did," Pupilli said of his folks who arrived here in 1904. He said a lot of other people arrived here from Yugoslavia in the early 1900s to work in the coal mines.

Mary Massa is another who's lived here all her life in the north section of town called Jacksonville. Her parents, and also her husband James' parents, came here from Levone, Italy.

"My father had a bakery here for years," Massa said of her dad, Martin Lanzone. The bakery put out 200 loaves of bread daily and 450 loaves on weekends and holidays.

The business district has dwindled almost nothing. Gambaiani's grocery store, the post office where Marjorie Natalie is postmaster, Bush's bar and the laundromat are all that remain.

Despite the lack of business activity, people like their hometown.

"I like the closeness of the people here," Natalie said. "Everybody is friendly." The post office is a popular place when people come for a morning chat.

"This is the only general store around here now," said Victor Gambaiani who, with his wife Delena, bought the store from James Perona 37 years ago. It's still known as Perona's market.

A popular spot in the store during the winter is the far end where a coal-burning, pot-belly stove gives heat.

Gambaiani — a Vermillion County commissioner — and his wife raised three boys while running the store. One is Larry, superintendent of Rockville Community Schools.

"I still enjoy going back to my father's store and seeing the people I grew up with," Larry said. "I worked in the store for years even on weekends when I was in college. This town has a lot of pleasant memories for me."

Bush's bar is the only place in town you can order a meal. The place has a family room where patrons can order breakfast or short order meals throughout the day. Catfish dinners and shrimp are weekend favorites.

"Both my husband and I are from this area," said Delores Bush, who took over the bar last year after moving from Indianapolis.

Blanford

Blanford Post Office

"We like it here because of the people and because it's much quieter than the big city."

John V. Albrecht grew up in Blanford, but he left years ago to work in Milwaukee. Now he's retired here, but not in the quiet atmosphere he had expected. Albrecht has been busy in the Blanford Action Committee — a group which exists to stop what they say is violent blasting from Peabody Coal Company's stripping operation at the Universal Mine.

"Their blasting has been shaking houses very hard," Albrecht said. Peabody, he said, told his group they'll make things right in eight or 10 years after they're finished stripping coal in the area.

"When they blast, our whole house shakes and pictures fall off the wall," he said. "You wouldn't believe it unless you were in the house."

Albrecht said his group doesn't want Peabody to leave — just mine the coal in a less damaging way. "Experts have told us there are alternative ways to get the coal," he said. "But the way they're doing it is cheaper."

An article by Dave Delaney, Terre Haute Tribune-Star, January 5, 1986, Tribune-Star Publishing Co., Inc.

CITY OF CLINTON

Clinton, named in honor of an early governor of New York, DeWitt Clinton, was laid out, probably, by William Harris, a resident of Martin county, Indiana, in 1824. Harris was a government surveyor. But the record of town and village plats at Newport shows that Clinton was platted and recorded by Lewis P. Rodgers, on January 8, 1829— probably a corrected and legal platting recorded of the original town. It is situated (the original plat) in section 15, township 15, range 9 west.

At first the growth of the town was very slow, indeed at the opening of the Civil war it only contained about two hundred and fifty inhabitants, but in 1868, when a railroad was an assured fact, it took on new life and vigor. But before railroad days it was the center of an agricultural district around it for a radius of fifty miles or more. Across the Wabash the people traded mostly at Terre Haute, fifteen miles distant from Clinton and always an absorbing factor in the country trade. Clinton stands on a level plateau of land extending from the western bank of the Wabash back nearly a mile to the hills, in which the great coal deposits are, which have for years been successfully worked. The population of Clinton, according to the 1910 United States census, was 6,289, but according to the 1912 city directory, carefully compiled, the city now has a population of 8,379. Aside from the mining element, the population is largely American. The commercial interests may be listed as between the extensive coal mining industry and the agricultural trade, with a considerable amount of money also put into circulation by reason of the vast brick and tile industries of the community, the paving brick alone being a large industry. But beyond question, the city thrives largely on its mining interests which are increasing yearly.

The transportation facilities are provided largely through the Chicago & Eastern Illinois Railroad and the Terre Haute, Indianapolis & Eastern Traction Company.

THE BEGINNINGS

The first mercantile establishment in Clinton was opened by John and Benjamin R. Whitcomb, who kept a small general store. Other early business men were John Payton, John R. Whitcomb, H.B. Cole, John Ferrel and John Marks. Later business men were James McCulloch, Otis M. Conkey, Jones & Chestnut, from Paris, Illinois, Leander Munsel, from the same place, Alanson Baldwin, of Baldwinsville, Illinois, who were extensive pork packers at Clinton. This city was for many years a noted pork market and shipping point for packed pork.

Lesser business was carried on by J.W. and Fielding Shepard, and Volney Hutchison, mechanics, who afterward moved into the country and became successful farmers; S.E. Patton, a cooper; H.F. Redding, carriage-maker and blacksmith, and others.

Many of the buildings occupied by these pioneers were still standing in the nineties, on the bank of the river, near the railroad bridge, where the old boat landing was, as monumental relics of that long-ago steamboat period. The scenes of the past ever and anon rise in the vision and memory of the older citizens of Clinton, who seem again to hear the shrill whistle of the steamer and the wharf-talk of river boatmen and roustabouts, as they loaded and unloaded the great cargoes of merchandise to and from the boats bound north and south from this landing place.

The population had not reached over one thousand eight hundred in 1890, but modern development, the growing industries, and general trend of the times of peace and real prosperity, will not long permit a city located as is Clinton to stand still, hence its present size and business enterprise.

EFFECTS OF CIVIL WAR

At the close of the Civil war there was a complete change in commercial and industrial life. It can only be compared in physical nature to an upheaval that obliterates old paths, landmarks and structures. Prior to the Civil War Clinton and the surrounding country had many industries. It was the era of the small industry under individual control. Such towns as Perrysville, Eugene, Mecca, Clinton and many others were centers of this kind of industry. In Clinton we had a wagon factory conducted by B.F. Morey, father of W.L. Morey. In that shop wagons were made complete, from end-gate to the tongue. And they were good wagons, too. They were like Holmes' wonderful "One-Hoss Shay," "that ran a hundred years to a day." They were like the characters of the men who built them-strong, close built and enduring. In connection with this wagon factory was the blacksmith shop, where the iron work was made, the paint shop where they were painted.

Today these wagon factories have all been brushed away by the big factories, owned and controlled by corporations backed by millions of dollars. We had a tan yard at the foot of Crompton hill, where an old man, named John Crompton, tanned hides and prepared them for the boot and shoe factory, conducted by John E. Ryan, on South Main street. Between these two, we used to get boots and shoes made, pretty high priced 'tis true, but built like the garments of the children of Israel for wear.

There was Harry Redding's famous cooper shop, where barrels and casks were made. There were the great pork-packing industries. There was Robert Chambers' cabinet shop, where furniture was made. There was Greenwat's blacksmith shop, where horseshoes were made, and Wiley's place, where cradles, bedsteads and coffins were made to order. There was the Mallory mill, where cane was ground and the juice was converted into sorghum molasses, which our mothers used in making ginger cake about three inches thick, as big as the oven would take in, and which was comparable only to the food of the gods. And there were saw-mills and shingle-mills and grist-mills all over this country. At Mecca, a woolen-mill used up the raw wool that was raised on the backs of sheep that roamed the hills of Parke and Vermillion counties. It was a Mecca indeed, for to it the mothers for miles around made their annual pilgrimages every fall, to lay in a supply of good woolen clothes for use in the family during the following winter. The motive power of this woolen-mill was water that had been accumulated by placing a dam across the Big Raccoon. Perrysville was a thriving, humming town and easily the best town in this county, doing an immense business in manufacturing and merchandising.

West of Clinton was the Indiana Iron Furnace, which employed a host of men, scattered a large pay-roll throughout the township, and which used up the iron ore found everywhere in the beds of the creeks.

In fact, the people were so self-dependent that they could practically get along for long periods without any outside aid. And yet all these industries were paralyzed and forever silenced by the after-results of the war. The fires died out of the smelting furnace, the boats came no more for their usual cargoes.

At this time Main street was only a second-rate affair. All the business was done along First street. The river bank was built up almost solidly in wood yards, coal yards, grain elevators, great warehouses, pork-packing houses, stores, etc. It was river commerce. I have seldom ever gone over into Illinois that I do not meet some old farmer who, half a century ago, brought his grain and pork to Clinton to be shipped off south in payment for the product of slave labor. There was no outlet for all this surplus product. There was no place to ship it and no way of getting it on to the markets of the world. And the industries, in and about Clinton, wilted at the blast of war as a sensitive plant will wilt in the hand. The men left the furnace to go to the front. Although they were all Democrats, they were all loyal to their country. The fires went out, never to light the midnight skies again. And today the place is almost a tradition. The flouring mill of William Hedges closed down, to never again turn a wheel and was later taken down, brought to town and rebuilt and burned in March, 1891. The pork-packing houses all closed down, never to re-open. The coal and wood yards and river traffic all fell into decay. The grain traffic alone held on until in the seventies, when the railroad came to its relief. Boys used to climb up into the warehouses and over the huge timbers to chase the bats and owls out from their hiding places.

INDUSTRIES OF CLINTON, 1912

Among the leading industries of the city of Clinton may be here cited the Clinton Paving Brick Company, which was established in 1893, with a capital of fifty thousand dollars; M.L. Morey, president; H.C. Dies, treasurer; J.W. Robb, secretary and manager; B.H. Morgan and M.C. Wright, directors. The first output of this extensive plant was in August, 1893, the capacity being forty thousand brick per day. The specialty is paving brick of a very superior quality. The company owns sixty-five acres of land, and thus produce their own raw material. They employ about sixty-five workmen, and run the year round. The output is nearly all sold in the great Middle West. The clay this company owns will furnish all that is needed for many years to come. It is one of the most extensive plants in this section of Indiana, and is the largest of any, save that at Veedersburg alone, which is the greatest in Indiana.

This has come to be almost a clay and cement age, and as timber becomes scarcer, the construction of almost all kinds of structures will be accomplished by the use of brick and cement materials. For street paving there is nothing now known so excellent as the proper grades of paving brick, and in this Clinton excels. For this reason the city is indeed fortunate in having this modern plant situated within her limits, furnishing employment for so large a number of men.

Other industries include the overall and skirt factory, in the south part of the city, which employs about seventy-five persons, mostly women; the Clinton Canning Factory, which institution puts up large quantities of vegetables; the ice company, making artificial ice of a splendid quality; the machine shops of Hays & Balmer and that of R.P. Shattuk; the hard-wood saw mills, located in the central eastern portion of the city, near the Wabash river front, the property of Butcher & Cooper.

Of the greater industry, that of coal mining operations, the chapter on Mining will treat.

The milling interests are well represented by the Clinton Milling Company, whose large plant is situated in the heart of the city, near the river front, where a fine grade of flour, meal, graham and feed is produced.

THE POSTOFFICE

Clinton has the most important postal business of any postoffice within the county. It is the only second-class office and is now looking forward with great anticipation to the time when it will become a free delivery office, the population of the city long since having passed the limit for such a change. There are four rural routes extending out from this office to the outlying country, and the parcel post is now installed and in active operation. Again, it is promised that the coming session of Congress will appropriate for a postoffice building not less than sixty-five thousand dollars.

There being a very large foreign element in and near the city, this has long been a good paying money order center, especially in foreign orders. The postal savings department of the office was established in October, 1911, and on December 13, 1912, the books showed an amount of $14,604 on deposit. The other business of the office, aside from money orders, amounted to $11,795, in the last fiscal year.

The postmasters of Clinton have included the following: The first was Dave Patton; then, commencing with James McCollough, who served from 1856 to 1860, the postmasters have been John A. Campbell, 1860-65; John Payton, 1865-69; John G. Campbell, 1869-72; Thomas H. Allen, 1873-77; John F. Leighton, 1877-85; George W. Edwards, 1885-89; Marietta Blythe, 1889-93; L.O. Bishop, 1893-97; W.H. Bonner, 1897-01; J.N. Frist, 1901-10; John O. Stark, 1910-14.

CHURCHES AND LODGES

Clinton has the following churches and lodges:

Roman Catholic, Sacred Heart, No. 548 Nebeker street.

Christian, northeast corner Blackman and South Seventh street.

Finlanders Lutheran, No. 326 North Eight street.

Methodist Episcopal, Blackman and South Fourth.

African Methodist Episcopal, 554 South Main street.

Presbyterian, northwest corner South Third and Mulberry streets.

First Italian Presbyterian, North Eighth and Oak streets.

United Brethren, No. 910 South Main street.

Fraternal Order of Eagles.

Columbian Federation Societies.

Grand Army of the Republic, P.R. Owen Post No. 329.

Knights of Pythias, Hazel Lodge No. 217; Victor Lodge No. 553; Uniform Rank No. 105; Pythian Sisters.

United Mine Workers of America, in which all the fifteen mines about the city are represented.

Masonic, Jerusalem Lodge No. 99; Royal Arch Masons, Chapter No. 125; Knights Templar, Commandery No. 48; Order of Eastern Star, Chapter No. 254.

Modern Woodmen of America, Camp No. 3105.

Independent Order of Odd Fellows, Unity Lodge No. 827; Clinton Encampment No. 143; Vermillion Rebekah Lodge No. 82.

Owls, Lodge No. 1199.

Improved Order of Red Men, Waukeena Tribe No. 175.

MUNICIPAL HISTORY

Clinton was incorporated about 1848-49, by special act of the Legislature, which empowered the trustees to prohibit the sale of intoxicating liquors. In about 1879 the place was incorporated under the general laws of the state, and was divided into five wards, from each of which there was elected one trustee, the term of office being for two years. The president was elected by the board and the members by the people. The records of the place have not been preserved complete, but such as have been kept intact show that the officers between 1880 and 1887 were as follows; Presidents-Neil J. McDougall, 1880-84; Decatur Downing, 1885; W.L. Morey, 1886-87. Clerks-D.C. Johnson, 1880; L.O. Bishop, 1881; Decatur Downing, 1882; J.M. Hays, 1883-84; Ed. H. Johnson, 1885-87. Other officers to the present have been as follows: The city was made a fifth-class city in 1895 and the mayors have been William G. Merrill, 1895; N.C. Anderson, 1896-98; C.M. White, 1898-02; D.C. Johnson, 1902-06; C.E. Lowery, 1906-10; H.M. Ferguson, 1910-11; M.M. Scott, 1911; M.J. Tucker, 1911 and present incumbent. Mayor Ferguson resigned October 16, 1911, and was followed by Scott, who resigned November 20, 1911.

The city officials in 1912 are: Mayor, Morgan J. Tucker; clerk, T.L. McDonald; treasurer, Arthur B. Roberts; attorney, John A. Wiltermood; board of health, Drs. W.D. Gerrish, C.W. Ashley, Ivan Scott; aldermen, first ward, Louis Antonini, second ward, James P. Tutwiler; third ward, William T. Reid; fourth ward, Lawrence W. Vogel; at-large, John R. Paine and H.S. Pinson; chief of police, W.D. Vanness; police, W.S. Vanhousen, James Buffo, A.M. Clark, David Bowser, Raphael Bunde.

The fire department consists of a volunteer company of about twenty men, with a chief and a driver of the city team; the former is now Carl Balmer and the latter (the only salaried man) is I.B. Hupp. The company is said to be one of the most efficient in all Indiana. The city owns a fine fire-fighting apparatus.

The board of education at present (1912) is: President, Dr. D.C. Schaff; secretary, Harmon K. Morgan; treasurer, Frank Slater; superintendent of schools, Prof. E.E. Oberholtzer.

The city has a fine public library, the gift of Andrew Carnegie, which building was completed in 1909, at a cost of thirteen thousand dollars. This library is held jointly by the city and Clinton township and a tax is levied for the purchase of books annually. The present board consists of: President, H.M. Ferguson; secretary, J.W. Strain; H.T. Harger, Roy Slater, Valzah Reeder, H.S. Pinson, Mrs. F.L. Swinehart, Miss Callie McMechen, Miss Bessie Vandyne. The librarian is Miss Faye Tillotson. The shelves of this new library are not well supplied with standard books, not even many of the state and United States government reports, but as time goes on doubtless the board will see to it that such works are added to the library, which now is really largely of interest to the school children and readers of fiction and the standard papers and periodicals. About $1,800 is raised annually by taxation for the purchase of books. The coming year it is expected the levy will furnish $2,800 for the extension of the library book stock. In December, 1912, there were 3,263 books on the shelves. The library was established in 1908 under the act of 1901-03.

THE WATER WORKS AND LIGHT PLANT

Up to about 1904 Clinton had no system of water works, but in that year the present system was installed. Wells were sunk to the gravel, in pure, living water, in the vicinity of the plant, which is near the heart of the

Dr. Bales-Veterinarian

business portion of the city and near the bank of the Wabash river. Bonds were floated in order to secure means with which to build the works, the cost to date being about $73,520. The plant was put in in 1910 under the direction of Superintendent W.M. Hamilton, who is still in charge. The total number of miles of water mains in the city now is thirteen. The plant was greatly enlarged in 1910 and is now supposed to be sufficient for a city of twenty-five feet, going fifty feet below the waters of the Wabash river, terminating in white gravel and sand, making a fine natural filter. The daily capacity of this system is two and one-quarter million. There are now ninety-two fire plugs or street hydrants, and in December, 1912, there were nine hundred customers. Water is sold both by meter and flat rate, the rates ranging from fifteen to thirty cents per thousand cubic feet. Three huge pumps are installed at the plant, but usually one is sufficient. In case of fire, another is set in motion and a pressure of one hundred pounds per square inch is realized in the business portion of the city. One of the mains extends about one mile out from the pumping plant. The present officers of the water works are the water committee of the city, with William Hamilton as superintendent, with Leslie Galloway and Jesse C. Patch as engineers, one for day and one for night.

ELECTRIC LIGHTING PLANT

While not a part of the municipal improvements, the electric lighting system in Clinton is here given. It is a private corporation, which organized and commenced operations in the summer of 1891, the turning on of the current being on July 1st of that year, and on the Fourth of July it was a feature of the city's Independence day celebration. It is known as the Clinton Electric Light and Power Company. Its first directors were J.E. Knowles, Daniel McBeth, B.H. Morgan, W.L. Morey, W.H. Bonner, J.W. Robb, secretary and manager, who has served in this capacity since then with a few years interim, and constantly since 1905. At first simply an arc system was installed, but in 1892 the incandescent system was put in operation. The plant is located on Vine street, near the water works plant of the city, close to the railroad and river front. They now furnish power to all the factories and mills in the city, save two newspapers, even furnishing the power for the roller mills and refrigerating plant. It is all home capital and is a financial success. The plant has three immense Corliss engines and three dynamos, though but one usually is employed, the others being for emergency and power extension when needed. The present president of the company is David McBeth; vice-president, Mark Nebeker, and J.W. Robb is secretary and manager; the other director is B.H. Morgan.

ITEMS OF INTEREST

Among the experiences of the people of Clinton, in years gone by, the following may be of interest to the present-day and future generations:

Here, as elsewhere in Indiana, the liquor question has ever been a thorn in the side of respectable citizens. Here has been fought many a hard contest between temperance and anti-temperance people. The saloon is still here and will likely exist until some state or national law wipes the business from the face of the commonwealth. One of the most remarkable movements along this line, in modern days, was the "Woman's Crusade" of 1874-76. In 1874 a band of praying women laid siege to a saloon, day and night, being on duty in divisions, by turns. The proprietor finally surrendered. In April, 1875, a company of ladies, headed by Mrs. Malone and Mrs. Kibby, marched in double file to the saloon owned by Tice & Melcher, to hold an interview with the proprietors; but on arrival found the fort evacuated and the doors wide open. The ladies guarded the place until evening and then retired. The next night one of the proprietors was arrested, and while he was in custody the citizens gathered at the point of contest and demolished everything that contained intoxicating liquors. The proprietor then sued fifteen of the citizens for $5,000 damages, but the case was compromised or dismissed. Other events of this crusade occurred, but of minor importance.

There are now numerous saloons doing business under a license system, while the work of the temperance press and pulpit, of temperance societies, including the Christian Temperance Unions, goes bravely on, with the hope of making public opinion in the state and county strong enough in the near future to forever do away with drinking places in the city.

NATURAL GAS

What was styled the Clinton Natural Gas Company was organized in the spring of 1887, with a capital of from two to four thousand dollars. The president was C. Mathews; secretary, W.H. Hamilton; treasurer, N.C. Anderson. The other directors were J.J. Higgins, Decatur Downing, J.E. Knowles, C.B. Knowles, and W.A. Hays. Drilling followed, but the word failure was finally stamped on their laudable efforts.

Above article was copied from the HISTORY OF PARKE AND VERMILLION COUNTIES INDIANA, copyright date 1913

TRACES, TRANSITION, AND TRANSPORTATION

Traces, what does that mean? Something that is left, a mark left by something or someone. Many, many years ago our State of Indiana, named from the name given to the early people that lived in our state..."Indian", thus Indiana. "Trace"...trails the buffalo herds left in their travels over Indiana to graze, feed, and flee from the Indians and early white men who hunted them for food and fur. It was a result of these "tracings" that the early Territory, Indiana, and the City of Clinton, got it's beginnings. Traces of the buffalo crisscrossed Indiana. These trails, the Indians followed on foot and horseback. Many Indian tribes were driven to this area by the early settlers, the white men from the original colonies. Many Indian tribes made this area their home. Their trails were followed by the White explorers, who were in want of colonies, settlements, and fur trading. They came on foot, horseback, and canoe. Thus began the exodus of the Indians and the buffalo from the Indiana Territory going West.

These traces and Indian trails crossed Indiana. White men came from various other Territories that were outside of the original colonies. They came from the Great Lakes area from forts and settlements of that area. They went down the Ohio River headed for the settlements of Vincennes (Sackville) or those in Kentucky. Many then pushed north...to Fort Harrison around 1811 which became Terre Haute. Early soldiers on the way to battle at Tippecanoe and Fallen Timbers (now Lafayette) liked what they saw and decided to settle after the battle with the Indians and the War of 1812 with the English.

Thus, early settlers came into Indiana, settling and clearing the land. They traded with the Indians, did fur trapping, and built cabins. They came upstream to Clinton from Fort Harrison seeking better homes and places to live. They also came upriver from Tennessee and Kentucky. Travel was indeed primitive at first. The Wabash River shoreline was inviting. There were high elevations both on the east and west sides of the river. The early settlers coming up in their canoes or log rafts found land to their liking beyond the higher hills.

The settlers found flat prairies that were covered with lush buffalo grass. There were wooded areas with various kinds of trees. This was important to their livelihood as implements. Many trees and vegetation had edible berries or nuts. However, they had to clear the woods for cabins, gardens, and crops before the land became usable.

Later, as time progressed, the settlers were befriended by many Indians who lived in this area. Exchange of ideas were traded. The Indians and settlers taught one another planting skills for gardens. During floodstage of the Wabash River, ideas were exchanged by them to better travel the river in the spring when it was high and good for travel.

Canoes, hollowed out logs, pirogues, and log rafts were modes of transportation to go downstream or upstream to trade or sell to the people living in the forts or settlements. All crafts were piled high with goods to trade, barter, or sell. Both Indians and settlers also carried backpacks with their goods along the trails and buffalo traces along the Wabash River shore.

The buffalo traces which crossed the area now known as the Wabash Valley crisscrossed in many directions. Constant travel north and south and east and west were the forerunners of our highways. These traces were widened by the covered wagons of the settlers going to seek new homes and land. The land rush and the gold rush (out West) brought many people to our fair Wabash Valley. It wasn't easy. It was rough with killing and sickness.

Clinton was laid out in 1828 by George Rodgers, government surveyor. It was platted and settled. It struggled and survived. There was very little population. The settlers farmed, hunted, fished, trapped, and mined for ore. Goods were sold and traded up and down the river. Later, keel boats, flat boats, and steam packetboats came. Clinton became a thriving river town. There were all kinds of goods and services.

All these modes of transportation helped Clinton to flourish and grow. A new method of travel began. The Wabash & Erie Canal was engineered from New York to Fort Wayne, to Lafayette, to Perrysville, and to Clinton. The canal and it's tow path ran on the eastern shore of the Wabash River near Lyford (then Hudnut). This did speed up goods to market in all directions from Clinton and to Clinton.

Up and down the river, cities and towns began to thrive and bustle. Clinton was no exception. The Industrial Revolution came along. With it came the inventions of ore smelting, steam railroads, and steamboats.

Clinton had no lock. It was called Clinton Locks because it was the largest river town. The lock was downstream between Atherton and Numa. It traveled thence into Terre Haute. Those new fangled steamboats were lots faster. The steam trains soon closed the Wabash & Erie Canal. Transportation in the state consisted of several thousand miles of track. They moved goods and people quickly. Clinton and the Wabash Valley prospered. Yes, there were bad times, too. There were bank closings, bankrupt railroads, and many other businesses were lost. However, the highway system running east and west through Terre Haute saw travelers and goods moving by wagon trains to the West. The invention of the gasless carriage came along about the time of the invention of electricity by Thomas Edison. There were railroad trains and interurban trains moving in and out of Clinton. Rails were going every direction. These two types of service competed and the railroads won out.

Wars came to America. The area boomed when the coal mines opened. Goods and supplies not needed here were shipped elsewhere. The advent of the automobile, however, caused the demise of the railroads. Highways spanned America. Goods were certainly moved more quickly by truck, automobiles, and rivers of the United States. Railroads began to dwindle after World War II. Even the transportation needs of Clinton changed. In about 1966, Clinton got an airport. It will handle prop, turbo, and small jet aircraft. Clinton has seen the modes of transportation go from foot to air. It has thrived and flourished. New industries have come in. Modern technologies have come along. We have lost some of our steam so to speak.

Train at West Clinton Junction

Transportation will help in the future. Perhaps the day shall come when the old Wabash will be dredged and become navigable again. Combined with all the modes of transportation, industry, and business, Clinton shall continue to grow immensely. *Submitted by James E. Graham*

CLINTON'S IRON BRIDGE

This is only the second of three bridges for highway traffic over the Wabash at Clinton and the west end was where the Four Season Fountain is now and it connected to Elm Street. It was used during the whole automobile era until 1964. It was built in 1900 and survived the 1913 flood and all the others until the fall of 1961. At that time an inspection by so called state bridge engineers pronounced the bridge to be safe. A few days later a fisherman, Andy Paloney, who had passed under the bridge in a boat reported that the under part of the bridge had some deterioration and was dangerous. Again the state bridge engineers came and examined the bridge and determined it to be safe. A few more days after that the eastern span fell into the river and a woman in a car and some men in a state truck went down with it. It was first reported that the woman in the car had struck the end of the bridge knocking it into the water, later others said that the bridge had began to move causing the woman to hit it.

The Army quickly brought in a portable bridge to cover the span and temporarily reopen the traffic until a new span was built, not as an iron span, but in the style more like the present bridge. The bridge was torn down when the present bridge was opened.

Ground Breaking Ceremonies for Clinton's New Bridge

In April of 1964 ground breaking ceremonies were held for the new bridge over the Wabash River to connect with Walnut Street. It is only the third bridge for highway traffic over the Wabash at Clinton, the other two were where the Four Season Fountain now is and connected with Elm Street. The bridge whose construction was about to begin is the present (1988) bridge.

A few months after the dynamiting of the catholic church two explosions occurred causing partial destruction of the piers of the Chicago and Eastern Illinois railroad bridge at Clinton. This was on April 19, 1910. The shock was felt in Dana, Hillsdale, and Terre Haute. The guilty ones were never captured although there were large rewards offered and expert detectives put into the case. The city offered one thousand dollars and the railroad offered three thousand dollars for information leading to the arrest of the perpetrators. Blood hounds were put into service, but all to no avail. *Submitted by Leo Reposh Jr.*

WABASH RIVER EXCURSION BOATS

They had paddle wheels at the back and one boat pushed the other. They were steam powered. They came up the river from Terre Haute to Governor's Island at Clinton and continued on to the mineral baths at Montezuma. Governor's Island had a dance pavillion and picnic area. According to Joseph Reposh, the first one was the Rainbow about 1913, and then during the 1920's, the Reliance, Reliable, and Defiance. He also says he saw steam tugs pulling barges that loaded and unloaded live hogs and mules at Clinton.

THE 1913 FLOOD

The Weekly Clintonian of March 27, 1913, says "The Wabash River continued to rise and on Wednesday morning, March 26, 1913, it had exceeded the 1875 mark by three inches." However, it went on to tell that this reading was controversial because people disagreed on whether or not the measure was positioned the same on this bridge in 1913 as it had on the previous bridge in 1875. It said that Soup Bone Hollow was inundated. Soup Bone Hollow was a low lying area near Feather Creek northeast of the railroad. It also said that the South Main Street grade was broken, and that Water Street south of Elm was inundated.

Problems also occurred at Montezuma where a grade was broken, and at Hillsdale where railroads were closed and threatened with washing out. Areas near Newport were flooded, but the town and the area around the courthouse were not threatened.

Many people and farm animals had to be rescued from flooded places throughout the area. Twenty families in the south part of Clinton were driven from their homes. Interurban traffic was stopped.

In the Weekly Clintonian of April 3, 1913, it said that the road east of the river bridge at Clinton was still impassable.

In regard to the railroad it says that piling and equipment was brought in and it was estimated by W.J. Jackson, Vice President and General Manager of the C. & E.I. Railroad that it would take at least another week to get the railroad across the Wabash River at Clinton back into operation. Both the grade and the bridge were damaged, and the repairs would take at least a week or longer pending further examination of the bridge.

The above statement about bridge repairs do not exactly make sense because in another article in the same paper it says that the eastern span was swept into the river while throngs of spectators watched, and that police almost had to battle spectators to keep them off the bridge as they waited for the eastern span to fall in. The center span was a draw bridge that would go up to allow boats to pass through. It also says that a train had passed over the bridge two hours before it fell in.

I remember a conversation several years ago with Dewey Allen, elderly former resident, who said that the force of the water was sliding the bridge off its piers and that the C.&E.I. put coal cars on the bridge to weigh it down and stop the sliding. It didn't work and the cars went with it. It pulled the tracks east of the bridge up on their side so they looked like a picket fence. Considering the second article and Allen's comments it seems obvious that a considerable amount of work was needed to repair the railroad and the bridge.

Flooded homes in Clinton, 1913

Railroad work crews use two cranes to set new beams in place to replace the span swept away by the 1913 flood.

CITIZEN'S BANK ROBBERY

Tuesday, Dec. 16, 1930, started out to be just another winter day in Clinton, clear and cold. At 9 a.m. Main street was beginning to shake itself awake as business houses opened their doors to the public. A few proprietors exchanged greetings as they sought their favorite coffee emporiums, and scattered early shoppers hurried to their destinations with scarcely a second glance at Christmas merchandise in the gayly decorated store windows.

There was nothing to indicate that within a few minutes the peaceful tranquility would be shattered and the day would become perhaps the most violent one in the city's history, with the next five hours a nightmare of robbery, murder, suicide, kidnapping, and auto banditry.

Although passersby failed to recognize the threat, the spark which was to touch off the crime explosion was already there—a shiny, new, black Buick sedan parked just north of the Citizens Bank in the Robb and Gilmour building at 141 South Main street. Five men sat tensely inside the car, waiting for the bank to open. In a few hours three of them would be dead, the other two in jail.

Lawrence Jackson, 1300 South Third street, recalls that cashier Willis Hedges came into the bank just a few minutes before it was due to open. Jackson and Pete Voto, another assistant cashier, were getting ready for the morning rush, and John Noland and Louella Cloutier, bookkeepers, were at their desks. John Moore, local shoe repairman and a patron, waited at the teller's window.

As Hedges went toward the rear room, he asked Jackson if the vault had been locked. The huge safe in the back had recently been fitted with a time lock and it was customary to set this before the bank doors were opened. The assistant cashier replied that it had been taken care of. It proved to be lucky for the bank—unlucky for Jackson.

At ten minutes past nine three rough-looking men, brandishing automatics, hurried into the bank, herded all six into the back room and forced them to lay face down on the floor. Another customer, a Mr. Hawley, the local Western Union operator who had just entered the bank, was made to join the others on the floor.

The leader, a large burly man, demanded that Jackson open the vault and the cashier got to his feet, but explained that the time lock would not allow the safe to be opened before 3 p.m. With an oath, the gunman slashed him across the head with his weapon drawing blood, and made him lie back down on the floor.

Returning to the front room of the bank, the bandits scooped up more than $15,000 in loose silver and currency, stuffed the money into sacks, and rushed outside to join their two companions in the waiting sedan.

Only a few minutes had elapsed since the bandits first entered the bank, there had been no alarm, and it seemed they were about to make a clean get-away. Fate, however, stepped in with the first of a series of coincidences which was to spell disaster for the robbers.

Ed Vansickle, whose barbershop adjoined the city jail on Mulberry street, had decided on a few hours of hunting that morning, and was to catch a ride with a friend at the Main and Mulberry street corner. With his shotgun cradled in his arm, Vansickle waited in plain view of the gangsters in the black sedan, and doubtless to them meant that he and perhaps others were aware of the holdup and were simply standing by until they attempted to escape.

With tires screaming, the big Buick headed south, and whether or not the menacing figure of Vansickle influenced their decision, the driver attempted to make a U-turn at the Mulberry street intersection. This was their first mistake, for the heavy machine struck the curb at the northeast corner, blowing out the right front tire, then careened northward at high speed with the wheel bumping furiously.

Only Police Chief Everett "Pete" Helms and Patrolman Walter Burnside were on duty that morning when someone came running in to tell them of the robbery. At about the same time Mr. Hawley was telephoning from the bank.

The city administration, headed by Mayor Henry Owens, employed only six policemen at that time. Four worked the night shift, while two took the 6 a.m. to 6 p.m. shift.

Rushing outside, Helms and Burnside climbed into an older model Oldsmobile owned by Cheek's Garage on Vine street, for their only squad car was being serviced and Cheek had loaned the department a replacement for the day.

Witnesses informed the officers that the bandits had headed out of town north on State Road 63 so they took off in pursuit. Although out of sight, the police were able to trail the get-away car because the flat tire was cutting deep grooves in the road.

The chase led north to the Fairview Road, west to Ninth street, north again out of Fairview and across the covered bridge, since destroyed by fire, to the Summit Grove road, then West again.

Traveling at a higher rate of speed than the disabled bandit car, Chief Helms and Officer Burnside were rapidly closing the gap, and, as their vehicle crested a hill, there, only a short distance ahead, were the bank thieves. They had stopped to change their smoking tire while one of the men, armed with a sub-machine gun, stood guard in the middle of the road waiting for the police car which they evidently felt sure was coming.

The fugitives had brought their car to a halt only a few yards beyond a dirt road which intersected the Summit Grove road at the Frist farm corner and Helms knew he must turn the borrowed patrol car down that dirt road for they could not pass the bandits and were carrying only side arms in the face of sawed-off shotguns and automatic weapons.

As they neared the intersection one of the gunmen shouted, "Get the one in uniform." Chief Helms was wearing civilian clothes while Burnside was in uniform, and they undoubtedly thought he was their greatest threat. The officers made the corner in a fusillade of bullets which riddled their machine and stopped out of range to await the gang's next move.

Although experiencing considerable difficulty with the battered rim, the bandits once more got their car headed west, and Burnside and Helms resumed the chase, keeping just out of range of the machine-gun trained on them from the rear seat.

During the hail of bullets at the crossroad, Burnside had felt a searing pain in his side and was knocked breathless. He told Helms he had been hit, but failed to find blood, although a huge welt had formed on his side.

It was later found that the slug had slammed into the door channel, expending some of its force, then was deflected into Burnside's Sam Brown belt further decelerating it, but there was still sufficient impact to bruise the skin and raise a painful welt.

Harlow Frist, a farmer, had watched the entire proceedings from a nearby hill, and during the shooting yelled "What's going on?" His curiosity might have cost him his life, for he discovered afterward that a bullet had pass through his coat.

Unable to get up speed because of the damaged wheel rim and possibly to confuse pursuers, the gunmen decided to change vehicles. At this point an elderly farmer, Jediah Frist, father of Harlow and Marshall Frist, Clinton, came along driving an older model Buick. He was promptly waylaid and put out alongside the road while the bandits transferred their loot, turned the car around and continued westward.

Selection of the Frist car was one more link in the inexorable chain of circumstances which proved to be the bandits' undoing. Sometime before, as a safety precaution, a governor had been installed on Frist's car which prevented the machine from traveling over 40 miles per hour, and at this moderate speed the commandeered auto tooled over the back roads toward Dana with the Clinton police following at a discreet distance.

Meanwhile news of the bank holdup was spreading like wildfire, due largely to the prompt action of Hazel Haase Cunningham, chief operator for the Indiana Bell Telephone Company's exchange here. Receiving word of the robbery only minutes after it occurred, Mrs. Cunningham phoned farmers and town authorities along the presumed route of flight appraising them of the situation.

Alarmed and curious citizens were also calling in to report or inquire about the strange behavior of the two cars and their occupants and this information was quickly relayed to officials ahead of the fleeing bandits.

Mrs. Cunningham was also able to advise the authorities of changes in the get-away vehicles, the number of bandits, and the general direction in which they were traveling. She later received the Bell Company's Silver Medal and $250 cash award for her services, and was included in a book "For Noteworthy Public Service," which listed winners of the Theodore N. Vail National awards, a Bell Telephone Company tribute to recognize unusual service during emergencies.

At the noon hour in Clinton, Mrs. Walter Burnside was assisting in preparing and serving WPA-provided food for school children at the First Baptist Church, one of several such stations. It was at this time she received word that her husband had been shot by the bandits without learning any of the details, and spent anxious hours waiting to learn how badly he had been wounded.

While the police car maintained its distance, another car drove up behind the officers near Tillotson Corner, an intersection on U.S. 36 west of Dana in Illinois, and the driver sounded his horn to signal he was going to pass.

Recognizing the occupants as Joe Walker of Dana, a former deputy sheriff; Homer Hann, Dana businessman, and Pete Scott, also of Dana, Helms and Burnside tried to dissuade them from getting too close to the fleeing bandits, but the driver kept going and drove up behind the Buick sedan. The gunmen stopped their car and the Dana group also came to a stop.

Walker, armed only with a revolver but apparently determined to make an arrest, started to approach the bandits, while Hann and Scott kept out of sight. As Walker neared the get-away car, one of the gunmen opened fire with a submachine gun, cutting him down mercilessly. He fell mortally wounded.

Pausing only long enough to see how badly Walker was hurt and to make arrangements to get him to a hospital, the Clinton police once more took up the chase.

Between Dana and Scottland, Ill., on U.S. 36, the bandits held up Wells Gelbert and his son driving a brand new Chevrolet truck. Forcing the younger man out, they transferred the stolen money and arsenal of weapons.

During the transfer there was another exchange of gunfire when Ernie Boetto and Charlie Clark, both of Clinton, joined the local officers. Boetto was armed with a rifle. In the brief skirmish, one of the bandits, later identified as E.H. Hunter, 47, a Terre Haute liquor runner, was wounded.

Although the truck made good time, the fugitives abandoned it near Sidell, Ill., in favor of a nearly new Model A Ford. This, too, proved to be a mistake for the car was nearly out of gasoline and, within sight of Sidell, the bandits were forced to pull off the road at the Les Moody farm home. One report indicated that Moody exchanged shots with the men when he became suspicious of their actions. At any rate he remained inside the house.

Brought to bay, the bandits attempted to hide in farm buildings and in the cornfield behind the house. By now a sizeable posse, led by Vermillion County Sheriff Harry Newland, had converged on the area and several hundred spectators watched as the officers close in.

The wounded Hunter was located first hiding in a hog pen. Three men had fled into the cornfield, but within a few minutes only one, identified as James Clark, 32, alias William Long, came out waving a handkerchief and surrendered to Burnside. He carried a sub-machine gun.

A search revealed the bodies of E.W. Landley, 65, formerly of Frankfort, Ind., and Thomas Bell, alias Herman Lamb, formerly of Pittsburgh, Pa., in the field. Both had been shot through the head and at first there was speculation that the two had been slain by Clark, but it was ascertained later that they had taken their own lives rather than face trial for their crimes. William Martin, 32, alias Walter Detrick, was discovered hiding in a corn crib and taken into custody.

All but $,800 of the loot was recovered on the spot after the gang was apprehended, but it was believed some was lost in the various transfers from one car to another. Most of the missing money was in currency, however about $1000 in silver and a similar amount in gold was included.

After Sheriff Newland had summoned an ambulance which took the critically wounded Hunter to a hospital in Danville, Ill., he and Deputy Raymond "Razz" Foltz, accompanied by Burnside, took the two captured gunmen to Newport for questioning by local authorities and Chauncey Manning, head of the Indiana Bureau of Criminal Identification. Later they were transferred temporarily to Terre Haute when threats against their lives were reported.

With two immediately dead as the result of the crime spree, the toll increased the following day when Mr. Walker died in the Vermillion County Hospital where he had been taken following the shooting. His fu-

neral was the largest ever seen in Dana at that time.

On Thursday, two days after the bank robbery, Hunter died in the Danville hospital bringing the violent five-hours' total to four dead. The bodies of Bell, Landley, and Hunter lay for days unclaimed in the morgue at Sidell, and eventually all three received pauper burials.

While in jail at Newport, the two prisoners remained uncommunicative, talking little, and refusing to answer questions. However, it was learned that the men had stayed in Danville, Ill., on the Monday night before the robbery, and that Hunter had driven the gang to Clinton the next morning. Hunter was also driving when the bandits switched to the Frist car after the holdup.

Arraigned in Vermillion Circuit Court on Dec. 23, 1930, both bandits pleaded "not guilty" and bonds were set at $100,000. The auto banditry charge was dropped since the bank robbery penalty carried a 10 years-to-life sentence upon conviction. The law firm of Sawyer and Aikman, pauper attorneys, was assigned to defend the prisoners, and trial date was set for Jan. 2, 1931.

A new speed record was set on that date when a jury to hear the case was selected in only one hour, and W.A. Saterlee, acting prosecutor for Prosecutor Homer Ingram at the time of the holdup, read the opening statements. Citizens Bank Cashier A.W. Hedges was the first of numerous witnesses to take the stand throughout the day.

Detrick and Clark, handcuffed and under heavy guard, seemed nonchalant as the trial wore on. Detrick, a "sheik"-type, cleancut, and well dressed, smiled broadly several times, but for the most part kept his eyes on the floor. Clark was not visibly affected as he scanned the courtroom closely and watched each witness intensely.

At 10:45 a.m. the following day, the case went to the jurors, and exactly 17 minutes later, the panel returned with a verdict of guilty as charged, and Judge W.C. Wait pronounced sentence. Both men served 22 years in prison for the crime.

Reports received at the Clinton police station following the robbery indicated that the five men comprised one of the worst gangs of bank robbers and criminals in the country.

James Clark, alias William Long, was a notorious underworld character. Known to police as Oklahoma Jack, he had been reported killed in a series of bank robberies in Kansas and Oklahoma. He was also believed to be the man who engineered the $600,000 holdup of a U.S. bank truck in Denver, Colo.

Walter Detrick, alias William Martin, had been sought in St. Louis, Mo., for numerous crimes. He was known to have participated in a Los Angeles theater robbery on July 15, 1929, and in the Proctor and Gamble payroll robbery in St. Louis on Mar. 5, 1929.

Landley, one of the two who committed suicide, was found to have been one of the men arrested in 1924 in connection with a bank robbery in St. Bernice. At that time he

had been held in the Vermillion County jail for about seven months, but was released for lack of evidence.

Thomas Bell, alias Herman K. Lamb, the second suicide, was considered the worst of the lot. He was the leader of the gang which robbed the Clinton bank and it was he who struck Jackson during the holdup. Bell was known to have led a $296,200 robbery at the Northwestern National Bank in Milwaukee, Wisc., on Dec. 8, 1924, and was the only one to escape arrest after that job. An escaped convict from the Utah State Prison, he was considered the brains of the holdup gangs with which he was associated.

Sometime later, local police received a letter from Tennessee authorities which indicated that Hunter's real name might be John M. McKee from that state. The tip had been provided by a relative of the dead gangster.

Following recovery of the $15,567 stolen from the Citizens Bank here, insurance agents Foster and Messick presented a $1000 reward to officers Helms and Burnside for their part in the dramatic episode, but they each retained only one-fourth of the amount and gave the rest to the widow of the slain Joe Walker.

Walter Burnside, now 73 years old, is one of the few still living who figured prominently in the events of Dec. 16, 1930. Sheriff Newland, Deputy Foltz, later a State Police Detective, and Chief Helms have since died, as have bank cashiers Hedges and Voto, farmer Jediah Frist and barber Ed Vansickle.

Mr. and Mrs. Burnside, who live at 1108 South Seventh street, came to Clinton from Scottland nearly 54 years ago. For 33 years, Mr. Burnside worked in the local coal mines.

Joining the police department in 1928, when 37 years old, Burnside served two years during Mayor John Paine's administration, then for five years under Mayor Henry Owens. During the early part of World War II, he served as head of a railroad guard detail at the Clinton C. & E. I. bridge across the Wabash river.

Returning to the police force under Mayor Clarence Wright in 1949, Burnside served 11 more years, retiring in 1960 under the present administration.

The Burnsides, who will have been married 55 years this June 16th, have two daughters, Mrs. Janet Shannon and Mrs. Jean Clarkson, both living in Detroit, Mich.

An article in The Daily Clintonian, November 20, 1972.

COLUMBUS DAY PARADE

Columbus Day, October 12, is the day that Christopher Columbus and his crew discovered America. In Canada, it is their official Thanksgiving Day, but in Clinton, starting in the early part of the 20th Century and continuing until 1970, Columbus Day was treated as Italian Day somewhat as Saint

Patrick's Day is treated as Irish Day. In the early years the celebration was conducted in the yard at Glendale School. It was later held at the Aragon Park, and the last year, 1970, it was held at Sportland Park.

Two important parts of the celebration were the parade and the queen contest. The parades started on Main Street and went to the celebration grounds.

Two other activities involved with Columbus Day were crock 'busting' and the greased pole. With crock 'busting', crocks were suspended from horizontal poles about seven or eight feet above the ground. A man would be blindfolded and given a big stick. He would try to find his way a few feet to the crock and swing the stick in an effort to break the crock. Some guys would miss by several feet, and others would make a direct hit. Whatever was contained in the crock would be his prize.

The other activity was the greased pole. It looked like a freshly cut utility pole placed upright in the ground and covered with about an inch of grease. Sacks with money in them were tied at the top of the pole and the object was to climb close enough to the top to remove the sacks.

The Lions Club conducted the celebration and Charles Edward Shannon was in charge of the last one in 1970. The Little Italy Festival was not an outgrowth of Columbus Day, but after a few years of co-existence, the Columbus Day Celebration was stopped.

EARLY 1913 NEWS

It is impossible to include all newsworthy things that ever happened in our history book, however a great number of such things happened in the first three months of 1913, so I will include a few of them as gleaned from the Weekly Clintonian which was a collection of each weeks biggest stories from the Daily Clintonian.

NEGRO KILLED AND NUMBER HURT AT JACKSONVILLE
January, 1913, Weekly Clintonian

What savored as a race riot at Jacksonville, the new mining camp west of the city, Friday, resulted in the instant killing of Clinton Hill, colored, late in the afternoon and the serious pounding of Brownie Ward, Ben Stewart, Rufus Anderson, and another negro known as "Tin Can" all colored drivers at the new Shirkie Mine. All the white persons involved were foreign.

The above paragraph is a direct quotation but the remainder is paraphrased. The new mine employed thirty foreigners and five blacks. When questioned about the incident the foreigners either could not understand English or pretended not to be able to understand it, so the information on what happened comes from Brownie Ward, one of those assaulted. It started when the foreigners decided that they were being cheated because they were paid for the amount of coal they dug and they felt that the scales were inaccurate and was shorting them. They decided not to work anymore until the condition was corrected, and they came out of the mine and sat down in a group. The black miners said that the others had no right to close down the mine without authority of the district officers (of the union, I presume). The foreigners had a committee to go to talk to mine engineer Stewart Shirkie but he was gone. It was considered part of the job of the black miners to stay and clean up the loose coal in the mine after the other miners had quit for the day so at this time that is what they did. Apparently the foreigners felt that since this was a sort of strike the blacks should have dropped everything and came out when they did. When the black miners came out they sat down and later they were attacked and slugged with heavy objects.

Two men, Gustaf Balch and John Johnkopski, were arrested and charged with riot. The witness, Brownie Ward, was struck on the head and crawled some distance before losing consciousness. He reported that he had seen Gustaf Balch strike Clinton Hill on the head with a scantling. When Brownie Ward woke up he found Clinton Hill's body lying nearby, dead.

Clinton Police Chief Vannest and County Prosecutor George D. Sunkel went quickly to the scene to investigate. It was considered a strong possibility that Balch would soon be charged with murder. Coroner Dr. I.D. White assisted by Dr. F.H. Beeler examined the body and determined that Hill's skull was crushed and that he probably died instantly. Hill was 47 years old and had a wife and five children. His father, Joshua, 90 years old, claimed the body and took it back to Burnett for burial.

Beauty Pageant Contestants around 1936. The girls on the left was a Baxendale and the girl on the right is Ilia Mae Rowley. The Baxendale girl won first and the Rowley girl won second in the pagent.

The Moose Lodge float in 1926 in the 4th of July parade.

Clinton 1947

RABID DOGS AT KLONDYKE
January, 1913, Weekly Clintonian

Klondyke Heights has had a mad dog scare for several days and it is reported two dogs afflicted with rabies have been active. A calf on the Frank Alfier farm is reported to have been bitten and was killed Sunday.

A pig at the Ot Webster place is said to have acted as if mad some time after being bitten and a cow near Klondyke Mine has been penned up pending developments after being bitten.

The people have been considerably alarmed over the rabid canines.

LICE AT UNIVERSAL
January 16, 1913, Weekly Clintonian

In this issue it was reported that twenty children in Universal School were infected with head lice which was doing considerable violence to their scalps. The article blamed the outbreak on foreign students. Students found to be infected with the lice were sent home and told not to return until they were rid of the lice.

MOVE THE COURTHOUSE TO CLINTON?

A series of articles in the early 1913 Weekly Clintonians dealt with a bill in the state legislature that among other things would have moved the Vermillion County seat to Clinton. The bill also had a part that would have affected the courts of both Parke and Vermillion Counties. Vermillion County at that time was represented in the house by State Representative Mark Lyday and Parke County was represented by a Mr. Spencer. Both counties were represented by a senator named Dr. J.F. Adams. As you know the courthouse in 1988 is still in Newport.

FATAL SHOOTING IN CLINTON
March 27, 1913 Weekly Clintonian

The same day that the first story on the 1913 flood appeared there also appeared a story in which a negro named Claude Taylor is said to have shot another negro, Mack Fossie, four times in the back and once in the front killing him in the home of William Booker in Clinton. He escaped the scene and had not yet been captured.

NON-FATAL SHOOTING IN CLINTON

Around the same time there was a dual at Main and Elm in Clinton between a policeman and another man. The policeman was wounded in the abdomen and hospitalized and the other man was wounded in the hand and escaped. A later article indicates that the other man was later arrested.

YOUNG FOREIGN MINER LOST IN KLONDYKE MINE

This too occurred early in 1913 and comes from the weekly Clintonian. The title seems to imply that the man was killed but this is not the case. Bayard Tuberosa actually got lost in the mine and was left by the other miners at quitting time. He tried to climb out of an air shaft but couldn't make it. His brother missed him and requested help to find him. Charles Wilson and Rudolf Finger went back in and found him asleep possibly overcome by gas. He could have fallen back down the air shaft and been killed or had he been left long enough would have died from the gas so he was lucky to survive.

STORIES FROM THE PLAIN DEALER

One of the other early newspapers to operate in Clinton was the Clinton Plain Dealer. Here are a few items from the Plain Dealer of January 18, 1907, front page.

A new Gas and Oil Company was organized in Clinton with H.H. Ferguson as President, David McBeth as Vice-President,

DRUM AND BUGLE CORP

World War I was concluded on November 11, 1918, and is called Armistice Day (Veteran's Day). During the 1920's the Clinton American Legion formed their Post No. 140 Drum and Bugle Corp which was active for many years and won many trophies for their performances. Their headquarters was on Third Street between Blackman and Mulberry in a house which later served as Dr. Fred Evan's office. Most of the corp's practice was done at Sportland Park.

COUNTY'S ONLY TRIPLETS (ABOUT 1905)

So far as anyone can remember, these were the only triplets ever born to Vermillion County parents. Dr. Henry Nebeker, prominent Clinton physician of a past generation, was so proud of having supervised their introduction to the world that he insisted on having his picture taken with them. Local coal miners did not work the day they were born and there was a general celebration in Clinton. Folks came from miles around to see the babies. Two of the triplets are still living and are well known here. They are Victor Tasso, driver for the 7 Up Bottling Co., and his brother, Matthew Tasso, now employed at Roselawn Memorial Park. The third triplet, Mary, died from pneumonia when she was nine months old.

They were the children of Baptist and Pauline Tasso.

Taken from The Daily Clintonian, June 12, 1963.

SNOW REMOVAL

If you are old enough you may recall that at least 40 years ago, when a heavy snow fell on Clinton, you would see a horse drawn, triangular, wooden snow plow doing a fair job of clearing the side walks all over town. I'm quite sure something like that would have been appreciated yesterday, (Wednesday, December 28, 1988) although a fine job was done of cleaning the streets so they would be passable.

From an article by George L. Carey, The Daily Clintonian, December 29, 1988.

The above described was a very simple and common device and is adequately described by Mr. Carey. The particular one he refers to was owned and operated by a man named Shepherd, father of professional baseball pitcher, Bert Shepherd. He was probably the last one in Clinton to use a horse for snow removal. *Submitted by Leo Reposh, Jr.*

ILLEGAL WHISKEY MAKING

Illegal whiskey making was like the coal mining industry, some of it was done for local consumption, other of it was done for shipment to the big cities for consumption there. It would be hypocritical to mention one industry without mentioning the other. This industry started during prohibition when manufacture and sale of alcoholic beverages was illegal, but it continued after prohibition was abolished and manufacture and sale of alcoholic beverages was again legal, because people were making money in that business and didn't want to give it up. This type of whiskey making was still illegal because it was unlicensed, untaxed, and in some cases very low quality and down right poisonous due to the use of such things as lead pipes or vats and the addition of carbide.

Whiskey is made by grinding fruit or grain and placing it into a vat, caske, or barrel and allowing it to ferment. Then the juice is placed in a still which is a copper or porcelain boiler and a fire or other heat source is placed under it. Then the steam passes through a cooling condenser and it is alcohol. This is according to Joseph Reposh who has some schooling in biochemistry.

Beer was another product that was produced by bootleggers during prohibition days. I believe that beer, called home brew, went out faster when prohibition was repealed than whiskey making did because due to its nature, quality is more important in beer. According to Joseph Reposh, beer is made from hops, malt, sugar, and yeast. First boil the hops. He says the buds of the hops are picked and used. Then put the juice of the boiled hops into a crock or barrel and put in malt, sugar, and yeast. The malt comes in the form of a syrup. Leave these

things in the crock or barrel about a week. It will rise and then fall. After it falls put it in a bottle and wait another week. Then it is ready to drink. *Submitted by Leo Reposh Jr.*

WINE MAKING AROUND CLINTON

Wine making in Clinton and vicinity was a different situation from whiskey making, because the legality of wine making depends on how much is made and what it is used for. Some people made large quantities of wine and sold it just as they did whiskey in probation days and afterward and this was illegal, but others made wine for private consumption in their homes and this is legally allowed. I believe wine making is a lost art locally because the older generations of European wine makers are now deceased, but there may be some younger ones who know how. Martin and Tilka Mohar used any available bottle to hold wine. I have been told by some German wine connoisseurs from Parke County that this is not good because wine needs to be stored in a certain color of bottle to filter out certain rays that will harm the wine, but since the wine was consumed by the same people who made it, I guess they only needed to suit themselves. The Mohar house was abandoned for sixteen years due to the death of Mr. Mohar and the illness of Mrs. Mohar and during all that time some wine was stored in the basement and was found in 1986. It was given away and its condition and use is unknown.

According to Joseph Reposh who has some schooling in biochemistry, wine is made by first picking the grapes, then they are ground. Stomping with one's feet is one of the lesser used methods for this. They are then put into a vat, barrel, or caske. The container is left open for fourteen to twenty days. During this time fermentation takes place. Next the juice is drained off and the juice is placed in a clean closed barrel which is laid down horizontally. Install a vacuum filter and put a bucket under it. In other words put one end of a pipe in the wine and the other end in a bucket of water so that both ends of the pipe are submerged. The impurities in the wine come out into the water. After thirty days remove the pipe and seal the barrel and let it age. Put it in bottles the following spring.

Submitted by Leo Reposh Jr.

According to a Clintonian article by Bonnie Jeffery there is a small winery operating in Clinton today, 1988. It is operated by Clee Sprague and his wife Chieko. This is called the Feather Creek Winery. *Photo by Bonnie Jeffery, Submitted by Leo Reposh Jr.*

CLINTON CITY GOVERNMENT

Clinton has a mayor and council form of government. These officials are elected every four years. There is also a city clerk-treas-

urer who is elected every four years. The elections are held the year previous to the presidential election year. Previously the elections for city offices were held in the off year election which is two years before the presidential election, but during the time Tubby Wright was mayor this was changed because some felt that the city elections did not get sufficient attention being incorporated with the other election. I, Leo Reposh Jr., have proposed that the city elections be moved back to be incorporated with the general elections, and Senator Ed Pease said that this will be considered in the next session of Indiana State Legislature. My reason for wanting the change was to save expense and because so many city officials resign to seek other elective offices.

In Clinton, the candidates for city office run on the major party tickets. In 1963, a local third party was formed and tried to capture the mayorship, but the election results had Democrat John Goldner the winner with third party candidate Elmo Magnabosco second and Republican Lloyd Ransford coming in third.

At the present time the mayor of Clinton is Ramon Colombo, the councilman-at-large is Mike Costello, the first ward councilman is Pete Arcamo, the second ward council woman is Lavonna Mattick, the third ward councilman is Ed Rieber, and the fourth ward councilman is Dominic "Tony" Costello. All these officials are Democrats, but the city clerk treasurer is a Republican, H. Marie Meadows.

The city has a city attorney who is Bruce Stengal, former county prosecutor, and this is an appointive office.

Since the time when the position of justice of the peace was abolished there has also been a city court with the judge elected in the city elections, and the present city judge is Carl Cloyd, a Democrat. The city judge is not required to be a lawyer and the present city judge is a former postmaster. A deputy prosecutor acts as prosecutor for city court. The previous city judge was Everett Lyday.

There are other city officials who are appointed. The Cemetery Superintendent is Rudy Bohinc. The Chief of Police is Ronald Hines, the Fire Chief is Everett Barker, the head of the street department is Ben Turchi, the head of the water department is Ronald Vorek, and the head of the sewer department is Enoch Jones. There is also a zoning board, a park board, and a board of public safety. *Submitted by Leo Reposh Jr.*

THE MAKING OF A MAYOR

The Mayor of Clinton, M.J. Tucker, had died and on April 29, 1924, the Clinton City Council was to meet and choose a new mayor. Public speculation reported in the Clintonian was that the Republicans were going to nominate Carl Zenor for mayor, although supposedly he was a Democrat. Also it was speculated that the Democrats would nominate someone and that the decision process would be long and difficult, because the council was made up of three Democrats and three Republicans. Another possible complication was that City Councilman Sam Kaa had started a business in another town and did not actually live in Clinton and therefore some felt he should no longer be allowed to vote on the city council.

After the meeting had been held it was reported that what happened came as a complete surprise. Democrat, John R. Paine, who had not been publicly mentioned as a possible candidate was chosen. He had been a city councilman at large and a local postmaster. Councilman T.L. Kibby nominated John R. Paine. Councilman B.F. Harrison who was Paine's cousin nominated Carl Zenor. Republican Councilmen B.F. Harrison and Alex Jones voted for Zenor, while Republican William Harden and the Democrats, T.L. Kibby, L.T. Shannon, and Sam Kaa voted for John R. Paine.

Apparently, the question of Sam Kaa's eligibility to vote never came up officially. I have some indication Sam Kaa may have been a nick name for a much longer name, and if it is the same person his out of town residence was temporary, and he continued his political career here.

In 1925 John R. Paine was elected to the mayorship the normal way. In the Democratic Primary he received 727 votes to 213 for John Zwerner. The Republican Primary went S.N. Sellers 819, C.E. Lowry 316, Ernie Boetto 280, Alex Jones 270. In the final election Paine got 1697 to Sellers 1360. *Submitted by Leo Reposh Jr.*

FRANKLIN DELANO ROOSEVELT AND WILLIAM HENRY HARRISON

Franklin Delano Roosevelt addresses local citizenry at the South Main Street Coliseum on Wednesday, October 13, 1920. At that time he was a Vice-Presidential candidate of the Democratic Party along with Presidential candidate Governor Cox. At that time it was Roosevelt's opinion that the ticket was in good shape in the cities but lagged in rural and small towns.

They were defeated by Warren Harding and Calvin Coolidge. Harding, Senator from Ohio, ran his front porch campaign from his home in Marion, Ohio. A short time later Roosevelt became ill and lost the function of his legs and later still (1932) he was elected President. In 1940 he became the first and only President elected to a third term and in 1944 he was elected to a fourth term but died in office April 12, 1945.

Franklin Roosevelt was the President with the longest administration, but the other President known to have visited our county, William Henry Harrison (passed through the county on his way to the Battle of Tippe-

---

CLINTON'S MAYORS - 1893-1983

1. Wm. G. Merrill May 1893 - May 1896 (R)
2. N.C. Anderson May 1896 - Sept. 1898 (R)
3. Dr. C.M. White May 1898 - June 16, 1902 (R)
4. D.C. Johnson June 16, 1902 - May 1906 (R)
5. C.E. Loury May 1906 - 1909 (R)
6. H.M. Ferguson Jan. 1, 1909 resigned Oct. 16, 1911 (D)
7. M.M. Scott elected by council Oct. 16, 1911 served to Nov. 21, 1911. (D)
8. M.J. Tucker elected by council Nov. 21, 1911 serving thru 1913. He was then elected Nov. 6, 1913 and served 1914 thru 1917. (D)
9. C.E. Loury again elected for years 1918 thru 1921. (R)
10. M.J. Tucker again elected for 1922 thru 1925. He died while in office Feb. 9, 1924. L.T. Shannon, councilman, and Sam Kaneznovich both served as mayor pro term until a permanent mayor could be selected. (D)
11. John Paine elected mayor by council April 29, 1924 thru 1925 and then elected for years 1926 thru 1929. (D)
12. Henry Owens elected for years 1930 thru 1933. The state legislature extended term 1 year. 1933 thru 1934. 5 years served. (R)

13. Dr. C.M. Zink elected for years 1935 thru 1938. He was re-elected for years 1939 thru 1942. (D)
14. Clarence "Tubby" Wright elected for years 1943 thru 1946 the state legislature again extended the term of office 1 additional year thru 1947. He was re-elected for years 1948 thru 1951. He was re-elected again for a record 3rd term 1952 thru 1955 - total 13 years. (R)
15. John Goldner elected for years 1956 thru 1959 - re-elected for years 1960 thru 1963 and re-elected for a 3rd term for the years 1964 thru 1967 - 12 years. (D)
16. Hugh L. McGill Jr. elected for years 1968 thru 1971. He was re-elected for years 1972 thru 1975. He was again re-elected for years 1976 thru 1979 - 12 yrs. (R)
17. Arthur Lindsey Jr. elected for years 1980 thru 1983. (D)
18. Don Natalie elected for years 1984 thru 1987. (D)

8 Democratic Mayors served 40 years
8 Republican Mayors served 50 years

Compiled by John Shepard

---

canoe) had the shortest Presidential administration. He made the longest inaugural speech and this was done outside in foul winter weather, and as a result he came down with pneumonia and died after a month in office which he spent being too ill to do much.

CENTENARY

This Vermillion County village on Indiana 163 is long past its heyday as an area coal town. But it still holds a few surprises.

Platted in 1910 and thought to be named after a now-gone church, Centenary has an impressive restaurant, a large and modern elementary school and an old-time general store, complete with comfortable chairs for local loungers and a wood stove for cold Hoosier winters.

Don't let the plain white front of The Old Homestead Restaurant fool you. It's downright elegant inside if you head for the left part of the room first.

There you'll find a large carpeted room with old wooden tables and chairs. There's a long, cherry wood bar in the back room next to a comfortable looking couch.

"Our trade comes from all over," said John Wilson, who runs the place with his

partner Carolyn Hatfill. The two have been a team at the Homestead one year.

"They say there's been a bar or restaurant at this site for over 100 years," said Hatfill. The two have rustled up a 17-item menu which includes frog legs, prime rib, catfish, oysters, shrimp, lobster and steaks.

"This is the Homestead and we're going to give it a homey look," Wilson said. "We want everyone to feel at home." Their main dining room can seat 70, while each of two other rooms can handle 40 diners each.

There's a spot for a band to entertain, but that doesn't get much use these days.

"We put toys in there for the little kids to play in," he said.

Modern, one-story Van Duyn Elementary School is located about a half-mile from the village of maybe a few hundred people. School started Aug. 22 and principal Jerry Shonk reports 312 youngsters grades K-6 showed up. About 10 percent of the students at the Consolidated school actually live in Centenary, he said. The rest come from the rural area around the community.

The school was built in 1961 and is identical in every way to Ernie Pyle Elementary School south of Dana, the principal said.

"We have an active PTO which has recently helped us purchase and put up playground equipment," Shonk said. The principal also said the PTO helped buy more computers for students.

"Five years ago we had eight computers," Shonk said. "Now we have 33 of them." Sixth graders Alta Dunkley and Cade Spires, both 11, have been computer students since the third grade.

"I'll probably use a computer as an adult," Spires said.

Beginning this fall, the school will have the services of physical education teacher Sue Claycomb on Wednesday afternoons, Thursday and Friday.

Claycomb will also coach the girls fifth and sixth grade basketball teams. She'll be inheriting last year's fifth grade team, which went undefeated.

Granny's is the name of the general store run by Wayne Flowers and his wife, Claytie, who prefers the name Granny. This is the only place in town where you can buy groceries and gasoline.

Granny's is an old-fashioned store with wooden floors and old-time glass and wooden candy counters. There's a woodburning stove toward the back of the store near the small hardware section and plenty of comfortable chairs for loungers who always seem to show up at various times during the day.

When you open the front door, you move an old cow bell hanging on a leather strap. That tells Flowers and Granny they've got a customer.

Sam Hedges, a 79-year-old retiree who has lived in the area all his life, recently took a seat in one of the chairs and proceeded to tell a visitor about life in Centenary years ago.

"The town wasn't all that much bigger years ago," said Hedges, a thin man dressed in bib overalls, white hat, shiny patent leather shoes and dark green shirt. "There were just a lot more businesses."

Hedges said there were so many taverns here during the coal mining days he can't recall them all. Two he did remember were the Blue Bird and the Yellow Dog. "This was quite a wild town back then," said Flowers, who occupied the chair next to him. Granny, seated near the others, said some of the old-timers told her women never went out alone at night back then.

Hedges said there was always a gob pile near the mines where people would pick coal for winter heat. "It must have been at least 75 feet high," said Hedges. The two big mines were Crown Hill No. 5 and No. 6. The gob pile was removed just last year.

Ray Hollingsworth, 79, is a retired miner who was once caught in a mine fire. "We got trapped behind a fire back in 1938," recalled Hollingsworth. He had been unconscious for some time and later his brother and others dragged him and 19 others out of the burning mine.

Strange as it may seem, English was a minority language in this town until the 1930s. Most people spoke Italian. "There were quite a few Serbians who ran taverns

Grocery Store and Firehouse in Centenary

here, too," added Hedges, who still likes to occasionally kick up his heels and dance.

"I like that good old-fashioned music," he said, "especially Dixieland. I always had a lot of friends here among all the branches of nationalities."

During a brief lull in the conversation, Flowers and Granny got up and put a record on the old-fashioned Edison windup record player. "Our son borrowed this record player the four years he went to Rose-Poly (now Rose-Hulman) in Terre Haute," Granny explained. The first record they put on the player was a quarter-inch thick version of "Sweet Georgia Brown."

Granny's place is also something of a museum for old-time farm equipment and miner's implements. Seven years ago, the Flowers bought two old saws from a fellow and fixed them up to the wall. Now the ceiling and walls are laden with all types of old-time tools and implements.

Flowers said a few years ago a fellow came into the store and admired all the old relics at great length. Then he told them he was going to do something for them. "He pulled out this harmonica and played for quite a while," said Granny with a grin. "Come to find out he was the state harmonica champion of Kentucky and Tennessee."

Right across the road from Granny's store is the Clinton Township Volunteer Fire Department where Gene Runyan is chief. Of the 17 firefighters, there is one woman on the force — Sherrie McFarland, who is also an Emergency Medical Technician.

Other businesses in town include Runyan's Salvage, Ted's Place operated by Ted Ruffattola, Dee's Tavern run by Delores Boling, and First Stop Tavern run by Robert and Rosie Finger.

There are a number of farms in the area. Some, like the one operated by Charles Sisson and his sons, Doug and Jeff, are large.

"We raise crossbreed hogs on our 1,200 acres," said Sisson, who said they generally raise 2,000 hogs per year. Sisson said some farmers make the mistake of jumping in and out of the hog business. "The time to get

into the hog business is when prices are low," explained the veteran farmer. "Then you stay in it."

Virginia Ybarrondo, 60, and her two grandchildren were recently sitting in the back yard of Ybarrondo's mother Antonette Gillio here. "I don't believe that business about you can't go home again," said Ybarrondo, who has been coming home to Centenary from southern California for four decades.

"Centenary will always be home to me," said Ybarrondo. "I look forward to this every year."

Article by Dave Delaney, Terre Haute Tribune-Star, August 31, 1986, Tribune-Star Publishing Co., Inc.

FAIRVIEW

You could say this town in Vermillion County is Clinton's shadow. But don't say it too loud. People here consider their community as a separate entity and an even better place to live than the neighboring city.

"This is the garden spot of America," says town board member Tom McLeish, a native of Clinton who has lived here 22 years since moving back to Indiana from Montana. "I'm not a politician, but the town board asked me if I'd serve on the board temporarily after this one fellow died. That was 18 years ago."

McLeish, like many residents, lives here but works elsewhere. In his case, his job is Clinton, where he runs Faraco's Art Jewelry at 215 S. Main St.

"This is a nice, clean town with lots of friendly people," McLeish said. "Fairview has a separate identity...most people are proud they live here."

Unlike many small towns, Fairview's population is increasing because of the home sites and subdivisions available. McLeish estimates that 80 percent of the new homes built in the last few years in these parts have been put up in Fairview. Many of those moving to the new homes are Eli Lilly

Turkey Run Bound

employees. Lilly's Clinton laboratory is located several miles north.

McLeish said most people who live here appreciate having a nice large lot. "Many of them are one acre," he explained. "I can practice golf in my back yard."

People here call the town Fairview, but on the map and the charter it's officially Fairview Park. It was platted in 1902 and adjoins the city of Clinton.

In 1913, it had a population of 700 people. Today, 1,202 live here.

Susan Crossley is water and street superintendent. "I could brag on Fairview forever," said Crossley, whose husband Harry helps her with the job. "I wouldn't leave her for anything."

The town has not been overrun by high technology, but Crossley said her department recently got a computer. "This has taken us out of the 1940s," she said.

More important to local residents, however, is that trash is picked up — free of charge — each Wednesday.

In a county where politics is an integral part of the society, someone once quipped that you have to be a registered Democrat to live in Fairview. Democrats do prevail.

Fairview Democratic precinct chairman Tom Lambert said the town contains a lot more Democrats than Republicans. "I'd say about 80 percent of the people here are Democrats," said Lambert. "This is a pretty nice little town."

Clinton Mayor Art Lindsay said the side-by-side communities of Clinton and Fairview get along quite well.

"As far as I'm concerned we're good neighbors," Lindsay said. "We help each other out," although he admits Clinton puts a lot more into the relationship.

"They don't have that much to share with us," Lindsay said. "However they help with snow removal and sometimes help pack chuckholes."

Fairview residents are proud of their well-maintained streets. "They should be," said Lindsay, who pointed out that Clinton streets get lots more use and are harder to maintain.

He also mentioned that Fairview residents use the Clinton streets since they shop and work there. "Clinton probably serves 15,000 people around here," said the mayor. "I suppose 70 percent of the people that work in Clinton don't live here. Many of our business people live in Fairview because it's cheaper to live there."

Lindsay also said Clinton sells water to Fairview in the summer when the town's wells run dry.

The Clinton mayor likes the looks of Fairview's new community center. "When they get that community center finished it sure will be nice," he said.

The Fairview Volunteer Fire Department has a nice new home and the town has a spanking new community building thanks to the work being done free by a number of local people.

"It cost us about $46,000 to put up the community building," said Bob Daniels, a town board member who runs Daniels Barber Shop in Clinton with his brother, Fred. Both have lived in Fairview all their lives.

A number of local people volunteered their skills and labor to build the building. Daniels said the community put on chili dinners, had auctions, got donations and received some money from the town board to put up the structure.

Harold Benskin, fire chief for 22 years, was one of those volunteers. "We've done most of the work ourselves," he said. Benskin said the place will soon be finished and will contain cooking facilities, a meeting room and the town's water office.

"People can use it for weddings, reunions and any type of meeting," the chief said.

Belva Daniels, Bob's mother, has lived here since she was three years old. "There's been a lot of changes here the past 50 years or so," she said. Roads were blacktopped, a park and town hall were built, and the fire department formed.

There were three or four grocery stores

here, but they're closed now. The last one to close was owned by Eunice Kennedy.

"I started working in the store in 1935 and closed it up in 1968," said Mrs. Kennedy, whose home is now the remodeled store building. "This has always been a nice town."

Kennedy said she closed the shop because of steep competition from large super markets that have popped up everywhere the last 20 years. She did it all in their little family store. "I even cut the meat myself," she said. "My dad taught me how to do it."

There are very few businesses in Fairview these days. However Professional Glass and Paint appears to be a solid one. "We do all kinds of glass work and have a lot of paints and do a lot of custom picture framing," said Randy Blackburn, son of owner Wayne Blackburn.

"We've really taken off on this picture framing," Blackburn said. "There's a real market for it." A number of the paints the store sells is of well-known Wabash Valley artist Salty Seamon. He said customers come from far and wide.

"This is a pleasant little community," said Wanda Vandeventer, a clerk at Blackburn's store. "The town board seems to take care of all our problems. We don't have water problems and the streets are good here."

The town park near the Blackburns' store is well-equipped with slides, a basketball court, swings, shelters and the tennis courts.

Don and Madeline Wilson are professional photographers who have lived here 15 years. "We've always thought of Fairview as a suburb of Clinton," said Mrs. Wilson. She and her husband operate Studio II in Terre Haute. Originally, they ran their business out of their house.

She said in the last decade or so local residents have been showing lot more price in their homes and yards. "People are really trying to improve their places," said Mrs. Wilson. "They're upgrading the town."

Fred and Juanita Gross have been in business 17 years selling truck tops and yard ornaments from their Lazy Daze business.

"Lots of people use our place to give directions," said Gross. "It's always being mentioned on the scanner or by CBers going by. I guess we're a landmark."

The place sells both painted and unpainted lawn statues. "We're also the largest truck cap sellers within about 70 miles," he claimed.

An article by Dave Delaney, Terre Haute Tribune-Star, May 18, 1986, Tribune-Star Publishing Co., Inc.

MY OLD HOME TOWN

My old home town, which for years has been known as Geneva, was originally called Vorhees. At about the turn of the century, Vorhees had a population of about 200 people, a Company Store and Post Office run by a Mr. Cummins; 3 saloons; 3 coal mines - one called the Peewee by the work-

ers and the other was operated for a while by Shirkie; and it also had a one room school house where Mr. Hatten James taught all 8 grades but as the population began to grow the school was closed and the children had to walk through the woods to the Sandytown School.

The 2 mines not only attracted the young men from the old pioneer families but they also brought many people of different nationalities to Vorhees. A small town grew up. A road which was later called the "slack road" was made, extending from the corner of the main road north to the Shirkie mine itself. Along the west side of this road, blocks of houses were built, and were soon filled with Irish, Scotch-Irish, Scotch, Dutch-Irish, Swedes and not a few Italians. Several families from Tennessee moved into the "Woods" near the Peewee Mine and quite a few people built houses along the railroad switch which led to the mine. (called Niggar Town). The first labor union, to my knowledge, to be organized in this county, was organized at one of these mines. It was called the Federation of Labor but was short lived around here, this occurred around 1890.

Boarding houses were to be found by men with no families - a family of each nationality would manage to accommodate boarders of their own nationality with the Swedes coming naturally to the Mungus (Magnus) Johnson home. There was 11 boarders sharing the same big room which had only six double beds - no room for any other furniture - but they were all happy. (At the Swede boarding house)

There was a large tract of land extending from what is now Washington Street in Fairview westward to the Feather Creek Free Gravel Road, which had been built between Clinton and Dana and through Vorhees. The south boundary of this land was what is now 4th street in Fairview and it extended north to the Peewee Woods and Norton's Creek. This land was owned by Decatur Downing who planted a large nursery in the west part of it. It had "Overseers" to "run" the nursery and they had authority to hire workers, sell trees, fruits, berries and etc. Among the first of these Overseers was Samuel Shannon, Sr. He hired quite a few workers among whom was the late Everett Shannon - called "Cotton Potter" by his many friends. During this time it was a big business for the vicinity. They shipped nursery stock, fruit and berries to other States, besides selling to nearby Terre Haute and Clinton, plus customers of the home town of Vorhees. In later years the family of James Downey, Sr. moved into the nursery but it never had as big an outlet as in former years. Then still later the land was sold and finally laid out into Gilbert's Subdivision of Fairview, although the nursery house was originally a part of Vorhees. Just what year the name was changed from Vorhees to Geneva I do not know, but during the time of the old Company Store and Post Office, it was Vorhees, Indiana. Although I have heard it said that one of the owners of one

of the mines had a daughter named Geneva and he wanted the town named for her. And so it was changed to Geneva.

By the time the Geneva mines were closing, mines at Lyford and all over the Clinton coal field were being sunk. Families were moving away from Geneva - some to Lyford, some to Clinton and still others to other mines. Soon Geneva looked almost like a ghost town; what houses had not been moved away were boarded up. The saloons were closed; the Company Store closed, boarded up and finally moved away. One saloon did try to struggle along for a while but finally it too closed. The 2 saloons were remodeled into homes and the 3rd remodeled into a church.

There was only a string of houses left, scattered along both sides of the Clinton to Dana road. Later we had another small country store run by Charles Willard and still later another one room school house was moved from Compton Hill to Geneva where the first 4 grades were taught with the older children going to Fairview School. But this school did not last long. Then all the Geneva children had to walk to Fairview School until the school buses were routed through Geneva.

Preacher John Phipps - he did not like to be called Rev. - came to Geneva to preach in the remodeled church. He and his wife and youngest daughter would drive a horse and buggy on Sat. evening to Geneva, stay all night and preach Sunday morning. Then after Sunday evening services, they would drive back to his farm south of Clinton. After his death, the people of Geneva built a small church on land donated by Arnold Davis. Several other Ministers came to preach at the new church, among them was Rev. John Wells. But the church did not prosper for long. The people began to go to other churches and some dropped out entirely. Finally the church was closed, boarded up and several years later torn down.

In more recent years Mary and John Chenhall ran a small tavern then later a grocery and gas station on the corner - the site of the old Company Store - later they remodeled the building into a dwelling house. Today there are only a few houses left in Geneva, but this is home to some very nice people including the Hinkle Bros. Excavating Company and the Geneva Golf Course owned by the Davis family. *Written by Christina Johnson Shannon*

UNIVERSAL

This Vermillion County community has been known by several names over the years...Chunn's Ford, Bunsen and now Universal.

But no matter the name, it has first and foremost been a coal town.

"Universal bought the mine from Bunsen," explained long-time Universal resident Howard Shew. "U.S. Steel eventually bought them out." He said the town's deep mines petered out somewhere around the 1930s ...

a fate that befell numerous mining communities throughout the area in the same period.

But coal mining remains the town's major industry. Now it's strip mining.

"The mine at Universal is the second largest of our seven Indiana mines," said James Russell, director of legal and public affairs for Peabody Mines, Evansville.

He said the Universal mine produces 2.5 million tons of coal yearly on a contract that runs through 1993. That amount figures to 25 percent of the tonnage produced by Peabody's Indiana mines. All the coal goes to Public Service Indiana's Cayuga's plant.

"Our payroll for the Universal mine is $20 million a year, including fringes (benefits)," Russell said. Peabody, which has run the mine since 1970, has approximately 330 employees at the Universal mine, he said.

Shew said that during the teens, Universal was a bustling community. "There were about 3,000 people living here then," he said of the community, which now numbers about 500 residents. Stores and businesses were cheek-to-jowl up and down Wood Avenue, the town's main drag.

What exists on that thoroughfare today is in stark contrast to times past. There are numerous empty lots and only a few businesses remain.

Hyde's General Store is the main business in town now. The post office is also an active spot on Wood Avenue. The main street also has a small park, with playground and baseball field.

Universal gets its mail daily from Terre Haute in one of the trucks from Bill Bybee's trucking service. Just a block from downtown is the Universal Volunteer Fire Department where Bill DaVitta is chief.

Another business is George Padish's Club Tavern, once the pay office for the local mine. "It was used as a hospital during World War I," Shew said. Today, the gray, two-story building is the town's only bar.

Many small Indiana towns have special days or annual festivals, and Universal is no exception. Bunsen Day is observed the Sunday before Labor Day.

"This is when every one from away comes back home to get together," said Minnie Hyde, a clerk at the post office. "We talk about old times."

Universal is kicking off a new celebration this spring with the Fathers Day Frolic, June 15-16.

"This is going to be a fund-raiser for the town," said postmaster Bonita Nolan, one of the festival's promoters. "It seems like a lot of other small towns have something like this...so we said 'why not us, too?'"

She said there'll be tournaments in horseshoes, bingo, bocci ball and euchre. A flea market and arts and crafts display are also planned.

How the funds raised during the festival will be used hasn't yet been decided. "Maybe we can fix up the park with the money," Nolan said. "Some have talked about building a tennis court."

Rose Calvetti Parsley is in her second

Universal

term as town board president. Others on the board are Pete Massa and Earl Clark. "In a small town everybody has to participate," said Parsley, on the town board since 1976. "If the local people don't get involved then the state will take care of you...and we don't want that."

She said the town has lost quite a bit of federal funding in recent times. "We don't have a lot to operate on," she said, "but then nobody does."

Parsley said Universal organized a police department three years ago and now has its first police car. Joe Hyde — who operates his family's general store — is chief. But these days his father, Charles, is pretty much running the show at the store while Joe works to complete his degree in political science from Indiana State University. Hyde, in and out of college for 17 years, hopes to receive his degree in December.

"We're real proud of our little town," said Parsley who pointed out the water system is working much better since a new well was sunk a few years ago. Virtually every street in town has been blacktopped. "I think we do a real good job on streets compared to some other little towns," she said. She said Peabody has been very supportive over the years and even clears snow from the community's streets for free.

One of the town's most active organizations in the Young Men's Club, around since the mid-1950s.

"We help the community and the children," said Paul Soyack, president of the 60-member group. The club was started by a group of young men, but today's members range from age 21 through senior citizens.

The club has its own clubhouse on 10 acres of land just outside the community. The complex includes a meeting room, bar, pool table and two outside pavilions.

The Young Men see to it that Universal's children have a Christmas party each year, Easter egg hunt, haunted house at Halloween

and a big Fourth of July blowout including fireworks.

Minnie Hyde has lived in this mining town all her life. "This is a nice little town," she said. "I like it here." But as has happened in so many other small Hoosier towns, people have abandoned village life and moved to the city.

She said at one time Universal had three grocery stores, a drug store, two movie theaters, several taverns and a furniture store. "Our post office used to be a bank, then it was an ice-cream parlor," Hyde said. "It's also been a gas station and grocery store."

Gladys Oard has lived in this area most of her life and was a teacher for 38 years at Universal School, which closed in the early 1960s.

"People like to vote for Terre Haute," she said with a smile. "I'll vote for Universal. Everybody here is my friend...we're one happy family." She said some of her students have gone on to become teachers, doctors, lawyers and into other professions.

Postmaster Nolan said the post office is one of the social centers of town. "You can learn a lot about what's going on around here by being in the post office early in the morning," she explained. "This is the gathering spot."

The general store is another popular place in this community. The old-time store with its wooden floors and glass candy counters sells all manner of goods including hardware merchandise. It also has a meat department and sells lunch to many, including employees at the nearby Peabody surface mine.

Mac Thornton is now retired in Universal after living in Chicago for years where he was connected with that city's fire and police communication department.

Farming is also a major business in the Universal area. Brothers John and Pete Massa have been working their fields for more than half a century.

"This has been a family farm since

1925," said John, who explained his father, Pasquale, arrived in this area from northern Italy in 1902.

The Massas, both retired, raise mostly corn, soybeans and wheat on ground they describe as "fair." These days, most of their land is rented out.

"We farm about 12 acres up near the house just for something to do," said John.

The brothers said many Universal residents work at Eli Lilly in Clinton, in Terre Haute or Paris, Ill.

Anna Davitto Econe of Portland, Oregon, was raised in Universal, but has been away for many years.

"I'm a coal miner's daughter and I married a coal miner," said Econe, who tries to return to the village of her youth every year. She was in town recently for her annual pilgrimage.

"This place used to be like an old western town," said Econe. "There were lots of killings...it used to be a wild place." She said times were always hard here until World War II. "The war gave us a chance to make more money," she said. It's a shame it took so many lives to give us a better life."

She recalled that the best section of town was where the company houses were built. "They were the only places that had running water and sidewalks," she recalled of those buildings, long-ago torn down. "There's not much here any more but beautiful memories."

Universal has produced a number of people who've gone on to big things in the world of sports and elsewhere. One of them is Fred Vanzo.

"He played blocking quarterback for Northwestern University," said long-time Universal resident Joe Virostko. "I never heard of that position before or since." Vanzo was drafted by the Detroit Lions and played with that National Football League franchise for a number of years.

Morris Nichols, Jerry Spurr and John Cavaletto were three Universal boxers who performed throughout the Wabash Valley. "We fought about every week," recalled Spurr, now a retired security guard, who also boxed in Chicago and Indianapolis.

He described himself as a semi-professional boxer. "Sometimes they'd give us $3 worth of credit for a bout," said the Universal street commissioner. "We didn't get no cash."

Vermillion County historian Martha Helt said Universal was first called Chunn's Ford, named after Major Chunn who camped here on his way to the Battle of Tippecanoe.

The town wasn't platted until 1911 and the first post office was established in 1912. Universal is near Brouillettes Creek, named for an early French trader. "According to stories he was captured by Indians," said Helt, "but an Indian maiden cut his bonds and he escaped."

The covered bridge that spanned the creek burned in 1967, she said, and the area's other covered bridge — called the Double S — is in bad shape.

"There used to be what they called the ghost town at Universal," said Helt, describing the coal company houses where the workers lived.

MUSICIAN HAS ENJOYED CAREER OF HIGH NOTES

UNIVERSAL — Joe Kriss lives alone here in a house full of memories.

The 81-year-old widower once had a musical career that reached its zenith in the 1930s when he joined famed clarinetist Benny Goodman to make music in both Chicago and New York City.

"Benny grabbed me after I had answered an ad," said Kriss, who played both saxophone and clarinet. Kriss outplayed 16 other musicians to get the job with Goodman.

Kriss has fond memories of performing with Goodman during the 1933 World's Fair in Chicago. The Universal resident — recalling what transpired more than half a century ago — said the police put famed stripper Sally Rand in jail after she lost part of her costume. "They later dressed her up as a bumblebee," he said. "Then we played 'The Flight of the Bumblebee.'"

Goodman then took Kriss with him for a 32-week engagement in New York City. Kriss has a large photo album filled with pictures taken during his musical heyday. One snapshot showed him with Goodman and Earl Sands of the Boston Symphony.

Kriss — who performed with numerous other Midwestern big bands — also worked in the Bunsen coal mine 17 years. The Universal resident spent three years at the Busch Conservatory of Music in Chicago.

This tiny Vermillion County community is also the home of accordion players Leno Monterastelli and Armondo Scioldo.

Monterastelli made records under the name Lee Monte. Scioldo played in dance bands for years and has performed at Clinton's Little Italy Festival since its inception.

"We had the same teacher, Armand Gatardi," said Scioldo who left Universal in 1936 for Chicago. As a hobby, he played in taverns on Saturday nights in the Windy City.

An article by Dave Delaney, Terre Haute Tribune-Star, May 26, 1985, Tribune-Star Publishing Co., Inc.

COVERED BRIDGES

These two covered bridges in Clinton Township were built by J.J. Daniels and cross Brouilletts Creek, named for an early French trader. According to the story, Brouillett was captured by the Indians and condemned to die. A friendly Indian squaw loosed his bonds, he made a flying leap into a canoe and escaped down the river.

The Chunn's Ford Bridge east of Universal was built in 1870 with a howe truss. Its length was 162 feet plus nine feet overhang at each end. Its width was 16 feet, and the height was 13 and 1/2 feet. It was a single span with a single roof, and it had cut stone abutments.

It was named for Major Chunn, a regular army officer who marched with Harrison to the Battle of Tippecanoe. He came to the county from Terre Haute prior to 1820 and was a great help in protecting the settlement from Indians. It was burned by vandals May 24, 1967.

The Double "S" Bridge or the S-Hill Bridge is located two miles northwest of Universal. It is called this because of a reverse curve in the road at the south approach to the bridge. It was built in 1879. It is 122 feet long plus 12 feet overhang at each end. It is 16 feet wide and 13 feet high. It has a single roof, cut stone abutments, one span, and a burr arch truss.

The area starting a few feet south of the bridge has been stripped of coal in recent years. The bridge has been replaced by a concrete bridge for use by traffic and a new road has been built to the south through the strip mine hills. The bridge remains as a historic landmark. It is not in very good condition.

Another bridge was nearby to the west called Indian Furnace Bridge and it was accidentally burned down prior to 1949.

Chunn's Ford Bridge

THE COVERED BRIDGE

For a hundred and fifty years, the covered bridge has been an old American landmark. Today it is becoming increasingly difficult to find even one, but only fifty years ago the traveler encountered countless numbers of them-at cities, villages, and country crossings.

The village bridge of the past century was the meeting place of town and country. In its dim interior men argued crops and politics while their womenfolk exchanged gossip and recipes and their children exclaimed over the gaudy circus posters that hung in the bridge long after the show had left town.

Out in the countryside a covered bridge was a good place to save a load of hay in a sudden summer shower. Farm boys found favorite fishing spots in its shade. It seemed as though a high-spirited mare could actually read the signs that were posted prominently over the bridge portals: "Five Dollars Fine for Riding or Driving Faster Than a Walk on This Bridge!" for often as not she would automatically slow to a sedate pace on coming in sight of the cool, timbered passageway. For years the covered bridge was the country cousin to the city amusement park's Tunnel of Love. The longer the bridge, the better. Just ask grandpa why they called them "kissin' bridges."

THE LAST AND LARGEST MINES

The most extensive coal mines within the county, or state, are the property of the Bunsen Coal Company, which corporation opened their works in the month of October, 1911, on section 31, township 14, range 9 west. The president of the company is T.H. Lynch; the secretary and treasurer, W.S. Wardley; the general superintendent, C.F. Lynch, and the superintendent, Charles Karral. The present machinist is George Finnigan. These mines are about six miles to the southwest of the city of Clinton. Three hundred and twenty men are now employed at the works, which are constantly developing and widening out. Twenty-six mules are used under the ground for drawing the cars to the shaft opening, from which it is hoisted by powerful, modern machinery to the surface and then dumped into the waiting coal cars of the Chicago & Eastern Illinois Railroad, which line transports most of the product to South Chicago. More than three and one-half million dollars have been invested in this plant, which now consists of Universal Mine No. 4, which is one hundred and sixty-five feet beneath the surface, and has a vein of four feet and eleven inches in thickness; Universal Mine No. 5, two hundred and thirty-six feet deep, with a vein thickness of four feet ten inches. These mines bear the geological numbers of four and five.

The output in December, 1912, was averaging about eighteen hundred tons per day, and it is expected that soon the two mines, which are very near one another, will have a daily output of three thousand three hundred tons daily. The motto of this company is "Safety, the First Consideration." The scientific care exercised about these immense coal-producing mines is indeed wonderful, even to the casual observer. Every appliance of safety, convenience and comfort is given the miners. The buildings consist of seventeen residences for the use of the officers and superintendents; the offices, power house, bath house, fan houses, boiler house, blacksmith shops, granary, mule barns, supply house, two tipples and two engine rooms. The bath house, as well as all other buildings around the plant proper, is constructed of cement and is fire proof. The bath house is built on modern plans for miners. Here are afforded hot and cold water, the year round. Here the miners and other helpers go and removing their good clothes, put on their rough working suits, the suits not in use being suspended high up in the spacious bath house, fastened by a strong chain and lock, the key carried by the miners, so nothing can be stolen, even to money in the pockets, as all are hung high up to the ceiling and no one but the owner can get them down. Upon coming from the mine the men go at once, if they choose, to this bath room, and there take a wash and shower bath before putting on their better suits, when they come forth not looking like ordinary miners, but neat and clean. One hundred and sixty-five miners, in December, 1912, were availing themselves of the free use of this bath house. The owners and managers of this plant have profited by the experience of the past methods employed in coal mining, and bettered every condition as far as safety and comfort is concerned, that is possible, under present conditions and knowledge. A high class of men are employed. From officers down, the mines are run by men of intelligence and sobriety.

At the site of the mines has been located a village, in which there are already numerous business houses and a postoffice called Universal, which was established in October, 1912. The coal company has no interest in this village, its site or business interests. They do not conduct the usual "mine store," out of which so much dissatisfaction has come in other mining places. Less than two years ago there was not a house on the present site of Bunsen; it has grown like magic and is destined to grow rapidly as the development of the mines increases. It may be added that both "hand" and "machine" mines are operated—Universal No. 4 is machine, while No. 5 is hand mined coal.

Taken from Parke and Vermillion Counties History, 1913.

EDUCATION

The subject of education is the all-important subject to any and all communities, and the early settlers of Indiana built it greater than they then knew, they laid the foundation for future growth of the educational facilities in the State.

The free-school system was fully established in 1852, which has resulted in placing Indiana in the lead of this great nation in educational progress. In 1854 the available common school fund consisted of the congressional township fund, the surplus revenue fund, the saline fund, the bank tax fund and miscellaneous fund, amounting in all to $2,460,600. This amount was increased from various sources, and entrusted to the care of the several counties of the State, and by them loaned to citizens of the county in sums not exceeding $300, secured by real estate.

In 1802 Congress granted lands and a charter to the people residing at Vincennes, for the erection and maintenance of a seminary of learning; and five years later Vincennes University became a reality!

In 1820 the State Legislature passed an act for a State University. Bloomington was selected as the site for locating the institution.

In 1862 Congress passed an act granting to each State for college purposes public lands to the amount of 30,000 acres; but as there was no Congress land in the State at that time, scrip was instituted, under the conditions that the sum of the proceeds of the lands should be invested in Government stocks, or other quality safe investment, drawing not less than five per centum on the par value of said stock, the principal to stand undiminished. The institution to be thus founded was to teach agricultural and the mechanical arts as its leading features. It was further provided by Congress that should the principal of the fund be diminished in any way, it should be replaced by the State to which it belongs, so that the capital of the fund shall remain forever undiminished; and further, that in order to avail themselves of the benefits of this act, States must comply with the provisos of the act within five years after it became a law, viz, to erect suitable buildings for such school.

March, 1865, the Legislature accepted of the national gift, and appointed a board of trustees to sell the land. The amount realized from the land sales was $212,238.50, which sum was increased to $400,000.

May, 1869, John Purdue, of LaFayette, offered $150,000, and Tippecanoe County $50,000 more, and the title of the institution was established-"Purdue University."

Donations were also made by the Battle Ground Institute, and the Institute of the Methodist Episcopal church. The building was located on a 100-acre tract, near Chauncey, which Purdue gave in addition to his magnificent donation, and to which eighty-six and one half acres more have since been added. The university was formally opened March, 1874, and has made rapid advances to the present time, and continues to grow for one hundred and fourteen years later!

The Indiana State Normal School (Indiana State University as we know it today) was founded at Terre Haute in 1870, in accordance with the act of the Legislature of that year. The principal design of this institution was to prepare thorough and competent teachers for teaching the schools of the State, and the anticipations of its founders have been fully realized, as proven by the able corps of teachers annually graduating from the institution, and entering upon their responsible missions in Indiana, as well as other States of the Union!

HOW MUCH DO YOU KNOW ABOUT OUR PUBLIC SCHOOLS?

What percentage of Americans feel that a strong educational system will best guarantee a strong future for America? (84%)

The most serious discipline problem in public schools is: (Absenteeism)

The average beginning salary for a mechanical engineer is $24,708. What is the average beginning salary for American teachers? ($12,769)

What percentage of public school teachers strike each year? (less than 1%)

What is the average number of hours a teacher spends on all school-related activities each week? (50)

How much will teacher Associations spend this year defending educators? ($20.3 million)

In 1970, 21 percent of the nation's high school honor students had used marijuana in some manner. What is the percentage for today's honor students? (4%)

The principal reason teaching is chosen as a career is: (Desire to work with young people)

What percentage of school students are discipline problems? (4.6%)

Teachers are hindered most from rendering the best instruction by: (Work load and extra responsibilities)

What percentage of public school teachers belong to a teacher or education association (NEA)? (80.3%)

The school lunch program for low-income children gets by on $1.20 per meal. The United States subsidizes top military officials at the Pentagon for meals in the amount of: ($14).

From: The 1982 Gallup Poll. The Condition of Education.

"Within the ivy-covered walls of the Clinton Public Library there is cultural pleasure, contentment and education for those who will enter there."

(Della S. Swinehart, one of the first trustees of the Clinton Public Library, appointed by the City Council on October 5, 1908.)

EARLY CLINTON LIBRARIES

The library movement in Clinton began before 1850. A wealthy man, William Maclure, proposed to donate libraries to working men's organizations, which were the first labor organizations in Indiana. Forty young Clinton residents organized a "Maclure Workingmen's Association."

They chose Hiram Bishop as the first librarian. He brought nearly five hundred books from Indianapolis and housed them in his own home. After his death in the 1880's, the books were given to the Knights of Labor. Thus rose, flourished and died Clinton's first attempt at a library.

Another effort was made in 1876 when a reading room was rented over John G. Campbell's Drug Store in the 200 block of Main Street. Books were donated and for a time there was great interest, but this attempt too was not long lasting.

In the fall of 1888, a third undertaking was made to establish a library. L.O. Bishop, editor of **The Argus**, gave the Epworth League of Clinton the proceeds of a special edition of his newspaper. Five hundred volumes were purchased with the donation of $200. These books were housed in the high school until the building was destroyed by fire in 1903.

HISTORY OF THE CLINTON PUBLIC LIBRARY

The drive to build the present Clinton Public Library began in October 1908 when C.H. Leeson approached the Clinton Commercial Club with the idea of establishing a free public library. Rev. Leeson researched the possibility of receiving a grant from Andrew Carnegie for the building.

A petition was prepared and circulated among the taxpayers of Clinton. When two-thirds of the taxpayers had signed, it was presented to the Common Council and a tax of one mill (1/10 cent) on each dollar was levied on all taxable property. The area included in Clinton Township but outside of the city of Clinton was asked to levy a tax of 2/10 of a mill. Andrew Carnegie promised to donate $12,500, and so the wheels were in motion to build a free public library in Clinton.

The first meeting of the library board was held on October 26, 1908. These first trustees included: H.M. Ferguson, Pres.; C.H. Leeson, Sec.; H.T. Harger, Treas.; A.F. Cunningham, Valzah Reeder, H. Sherman Pinson, Clara Wright, Callie McMechen and Della S. Swinehart. One of their first decisions was to establish the name The Clinton Public Library.

The lot on the corner of Fourth and Blackman streets was purchased from Belle Campbell for $1500. T.W. Dowdy was awarded the contract for the building, C.F. Fillinger, the contract for the lighting, plumbing, and heating.

Original plans called for a two story building with the upstairs to be used for club and lecture rooms. However, it was soon realized that the building could not be built for the budgeted $13,000. An alternate plan was proposed to erect a one story structure with a complete basement - the area of the exterior to be 45' by 60' covered with white enameled brick trimmed in Bedford stone.

On June 9, 1909, Faye Tillotson was selected as the first librarian with a salary of $40 per month.

Ground was broken in July 1909, and the cornerstone laid in October 1909. In the cornerstone was placed a sealed metal box containing a Bible, the latest copies of the Clinton and Terre Haute newspapers, an account of Cook's claim to have discovered the North Pole in 1908, and a history of the library movement as prepared by Rev. Leeson.

The Clinton Public Library opened its doors on Nov. 22, 1911 with 2400 books on the shelves. Circulation for the first six days was over 500 books.

THE CLINTON PUBLIC LIBRARY GROWS

As interest in the library grew, it was evident that more space was needed to accommodate both patrons and books. With the expansion of the children's section, the lower level was decorated to meet those needs in 1947. In 1952, a club meeting room was opened through the efforts of the Clinton B&PW and other local clubs.

In 1964, the library board assessed the condition of the library to be in need of major repairs. By October of that year access to the lower level from the street was completed, the inside painted, the woodwork refinished, new tables and chairs and card catalog added, and a new counter top installed. These improvements were made possible through the efforts of the Library Improvement Committee organized by the Clinton Lions Club.

The decision was made to move some of the adult sections to the lower level in order to increase the upper level work area for processing and circulating books in 1986. Shelving was replaced in the children's department, some added to the adult area and the circulating and card catalog files were refinished.

Today the library houses 31,157 items - books, periodicals, records, tapes, and videos and has a monthly circulation of more than 2700 items. It also offers services that include reading discussion groups, literacy programs, summer reading programs for school children, lunch bunch programs for pre-schoolers, and the availability of a meeting room to various organizations and interest groups.

The present library board includes: Jeff Thomas, Pres.; Yale Yeager, V. Pres.; Rosemary Stringfellow, Sec.; John Kyle, Treas.; Ruby Gallagher, Jerry Elmore, and Phillip Duncan.

Dolores Reagin is the head librarian. The support staff members are Stephanie Watson, children's librarian; Sheila Dugger, Jane Stevens, and Margo Fenoglio in addition to custodians, Vonnie Thompson and Mike Gozden.

Throughout the seventy-seven years since its opening, the Clinton Public Library has been committed to serving the people of this community, and hopefully will strive to continue expanding these services to meet the needs of all. *Submitted by Margo Fenoglio, March 28, 1988*

IMMIGRANTS

In 1878 an Italian coal miner entered the court house of Vermillion County on Indiana's border with Illinois, and declared himself ready to be an American citizen. This act in itself, although decades before the great waves of Italian immigration, was not a remarkable occurrence. But something caught the attention of Professor Edoardo Lebano of Indiana University as, one hundred years later, he perused the record of this miner's naturalization.

The newcomer's home town was in the north of Italy. And as it turned out, he was the first of a steady influx of northern Italians to Vermillion County over a seventy-five-year period.

In the early decades of immigration to this country, few Italians came from the northern regions such as Piedmont and Veneto. Most newcomers were fleeing the impoverished and backward south of Italy, particularly after a disastrous earthquake in 1908. Poor and often illiterate, at the bottom of the American social ladder, they usually stayed on the East Coast because they had no money for further travel. Immigrants from the more industrialized north of Italy, generally better educated and more prosperous, did not come to the United States in large numbers until after World War I; many then went to the West Coast and established vineyards. In Indiana's Vermillion County, however, an unusual situation had developed a generation earlier. For whatever reasons—economic, political, personal—sizable numbers of northern Italians had decided to leave home and seek a new life in America, settling in rural Indiana.

"How did they know about Vermillion County?" asks Edoardo Lebano. "And why did they come here from the north? That's what sparked my interest." Professor of Italian in Indiana University's Department of French and Italian, he undertook the study of this Italian immigrant community as his sabbatical research project in the fall of 1983, and expects to complete it during the coming summer.

The Italian flavor of Clinton, the county's largest town and home of most of the Italian population, is particularly marked. At one time, as Professor Lebano learned from a community spokesman, Joseph Airola, who arrived from Turin in 1920, Italians made up more than half the town's population. Clinton's "Little Italy Festival" on Labor Day weekend is one of only two or three fairs in Indiana honoring a specific ethnic group. A recently constructed "Immigrant Plaza," a municipal project long promoted by Mr. Airola, displays flags of the county's ethnic

groups and a statue of an immigrant by an Italian sculptor.

An intriguing comment by his colleague in the History Department, Professor Herbert Kaplan, first brought Professor Lebano to Clinton. As Humanist-in-Residence with the Indiana Library Association in 1979, Professor Kaplan had visited the library in the little town of Newport, the county seat. There he had noticed volumes of naturalization papers documenting the influx of immigrants to Vermillion County from 1856 to 1952. Professor Lebano soon found in these records, long neglected in a dusty basement, a means of restoring some life to the early days of an immigrant community in the rural Midwest.

Lebano's project has required endless hours of poring over nearly 3,600 Declarations of Intention. The records were microfilmed, then photographed in reduced size. Scrutinizing each one, Professor Lebano first sorted them by nationality, then alphabetized and arranged them by different categories to check for accuracy and avoid duplication. The analysis of each year's Declarations is a lengthy procedure.

The Declaration of Intention was the first step in the naturalization process. Why some immigrants filed immediately upon arrival in the county and some waited many years is another question that arouses Professor Lebano's curiosity. For example, of the seven Avenattis who settled in Clinton, one filed his Declaration after two years and all the others delayed citizenship for a long time, as much as forty-one years. In some cases it is evident that an immigrant had lived in other states before coming to settle in Indiana.

Until 1930 the forms were filled out by hand. Indifferent penmanship, combined with the imaginative spelling efforts of the American clerk or the immigrant himself, create many a puzzle for the researcher. Occasionally Professor Lebano finds that his knowledge of Italian dialect is useful, for instance in deducing that misspelled name reflects regional pronuñciation: "Tourain" for "Torino" (Turin). On the other hand, the Declarations suggest a good rate of literacy among these northern Italian immigrants. In 1912-13, for example, only 7 out of 136 could not sign their names.

The records after 1930, though helpfully typed, take just as much time to examine, Professor Lebano finds, because they are more complicated and include more information. As he sums it up, "All those children!"

The study covers the period from 1856 to 1952. During this time Vermillion County received almost 3,550 new citizens of foreign birth, the largest number coming during the first twelve years of this century. Italians accounted for one-third, or 1,178, of the total number who filed Declarations, with Austrians the next largest group (675) and then Scots. At least 77 percent of the Italians were from the northern regions of Italy.

Professor Lebano's demonstration that this Italian population was preponderantly from the north required some sleuthing. For the

Clinton Public Library

Citizenship Class-1936 Front: Judge Bingham and the class instructor. Some of the class members were-Mary Turchi, Maria Ruffatola, Mrs. Giovanini, Joseph Pupilli, Eli Latinovich, Mrs. Dom Garino, Minnie Lanzone, Joan Malone and Pete Arcamo

first few decades the Declarations give only the port of embarkation (Genoa, Le Havre, Antwerp from the north, Palermo And Naples from the south), and the immigrant's town, but no province or region. Gradually Professor Lebano has by now become familiar with a multitude of small towns and villages of Piedmont and Veneto.

The records themselves reveal social change. Italian women had been coming to Vermillion county for years, and virtually all Italian immigrants married women from Italy, preferably from their own towns. Only after 1922, however, did women, many of them well into middle age, start filing Declarations of Intention for themselves; apparently having the vote was an inducement. In the 1930s immigrants insisted that the clerk write "North Italy" after the name of their town, presumably so they wouldn't be thought to have emigrated from Southern Italy. And names can also tell a story. While living close together as a tight Italian community, immigrants commonly changed their names to the English form. For the first generation the same names appear over and over: Mary, Elizabeth, Teresa, Joseph, John, Domenic. The American-born children's names, on the other hand, are much more varied, about half Italian and half English.

The great majority of immigrants described themselves as coal miners on the Declarations of Intention. This represented another break with their pasts, for Italy has very little mining. Most immigrants were probably farmers in their homeland, but in the new country they had to go where the

work was. There are other examples of Italian immigrants seeking work outside urban areas and in occupations other than farming. In the mid-nineteenth century the cotton industry of the Southern states had brought in Italian workers; and in the late years of the century, other Italians from the northern provinces settled in Nevada to work in the silver mines. Professor Lebano has not yet determined how the Vermillion County Italians learned about mining jobs in Indiana, or whether they were actually recruited by the mine companies. Mining, however, was just a first step up the ladder, for typically the Italian residents of Clinton moved into other small-town occupations as soon as they could.

Professor Lebano finds in the old records a certain intimacy with his countrymen of the past. Far from "just cold statistics," he says, his study is "very interesting because you can construct the story of the family. I feel I have barely touched the surface." Eventually he plans to contact the Italian towns from which the immigrants came and, if they are interested, send them information about their Americanized "children."

After completing the statistical analysis, Professor Lebano plans to find out, from current phone books, how many Italians still live in Vermillion County. Then he will seek oral history, transcribed "*viva voce*" from the remaining first-generation immigrants and their children, for the second half of his study. Eventually, if the necessary funding becomes available, he would like to investigate Italian communities in other parts of

Indiana. Meanwhile, Professor Lebano believes that his examination of Vermillion County's "Little Italy," very possibly the largest concentration of Italian immigrants in the state (outside the Gary/Chicago area), can provide a useful framework for other studies of ethnic groups in Indiana.

IMMIGRANT STATUE

Few communities are fortunate enough to have a person like Joe Airola, and Clinton is now the poorer with his passing.

"He was an inspirational pillar from the very beginning of the Little Italy Festival," Ernie Gillio, LIFT board member and past president, said today. "Had it not been for Joe in the beginning many LIFT projects might not have been started or even completed," Ernie added.

"He was always there on the beginning of new projects - especially the Coal Fountain at the Immigrant Square and the grape vineyards on the Wabash riverfront," he added. Gillio is one of the original LIFT board members.

Not just Joe's efforts and guidance, but the many contributions of the entire Airola family toward the betterment of LIFT will stand forever.

In the late 1960s Joe turned over to LIFT the southwest corner of 9th and Clinton/Pike streets for the festival's use and development. The first and largest project on that corner was the Coal Fountain construction. Made of black granite, it continues to stand as a silent monument to the now-silent deep-

Immigrant Statue

shaft and strip coal mines which were the way of life for many immigrants for years.

The Immigrant Square is one of the most unique and picturesque locations in the Wabash Valley, and it is loaded with historic dedication. Thanks to the personal efforts of Joe and Josephine Airola, and a lot of planning by the LIFT board of directors, the special Immigrant Statue was designed in 1969 and created in Italy in 1970 by sculptor Carlo Avenatti. He is not related to any of the Avenattis who live in the Clinton area.

During 1970 the Airolas visited Italy to oversee the statue's construction progress, and they made visits twice weekly to the sculptor's working area. The project to commemorate the "old country" stirred interest in six Italian newspapers which ran pictures of Joe and the statue. The Airolas even accompanied the crated statue on the ship back to the United States.

After the statue arrived in Terre Haute by truck, Joe, in his familiar beige-colored Ford pickup, brought the statue back to its final resting place in Clinton. With the help of Dario Berto, Don Bonomo and Ernie Gillio, the statue was safely unloaded in one of Joe's garages and then uncrated.

Also accompanying the Airola's back on the return trip was an authentic bull's head fountain from Torino, Italy. Even though "nobody was supposed to have one of these but Torino," Joe and a relative in Italy persuaded Torino's mayor to grant permission to use the pattern. A new one was cast especially for Clinton's Immigrant Square.

Dedication of the statue, which represents the many foreign immigrants who came to Clinton from 1900 to 1930, was on May 30, 1971. Along with it were flown 28 specially manufactured flags representing the countries and the nationalities of the Clinton area in-

habitants. Joe himself unveiled the new bronze statue, and for years he single-handedly maintained the entire Immigrant Square in all its glory.

"He took care of the entire square for years," LIFT president Mick Cappa said today. "LIFT didn't have to worry about it for years until the summer of 1986 when Joe began to feel he physically could not do it anymore." He still continued coaching us with his knowledge, Cappa added.

If he could, the image on the Immigrant Statue would take off his hat and hold it over his heart. Clinton, and everyone, will miss its only Cavaliere of the Republic of Italy. Joe was, and always will be Clinton's "Knight."

Article by G.B. "Sonny" Carey, The Daily Clintonian, December 31, 1987

COAL INDUSTRY

Dave Lawson of 1125 South Sixth street worked for many years in the Clinton coal field and as the mines quit operation began hauling coal for a livelihood.

He came here from Knightsville, near Brazil, Inc., in 1914. Mines were beginning to play out in that area and more and more men began to hunt jobs in the rapidly-expanding industry here.

The Miami Coal Company had five mines operating in Clay County early in the 1900's, and in 1912 and 1913 sent Johnny Baird to Clinton to sink Miami six and eight. Later Baird supervised the sinking of mines 4, 5, 9, and 10 for the company.

Dave recalls that there were few houses south of where Matthews South School now stands, and that in walking to the Main street business section, he could cut across every block on the way.

Mining conditions in general were pretty poor, with bad air and in many instances water making work difficult.

When the United States Mine Workers of America was first organized in about 1898 dues were not checked off the miners' pay. The men went to the UMWA local and paid 50 cents per month for a working card. If the miner failed to have such a card by the third day of the month, the bank committeeman at the mine would not let him go down to work. After 1900, the union began to get stronger and conditions were improved. Dues in the UMWA at the present time run $7— $8 per month, Dave says.

When Dave started working in the mines at 11 years of age he was paid 75 cents per day for trapping. Fourteen was supposed to be the minimum age. Mule drivers and track layers received $1.75 a day and hoisting engineers for the company got $40 per month.

When the mines were working at full blast along in 1918, six miners work trains were operated daily. Four went south to the mines there and two went west to the Crown Hill mines 2, 5, and 6, Keller, and Klondyke. Miners from the north section of the city met at the railroad on Ninth Street,

others walked to a big barn used as a waiting room west of the present city park.

Some of the men often became disgruntled when trains were late or when the waiting stations were cold, and a few cries of "Home Go" frequently got the whole crew to turn down a day's work. When one or two emptied the water from their dinner buckets, over some real or fancied grievance, it could start a chain reaction which meant "home go" for everybody.

However conditions sometimes justified their dissatisfaction, for many times there were not enough coal cars to keep the men busy and there were days when perhaps three in a family got only four cars—about the average production for one man.

The Miami company abandoned its mines when it lost a large Chicago school contract which had been in force nearly 25 years.

An explosion at Dering 6 in which several miners were killed brought an end to operations there, and the Ferguson mines dropped off one by one. No. 5 and 6 closed down after loading machines were put in and it cost too much to operate the equipment. They were among the last of the deep mines to go, and only strip and wagon mines remained.

Fifty-six coal mines could be reached from Clinton, but all were not considered in the Clinton field.

When it was decided to build a new hospital here miners were checked off $1 each month and the first check-off amounted to $5,600. $22,000 had already been raised when it was decided to make it a county hospital. These funds were turned over, to the country for that purpose.

Archie Spears owned the Submarine Mine sunk during World War I. Mine run coal was sold for $6 per ton retail, but brought only $1.65 at the mine. Lump coal sold at the mine for $2.35.

In 1918 miners were being paid $2.56 per day, this was later raised to $3, then $5 and $7.50 with the scale gradually rising to the present wage.

Located on the Wabash River near Tecumseh, Submarine mine tunnels extended beneath the river and eastward giving the shaft its name.

The explosion which wrecked the Submarine and killed four miners about 1920 occurred around 8 a.m. Dave was called out because he had had mine safety training. John Stevely, deputy mine inspector, requested that Lawson take charge on top at the scene. Tommy Faulds, Matthew Kerr, and Dave Brown were also included in the group of rescuers.

Jimmy Needham, fire boss, was in the mine when the explosion occurred, but was not killed. Rescuers worked from 10 a.m. to 5 p.m. to get him out through an air course. Dr. D.C. Shaff, a local doctor for many years, went down into the mine at 11:30 a.m. and stayed with the rescue crew.

The mine worked the number four vein of coal at about the 200-foot level, and the entries extended back inside 2,500 feet from the shaft.

South of the Submarine were the Snow Hill mine and the Bardyke below Tecumseh, and the Grant at New Goshen, but these were not considered as being in the Clinton coal field.

The Eagle Mine, only about 100 yards from the Submarine, was owned by a brother of Archie Spears. Working in number five vein, the production output was 10-15 railroad cars daily. It was considered a small mine and the operation was all hand work.

North up the track towards Clinton was the Dering 6 mine, one of the biggest in the area when going full blast. An average of 3-4,000 tons of coal were mined each day, and most of the number four coal was shipped to the steel mills in the Chicago area.

Trains from the E.J. & E. Belt Railroad of Gary came down to pick up 75-100 cars at a trip. Some 15-20 "drags" of 50 cars each were made every 24 hours on the south line.

Matthew Wardrop and John Russell, local miners, were killed in an explosion at Dering 6. Buried under a slate fall, it took almost a week to get the two men out.

The Hall and Zimmerman mine, on up the track from Dering 6, worked the number five vein. A comparatively small mine, the work was all handloading and pick work. Lawson recalled that several shot firers were killed in accidents at Hall and Zimmerman.

The Miami Coal Company operated six mines in the area, four of them at Shepardsville. Mines number 4 and 6 were located on the south side of Shepardsville and number 10 and 5 on the north. Miami 9 was approximately 2.5 miles west and south of Shepardsville, while number 4, also southwest, was closer to New Goshen.

Lawson remembers John Beard, superintendent; Harry Moore, boss at No. 8, Joe Peel, boss at No. 6; Oscar Howard, boss at No. 10; Tommy Lewis, boss at No. 5; Bill Woods, boss at No. 4; and Cooprider at No. 9.

Number 9, biggest of the Miami mines during the 1920's to 1930's period, employed some 400 men at peaks. Production amounted to some 3,000 tons daily. Its closest rival, No. 8, employed between 350 and 375 men at peaks, and average daily tonnage would run about 2,500 tons.

No. 10 and No. 5 mines employed about 150 men and produced slightly under 2,000 tons per day, while No. 6 was a little over that figure.

Number four vein coal was considered best and this was produced at No. 4 and No. 10. Mines number 9,6, and 5 all worked the number five vein.

All work was done on a piece-work basis, and cars were sometimes hard to get. Some miners were forced to spend the entire day under ground to get one car, perhaps the next day might bring two. Four cars were considered a good day's work and would generally mean about $8 for the miner.

Archie Spear's Vermillion Mine was on the same railroad spur but west of Miami 9.

When work was beginning to get scarce in the mid-1920's the Vermillion operator declared that he could not meet the tonnage rate of 84 cents for screened coal and put his mine on a non-union basis. This meant a daily wage of around $7.50.

Although Spears was able to get all the men he needed for his operation, there was considerable bitterness in the local field and periodic fights. The bus taking miners to work was stoned on several occasions while going through Shepardsville.

Once during a strike a party of more than 50 miners from Illinois joined local union miners in staging a parade past the Spears home at Fourth and Elm Streets, but there was no violence and the marchers returned to union headquarters at Main and Mulberry streets above the Clinton Laundromat location.

The Dering Coal Company, with "Pap" Slattery as head bookkeeper, had its offices upstairs at Main and Blackman in the Staats Auto Supply building. Miami's office was in the former Evans building on Elm between Main and Third streets.

Some of the company officers included Henry Nichols, George Kamm, Hubert Ahlmeyer, and Charley Webster. Nichols and one of the others, armed with sawed-off shotguns, usually took the cash payroll to the mines. This often amounted to around $400,000, and as a general rule a second car filled with guards went along to protect the money. On one such run, Mr. Nichols' leg was shot off when his weapon accidentally discharged.

Oak Hill No. 1 and No. 5, south of Clinton, were owned by the Shirkie Coal Company which also owned two mines at Shirkieville. Both were right on the railroad southwest of the city.

The Abe Berry mine was sunk in the same area, but east of the C. & E. I. tracks. When the Oak Hill mines were abandoned later, Berry worked across the tracks into the old diggings.

Berry's operation was a wagon mine, sometimes called a gin mine since the cage was operated by mule walking in a circle and pulling a "gin pole" in windlass fashion.

There were also three small mines west and north of the city park and west of the railroad. Mr. Lawson recalled that during a big strike in 1922 when the mines were idle about six months, a Terre Haute paper company hauled thousands of tons of slack which had been dumped in the surrounding hills to its Terre Haute plant. It was understood the firm paid 15 cents per ton for the discarded slack.

The Crown Hill Coal Company, operated by S.C. Stultz and H.M. Ferguson, owned six mines in the area. Crown Hill 2 was located on State Road 163, near the Crompton Hill "Y", No. 3 and No. 4 were southwest of Crompton Hill, No. 5 and 6 were located at Centenary, and No. 7 Hazel Bluff.

Crown Hill 2 worked the number three and five veins of coal for the most part, but did mine some fourth vein coal.

Twenty-four men were trapped in a New

Year's Eve fire at Crown Hill 6, but only one life was lost in the spectacular blaze which dampened the enthusiasm of 1939 revelers.

As one of the rescue workers Lawson called the rescue squad from the U.S. Mine Bureau at Vincennes, and a mine rescue team from Bicknell also responded. Clinton firemen joined in the effort, and state police made numerous trips to the Vermillion County Hospital for blankets and to the Clinton Hotel where proprietor Harvey Moore prepared food and coffee for delivery to the firefighters.

Dave Lawson assisted in the rescue operations and suggested a path through old works in the mine which eventually saved 23 of the entombed miners. One man who left the main group in a desperate effort to escape was the only fatality.

The Crown Hill mine offices were located at Main and Mulberry in rooms above what is now Horney's Variety Store.

Bogle mines No. 1 and No. 3, operated by the Bogle family, were located south of Jacksonville. Number one worked in the fifth vein coal, while No. 3 worked the third vein. They were later sold to the Binkley Coal Company of which Ben Shull was superintendent.

Another mine considered in the Clinton field was located just north of Newport. It was a good sized, but shortlived mine and was abandoned after about five years. Dr. I.M. Casebeer was a stockholder in this venture.

Keller No. 2 and the old Klondyke mine were both located northwest of Clinton; while Bunsen No. 4 and 5 at Universal were operated by the U.S. Fuel Company. Tom Cokely and Dick Thomas were superintendents at the latter two mines, both of which mined fourth and fifth vein coal.

The Jackson Hill Coal Company had two mines. No. 5 was located in the river bottoms south of Shephardsville. Working number four vein the mine employed about 300 men and produced some 2,300 tons per day.

The mine was lost when the river broke through and drowned it out, leaving much good coal un-mined. Tom Faulds was pit boss, Lawson recalls.

Jackson Hill 6 was located west of Universal. It too employed some 300 men and had daily output of around 2,000 tons. Jesse Hamilton and Ott Wilson were superintendents at various times, and Cliff Connerly was head bookkeeper.

The Jackson Hill company was owned largely by the Colson family which also had holdings in Sullivan county. Offices were located in Terre Haute and the pay roll was delivered to the men at the mines.

Two mines operated in the Geneva neighborhood. One was called the Buckeye Mine while the second bore the name of the community.

Dozens of truck or wagon mines have flourished briefly over the years in the hills west of Clinton. Some of the present day mines of this type are the Big Oak north of Universal; Kelsheimers, along the Centenary

Crown Hill No. 6 Mine J.A. Switzer Hauling Props

road; Alex Ummel's near Geneva; and the Northwest Mine, between Blanford and St. Bernice. Jim Lawson and Loren Griffin also had a wagon mine, the Spring-Valley, located across the road from the Northwest mine. It operated in No. 6 vein.

Mr. Lawson's many years in the mines and the coal industry generally have left him a wealth of information on the subject and a vast store of personal recollections. He admits, however, that the dates and figures quoted in his comments could vary since they are drawn from memory and not written records.

One of the few local "old-timers' with an amazingly keen memory, Dave has seen the coal fields here mushroom, blossom, and wither. Perhaps his reflections on the industry, and those of men like him, may prevent this important slice of Clinton's history from passing into oblivion.

An article in The Daily Clintonian by W.W. Wake, December 24, 1963.

COAL MINING

In 1921, over 15,000 people lived in Clinton. Probably about three-fourths of them were miners. They were a tough breed. Their long coal dust-covered faces appeared daily coming from miles underground.

Clinton was bustling and economically sound but there were still many, many hardships.

Men risked their lives daily to raise the "black diamonds" from beneath the earth's surface.

Clinton and coal mining were one and the same. Today, coal mining is still a stronghold in the area but is nothing like what it was then.

Just a few years ago reminders of Clinton's most famous era stood everywhere. Today even those reminders have been erased, but the memories live on.

In 1918 six miner work trains were operated daily taking men to the south and west of town and there was a large barn near the railroad tracks which served as a waiting room. Miners from the Little Italy section met the train at the Ninth street crossing.

Thousands came to Clinton around the turn of the century looking for jobs in the new coal mines which had slowly been making their appearance in the area. Population in Clinton went from about 5,000 in 1911 to over 14,000 in 1920.

At its peak in 1920 there were 31 mines in operation. Some of the coal companies included: Dering Coal Company, Miami Coal Company, Shirkie Coal Company, Clinton Coal Company, Ferguson Coal Company, Jackson Hill Coal Company, Spears and Milward Vermillion Mine, Whitcomb's Monkey Mine, Keller's, US Fuel Company Mines, Bogle's, Eagle Mine, Buckeye, Oak Hill, Willow Grove, and Syndicate.

The smallest bi-weekly payroll was $150,000 and that was paid in cash. Between 300 and 600 miners were employed at each mine and 31 different nationalities were represented in the workforce. The miners worked only 200 days per year.

In 1923 and 1924, coal mining in Clinton took a sharp decline when then UMW President John L. Lewis obtained contracts for coal but none was available here at the union price set—and there was no market for coal at the producer's price.

The Miami Company abandoned its operations when a contract was lost from a large Chicago school. The contract had been in force almost 25 years.

An explosion ended work at Dering 6. A similar explosion at the Submarine in the late 1920's did not halt operations, but the Wabash River stopped workers when a giant cave-in flooded the mine.

Some say that Miami 10 halted operations in 1927, Miami 8 in 1930, Bogle's in 1935, Miami 4 (Binkley) in 1941, Bunsen 5 in 1921, and Bunson 4 in 1925.

Ferguson Mines No. 5 and No. 6 were closed after it was discovered the loading machines put in were too costly to operate.

Crown Hill 6 mine was halted in March of 1942 and was the last of the company's mines to go. They had about six years yet to run with the supply of coal available.

Some old-timers have said there is a vast supply of number three vein coal in local fields and some say it is inexhaustible.

The last deep shaft mine to close in this area was the Black Diamond Mine. Located on State Road 71 between Blanford and St.

Bernice, the Black Diamond was closed in 1964.

On March 29, 1976, the tipple and the coal chutes were nearly leveled by a fierce March storm and the mine—an irreplaceable part of our heritage—was gone forever.

Clinton's Coal Mining Heritage has been preserved and "brought back to life" with the Coal Town Museum which opens during the Little Italy Festival held over Labor Day Weekend in Clinton.

Coal Town is located on North Main Street in the old railroad station. Displays depicting miners in the "good old days" and some of the equipment used can be viewed.

Today, mining is still prevalent in the area with Peabody Coal Company's vast operations.

An article in The Daily Clintonian, June 19, 1987, by Jinanne Frazier.

DUST EXPLOSION CAUSES DEATH OF WILSON AT NO. 1

Such is conclusion of mine examiner Moore and the mine committee

Powder set off in can, this firing the dust

Unfortunate victim in twenty feet of good air when turns back into nearby room

William Moore, of Clinton, who succeeded William Edwards as deputy state mine inspector for the Clinton field and other territory adjacent, reports that an investigation into the death of Charles Wilson, the shot firer killed at Dering mine No. 1, a few days ago, convinces him there was a dust explosion following the accidental discharge of a keg of powder.

It also was revealed that the unfortunate shot firer, caught in the deadly gas and fumes, had made his way to a point within twenty feet of an entryway containing pure air, when he evidently became confused or faint and turned back into room 1, where he was found face downward. His two lamps and a pocket knife were found where his tracks led to within twenty feet of one of the main air courses not contaminated by the explosion. He had gone far enough after turning to get back into the room where he died to have gone to safety, had he kept ahead.

The finding of the mine inspector agrees with the conclusion of the mine committee, composed of John Carlson, William Yocum, and William Boyce.

They say that a keg of powder evidently had been exploded by a shot breaking through. While this powder explosion did very little damage, it is the conviction of the investigators that there was an immediate reaction in the form of a dust explosion which caused enough fumes to result in the death of Mr. Wilson.

The funeral of the young man was conducted under the auspices of the Clinton Lodge of Eagles, Monday afternoon, from the Presbyterian Church. Rev. Israel Lake of Hillsdale preached the sermon.

The inquest into Mr. Wilson's death was conducted at the office of the coroner, Dr. W.D. Gerrish, Monday evening, with Mr. Moore examining the witnesses. Nothing was brought out tending to change the mind of the examiner as to the cause of the shot firer's death.

The theory that a dust explosion resulted from the exploding of a keg of powder may be an important one in settling the question of damages going to Wilson's widow. There are notices posted at the mine to the effect that it is not operated under the Indiana compensation act which practically fixes in advance the amount to be paid for various kinds of injuries or in case of death. The law permits any company to elect to operate outside the schedule provided by the act, or within it.

When operating as the mine is operated, the amount of damages, where due, must be threshed out in the form either of a private settlement or through the courts. While a dust explosion may not mean negligence on the part of the mine operators, it has a tendency to point in that direction. One member of the mine committee, asked directly as to whether the mine was not in good condition in the matter of dust, said, "It was not just what it should have been in some parts," or words to that effect. It is taken for granted the company will attempt to show the mine was properly cared for in the matter of dust.

Both the mine committee and the mine inspector agree that the trouble would not have resulted had the keg of powder not been left out where it was. It should have been placed back instead of being out where the shot, breaking through the thin pillar of coal, set it off.

Taken from The Daily Clintonian, approximately 1912.

CROWN HILL MINE ACCIDENT

On December 31, 1938, a shaft fire trapped 20 men in the Crown Hill Six mine at Centenary for over 14 hours. One man perished.

Jesse Hayes, 35, a miner for 21 years, died of carbon monoxide poisoning in the mine that day. He left behind his wife and three children.

Of the remaining 19 men, only three have added a half century to their lives. Si Mattioda of Clinton, Roy Hollingsworth of Centenary, and Albert Colombo of Terre Haute can still recall that day 50 years ago that they thought was their last.

The other 16 men trapped in the mine that day, who are now deceased, included Lewis Reed, Flosis Shannon, Clarence Carty, Homer "Mousie" Hollingsworth, Howard Wright, Lloyd Beard, George Merritt, John Hrivnak, Roy Tyler, Frank Stewart, Tom Rayce, John Vearo, Harve Newport, Natale Muzzarelli, Steve Yeager, and James Graves, who ironically, was killed some years afterward in an accident at Blackhawk Mine.

Nearly 150 men had reported for work at

Miami 10 First Aid Team-Seated: David Howard and David Lawson. Standing: Albert Cain, Edward Geller, Thomas McWethy and David E. Blower.

the H.M. Ferguson-owned mine on that day, but the small group of men who were to be featured in the headlines across the nation, was in the wrong place at the wrong time.

The 20 men were mining coal from an east-west entry off the main south entries which had recently been extended to accommodate machine equipment. The entries were laid out in pairs so that air could be forced down one and return by the other. At approximately 30-feet intervals, breakthroughs were made so that air could also pass between the entries to service loading rooms off those passages. Temporary curtains made of canvas and light wood, called brattices, were placed at many of these passages so that the flow of air could be controlled to the various sections of the mine.

At approximately 11 a.m., a motorman drove down the South entry to get a load of cars from the 20 men in that area. Enroute he passed a pumping room, bratticed off, where unbeknownst to him a small fire set off by a ruptured electrical cable must have even then been blazing.

Finding the miners eating lunch and not quite ready for him, the motorman also decided to eat his lunch there before taking the trip back. That half-hour delay proved crucial, for when he again passed the pump stations the entire hallway was ablaze.

After several men at the mine entrance were notified of the fire, mine boss Tom Salmond began to gather a rescue unit. They entered the mine, some distance apart, and circumvented the flames. The rescue unit had penetrated the smoke-filled corridor several feet when Salmond, in the lead, complained of light-headedness and said he suspected carbon monoxide gas.

Salmond was overcome by the fumes and became unconscious. Two men dragged Salmond some distance along the tunnel, but they, too, were becoming affected and had to abandon Salmond, believing him either dead or dying. It was, in fact, reported at the tipple that the mine boss was dead, but other miners had made their way to him and pulled him to safety.

Hoping to avoid unnecessary anguish for families of the trapped men, and to keep hampering crowds away from the area, news of the fire was being kept quiet and other miners were told to go home. Clinton Volunteer Fire Department was contacted on a silent alarm and had delivered 1,100 feet of hose to the mine for use by company officials who still felt that they would be able to bring the blaze under control.

The 20 men, sealed off by a wall of flames, had been telephoned about their predicament and advised to remain where they were and brattice themselves off to conserve the air supply. Three mules, each of which would require as much oxygen as seven men, were taken to a more remote spot and curtained off, later becoming victims of oxygen exhaustion.

Pete Guerri, 84, a resident of Clinton Chateau, was part of the rescue team that day and recalled the awful nightmare which occurred 50 years ago.

"I had the Model Cleaners at that time. I was taking a steam bath when Pete Muzzarelli (Natale's son) came and told me his father was in the mine. I told my wife 'I'm going out to the mine'."

"After I got to the mine and saw what had happened I came back home to get my mine lamp and cap." Pete retired in 1937 after 21 years of mining. He started mining at the age of 11.

"Patty Lynch came up in the cage and requested volunteers. I threw the rope over my head and he said 'Pete, you don't work here anymore.' Then he told me I knew more about the mines than anyone he knew. He said 'Pete, we need a cager and I think you know the signals.' So I went down."

Pete knew the mines well. As a matter of fact, four years earlier had helped the electrician install the pump where the fire was now raging out of control. "I was down there, but I never saw the fire," Pete said. "The men came out and they had been hit by the smoke bad. You could cut it with a knife."

"I was down there for two or three hours before Ray Gilfoy relieved me. Later they needed me to help bring the bosses out, so I went back down," Pete recalled.

On commenting about the death of Jesse

Bunsen Mines #4 and #5.

Hayes, Pete said "Jesse and Roy Hollingsworth were checking for smoke by marking the walls." Chalk markings were made on the walls and if each following trip the mark could not be found the men knew the smoke was coming closer. "The old timers told them not to go. But they insisted. They were gone for some time and Mousie got worried and said "I got to go after my brother," Pete stressed as he relived that day.

Mousie found Roy unconscious from carbon monoxide gas and dragged the much-larger man painfully back to the group before nearly collapsing himself. "He didn't have enough strength to go back to get Jesse," Pete sighed.

The water which was used to fight the fire was pumped from a creek behind the Van Duyn farm home, over one half mile away. The Clinton Fire Department was assisted by a Montezuma pumper truck and a Terre Haute pumper. In bitter cold, and wading in nearly a foot of snow in slippery, pitch-black fields, the men ran hose lines from the mine to the creek.

A problem developed when it was learned that a double-male connector was needed to fasten the lines to the standpipe. None was available and a telephone call was made to Clinton Fire Department to see if one could be made. Harold Kendall, a member of the local force, contacted Joe Aimone, who at that time had a welding shop, and the piece was quickly fashioned and Kendall delivered it at 7 p.m., eight hours after the fire was discovered.

A crowd that was estimated at nearly 4,000 persons flocked to the scene. Newspaper press associations set up wire services to dispatch news and pictures of the tragedy to the world. A relative of one of the trapped miners called from Linton and said that he had heard the news via short-wave radio from the Big Ben Tower in England. This all took place while many people in the immediate area were still unaware of the situation.

Maps prepared by Cecil Harrison, surveyor for the Clinton Coal Company for nearly 30 years, were consulted to find what the rescuers thought would be their best route to save the trapped men. They decided to risk sending a rescue party through old entries five and six. They had been sealed off for 15 years and their condition was unknown. It was certain that there had been a large fall of slate and coal in the number six passage and it was thought to have extended into number five.

Removing the seal, and with fresh air being blown in behind them, the rescuers advanced several hundred feet through a comparatively intact tunnel until they encountered chest-high water and the cave-in. Bit by bit a hole was picked out through the blocked entrance and the brave men slithered through the narrow opening.

Some of that rescue squad included Frank Topolosek, Ed Lunstrum and Charlie Colombo, who is still living and now resides in Florida, Pete said. "Charlie did most of the work," Pete commented.

It was 1:20 a.m. Sunday, January 1, 1939, when the first survivor, John Vearo, was blanketed against the cold and arrived at the top. A mighty cheer arose from the crowd.

Some of the remaining men were able to leave the mine on their own feet, while others were carried on stretchers. Hope had been abandoned for George Merritt, but the searchers found him also, somewhat revived from the air being pumped in, and about 200 feet beyond the point where Hayes had died. He was sitting up, in a dazed condition. Merritt was the last survivor to reach the top, 18 hours after the nightmare had begun, at 5:30 a.m.

Today, records at the Clinton Firehouse for the last day of 1938 show a very brief entry: "Crown Hill Six mine fire." A list of the members of the department who answered the alarm follows: Tony Fenoglio, Bill Shepard, Dow Mitchell, Ray Graves, Wayne Peer, Wilford Doolin, Roy James, John Guerri, Harold Kendall, Clarence "Tubby" Wright, Driver Cappy Dunlap, and Herschel Cheek, who is the only living member. Cheek resides at 145 South Third Street, Clinton.

Article by Cindi Marietta from December 30, 1988, The Daily Clintonian, which was taken from articles in The Daily Clintonian on December 31, 1963, and January 3, 1939, and a personal interview of Pete Guerri.

COAL MINES

The Black Diamond Mine was located north of Jacksonville at the bottom of a hill near Brouillett's Creek. This was a small wagon mine meaning it did not have a railroad spur, but depended on wagons or trucks to transport the coal to the user and the coal was used locally to heat homes and other buildings. Black Diamond changed ownership and names many times. We normally called it Northwest Mine. After it went out of business it was used by LIFT as a tourist attractions.

The other five are larger mines with railroad spurs to ship the coal out for possible industrial use or to heat homes in distant cities. These are shaft mines as opposed to a slope mine or a strip mine. Archie Spears was the mining engineer in some of these mines.

Crown Hill Two was close to where Paradise Bowl is now. Crown Hill Three was in the powder mill area south of Wal-Mart. Crown Hill Five and Six were in the Centenary area. Crown Hill Seven, was on the road between Hazel Bluff and Universal.

Mid Continent Coal Corporation operated a strip mine in the vicinity of Spangler Road near Centenary around 1937. They had a railroad spur into this mine to ship coal out for use in distant places.

Another type of mine was the slope mine which was a small operation where miners started at the bottom of a hill and tunneled back into the hillside to retrieve coal. *Submitted by Leo Reposh Jr., RR 3, Box 768, Clinton, Indiana*

NORTON CREEK COAL MINES

The "Norton Creek Coal Mines" are located on the line between Clinton and Helt townships, on section 5 of Clinton Township, and section 32 of Helt Township. Their development commenced in December, 1884. F.A. Bowen was the proprietor, and Charles P. Walker, of Clinton, the superintendent and manager. In the spring of 1885, under the general laws of Wisconsin the "Norton Creek Coal Mining Company," was organized, with a paid up capital of $40,000, with its general office at Milwaukee, Wisconsin. H.M. Benjamin, of that city, is the president of the company, and Charles P. Walker, of Clinton, superintendent and treasurer, and general agent for Indiana. Connected with the property are 255 acres of land. The mines are about two and one-half miles west of the "Eastern Illinois Railroad," and connected by a spur track. The company also own the old "Briar Hill" mines, on section 9, Clinton Township, but they are not now operated.

On the southeast portion of section 5 is located the company's large mercantile establishment and local office, which, with twenty-seven tenement houses, constitutes quite a village, called "Geneva," named in honor of a daughter of Superintendent Walker. The sale of coal in 1886 reached $160,000, and the mercantile establishment $42,000. Near the mines are several tenement houses, and at the Briar Hill mines eleven houses. All are occupied by employees of the company. The business is increasing, owing to the excellent quality of coal produced. Commencing with the winter of 1887-'88 an average working force of 300 men are employed.

Taken from 1888 Vermillion County History

MYSTERIES

WOLF MAN MURDER

This case occurred about 1930. No names other than that of the arresting officer will be used. Magazines printed different versions of the story and even listed other local police as the arresting officers. The Clintonian compounded the offense by reprinting the stories in 1969. There are a number of mental disorders involving sexual perversion. This one involves a young man who was only interested in male children and was prone to use force.

My mother and a little boy were playing near the street. This man came along and made conversation with them. Then he asked the little boy to come into a coal shed with him. The boy said "No" and distanced himself from the man. When Mom questioned him about the man he said, "He wants to kill me."

Later, on a Halloween night, a boy whose family were acquaintances of both my parents, but not the previously mentioned boy, was found crawling home from a Halloween party badly injured. Apparently he had been slugged with a rock held in a hand. The boy was taken home and died there.

Much later the young man came to Central School grounds and Mom saw that he was drawing attention. One boy was bold enough to tell her that the man was exposing himself. A teacher in an upstairs window saw him and also saw Police Officer Walter Burnsides up the street. Burnsides could not see the man and the man could not see him. She yelled for Burnsides and the man bolted toward home. Officer Burnsides was barely able to keep him in sight part of the time. When the man reached the vicinity of his home which was in Mom's neighborhood Grandma saw him, and he stopped and started watching some men working on a water pipe. Officer Burnsides caught up and accosted the man. He said, "I've been here watching these guys work for hours." The men said, "He is lying, he just got here", so Burnsides took him into custody. He was convicted of the murder of the boy, his sentence was not death nor life in prison and he was only about 17 years old so Mom figures he may have been again walking the streets of Clinton at the time the Clintonian printed the articles in 1969, in fact he might be now. *Submitted by Leo Reposh Jr.*

FORREST DUGGER MURDER CASE

Another unsolved murder took place in 1962. Forrest Dugger was an attendant at the Hoosier Pete gas station on the southeast corner of 4th and Vine Streets in Clinton and was on evening duty not later than 9 p.m.

His body was found lying outside the gas station dead of a single gun shot wound. He had money in his pockets and money was in the cash register. Nobody heard a shot. If it was known at what range he was shot it was not made public. There was never a single clue made known to the public. In conversations people went over a list of suspects, but it was simply a list of local people known for misbehavior.

A few years later a rusty gun was found across the street in a hedge at the post office. We thought, finally a clue. Then the police announced it was not the gun that killed Forrest Dugger, so it remains as a completely unsolved murder. *Submitted by Leo Reposh Jr.*

FRED CALL MURDER CASE

In 1958 Fred Call's body was found along Water Street near Blackman St. in Clinton dead of a tremendous blow to the head. Word spread fast and a crowd gathered, and my father among others saw the body early in the morning. At noon half the Clinton High School student body came to the scene.

A few days later a man was arrested. He said that Call had been in a car with him at that spot the night before the body

was found, that they had argued and he had pushed Call out of the car and drove away. He said that Call received no significant injuries in the altercation. He was put on trial but found not guilty of murder or any other charge.

Technically this is still an unsolved murder, but it wasn't regarded as such by many because although the jury was unconvinced of his guilt many were unconvinced of his innocence. *Submitted by Leo Reposh, Jr.*

THE WOMAN IN BLACK

Roughly during the days of prohibition there were rumors that lasted for the duration about the woman in black, who roamed at night and scared and sometimes assaulted people. In 1979, a woman wrote a letter to the Clintonian about an experience she had as a small child. She and her grandmother and her aunt were walking home from the Baptist Church at 5th and Walnut. They had just crossed the railroad on the east side of North Main Street. They passed the Potter Hotel which had a high porch. Right after they got by, a dark figure arose from the porch and seemed to start following them. They turned toward Water Street and it still seemed to follow. The child and the two women were all scared. The child broke into a run and yelled for her grandfather at home and he heard and opened the door. She ran in and the two women who were slower came in a few moments later. The black figure went into a nearby house. She says that her grandma later learned that the woman in black was watching a wandering husband.

My dad, Leo Reposh, said that one night he and John Rozina and Mike Fossi were on Anderson Street near Feather Creek bridge when they looked back and saw the woman in black behind them. They ran and separated at 12th Street and all continued home without looking back anymore. He theorizes that she was someone avidly against alcoholic beverages and she was spying on bootleggers and possibly looking for a chance to assault them as, rumor said, she did.

In 1928, my mother, Ethel Reposh, was briefly abducted by a woman in black in daylight on her way home from Columbia School. The woman was leading her away from home. A Mr. Voto saw her and told her in Italian to let my mother go and his daughter would take her home. She did, and we know who she is. *Submitted by Leo Reposh, Jr.*

UNSOLVED MYSTERY

Linda Stull was born in Michigan. Her parents went their separate ways leaving her and her three brothers in a group home. Her mother went away to work and then met and married a Clinton man and they settled in this area. They retrieved Linda and one brother from the group home to live with them. The brother died of a congenital illness and then they retrieved the

other two brothers. Meanwhile the mother and stepfather produced three more children of their own. While Linda was very young she was loaded with duties of caring for the small children and other household duties while both parents worked. By the time she had become a teenager the little children did not require so much attention anymore, but she said she was doing terrible in school. Then she became a teenaged mother and dropped out of school. She was able to take pretty good care of her own child, worked in her family's shop, and also had another job.

Her younger brother had a paper route and in the summer of 1977 he went away to Boy Scout Camp. Linda did the collecting for his paper route and this is when she disappeared. She first collected from the northern half of the route, then she returned home and left the money, and then proceeded to collect from the southern half. When she left it was the last time her family ever saw her, period. She never returned. She was expected to be home about 7 pm. At about 10 pm the family called police and were told that if she didn't return by morning they would start to look for her. The family wasn't satisfied and started to look for her. At midnight her stepfather found her bicycle in Sportland Park. A policeman on routine patrol saw him in the park with the bicycle and questioned him, and at that time the police began to take the case seriously. This was only about five hours after her disappearance. The response by police, news media, and other groups was remarkable with people searching the wooded areas near the west side of town, helicopters searching as far as West Terre Haute, and the television stations putting her picture on T.V. The family retraced her collection route to see where it had ended as this would possibly reveal where she had met whatever caused her to disappear. They found that she had completed the route., Our most accepted theory was that upon completion of the route she had gone to the park deliberately to meet someone or else had gone to the park to watch a ball game and met someone by chance, and that she had left in a car with them expecting to return soon. The family learned the identity of a few of her male acquaintances whom they had not been aware of before, but as far as is publicly known no one was questioned except Linda's mother and stepfather both of whom were given lie detector tests. A fortune teller told members of the family that Linda was dead and that her body was concealed by water. Police officer Guinn said he had examined several area ponds and found nothing. There were numerous theories and some sightings claimed, but some were disproven and others remained.

The mother and stepfather separated a year later and she took the other children to Florida. Some people said that Linda had disappeared and was with the others in Florida, but the mother died there and the other children returned to this area, and they assure us that Linda was not with them in Florida. No new clues to her whereabouts have surfaced in eleven years. *Submitted by Leo Reposh, Jr.*

BUSINESSES

CLINTON HOTEL

This information on the Clinton Hotel was borrowed intact from "Clinton on the Wabash" by Louise Hitt Booth. The Clinton Hotel was located at 307 South Main Street which was the southwest corner of Main and Blackman. It was owned by Charles and Henry Meyer who were brothers. The European Plan was used (no meals provided with the cost of the room). Prices were listed as being 50¢ and up per night. There was a dining room and a popular lunch counter. This hotel burned in 1956, removing one of the towns best landmarks. The building was replaced by the J.C. Penney Store. This company left Clinton in 1985. The Clinton Hotel was never replaced.

RIVERSIDE MILL

Riverside Mill was a grain mill located on Water Street in Clinton between Mulberry and the railroad. This mill was operated by Clifford Andrews assisted by members of his family and employees. He came to Clinton from Lafayette. He was not the original owner of the mill. The mill bought grain and the biggest part of the grain was shipped out by rail to distant places. They also sold feed for livestock and other farm needs, as well as doing custom grinding and blending. At that time Mulberry Street ran straight through to 9th so Mulberry Street had a lot of traffic of grain trucks and tractors pulling wagons to the mill from farms west of town. When Clifford Andrews died the mill went out of business. Clifford Andrews liked to write funny things and put them in the newspaper. He used to sign them "Fare, Fat, and 55".

After the mill was abandoned it caught fire and was torn down in 1976. *Submitted by Leo Reposh Jr.*

CLINTON HARDWARE COMPANY AND CLINTON STOVE COMPANY

Clinton Hardware Company was a store run by Harlan and Lewis and located on the northwest corner of Main and Mulberry. Harlan and Lewis later parted company and in my younger days Grace Lewis Walker ran the Main Street store called Lewis Hardware and S.O. Harlan ran the north 9th Street store called Harlan Hardware.

The stoves were manufactured at the Clinton Stove Company located on Western Avenue just east of the railroad on the north side of the highway. Howard Pierce in a 1979 newspaper article says The Clinton Stove was one of the finest stoves made and sooner or later most Clinton people owned one of them.

The Clinton Stove Company building

was more recently used as a used auto parts warehouse called West Side Auto Parts and is now a storage garage for White Excavating. About 1976 a train wreck occurred and a loaded coal car went through the west wall of the building and turned over. An old fashioned rail mounted steam crane was brought to the scene and worked together with a modern White Excavating crane running on rubber tires to pull the car out of the building. The fire from the smoke stack on the steam crane was a show in itself. *Submitted by Leo Reposh Jr.*

CLINTON PAVING BRICK COMPANY

Among the leading industries of the city of Clinton may be here cited the Clinton Paving Brick Company, which was established in 1893, capital of fifty thousand dollars; M.L. Morey, president; H.C. Dies, treasurer; J.W. Robb, secretary and manager; B.H. Morgan and M.C. Wright directors.

The first output of this extensive plant was in August, 1893, the capacity being forty thousand brick per day. The specialty is paving brick of a very superior quality. The company own sixty-five acres of land, and thus produce their own raw material. They employ about sixty-five workmen, and run the year round. The output is nearly all sold in the great Middle West. The clay this company owns will furnish all that is needed for many years to come. It is one of the most extensive plants in this section of Indiana, and is the largest of any, save that at Veedersburg alone, which is the greatest in Indiana.

This has come to be almost a clay and cement age, and as timber becomes scarcer, the construction of almost all kinds of structures will be accomplished by the use of brick and cement materials.

For street paving there is nothing now known so excellent as the proper grades of paving brick, and in this Clinton excels. For this reason the city is indeed fortunate in having this modern plant situated within her limits, furnishing employment for so large a number of men.

Other industries include the overall and skirt factory, in the south part of the city, which employs about seventy-five persons, mostly women; the Clinton Canning Factory, which institution puts up large quantities of vegetables; the ice company, making artificial ice of a splendid quality; the machine shops of Hays & Balmer and that of R.P. Shattuk; the hard-wood saw mills, located in the central eastern portion of the city, near the Wabash river front, the property of Butcher & Cooper.

The milling interests are well represented by the Clinton Milling Company, whose large plant is situated in the heart of the city, near the river front, where a fine grade of flour, meal, graham and feed is produced. *Submitted by Leo Reposh Jr.*

CONSTANTINO BAKERY

The Constantino Bakery was located on the southeast corner of 8th and Anderson Streets in Clinton. The brick house in which it was located is still there, and the baking was done in the basement. According to Louise Hitt Booth's book, "Clinton on the Wabash" the owner was Peter Constantino and he had a wife named Adele and children named Arturo, born 1897, Ines, born 1900, and Palmari, born 1903, all born in Italy and they came to America in 1908. She says that another source says Mr. Constantino's name was Paul Rollo Constantino. Be that as it may, and considering the fact that many Italian bakeries operated in Clinton at one time or another, that the significant thing is that they delivered bread to people's homes twice a week in a little truck. They deserve to be remembered for that. There is nothing better than fresh Italian bread.

The funny thing is that the woman who delivered the bread, Mrs. Constantino, I presume, was always called puna tete. From the time I was age three until age thirty I thought that was her name. At that time someone told me that puna tete meant bread woman in Italian and that Palmari meant baker boy. They were only half right because Palmari was the young man's proper name. *Submitted by Leo Reposh*

CLINTON TELEPHONE COMPANY

John Horney was born in Ferdinand Township, Dubois County, Indiana, on August 29, 1863. His parents, Zacharius Horney and Victoria Pfaff Horney, were immigrants from Alsace-Lorraine who came to America in about 1848. They settled on a farm near Ferdinand.

His father died in 1871 and his mother remarried in 1872. John, then age nine, and his brother, Albert, then age 11, went to work in the Rosemont Coal Mine near St. Anthony. John saved money from his mining wages until he saved enough to leave Dubois County by train and came to Clinton Locks (now Lyford) in about 1878. He worked in a coal mine there for some two years, then went to work on a farm near Veedersburg in late 1882. There he met Carrie May Harrison, daughter of Eli Harrison and Margaret Arthurs Harrison. Carrie was a divorcee and John was a Catholic. When the Catholic Church refused to marry them, John became a Presbyterian and they were married at Rockville on August 31, 1884 and moved back to Clinton Locks.

John then went back to work in a coal mine and the young couple bought a house on Nebeker Street where they kept boarders until early 1887. By then they had saved enough money to open a restaurant and bakery business in the city of Clinton.

In 1892, John and Carrie went to the World's Fair in Chicago. There he saw one of Alexander Graham Bell's inventions—the telephone. There were none in service in Vermillion County and only a few in Terre Haute.

Although fascinated by the telephone, he had to devote all his time to the bakery and restaurant business. In late 1894, however, he was bitten by a mouse and was severely blood-poisoned. While recuperating, he began thinking about the telephone again. He rented a room in the 100 block on South Main Street, across from his bakery, where he set up a "tinker shop" and made his own telephones. The first two connected the bakery to their home. Later, Dr. Aikman asked John to set up a telephone line between the doctor's office and residence. Dr. C.M. White, Dr. H.E. Washburn, Mr. Swinehart, and Matt Scott soon followed.

When about twenty such lines had been installed, Dr. Aikman suggested that John interconnect these lines so they could talk to each other. The first such "exchange" in Clinton used a butcher block as the base. This was a quite crude installation, but it served its purpose until 1898 when John bought a 25-line Kellog Telephone Company switchboard. He installed it in Mrs. Ada Layton's home on Mulberry Street back of the Lewis and Staats Hardware Store.

As the number of telephone customers increased, John added a room, bought some more switchboard sections, and in 1900 hired Cora Newell (later Cora Evans) from Hillsdale as Chief Operator. He also constructed "long distance" lines between Clinton and Lyford, Hillsdale, St. Bernice, Dana and Terre Haute.

The Clinton Telephone Company continued to grow rapidly in the little building on Mulberry Street. By 1906, the company served more than eight hundred lines in Vermillion and Parke counties.

During the early 1900's, John invented the "harmonic ringing system" for the switchboards with which party-line customers heard only their own ringing code.

In 1906, Indiana Telephone Company, predecessor to Indiana Bell, bought the Clinton Telephone Company from John and retained his as its manager.

In 1909, John began to be interested in automobiles and again began "tinkering" with the "horseless carriage". He resigned from Indiana Bell in 1913, and set up a small garage in back of his residence at 115 South Fifth Street.

The garage business began to prosper and took over most of the back yard until his wife insisted he move his business elsewhere. He leased a building on Mulberry Street (across from his first telephone building) and started an automobile repair. Among a number of his inventions was a method for re-magnetizing the circular magneto in Model T Fords. Later, he began re-charging and rebuilding storage batteries. He also invented a number of tools used in the battery and automobile business. He was always trying to find a better way to do things. (This inventiveness characteristic apparently was inherited by his grandson, Robert Lawrence Bence, who graduated from Clinton High School in 1924 at the age of 15, went to Purdue University, joined the Navy, retired as a Captain, and became an executive of Southwestern Bell Telephone Company, where he invented a number of systems including the "talking computer" later manufactured by IBM).

John Horney continued to work until his death on February 20, 1942. He was a Mason, he was active in the Presbyterian Church, and was well known for his philanthropies and his multitude of friends. *Submitted by Robert L. Bence*

PESAVENTO HALL

Chris Pesavento's Saloon in the 400 block of North Seventh Street in 1920. There was a dance hall upstairs. On the left side was a miners' supply store which also sold ammunition. Some years later this was the Honeymoon Cafe run by Eli and Lotti Delich who resided in the part that was the miners' supply store.

The following is from Louis Hitt Booth's book, **Clinton on the Wabash**.

Pesavento Hall was owned by Chris Pesavento in 1912 and was located on North Seventh Street at Oak Street. He opened this place of business in 1904. Since the miners' train stopped only one block from his store, Pesavento added miners' supplies to his inventory. A majority of the Miners' Locals (there were 22 at the time according to one source) met upstairs in the hall, which will long be remembered as the scene of many happy occasions, such as wedding celebrations and lodge dances. The Hungarians would string fresh fruit around the heads of beautifully costumed dancers. The best beau had to pay a fine in order to get the fruit from the head of his sweetheart. If he refused to pay, the lodge judge would put the young man in a jail to sit out a few dances. All the earnings from these dances were put into a welfare fund for the members. Besides, Croatian, Serbian, and Polish music that swelled the walls of the hall, there were the merry wedding dances of the Lithuanians, whose men broke a china plate with silver dollars in order to dance with the bride. The contributions often gave the newlyweds a good financial start. Also this hall was the scene of the Italian Mardi Gras, sponsored by the Societa Veneta and was called "L'Ultimo di Carnivale." During it, the Italians sang the "old country" songs and danced the Murfina, an old folk dance.

A Slovenian Lodge held similar activities in Clinton and is still in existence. Rudy Bohinc is the Secretary-Treasurer (1988).

CLINTON RAILROAD STATION

According to the 1913 Vermillion and Parke County History Book the Chicago and Eastern Illinois Railroad was completed through Vermillion County in 1868-69 when leadership of the efforts was taken up by Joseph Collett Jr. A two percent tax was approved in the county to help pay for the construction. Actually only a 1% tax was used because the other 1% was to be used if necessary and it was never deemed necessary. The railroad opened in 1870. With the exception of Clinton the railroads missed all the cities in Vermillion County. Most of the river towns suffered. This section was owned by Collett, O.B. Davis, Nathan Hardy, William E. Livengood, Joseph B. Cheadle, and others, local people.

On May 1, 1880, it was leased to C. & E. I. They now own and operate it. The principal stations were Clinton, Summit Grove, Hillsdale, Opeedee, Newport, Walnut Grove, Cayuga (Eugene), Perrysville, Gessie, and Rileysburg.

Chris Pesavento Saloon. Upstairs was the dance hall and next door was miner supplies and ammunition

Clinton railroad train station of the Chicago and Eastern Illinois Railroad.

The Chicago and Eastern Illinois Railroad offered passenger service, for example, from Clinton to Cayuga, but most of the Clinton passengers went to Chicago. Service was also available to Terre Haute and points south all the way to Florida. According to John Shepard Jr., the last express agent, parcel express was available through the Clinton Railroad depot until November of 1967. He says that passenger service was discontinued shortly thereafter. The last person to handle the passenger business was Simon Maher.

During the summers of 1962 and 1963, I worked nights at the Speed Grill near the train station and each night the passenger train would stop there about 1 a.m. A local taxi would be waiting most evenings at the station and he would almost always get a passenger.

The Chicago, Milwaukee, Saint Paul, and Pacific Railroad had a roundhouse at St. Bernice, Vermillion County, Indiana, which was for repair and maintenance of trains. This railroad used almost all old time steam trains with only a few diesels showing up just before it closed in the early 1950's. However, the C. & E. I. used streamlined diesel engines somewhat earlier with the square looking diesel engines used as switch engines.

After the passenger and parcel express service went out of business LIFT took over the station. It became a coal mining museum and remains so. *Submitted by Leo Reposh Jr.*

OLD JAIL AT COLUMBIA PARK

The old jail is located in the middle of the 800 block of Anderson Street at the southwest corner of Columbia Park which was the school ground of Columbia School. It contained a cell and a small space with a desk. This small jail was of greatest ad-

vantage to the person who may be arrested for intoxication, because the alternative was to be walked to the main jail twelve blocks away. Main jail was at the 100 block on Mulberry Street. Among the obvious problems of walking prisoners to the main jail was that if a policeman had an appetite for brutality the walk gave him an excellent opportunity to beat the prisoner.

The older jail became obsolete with extensive use of police cars. *Submitted by Leo Reposh Jr.*

ADVERTISEMENTS IN THE SATURDAY ARGUS

On December 10, 1898, the Saturday Argus (a Clinton newspaper) printed a Christmas edition which was mostly a shopper's guide. It contained a number of stories which are virtually impossible to read, but the advertisements which make up most of the paper have larger print and are easier to read. Listed below are some of the businesses advertised.

Washburn and Nebeker - clothing and push food market; C.W. Satterlee & Son - all-night restaurant; Smith and Curtis - groceries, dishes, and pans; R.H. Swinehart and Sons - hardware, harness, stoves, ranges, furnaces, bicycles, guns, and ammunition; G.M.C. Bartmess - jeweler and optician; W.H. Bonner - fire, life, and accident insurance; F. Alfier and Family - staple and fancy groceries; J.P. Tutwiler - groceries; Andrews and Bullock - farm machinery; B.H. Kellogg - jeweler; Moore's Air Tight Heater at R.H. Swinehart and Sons; Morgan's Cash Emporium; Post Office Book Store - J.N. Frist, Prop.; The Leader - department store; Truitt and Blythe - a store; Tursher and Staats - meat of all kinds; Scott and Martin - clothing; The Murray Grocery Company; George B. Tillotson - fine livery and boarding stable; Wilson and Crane - drugs, school supplies, etc.; Crabbs Blue Front Cash Grocery;

McBeth and Wilson - hardware, stoves, buggies; The Morey Company - lumber; Craft and Swinehart - bicycles; Charles Whitcomb and Company - lumber and hardware; Scott and Paine - staple and fancy groceries.

The advertisements contained various forms of Christmas greeting, pictures of some of the merchandise, and Christmas pictures such as Santa Claus lithographs. *Submitted by Leo Reposh, Jr.*

MODERN DAY BUSINESSES

The business life of Clinton has been like a tide. It comes in and it goes out. Clinton has flourished and floundered. It has, however, come back.

Rivertrade flourished in it's infancy. Keel boats, flat boats, canoes, paddle boats, and then shallow draft steamers. Clinton most certainly flourished as a rivertown. Docks abounded along Water Street. The foot of Blackman Street was our riverside dock area. Some of the businesses were pork packing houses, tanneries, and barrel makers, to name a few. This was a busy, bustling town when the farmers, the trappers, and fur traders came to town to sell, swap, or barter. Clinton along it's riverfront was a very busy place. The needs of the people changed when the river became less navigable. The Wabash and Erie Canal failed at the advent of the railroads. Times and people's needs changed.

Water (First) Street businesses moved up to Main (Second and High) Street. It was a busy, bustling street, unpaved, dirty, and dusty during dry spells and muddy and almost impassable during the rainy season. Agriculture, farming, etc., also had a hand in changing our town. The railroad trains, later, and the electric interurban trains made Clinton a very busy place. A boom came with coal mining. Population increased several fold. The coal mines and the miners needed supplies. New businesses came in to fill the needs. Families came to Clinton so more ladies and children graced our town. Wars also had an impact upon Clinton business life. Thus, we can see Clinton business has changed. People have come and gone, so have the businesses over the years. Coal mines closed and work forces departed. Local citizens who grew up in the area left town. Many returned in later years to again call Clinton home. Ninth Street and Main Street were the two business streets. However, intermingled throughout town were "Mom and Pop" business places. Times of Clinton have changed. We are aware the changes have also changed our needs. This brings us to modern day Clinton in the year 1988.

Business is as usual for the citizens, diversified and complex. There are many types to fill the supplies and demands of it's people. Clinton is a bedroom city with transient citizens. This results in the need for various shops, stores, and industry. Herewith is a listing of these that are needed by present day Clintonians. Businesses are listed by street area.

WATER STREET — Public Service Indiana; Hoosier Ready Mix; and Clinton Skateworld.

MAIN STREET (North to South) — Clinton Tanworld; Dairy Queen; C.B. King Specialists; Marshall Pontiac-Olds-Buick; Jim Curtis Garage; Speed Grill; Bag & Save; Lowry Shell Service; Little House Tavern; Ste-Mar Hardware; Half Time Specialties; Robertson Antiques and Used Furniture; Lucky Strike Bowling Alley; Clinton License Branch; LaRue's Restaurant & Lounge; Gillis Pharmacy; Faraco's Art Jewelry Shop; Nannie's Nook Flowers & Gifts; Henry Antonini, Attorney; Dr. D.D. Guha; First Citizens State Bank; G.C. Murphy Company; Goodwill Store; Horney's True Value & Variety; Jan's Hallmark; State Farm Insurance Agency; Shuee & Sons TV & Appliances; Silver Scissors Clothing Boutique & Toning Center, Silver Scissors Salon; Tony's Barber Shop; P & T Video; Beardsley & Stengel, Attorneys; Wright's Apartments; Burks Restaurant; Clinton Discount Sales; V & S Ceramics; Uran's Rooms; Connie's Creative Crafts; Walker's Pizza; Rosenblatt's; Vermillion County Hospital Services, Inc.; Clinton Cable TV Co., Inc.; Clinton State Bank; Clinton Color Crafters; The Daily Clintonian; Valley Oil Service Station; Clinton Chateau Apartments; Clinton Nursing Home; Vermillion County Center of Hamilton Center, Inc.; Vermillion County Alcohol & Drug Service; Visiting Nurses Association; Dr. John Albrecht; Dr. Michael Berger; Dr. Joel Elias; Dr. Elpidio Feliciano; Dr. Anna Zimmerman; Vermillion Convalescent Center; and Ron Frink Construction.

ELM STREET (East to West) — Mike's Motor Co.; Druthers Restaurant; The Coffee Club; Powell's Pharmacy; Tuxedo's & Lace; Layton's Refrigeration, Heating & Cooling; Clinton Ford Mercury Sales; Wilson Insurance Agency; Conrad Studio; Sharp Mini-Mart; Harold R. Rieches, CPA; Ninth Street Carwash; Rayce Laundromat; Scott Oil Co.

BLACKMAN STREET (East to West) — Cottrell's Taxi Service; A & G Gift & Ceramics; Teleview House; Indiana Furniture Company; Paper Back Rack; Clinton Paint & Carpet, Inc.; Robb & Gilmore Agency; Dr. Charles Rutan, Optometrist; Sawyers Flowers; Fashion Shop; Linkon Auto Parts; Stevenson Lumber Co.; Clinton Public Library; J. Graham Services, Incorporated; Frist Funeral Home; Savage Tax & Accounting Service.

MULBERRY STREET (East to West) — Thomas & Thomas, Attorneys; Miss Carol's Beauty Salon; Daniel Brothers' Barber Shop; Strings & Things; Theda's Beauty Shop; and Uptown Coin Laundry.

VINE STREET (East to West) — 500 Service Station; Karanovich Funeral Home; Valley Federal Savings Bank; Laurel Lee's Beauty Shop; U.S. Post Office; Malone Realty & Insurance; Barrato Salami House; Stanley Upholstery & Supplies.

NINTH STREET AREA (South to North) — Pizza City; Tropical Splendor Tanning; Clinton IGA; Western Avenue Liquors; Humphrey & Son Garage; Heritage House of Clinton; Vermillion County Emergency & Convalescent Ambulance Service; Simpson Calico Corner; Simpson Refrigeration; Valley Oil Co.; Hook's Drug Store; Scott's Service Station; Clinton Auto Parts; Mills Restaurant; Rick's Paint & Body Shop; Curls Unlimited; Reed Appliance Repair; Century 21 Marietta Realty; Terra Villa Restaurant; Bello Shoe Repair; Magee's Clinton Marine Sales & Service; 9th St. Sales and Service; Dr. Kent Cammack, DDS; James Gallagher; Attorney; Dr. Duane Binder, Chiropractor; Avenatti's Building & Remodeling; Bonnie Jean's Salon of Styles; Michael D. Burton, Attorney; Divan Welding; Gemini Lounge; Rainbow Day Care Center; Western Indiana Private Industry Council; H & R Block; Waters & Associates Realtors; Rainbow Christian Bookstore; Prudential Insurance; Andrews Heating & Air Conditioning; Bynum Water Conditioning; Cheek's Tavern; West Floor Covering; Fossi Bakery; Ninth Street Liquor Store; Paradise Donuts; North Pole Tavern; Battaglia's Restaurant; Dreamland Cafe; Pastore Brothers Lumber; M & M Lawnmower Sales and Service; M & M Ninth Street Laundry; Ninth Street Feed Service; Giacoletto Sporting Goods; Columbus Co-op Store; Clinton Family Dentistry; Mishler Insurance; Lowry Wholesale Beverage, Inc.; Ice Cream Station; Brandys Restaurant; The Castle; Moulton's Service Center; and Professional Glass & Paint.

HIGHWAYS 63 AND 163 AREA — Two Broke Tramps II; Straley & Sons Automotive; Sportsman Center; Frederick's Gift Shop; Giuseppe's Restaurant; Supreme Submarine; Major Construction Co.; Shepard's Gas & Appliance, Inc.; Countryside TV & Appliances; Dr. William Somerville, Veterinarian; Dr. G. Thomas Cloyd; Dr. Jeffrey L. Snoody; Paradise Bowling & Pizza; J.R. Rumpza Chevrolet, Inc.; Renatto Inn; Wal-Mart; The Strand; Dump Trucks, Inc.

HIGHWAY 63 NORTH — White Airport and White Construction Co.; Eli Lilly Clinton Laboratories; Terrecorp; Standard Asphalt; Mack Readymix Concrete; Kanizer Excavating Co.; Corner Stop; Uselman Packing Co.; and Mid States Railcar, Inc.

OTHER BUSINESSES — Berto's Garage & Radiator Shop; Steve Nagy Repairs; Indiana Sportswear; Pam Hastings Ceramics; ABC Nursery; Vrzina Construction; Robert Beard Plumbing; Wallace Builders; Model Cleaners; Able Valley Disposal, Inc.; Lubovich Excavating; Perry's Backhoe Service; Hinkle Brothers Excavating, Inc.; Martin Marietta Aggregates; Kite & Company; Potter Specialty Business Cards; Yogi's Tree Service; Foltz Video Productions; Welker Construction; Mid America Appraisal Services, Inc.; Fairway Court Apartments; Spendal Meats; Lazy Daze Camper Sales; Valley Pre-School, Inc.; Joyce's Pretty Punch Embroidery; Bowman Tax & Business Planning; Arkie's Asphalt Paving; Kenly, Inc.; A Oaks Septic Tank Service; Dapper Pooch Salon & Boutique; Wilks Realty; Valley Security & Maintenance Co.; Gilbert Vacuum Cleaner Repair; Bronz Bodies Tanning; Dr. J.F. Swaim; Dr. Antolin Montecillo; Clinton Apartments; Michael Smith, Architect; Causey's Sewing Service; Tex's Tack; Donna's Designs; Hair Junction; Willy's Styling Center; D & B Self Storage Center; Russell's Termite & Pest Control; Kelley's Cleaning Service; Ballock Construction; Shull Electric; Alderson Cleaners; S.F. Construction; J & S Painting; and Morgan's Tree Stump Removal.

COTTAGE INDUSTRIES — There are numerous industries located in homes scattered throughout Clinton such as beauty shops, sewing/alteration shops, cake decorators, carpenters, etc. Apologies are in order for those missed.

It takes many varied types of businesses to meet the needs of the City of Clinton and it's people of 5,000 plus population, in the year 1988.

What will the future bring? What will be our needs? Our future is before us, may it be fruitful. God has blessed our forefathers as He will continue to bless us. His will be done. It is really not THE END only ..... The beginning. *Submitted by James E. Graham*

CLINTON TOWNSHIP HOMES

ULYSSES WRIGHT HOME

The house on the north west corner of 5th and Vine in Clinton is now occupied by Del Reininga. Prior to 1964 it was occupied by Mr. and Mrs. Harold Malone and family, and before that by Mr. Malone's aunt, Nellie Malone Wright. This house was built by Ulysses Grant Wright to be the home of his bride, Nellie Malone, and himself and it was for the remainder of their lives. He was president of the First National Bank in the middle block of Clinton's Main Street. According to a 1922 city directory.

Ulysses Grant Wright was the son of John Wright and Mary Chunn Wright, John's second wife. His first wife was Margaret Nichol and they had six children: Evalyn, Angeline, Laura, Silas, Lucius, John O. and Narcissus. Narcissus married James Paine (see related articles on their descendants, Ethel Reposh and Charles Donald Paine). John Wrights second wife Mary Chunn was the daughter of Major John T. Chunn and Mitilda Chunn. Major Chunn was a veteran of the War of 1812 and the Battle of Tippecanoe. Ulysses Grant Wright's sisters and brothers were Margaret, David, George, Maria who married Frank Van Duyn, Naomi, Benjamin, and William.

John Wright was born March 22, 1818 in New York, and came to Clinton in 1820. He was the son of George and Anna Handy Wright. George Wright was born March 10, 1774, in East Windsor, Conn. the son of David and Mary Wright. David was a private in the Revolutionary War in the Conn. Militia, possibly a minute man and saw action. David was born Feb. 24, 1742, the son of Jonathan Wright Jr. and Abiah Keep Wright. Jonathan Wright Jr. born 1710 in Windsor, Conn. was the son of Jonathan Wright and Experience Edwards Wright. Jonathan Wright was born Dec. 18, 1686, in Northampton, Mass., the son of James Wright and Abigail Jess Wright. James Wright born 1639 in Springfield, Mass. was the son of (Deacon) Samual Wright and Margaret Wright. Samual was born 1614 in London, England, died 1723 in Northampton, Mass. He is the one who came to America. He is the son of Nathaniel Wright christened Jan. 28, 1581, and Lydia James Wright born Durham, England. Nathaniel was the son of Lord Sir John Wright born 1544, and either Enfell Linsell or wife no. 2, Bennett Greene. Sir John was the son of John Wright born 1522 and Alice (Rucke) Wood Wright born 1520 in Wrightsbridge, Essex Co., England. John Wright was the son of Sir John Wright born 1488 in Kelvedon, Essex Co., England, and Olive Hubbard Wright, 1492, Kelvedon. Sir John Wright was the son of Devine Reverend Sir John Wright who died May 9, 1509, and his wife Agnes. His father was Sir Henry Wright of England. *Submitted by Leo Reposh Jr.*

H.M. FERGUSON HOUSE
According to James Graham this house at 509 South 5th Street was the home of H.M. Ferguson. It is a grand old house with a separate garage with an upstairs, and a gazebo in the yard.

Strangely, there is not a specific article in earlier history books on H.M. Ferguson, but he was the owner of the Clinton Coal Company, according to Louise Hite Booth, he was also once president of the Clinton Library Board, and according to John Shepard he was Clinton's first democratic mayor from January 1, 1909, until he resigned October 16, 1911. *Submitted by Leo Reposh Jr.*

HEDGES-AIMONE— SHORTRIDGE HOUSE
The Dr. Isaac Hedges house, 145 S. 5th Street, Clinton, was erected in 1875. Dr. Hedges was a well-known physician and prosperous business man born in 1819 and died in 1883.

The original builder of the house was George Edwards, the first man from Vermillion County to join the Gold Rush to California.

The house was considered one of the finest residences of the time and is an excellent specimen of the architecture of the period. It is included in the book compiled by Wilbur Peat, Indiana Houses of the Nineteenth Century published by the Indiana Historical Society.

The Hedges family occupied the house until the death of Miss Jennie Hedges in 1961. Upon her death, it was purchased by Johnny Aimone. Johnny and his family

Ulysses Grant Wright house at 5th and Vine in Clinton

Home of H.M. Ferguson at 509 South 5th Street in Clinton.

Hedges-Aimone-Shortridge House at 145 South 5th Street in Clinton.

lived there until his death due to a motorcycle accident in 1969.

Johnny remodeled the kitchen into a very workable, attractive, country kitchen. He decorated one bedroom for his three sons, Joey, Michael, and Tony. It had three closets all across one wall, window seats, a blackboard on a wall and bookshelves. His office was papered with old maps of the world. He had the house sided with gray aluminum siding to resemble the narrow wooden siding it originally had.

Upon his death, it was purchased and occupied by Henry and Betty Shortridge and son, Marty.

They have finished decorating the house and have had the outside trim stripped completely and painted white. It now has wine-colored awnings hanging over the front porch entrance-way where the original awnings used to be.

The stairway has been stripped and rubbed with tung oil and lemon oil. The steps are carpeted in blue. The risers of the steps are their natural color and are not covered. The newel post is beautifully designed, using three different kinds of wood.

The dining room is lovely with red-flocked wallpaper and red carpet. Mr. Aimone had installed beams across the dining room ceiling which were taken from the old Fairview School. The room contains one of the three original chandeliers in the house. They are all made of a custard-glass-like material with different designs like coat-of-arms on each.

There is a spiral stairway leading from the kitchen to the back part of the house which contains a bedroom, pantry, small storage room and the bathroom. It was said to be the servants quarters in early days.

The house is in magnificent shape after its 113 years in existence.

METHODIST CHURCH

The first Methodist Society formed in Vermillion County was organized at the home of John Vannest, the first settler in the county. The Class comprised Mr. Vannest, his half-brother, George Rusk, James, Amos, and Joseph Reeder, and the Brannon family. The meetings were held in the barn every four weeks. Itinerant Methodists ministers of pioneer time were noted for their deep convictions, powerful preaching, and their energy and daring in threading the wild woods and prairies in search of the isolated settler for the purpose of preaching the gospel and organizing Methodist classes. They believed that sinful men could be transformed by Jesus the Christ.

History tells us that when a small number of pioneers banded together under the Reverend John Gerrish and built a small house of worship in 1831, they were erecting the first church in Vermillion County. Although a Presbyterian church, the Methodists had aided in the building of it, and consequently used it as their place of worship, too. Records differ as to its location. Some say that it was a frame structure located at the corner of Walnut and Main

Streets. Methodists worshipped here for 20 years. The town of Clinton was growing so in 1852 a larger and more substantial building was erected on the opposite corner on land donated by Mr. Benjamin Whitcomb. It was in this church building that S.P. Colvin preached when the Civil War broke out. His circuit included Clinton, Salem, Centenary, Center, and Trinity Churches. Seventy-five percent attended church at this time. A big revival followed the opening of the church and there were many conversions.

CENTENARY METHODIST CHURCH

November 8, 1967, marked the 100th anniversary of the Centenary Methodist Church, with David M. Bonner as minister. He also serves at Center, Salem, and Fairview churches. On November 8, 1867, ground was broken. The first church of which there is any record was erected in 1868 on the present site on SR 163, with the land donated by Jackson Dowdy. Dedication ceremonies were held about the middle of June, 1886, with Reverend William B. Rippitoe as pastor. By 1874, the membership had grown to 40. Sunday School was organized with a membership of 35, with Amon Dowdy and Mr. Darby among the first Sunday School superintendents. Again in 1907, when Reverend Morgan was pastor the membership increased, and almost as great an interest was manifest as the years Reverend Travis was pastor.

About the year 1903, the church was remodeled. The two doors were replaced by one double door, and at this time, the bell was purchased and placed. Reverend Hickman was pastor at the second dedication in 1903. Sometime in the 1890's an organ was purchased, this being replaced by the present piano about 1910. Reverend R.S. Guinn was pastor from 1903-1934, and was replaced by Reverend Harold Hotchkiss who served from 1936-37.

In June, 1938, the Centenary church was virtually destroyed by a storm. The church stood idle for two years. In 1940, Reverend Hugh VanLieu became very interested in the church and began to rebuild the membership. The church was re-opened and the first service was held July 28, 1940, with an attendance of 79. In June, 1948, the church held its third dedication. This same year—1948—Centenary was placed under the charge of Clinton First Church with Dr.

George P. Burdon, pastor, who served from 1948-52.

On April 27, 1956, ground was broken for a new 20 x 40 addition on the north side of the church. The new addition was used for Sunday School classes and educational facilities.

In May, 1960, Reverend Skidmore retired from the ministry and was replaced by Reverend George Quinn. On August 8, 1961, ground was broken for a new addition. The corners of the north side and south side of the vestibule were built to make an all-purpose room, two restrooms, and a hall used for storage and coat rack.

Centenary eventually became a part of what is now Wayside United Methodist Church.

FAIRVIEW PARK METHODIST CHURCH

In the spring of 1907, a group of Fairview Park people and other interested people, led by Robert Gosnell, Reverend Charles Leesen of Clinton First Methodist Church, and District Superintendent Dr. Walker met at Mr. and Mrs. George Tillotson's home to discuss and later make plans for a new church. The Fairview people had been holding church services in the old Fairview Park School. Land was donated by Sarah Downing. It was a piece of land at the corner of what is now Fourth and Lincoln Streets. An official board was appointed as follows: Owen Clark, John W. Smith, George Tillotson, Robert Gosnell, George Hammerley, and James Crumley, with Miss Grace Tillotson as secretary.

The blueprint for the church was made and the contract let to Mr. Wylie Evans. On October 18, 1907, the cornerstone was laid and work begun and later completed by Tom Dowdy. The church was dedicated April 12, 1908.

Reverend Leesen, who had charge of the finances, reported the total cost of the building was $3,052.36 of which $1,825 was paid, leaving a balance of $1,227.36. The dedication ceremonies were in the forenoon with a meeting in the afternoon. Dr. Walker was the speaker. Solicitation was made for money to meet other expenses and $105 was donated. Then all the members of the society were enrolled as charter members of the new church.

The building consisted of an auditorium, one class room a brick walled basement of one room and a coal bin. The first seats were chairs which were later replaced by

CLINTON AREA CHURCHES - 1988

Asembly of God
Baptist Church
Church of the Nazarene
Fairview Park Church of Christ
First Baptist Church
First Christian Church

First United Methodist Church Calvary
Jehovah's Witnesses
Sacred Heart Catholic Church
True Gospel Tabernacle
United Presbyterian Church
Wayside United Methodist Church

pews. The musical instrument was a reed organ until it was replaced in June, 1917, by a new piano, presented by the "Rose Circle" Sunday School class. The electric organ was given by church members, friends, and other music lovers in December, 1949.

The Boosters' Class, comprised of both men and women, worked hard to make money for the church and to furnish it. Among its first teachers were John Helt and Harlow Little. Its name was later changed to "Builders Class." Mamie Smith taught this class for 35 years. After her retirement, Hazel Foltz became the teacher and as of 1979 she has taught about eleven years. In 1934, this class was instrumental in remodeling the basement and adding two new class rooms to the auditorium and other improvements as well.

The "Ladies Aid" was organized about 1906, before there was any church built in Fairview. It was a group of women who met every Thursday at each others homes and quilted. They sold quilts and the proceeds were used to help build the Fairview Park Methodist Church. In about 1940 or 1944, this group changed its name to the "Willing Workers" who with Martha Shew as president (1979) still meet every Thursday in Wayside Church to quilt and they still contribute generously to their church.

The Fellowship Class and men's organizations and other Sunday School classes have contributed much down through the years and have accomplished much toward the improvement of the church.

In the fall of 1966, a very dynamic young woman, Patti Jarvis, came to work in our charge. She was a student of Christian Theological Seminary in Indianapolis, as was our pastor, David Bonner. On the weekends she lived in Fairview and worked in our churches. Patti made many contributions to our church program, such as helping train teachers, giving sermons, producing programs, crafts, assisting in workshop services, directing and assisting in our planning process for the new congregation and many other ways, especially including music. She played the guitar, organ, and piano and she sang and directed the choir at Fairview. Most of all Patti was our friend and became very dear to us. She completed her Master of Divinity Degree at Christian Theological Seminary and married. She and her husband served a three-year tour of teaching and preaching in Kenya, Africa. They are now living in West Virginia and are serving the Methodist—Patti as a minister and her husband in an administrative position.

Written in 1979.

Fairview Park Methodist Church is now a part of the Wayside United Methodist Church.

GENEVA CHURCH

The Geneva Church could be called a small root of the Fairview Park Methodist Church. Very little can be learned about this little church except of my own personal memory verified by my old friends. It was located in the village of Geneva about a mile and a half from the Fairview Church. It was organized by a minister named John Phipps in about the year 1908. He was the first preacher to preach there and he continued his ministry there until his death. The church was held in what was formerly a saloon building. The men of the community repaired the wooden bridge which led from the road to the front door. They then repaired the building itself.

After John Phipps' death, other preachers came in from time to time to preach. Among them were frank Simmons, James Butcher, John Wells, and George Potter. Through the efforts of George Potter, the Geneva Church became a member of the United Brethern Union. A small new church was build on land donated by Arnold Davis—probably about 1912. This church was short lived for people lost interest in it and it closed its doors. Most of the few remaining members went to Fairview Park Methodist Church.

The last Sunday School superintendent of the Geneva Church was Arnold David. The last Sunday School teachers were Arnold Davis, Mrs. George Gilmore, and Amanda Harden. *Written by Christina Shannon*

FINLANDER LUTHERAN CHURCH

The 1913 Parke-Vermillion County History Book lists a Finlander Lutheran Church in operation at 326 North 8th Street.

A physical examination of that block indicates that 326 would be the only vacant lot now existing in that block. This is next door to the former home of a prominent Finnish family, the Lahtis. This lot slopes upward toward the back, and I remember a structure at the top of the slope still there in 1961. It was a wooden structure with a light above the front door. Mrs. Martha Lahti says that it was a Finnish school for seven or eight years and then the negro school on south Main Street disbanded and moved into the building. *Submitted by Leo Reposh, Jr.*

AFRICAN METHODIST EPISCOPAL CHURCH

The African Methodist Episcopal Church of Clinton, was organized in 1876, by Rev. W.S. Langford, of Rockville, at the time, who was also pastor for a while. The class, led by George Harris, started out with only six members, with Mrs. Lida Brown as class-leader. Stewards, William Bowen, John Cooper, Elbert Brown, John Bowen and John Walker. Sunday-school, of about fifteen pupils generally, is superintended by James Bowen.

The pastor is Rev. W.R. Hutchison, now a resident of Lost Creek, Vigo County; this is his third year. The church building, 26 x 30 feet in dimensions, was erected in 1881, at a cost of $250, and is free from debt. It was located at 544 South Main Street.

CLINTON CITY SCHOOLS

The first school in Clinton Township was Davidson Hill School at what we now call Crompton Hill, but it was abandoned long before Crompton Hill School was built and students from that neighborhood had to go to Hazel Bluff School. Teachers at Davidson Hill School were H.W. Curry, Tom Kibby, and C.M. Leggett. (See a separate article on township schools.) In the city itself there was a military farmers school that started in 1860 and also has a separate article.

In 1871 a new school was built on Blackman Street between Third Street and Fourth Street and it was a grade school (1-8). In 1872, it was added to. This information comes from Frank L. Swinehart. In 1884, a high school was established in the same building. According to a former teacher, Glenn Morgan, at first Mr. Tomlin taught all high school classes. Later Mr. W.A. Kearns became his assistant. Classes offered were botany, geology, rhetoric, physical geography, algebra, geometry, and higher math. Latin was offered as an extra and was taught in the evening. High school was three years so the first graduating class was 1887. The first graduates were Alice (Bechman) Hoagland, Edward Cunningham, Blanch Hupp, R. Seymour Mathews, and Daisy (Robinson) Scott. High school was three years so the first graduating class was 1887. The first graduates were Alice (Bechman) Hoagland, Edward Cunningham, Blanch Hupp, R. Seymour Mathews, and Daisy (Robinson) Scott. High school was then lengthened to four years so there was no graduating class in 1888, but in 1889 and thereafter there was always a class. In 1892, the school was again enlarged. By 1899 there were three teachers in high school, H.E. Schell, Supt.; William F. Clarke, Principal; and Mr. Joseph Strain. In 1901, a new building was built on the corner of 3rd and Blackman to house a junior and senior high school. They were believed to be bums taking refuge from the cold. During Christmas vacation of 1903 it burned down. The remains of two persons were found in the ashes. It was replaced with a new one on the same spot that opened in late 1904. In the fall of 1907 the first high school athletic association was formed. Both boys and girls had basketball teams in 1908-1909. (See separate story on athletics.)

In 1907 Columbia School was built with four rooms, a brick building in the 400 block of North Eighth Street. It was where Columbia Park and the water tower are now located.

In 1906-07 high school enrollment was 66, in 1907-08 it was 99, and in 1908-09 it was 199.

In 1912, Mathews South School was built, and in 1913, Glendale School was built. Both were grade schools built on the same plan. In 1919 a new high school was built at 3rd and Mulberry, and in 1920 a new junior high was built at 4th and Mulberry.

In 1906, a catholic school was started on 6th and Nebeker and there is a separate article on that. There was a Finnish Lutheran School on North 8th Street which later became a negro school and there is a separate story on that. The Clinton Township Schools are covered separately and there were sixteen of them operating simultaneously. The township schools were under a different jurisdiction and an arrangement was made for the township to pay the city school system for the township students to attend Clinton High School.

From 1900 to about 1930 population grew and there was always a need for more school space, in fact a former church building on Blackman was used for extra classrooms, 1907-1917, but afterwards population began to decline and Columbia School which had been operating the first four grades closed down in 1930. The students were divided between Glendale and Central. In 1936, the original 1871 school was torn down. Central school was moved into the 3rd and Blackman building. A new gym was built at 4th and Blackman. It was for basketball games, physical education classes, and other activities and downstairs it had facilities for home economics and industrial arts. These had been housed in the 1905 building into which the grade school was moved.

In 1946, the junior and senior high schools traded buildings, but actually they shared many of the facilities both before and after.

In the fall of 1960, Central School moved into a new building on a square block bordered by 8th, 9th, Mulberry, and Blackman Streets. This vacated the 3rd and Blackman building which was again used for high school classes and also the school offices were moved into there from the former dwelling that was used in the middle of the 200 block of 4th.

During the 1960-61 school year the new South Vermillion School Corporation was formed thus abolishing the Clinton City Schools, the Clinton Township Schools, and the Helt Township Schools.

The Superintendents of Clinton City Schools were: James Tomlin 1886-1891; W.P. Hart 1891-1894; H.P. Leavenworth 1894-1899; H.S. Schell 1899-1902; William F. Clark 1902-1906; Charles C. Coleman 1906-1907; Orville C. Pratt 1907-1911; E.E. Oberholtzer 1911-1913; James Wilkinson 1913-1916; Donald DuShane 1916-1918; George McReynolds 1918-1931; L.E. Michael 1931-1934; Earl C. Boys 1934-1961. *Submitted by Leo Reposh Jr.*

FARMERS INSTITUTE AND WESTERN UNION SEMINARY

The seminary known as the Farmers' Institute was opened January 9, 1860. It was located on hills overlooking the Wabash River where Riverside Cemetery is now located. The students were housed in one huge three-story structure consisting of the central part and two wings extending on either side. The well-ventilated sleeping rooms had no heat. Two boys were assigned to one room. The entire school covered sixteen acres of ground. It accommodated 150 students, all boys.

The Institute kept horses, cattle, poultry, and bees. These animals provided some of the food supply and were used as part of the students training in animal-husbandry.

It was an industrial and disciplinary boarding school for male students with military and agricultural exercises. It was plain in character and farmer-like in its accommodations. The students' wardrobe consisted of a uniform, overcoat, overshoes, a pair of heavy boots, a pair of light slippers, four shirts, four pairs of socks, two light summer and one dark winter cravat, and an umbrella. They were allowed a washing of six pieces of clothing per week. The boys under fifteen years of age had to deposit spending money with the disciplinarian and could not spend it without his consent.

The cost per year was $150 for boarding students. A limited number of day students was accepted at $20 per annum. There were two courses of study; one for regular students who intended to graduate through the classics, and another for those who were irregularly entered. (**Circular of the Farmers' Home Institute** (Terre Haute: Daily and Weekly Wabash Express Power Press Print, 1860)

The institute was closed in 1861 due to the Civil War.

During the Civil War the Farmers Institute was used as a Union Army Training Center.

The town board got possession of the school and in 1866 it re-opened with two sections, high school and grammar (junior college). High school offered reading, intellectual and practical arithmetic, geography, penmanship, grammar, composition, and vocal music. The junior college offered orthography, reading, arithmetic, algebra, geometry, trigonometry, surveying, bookkeeping, chemistry, analysis, physiology and health, history, natural philosophy, rhetoric, botany, astronomy, and Latin. Tuition-$10 per term.

In 1871 under the professorship of John R. Whitcomb and Charles M. Taylor the school was opened to women and became known as Western Union Seminary. In 1876 the town took its support away and opened a school in the Old Sons of Temperance Hall. The seminary building was sold to Dr. Bogart and was divided and moved forming a number of dwellings and the central part was made into an opera house located at Main and Vine.

(Page 1 is lifted directly from History of Education in Clinton by Desree B. Brown while page two is a blend from Ms. Browns second page, and from Historic Scenes compiled by the Vermillion County Historical Society in 1974, and another article by Louise Falls.) *Submitted by Leo Reposh Jr.*

WASHINGTON SCHOOL

A negro school was located at 326 North 8th Street. This building formerly housed the Finlander Lutheran Church. It was a one-room school. Two of the teachers were Fern Jamison and a Mr. Tuttle (Tuggle). The children of James "Cherokee" Shelton and Kate Shelton of the 1200 block of White Street went there. A distinguished alumnus of the school was their son, James Henry "Buster" Shelton, who was a commercial artist and his services were greatly sought locally before he moved away to the city.

In 1928, when Ethel Reposh started to Columbia School, she passed this structure each day and the school was no longer in operation. At that time, Jesse Anderson and Walter Stewart, two neighborhood Negro children, attended Columbia School. *Submitted by Leo Reposh, Jr.*

CLINTON HIGH SCHOOL SMOKE STACK

The heating plant and the accompanying smoke stack has been a part of the Clinton school block, bounded by 3rd, 4th, Mulberry and Blackman for many years. During the 50's a sort of vandalism started in which members of each year's senior class would paint the year of their graduation on the smoke stack. The following year's class would paint it just above the previous. This was done at night and in secret. One class seemed to have difficulty going higher so instead they painted theirs at the bottom. My class in 1961 had some persons who wanted to put the number at the top so no one could go higher. Meanwhile another group painted our year above the previous, the normal. The other group was not satisfied and eventually did put our number at the top so it was on the stack in two places. Now, 1988, all those numbers are gone. The oldest that can be seen is 1962. In 1977 when the high school moved the custom stopped. *Submitted by Leo Reposh Jr.*

1926-27 - CLINTON SCHOOLS

Superintendent, George W. McReynolds; Secretary, Nema O. Carlin; Attendance Officer, Henry C. Drake; Supervisors, Essie Long, Paul Kelly, Marie Randolph, and Katherine Slimpert.

Senior High - Principal, L.E. Michael; Mary Balch, Esther Clayton, Phoebe Conley, Clyde Cunningham, Rosalie Deardorff, Mary Fordice, Thelma Hall, Helen W. Johnson, Marian Livingston, Margaret McWethy, M. Blossom Mainard, Thelma Medill, Glen Morgan, Fred Reeder, R.M. Strwalley, Blanche Warren, Edna West, Helen Wood, and Ruby Wright.

Junior High - Principal, Earl C. Boyd; Phoebe Brugh, Ruth Campbell, Ruth Delp, Melba Donaldson, Jewel Ferguson, Alvin Hayes, Kathleen Nurnberger, Paul Pruitt, Florence Salaroglio, Mildred Treagar, and Mayme Williams.

Central School - Principal, Margaret

Martin; Agnes McGinty, Ruby Martin, Mabel Acord, Marie Wood, Gertrude Ewing, Marie Goad, Fern Friskney, Ruth Hicks, Rosa M. Johnson, Thelma Roberts, Marian Davisson, Gladys Malone, and Bernice Templeton.

Columbia School - Principal, Verne Kutch; Mable Hicks, Alice O'Herron, and Eleanor Purks.

Washington School - Fern Jamison (grades 1-6).

South School - Principal; Helen Porter; Beulah Jones, Lena McCullough, Mabel Clearwaters, Irene Clemenz, Ruth Wood, Marietta Alverson, Elnora Switz, Louise Altenberger, and Jane Zell.

Glendale School - Principal, Cecile Wright; Belle James, Lois E. Morton, Olive Gauchat, Edna Rice, Hester Asdell, Inez Sroitz, Lucille Lewis, Susie Satterlee, and Miriam Bales.

Clinton High School Smoke Stack

CLINTON SPORTS

CHAMPIONSHIP FOOTBALL AT CLINTON HIGH SCHOOL

Football is said to have started at Clinton High School in the fall of 1915 with a football contributed by a lawyer. Interscholastic football started in the fall of 1916. It is also said that Clinton won three state football championships, but it isn't true, it was five. At that time the Indianapolis Times Trophy was the symbol of the state championship and Clinton won it five (5) times.

In 1920 with coach M.E. Morgan, Clinton was chosen by Heze Clark for a tie for the "state's most outstanding team". The team they tied with was Wabash. Two Clinton players were chosen for the all-state first team, Ralph Anderson and Herbert Keltz. Their season record was:

C.H.S. 6 - Linton 0
C.H.S. 8 - Garfield 14
C.H.S. 27 - Brazil 0
C.H.S. 35 - Bloomfield 0
C.H.S. 32 - Paris, Ill. 6
C.H.S. 26 - Sullivan 14
C.H.S. 7 - Robinson, Ill 14
C.H.S. 54 - Princeton 0

In the fall of 1924 in coach Paul "Spike" Kelly's first year as coach at Clinton they did it again. This time the tie was with Elkart for the championship. Incidentally, in the fall of 1923 Clinton played Rose Poly Tech to a 6-6 tie. The 1924 record was:

C.H.S. 28 - Oblong, Ill. 0
C.H.S. 13 - Garfield 0
C.H.S. 43 - Georgetown 7
C.H.S. 19 - Marshall 3
C.H.S. 13 - Robinson 25
C.H.S. 101 - Sullivan 0
C.H.S. 40 - Oakland, Ill. 0
C.H.S. 14 - Gerstmeyer 7
C.H.S. 13 - Brazil 0

Clinton gave Georgetown, Ill. and Brazil both their only defeat of the season. Andy Graham made all-state as right halfback. George Van Hoosier made all-state second team, John Wardrope and John Magnabosco made all-valley. Other players were Tony Ave, Dante Pesavento, Attilio Rigoni, Raymond Evans, Ralph Bates, Fred Faulds, Harold Kendall, Harold McKinny, Dan Bell, Darrell Overpeck, Joe Gatharum, James Wallace, and Orville Melbourne.

1928 was the biggest year yet, as Clinton won the state championship in addition to the Wabash Valley Championship, and championship of the Big 10 conference in their first year in that conference. It was made up of teams from all over the state. Coaches were Spike Kelly, Tiny Pierce, and Hal Stanton. The record was:

C.H.S. 19 - Elwood 6
C.H.S. 6 - Muncie 0
C.H.S. 28 - Georgetown 0
C.H.S. 22 - Bicknell 7
C.H.S. 13 - Evansville Central 7
C.H.S. 33 - Robinson, Ill. 0
C.H.S. 37 - Gerstmeyer 0
C.H.S. 40 - Garfield 0
C.H.S. 18 - Linton 0
C.H.S. 40 - Brazil 0

Players were John Stanisha, George Clayton, Marvel Calvert, Max Malone, Bill Wilson, Tony Sungalia, Robert Brown, Bruno Ave, Charles Sturgeon, John Trevarthan, Ettore Antonini, James Howard, Paul Coburn, Charles Bates, Frank Michalski, Earl Hayslett, Andrew Vorek, Charles Shannon, Pete Nedimovich, Reno Divan, Captain Roy Cogan, Russell Fife, and Clifford Marsh.

In 1931 there is said to have been a political upheaval in Clinton government and coach Spike Kelly among several others departed. John Magnabosco replaced him as head coach. In the fall of 1931, the Big 10 conference had been enlarged and became the Big 15 conference and Clinton tied with Marion for the championship of the Big 15 with an impressive 9 wins, one loss, and one tie.

In 1932 Clinton again won the Times Trophy for state championship. Their record was:

C.H.S. 25 - Jasonville 0
C.H.S. 13 - Sullivan 0
C.H.S. 25 - Wiley 0
C.H.S. 25 - Paris, Ill. 0
C.H.S. 19 - Bicknell 0
C.H.S. 6 - Evansville Central 8
C.H.S. 33 - Indianapolis Cathedral 0
C.H.S. 19 - Evansville Memorial 6

Chris Dal Sasso made the all-state first team for the second straight year.

Football

Joe Gili, George Bibich, William Thompson, Louis Antonini, Captain Chris Dal Sasso, Ward Watson, Arveno Antonini, Frank Harden, Oliver Hayck, Tony Campagnoli, Bruno Dal Sasso, Charles Colderbank, William Jones, Fred Vanzo, Coach John Magnabosco, Edward Purcell, John Jones, Charles Lewin, James Moudy, Sloucho Karanovich, Eugene Poletto, Clarence Abriani, Max Mitchell, John Goldner, Victor Valerine, Wayne Jenks, John Roe, Lynn Dallagiacomo, Donald Hays, Dale Miller, Assistant Coach M.E. Frump, Julius Skinder, Pete Scaggiari, Warren Weir, Charles Macnair, Marion Neidlinger, George O'Keefe, Maynard Malone, George Howard, Bernard Reynolds, Robert Goldner, Thomas McCrea, Samuel Frantz, Wayne Sims, Atiglio Campagnoli, Clyde Coburn, Assistant Coach Mark Williams, Student Manager Edward Auer, Herbert Jones, Louis Short, Verlin Ross, Allan Watters, Harold Faught, John Melbourne, Harold LaVanne, Americo Ave, James Justice, Lyle Marshall, Condido Mattioda, Pete Fossi, Truman Anderson, Chester Adams.

The 1933 season was exciting because four major teams finished the regular season undefeated. They were Clinton, East Chicago Washington, Whiting, and South Bend Central. Provision had been made before hand to play an additional game that year under such conditions. The extra game with E.C. Washington ended in a tie. The sports writers voted this time on who should be champion and announced on Dec. 20 they chose Clinton again. The season record was:

C.H.S. 39 - Sullivan 0
C.H.S. 38 - Wiley 0
C.H.S. 38 - Bloomington, Ill., Trinity 2
C.H.S. 44 - Jasonville 0
C.H.S. 43 - Evansville Central 6
C.H.S. 6 - Westville, Ill. 0
C.H.S. 19 - Indianapolis Cathedral 0
C.H.S. 30 - Bicknell 0
C.H.S. 18 - Evansville Memorial 2
C.H.S. 6 - East Chicago Washington 6

Semi-Pro Football

About 1933 when Clinton's outstanding high school football players were getting out of college or high school the Diana's semi-pro Clinton football team was organized. It had some success winning over half its games. The Diana's semi-pro basketball team was also formed. *Submitted by Leo Reposh Jr.*

FOOTBALL

Another article in this book indicates that the Clinton Wildcats' football teams shared two Indiana State Football Championships and then won three State Championships all to themselves in the seasons from 1920 to 1933 and in addition to that sometimes they won the Wabash Valley Championship the same season. The Wabash Valley included a large area of Illinois. The boundary was approximately midway between Clinton and Saint Louis, so they were champs of a large area. However, Clinton's phenomenal success at football was not restricted to that time period.

In the fall of 1951 the Clinton Wildcat Football team—Mike Dick, Jim Hutson, Joe Massa, John Enrietto, Fred Bates, John McLeish, Pat Bennett, Chuck Eaton, Philip Gutish, Chuck Schelsky, Gene Dick, Eddie Bumgardner, Lloyd Rivera, Ted Lobbia, and Warren Foster—coached by Thorval Mattax assisted by Mr. Burch, Mr. Hall, and Mr. Burton, compiled a record of nine wins and one loss. According to a Clintonian report at the end of the season they were the top scoring team in the state with 383 points for the season. According to the records given in the 1952 year book the scores don't quite add up to 383 points, but I do believe that they were the top scoring team in the state that year. The record was: Linton 13, Clinton 6, which was their only loss; Clinton 38, Dugger 6; Clinton 47, Gerstmeyer 7; Clinton 67, Westville 6; Clinton 14, Garfield 7; Clinton 40, Bicknell 0; Clinton 52, Sullivan 0; Clinton 33, Wiley 6; Clinton 31, Danville, Ill. 13; Clinton 26, Brazil 0. Linton, the only team to beat Clinton went through undefeated and won the Western Indiana Conference Championship.

The following year the Clinton Wildcats won the Western Indiana Conference with an over-all record of 7 wins, 1 loss and 2 ties, and a conference record of 6 wins and 1 tie.

In the fall of 1973 the Wildcats had a high scoring football team who won 7 games while losing 3. Two of their losses were to Terre Haute South and to Greencastle who both finished their seasons undefeated. Clinton scored 74 points against North Vermillion, 73 against North Central and 61 against Linton.

The following year the Wildcats went through their season of 1974 undefeated and won the Western Indiana Conference. Their record was: Clinton 13, Brazil 0; Clinton 33, Schulte 0; Clinton 25, Owen Valley 14; Clinton 20, West Vigo 7; Clinton 48, North Vermillion 0; Clinton 47, Sullivan 8; Clinton 25, South Vigo 0; Clinton 35, Greencastle 34; Clinton 42, North Central 6; Clinton 27, Lebanon 6. Brazil who was Clinton's first opponent then won all the rest of the games (9) on their schedule defeating their eight common op-

ponents by nearly identical scores to those of Clinton.

The local school won two more Western Indiana Conference Championships before the conference was disbanded. *Submitted by Leo Reposh Jr.*

BASKETBALL AT CLINTON HIGH SCHOOL

In the fall of 1907 the first high school athletic association was formed. Both boys and girls had basketball teams in the 1908-1909 season. Girls basketball players uniforms consisted of long dresses. Girls basketball was dropped and didn't restart until recently at South Vermillion. The early teams would play church teams, teams sponsored by businesses, college teams, any opponents they could get. The first games were played in a field in 1908. The first indoor games were played in a theatre at 9th and Vine. Later they were held in Wabash Garage on Blackman between Main and Water. This was later Osmon's Furniture warehouse. The games were held at Dice Garage from 1914 to 1920 when a citizen group headed by Guy H. Briggs built the Coliseum in the 700 block of Main Street, and games were held there until 1936 when the gym at 4th and Blackman was built.

Clinton had many good basketball teams, but one standout was the 1921 team that won the Wabash Valley Tournament in Terre Haute. The coaches were M.E. Morgan assisted by Principal Charles Zimmerman. The players were: Ralph Anderson forward; George McNair, forward; Harold Mills, center; Van Reeder,?; Owen Curtis, guard; Paul Kutch, guard; William Cooper, guard; and Dain Miller, forward. Their record was:

C.H.S. 46 - Farmersburg 5
C.H.S. 40 - Stauntan 7
C.H.S. 25 - Bloomingdale 18
C.H.S. 18 - Glenn 5
C.H.S. 20 - Normal 15
C.H.S. 14 - Garfield 16
C.H.S. 18 - Sullivan 16
C.H.S. 47 - Perrysville 18
C.H.S. 13 - Brazil 19
C.H.S. 25 - Rose Poly Freshmen 20
    Wabash Valley Tournament
C.H.S. 25 - Bloomingdale 10
C.H.S. 20 - Cayuga 17
C.H.S. 17 - Sullivan 13
C.H.S. 30 - Freelandville 27
C.H.S. 20 - Garfield 37
C.H.S. 15 - Brazil 14
C.H.S. 30 - Sullivan 22
C.H.S. 20 - Normal 43

The official forgot or neglected to file the necessary papers and therefore they were not permitted to participate in the state (district) tournament.

In the early days of the state tournament many, probably more than half, of the schools did not participate so our district tournament had schools in it from over a wide area and the winner went on to the finals. Gradually more teams joined until our district was made up only of Parke and

Vermillion County teams, and the name was changed to sectionals.

In 1930 the Wildcats were runners up in the now much larger Wabash Valley tournament with coaches Spike Kelly and Tiny Pierce. They also won the sectional. Players were: Bruno Ave, F; Robert Brown, G; Ettore Antonini, C; Tony Sungalia, G; Tony Gatherum, Captain; William Minett, G; John Ousky, F; Ralph Harris, G; Guy Wardope, C; and Charles Burton, F.

Among other successful seasons were 1943, 1947, and 1950 when the teams won the sectionals and regionals and participated in the state semi-finals. *Submitted by Leo Reposh Jr.*

1947 BASKETBALL TEAM

Clinton's 1947 Boy's High School Basketball team may have been the best team they ever had. They were Coach Robert Burton, Wayland Archer, Richard Glover, Johnny Goodman, Bill Povlin, Eugene James Ferrare, Bob Delp, Claude James, Johnny Murphy, Waite Archer, and Bob Dagley.

Waite and Wayland Archer were twins. One was a forward and did a lot of scoring while the other was a guard who did a lot of ball handling. These were the first of Indiana's famous basketball twins, the others were Arley and Harley Andrews of Terre Haute Gerstmeyer, and the Van Arsdale twins of Indianapolis Manual.

Clinton's 1947 percentage of games won was slightly short of the record of 1968, but this was due to the luck of the draw in the tournaments. The 1947 team won twelve out of 16 regular games losing to Linton, Gerstmeyer, and twice to Garfield. They won the Vermillion County Preliminary of the Wabash Valley Tournament, but in the first game of the 16 team Wabash Valley Finals they again ran into Garfield's brick wall. Garfield accounted for three of Clinton's defeats.

In the state tournament Clinton won the sectional by beating Newport, Dana, Rosedale, and Tangier, and then won the Clinton regional by defeating Covington and Crawfordsville. Next they went to the semi-state at Butler Fieldhouse, Indianapolis, where they played Shelbyville and lost.

Shelbyville continued to win and made it to the final game where they met Clinton's old nemesis, Garfield. Shelbyville's star player was Bill Garrett who went on to be Indiana University's first black basketball player, Garfield's star player was Clyde Lovellette, who went on to star on Kansas's NCAA Championship team, play pro basketball and be Sheriff of Vigo County. Shelbyville own the game and the Championship of Indiana giving Garfield its only defeat of the season. Clinton could undoubtedly have gone farther in the tournaments if they hadn't run into these two teams so early. *Submitted by Leo Reposh Jr.*

VERMILLION COUNTY BASKETBALL TOURNAMENT

For many years the Vermillion County

high schools participated in the Wabash Valley Basketball Tournament. The first stage of which was the preliminaries producing sixteen winners who then went on to the finals in Terre Haute. Later the finals were divided and there were four quarter finals of four teams in each with the four winners going to the four team finals. The Vermillion County schools were accommodated by being allowed to have the seven county schools in our own separate preliminary at a time when most preliminaries had ten teams. This enabled us to give our preliminary an additional designation, "Vermillion County Tournament". The Clinton Wildcats, for the obvious reason that they had by far the biggest enrollment of all the schools, won about eight out of ten of these county tournaments even in years when some of the other county teams were able to beat them at other times of the season.

An exception to Clinton's domination of the county tournament came in the 1951-52 season. Clinton won their first three games of that season and then were hit with a 44-34 defeat by Dana. At Vermillion County Tournament time Dana came in as the favorite to win it, but Hillsdale's Hilltoppers eliminated the Clinton Wildcats 52-51 in the second round and then went on to beat the Dana Aggies in the final game to take home the county trophy. Hillsdale was eliminated from the finals by Brazil. Dana was runner-up in the sectional also, to Rosedale, even though they were expected to win it all.

The following season Dana again defeated Clinton in the early season, and in the county tourney, Clinton and Dana were paired in the first game. This time Clinton scraped through 49-48, and went on to beat Newport and Saint Bernice for the trophy and then beat Brazil and Sullivan to make the final four where they lost to Wiley.

In the last county tournament held, in the final game the Cayuga Indians beat the Wildcats, 67-40. Final game, final revenge. *Submitted by Leo Reposh Jr.*

TENNIS

The 1987 South Vermillion Girls Tennis Team was dubbed by Leo Reposh, Jr. as the "South Vermillion International Tennis Team", because in addition to the local girls the team included Francesca Jessica Emanuel of Torino, Italy; Carla Sivatte of Barcelona, Spain; Adriana Guzman of Colombia; Pia Bergman of Finland; and Ana Cabillo of Spain. *Submitted by Leo Reposh Jr.*

LOCAL SPORTS TRIVIA

During the late 1970s Clinton had a young man, David Peperak, who had first driven sprint cars in another organization and then switched to the United States Auto Club Sprint Division. In the Tony Hulman Classic of 1983 he set a new speed record on the Terre Action (dirt) Track. The old record had been set nearly twenty years earlier by three time Indianapolis 500 winner, Johnny Rutherford.

In another type of auto racing, David Thomas of Klondyke set a number of world speed records in this class at Indiana's Bunker Hill Drag strip near Kokomo, Indiana, in the early 1980s.

In 1975 Clinton High School had the largest high school football player in the state of Indiana, Robert Young, weighing 350 pounds, and at the same time had the state of Indiana's tallest high school basketball player, Mark Wasson, who was only slightly less than seven feet tall. Wasson graduated in 1976. *Submitted by Leo Reposh Jr.*

An all-girls band in Clinton. Katherine Lowery is in the center. Jeannette Rowley and Ilia Mae Rowley are the two girls on the right.

CLINTON ORGANIZATIONS - 1988

American Legion Auxiliary
American Legion Post 140
Business and Professional Women
Business and Professional Women
    Past Presidents
Christian Women's Fellowship
Clinton Adult Tutoring Service
Clinton Boat Club
Clinton Chamber of Commerce
Clinton Golf Association
Clinton Jaycees
Clinton Lionesses
Clinton Lions Club
Clinton Optimists Club
Clinton Photography Club
Clinton Volunteer Fire Department
Dreamland Pleasure Club
Eagles Auxiliary
Eastern Star
Fairview Park Home Economics Club
First United Methodist Women's
    Organization
Fraternal Order of Eagles
Grandmothers Club
Half Century Auxiliary

HalfCentury Club
Hospital Guild
Independent Order of Odd Fellows
Italian Singers
Jerusalem Lodge 99 F & AM
Jobs Daughters
Kappa Delta Phi Sorority
Missionary Circles First Baptist
    Church
Moose Lodge
Optimists Club
Phi Beta Psi Sorority
Pocahontas Club
Rotary Club
Sacred Heart Men's Club
Senior Citizens Center
Sigma Delta Pi
Tri Kappa Sorority
United Presbyterian Women
Veterans of Foreign War
Veterans of Foreign War Auxiliary
Wakofe Club
Wayside United Methodist Women's
    Organization
Women of the Moose

Columbian Rebekah Lodge 425-Covered wagon days held in old I.O.O.F. Hall. Row 1: Jeanne Bain, Clara Mindeman, Gertrude Reed, Sue Beard, Martha Wright, Lillian Stout, Lola Campbell, Marcella Vicars, Nora Miller, Vera McWethy, Clara Draper, Jessie Fox, Mabel Ray, Florence K. Miller, Carrie Osman. Row 2: Pauline Cornwell, Lucille Jones, Mary Nell Allen, Pearl Ernhart, unknown, Minnie Myers, Alice Foncannon, Nellie McCown, Minnie Price, Pearlie Jones.

Royal Neighbors Float-1st place Columbus Day Parade-1964 Kay Lubovich, Paulette Cappa, Joyce Karanovich, Mary E. Massa and Waunita Barratto.

A.O.U.W.

The A.O.U.W. organized here eight or ten years ago; soon had thirty or forty members, but in about a year they practically disbanded. Perry Jones, superintendent of a coal mine in the vicinity at the time, was master workman of the lodge. He moved away some years ago. Probably he constituted the soul of the lodge, and when he went away the body died.

Taken from 1888 Vermillion County History

REBEKAH LODGE

Vermillion Lodge, No. 182, Degree of Rebekah, was organized July 9, 1877. It has at present about forty active members. The officers are—Mrs. Anna Davis, Noble Grand; Miss Ella Bishop, Vice-Grand; Mrs. Katie McWethy, Treasurer; Lillie Birt, Recording Secretary; Miss Lulu Allen, Permanent Secretary.

Taken from 1888 Vermillion County History

CLINTON ENCAMPMENT

Clinton Encampment, No. 143, was chartered May 16, 1876. Present officers—W.H. Hill, Chief Priest; W.H. Cale, Senior Warden; Harry Swinehart, Junior Warden; J.M. Blagg, High Priest; W.F. Wells, Permanent Secretary; Ed. H. Johnston, Scribe; J.H. Black, Treasurer.

Taken from 1888 Vermillion County History

AMANT LODGE, I.O.O.F.

Amant Lodge, No. 356, I.O.O.F., was instituted November 16, 1870, with about twelve members, who have increased to about seventy-five. The present officers are—A.V. McWethy, Noble Grand; J.H. Black, Vice Grand; Frank Swinehart, Recording Secretary; W.H. Hill, Permanent Secretary; John H. Birt, Treasurer. The past grands number twenty-three. The lodge has an unusually nice room for their meetings.

Taken from 1888 Vermillion County History

JERUSALEM LODGE, F. & A.M.

Jerusalem Lodge, No. 99, F. & A. M., received its charter May 29, 1850, and has ever since then been kept alive. The charter members were—Sylvester Redfield, Worshipful Master, who afterward moved to Nebraska, John N. Perkins, Hiram Barnes, John R. Whitcomb, Benjamin R. Whitcomb, William S. Price, James Gazsoway, James McCulloch, Nathan Sidwell, J.J. Moore and William Barrick. The present membership is fifty-six, with these officers: James Robert, Worshipful Master; Robert B. Bailey, Senior Warden; Jasper Frisk, Junior Warden; N.C. Anderson, Treasurer; D.A. Ranger, Secretary; H.B. Dudley, Senior Deacon; John Horney, Junior Deacon; and William Hughes, Tyler.

Taken from 1888 Vermillion County History

P.R. OWEN POST, G.A.R.

P.R. Owen Post, No. 329, G.A.R., was instituted April 15, 1884. (See a preceding page for a sketch of Dr. Owen). The Post was organized by Captain R.B. Sears, of Newport, mustering officer, with about twenty-five or thirty members. They now number fifty-four, and are in prosperous condition. Officers—L.H. Beckman, Post Commander; Cornelius Quick, Senior Vice Commander; T.B. Wells, Junior Vice Commander; S. Weatherwax, Adjutant; J.H. Wilson, Quartermaster; William Kelp, Chaplain; D.A. Ranger, Quartermaster Sergeant; Enoch Whitted, Sergeant.

Taken from 1888 Vermillion County History

SOVEREIGNS OF INDUSTRY

Council No. 3, Sovereigns of Industry, was organized May 5, 1874, with twenty-five members. James A. Greenwalt was elected President; David McBeth, Vice-President; J.C. Campbell, Secretary; T. Victor, Treasurer; S.B. Blackledge, Lecturer; J.C. Hall, Steward; D. Moore, Inside Guard.

Taken from 1888 Vermillion County History

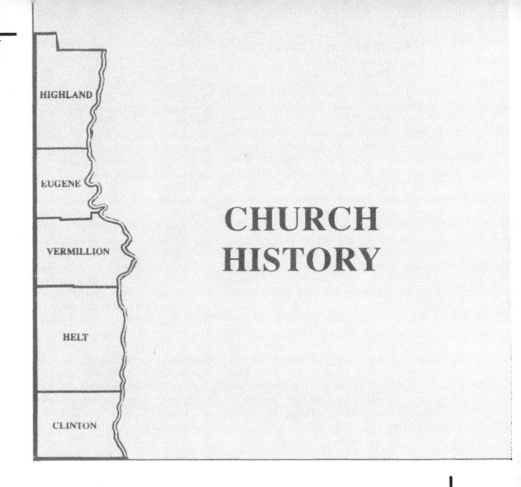

CHURCH HISTORY

St. Joseph Catholic
Church-Universal

127

BETHLEHEM UNITED METHODIST CHURCH

The Bethlehem Church of the United Brethren in Christ was organized in 1858 in the old Wright School House in Clinton Township, Vermillion County, Indiana. The school house stood just south of what later was the engine room of the Bunsen Mine. Reverend John Burtner, pastor of the New Goshen circuit was the first preacher in charge of the fledging church.

Charter members were: Noah Hedges and wife, Columbus Hedges and wife, Marion Wright and wife, Sarah Shew Hedges, John A. Hay, Mary A. Hay, Abraham Foltz and wife, Mary Probst Foltz, William Hedges, Maria Shew, Pamelia Shew Tennis, Geneva Shew, Riley Shew, Matilda Shew Ellis, James F. Wright, Levi Wright, Mary Lenhart, Louis Rhyan and Sylvanus Rhyan. They worshipped in the school house until the summer of 1868, when a new frame church was built on the corner of the Range line Road on one half acre of land donated by Henry and Irene Shew. On February 25, 1869 the land was deeded to trustees; William Hedges, Henry Ryan and John A. Hay and those following, with the stipulation that the land was to be used for a church only and if at any time it ceased to be used for a church, it would revert back to the Shew family heirs. Reverend A.J. Newgent of the New Goshen circuit was pastor. William Hedges, Noah Hedges, Columbus Hedges, Henry Rhyan and Sylvanus Rhyan made up the Board of Trustees. The Church was dedicated on August 8, 1869 by Reverend Samuel Mills. The estimated cost of the frame church was $1,000.00.

About 1913, the U.S. Steel Company sank the Bunsen mines and the town of Universal was born. By 1915 the population had increased in the community and plans for a larger church were started.

The Bethlehem Church and Sunday school possesses a somewhat cosmopolitan membership, having on the church, or Sunday school rolls, people of English, Scotch, Irish, German, Belgian, French, Italian, Swedish, and Hungarian descent, all of whom assimilate most agreeable, and give evidence of an excellent spirit of cooperation and good fellowship.

In 1919, with Reverend C.K. Saylor as pastor, the frame church was moved over to the south side of the church lawn and construction on a brick church was begun in its place. Services continued there until the new church was completed in 1921, under the pastorate of Reverend H.A. Barton. The Board of Trustees were: Warren Wright, Gurney P. Foltz and Ray C. Foltz. The estimated cost of the brick church was $16,000.00. Dedication services were held on February 26, 1921 with the conference superintendent, Reverend J.C. Shannon, presiding.

In April 1935 the Leaders Class was organized and in 1988 celebrates fifty three (53) years together. Charter members were: Rachel Bozarth, Rovine Eaton, Donald Foltz, Thelma Foltz, Leone Hughes, Margaret Martin, Gladys Oard, Bessie Phillips, Melvin Searing, Doris Spurr, Helen Spurr, Meda Wright and Mary Johnson, teacher.

In 1946 the United Brethren in Christ united with the Evangelical Church and was then known as the Bethlehem Evangelical United Brethren Church.

In 1968 the Bethlehem Evangelical United Brethren Church united with the Methodist Church and is the remaining Evangelical United Brethren Church known now as the Bethlehem United Methodist Church, and is located one-half mile west of the town of Universal.

Newport United Methodist Church

When Indiana was still a portion of the Northwest Territory, the site that became the town of Newport was occupied by early settlers and Indians. They had chosen this area because of its abundant springs and its elevation above the nearby Little Vermillion River, and the Wabash River, just a few miles to the east. Also, the site was on the River Road that connected Fort Sackville (Vincennes), Fort Harrison (Terre Haute), and Fort Ouitanon (Lafayette).

Early itinerant preachers or ministers brought the gospel to these early settlers, and for a time Newport was served by the Vincennes Methodist Church, established in the 1700s. These circuit Riders were dedicated, strong and intrepid. Between 1810 and 1832 the following Methodist circuits included the Newport area:- Vincennes, Ft. Harrison, Honey Creek, Vermillion, Eugene, and Pine Tree.

The meetings were held in various homes until the first church building in the town of Newport was built in 1838, on the east side of South Poplar Street, Lot 40. This lot was deeded to the Methodist Congregation by Stephen S. Collett. Trustees were Nathaniel Jones, Robert Nixon, Adam Zener, William Blair, Silas Winchel, Squire Howell, and Thomas Lyon. About the same time, Lot 63 was purchased from Sam Tate to be a parsonage site; this was on south Main Street. Trustees in addition to those already named were:- Charles Gordon, James Naylor, and James Harper.

In 1853 the congregation felt the need for a new church building and Lot 38 was purchased, corner of Market and Poplar Sts. Joseph Hicks was hired to build it, taking as part payment the older building on Lot 40. Trustees in this year were:- James Hopkins, Simeon Chipps, Samuel Davis, Ure Aston, and M.P. Lowry. Mr. Hicks moved the old building to Lot 48, on the west side of the town square (across the street south from the present postoffice). Having served there as a blacksmith shop for many years, it later was used as the L.J. Place Hardware Store, and a third story was added. Still later it was remodeled and modernized - third story removed - into a printing shop, housing the Newport newspaper, The Hoosier State, Donald L. Collings, Editor; the second story was used for apartments. After 150 years the building still stands.

The new church on Lot 28 was finished in 1853, a beautiful frame building that served this Methodist congregation for many years. In community emergencies this building also served as a Court Room - the Court House was being rebuilt after a fire - and as a schoolhouse - after the Seminary on the hill burned, in 1886. The church added an 18 foot extension in 1879. In 1882 a parsonage was built on East Market Street, north side - that house still stands, first house east of the Lions Community Park.

In 1893 the present brick building was erected on Lot 90, northwest corner Market and George Sts. Trustees at that time were:- John W. Parrett, R.H. Nixon, Elias Pritchard, Abel Sexton, Hiram Cady, and H.H. Conley. The cost of this new church building was reported as $5,225. (The Hoosier State, Newport's newspaper, a weekly reported that the trustees were $100 short of the full amount needed, in order to have it entirely paid by the dedication date, so John W. Parrett added another hundred, making his total contribution $1200. The Rev. Mr. Parrett was over 90 years old at this time, he had been assigned to the Newport Church in 1850, and had married a Newport girl, Lydia Zener; in later years they retired to Newport. In 1887 John W. Parrett was credited with saving the Methodist-associated De Pauw University, by contributing the $1700 needed to raise $5,000 thereby insuring a bequest of Washington DePauw to the Greencastle campus.)

The old frame church building on Lot 28 became the Newport Opera House, and in 1925 it was converted into a residence which still stands.

A nearby country Methodist church, Memorial Chapel, had to be abandoned when, early in World War 2, the federal government took huge acreage of Vermillion Township for the location of Wabash River Ordnance Works. Several members of that congregation who remained in Newport area did attend Newport Methodist - Conference had urged the Memorial Chapel memberships be moved to Newport - but most of these farm families did re-locate further away, in order to find farm land. Lectern and chairs from Memorial Chapel were included in the worship center, and later an extensive enlargement project added a dining room and kitchen, utilizing building materials from the torn-down Memorial Chapel. Later, a roomy half-bath was built into existing space, and still later, to meet

government specifications for public meeting places to be accessible to handicapped persons, a ramp with handrail was constructed. These facilities have been used for the local site of the national nutrition program for senior citizens. Also, various youth groups, including Scout troops, hold meetings there. A great effort is always made to help in all commendable community projects.

Although usually referred to as "the Methodists" this church, as part of the Indiana Conference, was officially The Methodist Episcopal Church until May 10, 1939, when the correct name became The Methodist Church. In 1968 this denomination and the Evangelical United Brethren Church united to become the present The United Methodist Church. The Newport congregation is now served by the Rev. Mr. Jon Overbey, Clinton R.R., and is part of the Terre Haute District, Dr. Richard Armstrong, Superintendent, and of the South Indiana Conference. Local governing body is the Administrative Board. Present trustees include Kenneth Collins, Maynard Hollingsworth, Arthur Allan, Keith Youmans, Thomas Clarey, and Donald Moody, Jr.

Administrative Council and office holders include, alphabetically, Arthur Allan, Mary Allan, Beverly Arrasmith, Martha Clarey, Thomas Clarey, Jeanne Collins, Kenneth Collins, Margaret Duzan, Lorraine Greene, James Haverkamp, Mary Jo Hegarty, Ada J. Hollingsworth, Maynard Hollingsworth, Vicki Howard, Jane Lewis, Evelyn McMasters, Donald Moody, Jr., Ruth Moody, David Norman, Dorothy Rusk, Bill Rusk, Judith Stein, Michele Stein, Clair Van Sant, Freda Van Sant, Thelma Wickens, Keith Youmans, and Virginia Youmans. Youth members assisting as acolytes and ushers are:- Kevin Collins, Kirby Collins, Scott Moody and Sheri Moody.

THE SALEM UNITED METHODIST CHURCH

Five years after Indiana became a State, Vermillion County effected the first Methodist denomination. Helt Township (so named after the John Helt family) is the second from the Southern line of Vermillion County, and extends from the Wabash River West to the State line of Indiana and Illinois. It contains seventy-two square miles. Originally one-fourth of its area was prairie and three-fourths timberland. Most of the prairie land is a rich black soil while the remainder of the county is rich bottom land of the first and second variety. Especially the lower bottom lands are rich, much of it being subject to inundations, which leaves a sediment equal to the soil found in the celebrated valley of the Nile in Egypt.

It was here on Helt's Prairie that the church known as The Salem Methodist Episcopal Church, one mile North of Sumit Grove, was formed where preaching after this faith was had by Reverend Chamerlain in 1821-1822. The next preacher was Reverend Dr. William B. James, a Virginian, who lived at Mansfield, Ohio, Butler County, (where he started the First Method-

ist Church that still stands today) came to this County in October 1822, when he preached in the log barn of John Helt and later in a small log cabin school house with split-pole seats. He also practiced medicine. The records of the clerk's office in Romney, West Virginia, show that permission was given January 1797, to William B. James to perform the marriage ceremony according to the form of the Methodist Episcopal Church. (Jesse James is a direct descendant from this Reverend Dr. William B. James.) He preached and practiced medicine until 1826, when he started for New Orleans with a boat load of corn, and died en route.

Thanks to Reverend James, the "Helt's Prairie Class" had started the first Church in Vermillion County. One of the principal members was Phebe Ryerson. At the age of 12, she had never heard one pray. She attended the Helt's Prairie Class Meeting, and when the expected preacher did not arrive, the class leader sang and prayed, which was the means of her conviction and conversion and she remained a zealous member of the church all her life. A short time before her death, the autumn of 1874, age 79, she willed one thousand, five hundred dollars to the missionary society, five hundred dollars to Asbury (now

DePauw University), two hundred dollars to the Biblical Institute at Evanston, Illinois, two hundred dollars to the educational fund of the County, besides other sums to various individuals.

November 20, 1845, James Harper, Sr., and wife Elizabeth, donated the land for the erection of a frame house. This was completed in 1846, and dedicated to the Lord. The name Salem, taken from the Bible, (Genesis 14:18, and Psalm 76:2) stands for PEACE. Psalm 76:2 is the Jewish interpretation that Salem is JeruSALEM!

In 1878, this frame building was sold and the brick structure erected by the congregation on the old foundation. The architecture is Early Gothic and Romanesque Revival. The brick structure was completed the same year, and the funeral for the first and only execution in Vermillion County was held at Salem Church.

The Women's Missionary Society was organized in November 6, 1881 with 20 members. Today it still continues, and is known as The Salem United Women.

In 1978, one hundred years later, an educational unit was added.

The Church was placed on The National Register of Historic Places, February 22, 1977!

THE UNITED PRESBYTERIAN CHURCH OF CLINTON, INDIANA

Perhaps the uniqueness of the present United Presbyterian Church, 3rd & Mulberry Streets, Clinton is that two completely separate churches, each with its own proud heritage and distinctiveness, became one church as the result of the merger in 1962 of the First Presbyterian Church and the Hillcrest Presbyterian Church, 5050 North 8th Street.

On September 20, 1834, the first Presbyterian church in Vermillion County was organized in Clinton, and appropriately named the First Presbyterian Church of Clinton. It is one of the oldest in this part of Indiana. The first minister was the Rev. John Gerrish who conducted services in the old Union Meeting House. A church building which was erected in 1846 was occupied until 1895 when it was sold to the school board. While a new sanctuary was being built, services were held in the Opera House. It was during this period, in the year 1891, that the church supported a Women's Home and Foreign Missionary Society for the purpose of study and financial support of missions, as well as for joining together in Christian fellowship.

On August 9, 1896, the present church building was dedicated. One of the lovely stained-glass windows which enhances the beauty of the sanctuary was a gift to the church from Mrs. Martha Ann Whitcomb Matthews, wife of the Indiana governor, Claude Matthews, in memoriam of him and their son, Seymour. In 1902 the lot north of the church was sold and the proceeds used to finance the building of the manse. During the years 1914-1915, the north wing was added and the present pipe organ installed. An Inaugural Organ Recital was given by Mrs. Dena Hutchinson in dedication of the organ. Mrs. Hutchinson served as organist from 1915 to 1962. Mrs. Ruby Carmichael of the Hillcrest Presbyterian Church succeeded her, playing until she retired in 1984.

In 1910, Mr. J.W. Robb, a church Elder believed the church should serve the needs of the many new citizens coming to Clinton from across the seas to work in the mines. He presented a plan for an "Italian Mission" to the Crawfordsville Presbytery which gained their support and Hillcrest was begun.

In the early 20's another women's organization named the Furnishing Society of the Presbyterian Church came into existence, and as the name implied, a variety of needs were furnished - items ranging from contributions toward the minister's salary to the purchasing of a pump for the manse cistern. In 1947, this organization disbanded and became the Presbyterian Women's Organization, later becoming the United Presbyterian Women's Organization when the two churches merged in 1962.

In 1944 Rev. Roy C. Linberg came to Clinton to serve as pastor to both the Hillcrest Community Center and the First Presbyterian Church. In 1957 Hillcrest became a Church with its own officers and Rev. Linberg was no longer the pastor of the First Church, only Hillcrest.

In 1962, after many joint meetings of the Sessions of both First and Hillcrest Churches, the two were united to become the United Presbyterian Church of Clinton meeting in the building of the former First church. The Session of the new united church included Elders Ray Medlock, James Ferguson, Noland Wright, John Fenoglio, Tom Craig, Paul Holbert, Ed Shannon, Agnes Renwick, John Kyle, Dorothy Brown, Louis Causey, and Martha Gray. The Deacons included Alice Nardi, Wayne Moore, John Strain, Mabel Pugh, Ronald Wright, Walt Laney, Don Gardener, Carl Hanks, Edith Vignocchi, Earl Turner, Frank Foncannon and Claude Vietti.

It was a new church with two long and proud traditions, and its congregation continued to provide good fellowship and dignified worship of God in its belief that still "We Are Laborers Together With God". The Church celebrated its 150th Anniversary all year long in 1984.

Wayside United Methodist Church

When the Center-Fairview-Salem Methodist Churches met for a joint fourth-quarterly conference on February 11, 1966, they were all in deep trouble. Because of low income, small memberships and general inactivity, they were told it might be difficult, if not impossible, to get a pastor to accept leadership in three small, poor rural churches.

A group of lay people known as the Unified Christian Fellowship worked hard in exploring the needs of all of the churches of the community with the assistance of a young, eager minister, Rev. David Bonner, who had been assigned to the Center-Fairview-Salem charge.

The national merging of the Methodist Church and the Evangelical United Brethern Church was imminent, and had a big bearing on the local situation. The parishes were being re-aligned: Dana-Bono remained the same, together; Clinton First remained the same, alone; Center was closed; Centenary was closed; Fairview was closed; Salem remained; Jonestown EUB was closed; and Bethlehem at Universal remained. The UCF, as such, no longer existed, but many of the persons who had been involved with it were now busily working to help bring

about the formation of a new congregation out of the membership of the dissolved churches. Out of the membership of the Center, Fairview, Centenary, Jonestown, and any who cared to join from the Bethlehem or Salem group, was born the membership of the new Wayside United Methodist Church. After a complete canvassing of the membership of Center, Centenary, Fairview, Salem, and Jonestown, a chartering service was held for the new Wayside United Methodist Church in the Fairview building on May 5, 1968, for a new membership of 240. Wayside was one of the first three churches chartered as a "United" Methodist Church.

A contest was held to choose a name for the new church and the name "Wayside" which was submitted by Marie Myers was chosen.

Now there was a new church, it had a name, but there was still no place for this body to call home, except to continue to meet in the Fairview building, which was much less than adequate. A committee was elected, not appointed, for the purpose of locating and purchasing a suitable site for the building of a new parsonage and eventually a church building. The committee located and purchased some eight acres on Highway 63, and plans advanced for the construction of the parsonage.

The church family changed, and under the gentle but determined leadership of Rev. Charles Flory, the parsonage was built, with completion in September, 1970. The church building was started soon after, and was completed and consecrated on November 19, 1972. The newest portion of the Centenary building was moved to the Wayside acreage, and set up to be used for an educational unit. In 1982 and 1983, this building was enlarged, remodeled, refurbished to furnish more needed class space and storage space for yard-care tools.

In May, 1983, just prior to annual conference, Wayside United Methodist Church voted to become a single point charge.

In 1984, a mobile classroom was provided by the South Indiana Conference on a loan basis. It is still being used by two adult Sunday School classes.

Since the chartering, there have been six pastors serve at Wayside; David Bonner, Charles Flory, Howard Allen, C.E. (Gene) Gilbreath, Hollis Huber, and presently, Patrick Walden. We have had the pleasure of having two interns serve here, Priscilla Pope and Sam Chizmar.

On the Wayside United Methodist Church letterhead you will find this slogan, "Let Me Stand By The Side Of The Road And Be A Friend To Man". *Submitted in part from a history by Esther L. Foltz*

HOPEWELL FRIENDS CHURCH

About one mile up the hill from Quaker Point is the Hopewell Friends Church. On the western edge of Vermillion Township the early settlers were mostly members of the Society of Friends, or Quakers. Most of these people came originally from the Carolinas or Virginia or other slave holding states. Their abhorrence of slavery was one of the main factors in causing them to leave their home state. Richard Haworth and his family came in 1822 from Clinton Co., OH. Richard's wife Susannah was a sister to William Henderson the father of John Henderson. Jonathan Haworth, a cousin of Richard, also came from Ohio at the same time. Richard Henderson and his son Isaac brought their families two years later. Other settlers were named Brown, Canaday, Gibson, Folger, Branson, Pugh, Walthall and Howard.

In the early 1820s meetings were held in the log house of John Haworth just a few rods northwest of the present Hopewell Friends Meeting. Their meetings in the summer time were held on alternate Sundays at Vermilion Grove, Illinois at the home of another John Haworth who was known as "Yankee John" to distinguish the two men. The first church was built of hewn logs with only one door and three windows. This building also served as a schoolhouse at a time when there was no public provision for schools. In 1831 another room, frame, was built on to the east side of the log building with an opening between that could be opened or closed by raising or lowering a large shutter to separate the men and women when meetings for business were held. In 1840 the log part was replaced with a frame room.

In 1843 Dillon Haworth and wife Mary deeded a four acre tract for the benefit and use of the Society of Friends which was no doubt the site for the Meeting House and cemetery.

In 1873 the north part of the present structure was erected by William Erving of Parke County. At this time Hopewell achieved Monthly Meeting status and was part of Vermilion Quarterly Meeting.

In the early days there was no music. The introduction of a musical instrument was accomplished in 1869 against very strong protest. Little by little objections gave way, but it was not until revival fires broke out that congregational singing and song books with notes came into use. Early services were unprogrammed and attenders sat in silence until they were moved by the Spirit of the Lord. Although this silent waiting is still part of Friends worship, Hopewell began to "record" ministers for service as pastors about 1901.

In 1901 the church was remodeled and the south room (now known as the Henderson Room in memory of John and Dinah Henderson) was built by Noah Dixon and Benjamin Linton. The parsonage just

Hopewell Friends Church

north of the church was erected in 1900. In 1953 the church basement was added and in 1980 extensive remodeling was begun by Allan Harvey, including a new church entry with a library and classrooms.

In the 1888 history of Vermillion County the Hopewell membership was given as 230. Although membership has declined over the years the members continue to claim the promise of Matthew 18:20, "For where two or three are gathered together in my name there am I in the midst of them."

TENNESSEE VALLEY BAPTIST CHURCH

The Tennessee Valley Baptist Church was organized August 17, 1872, by 12 members, all coming from the state of Tennessee.

The charter members were Thomas Dugger and wife, Benjamin Dugger and wife, James Dugger and wife, Henry Howard and wife, Jennie Lewis and husband, John Dugger and Rosamond Pierce Underwood.

With much hard labor and sacrifice the church was completed and dedicated November 15, 1875. It was named the Tennessee Valley Baptist Church by the eldest

member, Deacon Thomas Dugger.

The early members built well, for although there have been many remodelings, the original church still stands. Records mention putting a solid foundation of stone under the church, of recovering, of painting and other evidence of their good care. In 1928, a major task was carried out. It was in that year the church was raised and a basement put under it. Other improvements have been made, sure evidence that the concern of the forefathers of this church have not been lost by succeeding generations.

On December 12, 1875, the church organized a Sunday School and this has been in continuous operation since that time. There have been times when the church lacked a minister but even then the school was carried on instilling in each one the love and reverence for our Lord.

The first pastor was Rev. William McMasters, who served the church 13 years. During this time the membership grew from twelve to nearly one hundred. Appearing on the church records today are the names of grandchildren and great-grandchildren of these first settlers, faithfully keeping alive the Spirit and tradition of Tennessee Valley Baptist Church.

The Tennessee Valley Baptist Church-Hillsdale, Indiana

CAYUGA UNITED PRESBYTERIAN CHURCH

The first recorded meeting of any church congregation in Eugene Township was a Presbyterian meeting in a log house of William and Jane Thompson which stood about two hundred yards northeast of the present Cayuga Presbyterian Church. This meeting was in 1823. The congregation of fourteen members named the church "Vermillion River and County Presbyterian Church."

In 1859, Eugene had a church built which was jointly used by the Methodist and Presbyterian congregations. The Presbyterians began using the Eugene Opera house in 1886 until construction of their own building in 1889. The site for the present church was given in 1901 by John S. Grondyke, and the new Cayuga Presbyterian Church was dedicated Sunday morning, December 13, 1902. The total cost was $6498.00 and the remaining debt of $2,100 was more than raised at that dedication ceremony.

The Cumberland Presbyterian Church located in Portertown moved to Cayuga in 1889 and in 1907 united with the present church. The Eugene Church building was dismantled in 1917 and the material largely used in building the present Manse.

The church was considerably improved and modernized in the depression year of 1933 by digging out the basement, installing a kitchen, dining room, recreation room and fireplace. An entry ramp and the enclosure for the basement stairway are the most recent improvements to the exterior of the church.

THE RILEYSBURG CHURCH

In the year of 1889, the New Light Christians began regular preaching services in the Rileysburg school house located on the East side of the Rileysburg road just South of the railroad tracks. In 1898, a small group of men formed the Rileysburg Hall Association and built the Rileysburg Hall on the West side of the road directly across from the schoolhouse. Various denominations began holding church services in the hall at somewhat irregular intervals, sharing the time with community projects such as debates, minstrel shows, plays, dinners and lodge meetings.

In 1915, feeling the need of a religious awakening in the Rileysburg area, L.A. Krauel secured two men from the Moody Bible Institute to evangelize the community. December 25, 1915, marked the date of the first invitation to accept Christ in the Rileysburg Hall. On January 20, 1916, twenty people came together to form The Rileysburg Congregational Church. They changed the name of the church to The Rileysburg United Brethern Church in 1927,

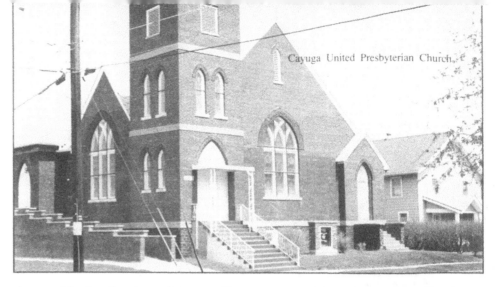

Cayuga United Presbyterian Church

along with the Gessie and Perrysville churches. The three formed a new church union in 1968, Rileysburg again changed its name to become the Rileysburg United Methodist church. In 1970 Rileysburg became an Independent Christian Church. Ministers over the last decade have traveled from Lincoln Christian College to help keep its original premise alive.

Although only memories remain of the one bustling Rileysburg community with its tile factory, general store, Riley Station, barber shop, post office, and blacksmith shop, The Rileysburg Hall remains. The original Hall erected in 1898 has, however, changed a little with the times. Kerosene lamps have given way to electric lighting. The Wabash King Stoves (Manufactured in Perrysville) have been replaced with gas floor furnaces. The entrance ticket booth has disappeared. The idea of a kitchen built under the stage was never made reality, but donations from the Ladies Aid Society (The result of many suppers) lined the aisle with carpeting, and adorned the stage with curtains. Padded pews replaced the straight-backed wooden chairs. The pews were purchased and restored in 1946 from the Hopewell Methodist church after a tornado destroyed their building. The stage has been divided into classrooms and the wooden siding replaced with aluminum.

Meetings are still held every Sunday morning. Although its membership is small in number, the feeling of family and love in Christ remains strong. Many ministers and families have passed through its doors always taking a little piece of Rileysburg with them as they leave.

Feeling the need of a religious awakening in the Rileysburg area, we remain.

SACRED HEART CATHOLIC CHURCH

In 1883, Clinton was a mission of Montezuma with Rev. T.O. Donaghue as mission priest and remained a mission until 1889 when Rev. Joseph T. Baur was commissioned to organize a parish. Due to the rapid growth of the congregation the present property at Sixth and Nebeker streets was secured. Here St. Patrick's Church was erected in the spring of 1894.

Clinton grew rapidly and with its growth the Catholic population increased making it necessary to build a larger church. In 1908, Rev. Wm. A. Maher initiated the move for the erection of the present church building modeled after the Cathedral of Thurles in Ireland. The name was then changed to Sacred Heart.

The old church was converted into a school with the Sisters of St. Francis from Oldenburg, Indiana, in charge. A new school building was completed in 1957 and has continued to flourish through the years. In 1986, the parish was proud to celebrate 80 years of excellent education.

Today the parish community consists of 1300 people and continues to provide spiritual growth and involvement in the community.

ST. JOSEPH'S CATHOLIC CHURCH

St. Joseph's Catholic Church in Universal was established during the summer of 1917. Reverend Clement J. Thienes of St. Mary-of-the-Woods began saying Mass in the second-floor of Joe Marietta's building. The white frame building on Wood Avenue was dedicated in June, 1920. The cost of the structure was $2,500.00.

Though the exterior looks basically as it did when originally built, the interior was given a modern look beginning in 1950. The pot-bellied stove gave way to a furnace, hardwood oak floors replaced the rough planks, stained glass windows were installed, and an oak altar replaced the high, white one. The focal point above the altar is a large cross acquired from Germany by Reverend Robert Wilhelm. The cross is hand-carved from one piece of wood and had been used in a Passion Play in Germany.

Being a mission, there has been no resident pastor. It has been administered by priests from St. Mary-of-the-Woods; St. Patrick's, Terre Haute; Gibault School; St. Leonard's, West Terre Haute; St. Ann's, Terre Haute; and Sacred Heart, Clinton. The church is cared for by the Altar Society which was formed in 1928.

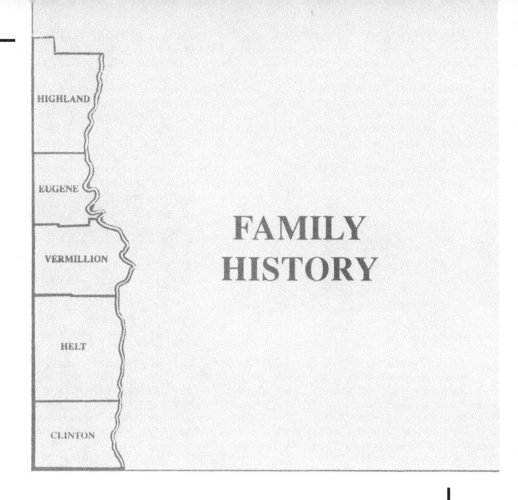

FAMILY HISTORY

HIGHLAND

EUGENE

VERMILLION

HELT

CLINTON

Foncannon Reunion

ELI THEODORE ADAMOVICH,

was born on Jan. 22, 1891, in Yugoslavia, the second eldest son of Theodore and Anna Adamovich in a family of 11. The parents are now deceased. He left his native country in 1916 coming to American to make his fortune. He worked in Austria and Germany on the railroads to make money for passage fare, passport, and some money to live on till he could get a job.

Eli T. Adamovich Family: Eli, Louis Vocatore, Germaine, George, Merle, and Nick

He landed in New York City and traveled from there to Minnesota to work in the ore mines. He soon left there and went to Detroit staying only a short time, then came to Clinton. He made Clinton his home for the rest of his life. He died in 1970 at the age of 70 years. He worked in several coal mines here. He has some sisters and brothers still living in Yugoslavia.

He married Germaine "Mary" Wailly Adamovich and had a total of six children and one stepson, Germaine's son from a former marriage. All are living in this area except for one who is in California. Three are deceased.

(see related article—Germaine "Mary" Wailly Adamovich)

GERMAINE "MARY" WAILLY ADAMOVICH,

was born on Nov. 13, 1903, in France, the daughter of John B. Wailly and Jeanie Wailly who were born in France. John B. Wailly was co-namer of Sportland Park in Clinton for which he received $5.00. They are now deceased.

John Wailly Family

They arrived in this country in the early 1900s in New York City and then came to this area, first settling in the Mecca area and then coming to the Centenary area. Their family consisted of four sons and three daughters.

Germaine married Eli T. Adamovich in Blanford and had a total of six children, and one stepson, Germaine's son from a former marriage. All are living in this area except for one who is in California. Three are deceased. Germaine remarried in 1947. She passed away at the age of 53 in 1956 in Clinton.

(see related article—Eli Theodore Adamovich)

136

GEORGE AND MYRTLE LOUISE ADAMOVICH,

George Adamovich was born June 24, 1923 at R.R. #2, Clinton, IN, the son of Eli Theodore Adamovich and Germaine "Mary" Wailly Adamovich. He was second eldest of seven children. Their parents are now deceased.

George grew up in the area of Clinton where he graduated from Clinton High School mid-term 1942-1943 school year. Upon graduation he was inducted into the U.S. Navy where he spent three years of almost all overseas service, seeing many countries, but having only limited action.

George and Myrtle Adamovich

After being discharged from the U.S. Navy in 1946, he was employed by the Chicago, Milwaukee, St. Paul and Pacific Railroad located at West Clinton. He spent five years learning the machinist trade.

On Oct. 5, 1946, he married Myrtle Louise Duell whom he met a few months earlier. She was the second eldest child of Daniel Marion Duell and Anna Marie Roberts Duell. Her parents are now deceased. Myrtle was employed at the Vermillion County Hospital as a nurses aide. This is where he met her.

George was then called back into service during the Korean War from January 1951 to April 1952. He served aboard the Battleship U.S.S. Wisconsin B.B. 64 again seeing many countries and also seeing much action off the coast of Korea.

In 1959, they made application for the adoption of a child which came to pass in 1961. They received a daughter born May 2, 1961. She was just nine days old. She was named Vikki Sue Adamovich. She is now Vikki Sue Dugger, wife of Allen Dugger. Application was made again for the adoption of another child, this time a son who was 13 months old. He was named George Wayne Adamovich.

George and Myrtle have resided at 361 Jackson Street, Fairview Park since 1952. George is now employed at the Eli Lilly Clinton Laboratories Plant working in the maintenance department.

NELL ALLEN,

was born Apr. 10, 1917, in Clinton, IN, one of four children of John Harrison Jackson and Reba Paine Jackson. She is the granddaughter of Nathan Robert Jackson and Martha Alice Craig Jackson and of Henry Washburn Paine and Kizzie Spainhower Paine.

Nell has three sisters—Neola Davitto, who lives in a local nursing home, Ethel Reposh (see related story), and Martha (Mrs. Jack) Dreher of Terre Haute. She has two sons residing in Clinton—Galen Harrison Brown, employed at Uselman's Meat Packing, and George Ross "Buddy" Sanquenetti, who is a paramedic and operates the DeVerter ambulance in Clinton. She has nine grandchildren. She is a retired drycleaning and clothing repair employee.

James Earl Paine and Narcissus Wright Paine, great-grandparents of Nell Allen

Nell Allen attended school at Poe, IN, (Allen County), and at Columbia School, Glendale School, Clinton Junior High School, and Clinton High School. *Submitted by Leo Reposh, Jr.*

ARRASMITH,

The Arrasmith family was founded here by two brothers, Alexander and Alva.

Alexander Arrasmith was born in Kentucky in 1795 and in 1822 came to Eugene Township with his wife Jane and four year old son, Richard. He lived one-half mile south of the railroad on the first road west of the brickyard. They had four additional children, Rebecca, Thomas G., James A. and William B.

Thomas G. was a wagon maker. James A. built one of Cayuga's early hotels, in 1887, and operated it until it burned down in December, 1891.

Alva Arrasmith, Alexander's younger brother, was born in Kentucky in 1808. He came to Indiana in 1828-1833, then moved to Vermillion County in 1851. He lived four miles southwest of Cayuga. Alva was a Trustee of the Eugene Methodist Church and Alexander was a life long member. Alva was married to Dorothy Waller Goodloe Mitchell. They had nine children. One son, John Wesley died in a Confederate prison in Florence, AL.

Another of their sons, Thomas Tarquin Arrasmith, was married to Eliza Jane Butler of the Henderson Chapel area. Their children were Elsie, married to Arthur Betson (father of Carl Betson), Effie, married to Samuel King, parents of Iva Jordan, Archie and Doyne King, and Pearl Arrasmith, married to Minnie Kyger. Their children, Charles and Thomas Alva still reside in Vermillion County, and their daughter, Charlotte (Shaw) lives in Fountain Co., IN.

MARGARET BATES,

was born in Paris, IL, in 1909 to Charles Roy and Stella Hoskins McKinney. There were three children in the family—Harold, Margaret and Joy. When the children were young, the family operated a grocery store on the Clinton-Paris Road. They also lived in Jacksonville, IN, where they owned a store. In 1914, they moved to Centenary. Here Margaret started school in the wooden building. The father farmed and worked in the mines.

The McKinney family moved to Clinton in 1922. Here sister Joy was born in 1925. All of the children graduated from Clinton High School. Harold attended Indiana State Teacher's College (now I.S.U.). Margaret received her Bachelor's and Master's Degree in Education. Joy went to business college and became a secretary.

Margaret began her teaching in 1930 in a one-room school at Syndicate. Her second year was taught at Smith. Later she taught at Jacksonville, Centenary, and in the Clinton City Schools.

Margaret and Warren Bates

In 1934, Margaret married Warren Bates, son of Reverend Lynn and Mrs. Bertha McDonald Bates. Warren's father was a minister at Fairview Methodist Church, and his mother was a retired school teacher. Warren was a barber on 9th Street for many years. He had a brother Robert who also was a barber.

Margaret and Warren had a daughter Phyllis born in 1936. Phyllis graduated from I.S.U. and became a teacher in the Highland and Griffith, IN, Schools. She taught Art for many years. She married Dr. Peter Ferrins and they live in Munster, IN. Phyllis is now working as a Realtor.

Margaret's brother, Harold, married Betty Jane Carmack of Newport. They moved to LaPorte, IN, where Betty still lives. They had four children— Paula, Charles, Marilyn, and Susan. Harold is deceased.

Her sister, Joy, married Richard Whitlock of Terre Haute. They have three children—Rick, Joy Ann and April. All of the children graduated from I.S.U. Rick works at Gibault School for Boys. Joy Ann taught school for several years, but is now working at Conservatory of Music. April is attending Butler preparing to become a pharmacist. Richard retired from Eli Lilly and Joy retired from Pfizers in 1987.

Margaret completed her teaching at the Glendale School where she taught the second grade for 20 years. She retired in 1974. Warren died in 1975.

Margaret and Warren were members of First United Methodist Church of Clinton. Margaret has taught Sunday School for many years. She is a member of Delta Kappa Gamma, Sigma Delta Pi, Y.W.C.A., Retired Teachers, and Vermillion County Historical Society.

CHARLES (CHARLIE) BALES AND SVANNAH MAUDE WRIGHT BALES,

Svannah Maude was the second daughter of John and Rosa Wright. She was born Jan. 10, 1890, in rural Clinton, IN. She died Dec. 7, 1965, and is buried at Spangler Cemetery in Vermillion Co., IN.

Svannah married Charlie Bales. Charlie was superintendent at Big Oak Coal Mine.

Charles Bales, Peter Wright, David Wright, Jeannie Wright, Rita Wright, and Svannah Bales

Svannah and Charlie had only one son, Homer Kenneth Bales, born Dec. 13, 1908. He died in 1971. Homer married Mary Doan of Clinton, IN.

When I was a very young child, our family would go visit Aunt Vannah and Uncle Charlie. She made the best jelly. Being a kid I would always ask for jelly and bread. So one day Aunt Vannah asked if we would bring a loaf of bread with us next time, because I guess I would eat all her bread and all her jelly. It sure was the best jelly I ever had. *Submitted by Edna Wright*

ANTONIO AND CAROLINA (BERTI) BAZZANI,

From Italy With Love is the name of a fictionalized account of the Tony and Carolina (Berti) Bazzani family, written by their granddaughter Karen (Bazzani) Zach. In her book, Karen relates the meeting of the Bazzani's when Tony was a man of 30, gone home to his small village (Lotta) in Northern Italy to visit his parents, Guiseppi and Luigia (Freschi) Bazzani. While there, his eyes, as well as his heart alit on the young lovely Carolina, daughter of neighbors, Rinaldo and Possidonia (Galli) Berti. Sounds like a natural happening? Not when the female is only 15! Besides the age difference, a major deterrent in the relationship was the fact that Tony wished to take Carolina back to America.

Tony was born July 10, 1883, the son of share cropper farmers. His older siblings, John, Louie and sister, Frances had gone to America when Tony was young. He, too, decided America was the place to seek his fortune. Tony's other siblings were: Rosa and Maria.

Carolina, too, was from a large family. She was the first born in "the house Rinaldo built." All the Berti children (Tomaso, Helena, Medaudo, Mario and Anna) remained in Italy but brother Ermette who raised his family in France.

Since Tony had not received American citizenship, he was forced to serve in the Italian Army during WWI. Thus, his "visit" lasted almost six years. The couple eloped in June of 1915. Their first child, Mabelia Alicia (Alice) was born Oct. 16, 1916. She was named after a character (Alias) in one of Carolina's "cheap books." One other child, Fernando (Aug. 20, 1919) was born/died in Italy. Upon completion of Tony's service and the governmental approval to emigrate, the Bazzani's embarked upon the ship, Tarmina. The process into America should have been quick and easy since the Bazzani's had purchased second-class passage; however, due to a railroad strike, the family spent two weeks of unbelievable hardship in the condemned Castle Garden facilities on Ellis Island when they finally arrived in "Tony's America" on Carolina's 21st birthday. Their name has been placed on the Wall of Immigration at Ellis Island.

Tony and Carolina lived in Universal for many years while he worked in area mines. Carolina worked at odd jobs, including baking and sewing. Fernando II (later name was legally changed to Fred) was born exactly one year to the day his brother of that name was born/died. Both Fred and Alice are graduates of Clinton High (where Tony and Carolina later moved to 230 N. 9th Street). Alice graduated from St. Anthony's School of Nursing and worked at the Clinton Hospital many years. Her husband, Harold Certain was a maintenance man and welder at Lusterlite, Paris, IL. Their son, Frank and wife Jeanie (Nestler) now live in the 9th Street home. Frank and Jeanie have Michelle and Anthony. Harold and Alice's other son, Tom

and wife Jackie (Cooke) live in Portland ME and have three children, Geoff, Michael and Lindsay. Fred married Kate Smith and moved to her hometown of Waveland where he served as Rural Mail Carrier for over 25 years. Children: twin sons, Larry and Garry and daughter, Karen. Their family is included in the Montgomery County Family History Book by Turner Publisher.

Tony died Nov. 18, 1961; Carolina passed away Jan. 8, 1980. Both are buried in Rose Lawn cemetery, but the roots of "The Lover of America" continue to grow! *Submitted by Karen Bazzani Zach*

MARY ELIZABETH BELL,

is listed in Who's Who in American Education, 1963-1964. After graduating from Dana High School in 1929 she received her B.S. degree from Indiana State University in 1939. She acquired an M.S. degree from Butler University in 1949 and Ed. D. from Indiana University in 1957. She taught in the Indianapolis schools from 1930 until 1953. Then she went to Kettering, OH to become Director of Elementary Education. From there she went to the University of Arizona as Associate Professor of Education and in 1961 she became Associate Professor at Murray State College.

DAVID BENNETT,

was born Dec. 8, 1853, in Ohio, the son of Joseph and Elizabeth (Hart) Bennett-both born in Pennsylvania and died in Wauerly, KS. Joseph and his family lived in Pennsylvania for 31 years; and in 1852, the Bennett family moved to Ohio until about 1866.

Clarence Bennett

They came into Vermillion County for a short stay and then moved on to Douglas Co., KS. Joseph lived in Coffey Co., KS, until his death, Sept. 28, 1897.

David came back to Highland Township to farm and married Canthey (Kate) Milum in July 15, 1877. She was born Aug. 26, 1859, in West Virginia, daughter of John B. and Clara J. (Howell) Milum. They lived in Champaign Co., IL, until 1872, then moved to Highland Township.

Born to them were five children, Robert born Mar. 7, 1878, married Elizabeth May Dennis; Ernest born Feb. 20, 1881; Clarence born Nov. 21, 1882, married Furn Sanders; Nellie Louise born Nov. 3, 1884, married Fredrick Prather; Bessie June born June 10, 1891, married Victor H. Jones.

David and Canthey lived in Highland Township until their death. Canthey died Jan. 26, 1933, and David lived with his daughter and family until his death in 1942.

FRANCIS AND IVA DUNIVAN BENNETT,

Francis Marion Bennett was born Nov. 27, 1884, the son of Joseph and Julia A. Millikan Bennett, in Vermillion County near

Stumptown, where he spent most of his lifetime within a few miles near the communities of Stumptown and Quaker.

Francis and Iva Bennett

He attended grade school in the one room school at Stumptown and graduated from Newport High School in 1916. The following year he married Iva Belle Dunivan, Sept. 12, 1917, and soon after went into military service. To this union were born ten children—Roy of Kingman, IN; Francis Ray of Covington, IN; Ruth Edna Crist of Perrysville, IN; Iretta Belle Shepard of Dana, IN; Norman Earl of Dana, IN; Robert Clay of Corona, CA; Joe Allen of Eugene, OR; Anne Irene Hall, Fairfax, VA; Eileen Gay Krablin of Little Rock, AR; and Mary Sue Parks of Georgetown, IL.

Francis worked his entire life as a farm laborer and a tenant farmer, much of the time for Bert Cook. Francis and Iva raised their ten children on the Cook farm in the Quaker Community, close to the Hopewell Friends Church where Iva and Francis were involved in teaching Sunday School.

Upon retirement Francis and Iva moved to their country home only about a mile down the road, caring for the sick, raising a superb garden, and enjoying their 30 grandchildren and 33 great-grandchildren. In 1964, they moved to Dana. After Iva's health deteriorated, it was necessary to move her to the nursing home in Chrisman, IL. Francis joined her there shortly before her death, Sept. 13, 1979, one day following their 62nd wedding anniversary. Francis called the Chrisman Christian Village home for six more years, where he died May 7 1985, following a brief illness.

NORMAN EARL (BUD) AND ROSALIE HICKEL BENNETT, Norman

Earl (Bud) Bennett, was the sixth child (Oct. 4, 1931) of ten children born to Francis and Iva Dunivan Bennett in the Quaker community near Dana, In. He attended both grade school and high school in Newport, IN, graduating in 1949.

After graduation from high school, he worked as a farm laborer prior to entering the U.S. Navy in April, 1952. During his four years of service he enjoyed being stationed on the East Coast and a world cruise seeing many foreign countries and historic places of interest. June 19, 1954, he married Rosalie E. Hickel of Paris, IL. Rosalie was a student nurse at the Paris Hospital; the last class to graduate from that school of nursing. Following graduation and completion of her state board exams, Rosalie joined Bud in Key West, FL, an R.N.

February 3, 1956, they became the proud parents of a son, Norman Bruce, two months prior to Bud's discharge from the Navy. The family moved back to the Quaker Community. Bud worked as a laborer for Lindsey Joe Moore and Rosalie as an R.N. at the Vermillion County Hospital. In 1959, Bud chose to attend Hobart Trade School in Troy, OH, for six

months; later moving to Tilton, IL, working as a welder for the Hyster Co. in Danville, IL, and Rosalie working at Lakeview Hospital.

In 1960, they bought their first home in the Westville, IL, Community and on Sept. 5, 1963, their daughter, Jo Lynn, was born.

In the spring of 1965, they moved back to the Quaker Community, having purchased the country home of his parents, where Bud and Rosalie still reside. Bud is now a maintenance mechanic for Public Service Cayuga Generating Plant and Rosalie is employed at the V.A. Hospital in Danville, IL.

Their son, Bruce, is married to the former Tina Young of Clinton, IN, where they reside. Bruce has one daughter, Breaha, born Nov. 2, 1982, and a step-son, Billy Jones. Bruce is a maintenance mechanic for Inland Container Corporation, Newport, IN.

Jo Lynn resides in Bedford, TX, a suburb of Dallas where she is employed at the Texas University, Arlington Campus in the horticulture department.

RAY MERRILL BIGGS AND IRMA BLY MACKEL BIGGS, now of Venice, FL,

grew up in and around Clinton and raised their family in Lyford. Ray was born Aug. 26, 1917, in Fontanet, IN, the only child of Earl Ray Biggs and Maude Susan Muncie. His grandparents were Reuben Wesley Muncie/Mary Jane Jacks and Sterling Biggs/Ida Mae MacNiel. Irma was born June 29, 1917, at home at 1401 So. 4th St., Clinton, the first child of Frederick Julius Mackel and Fleeta Belle Cunningham. Her only brother is Dr. Frederick O. Mackel of Ft. Wayne. Her grandparents were Charles Frederick Mackel/Lucy Matilda Fortner and John Cunningham/Martha Bradbury.

Ray and Irma Biggs

Ray and Irma met at Clinton High School where they played violin and piano in the orchestra, and graduated in 1936 and 1937. Irma attended Brown's Business School and worked at Murphys and Bonocorsi's. Ray attended Indiana State Teachers College and worked at Krogers and the Terre Haute Boilerworks. They married Dec. 10, 1939, in Clinton and lived in Lyford near his parents. In 1943 they built on US 41 across from Varda's Tavern, where they raised their family until 1964. Their first child, Larry Ray Biggs, was born Mar. 8, 1942 in Clinton. He lives in West Terre Haute with his wife, Carolyn Sue Vermillion, and two children, Leticia Lynn (Tish) and Wade Alan Biggs. Their last child, Linda Gail Biggs, was born June 17, 1946, in Lyford. She lives in Stone Mountain, GA with her husband, Chester Lee (Chet) Fields of Fairview, and two sons, Steven Ray Fields (born June 20, 1966, in Terre Haute) and David Lee Fields (born Aug. 1, 1971, in Bremerhaven, W. Germany).

During their lives in the Clinton area, Ray worked in the coal mines, starting in 1939 as a blacksmith at Saxon Mine and finishing as Chief Electrical Engineer at Viking Mine when it closed in 1964. He was an active Mason from 1947, serving in 1951 as both High Priest and Master of Jerusalem Lodge #99. He and Irma both took active roles sponsoring and supporting groups such as Job's Daughters, DeMolay, Band Boosters, and First Christian Church. Irma also was active in Parke Homemakers Home Ec Club and spent much time sewing, canning, doing leathercraft, and chauffeuring the kids to various activities.

Upon moving in 1964 to St. Clairsville, OH, Ray became Master Mechanic of Franklin Mine. Irma took up an interest in organic gardening, and they renewed their interest in square, round, and folk dancing. Ray retired with lung problems in 1979, having worked his way up to maintenance Superintendent of five mines.

They moved Dec. 10, 1978, to Venice, FL. Ray revived a passionate interest in woodcraft, and Irma discovered a talent for wood finishing. Much time was devoted to caring for their mothers until their deaths in 1985 and 1988. Now that ill health keeps Ray and Irma close to home, their special pleasure is calls and visits with family and friends, many of whom still call Clinton home. *Submitted by Linda Fields*

THE BISHOP FAMILY, Max L. Bishop

was born in Vermillion County, Feb. 6, 1916, the eldest of three sons of Leo and Alberta Davis Bishop. He grew up on a farm south of Newport, graduating from Newport High School in 1934. Helena Cramer was born in Newport, Jan. 6, 1916 to Roy and Jessie Reed Cramer. She, with one brother, Frank, grew up in Newport, graduating from Newport High School in 1934 and Terry Haute Commercial College in 1936. Max and Helena were married Nov. 14, 1936. They moved to Danville, IL, then returned to Vermillion County in 1942 where they have since farmed. They came to the Dana area in 1944.

The Max Bishop Family; Row 1 - Cary Marshall, Graham Bishop, Jacob Lieser, Joshua Bishop. Row 2 - Sue Marshall, Max Bishop, Helena Bishop. Row 3 - Gary Marshall, Cheryl Estrick, Jennifer Lieser, Wandalene Bishop, Anita Bishop, Marian Bishop, Kelly Bishop. Row 4 - David Bishop, James Estrick, Rick Lieser and Kyle, Garry Franklin Bishop, Kevin Bishop, Brian Bishop, Ronald M. Bishop

They are the parents of 1. Ronald M. of Rosedale, Rte. 1, born Apr. 20, 1938, married Mrs. Marian Wier. He has one daughter, Carla, who married Frank Cirey and they have a daughter, Brittianie Anne. Carla's family lives in Minot, ND. 2. Garry Franklin born Oct. 25, 1940 married Wandalene Haga. They are the parents of two daughters: Jennifer Lynn, who married Rick Lieser and has two sons Jacob and Kyle; and Cheryl Elaine, who married James Estrick. This family now lives in Greenley, CO. 3. Marcia Jo Kyle, (1947-1977) mother of three sons David, Kelly and Brian. 4. Sue Ann, born July 6, 1950, married Gary Marshall. They are the parents of Andrew (1872-1983) and Cary Michelle. 5. Kevin Alan born May 14, 1955, married Anita Breedlove. They are the parents of Joshua and Graham. In 1977, after the death of their daughter Marcia Jo Kyle, they adopted their three grandsons David, Kelly and Brian.

They have been progressive farmers always looking for new ways of improving their farming methods and are still farming with their son Kevin and son-in-law Gary Marshall.

They have been long time members of the Dana United Methodist Church where they both are presently serving on Church and Parsonage Boards. They are members of the Vermillion County Historical Society. Max was a member and President of the Dana Town Board for several years, a former member of the Dana Fire Department and a member of the K of P Lodge. Helena is presently a Trustee of the Vermillion County Library Board. Helena has always been interested in history. She compiled the History Book "Dana's One Hundred Years' in 1974 for Dana's Centennial as well as "Our Hundredth Year 1878-1978" history of the Dana United Methodist Church.

Max's ancestors, Davis, Hood, and Aye came from Tennessee and Virginia to Helt Township, some as early as 1823. We have exhorters license for John Aye, Max's great-great-great-grandfather, a Circuit Rider who preached on Helts Prairie in 1824.

The Bishop and Thomas families came from Kentucky to Opeedee near Newport. Helena's family the Cramers and Cobles came to Parke County from Pennsylvania and Ohio in the 1850's. The Reeds came from Stokes Co., NC to Columbus, IN in the 1840's and on to Parke County in 1904.

Our ancestor's choice of Vermillion County was just Great!

DANTE AND ORFINA BIZZY,
Dante Bizzy (1882-1957) came to America from Italy in 1902. He worked in the mines in Kansas before coming to Vermillion County. While in Kansas he married Orfina Bonhivert Ginardi (1883-1975). She had two sons by a previous marriage, Homer L. Ginardi (1900-1974) and Joe Ginardi Bizzy (1904-1936). Their son, Danty C. Bizzy now lives in Blanford.

Dante and Orfina Bizzy

Mr. and Mrs. Bizzy were in business at the corner of Second Street and what is now State Road #163 for many years. Mrs. Bizzy ran the restaurant and Mr. Bizzy was a miner.

Danty C., their son, worked at Interstate Coal Mine before going to Brazil, IN, to work at the Clay Plant.

In 1931, Danty C. moved to Michigan and worked at various jobs, including Detroit Edison Power Plant retiring after 36 years and returning to Blanford in 1974 to live.

He has two children. A son, Harold (1928) lives in California, and his daughter, Evelyn M. Bizzy Humes (1938) lives in Michigan. He has ten grandchildren and five great-grandchildren.

Danty C. is man of many talents, his most treasured one is making friends and nurturing each friendship.

GEORGE M. BOATMAN,
(born Nov. 10, 1869, Parke County, died Sept. 22, 1951, Clinton) was born in Florida Township and was the great-grandson of William C. and Elizabeth Boatman who moved to Parke County from a farm near Crab Orchard, KY in 1826. His grandparents were John Boatman (born Apr. 19, 1811, Lincoln Co., KY, died July 22, 1881, Parke County), and Eveanna Madoritha "Dolly" Lenderman or Leenderman (born June 14, 1817, Wilkes Co., NC, died Sept. 12, 1876, Parke County) who lived on 160 acres in Parke County after their marriage Mar. 23, 1839. They received a "Land Patent" on sheepskin signed by President Tyler in 1841 which is in possession of one of the great-granddaughters. John was the father of seven children by his three wives. His youngest son, Samuel, was born three months after his 65th birthday. John was a farmer, an excellent furniture maker, and a preacher in the Christian Church.

George M.'s parents were Leonard C. Boatman (born Apr. 4, 1841, died Jan. 26, 1928, Florida Township, Parke County), and Malinda Jane Laney or DeLaney Boatman (born Jan. 7, 1849, Parke County, died Apr. 13, 1926, Independence, LA) who resided in Parke County, IN, except for a brief time when they owned a plantation near West Point, MS.

George M., the eldest of nine children, married Gail H. Davis on Feb. 3, 1898, Parke County. They had one son, Fred H., born Aug. 23, 1901. George M. was a mechanic at the coal mines near Lyford, IN. Gail H. was born 1878, and died June 16, 1913. George M. married Bessie Patton Lake (born June 12, 1876, Scotland, died Apr. 24, 1950, Clinton).

Bessie Patton Lake's first husband was James E. Lake (born September, 1872, died Oct. 8, 1914). They were married Jan. 22, 1896, Parke County. Their son was John Roy Lake (born Mar. 6, 1903, Parke County, died June 12, 1986, Terre Haute). His first marriage was to Helen and his second marriage to Francis.

George M. and Bessie Patton Lake Boatman lived at 331 Walnut Street, Clinton, until their deaths. This marriage produced one daughter, Georgia Margaret Boatman (born Nov. 11, 1916, Clinton, died Aug. 27, 1969).

Margaret married Leslie M. Hogue (born Jan. 30, 1911, West Terre Haute, IN, died Mar. 20, 1978) on Aug. 12, 1941.

Les and Margaret lived at 331 Walnut Street, Clinton, and also in Fairview later. Margaret was a registered licensed nurse in Clinton and Les worked many years for Montgomery Ward and Company in Terre Haute. They had two children, Michael, now living in Wisconsin, and Susan, whose married name is Dodson, living in Universal.

Leslie M. Hogue's second marriage was to Lucille Lewis Gilfoy of Clinton.

Also, of the large Boatman family was George M.'s youngest brother, Fredrick Yancey Boatman

(born Mar. 29, 1886, Parke County, died Apr. 7, 1934, Clinton.) Fred, a prominent builder in Clinton married Ethel Marshall (born 1886, Parke County, died Nov. 16, 1973, Clinton), on June 26, 1913, Clinton. They lived at 434 Elm Street, Clinton. For many years, Ethel and their son, Leonard Marshall Boatman, operated Marshall's Wallpaper and Paint Store at 346 South Main Street, Clinton. Marshall and his wife Bertha Maria Caniparoli Boatman, a retired registered nurse, live at 956 South Third Street, Clinton.

Another brother, James Arthur Boatman, (born Apr. 20, 1874, Parke County, died Feb. 18, 1937, Clinton), was a builder and contractor in Clinton. James first married Madge Coleson of West Point, MS, and his second marriage was to Ethel Bishop (born 1880, died 1950, Clinton).

Other brothers of George M. Boatman were Charles Overton and Chester Bruce. Sisters were Ella Ann; Cora Alice who first married Howard Mansel Luce of Clinton, and second marriage was to Jasper Black of Rosedale; Eva Jelaney who first married Roy Coleson of West Point, MS, and second marriage was to Dr. Luther Layton Ricks, M.D., Independence, LA; and Mary Letha Boatman married to Dr. Charles William Griffin, D.C., Rosedale, IN.

GUY H. BRIGGS,
was born Oct. 9, 1874 in Vigo County and received an education in grade school and on the farm. On Dec. 15, 1895, he married Thursa Reeder. Thursa was the daughter of J.W. and Elizabeth Smith Reeder and was born on Oct. 7, 1872. Thursa was first married to Bert Wright and they had one daughter, Mary Wright Louden. Bert Wright died at age 20.

Guy Briggs started out as a small farmer, but was extremely successful, eventually expanding his holdings to over 3,000 acres in Vigo County, as well as 170 acres in Clinton Township and 135 acres in Eugene Township in Vermillion County. Mr. Briggs was in the real estate and plotted and built Shepherdsville on his own land. He named it after his aunt, Mary Shepherd. The town elected to be spelled Shepardsville. Guy was supt. of Sunday School at Trinity Church. He was also elected Fayette Township Trustee, which made all of this more interesting, because his education was in grade school. He conducted the 1908 Fayette Township High School Commencement.

Guy H. Briggs

Mr. Briggs went into the construction business and built part of Hwy. 41 to Rockville, as well as part of 163 to Centenary, IN. Later, Mr. Briggs moved to Clinton where he was in the insurance and real estate business. After moving to Clinton, Guy became very active in civic affairs including being a committee member of the building of the First United Methodist Church at 4th and Blackman. He built the coliseum so that the schools would have a place to play basketball. During W.W.I, he organized the Liberty Guard, as his daughter has a certificate from Gov. Goodrich so stating. During W.W.II he was director of the Vermillion County ration board.

Guy and Thursa were the parents of two children, Herbert Ray, an Indianapolis lawyer, and Ruth Marie Briggs Gerrish.

Mr. Briggs was a jovial and entertaining companion socially, and held affiliations with the Elks, Moose, Lions, Mystic Shriners, Knights of Pythias, Odd Fellows, Half Century Club, Redmen, Modern Woodmen and Knights Templers. He was also a 32 degree Mason. *Submitted by Leo Reposh, Jr.*

CARL AND EVELYN BROWN, Carl E. Brown was born on May 2, 1921 at Bono, IN and is the son of Sheldon C. and Erie Brown. He is a Dana High School graduate, a WWII U.S. Navy veteran, and received a M.S. Degree from Indiana State University.

Mr. Brown was a Railway Postal Clerk on the New York Central Railroads between Chicago, IL, Cincinnati, OH, and Cleveland, OH, and St. Louis, MO. This consisted of sorting mail to railways that supplied towns and to other towns that supplied smaller towns and villages. City mail was worked by reading the street number and a street in a town such as Indianapolis, Chicago, or Cincinnati and sending it to the correct sub-station within the city.

Carl and Evelyn Brown

Mr. Brown is retired, a member of the Indiana Retired Teachers Association, President of the Vermillion County Retired Teachers, Vice President of the Collett Home Board, Cayuga, IN, a member of the Vermillion County Hospital Foundation, a member of the American Legion, and The Knights of Pythias.

Mr. Brown is a retired school teacher and Industrial Arts Department Chairperson from Pike High School in Marion Co., IN. He also was Junior Class Sponsor for many years.

Carl and his wife were married on Apr. 3, 1955 in the New Brunswick Christian Church near Lebanon, IN. Mrs. Brown is the former Evelyn E. Reed, daughter of Walter and Goldie Reed. She is a graduate of Pinnell High School, Lebanon, Central Normal College, Danville, IN, Butler University, Indianapolis, IN, Indiana State Teachers College, Terre Haute, IN and did additional graduate work at the University of Southern California, Los Angeles, CA.

Evelyn was born in Milledgeville, IN on Apr. 9, 1918. Her teaching experience was in Boone and Marion Counties. She retired from the Washington Township School System in Marion Co., IN with approximately 36 years of teaching experience.

At an early age Mrs. Brown was a member of a wining state music memory team and served many years as a teacher and a pianist in her local church. She was a charter member of the Harrison Township Home Extension Club and a member and officer in the Lebanon B.P.W. She was secretary and treasurer of the Boone County Teachers and served in many professional capacities in Marion County as well as secretary in a division of the State Teachers Association.

Evelyn is a member of the Indiana Retired Teachers Assoc., A.A.R.P. and Beta Chapter, Delta Sigma Kappa, Danville Fidelis Alpha Chapter, Alpha Delta Kappa, West Indianapolis, Happy Homemakers Club, Towne and Countrie Club, As you Like It, and the Vermillion County Retired Teachers Association. Mrs. Brown served as president of the first support group of the Ernie Pyle State Memorial, 1984-1986. She did clerical work at the Wright Patterson Air Force Base in 1945.

Mr. and Mrs. Brown have traveled extensively in the United States and Canada. They enjoy traveling, fishing, and growing several hundred mums each summer and fall. Evelyn enjoys crocheting, painting, and music.

The Browns are members of the Montezuma Christian Church.

GALEN AND CAROLYN KYLE BROWN, Galen Harrison Brown was born Mar. 8, 1936 in Clinton, the son of Escoll C. Brown and Nellie May Jackson Brown (now Allen). See related story on Nell Allen. Escoll C. Brown was a barber in Clinton and later in Rockville and operated a horse farm near Rockville. Galen is the grandson of Galen Brown and Margret Middlebrook Brown who resided at Hillsdale and of John Harrison Jackson and Reba Elizabeth Paine Jackson who resided at Clinton. Galen attended school at Fairview, Crompton Hill, and at Van Buren in Clay County. He was a member of Indiana Vocational Technical College's first graduating class in 1969. He served a number of years in the United States Army having been stationed in both Germany and Korea. He is skilled and employed in the meat processing business.

Front: Bob Stull, James Stull. Middle: Linda Stull, Santa Claus, Reba Paine Jackson. Back: Kimberly Lynn Brown, John Harrison Brown, Vincent Edward Brown.

Galen Brown was married to Pat Mankin and they have a daughter, Gail Lynn Rusk of Dana. Later, he was married to Virginia Thomas and they have three sons, Timothy Gale Brown, Thomas Dale Brown (twins), and Ronald Eugene Brown. He was married to Mary Stull producing children, Vincent Edward Brown, John Harrison Brown, Kimberly Lynn Brown.

Carolyn Kyle Brown was born Nov. 30, 1936, in St. Bernice, the daughter of Clarence Edward Kyle and Mary Lloyd Hopkins Kyle. She has three brothers James, Ronald, and Terry. Terry served in Vietnam. She has three sisters, Arlene Craddle,

Nancy Kyle, and Ethel Runyan. She attended school at St. Bernice where she was a high school majorette. She graduated in 1954. She married David Williams and they have three sons, Charles Edward, Robert Richard, and Scott Andrew; and a daughter, Lori Williams Stevens. Another son David James Williams, was killed in a shooting accident.

Galen Harrison Brown and Carolyn Kyle Brown were married in 1984, and reside in Clinton. Carolyn has had a number of jobs including clothing manufacturing and nursing home work. She is an outstanding seamstress. The Browns attend the St. Bernice Nazarene Church. *Submitted by Leo Reposh, Jr.*

MARTHA ELLEN BROWN, born Sept. 7, 1930 in Vermillion Co., IN, married William R. Moore of Danville, IL on Aug. 17, 1957. They live in Danville, IL. She has taught high school and college. He is an industrial controller. They have two daughters: Mary Ann, an artist, married to Richard J. Tori and living in Naperville, IL and Nancy Louise, an artist, living in Danville, IL. *Submitted by Mary L. Smith*

SHELDON AND ERIE BROWN, Sheldon C. Brown (1888-1971) a World War II veteran and Erie Branson Brown (1893-1976) were married on June 2, 1917. Mr. and Mrs. Brown were both from farm families in the Dana area. Mr. Brown, the son of Thomas and Nellie Russell Brown and Erie Branson the daughter of Thomas and Martha Mater Branson were both from farm families north and west of Dana, IN in Vermillion County and were lifelong members of the Dana Community.

Shell and Erie Brown

The Brown's lived in Dana but owned the farm at the northwest corner of U.S. 36 and State Road 63.

Mr. Brown was a graduate of Dana High School and attended Indiana State Normal at Terre Haute, IN. He was a Railway Postal Clerk for over 40 years and was a member of the American Legion, the Knights of Pythias, and the Masonic Lodge.

Mrs. Brown was born in and attended Parke County Schools. She was a member of the Eastern Star, Pythias Sisters, the American Legion Auxiliary, a Rebecca, and the Baptist Church. She was a cook at the Dana High school for many years and will be remembered for helping plan several Athletic Banquets for Dana High School.

Mr. Brown's work was on many of the railroads in the midwest but primarily on the New York Central Railroad between Cleveland, OH, and St. Louis, MO. His work consisted of sorting mail to other towns that supplied mail to smaller towns. Much studying was required as this was all done by memory. The railway mail cars would have up to 12 railway postal clerks working up to 15 states and three large cities to general scheme. Working city mail consisted of reading the street address and sending it to the correct zone or substation in a city such as Cleveland, OH or New York, NY.

Mr. and Mrs. Brown were the parents of three children, Mary Louise Brown Smith, Dana, IN, Martha Ellen Brown Moore, Danville, IL, and Carl E. Brown, Dana, IN. Their grandchildren are Gary and Dennis Smith, Debbie Smith Jukes, Mary Ann Moore Torri, and Nancy Louise Moore. Their great grandchildren are Dawn and Larry Jukes and Erin Smith.

WILLIAM C. BROWN,

was born in Scotland in 1800. He came from Maryland with his family of six or seven children. He was a foundry manager and furnace maker. He worked at the Indiana Furnace in Clinton Township. He had five sons in the Civil War and one died at Gettysburg. *Submitted by Ernestine Brown*

CAROLE KATHLEEN KUHNS CANADA,

was born Apr. 22, 1938, to Herman Kuhns and Ruby Pauline Nolan Kuhns. Carole married Jerry Lee Canada on Sept. 29, 1956. They had Jeffrey Lynn Canada on July 8, 1957, Jill Luann Canada on May 28, 1960, and Jan Lenette on Mar. 25, 1963. Carole and Jerry have four grandchildren.

ISAAC CARMACK,

The Carmack family came from Tennessee in 1830 and entered land in Sections five, nine, and 22; son Alfred in Sections nine and 31. Son Andrew came in 1842 and entered Sections nine and ten. Andrew's oldest son William Pinkney's home was in Section five which was almost in the center of the Wabash Ordnance Plant. The Carmack Cemetery is nearby. Isaac and Mary are buried there as are several other Carmacks. The Carmack family tree is well mingled with other pioneer families such as Asbury, Betson, Castle, Clearwater, Lowry, Newlin, Spellman, Weatherman, Wiltermood and Zener.

William Pinckney and Mary Elizabeth Asbury Carmack

Isaac Carmack, 1788-1863; Mary Campbell, 1795-1884.

Lucinda, 1811-1872, married Julius Bogard, 1811-1891.

James Alfred, 1814-1879. James A. married first 1840 to Eliza Ann Rhodes. Mary Jane, 1841-1928, married 1859 to Zera Castle, 1835-1917. James A. married second 1845 to Delila Jane Moore, 1820-1851. Eliza Ann, 1849-1919, married 1872 to Melvin Zener, 1844-1908. James A. married third 1852 to Mrs. Sarah Bond Lowry. James A. married fourth 1865 to Jane Haymaker.

Andrew, 1816-1895. Andrew married first 1840 to Rachel Nichols, 1822-1860. William Pinkney, 1841-1915, married 1866 to Mary E. Asbury, 1847-1942. Ida M. 1866-1955, never married. Sara E. 1869-1955, married 1893 to Quincy Clearwater,

1863-1905. Wayne, Forest, Dorothy, and Birch. Rachel J., 1872-1925, married 1898 to Wm. R. Bowen. Opal, Gordon, Ethelyn, Lucille, Olive, Kaith.

Fred O., 1874-1946. Fred O., married first 1896 to Rose Betson, 1876-1913. Hazel, 1898-___, married 1920 to Harlow Myers. Louise, 1905-1929, married 1927 to Robert Halsey. Everette, 1911-___, married 1930 to Josephine Hoover. Howard, Robert, Fredrick, Mervin, Rose L. Fred O., married second 1914 to Sylvia Douglas. Elsie May, 1915-1958. Orin D., 1917,___. Richard, John, Thomas, Tony, Christine.

*Elsie Lenore, 1877-1939, married 1899 to Woodruff Weatherman. Lowell, Lulu, Harold, Wm. Walden, Vernon, Melvin.

William Rollin, 1879-1959. Wm. R., married first 1904 to Blanche Westbrook, 1884-1911. Enid, Bernice. Wm. R. married second to Florence Newlin.

Robert R., 1881-1969. Robert R., married first 1910 to Elsie Jackson, 1885-1937. Marvin J., 1913,___. Robert R., married second 1939 to Maud Jackson, 1887-1965.

Carrie Bell, 1884-1973, married 1912 to Everette P. Brown. Jeri, Wilma, John H.

Mabel Fern, 1886-1952, married 1912 to Emmett Hollingsworth, 1886-1930. Irwin, Margaret, Barbara.

Paul E., 1889-1975, married 1912 to Flossie Wiltermood, 1895-___. Betty Jane, married 1936 to Harold McKinney.

Mary Gladys, 1893-1980, married 1927 to George W. Jackson. Mary Kathryn.

*See Wood Weatherman. *Submitted by Isabel B. Weatherman*

CARSMAN,

The John and Helena Carsman family of Vermillion Co., IN, both having immigrated from Germany in 1856, were married Apr. 19, 1880, and made their home in Cayuga. Six children were born (picture left to right by age), Henry, Edward, Alex, Frank, Clara, Lucy. Henry was a grain mill operator in Cayuga. Edward was chief facility accountant with the New York Central Railroad, residing in Hammond, IN. Alex was signal maintenance superintendent of Big Four Railroad, residing in Terre Haute. Frank was a grocery store owner and had interest in a bank in Ridge Farm, IL. Clara worked at Auto Sales of Cayuga. Lucy, married, lived in Marion, IN.

Henry, Edward, Alex, Frank, Clara, Lucy. All are 70 and over.

All in the picture have passed on with the exception of Clara, who lives in a nursing home in Terre Haute.

The pork industry and farming brought this family together in Cayuga and Eugene. The families of John and Helena both came to the United States for political freedom. Each family took the only transportation available, coming from New

York City via the Hudson River and Erie Canal to Lake Erie and Toledo, and then via the Wabash-Erie Canal by canal boat to Lodi.

John Gottfried Carsman was born in Germany Mar. 3, 1853. John's father was a soldier for the German emperor, picked for his horsemanship and physique to be with the elite guard which protected the emperor, William II. John's father died while in service, and John was adopted by John Frederick Kinderman. Not until later was John told that he was a Carsman.

Helena Heidbrider was born in Germany, the daughter of a politician. He was said to be chief of police in Berlin. She immigrated with the Wittenbergs, who were lawyers. They all settled in Lodi, IN, and shared a home which the Wittenbergs had had built for them.

John worked 45 years as a laborer and section foreman on the C. & E. I. Railroad. He died when a passenger train derailed while he was working as a crossing tender at Curtis Street in Cayuga, Mar. 29, 1924. *Submitted by Joseph E. Carsman, son of Edward Carsman*

JOHN ALLEN CHEESEWRIGHT AND PATRICIA LEE RUNNER CHEESEWRIGHT,

John Allen Cheesewright was born Apr. 8, 1936, in Edgar Co., IL, the son of Arthur W. Cheesewright and Marie Wagner Cheesewright. He has one sister, Janice Marie Cheesewright Wohlfort of Richmond, IN. John grew up in Dana, IN, where he graduated from Dana High School in 1954. He entered Purdue University and graduated in 1958 with a degree in General Agriculture. He met his wife, Patricia Lee Runner Cheesewright, the only child of Helen Marie Carlson Runner McKinley and Orville Charles Runner, in Lafayette where they were married Sept. 1, 1957. After John's graduation from Purdue, they moved back to Dana where John farmed with his father.

John Cheesewright

Pat was born and raised in Lafayette where she attended local schools and graduated in 1954 from Jefferson High School. She was taught baton twirling since 1952 and is a certified coach and judge for the United States Twirling Association.

In 1958 they became parents of a daughter, Kay Lynn Cheesewright Duke, in 1960 the parents of a son, John Kelly, and in 1962 the parents of a daughter, Kristine Lee Cheesewright Fangman. In November, 1987, a son, John Perry Duke, was born to Kay and William Collins Duke.

Pat and John are members of the Bono United Methodist Church where John has been Sunday School Superintendent for many years. He also belongs to Knight's of Pythias Lodge, Farm Bureau, and has been active in county politics. Pat is a member of the Dana 49'ers Club, the Towne and

Countrie Garden Club, the "As You Like It" Club, Bono United Methodist Women, and a board member for the Indiana Baton Council.

KATHERINE LAQUETIA (MORRIS) CHRISTENSEN,

was born Aug. 19, 1958 at Vermillion County Hospital in Clinton, IN. She is the eldest daughter of Nelson Eugene Morris and Hazel Jewel Durham (last name known as Ray). At the age of three months, Kathy was dedicated at the Assembly of God Church on North Main Street and resided at the southwest corner of Elm and Third Street for only a short time (as a young child.)

Her grandparents, Josephine Earl and Nelson Lewis Morris, an electrician, lived in Rosedale, IN in the 1950's. Katherine's other grandparents, Homer and Ruby Durham, did not move to this area until 1967.

In 1979, Kathy married Dale Alan Christensen and became a resident of Coal City, IL. She has one son, Joseph Michael Christensen and three step-children, Kristin Ann, David Alan, and Susan Lynne Christensen.

Katherine L. Christensen

Now attending Joliet Junior College, she is pursuing a career in computer programming and writing.

The theme below, written by Katherine, honors all the unforgotten borrowed places in her life from Vermillion County and it's surrounding country acreage.

Borrowed Places

Resting comfortably in a recliner, I admire the collection of artwork on the smooth, plastered walls. However, across the room one piece captures my attention. A wooden, oak frame tenderly embraces an oil painting of a peaceful, scenic nature. I begin to see structures, hear sounds, and feel familiar emotions as my mind lulls back to my past of borrowed places.

In a small town, a withered, weather-beaten old house, consisting of a story and a half, sits beside an alleyway with plumply-pitted potholes. This house is certainly a treasure chest of unforgotten memories. Along one side of the yard, two bushes conceal ripe blackberries. Proudly, the conventional outhouse stands tall in the midst of the acre lot. Who would ever know a family of six lives here, except the past of borrowed places?

There are stables on the outskirts of a city behind a place called Demming Park. Within these stables, a little girl carefully brushes a fully-grown Appaloosa. Down the hill away from the barn dwells an enormous, huge tree in the middle of a sparsely graveled driveway. This green giant, an ever-dedicated nanny, patiently watches the barefoot youth mount her faithful four-legged creature. She continues her usual journey around the king-size body and then proceeds towards the beaten path of the pas-

ture. There is no confusion here. Freedom is a friend. Friends are plentiful among these borrowed places.

Dirt roads wind through hills of fenced country pastures. Within the wooden posts and rusty barbed wire, wild flowers and endless weeds outstretch their arms to the warmth of Heaven. Meanwhile, a contented squirrel quietly plays on the boulder near a pony. Where do fears exist in this protected acreage of borrowed places?

Around the edges of a pond are large rocks, some of which are engulfed in rainbows of flowers. This pond is like a mirror. Therefore, by looking within this mirror, I not only see my face but also my soul. When I search this inner sanctum, I find answers and receive assurance for my tomorrows. Many of life's decisions are made here at my borrowed places.

As my mind returns to reality, I find myself staring at this framed phantom. The peace and serenity of each location have been captured and placed on the canvas. At one time, they were a genuine reality but now are only a temporary place in time. The warmth, love, and happiness obtained from the strokes of the brush are the painter's life. I should know; I am this painter — from those borrowed places. *Submitted by Katherine L. Christensen*

ALONZO CITY, son of Miles and Emma, was born in Linton, IN, in 1911. He went to East Union School. He married Emily Symmonds Gutierres in 1932. Emily is the daughter of William and Orilla Smith Symmonds, born in Perth, IN, in 1903. She married Raymond Gutierres in 1919. Charles Ray was born in 1924. Raymond was drowned in 1926. They moved to Universal in 1940. Joyce was born in 1941.

"Lon" worked for Like-Nu Motors, Stran Steel, and retired from Alith Corporation, Danville, IL, in 1974. He also played guitar for dances in his younger years, and ran the Universal Garage.

Emily died in 1973 and was buried at Walnut Grove Cemetery in Clinton.

Alonzo was remarried in 1979 to Constant Strawser Jorden Rankin, who had three grown children. They are Ed Nelson Rankin, Judy Rankin Akers, and Shirley Jorden Christian.

Lon died in 1987 and is buried at Walnut Grove Cemetery in Clinton.

Charles Ray "Duck" Gutierres went to East Union School, Universal School, and Clinton High School. He married Kathern "Kate" Woodward of Georgetown, IL, in 1951. Pamela was born in 1952. Duck worked for Allis Chalmers, Indiana State Highway Department, and retired from Peabody Coal Company in 1986. Kate worked for the Vermillion County Hospital. They live on Kelly Hill outside Universal.

Pamela went to Universal School, Van Duyn School, and Clinton High School. She married Tony Chapman of Klondyke in 1969. They had two sons—Tony Ray and Troy. Both boys now attend South Vermillion High School. She divorced and married Rene Daniels of Klondyke in 1979. They now reside in Klondyke.

Joyce attended Universal School and Clinton High School. She married Harry Otto Reagan of Worthington, IN, in 1958. They lived in Illinois where Annette was born in 1959. They moved to Virginia and back to Universal. Meta was born in 1965. She divorced and married Donald Hall of Melcroft, PA, in 1969. They lived in Universal and

Terena was born in 1972. He adopted Meta. They divorced in 1981. Joyce and girls lived in Universal until 1985. She, Meta, and Terena moved to rural Parke County, where they still reside.

Annette Reagan married Charles "Chuck" Kernstein of rural Vigo County, in 1981. They now reside outside North Terre Haute.

Meta has worked for Parke County Ambulance Service, Wal-Mart, and Melita Corporation. She has also attended St. Mary's of the Woods College, and Indiana State University.

Terena has attended Van Duyn School, South Vermillion Middle School, Mecca School, and is now attending Riverton Parke High School.

BENSON CITY, was born in Linton in 1917. He married Evelyn Stewart of rural Vigo County in 1934. They had one son, Robert Benson "Benny", in 1935. Benson went to East Union School. Benson moved his family to Universal in 1939. He entered the U.S. Navy during World War II and served in the Pacific. He worked as a miner for Snowhill and Pyramid Mines, and also at the Newport Army Ammunition Plant. They lived in Universal until 1955. From 1955 to 1976, they lived in Terre Haute. When they retired from Ann Page Foods of Terre Haute, they moved to Clinton where they still reside.

Benny, son of Benson and Evelyn, went to East Union School, Universal School, Clinton High School (1952), and Indiana State University (1956). He worked for Pepsi Company while in high school and at Ann Page as a chemist. In approximately 1969, he worked for the U.S. government as a chemist. He married Jan Stewart of Jasonville in 1958. They lived in Universal. They divorced and he married Evelyn (?), who had two daughters, Leigh and Lynn. They moved to Houston, TX, where he died in 1972. He is buried at Walnut Grove Cemetery.

ELMER CITY, was born in Linton, IN, in 1899. His parents were Miles and Emma City. Elmer and his wife had four children: Benson, Damon, Emma Jean, and Beatrice. Elmer was a miner and moved approximately the same times and places that his father's family did.

Elmer lost his wife young, just after the birth of Beatrice. Elmer was called "Chalk-eye" by most of his friends. He played the guitar for a lot of country dances in his younger years.

In the early 1940's, "Chalk-eye" moved to Terre Haute and lived there until he retired. He moved to Universal in the early 1960's and lived there until he died.

Damon City lived in Vermillion County until he entered the U.S. Army during World War II. He married Thelma Halderman of Worthington, IN, and worked for Crane Naval Ammunition Plant until he retired. His children are Mary Dee, Dewey, Zenobia, Diane, and Jeff. He died in approximately 1983.

Emma Jean went to East Union School and Universal School. She married Leroy Inman of Worthington, IN. They had four children: Jack, Eugene, Penny, and Randy. She divorced and married Walt Disney of Martinsville. They have two children, Walt II and Walinda. They now reside in Martinsville.

Beatrice "Beady" City went to East Union School and Universal School. She married John Halderman of Worthington and moved all over this country as he was a carrier man in the Army. They had four children: Nancy, John, Susan, and Terry. She divorced and married Thomas Tow of California. She is an LPN and her family are still there.

MILES CITY, was born in Linton, IN, in 1872. His parents were Joshua and Martha Seacrest Citty.

The City family emigrated to the United States from the black Forest of Germany in 1710. The original name was Zestin. Over the years it has been changed from Zestin to Zetty, Setty, Citty, and finally to City.

Miles married Emma Hoops in 1890. They had six children but raised only three: Rosco, Elmer, and Alonzo.

Miles was a miner and followed the mines. In 1920, he and his entire family moved from Linton to Indianapolis. Then in approximately 1922, they moved again to northern Vigo County. They moved again in 1925 to a now defunct town of Easytown where Miles worked in that mine until he retired.

Emma did home sewing and she died in 1934. She is buried in Shirley Cemetery just north of the old town.

Miles and the rest of his family moved to Universal during the years of 1939 and 1940. Miles lived there until his death in 1948. He is buried beside Emma.

Miles' Rosco joined the United States Calvery, Black Horse Division. He was shot while watching a fight on the street in Hawaii. The bullet hit his spine and he was paralyzed. He was sent to California and later home. He developed TB of the bone. In spite of this he married, but he only lived a short time and he died in 1924. He is buried in Barthalomew Cemetery in northern Vigo County.

HARRY CLEMENZ, and Edith West were married in March, 1923. Harry, who was born in Lawrence County, June 12, 1900, was the son of William and Mary Lou Kerchmier Clemenz. Edith, born in Fountain County, Feb. 22, 1903, was the daughter of Charles and Cora (Hale) West of Parke County near Tangier, IN.

Harry and Edith moved to Vermillion County after they were married. Harry worked for the C.& E.I. (Chicago and Eastern Illinois) Railroad as a car inspector until he moved to Phoenix, AZ, in 1943, and worked for the Southern Pacific Railroad until he retired. He died Nov. 8, 1985, in San Diego, CA, and was buried in Phoenix.

Harry and Edith lived in Fairview and Clinton and had a daughter, Martha Ann, born May 19, 1924, and died July 25, 1925. She died of an illness called Summer Sickness. Charles William was born May 7, 1926, and Barbara Jean was born July 16, 1932, all in Clinton.

Charles and Patricia Peterson were married July 1, 1944, in Clinton. Charles served in the U.S. Navy during World War II. Charles and Pat had four children, Michael Lee, born March, 1946; Karen Sue, born December, 1948; William Ernest, born Feb. 14, 1950; and David Charles, born in southern Indiana, September, 1953. Charles and family later moved to Indianapolis where he was employed by Johnson Controls until his death, Feb. 5, 1977. He died of Leukemia.

Barbara married Bob Potter in 1950. They had a daughter, Donna Kay, born Jan. 6, 1952. They divorced in 1952, and Barbara married Tony Davitto of Universal, IN, Feb. 20, 1953. Tony adopted Donna in 1953. They built a home where the old Woodsy Grocery Store used to be, in the middle of the 1200 block on the west side of Fifth Street. They had a son, Ricky Allen, born Feb. 17, 1954. Tony was employed with Dupont, Dana Plant, until it closed in 1957. They moved to Idaho Falls, ID. Tony worked for Phillips Petroleum Company at the National Reactor Testing Station at Arco, ID, until 1962, when they moved back to Indiana and settled in Danville, in Hendricks County. Tony was employed by Link Belt (Bearing Plant) until he retired in 1980.

Edith West Clemenz divorced Harry and married Farris G. Pyle of Parke County in 1955. She moved to Rockville and lived until her death, Dec. 30, 1980.

Bob Potter died April, 1987, in Taylor, MI.

ROBERT CLINGAN, was born Aug. 26, 1916 to D. Earl and Flossie Clingan at R.#1 Perrysville, IN, on the farm purchased in 1900 by his grandfather, Dennis Robert Clingan, he graduated from Perrysville High School and in 1935 was married to Letha Mae Jordan of St. Bernice. She is the daughter of Wallace and Hazel Shuey Jordan.

A son, Wallace Earl Clingan was born in 1938. He also graduated from Perrysville High School in 1956. In 1959, he was married to Mary Janelle Crisp, the daughter of L.D. and Maxine Crisp of Perrysville.

Two children were born to this union, Jenifer Noelle in 1962 and Dennis Eric in 1964 and they each were graduated from North Vermillion High School.

In 1983, Jenifer was married to Kurt Dinsmore and they reside in Albuquerque, NM, where she is a radiologist and is going to New Mexico University with a business major and Kurt is a detective on the Albuquerque police force.

In 1985, Dennis moved to Albuquerque and is a machinist at Sandia Labs.

CLOVER, The James Clover family first settled in Vermillion County in 1820, and built a log cabin on the northwest corner of what is now Spangler Cemetery, west of Clinton. They were descendants of Clover's from Pennsylvania.

One of the sons, Joseph A. Clover, was three at this time. The family later built a two-room house a quarter mile north along the foothills and moved into it, later adding more rooms and an upstairs. It was known as the Buckhorn House because of the deer antlers hung outside. After clearing fields, farming was the principle vocation. Attending Church and neighborhood gatherings were the social part of life.

Home of William R. Clover (later Howard R. Clover)

In 1840 Joseph Clover married Druscilla Reeder. They had five children, one of which was William R. Clover. He, too, farmed, mined, (on his own property) and kept bees, as his father had done. He married Mary Alice Ross in 1875. To start housekeeping, they built a two-room house, with summer kitchen addition, on top of "Clover" hill. As the family grew to eight children, they added rooms, hallways and an upstairs, making a ten-room house with large front porch. The four daughters were teachers and nurses and three of the sons chose various occupations. Some served in World War I. One, Howard R. Clover, chose to remain on the farm.

Howard married Nora Ford of Center neighborhood in 1914. She was the great-granddaughter of Augustus Ford, one of the first settlers of Helt's Prairie, who fought in the War of 1812. There is a monument in his honor in Helt's Prairie Cemetery.

Howard and wife lived in a six-room house near the larger one, moving in with the grandfather in 1925. They attended the old Centenary Methodist Church. He farmed, mined, kept bees, had a dairy and raised cattle. There were three daughters and one son in this family. Two of the daughters married and moved away, later. The other daughter, Helen, and brother Paul C. Clover (of Paris, IL) ran the farm after the death of their father in 1972. Helen and her husband, Harry L. Ahlemeyer, later bought the farm (which they named "Clomeyer") and are present owners, with tenant farmers.

The large Clover home was empty for several years after Howard Clover's death. It and the smaller house deteriorated to the point it became necessary to demolish them. This was a sad decision because both houses had many happy memories, and served the Clover family well for three generations.

The Ahlemeyer's now live in Indianapolis. He is retired from Cummins. They spend a lot of time at the farm where they have modernized a small cabin, formerly the dairy-house. They have a daughter, Harriet MacKinnon, who lives with her husband and twin daughters in Westfield, IN, and a son, John H. Ahlemeyer. He built a house on his property at the farm, where he lives with his wife, daughter and son. He is employed at Eli-Lilly at Clinton, and helps manage the farm in his spare time.

COFFIN, The first of name of Coffin in America was Tristram who at the age of 34 with his wife, Dionis and five children, emigrated to Salisbury, MA from England. In 1659 Tristram, with a group of nine Salisbury men, went to Nantucket Island. With these nine others he purchased the Island.

Dr. William Coffin, son of Tristram Coffin, and his wife, Eunice Worth, came to Vermillion County from North Carolina in 1822. They went to Eugene Township in 1823. William Coffin entered several tracts of land from the U.S. Government at the time of their settlement. Most of the area at that time was dense forest-populated with wild animals and Indians.

Coffin Homestead

Vermillion County was not established until

1824 with four townships. Eugene was then a part of Vermillion and Highland Townships. So at the time the Coffins settled, neither county nor township was established. Dr. William Coffin was 25 years old when he settled in Eugene Township and for ten years was associated with a Dr. Scott of Newport in the practice of Medicine. In 1849 he journeyed across desert plains via ox team to the Gold Diggings in California, leaving his family in Eugene Township. He died in California.

Simpson Worth Coffin, son of William, was 20 years old when his father became one of the "49'ers". At the time of William's death he was the owner of 480 acres in Section 8 and 17 in Eugene Township.

Great-Grandfather Simpson was born May 10, 1829 on the old homestead commonly known as the Collett Farm which is South and East of the Collett Home. He was a farmer and was educated at Indiana University and Wabash College. He was a member of the Masonic Lodge, (being the sixth member raised,) was a friend of Joseph Collett (Collett Home benefactor) and was named by him to be one of the first board managers. When almost 80 years old, Simpson died on Dec. 5, 1909. At the time of his death he was one of the oldest continuous residents of Eugene Township.

Simpson Worth and wife were the parents of two sons and one daughter. Belle (born 1864, died 1930) was a merchant and early teacher in the county schools. My grandfather, Milton Worth Coffin, was the eldest born (born 1857, died 1940). He was the 13th member of the early Presbyterian Church and a Charter Member of the Order of Eastern Star in 1903. He and his wife, Emma, had three children: Blanche, who died in infancy in 1890; Gladys Coffin Thomas, my mother, died in 1978; and Eliazabeth Coffin Wiggins, youngest, now resides in Indianapolis after spending many years as an abstractor in Vermillion County.

The only descendants of Simpson Worth Coffin now living are one granddaughter, Elizabeth, three great-grandchildren - Kenneth Coffin Wiggins of Speedway, IN; William Charles Wiggins of Indianapolis, and myself, Anabeth Thomas Jenkins Lallish of Cayuga, IN.

There are five great-great-grandchildren: Janet Lynn Jenkins Martin, Georgetown, IL; William Thomas Jenkins, Danville, IL; Gregory Joel Jenkins, Indianapolis (Carmel), IN; Kenna Wiggins Fetherolf, Speedway, IN; Andrew John Wiggins, Speedway, IN.

There are great-great-great-grandchildren as follows: Jeffery Scott James, Georgetown, IL; Brian Thomas James, Oakwood, IL; Ryan Scott Jenkins, Danville, IL; and Evan William Jenkins, Danville, IL.

The Coffin Homestead remains in our family, having been in our family, for 185 years (no original buildings remain). No remaining residents with the name of Coffin reside in Eugene Township or Vermillion County. *Submitted by Anabeth Thomas Jenkins Lallish*

JAMES COLE,

JAMES COLE, was born in Essex County, England, in 1590, and died in Hartford, CT, in 1652. He was married to Anne Edwards in 1625 at St. Dustans, Stephany, England. James and Anne immigrated to Hartford, CT, in 1635, where he was a follower of Thomas Hooker, the famous Colonial clergyman who was one of the founders of Hartford. Children were John and Samuel.

John Cole, was born in London, England, (?)

date, and died in 1685 in Hartford, CT. He was married to Mary B. in London in 1613, and died in London in 1685. Samuel Cole, born and died in Hartford, CT, dates unknown, was married to Mary (not certain). Samuel and Mary had a son, Samuel.

John Henderson Cole

Samuel Cole, was born in 1673 in Hartford, CT, and died in 1760 in Norwalk, CT. He was married to Mary Kingsburg, who was born in Wilton, CT, and died in 1746 in Norwalk, CT. Samuel and Mary's son was Caleb.

Caleb Cole was born Feb. 8, 1703, in Hartford, CT, and died in 1780 in Sharon, CT. He was married to Ann Whitney St. John on Dec. 20, 1742. Children of Caleb and Ann were David, Ann, Joseph, Thaddius, Matthew, Rebecca, Abigail, Samuel, Mary, Racheal, Zeburon and Erastus.

Matthew was born at Sharon, CT, on Jan. 22, 1746 and died in 1826. He was married to Lois Tyler at Baliton, NY. Matthew was a Captain in the American Revolution and commanded a Company when Tyron invaded the Colony. Their children were Timothy Tyler, William, Erastus, Calvin, Milo and Almira.

Milo Cole, was born in 1802 in New York, probably in Broome County. He married Mary Ann Lacey. She was a daughter of Daniel and Elizabeth Pettit Lacey who came from Dryden, NY, through Ohio into Vermillion Co., IN. Mary Lacey had two brothers, Daniel and Benjamin. Milo died on Jan. 21, 1844, and Mary in 1880 in Vermillion County. Their children were Oliver, Matthew, Elizabeth, Eli, John, Anna, Mary, Calvin, Benjamin, Daniel.

Calvin Cole was born in Ohio on Mar. 27, 1838. He married Hannah Elvira Swem on Apr. 4, 1860. Calvin enlisted in the Union Army Feb. 15, 1865, and was discharged June 17, 1865. He served another year and was paid $400.00. With part of this money, he bought 40 acres of land in Highland Township, Section 5, Twp. 18, Range 10. Children of Calvin and Hannah were Charles, Levi, William, John, James, Chauncey, Rollo, Eva, Lida, Lee, Grover.

John Henderson Cole was born Mar. 14, 1867, and died Aug. 6, 1952. He married Lillian Ellen Adams on Mar. 26, 1899. John farmed and was Township Assessor and a life long Democrat. Children are Edgar, Tessie, Mary E., Ima Lee, John, Paul, Wayne, Gladys.

Mary E. Cole, was born Dec. 21, 1904, and married Harry Green in 1930. She had one son, John Stanley born in 1931 and died in 1953. She married Norman Skinner on Oct. 1, 1941. Children are Norman L., born Nov. 27, 1942, and Curtis, born Nov. 16, 1945. Children of Norman and Dorothy (Mitchell) are Norman L. and Nicole Skinner. Children of Curtis and Candace are Cory and Chad Skinner.

DORIS MARIE COLLIER,

DORIS MARIE COLLIER, was born July 18, 1910 in Plainfield, Hendricks Co., IN, to Orlie Thomas and Bertha Nolan Collier (See related biography). She attended Bono School in the elementary grades but graduated from Dana High School in 1925 at the age of 15. After a year at Indiana State Teachers' College, she taught elementary grades in Dana and in Clinton until 1935 when she began teaching in Hebron, Porter Co., IN. Doris (Dorie) was married to Monte Carson Morrow June 12, 1938. They resided in Hebron, IN, where their two children Melinda Jane and Charles James were born. On Oct. 29, 1976, after a teaching career of 45 years, Doris died in Hebron, Porter Co., IN, where she is buried. *Submitted by Pauline C. Shrine*

PAULINE COLLIER,

PAULINE COLLIER, the second daughter of Orlie Thomas and Bertha May Nolan Collier (see related biography), was born at Plainfield, IN, Oct. 29, 1912. By Thanksgiving that year Orlie had deserted his little family so they moved back to the Nolan family farm west and adjacent to the present Ernie Pyle School in Helt Township, Vermillion County. There they stayed with Grandpa Alfred and Grandma Sarah Florence Osmon Nolan (See related biographies) for at least a year when Mother Bertha moved into Permelia Peyton Alberts' three roomed cabin and was her companion for the next eight years. By the time Aunt Millie died, Pauline was in the fourth grade at Bono School, where Bert Helt, the principal, pulled a couple of her teeth by fastening them to a string tied to his office door. He also taught her to count to 20 in Latin. (Maybe that was the reason she later made A's in Latin.) Upon their moving to Dana, Lillie Malone was her teacher for her second semester of the fourth grade.

It was Pauline's responsibility to do all the marketing for the boarding house Mother Bertha established on West A Street there in Dana so she became well acquainted with Orville Starr, the manager of the A & P, with Dave Reed, who assured her his beef was, "As tender as a women's heart!" and with Tim Clark, the grocer, who had the freshest coconut in town. While Sister Doris was the housekeeper, Pauline became the lackey boy, dishwasher, etc. Sometimes there were 15 or 20 dinner buckets to "fix" for construction workers for route 36, coal miners, etc. It never dawned on Doris or her to complain because they "were saving for college."

Although she has a scholarship from Jacksonville, IL, Women's College and had been accepted at the Union Hospital in Indianapolis, she finally graduated from Indiana State Teacher's College in 1934 with a BS degree in math and English. After a year doing social service work in Lake County, she taught a year at St. Bernice.

On Dec. 28, 1935 "Polly" married Charles William Shriner, whom she had met in college, and lived east of Huntington where their children, Jerry Alice, Jane Ann, William Nolan, and Betty Pauline were born. Polly helped with the truck farming until 1955 when Jerry left for Purdue. At that time Polly was drafted to teach in the local school. By the time the other three children had finished college, Bill and Polly were spending time three weeks each, every summer hiking the Appalachian Trail and canoeing and fishing in the Quetico Provincial Park. In 1965 they also spent three weeks in Equador where their son and wife, Bill and Joy, were Peace Corps volunteers.

In 1976 Bill and Polly retired from the Huntington County School and now winter at Melbourne

Beach, FL, where they hike and snorkel. They have 15 grandchildren and two great grandchildren. *Submitted by Pauline C. Shriner*

EDWARD EUGENE "GENE" CONARD AND SALLY BARRICK ROSE CONARD,

Gene was born in Vermillion County in a farmhouse just outside of Dana. He was born to Harley P. and Pearl Ely Conard on Apr. 25, 1926. He attended school in St. Bernice for six years and then in Dana where he graduated in 1944. Upon graduation he entered the Navy where he served two years in the Pacific. He moved to Kokomo, IN in 1946 where he worked for eight years at The Globe American Corporation. He then moved back to Dana where he drove a truck until 1958 when he was burned over 80% of his body. He was in the hospital almost two years. He has been employed as Supervisor of the guards at the Inland Container Corporation for Advance Security for the past 12 years.

Edward "Gene" Conard Family

Sally was born in Danville, IL on Aug. 6, 1934, to Viola Sparks Barrick and Paul G. Barrick. She moved to Urbana, IL in 1937 where she lived with her grandparents. She attended schools in Urbana, IL. She received her GED from Indiana in 1975 and attended Indiana State University for one semester. She worked at General Electric in Danville, IL for 15 years.

They were married in 1954 at the Dana United Methodist Church. They are the parents of two children and the grandparents of four. They have a foster son and a foster granddaughter.

Louwanna Marie Conard was born Dec. 26, 1954, at the Vermillion County Hospital in Clinton, IN. She has two sons, Eric and Matthew Wallace.

Charles Eugene Conard was born on Nov. 9, 1956, at St. Elizabeth Hospital in Danville, IL. He has a son, Christopher Eugene, and a daughter, Danielle Marie.

Robert Eugene Conard, foster son was born Feb. 17, 1950, son of William and Irma Morgan Conard. He has one daughter, Sandra Jean.

They are members of the Dana United Methodist Church. Gene is a Trustee and Sally is on the Board. Both of them were very active with their children in Boy Scouts, Girl Scouts, Band Boosters, 4-H, and Little League as well as Babe Ruth. Gene holds a Life Membership in the Clinton Moose Lodge, K of P in Dana and is also a member of the American Legion, Cayuga, IN. Sally is a past president of The Vermillion County Homemakers, a charter member of the Hospital Guild at Clinton, and is a member of the Dames Club in Dana.

They have lived in the same home since 1960 in Dana.

ROBERT EUGENE CONARD AND SOPEE VUTIVUT CONARD,

Robert was born in Clinton, IN on Feb. 17, 1950, the son of William E. and Irma Morgan Conard. He lived in northern Indiana for awhile but came to Dana to live with his Uncle and family, Gene and Sally Conard. He became their foster son and attended South Vermillion schools, graduating in 1969. He worked at General Electric in Danville, IL and then joined the Army. He was in the Army for 15 years and retired on a medical retirement. He attended Indiana State University and he is now employed for the Postal Service in Terre Haute, IN. He is a member of the Dana United Methodist Church.

Robert, Sopee, and Sandra Conard

He has two brothers, Roger Dale and William Richard Conard, of California. He also has three half sisters and one half brother.

Sopee Vutivut was born in Bangkok, Thailand, on Dec. 23, 1950, the oldest of five girls. Her parents are Choom and Sally Vutivut. She attended school in Thailand and graduated from there. She is employed at Sears in Terre Haute, IN.

They were married on June 2, 1972, in Bangkok. They have one daughter, Sandra Dean, who was born on Dec. 30, 1976, at Fort Campbell, KY.

They decided to settle in Indiana after their military career ended. They bought a home and plan to remain hoosiers.

CHARLES EUGENE CONARD AND DEBBIE MARIE SHEEHY CONARD,

Charles Eugene Conard was born on Nov. 9, 1956, in St. Elizabeth Hospital, Danville, IL. He is the son of Edward "Gene" and Sally Conard. He attended South Vermillion Schools and graduated in 1975. Upon graduation he entered the Marine Corps. He is making a career of his military service and has 13 years of active duty. He holds the rank of Gunnery Sergeant and is a Weather Forecaster. He is an Eagle Scout and is still active in Scouting with his son. He is a registered Sports Official and he is active in sports. He is a member of the Dana United Methodist Church. While active in the MYF he was able to take two bicycle trips over 1000 miles each. He also was a Boy Scout Camp employee.

Charles and Debbie Conard

Debbie was born on Aug. 10, 1958, in Northern Indiana. Her parents are Henry and Agnes Sheehy, her grandparents who adopted her. Her mother Kathy Sheehy Trantham Winkler, lives in northern Indiana. She attended schools in norther Indiana and graduated from South Vermillion High School in 1976. Debbie has one sister and one brother.

They were married on Aug. 6, 1977, in San Clementee, CA. They have two children: Christopher Eugene, born in South Carolina on Dec. 19 1978, and Danielle Marie born May 14, 1984, at Chanute Air Force Base, Rantoul, IL.

They have lived in California, South Carolina, Hawaii, Indiana, Illinois, Japan, and now they are back in Beaufort, SC.

Being in the military is a family career so Debbie generally finds employment on whatever base they happen to be.

WILLIAM RICHARD CONARD AND MINNIE PHIPPS CONARD,

moved to Vermillion County in 1909 from Oden, IN. He farmed in this area for many years on shares. They are the parents of four children. She died in April, 1934, and he died in September, 1956. They are both buried in the Bono Cemetery.

They farmed three or four farms in the area. He retired from farming in the early 40's. He and his son, Harley, shared in the farming chores and in his later years he lived with them in their home in Dana.

William, Minnie, and Harley Conard

Their oldest son, Harley, married Pearl Ely in 1921 in New Jersey. They were the parents of two sons, William Ely Conard and Edward Eugene Conard. Harley worked on the railroad in New Jersey after serving in the Army in World War I. He had his right arm severed in an accident in 1920. After his marriage they moved to Indiana where he joined his father in farming. He was killed in a car accident in 1966, and Pearl died in December of the same year. They are buried in the Bono Cemetery.

Elmer Jay, their second son, lived and worked in the area for many years as a Car Salesman. He retired and moved to Sullivan where he died in July, 1977. He was married to the former Ruth Prather. She was a cook for many years at schools in the area. She is a member of the Dana United Methodist Church and is now residing at the Millers Merry Manor Sullivan, IN.

Lena Conard, their eldest daughter, married Carl Longfellow. Early in their married life they moved to Kokomo, IN where he worked as a carpenter and a laborer in the steel mill. She was a housewife except during World War II when she worked outside of the home. They had one son, Bobby, who died at the age of eight. Carl died in 1954, and Lena sold their home which they had built. She moved in with her sister where she lived until her death in 1971. They are all buried in the Bono Cemetery.

Thelma Conard the youngest daughter and child,

graduated from Helt Township High School, Bono. She married John F. Foltz. They lived in the St. Bernice area for several years where he worked and she was employed by Dr. Green as his office secretary. In the early 40's they moved to Kokomo, Indiana. John went to work in the Steel Mill and Thelma worked in the dispensary at the Globe Amercan Corporation. Later she worked for Firestone, she retired with over 20 years service. John retired from Continal Steel at 65 years of age and has enjoyed his beautiful flower gardens.

They had three grandsons, four great-grandsons, two great-granddaughters, and eight great-great-grandchildren.

JANE CONN, In the summer of 1968, Jane Conn moved to Perrysville from Anderson, IN. Her son, Mike and daughter, Cindy were with her. Her daughter Lois was already residing in Perrysville.

Mary Jane was born June 10, 1922, in St. Paul, MN to Charles Henry and Amanda Alma Graham. Jane grew up in East Alton, IL. In 1943, she married Marvin S. Conn. Jane still lives in Perrysville where she has been the librarian at the Perrysville Branch Library since 1970.

William Charles (Bill) was born Jan. 24, 1945, in Anderson, IN. He is the oldest of four children. He served in the U.S. Army for 20 years, which included two tours in Vietnam. He has three sons. Anthony Randall from his first marriage and William Charles Jr. and Roger Dale from his marriage to Linda Turbitt of Maryland. He now lives in Delaware.

Lois Ann was born Aug. 29, 1947, in Anderson, IN. She married Samuel Lee Reed in 1965. They were divorced in 1974. They had two children, Lee Allen and Teresa Lee. Lois currently lives in Lawton, OK.

Kenneth Graham (Mike) was born Nov. 30, 1953 in Anderson, IN. He attended and graduated from North Vermillion High School in 1971. He currently resides in Covington, IN, with his wife Aleta M. and his stepson Jason E. Wheaton. He is a former member of Mensa and is also a private pilot.

Cynthia Kaye (Cindy) was born Sept. 5, 1958 in Anderson, IN. She attended Highland Elementary in Perrysville and graduated from North Vermillion High School in 1976. She was a member of the National Honor Society and was in Who's Who in American High Schools of 1976. Cindy served in the U.S. Army for two years and is still in the U.S. Army Reserves. She is living in Hopewell, IL with her husband, Bill Good and their two children, Michelle LeAnn and Leigh Thomas.

JOHN WILLIAM COOPER AND REBECCA WOLFE COOPER, my great-great-grandparents were born in Hampshire Co., VA (West Virginia) in the 1790's. The Wolfe family was in Ross Co., OH, by 1800; the Coopers by 1813. Deeds made in 1827 by John and Rebecca selling his inherited lands in Hampshire County, and hers in Ross Co., OH, give their residence as Vermillion Co., IN. A deed made by Rebecca in 1847, gives John's death as 1847, her as his widow, and a son-in-law as co-signer of the deed.

John Cooper and his brother were surveyors and are reported to have worked for the government in plotting out the new country, moving west as the new country developed. In 1847, there was a great movement of people from Vermillion County to Iowa. Son David and John's brother were in the caravan. The Coopers settled there in Washington and surrounding counties.

Albert Taylor, Sarah Angeline Rhoten, James Thomas, and Marion Marcus.

John and Rebecca are reported to have had 16 children, but I have found only 11. All were born in Ross Co., OH. Most of them were married in Vermillion County, namely:

Sarah b. Apr. 20, 1816; d. Oct. 30, 1853; m. May 29, 1830 to Goldstein Nutterfee.

Elizabeth m. Jan. 23, 1827 to William Swann.

Nancy m. Aug. 22, 1832 to Benjamin Pier. Only information is they sold acreage in 1838 to John Cooper.

Mary Ann b. ca 1823; d. after 1887; m. Feb. 14, 1887 to Abraham Shannon.

David b. Mar. 20, 1820; d. after 1887; m. Apr. 6, 1843 to Rebecca Malone.

Theodosia b. ca 1824; m. Feb. 14, 1841 to Orison Kellogg, a widower living in Chicago in 1887.

Charlotte m. Aug. 30, 1846 to Seth Goodwin. Husband in 1887 was Jerome Chandler.

Margaret m. to Simeon Barrister.

John William, no information; living in California in 1887.

George died as a youth.

My line comes down through Rebecca Jane who married David Frazier Taylor of the Dana-Clinton area.

Rebecca b. Mar. 8, 1826; d. Dec. 6, 1908 in Dallas Co., MO; m. Nov. 10, 1844 to David Frazier Taylor. David was a cooper by trade.

They had eight children, seven growing to adults, namely:

Eliza Ann who died as an infant.

Rebecca m. Jesse Foose; the only one in the family to live her entire life in Vermillion County, living to be in her 90's.

Sarah A. Mariah m. William Meade in Missouri.

James Alexander died as a youth at age 18.

Martha Jane m. William Myers in Vermillion County.

Levi Calvin m. Susan Munholland in Missouri.

Georgia Ann m. William Willhoite in Missouri.

Albert (my grandfather) b. Dec. 15, 1851, Vermillion County; d. May 19, 1939, Vinita, OK; m. Sept. 22, 1872, Dallas Co., MO to Sarah Angeline Rhoten, a native of Parke County.

The Taylors moved in 1880 to Dallas Co., MO. In 1906 Albert with his two sons, James and Marion, both born in Vermillion County, and their children moved to Indian Territory in October before Oklahoma statehood the next year. Albert also had a son Elmer and a daughter Gertie, born in Missouri, who came to the Territory with them.

Sources of information: Records of Rebecca Foose; Marriage records in Vermillion County; Probate of Thomas Cooper, Jr.'s will in Hampshire Co., WV; Probate of David Wolfe's estate in Ross Co., OH; History of Washington Co., IA, 1887, biography of David Cooper; Family records of Lucille Webb, of the Cooper-Nutterfee line; Hampshire County census of 1784; Ross-Fayette Co., OH, census of 1820; Vermillion Co., IN, census of 1830, 1840, 1850; Washington Co., IA, census of 1850, 1860.

DOMINIC ANTHONY COSTELLO, was born July 18, 1908, in East Mineral, KS, to Italian parents — Julia and Andrew. In the early 1900's many families followed the coal mines in order to make a living — and so the Costello family came to Clinton, IN, because of the many mines in the area.

Dom became a great boxer in Clinton's books. His career ended when he married Martha Louise Miller on Sept. 2, 1935. She was a school teacher at Blanford at the time but the marriage was kept a secret for fear of losing her job!

Dominic Costello

Four children added to the Costello family. Martha L. known as Marna in 1937, Dominic Anthony in 1940, better known as Tony, the Barber; Patrick Michael (Mike) in 1952 became a teacher and coach, and Gina Marie was born in 1955 and has become a nurse.

Highlights of the family where when Dom was elected Sheriff of Vermillion County in 1949. Martha says, "we were in jail ten years! Honestly we had a happy family life — feeding the prisoners, returning runaway dogs and taking telephone calls for many people (telephones were scarce then). Honestly there was never a dull moment."

Dom served as treasurer and was elected in 1954 to Executive Committee of Indiana Sheriff's Association. He was always ready to listen and to help others.

Now it is up to the grandchildren to keep the family name in good shape. To name a "few" they are Jamee Burdick and her two children, Brooke and Michael; Angela and Dominic; Andrew, Patrick, and Julia Marie; all of Clinton; and Kylee Marie of Rockville.

CRANES, Benjamin and Miriam Fisk Crane and eight of their 13 children came from Vermont to Vermillion Co., IN, in 1839. They were farmers, businessmen, tanners of hides, speculators, ran hotels and grocery stores.

The children who came to Indiana:

Erastus G. Crane and Laura Temple. They have five children. He helped start Center Church in 1853 and donated land for second Bales school house in Helt Township. He helped raise his brothers' children.

Benjamin and Sarah Crane lived in Newport, IN, and later in Danville, IL, where he was a merchant. He was a Presbyterian. They had three children.

Sylvanus B. Crane ran a hotel and grocery store and a distillery in Muscatine, IA. He's a charter member of Hawkeye Masonic Lodge and Muscatine Agriculture Society. He married Philina T. Taull of Iowa. He had one child.

Leander Crane married Mary Ann Richardson and lived in Newport with their two children. After her death he went to Muscatine, IA and worked as a stone cutter.

Carlton W. Crane was in business in Newport, IN. He first married Maria Sible, and after her death he married Barbara Hopkins. He had eight children.

Miriam Julia Crane married Archibald Wishard. They had three children. She helped raise her relatives. She later married Andrew Whitesell.

Mariam Elmira Crane married William I. Nichols. They had a son who is buried at Higbee Cemetery, Helt Township.

Joseph Dunbar Crane married Mary Smith. They had no children. He's in business in Danville, IL.

Descendants of this family went into Illinois, Kansas, Missouri, Oklahoma, Texas, Washington, and California.

Some descendants still live in Vermillion Co., IN. *Submitted by Ernestine Brown*

CHARLES WILLIAM CRIST AND IRMA LEE PRATHER CRIST,

Irma Lee Prather is the youngest daughter of Dewey and Mabel Wilcoxen Prather born in Rileysburg on Nov. 15, 1925.

After attending school in Rilesburg, she graduated from Perrysville High School in 1943. She graduated from Indiana State Teachers College (now Indiana State University) with a degree in Home Economics and Commerce in June, 1947. Later she returned for an elementary degree. She accepted a position as secretary to the Dean of Women on campus and later worked as secretary to the Supervision Teachers in Mishawaka, IN.

Irma Lee was married to Charles William "Bill" Crist on Dec. 19, 1948.

Bill, born May 12, 1927, the only son of James Riley and Moyne E. Neal Crist, was reared in Clay Co., IN. A graduate from Lewis Township High School (Coalmont, IN). His college education was interrupted when he enlisted in the United States Navy during World War II and served as a Pharmacist Mate. After his tour of duty, he continued his education and graduated from Indiana State Teachers College with a Bachelor of Science degree and a Masters degree in Mathematics and Physical Education.

Bill taught Math and coached at Main Junior High School in Mishawaka, IN for two years. He then moved to Rileysburg and entered business with his father-in-law and managed the family implement and farm supply store for 14 years.

A son, James Dewey, was born Feb. 15, 1951 in Mishawaka.

Their oldest daughter, Joyce Margaret, was born Feb. 25, 1953. Lynn Kathleen, their youngest child, was born June 21, 1958.

In 1964, Irma Lee became the first kindergarten teacher in the Highland Elementary School. She taught there for 12 years before teaching Home Economics and Business classes at North Vermillion High School. Irma Lee retired in 1985 after 21 years in the School Corporation.

Bill returned to teaching in 1965 in the North Vermillion School Corporation teaching Junior High and High School Mathematics. He also served the school as a coach and was Athletic Director from 1966 to 1971. Bill retired from the school corporation in 1987 after teaching 22 1/2 years.

Both work for The Rileysburg Church and other community activities.

Irma Lee and Bill's children all graduated from North Vermillion High School and Indiana State University. Their son Jim presently resides in Morocco, IN, and he teaches Social Studies and coaches at North Newton High School.

Joyce married Kenneth Lyle Olsen on Dec. 27, 1975, in the Rileysburg Church. They make their home in Attica, IN. She teaches in the Attica Elementary School and Ken teaches at Fountain Central High School. They have two sons, Kevin James, born May 15, 1980, and Keith Andrew born Apr. 2, 1983.

Lynn now lives in Indianapolis, IN where she works as a Registered Nurse in St. Vincent Hospital.

Bill and Irma Lee are enjoying their retirement and are pleased to remain active in the community.

REX AND LUCILE CROWDER,

Rex Crowder has been a Shell Service station operator in Perrysville since July 19, 1933. In January 1929 he married Lucile Rhodes. He served on the Vermillion County Hospital Board 16 years and on the Highland Township advisory board eight terms. He is a charter member of the Lions Club. He graduated from Perrysville High School in 1924. They have two sons James Robert and Rex Jr.

James Robert, May 8, 1932, attended Perrysville Schools, graduating in 1950. He graduated from barber school at Indianapolis, and opened his own shop in Cayuga in 1951. He married Marcia Heidrick in June, 1953. In 1976 he closed the barbershop, became an insurance agent and a Realtor. Marcia graduated from Perrysville in 1950. She is secretary in their office. They have two sons, Daniel Alan and Thomas Lane.

Rex Crowder

Daniel Alan, July, 1954, attended Cayuga school, and graduated from North Vermillion in 1972. He graduated from Indiana State University in 1976 majoring in accounting. He married Luann Hollingsworth, March 1976. She graduated from North Vermillion in 1972, also Ivy Tech in 1976. In 1978, Dan was a comptroller for American Fletcher National Bank in Deerfield Beach, FL. In 1981 they came back to Indiana and opened an accounting office in Brownsburg. Dan enrolled in Indiana University School of Law, graduating in May 1985, and was admitted to the Bar October, 1985. They have two sons, Matthew Alan, Mar. 8, 1980, and Michael Robert, Jan. 29, 1982.

Thomas Lane, June 1957, attended Cayuga School, graduated from North Vermillion in 1975, played basketball, and was on the track team. He attended Indiana State University and was on the basketball team led by Larry Bird that went to

NCAA in Sale Lake City, UT, 1979. He returned to ISU, received a degree in mechanical engineering, and is a design engineer for Hyster Plant in Danville, IL. In January 1980, he married Karen Stark. She graduated from ISU in 1979. She is a licensed CPA and is a manager with Kesler and Company in Danville, IL.

Rex Jr., Jan. 18, 1935, attended Perrysville Schools, graduating in 1953. He attended Indiana State University graduating in 1957, B.S. degree in education, M.A. degree in 1963. He married Violet Kathryn Heath in June 1959. She has a B.A. degree from Douglas College/Rutgers University. Since 1965, Rex, Jr. has been Assistant Director of Educational Placement in ISU. He is director of the Career Center there. They have three children, John, Anne, Mark.

John, September 1960, graduated from South Vigo High School in 1978. He graduated from Rose Hulman, 1982, with a degree in chemical engineering. He is presently on Inter Varsity Christian Fellowship Campus Staff at Indiana and Depauw Universities.

Anne, August 1964, graduated from South Vigo in 1982, received B.S. degree from ISU in 1986, in elementary education with math endorsement. She was president of Mortar Board Honorary.

Mark, May 1966, graduated from South Vigo in 1984. He is presently a senior at Rose Hulman, majoring in chemical engineering. He was elected to Blue Key Honorary. *Submitted by Lucile Crowder*

DONALD E. HESKETT AND PATRICIA ROSE HESKETT CRUM,

Donald E. was born on Dec. 25, 1935, and Patricia Rose was born on Jan. 7, 1940, to Milo Everett and Wauneta Mitchell Heskett of Summit Grove.

Both Donald and Patricia have lived most of their lives in and around Summit Grove.

Donald graduated from Hillsdale High School with the class of 1954. December 18, 1954 he married Ruby Dean Love, daughter of Dan Dewey and Iris June Knoblett Love. Ruby, the eldest, has a brother and sister.

Donald and Ruby are the parents of two sons, Ronald and Robert, two daughters, Teal and Sara. They are the owners of Heskett's Greenhouse in Summit Grove and Donald is employed with Shelton Hannig Construction Co. at Eli Lilly Co.

Patricia Heskett Crum and Donald Heskett

Patricia graduated from Hillsdale High School with the class of 1958 and from St. Elizabeth Medical Secretary School in 1959. She was employed as the first Medical Secretary at the Vermillion County Hospital. June 17, 1961, she married Lawrence H. Crum, Jr. the eldest son of Lawrence Homer and Hazel Stewart Crum of R.R.1, Dana, IN. Lawrence (Larry) has two brothers, Tom and Jim and one sister, Naomi.

Lawrence and Patricia are the parents of two sons, Michael and Mark, and one daughter, Mila. They are members of Salem United Methodist Church, and Patricia is serving her fourth year as President of Terre Haute District United Methodist Women. Patricia is also chaplain of the Estabrook Chapter D.A.R. of Parke County. Her daughter, Mila, is also a junior member of the D.A.R. At the present Patricia is President of the Historical Society of Vermillion County.

They reside at R.R.1, Hillsdale on a small farm and Lawrence is employed with Turner Coaches and Charters of Terre Haute, IN.

Donald and Patricia's parents are both deceased, Milo having passed away Jan. 29, 1988, and Wauneta passed away July 18, 1983 and are buried at Helt's Prairie Cemetery.

DARRELL D. DAVIS, was born Apr. 3, 1916, in Geneva, northwest of Clinton, IN. He was the fifth child of Oliver A. and Etta A. (West). Their other children were Dorothy L. (Pell), Mamie V. (Durand), George—died as a young child, Irma V. (Divan) and James O. Oliver was a coal miner and spent his entire life in Vermillion County.

Oliver A. Davis was born Jan. 10, 1881, in Vermillion County and was the second child of Arnold W. and Martha J. (Shannon). Arnold W. was a coal miner and farmer and also spent his entire life in Vermillion County. Their other children were James Q. and Lottie H. (Daughterty).

Arnold W. Davis was born May 4, 1854, in Vermillion County, and was the sixth child of Silas and Caroline (Mitchell). Silas was a cooper and farmer, born in 1818, in Ohio, and came to Vermillion County in 1823. Their other children were Emily (Potter), Josephine (Nolan), Silas Jr., Charles, Frank, George, William, and Phillip.

In 1937, Darrell married M. Elizabeth (Taylor). They had five children, Irma L. (Kibbe) of California, Mary E. (Carr) of California, Carol A. (Lokken) of Washington, David O. of Florida, and Janice G. (Black) of Indiana.

As a young man, Darrell worked as a coal miner and farmer in Vermillion County. In 1941, he moved to Valparaiso, IN, and worked in a supervisory capacity manufacturing permanent magnets for the Indiana General Company for 40 years.

M. Elizabeth died in 1959, and Darrell married Betty M. (Oplinger) in 1961. Her daughter is JoAnn (Whalls) of Indiana. Upon retirement in 1981, they moved back to Vermillion County.

He is a member of the F & AM of Porter County and a 32nd degree Mason of South Bend. He holds a gold card in the American Federation of Musicians, and is a member of the Valparaiso Eagles and the Clinton Moose Lodge.

Darrell and his wife, Betty, now reside on the 25 acre family home place located in Geneva, that was purchased by his Grandfather Arnold W., in 1899. At present, Darrell and Betty have 25 grandchildren and 24 great-grandchildren.

THE MARTIN DAVITTO FAMILY, Martin and Pierina Tidor Davitto were married Oct. 21, 1922, in Terre Haute, IN. Martin came to the United States from Corio Canavasi, Casa Gat, near Torino, Italy, in 1912. He worked in the Bunsen #4 and Bunsen #5 mines and had their home built in Universal. He then returned to Italy and brought Pierina to the United States in 1922. Martin was one of six children of Tony and Oson Chichilda Davitto. Martin had also worked in the mines in Germany.

Martin became a U.S. Citizen in 1939, and Pierina became a citizen in 1953. Martin was born Dec. 4, 1885. They had three children, Tony was born July 5, 1923, Rose Mary was born July 24, 1924, and Renaldo David was born June 30, 1934.

Tony served in the Army Air Corps during World War II. Tony also worked in the mines for two and one half years. He also worked for E.I. Dupont de Nemours at the Dana Plant until its closing in 1957. He moved to Idaho Falls, ID, and worked for Phillips Petroleum at the National Reactor Testing Station at Arco, ID. He then came back to Indianapolis to work for Link Belt until he retired in 1980. Tony married Barbara Clemenz Potter, Feb. 20, 1953. They have a daughter, Donna Kay, born Jan. 6, 1952. She was adopted by Tony in 1953. They have a son, Ricky Allen, born Feb. 17, 1954. They both were born at Vermillion County Hospital.

Donna Kay married Thomas M. Coleman of Indianapolis, IN, in 1970, and they have three sons—Eric James, born Oct. 24, 1970; Brian Anthony, born Aug. 24, 1972; and Jeremy Matthew, born Oct. 7, 1980. Tom is making the United States Air Force his career and is due to retire in 1991. He is stationed at Grissom Air Force Base near Peru, in Miami County. They live in Walton, IN, in Cass County. Eric, Brian, and Donna all work on the Air Force Base.

Ricky Allen married Jill Mendenhall of Hendricks County, June 5, 1976. They have a daughter, Emily Renee, born July 8, 1983. Tyler Martin was born July 29, 1985. They live in Brownsburg, IN and Ricky works for Allison, Division of General Motors, in Indianapolis, IN. Ricky and Donna both graduated from Danville Community High School in Danville, IN.

R. David married Judith Kelsheimer, Nov. 19, 1953, and they have a daughter, Diane Renee, born Jan. 5, 1964. Diane married Ron Straw, May 25, 1985, and was divorced. She later married Robert Lynch, Nov. 21, 1987. Bob is employed by Eli Lilly of Clinton, and Diane is a beautician at the Hair Junction of South Fifth Street in Clinton. They have a daughter, Laney Renee. They moved to rural Paris, IL, in 1988. David and Judith rebuilt the old John Vero home in Hazel Bluff and have lived their since 1959. David also served in the Army and Army Reserve for a total of six years. David was employed by Mikes Motors for 15 years and now works for Peabody Coal Company of Universal and also farms in his spare time.

CHARLES WILLIAM DITTO, was born Jan. 21, 1919 in Mooresville, IN, the son of Leroy and Eva Marie Lewis Ditto. Charles was the eldest of three children and grew up in the rural Dana "Horseshoe area". He began school at Stumptown, IN and later attended Quaker school through the seventh grade. Beginning in the eighth grade he attended Newport High School and graduated with the class of 1937. During High School Charles was active in Band and Track. In his senior year he placed fist in the mile and second in the half mile run.

After graduation he spent some time in the C.C.C.'s in St. George, UT. He came home and worked in the coal mine with his father until 1940 when he went to Gary, IN and worked in the Steel Mills, until World War II was declared. He returned home in 1942 to work at the Wabash River Ordnance Plant, until inducted into the United States army in October 1942. On June 1, 1944 he shipped

out for the South West Pacific and was attached to the 13th Air Force. After the war was ended he returned from the Phillipine Islands, where he had served, and was discharged from service in January of 1946.

Charles W. Ditto

On Feb. 12, 1946 he was united in marriage with Hazel Snyder, daughter of Andrew and Lulu Golly Snyder, at Camden, NY. To this union was born one daughter, Pauline Marie. Pauline is now Mrs. Linn Stevenson. They reside in the Peoria, IL, area and have one son, Kevin Linn.

In 1946 he started farming, and in 1950 he also began driving a tank truck for Standard Oil Company. He later drove for Mobil Oil Company until 1968. The family then moved to Mechanicsburg, IL, and became caretakers of a Nazarene Church Camp for two years. They returned to Eugene and he now works for Colonial Brick Corporation.

Charles has lived in Eugene since 1954. When this life is over, he will be laid to rest in the Thomas Cemetery at Newport, and become a part of the fourth generation of the Ditto family to be buried there.

CHARLES WAYNE DOWERS AND JOANNE MCCORD DOWERS, Charles "Wayne" Dowers was born Mar. 9, 1927, to Charles A. and Beaulah Lettie Brown Dowers at their home a mile west of Cayuga. This home was shared with Charles A.'s parents, James A. and Ellen Holdaway Dowers. In 1933, on March 7, Wayne's brother, Marvin Lee, joined the family. In 1938, Charley and Beaulah moved and established their own home on the northwest edge of Eugene. Wayne and JoAnne still reside on a section of this property in a house built by Wayne, his father, and brother in 1952. Wayne and Marvin attended school at Eugene and were graduated from Cayuga High School in 1945 and 1951, respectively. Wayne served in the U.S. Army from 1954 to 1956. Wayne lost his brother in death in 1956; his father passed away in 1962, and his mother in 1973.

JoAnne did not live in Vermillion County until 1968, but grew up just across the Wabash River in Fountain County. She did, however, graduate from Perrysville High School in 1956. In 1960 she earned her B.S. degree from ISU, then Indiana State College, and in 1970 received her M.S. She taught English as JoAnne McCord, JoAnne Wallace, and JoAnne Dowers in the North Vermillion School Corporation (both Newport Elementary and North Vermillion High School) since its beginning in 1964.

Wayne began his life's work in construction at the gravel pit north of Cayuga where his father worked. Presently he is employed as an operator for Dennis Trucking in Terre Haute. He has been a member of Local 841 IUOE for 42 years. Also he enjoys being a small, part-time farmer and gardener.

Wayne and JoAnne were married on Jan. 24, 1975, at the Cayuga Church of the Nazarene where they are currently active members. They have an adult son, John Joseph. From a previous marriage Wayne has two daughters, Dawn Alison Dowers (Mrs. Jack) Thompson of RR 2, Kingman, and Lisa Gail Dowers (Mrs. Bradley) Mitchell of Pecatonica, IL. Jack and Dawn have given Wayne and JoAnne four granddaughters: Alison Gail (12 yrs.), Leann Rachell (eight yrs.), Erin Renae (two yrs.), and Kayla Diann (ten mos.). Brad and Lisa have added two grandsons: Gregory Michael (four yrs.), and Douglas Scott (one yr.). From the former marriage there was also a son, Gregory Wayne (1951-1953).

JoAnne's parents, Joseph Douglas and Maxine Myers McCord, still live in Fountain County. Wayne's closest relatives beyond his children are two aunts who both reside in Eugene: Estella Collier, his mother's sister, and Esther Grumley Gragg, his father's sister. Although often asked, he is not closely related to any of the other Dowers of Cayuga.

MARTHA JEAN JACKSON DREHER,

was born Oct. 21, 1925, the fourth daughter of John Harrison Jackson and Reba Elizabeth Paine Jackson at 203 North 8th Street, Clinton, IN. Her three sisters are Neola Davitto (See related story on Neola's daughter, Elizabeth West), Nell Allen (See related story), and Ethel Reposh (See related story) all of Clinton.

Martha Jean Jackson Dreher

Martha attended Central School briefly, then attended Glendale, Fairview School, and Clinton High. She is a graduate of Smart Appearance Beauty College in Terre Haute.

In 1960 she left Clinton and moved to Terre Haute. She is married to a hard working man, Jack Dreher, and they live in a new house over looking the Wabash River. Jack is a graduate of Gerstmeyer High School and a native of Terre Haute.

The picture was taken in 1936 when Martha was 11 years old and a sixth grade student at Fairview School. *Submitted by Leo Reposh Jr.*

ROBERT E. DOAN AND JOSEPHINE R. MILLER DOAN,

Robert Eugene Doan was born Feb. 7, 1923, in Mecca, IN, the son of Robert O. and Eva G. Lawson Doan. He is the seconded eldest of seven children. Robert attended grade and high school in Mecca. After graduation he got his first job at Wabash River Ordnance Works which was just building a plant near Newport, IN.

February 3, 1943, Robert entered the U.S. Air Force and served three years during World War II. Most of these years were in the South Pacific area with the 386th Air Service Squadron.

Mr. and Mrs. Bob Doan

After discharge from the Air Force in February, 1946, he returned to his home town and to his former employment. About this time he met and married Josephine (Jo) in September, 1946. They are the parents of a son, Robert Joseph, born a year later.

The couple lived in Clinton for the first five years, then moved to Dana in 1951. Here they became an active part of the community. She worked several years at the Dana News and is presently employed at the Daily Clintonian (18 years).

They are members of the Dana United Methodist Church. Bob is a member and Past Master of Asbury Lodge 320 F&AM, member and Past Chancellor of Dana Lodge 247 Knights of Pythias, member Scottish Rite, Valley of Terre Haute, member Zorah Shrine and Secretary/Treasurer of the Dana Community Volunteer Fire Department.

Bob and Jo have one granddaughter Jessica of Crawfordsville, IN.

HARVEY H. AND MARIE ADAMS DODD,

Harvey was born in Mountain Grove, MO, on Jan. 16, 1936, the son of William and Lucy Kemper Dodd. He is the eldest of two children. He grew up in Arkansas and Missouri but moved to Cayuga in 1952 where he graduated from Cayuga High School in 1956. In October 1959 he married Marie Adams. Marie was born Mar. 2, 1941 to Gordon and Virginia Adams. She was born and raised at Georgetown, IL where she graduated high school in 1959.

The couple made their home three miles southeast of Newport, known as O.P.D. Road, where they raised four children and have one grandchild.

Cheryll Dodd, born Dec. 19, 1960, in Gary, IN, is employed by Indiana State University where she is also working on a degree.

Randy Dodd, born Dec. 4, 1962, also born in Gary, is stationed at the Little Rock, AR Airforce base.

Patricia Dodd Bayles, born Aug. 5, 1965, resides on O.P.D. Road and is employed at Indiana State University.

Bruce Dodd, born Oct. 27, 1966, works and resides in Urbana, IL.

Jordan Michael Bayles, the son of Patricia, was born Jan. 5, 1986 and is the first grandchild of Harvey and Marie.

FOREST TURNER DOWNS,

was born Jan. 11, 1915, at Newport, and died Dec. 19, 1982, at Mesa, AZ. He was the son of Leander Downs and Nancy Ellen Maxwell Downs. On Dec. 27, 1935, he married Frances Olivene Louise Lewis, the daughter of Cecil James Lewis and Sarah Van Huss Lewis. She was born Oct. 12, 1913, in St. Bernice.

They were married at Terre Haute, and are the parents of five children - Phyllis Kay, born Oct. 6, 1936, in Clinton, married David Carl Sproul on Mar. 27, 1959; Marlene, born June 16, 1938, in St. Bernice, married Gerald Wayne Holdcraft on January, 1968; Elaine Joyann, born Jan. 5, 1940, at Tennessee Valley; Cecil Lee, born Mar. 15, 1942, at Tennessee Valley, married Wanda Gail Zelhart on Dec. 14, 1974; Archie Ray, born June 14, 1943, in Clinton, married Carolyn Grosman in 1966, and Cho Une, in 1984.

Their grandchildren are - Michael David Sproul, born Aug. 10, 1963, in Pennsylvania, married Elma Phillips, June, 1986; Donald Wayne Holdcraft, born Aug. 25, 1968, in Phoenix, AZ; Stephen Ray Downs, born Nov. 17, 1970, in Phoenix, AZ, died August, 1976, in Saginaw, MI; Nathan Carl Sproul, born June 19, 1972, in Denver, CO; Marea Kay Sproul, born Apr. 27, 1975, in Phoenix, AZ; Johannah Beth Downs, born Jan. 18, 1977, in Mesa, AZ; Jonathan Ray Downs, born Sept. 21, 1978, in Phoenix, AZ; Joel Downs, born Dec. 8, 1979, in Mesa, AZ; Jennifer Lynn Downs, born Mar. 30, 1981, in Mesa, AZ; and Joshua Lee Downs, born Feb. 14, 1983, in Mesa, AZ.

LEANDER DOWNS,

was the son of William Downs and Rachael Kahler Downs. He was born Mar. 4, 1886, in Pulaski or White Co., IN, and died Jan. 17, 1945, at Hillsdale, IN. On Jan. 19, 1910, he married Nancy Ellen Maxwell, the daughter of John Lafayette Bush Maxwell and Hannah Santilla Dark Maxwell. She was born May 25, 1888, in Vermillion Township, and died Oct. 15, 1957, at Worthington, in Greene Co., IN, and was buried in Hopewell Cemetery. They were the parents of six children - Willard, born Mar. 7, 1912, in Dana, died Mar. 9, 1912, in Dana; Willis, born Mar. 7, 1912, in Dana, died Mar. 9, 1912, in Dana; Forrest Turner, born Jan. 11, 1915, in Newport, died Dec. 19, 1982, in Mesa, AZ, married Frances Olivene Lewis on Dec. 27, 1935; Otis Maxwell, born Oct. 1, 1916, in Newport, married Naomi Ruth Clevenger on June 17, 1942; Harley Archie, born Jan. 24, 1919, in Newport, died Aug. 27, 1970, in Flint, MI, married Wanetta Harmon on Sept. 17, 1942; Warren, born Oct. 20, 1920, in St. Bernice. (see related article - Maxwell Family)

Added by granddaughter, Marlene Downs Holdcraft. Grandma liked to say little poems she made up - and laughed with us. She had one that was in an autograph book:

He walked her home
because it was late
He went ahead to open the gate.
She wanted to thank him
but didn't know how
For he was the farmer and she was the cow.

WILLIAM DOWNS,

was the son of John Downs and Mary Jane Hines Downs. He was born Apr. 9, 1835, in Caldonia in Marion Co., OH, and died Mar. 27, 1910, in Dana, IN and was buried in Hopewell Cemetery. He lived in Ohio, Indiana, and Illinois. He was married to Frances Mary Berry at Indian Creek in Pulaski Co., IN. She was the daughter of Thomas Berry and she was born in Marion Co., OH. They were the parents of seven children - Ira, born in Eugene Township, April, 1861, married to Ida Isks; Charlie, Alice, and four with unknown names.

On Mar. 16, 1882, he married Rachael Kahler, daughter of George Kahler and Rebecca Decker Kahler. She was born Jan. 4, 1852, in Pulaski Co. IN, and died Mar. 19, 1932, in St. Bernice, IN, and was buried in Hopewell Cemetery. They were the parents of seven children - Mary R. was born March, 1885, and was married to Matthew Payton and Jack Canaday; Leander was born Mar. 4, 1886, and died at Hillsdale, IN, on Jan. 17, 1945, and was married to Nancy Ellen Maxwell, Jan. 19, 1910; Grace Josie was born April, 1888, and was married to Benjamin Jones; Wibert was born Sept. 17, 1889, and died Dec. 9, 1962, and was married to Iva Jones, Apr. 16, 1929; Albert was born Apr. 7, 1891, in Eugene, and died June 3, 1959, and was married to Ethel Jones, May 24, 1913; Aaron H. was born October, 1892, and was married to Jessie ?; Katy Golden, deceased.

PAUL JAMES DUCHENE AND NORMA JEAN BONOMO DUCHENE,

Paul James Duchene was born Sept. 11, 1922, in Mecca, IN, the son of Paul John Duchene and Maudie Jemima Hollingsworth. He has one sister, Dorothy Irene Duchene (Joy), born Apr. 27, 1924, in Clinton, IN.

He attended Lincoln Elementary School in Muncie, IN, and Central and South Elementary Schools in Clinton, IN. He graduated from Clinton High School in 1941. Following graduation he enlisted in the United States Army, 30th Infantry Division, and was stationed in Europe during World War II.

Paul and Norma Duchene

Returning home to Clinton, he married Norma Jean Bonomo, born Apr. 2, 1927. The couple was wed in 1951 at the Sacred Heart Church in Clinton. Norma Jean is the daughter of Carlo Bonomo, a native of Italy, and Rose Gugliemetti of Syndicate. Paul worked at Quaker Maid in Terre Haute, at the Du Pont Plant near Newport, IN, and was employed at Anaconda Aluminum Company in Terre Haute for 21 years. He was a Boy Scout, an Eagle Scott, and a Boy Scout Leader. He was an Indian relic collector and was listed in the Who's Who for Indian Relics. He was a member of the Indiana Archaeological Society, American Legion, Veterans of Foreign Wars, The Redskin, and Genuine Indian Relic Society. He died May 31, 1979, in Clinton.

Norma attended Glendale Grade School. She graduated in 1946 from Clinton High School. She was a Girl Scout Leader and is a member of the Sacred Heart Church. She still resides in Clinton, IN.

The couple had two children - Rose Jean Duchene (Roberts) (Shew), born June 21, 1952, and Paul James Duchene II, born May 15, 1953, in Clinton. The couple have five grandchildren - Joy Lynn

Roberts, born Feb. 3, 1973; Robert "Bobby" Roberts, born Dec. 7, 1976; Sara Rose Shew, born Nov. 10, 1986; Brian Paul Duchene, born Aug. 19, 1974; and Anthony William Duchene, born Sept. 4, 1975.

PAUL JOHN DUCHENE AND MAUDIE J. HOLLINGSWORTH DUCHENE,

Paul John Duchene born July 14, 1895, in Yeddo Co., IN the son of Noah Duchene of France and Clara Marie Stickle of Clay Co., IN. He had one brother, Noah Alfred Duchene, born July 22, 1900. They owned and operated a coal mine west of Clinton. Due to ill health he later worked at the Clinton Hotel until his death Dec. 8, 1946. He had two sisters: Leona Josephine Duchene (Whitworth), born Apr. 25, 1912, in Lodi, IN and Norenna Blanche Duchene, born July 22, 1903, in Vermillion County. His sisters along with their mother operated a small grocery on Crompton Hill in Clinton in the early 1900's. July 23, 1921, he married Maudie Jemima Hollingsworth, born Mar. 19, 1904, in Vermillion County, daughter of Elizabeth Ann Raine (Hollingsworth) (Steedman) of Grape Creek, IL and James Madison Hollingsworth of Newport, IN. She attended Shanks School in New Goshen, IN. She worked at the Vermillion County Hospital and was a member of the local Moose Lodge. She died Feb. 7, 1966, in Vermillion County. She had three sisters: Margie Ann Hollingsworth (Pollom) born Oct. 25, 1911, in Davis Co., IN, Mabel Marie Hollingsworth (Rueben) (Kirts), born Jan. 31, 1908, in Vermillion County; Mandy Irene Hollingsworth, born Jan. 3, 1917, in Vigo Co., IN. She died Mar. 27, 1918, of German Measles. The couple had two children, Paul James Duchene born, Sept. 11, 1922 and Dorothy Irene Duchene (Joy) born Apr. 27, 1924.

The couple are survived by five grandchildren: Sheri Lynn Joy (Leverenz) born Feb. 17, 1945; Tona Sue Joy (Horn) born Oct. 20, 1948; Larry Alan Joy, born Jan. 6, 1950 in Terre Haute, IN.

Paul and Maudie Duchene

Rose Jean Duchene (Roberts) (Shew), born June 21, 1952; Paul James Duchene II, born May 15, 1953, in Clinton, IN. There were ten great-grand-children descendants: Lori Lynn Leverenz, born Jan. 22, 1967, in Danville, IL; Scott Alan Leverenz, born Feb. 9, 1975, in Danville, IL; Amy Sue Horn, born Oct. 19, 1970, in Evansville, IN; twins, Golden Raise Joy and Ginger Mae Joy, born Oct. 17, 1978 and died November, 1978 in Terre Haute, IN; Joy Lynn Roberts born Feb. 3, 1973; Robert John Roberts, born Dec. 7, 1976; Sara Rose Shew, born Nov. 10, 1986; Anthony William Duchene, born Nov. 11, 1975; Brian Paul Duchene, born Aug. 19, 1974, in Terre Haute, IN. *Submitted by Sheri Joy*

CLARENCE AND FLORA BEDINGER DUNHAM,

were residents of Vermillion County from 1910 to 1956 when they retired from farming

and moved to a daughter's home in Lisbon, IL. Six of their seven children were graduates of Perrysville High School, and numerous descendants still live in Vermillion County.

Clarence Elmer Dunham was born Jan. 13, 1872, in Logan Co., IL, eldest son of Quincy and Laura Belle Alsop Dunham. In 1881, Quincy, a Civil War veteran, died in a smallpox epidemic. Soon thereafter the family moved, first to Iroquois Co., IL, then to Vermilion Co., IL. On Christmas Day, 1894, Clarence married Flora Bedinger in Hoopeston and they lived there on a farm until 1910 when they moved to another farm owned by Clarence's mother on the Sand Prairie west of Perrysville. When his mother died in 1914, the farm was sold, with Clarence buying the north 180 acres.

This acreage was distinguished by its unique barn, built in a style known as the Pennsylvania barn. It was a rectangular structure built on a south-facing slope. The milking parlor and stables were built into the slope for winter warmth and summer coolness, with the threshing parlor and haymow at ground level above. A long south-side forebay provided an outdoor shelter for livestock. Beams and rafters were all hand-hewn and hand-pegged, and the first floor walls were built entirely of stone. This landmark was accidentally burned in the late 1950s.

Clarence Dunham was a farmer throughout his working life, and a staunch Republican. He was a descendant of Peter Banta, a scout in the Revolution. Clarence died June 30, 1958, in Lisbon, IL.

Flora Bedinger was born June 16, 1875, at Eugene, IN, eldest daughter of Elbert T. and Lucy Smith Bedinger. Lucy Bedinger died of tuberculosis in 1881 and Flora was sent to be a foster child in the home of Luther and Deborah Riggs near Hoopeston, IL. There she was later married, living her adult life as a farm wife and mother. A descendant of Revolutionary soldier Christopher Bedinger, she was a member of the Christian Church and a charter member of the Royal Neighbors Lodge and the Sand Prairie Club in Perrysville. Flora died July 3, 1959, in Lisbon, IL, and is buried beside her husband at Sunset Memorial Park in Danville, IL. Children of Clarence and Flora Bedinger Dunham were:

Edna Viola (1895-1987), married 1917 Edwin Leigh Jones of Perrysville (1895-1951). Their children were Mildred Florabelle, Edna Louise, Edwin Leigh and Daniel Victor.

Laura Goldie (1897-1976), married first Chester Cromwell Wrenn in 1928, and second, James Williams in 1970. Her daughter was Carol Mae Wrenn.

Estella Pearl (1899-1987), married 1929 Clarence Oliver (Jack) Holmes (1890-1953). Their children were Robert James and John Dale.

Russell Elmer (1900-1954), married 1923 Edith Alice Wilcoxen (1902-1954). Their children were Eleanor Jean, Richard Vaughn, Orde Eugene, Melvin Lloyd and Kathryn Sue.

Leah Ivy (1903-1982), married 1931 Bernard Michael Lynch (1898-1957). Their sons were Bernard Gregory and Raymond Patrick.

Clarence Glenn Preston (1910-1977), married 1931 Genevieve Claire Kell (1912-1971). Their children were Norma Lee, Morris Glenn, Charles Leroy, Clarence David, John Franklin, Paul Dan and Paula Diane.

Julia Lucy Virginia, born 1913, married 1937 Paul Chrysto Young (1912-1971). Their children were Alan Duane, Linda Lou, James Douglas and Paul Leslie. *Submitted by Kate Dunham*

JAMES ALEXANDER ELDER, section three, Helt Township was a native of Brown Co., OH, a son of Samuel and Mary (McCane) Elder, his father a native of Westmoreland Co., PA and his mother from Ireland. His grandfather, Samuel Elder, was also a native of Ireland and came to America soon after his marriage. Samuel Elder, Jr. left his native state in 1816 and moved to Ohio where he lived until 1832 when he moved to Vermillion Co., IN and settled in Helt Township where his wife died in 1852. In the summer of 1869 he went to New York to visit friends and died there on July 6th of that year.

James A. Elder was reared on a farm in Vermillion County and was educated in the log cabin school. He always devoted his attention to farming, and was as a result of economy and good management, successful, owning a fine farm of 423 acres in Helt Township and an additional 143 acres in Edgar Co., IL. He made a speciality of stock raising, and had some very fine graded varieties of both cattle and hogs. He took pride in having his farm and stock equal to any in the county, and devoted his entire attention to improving his property. He took an interest in the managerial welfare of the county, but preferred to leave the duties devolving on an office-holder to those who had such aspirations, his time being taken up with his own private business, although he served three terms on the board of county commissioners (as of 1888). Mr. Elder was married Apr. 1, 1852 to Euphamis Sheely, daughter of George Sheely. She died the following August, and Jan. 18, 1855, Mr. Elder married Mary, daughter of James Morgan. To them were born two children - George and Harriet. George married Mattie Temple, and Harriet is the wife of Oscar Gibson. Mrs. Mary Elder died on Nov. 10, 1862. On Mar. 26, 1864, Mr. Elder married Mrs. Julia A. Dicken Fisher, daughter of Richard Dicken, who died on Dec. 13, 1875, leaving two children - Clara A., wife of Fisher McRoberts, and Samuel. Samuel married Lucy Grant Martin and after her death married Margaret Irene Pinson. On Feb. 1, 1877, Mr. James A. Elder married Susan R., daughter of Adna Beach. He and Susan were members of the Presbyterian Church. James A. and Susan moved to Dana when their son, Samuel was 21 years old, and they gave the farm to him. James died on May 1, 1901 and is buried in the Elder cemetery along with other family members and neighbors.

Source: 1888 History Of Vermillion County (in addition to family information) *Submitted by Dorothy Elder*

JAMES PINSON ELDER AND DOROTHY RUTH WALTERS ELDER,
James Pinson Elder, Helt Township, was born to Samuel and Margaret Irene Pinson Elder on Oct. 11, 1908. He graduated from Bono High School in 1926 and attended Indiana University where he met and later married Dorothy Ruth Walters of Bedford, IN, on July 13, 1929. Dorothy, born on Nov. 10, 1909, is the daughter of Clarence Lambert and Elma Clarice Redman Walters. Dorothy's mother was Secretary Treasurer of the Indiana Limestone Institute and her father owned and operated a Business College in Bedford.

In 1937 James and Dorothy moved to Dana to farm with his father. Samuel died in 1942 and Jim took over full responsibility of the farming operations of 325 acres, raising grain, hogs, sheep and cattle. Jim attended several Purdue University Intensive Short Courses in Agriculture. He took

special pride in producing certified seed and was active in state seed improvement programs. He was a leader in soil conservation practices, being one of the first supervisors of the Soil Conservation District. For many years, he was a top producer in the Five Acre Corn test program. The Elders were recognized for "Century Ownership" in 1948 because the farm had been owned and operated by the same family for 100 years or more. Jim's great grandfather, Samuel, received the deed to the farm in 1832, when he arrived here from Ohio, and formerly from Westmoreland Co., PA.

Jim was very active in community affairs, a member of Vermillion County Farm Bureau, Purdue Alumni Association, Asbury Lodge 320, F&AM Dana, Scottish Rite and Zorah Temple of Terre Haute, and Knights of Pythias 247, Dana. He was a Republican member of the Vermillion County Council for several terms. When Jim died in 1964, he was interred in the Redman, Walters, Elder family crypt in Washington North cemetery in Indianapolis.

Dorothy has been an active community leader for many years, serving as president of the Parent Teachers Association, 4-H leader, and Girl Scout leader. Dorothy's involvement also includes As You Like It Club, Garden Club, Delta Kappa Gamma, Dana Bridge Club, County Library Board, County Historical Society, Sigma Kappa Alumni, Purdue University Alumni Association, Mothers' Club, Vermillion County Chorus, Federation of Clubs, Hospital Volunteer Guild, and numerous Ernie Pyle Memorial activities.

During World War II when the Newport Munitions plant brought many people to Dana, and housing was scarce, Jim and Dorothy arranged for roomers to live in their upstairs, giving them kitchen privileges and making them feel at home.

Dorothy spearheaded the establishment of the Indiana State Memorial for Ernie Pyle. Ernie was born in the west farm house on the Elder farm which was donated to the State of Indiana by the Elder family. The Indiana State American Legion organization, with the leadership of the Dana Legion assisted the Indiana Legislature in establishing a State Memorial, including moving and renovating the birthplace home from the Elder farm to its current location on Main Street in Dana. Dorothy presented the key to the home to Governor Otis Bowen during the dedication ceremonies in Dana.

The Elder daughters include: Mary Jenet Elder Penrod, PhD, resides in Indianapolis and is married to Walter J. Penrod. Their children are Kathryn, Sharon, Susan, Marilyn and Jim. Kathryn Ann Elder Kaiser, resides in San Diego, CA and is married to Thomas G. Kaiser. Their children are Gregory, Jim, and Lindy. Bette Louise Elder resides in Indianapolis, IN. Jim and Dorothy Elder have certainly had a positive impact on the lives of their children, their friends, and the community. *Submitted by Dorothy Elder*

SAMUEL E. ELDER AND MARGARET IRENE PINSON ELDER,
Samuel Elder was the son of James Alexander Elder (Oct. 2, 1822 - May 1, 1901) a prominent farmer in Helt Township, and grandson of Samuel Elder who came to Indiana in 1832 from Brown Co., OH, after moving there in 1816 from Westmoreland Co., PA.

Samuel was given the deed to the farm southwest of Dana on his 21st birthday in 1892 by his father, as he and his wife had retired from farming and purchased the brick home on West A street in Dana, the present home of Dorothy Elder. Samuel was

married to Lucy Grant Martin (May 9, 1871 - Apr. 17, 1905) by A.D. Rippetoe, Oct. 5, 1892. They lived in the farm house until they moved into their new home on West A street in 1896 where they lived until her death in 1905. No children were born to this marriage. She is buried in the Bono Cemetery.

Samuel married Margaret Irene Pinson, the daughter of Thomas Phillo and Direxa Shew Pinson on Jan. 9, 1907. The marriage was performed by Rev. H.M. Brooks of Paris, IL, former pastor of the Christian Church in Clinton. They were married at the family residence at the corner of Third and Walnut in Clinton. "The bride carried a bouquet of bride's roses and looked lovely in her wreath of hyacinths and gown of white embroidered Japanese silk, trimmed with baby Irish lace, with demi train, showing the work of an artist in its design. The groom was handsome in a becoming evening suit of black."

Margaret had taught school in Newport, Toronto and Clinton after receiving her education at the Indiana State Normal School in Terre Haute (founded in 1870). She was called Maggie by her family and friends and Miss Pinsey by her students. It was noted in the newspaper account of the wedding "perhaps a more pathetic scene is seldom witnessed than when she kissed good-bye to her little charges, their love for her amounting to almost idolatry."

Margaret and Samuel moved into his white frame house on West A street, and in 1910 moved to the farm homestead, after which they built the brick home on State Road 71 in 1921-22, which they continued to call home. They were among the first in the community to have their own electricity producing Delco plant.

Samuel was a prominent farmer, banker, and was active in numerous organizations, always working for the benefit of the community. Margaret was also active in community and church activities. She was a life long member of the As You Like It Club, and a member of the Merry Housewives. Margaret was very proud of the fact that her ancestors came to America on the Mayflower, her lineage being traced to John and Priscilla Mullin Alden.

Their only son, James Pinson Elder was born on Oct. 11, 1908. He graduated from Bono High School in 1926, going on to Indiana University. He learned to play basketball as well as the violin, and enjoyed farming with his father. A verse which hung prominently in the kitchen - "The world is like a mirror, reflecting what you do, and if you face it smiling, it will smile back to you", was exemplified in Jim Elder's life. He married Dorothy Ruth Walters of Bedford, IN on July 13, 1929 and they moved to Dana in 1937 to farm with Samuel and Margaret.

Samuel's farm employee (and family) lived in the home on the "west place". This is the home in which Ernest Taylor (Ernie) Pyle was born on Aug. 3, 1900 to William C. and Maria Taylor Pyle, who were at that time working for Samuel Elder.

After Samuel died in 1942, Margaret continued to live in the brick house on 71 and James operated the farm. Margaret died on Jan. 28, 1957 and is remembered as a fine teacher, and able community leader, and friend to many people. Both Samuel and Margaret are buried in the Bono Cemetery. *Submitted by Dorothy Elder*

HAROLD WILLIAM ELLIOTT AND GERTRUDE MAY WRIGHT ELLIOTT,
the third child of John and Rosa Wright was Ger-

trude May, who was born Oct. 5, 1889. She married Harold William Elliott, Jan. 27, 1912. They lived in Gaylord, MI. She died Apr. 17, 1968. They had two children.

Harold William was born Apr. 14, 1937, and married Gail Diona White on June 25, 1959. Harold William and Gail had three sons, Thomas Harold, James William, and Robert Kenneth.

Harold and Gertrude Elliott

Thomas Harold was born June 7, 1963, and on Dec. 10, 1982, he married Sheryl Marie Bohn. She was born Aug. 18, 1962. Thomas Harold and Sheryl have two children, Steven Robert, born May 6, 1983, and Sherrie Ann, born Mar. 9, 1985.

James William was born July 11, 1960, and on June 30, 1984, he married Marla Kaye Giddens. She was born Aug. 28, 1959. James William and Marla have one son, Ryon James, born Dec. 27, 1985.

The last son of Harold William and Gail is Robert Kenneth, born Apr. 6, 1968.

Marylu Elliott, daughter of Harold William and Gertrude May, was born Sept. 29, 1938. She married Wayne Phillip Boshka on Jan. 30, 1965. Wayne Phillip was born Aug. 28, 1931. They live near Chicago, IL.

Aunt Gertie would send me boxes of clothes because my Dad worked on W.P.A. and didn't have much money to buy me clothes. *Submitted by Edna Wright*

EVERETT

Fred and Lillian, Clifford and Ethel

FREDERICK ANTHONY FABLE, born Oct. 30, 1817 at Philadelphia, PA, died Aug. 28, 1900 at Eugene, IN. His father was born in Germany and his mother in Pennsylvania. Mr. Fable was one of the early pioneers of Eugene township, having settled in Eugene in 1842. He came here when the pork packing industry at Eugene was in full blast and for many years operated a cooper shop with ten or 12 men employed furnishing barrels for the packing establishment. He learned the cooper trade as an apprentice in Cincinnati. He married Frances A. Moore on June 15, 1850.

Fred A. Fable II and Anna Mary (Mollie) Fable - 1955

Born to this union, two daughters and four sons of which George Henry Fable was the youngest. The mother of these children passed away in February, 1864. A second marriage to Susan A. (Perrin) Fable resulted in a daughter, Parolee Fable who was born July 24, 1866, died Feb. 5, 1941.

Mr. Fable was one of the energetic and prominent pioneers who materially aided in shaping the future of this township. In the early days, he was one of the leading Democrats in this end of the county and very popular with all classes. As trustee of Eugene Township for 13 years, he was in a position to advance the cause of education, and did so with an unselfish purpose. Mr. Fable was a Mason and held membership in the old lodge at Eugene which was obliged to abandon its meetings and surrender its charter during the Civil War as most of the members were at the front fighting for the Union. His funeral was conducted from the Eugene residence by Rev. A.V. Brashear of the Presbyterian Church.

George Henry Fable was married to Sarah Higgins, Aug. 20, 1882. Children were Fred Anthony Fable II, born Nov. 7, 1883 in Eugene, IN, died Oct. 26, 1962; three daughters, Georgia (Zell), born Nov. 6, 1885, died Aug. 28, 1969; Maude (Wright), born Feb. 4, 1888, died Apr. 3, 1971; Ruth (Bartley), born Mar. 18, 1896. Sarah (Higgins) Fable, mother of the children named above was born Aug. 7, 1860, died Sept. 9, 1898. A second marriage to Rose (Smith) Fable on Dec. 29, 1900 a son, Russell Fable, born Nov. 16, 1904, died Sept. 7, 1982.

Fred Anthony Fable II, married Anna Mary (Lashley) Fable, June 3, 1902, parents of Helen (Mitchell), born Oct. 6, 1903, died Oct. 11, 1983; Hazel Fable, born Apr. 19, 1905; Lashley, born June 7, 1907, died Sept. 23, 1978; Annabelle (Gibbs), born July 27, 1908. Anna Mary (Lashley) Fable, known as "Mollie", mother of the above children, was born at Bellaire, OH, Nov. 30, 1880, died Oct. 31, 1975.

For many years George Henry Fable operated a hardware business in Cayuga. He was joined by his son Fred A. Fable, who in the early 1900's added the sale of automobiles to the hardware business. This business became the Ford dealership in 1928 which continued at the same location. He was joined by his son-in-law Marshall Gibbs until his death. Mr. Fable, enthusiastic booster and instrumental in the organization of Cayuga Lions Club, in which he worked faithfully for the remainder of his life, also a member of Cayuga Masonic Lodge No. 584, F. & A.M. for many years.

Russell Fable married Ruth (Anderson) parents of Larry of Somers, NY, Vaudene (Pedigo) of Williamsburg, VA, and Robert of California.

Lashley Fable married Katherine (Boyd), Dec. 25, 1932, parents of William Boyd Fable, born Nov. 12, 1938 and John Lashley Fable, born Jan. 27, 1942. Katherine (Boyd) Fable was born Mar. 25, 1906 at Cayuga, IN.

William Boyd Fable was married to June (Garlick) Fable July 1, 1963 at Concord, CA, parents of Robert Karl, born July 9, 1967 at Concord, CA and Scott Edward born Jan. 1, 1975 at Concord, CA.

John Lashley Fable was married to Barbara (Knight) Oct. 23, 1965 at Lake Worth, FL, parents of Nicole Allison Fable, born Mar. 16, 1971 at West Palm Beach, FL. *Compiled by Hazel A. Fable*

VIOLA CHAPMAN FARRINGTON, was born on July 18, 1915, rural Colon Township, St. Joseph Co., MI. She was the daughter of L. Jay Chapman and Katie Hafer Chapman. She graduated from Colon High School in 1933.

She came to Indiana in the first part of April, 1945. She was the wife of Gerald Farrington. They moved to the Krekler farm, the first farm north of Clinton, IN. Later having bought the old Krekler farm, known as Hazel Bluff Farm, they moved there.

She came to Clinton, IN with four children. The fifth one was born at Vermillion County Hospital on Nov. 24, 1946.

She moved to the city of Clinton, IN, in February 1969. She retired from Meis store in Terre Haute as an alteration lady after about ten years.

The oldest daughter now lifes in Denver, CO. The two middle boys live within three miles of Clinton. The middle daughter lives at Hillsdale, IN. The youngest boy lives at Plainfield, IN and works as a mechanic for Public Service Indiana.

She now has six grandchildren and one great-grandson.

ANTON J. FENOGLIO AND RUTH A. HARBRUEGER FENOGLIO, Anton Joseph Fenoglio was born Jan. 3, 1908 in Clinton, the son of John and Joan Fenoglio. Ruth Augusta Harbrueger was born July 17, 1909 in Terre Haute, the daughter of Conrad and Carrie Harbreuger. Tony graduated from Clinton High School in 1926. He played baseball with the Diana Sweet Shop baseball team in the late 20's and early 30's. He was later active in refereeing area high school basketball and football and umpiring baseball games for many years. Ruth graduated from Wiley High School in 1927 and from Union Hospital School of Nursing in 1930.

They were married in Clinton on Oct. 4, 1936. Ruth worked as an R.N. at Vermillion County Hospital from 1932 to 1936. Tony worked as a teller at the Clinton Trust Co. (later known as the Citizens State Bank) from its opening in 1933 until 1941. He worked at the Newport Army Ammunition Depot from 1942 until 1948.

They had one son, John Conrad, born July 28, 1937 and one daughter, Alice Marie, born Oct. 24, 1941.

Tony operated the Dreamland Dance Hall above 559 North 9th Street and later the Aragon Ballroom at 447 North 9th Street until 1947. In 1947 they purchased the Happyland Swimming Pool at 1500 North 7th Street. They renamed it Aragon Park made it the mecca of heat-escapees in the days before everyone had home air-conditioning and backyard or municipal swimming pools. They moved the hardwood floor from the Aragon Ballroom to The dance floor at Aragon Park and continued the tradition of hosting large crowds of dancers almost every Saturday night. Leo Baxter's band was a fixture there for many years. Lu George and Jimmie Adami as well as touring bands led by Russ Carlisle, Don Regan and others played there. Tony also sang with the Elk's Chanters of the Terre Haute Elks Lodge #86.

In the early 50's they began serving banquets at the newly built dining room at the swimming pool. In 1956 they purchased the former home of Joe Vietti at 1600 No. 7th Street which was then operated as the Castle Restaurant. They operated both the Aragon Park Swimming pool and the Argon Castle Restaurant until Tony's death July 25, 1964. Both were sold later that year and Ruth resumed her career as an R.N. at the Vermillion County Hospital until she retired in 1976 just before the original hospital building was left and the newly constructed building occupied.

Both Tony and Ruth were active members of the Presbyterian Church in Clinton. Tony was one of the founding members of the Lions Club and a longtime member of the Clinton Volunteer Fire Department.

JOHN CONRAD FENOGLIO AND MARGUERITE PASAVENTO FENOGLIO,

John "Jack" Fenoglio was born July 28, 1937 in Clinton to Anton and Ruth Harbrueger Fenoglio. He has one sister, Alice Sink, who lives in Rockville with her husband and son Joe.

Jack grew up, attending elementary school in Clinton, and graduated from Clinton High School in 1955. Graduating from Rose Polytechnic Institute in 1959 with a B.S. degree in chemical engineering, he was commissioned a second lieutenant in the Army Corps of Engineers. Eventually he became captain in the Army Reserve.

After working in the technical department in Anaconda/Arco/Alcan in Terre Haute for 28 years, he with two other Alcan employees formed Specialty Blanks Inc. in 1987, a company which blanks and anneals aluminum circles. He serves as Vice-President of that company.

His interests are Boy Scouts of America, which he has served as Cubmaster, Scoutmaster, and Council Commissioner. He is a member of the Indiana Society of Professional Engineers, Wabash Valley Rose Tech Club, Alpha Tau Omega Fraternity, and has served on the South Vermillion School Board and the Little Italy Festival Board.

Marguerite "Margo" was born in Clinton to Dan and Josephine Masarachia Pesavento on Apr. 22, 1936. She attended school in Clinton graduating from Clinton High School in 1954. After graduating from Indiana State College in 1958, she taught at Central Elementary School in Clinton. She was a member of Chi Omega Sorority in college.

In 1981 Margo joined the staff of the Clinton Public Library.

The couple are members and have served as elders in the United Presbyterian Church.

Married on June 12, 1960 in the Hillcrest Presbyterian Church, they have two children who were raised in Clinton and graduated from South Vermillion schools. Anna Maria, born June 11, 1961 is a graduate of DePauw University and works as a radio account executive in Minneapolis, MN. John was born on Aug. 23, 1965 and graduated from Indiana University. He is living in New Castle, IN and serves as District Executive for the Boy Scouts of America.

CHET AND LINDA FIELDS, of Stone Mountain, GA still call Clinton their hometown. Chester Lee (Chet) Fields was born in Chicago Feb. 11, 1947, the only child of the marriage of Richard C. Fields (originally of Hazard, KY and now of Sierra Vista, AZ) and Martha Jean Childers of Vermillion County. His childhood included many moves in Clay and Vermillion Counties. He was very active in Boy Scout Troop 63, PUSH Little League, and First Christian Church. He graduated from Clinton High School in 1965 and attended Purdue University before spending eight years as a CTM in the U.S. Navy. He grew up with sister Pam Cottrell, still in Clinton, and brother Jim Cottrell, now of Idaho. Their father, Hank Cottrell, died in the Home Packing explosion in January 1963. Chet has four other sisters and three brothers on his fathers side. Linda Gail Biggs is the daughter of Ray Merrill Biggs and Irma Bly Mackel and was born June 17, 1946 at home in Lyford. Her only brother, Larry Ray Biggs, now lives in West Terre Haute. Linda's interests include 4-H, piano, Band, Job's Daughters (Past Honored Queen) and Christian Youth Fellowship. She graduated from CHS in 1964 and attended Indiana State University before marriage.

Chet and Linda Fields

Chet and Linda led a nomadic lifestyle for several years. Steven Ray Fields was born June 20, 1966, in Terre Haute. That summer they lived in St. Clairsville, OH where Chet was mechanic in a mine. Back at Purdue, Linda did dressmaking and Chet entered the Navy for electronics training. After moves to San Diego, Oakland, and Alameda, CA, Linda spent a year at Ohio University (Belmont County) before joining Chet in Japan where he worked in Yokosuka. They lived in Hyama and Yokohama and Linda studied Pattern drafting and taught English at Kanto Gakuin University. After four months in Norfolk, they were sent to Bremerhaven W. Germany, where David Lee Fields was born Aug. 1, 1971. They were assigned to the Maryland suburbs of Washington DC from November 1972, until Chet's discharge in May 1975. Life there centered around activities at Temple Hills Baptist Church and Prince George's College, where both attended classes.

After the Navy, they lived one year in New Orleans and three years in Baton Rouge. Linda sold the Dale Carnegie Course and pianos before settling into the mortgage business as processor and originator for the past 12 years. Chet attended University of New Orleans and LSU and worked for Radio Shack and Magna Fun Corp. before becoming electronic field service technician for CompuScan. In August, 1979, they transferred him to Atlanta and the family moved to Stone Mountain, GA, where Chet was promoted to District Manager and then to Regional Manager. Linda continued her Mortgage career and is proud that, although it took 23 years,

she graduated from Mercer University in June, 1987. She also teaches Sunday School at Pine Lake Baptist Church. Chet's interest have included Scouting, Kiwanis, hunting and fishing. Steve is working and finishing college and just finished Army jump school. David is a high school student with a passion for evangelism and an impressive resume for plays and musicals. Regardless how long we live in Stone Mountain, we'll always think of Clinton as home. *Submitted by Chet and Linda Fields*

FILLINGER FAMILY, Henry Lewis Fillinger was a grandson of Ludwig Fillinger who had come to America from Germany on the English ship 'Winter Galley' in 1738. Henry and his wife Nancy Davis, a daughter of John Davis of Montgomery Co., VA, moved from Blacksburg, VA to Parke County in 1839 and to Vermillion County during the Civil War. They had ten children. Their fifth child was John Ballard Fillinger. On John's return from the Civil War he met and married Catharine Roseann Hood on Feb. 24, 1869. Catharine was the daughter of Rebecca Aye and Thomas Simmons Hood. She was born Oct. 10, 1851 and died in August 1939. They had seven children. John served as Helt Township Trustee. Their second child Halbert Lewis Fillinger served in the National Guard during the Spanish American War. On June 8, 1899, Hal married Emma Southard, daughter of Huston Southard and Sarah Jane Langston Southard. Hal went into the hardware business with his father in the early 1900's. After Dana's big fire in 1913, he rebuilt the store and was a merchant through the 1920's. He was an architect and a professional engineer. He served as County Surveyor for many years and was the architect for the Court House in Newport as well as many schools and homes in the area. Hal and Emma had two children, Halbert Ernest Fillinger and Norma Fillinger Connell.

FOLTZ, During the 1870's, two of seven Foltz brothers came to Clinton township in Vermillion County. They were Abraham, married to Polly Propst, and Gideon, married to Cynthia Strole. They left Virginia, a Confederate state, because of hard economic times following the Civil War. A disastrous flooding of the Shenandoah River, where Gideon operated a gristmill, also prompted their leaving.

Abraham raised a son, Frank, and two daughters, Sarah and Kate.

Gideon raised seven sons and four daughters. The eldest daughter stayed in Virginia. Six of his sons and two of his daughters married and raised families in Clinton township.

Philip married Theresa Wright and raised Robert M., Gurney, Floyd and Ray.

Harden married Kate Foltz and raised Beulah (m. Charles Haymaker).

David married Mary E. Whitesel and raised Albert, Grover, Verna, Laurin, John and Samuel. The daughters were Jessie (m. Almond Satterlee), Clara (m. Ray Dyer), and Eva (m. David Bledsoe).

John married Louisa Walter and raised Solon, Addison, Claude, Lola (m. Charles Case) and Edith (m. Fred Myers).

Luther married Sciota Ike and raised Paul, Ivan, Ira (Raymond or "Razz"), Lloyd and Glenna (m. John Houser).

Joseph married Laura Fuquay and raised two daughters, Jenny (m. Elza Tweedy), and Faye (m. Raymond Downing).

Mary Ann Drusilla married Charles Walter and raised Fred, John, Omer, Sadie (m. Sam Dugger), Nell (m. John Foster) and Mary (m. Ben Jones).

Bettie Lee married Edwin Hedges and raised Cecil, Herschel, Edna (m. Herman Hedges) and Veda (m. Aubrey Kelley).

In the new and growing country, most of these men farmed some and were carpenters; and as the coal mines opened up many helped to sink and work these mines. Nearly all of these Foltzes were Democrats.

As the next generation came during the depression of the 1930's, many had to leave Vermillion County for a better opportunity. During W.W.I and W.W.II and the Korean conflict, many served their country in the armed forces. Some attended church; most made some contribution to their community. One served in law enforcement and one served in the state legislature.

At the present time, 1988, there are some relatives and descendants of these original settlers living in Vermillion County, but many have scattered. Few live in the county who bear the "Foltz" name. Paul and Hazel Foltz have four of their five sons who live in Vermillion County. Kenneth who married Esther Frist, had four children, Carolyn, Margaret (Peg), Ronald and Sue. None of them live in Vermillion County.

Dale, who married Dorothy Travis raised Warren, Mary Ann, Eleanor, Dean and Amy.

Donald, who married Jean Uran raised Julia and Tim.

Max, who married Barbara Shoemaker had four children; Randall, Vickie, Cynthia and Dirk.

The son not residing in Vermillion County, Leon, lives in Indianapolis. There was also a daughter, Eleanor (m. James E. Murray), both deceased.

Robert N. who married Genevieve Runyan Uhrin has no children. He is a descendant of Philip.

Frank, a descendant of Abraham, married, but no children.

Gene, who descended from a brother of the original two, Abraham and Gideon, married Loretta Weatherly and has three daughters, Kay Lynn, Natalie and Diana Jo.

Most of this generation graduated from high school, and some were privileged to acquire some higher education. There have been four Foltz wives who have taught in Vermillion County. They are Alma (Mrs. Ivan), Minnie (Mrs. Solon), Bertha (Mrs. Gurney) and Jean (Mrs. Don). There are others teaching in out-of-county systems. They have, no doubt, had some influence upon the community.

DONALD E. FOLTZ, was born in Clinton Township on Dec. 29, 1924, the fourth child of Paul and Hazel Walther Foltz. Grades one through five were spent in the one-room Spangler School, followed by grades six through eight at Fairview School. Don graduated from Clinton High School as a winner of the Sam Stultz award for 32 A's. He enrolled in Purdue University and worked his way through college as a fireman in the Chicago, Milwaukee, St. Paul, and Pacific Railroad at West Clinton, Purdue Dairy Farm and Purdue Home Economics Cafeteria. At Purdue, Don was Editor of the Purdue Agriculturist, Ceres - President, member of Alpha Zeta and Sigma Delta Chi honoraries, and a member of Acacia fraternity. He was selected to represent the university as a Danforth Fellow and as a nominee for Rhodes Scholar. Don graduated

summa cum laude in 1942 and began working for Indiana Certified Seed Service. He next became Assistant County Extension Agent in Vigo County. Don was selected for the National 4-H Fellowship for one year of study in Washington, D.C.

Donald E. Foltz

Korea intervened, and after Officer Candidate School at Fort Benning, he served in combat as a Second Lieutenant in the Infantry. After the truce Don enrolled in the University of Maryland where he received his master's degree. He returned home to farm and serve as Vermillion County State Representative in 1955, the first Korean Veteran in the Indiana Legislature. Don was selected outstanding freshman legislator. He was re-elected in 1957, 1959, and 1961, serving as Majority Leader in 1959. During those years Don sponsored legislation which created the Purdue School of Veterinary Medicine, the School Reorganization Act, and the creation of the State Department of Administration.

In 1961 Gov. Matthew Welsh selected Don to serve as Director of the Dept. of Conservation. During his four years as Director, he added over 30,000 acres to the state conservation system including Raccoon Recreation Area along with the other long-range reservoir development for multiple use. Don also changed the Department from patronage to merit system, moved the Indiana State Museum out of the State House basement into its own building, and left a long-range plan which guided the Department until it was completed. While in state government, he obtained a bank charter and led the formation of the Clinton State Bank where he served as president for many years. When the Wabash River bridge fell in, Don worked with Gov. Welsh to obtain the temporary and permanent replacements. He also was largely responsible for the relocation of State Road 63 west of Clinton. On Don's 40'th birthday Gov. Welsh came to Clinton to dedicate the new bridge and open the new bank. Gov. Welsh made Don a Sagamore of the Wabash.

With the Change of administration, Don went to work for Hulman & Co. spending the month of May at the Indianapolis 500 Race for over 20 years. Don's very active community service includes serving as chairman of the building committee for the Wayside United Methodist Church and parsonage. He has served several years as president of the Wabash Valley Association, is a life member of the Vermillion County Historical Society, and member of the Purdue Alumni Board. Don served as president of the State Purdue Agricultural Alumni, president of West Central Indiana Economic Development, secretary of the Swope Art Museum Board, and president of the Swope Board of Overseers. He is a member of the State Farm Advisory Board, Jerusalem Lodge #99, Scottish Rite, served on the Boy Scout Council and as a Junior Achievement

advisor. Don worked with the Terre Haute Committee for Area Progress, the Leadership Terre Haute Committee, the Research and Conservation Development Committee, State President, Regional President and National Representative to the Extension Advisory Boards. Don was a recipient of the Certificate of Distinction from the Purdue Ag Alumni Assoc.

Don served as president of the Hamilton Center Board for three years before they selected him to be the Chief Executive Officer of the six-county mental health facility in 1986. He has always been actively involved in the farm where he lived with his wife and two children. He has acquired over 1000 acres in the Clinton Township area which his son now farms. His recreation time is usually spent traveling about the world.

JEAN URAN FOLTZ, JULIA ELLEN FOLTZ, TIMOTHY CLINTON FOLTZ, Jean Uran was born at home in Terre Haute on Oct. 29, 1930, the first child of Kenneth and Millicent Gebhart Uran. She graduated from Wiley High School as a member of the National Honor Society and enrolled in Purdue University. While at Purdue, Jean was selected to be on the Student Union Board, Omicron Nu, Kappa Delta Pi, Gold Peppers, May Queen Court, Mortar Board - President, and Vice President of Chi Omega sorority. Following graduation, Jean returned home to teach English at Thornton Junior High School. During that year, she married Donald E. Foltz on Feb. 14, 1953 just before he left to serve in the Korean War. In June of 1953 Jean went to work for WTTV - the only television station in Indiana - doing a 30 minute, daily cooking program called "Welcome Home". When Don returned from Korea, Jean went with him to Washington, D.C. and obtained her master's degree from the University of Maryland. Upon graduation they returned to their farm home and Jean taught Home Economics and managed the cafeteria at Gerstmeyer High School for five years. She was a charter member and served a term as president of the Towne & Countrie Garden Club. Jean also served as State Conservation Chairman and State Secretary of the Garden Clubs of Indiana. She was selected to serve a term as president of the local Tri Kappa chapter before becoming a Tri Kappa Associates member.

Donald E. Foltz, Jean Foltz, Tim Foltz, Julia Foltz

Jean left teaching for nine years to be with their two children. When they entered school, she began teaching science for the South Vermillion School Corporation and has for over 20 years.

Julia Ellen was born on July 31, 1959 and attended Van Duyn Elementary and Clinton High Schools. She was a four-year band member and spent a summer in Lima, Peru as a Spanish exchange student. Julia participated in 4-H for ten years and received many awards including the

Tenure award and being a delegate to the National 4-H Conservation Camp in Washington, D.C. Julia attended Vincennes University for two years where she was a member of the Roaring Twenties swing choir. She graduated from Indiana State University and taught three years in McAllen, TX. Julia is working for the Vigo County School Corporation and received her master's degree from Indiana State University in 1989. She is a member of Tri Kappa, Vigo County Teachers Association, Indiana State Teachers Association, and the National Education Association.

On Oct. 18, 1961 Timothy Clinton was born. He attended Van Duyn and Central grade schools and South Vermillion High School where he lettered in Cross Country and Swimming and was a member of the National Honor Society. Tim was active in Boy Scouts for eight years and became an Eagle Scout, attended Philmont Camp in New Mexico and the World Jamboree in Pennsylvania. Tim participated in 4-H for ten years winning many awards including the Tenure award. He was selected for Who's Who in American High Schools. Tim went to Purdue University where he was a committee chairman for Ag Expo, served on Ag Council, and was selected for Ceres. After graduation Tim returned home to operate the family farm. He has served on the Vermillion County Extension Board the county Research, Conservation, and Development Committee, and a term as president of the Vermillion County Purdue Ag Alumni. He has worked with REACT, the Blanford Sportsman Club, and bowled with the Wayside United Methodist Church league.

KENNETH FOLTZ, On Oct. 6, 1935, Kenneth, eldest son of Paul H. and Hazel Walther Foltz and Esther, second daughter of Harry H. and Mable Boyd Frist, were married at the M.E. Parsonage in Newport by the Rev. E.T. Miles.

Kenneth had been working for and with his father in his farming operation, and the young couple settled into what proved to be a lifelong occupation in agriculture in Clinton Township.

After living with Kenneth's family a few weeks, the couple established their first home in the "little house on the corner", at the intersection of the Sandytown road and the Range Line. The following spring, they moved to what is known in the family as the "Baringer Place". There in 1937, their first child, Carolyn was born, and in 1939 Margaret Anne (Peggy) followed. In 1942, after the death of Mr. and Mrs. Everett Dowdy, their heirs decided to sell their 43 acres, and Kenneth and Esther bought it. They moved into the property on September 17, and on October 3, their son Ronald was born there. In 1944 Sue was born at the Vermillion County Hospital, completing the family unit.

Kenneth Foltz Family - 1951, Kenneth, Ron, Carolyn, Peggy, Sue, Esther

In the late 1940's they purchased a six acre tract

from Fred Gregg, and in the early 60's they sold this tract to Charles and Patricia Sisson. In 1950, Kenneth and his brother Don bought 36+ acres from William Farrington, plus a six-acre plot that lay in the corner of that tract. In 1957, Kenneth bought Don's interest in this place. In 1964, Kenneth purchased from the heirs of Tom Smith, a small plot, and in 1967 he purchased from Joe and Caroline Bonacorsi a plot of 27 acres, both acreages joining the Dowdy place on the south. In 1973, after his father's death, Kenneth purchased the "Baringer Place" from his mother, leaving her a life-estate in the house and yard. Thus, they accumulated a modest 222 acres.

As a couple, Kenneth and Esther made conscious effort to be contributors to the community, and raised their family with the same ambitions and attitudes. Both have been active in church, Farm Bureau, Soil Conservation District, Home Extension club, 4-H leader, school connected activities. Their children were active in 4-H, Junior Leaders, Student Council, school music groups, cheer-leading, church youth groups, etc.

In 1957, Carolyn married Montelle H. Lowry, a professional painter, decorator and interior finisher. They had three children.

In 1960, Peggy married Frank W. Hughes, a high-school science and math teacher. They had two children.

In 1964, as a Junior at Indiana University, Ron joined the Peace Corps and spent three years there as an agricultural advisor, working with youth.

Also in 1964, Sue left her nurse's training at St. Anthony's Hospital to marry Jeff Skjordahl, who was at that time in the U.S. Air Force. They had two children, and then Sue completed her training and received her R.N. Jeff finished his degree in engineering at Rose-Hulman.

As a result of Ron's three years in Brazil, an orphan, one Loureno Batzner by name, came to the Foltz home, where he lived with "Kenna and Ma" while acquiring a high school and college education. He is now back in Brazil, helping and teaching his own people.

Ronald was killed in a traffic accident in June of 1972.

Kenneth and Esther have enjoyed the fellowship of their family, their seven adult grandchildren and now they have two great-grandsons, of which there is no equal!! Just ask them.

Kenneth and Esther worked hard, together, except for one area; they espoused opposite political parties, a fact that was never allowed to become a problem, because neither expected the other to forsake their heritage.

MAX LEROY FOLTZ AND BARBARA ANN SHOEMAKER FOLTZ, Max L. Foltz was born at home on Range Line Road, Aug. 19, 1931. He was the sixth child of Paul and Hazel Walther Foltz. He attended grade school at Fairview School and graduated from Clinton High School in 1951. He worked on the family farm until he was called into the army in 1954.

Max married Barbara Shoemaker, Oct. 31, 1953. Barbara was the first child in the family of Chancie and Sylvia Rudisill Shoemaker. She was born on June 17, 1934, in Lyford, IN, and lived there until the seventh grade. In 1946, the family moved east of Boonville, IN, and lived there until 1951, when they returned to Clinton. Barbara graduated from Clinton High School in 1952.

Max and Barbara met at Fairview Methodist

Church, where they married a year and a half later, Oct. 31, 1953. Both are members of this church which was later the Wayside United Methodist Church.

Randall Allen, their first born, was born on Sept. 25, 1954. When Randall was three months old, Max was shipped out to Korea where he served in the army until May, 1956. In the fall of 1956, he started work as a cement mason in Terre Haute. The next summer a daughter, Vickie Lynn, was born June 11, 1957. A third child, Cynthia Louise, was born a year and a half later, arriving on Christmas Day, 1958. Four years later the fourth child, Dirk Paul, was born on Dec. 12, 1962.

Barbara worked as a free lance artist from 1965 until 1975, when the Foltz Photography Studio was opened in Clinton. In 1983, Barbara joined her studio with Smith's Studio in Terre Haute, calling it Smith Foltz Photography. The same year the studio in Clinton was opened, Max went to work at Ziegler Coal Company in Murdock, IL, where he worked until the mine closed August, 1986.

Max and Barbara live on Range Line Road in the house that his father built for his mother before they were married in 1911, and the same house where Max was born.

Randall Allen married Brenda Kay Thompson, Nov. 9, 1984.

Vickie Lynn married Robert Anthony Peperak Apr. 9, 1976. They have one child, Joseph Anthony.

Cynthia Louise married Keith Pruett, Feb. 18, 1977. They have two daughters, Brandy Ann and Lindsay Michelle.

Dirk Paul married Anna Aqualine Poletto, June 6, 1987.

PAUL AND HAZEL WALTHER FOLTZ, Paul H. Foltz, the second child of Gideon Luther and Sciota Ike Foltz, was born on Easter Sunday, Apr. 6, 1890 in a log cabin which has since been moved and restored by his son Donald. Paul was born on Range Line Road and lived there most of his life. He attended Sandytown School and then Columbia School in Clinton completing the sixth grade. As a young man he worked carrying ice, doing farm work, and doing carpentry work with his uncles and cousins. Paul began working for the Klondyke Coal Mine before his marriage to Hazel Walther on Easter Sunday, Apr. 16, 1911. He worked for Clinton Coal Company for 31 years at the Crown Hill # 5 and Crown Hill # 6 mines. Paul also began to buy farmland. The family farmed and operated a dairy, delivering milk in Clinton for a number of years. Paul was a charter member of Farm Bureau and served as president of the Clinton Township group. He was a lifelong Methodist belonging to the Centenary Church, then Fairview, and later a charter member of Wayside United Methodist Church when the churches merged. Paul held many church board positions during his lifetime. Paul died on Apr. 15, 1971, one day before their 60th wedding anniversary. He is buried at Rose Lawn Cemetery on old highway # 41.

Hazel was born on Sept. 1, 1889 to Henry and Elizabeth Conrad Walther on R # 3, the youngest of seven children. She attended Hazel Bluff School and Clinton High School. A few years after marrying Paul, their son Kenneth was born on July 20, 1913, followed by a daughter Eleanor on May 22, 1916. Four more sons were born - Dale on Aug. 10, 1922, Donald on Dec. 29, 1924, Leon on Feb. 16, 1927, and Max on Aug. 19, 1931. Over the years all six children married and gave Paul and Hazel 20 grandchildren, 21 great grandchildren, and two great, great grandchildren at the last counting. Hazel is a charter member of Clinton Township Farm Bureau and has been a member of Clinton Township Demonstration Club for 60 years. She is the oldest member of Wayside United Methodist Church where she taught a Sunday School class for many years.

Paul and Hazel Foltz

At the time of publication she is 99 years old, lives alone, and is of very sound mind. Hazel remembers all the changes in her life, from going to church in a horse and buggy to riding in an airplane and watching men land on the moon. They put in their first telephone in 1912 and watched an airplane land at the Sam Stultz place in 1917. Their first car was a 1917 Ford that cost $395.00. Women's suffrage became law in time to vote in the fall of 1920 and Hazel has voted in every election except for one primary. Electricity came up Range Line Road in 1923, but stopped a half mile from their house. Paul finally arranged for electricity in 1926 and they bought a washer, cream separator, iron, and sweeper. In 1930 Paul traded a cow to get their first radio. They dug a basement in 1937 and put in a furnace to replace the coal stove. In 1938 Paul traded a heifer for their first refrigerator. Range Line Road was blacktopped in 1939. When grandpa came to live with them in 1946, a modern bathroom was added to the house. In 1952 Paul and Hazel remodeled the house across the road on land they had purchased. The house had been built by Christopher Beringer, son-in-law of Fredrick Spangler before the Civil War with home grown lumber. Removing wallpaper during remodeling uncovered newspapers of Abraham Lincoln's death. They purchased a television in 1953. The heat wave and drought of 1988 saw the addition of an air-conditioner. Hazel had lived her entire 99 years in just four houses and they are located within four miles of each other, 75 years on Range Line Road. She has lived almost half of the time that the Unites States has existed.

JOHN FOX, was one of the most respected citizens of the Gessie community. He lived one mile north of Gessie, near the cross roads (Steven Hicks Family resides there now).

He was born May 10, 1751, in Hesse-Cassel, Germany and came to America and settled near Fredic, MD.

John Fox married Susan Hilligas. They came west with five children and settled in Vermillion County near Gessie, IN.

The childrens names were Anna, Mary, Catherine, Margarite and John Daniel.

Anna married Philander Goff. A daughter was Eva Goff Hicks, who was married to Daniel A. Hicks. Their sons Jene, Carl and Ray are residents of this area.

John Fox was a successful farmer. At the time of his death his farm consisted of 186 acres.

BEULAH L. THOMAS FRIST, the older daughter of James L. Thomas and Golda Nolan Thomas, was born in Helt Township on June 13, 1920. She has a sister, Madge L. Lake who now lives in Helt Township.

Beulah graduated from Hillsdale High School in 1938 and Indiana State University in 1942. She attended graduate classes at Indiana State and Butler University. Beulah taught in the high school at Perrysville in Vermillion County, at Pike Township High School in Marion County and the Indianapolis Schools 101 and 108 for a total of 27 years until retiring in 1980.

Beulah married Harold Frist on Dec. 12, 1942, and they have one daughter, Lisa Ann.

Beulah is a member of the Avon Methodist Church.

HAROLD B. FRIST, the older son of Marshall A. Frist and Marjorie Blakesley, was born in Helt Township on Oct. 28, 1920. Harold was graduated from Clinton High School in 1938. In 1942 he graduated from Rose Polytechnic Institute where he was a member of the Tau Beta Pi Honorary Fraternity. He and Beulah L. Thomas were married Dec. 12, 1942 and have since lived in Indianapolis. Harold worked for the Allison Division of General Motors for 38 years retiring as Superintendent of Quality Engineering in 1980. He is a member of the Avon Methodist Church.

Harold and Beulah have one daughter, Lisa Ann, born Nov. 14, 1955.

LISA ANN FRIST, is the only child of Harold B. Frist and Beulah L. Thomas Frist. She was born in Indianapolis on Nov. 14, 1955. Lisa graduated from Ben Davis High School in 1974 and Franklin College (cum laude) in 1978. She has done graduate work at Ball State and the University of Indianapolis where she received her masters degree. Lisa taught school as an art teacher at Pendleton Middle School and at Custer-Baker Middle School at Franklin, IN. Lisa, who is a member of the Avon Methodist Church, lives in Greenwood, IN.

MARJORIE BLAKESLEY FRIST, was born Sept. 10, 1901 in Helt Township. She was the oldest child of L. Bruce and Eva James Blakesley. Her sister, Marzelle, born July 3, 1913 now lives in Fresno, CA.

A brother, James Wesley, was born Apr. 4, 1916 and died on Aug. 16, 1940.

Marjorie graduated from Hillsdale High School in 1918. She was a member of the Clinton Mothers' Club and an active member of the Clinton Methodist Church and the various women's organizations of that church.

Marjorie died on Mar. 5, 1982 on her way to a World Day of Prayer meeting at the Clinton Christian Church and was buried in Helt's Prairie Cemetery.

MARSHALL A. FRIST, was born Mar. 1, 1897 to Jediah and Elizabeth Helt Frist in Helt Township. He graduated from Clinton High School and served in the Army in W.W.-1. On Dec. 14, 1919 he married Marjorie Blakesley, daughter of Lawrence Bruce and Eva James Blakesley. To this union, Harold B. was born on Oct. 28, 1920 and Wayne Edward was born on Aug. 19, 1925.

Marshall graduated from the Cincinnati College of Embalming in 1924 and started working for his uncle, Jasper N. Frist, at the Frist Funeral Home in Clinton. After 40 years he sold his interest in the business to Harold B. Mack.

Marshall was a member of the Clinton Methodist Church and several other organizations of the community. He and Marjorie had four grandchildren.

Marshall Frist died on June 20, 1966 at the age of 69 and was buried in Helt's Prairie Cemetery.

PATRICIA J. (PAT) FRIST, was born in Vermillion Co., IN, May 19, 1932, the daughter of Harry H. and Mable Boyd Frist, and the youngest of five daughters. She attended school at St. Bernice but graduated from Clinton High School. She also graduated from Mi-Lady Beauty Academy at Terre Haute, and through her jobs has attended schools in banking and has taken several classes to further her education in insurance.

Among places of employment, she was one of the original employees who opened the Clinton State Bank in November, 1964. For several years, she was employed in Lang Helt's Clinton Insurance and Real Estate Office. Presently she is employed at Sycamore Agency at Terre Haute, IN.

Patricia J. Frist

The sisters of Pat are: Emily (Mrs. Sam) Saxton, Esther (Mrs. Kenneth) Foltz, Shirley (Mrs. Melvin) Jones, and Myrtle (Mrs. Royce) King (deceased).

The parents of Harry Frist were: Jediah Frist and Elizabeth Helt Frist. Parents of Jediah were: Jediah R. Frist and May J. Pierce Frist. Elizabeth Helt Frist was a descendant of Michael Helt, who was one of the original Helt's prairie settlers, Her parents were Charles B. Helt and Sarah Taylor Helt. Charles Helt's parents were Michael Helt and Elizabeth Aye Helt.

The parents of Mable Boyd Frist were Albert E. and Emily Skidmore Boyd. The parents of Albert E. Boyd were Ellis Delivan Boyd and Rebecca Bales Boyd. Elizabeth Skidmore Boyd was a descendant of John Skidmore who also was one of the early settlers of Helt's prairie; her parents were George Skidmore and Amanda Gooden Skidmore. The parents of George Skidmore were John Skidmore and Jane Hopper Skidmore (Jane being John's second wife and a sister to his first wife).

The Helt, Skidmore and Ford families came together from Ohio and settled in Natural Prairie which is still known as Helt's Prairie, north of Clinton approximately five miles. They came down the Sciota River in Ohio, down the Ohio River, and up the Wabash River.

Jediah Frist came with his family at a very early age to Vermillion Co., IN, from Delaware. He was the brother of Jasper N. Frist, the founder of Frist Funeral Home, and he was the father of Marshall A. Frist, who was also a part owner of Frist Funeral Home at one time.

Pat is an active member of Clinton First United Methodist Church and has attended there for approximately 40 years. She has been an active member of choir for approximately 30 of those years. She has also been a member of the Esther Circle and held various offices in the church. She is also a member of Ft. Harrison Chapter of Daughters of American Revolution, Farm Bureau, an MAL member of Delta Theta Tau, and currently on the board at Helt's Prairie Cemetery. She is a licensed cosmetologist and licensed insurance agent.

WAYNE EDWARD FRIST,

was the second son of Marshall and Marjorie Frist. He was born Aug. 19, 1925 in Clinton. He graduated from Clinton High school in 1943.

After serving in the Navy as a pharmacist's mate, he moved to Boone, IA, where he worked for John Deere Mfg. He and Ruth Eddy were married and had three children: Merschell, Michael and Joan Marie.

Wayne died in 1963 and was buried in the Boone Cemetery.

LEO FULTZ AND CARMIE SMITH FULTZ,

Leo Fultz was born Apr. 22, 1905 near Cayuga the youngest son one of eight children of John Milton and Cora May Onley Fultz. His grandparents were Jacob and Mary Louise Murray Fultz of the Pioneers in Vermillion County since 1826 as First Land Owners.

Adept, one day at a time, he had lived over 80 years in Vermillion County in and around Eugene and Cayuga. A family man he married Dora Richmond and is the father of Richard and Joan. He let her get away.

Front: Leo Fultz, Carmie Fultz, Jeanie Lamb. Back: Freda Gascon, Mack Fultz, Nikke Baker.

September 16, 1945 he married Carmie Smith, daughter of Amanda Scott and Clarney Smith at the first house south of where his father would have been born had the house not burned.

They farmed 200 acres, accumulated a herd of cows, at one time furnished milk to school children at Cayuga, Eugene and Perrysville schools.

They have three daughters and a son, Nikke, Freda, Mack and Jeanie, all married and are parents and grandparents of 14 grandchildren and more.

They moved in 1951 to Highland Township north of Eugene and built a brick home on 233 acres they own which is farmed by Mack, who bought the farm next door with his wife, Brenda and two sons, Mark and Mike. They own 100 acres north of Eugene past the curve in the road.

They attended the Cayuga Presbyterian Church in Cayuga since their children were baptized there

Mar. 25, 1951 by Rev. Trickey. The same one she attended since 1922.

Nikke and Freda graduated from Indiana State University June 4, 1970 and June 13, 1979. Jeanie married Kerry Lamb. They own a home at Chester, VA and are active in the nearby Methodist Church. Nikke married Jake Baker. They have seven children and live north of Perrysville. Freda married William A. McLain. They are the parents of Anne, Eleanor and Billie Jo McLain. Today she is married to Raymond Gascon. They own a home at Port Alleghany, PA, and are the parents of one daughter, R.G. and one son, Zechariah.

Carmie was a typist at the Indianapolis Senate 1932. She did stenographic work for Civil Service in Washington, D.C., five years at the U.S. Treasury, one year at the Securities & Exchange Commission, and one year at the Quartermaster General's Office.

She is a 50 year member of Eugene Township Home Economic's Club. She served as President of United Presbyterian Women and attends church and Sunday School at the Cayuga Presbyterian Church.

VIRGINIA WALTHALL GAINES,

was born Nov. 30, 1925, in Ventura, CA. She was one of eight children born to Clinton and Anna Opal Nichols Walthall, from Quaker, a small town northwest of Dana.

Virginia grew up in and around Newport. She graduated from Newport High School in 1945.

She married Ralph A. Gaines, Dec. 26, 1945. A daughter, Carolyn, was born in 1949, and another daughter, Mary, was born in 1950.

Virginia is now employed as head cook at Newport Grade School, and is an active member of The First Assemby of God, in Cayuga.

MARSHALL GLICK GIBBS,

was born on July 1, 1908, in Indianola, IL. On Aug. 11, 1935, he married Annabelle Gibbs (Fable) in Cayuga, IN. Marshall is the eldest of three sons and two daughters of Fred H. Gibbs and Rosa Lena Gibbs (Glick) of Indianola, IL. Annabelle is the youngest of three daughters and one son of Fred A. Fable and Anna Mary (Mollie) Fable of Cayuga, IN.

Anthony A. Gibbs, Linda K. Gibbs, Michele L. Gibbs, Annabelle Gibbs, Marshall G. Gibbs

Marshall G. Gibbs is a graduate of the University of Illinois at Champaign, B.S. 1932, and Indiana State University, Terre Haute, M.S. 1965. He was a teacher and counselor in the Cayuga and North Vermillion School systems for 23 years. During most of that time he was also associated with his father-in-law, Fred A. Fable, in the Fable Motor Company Ford Dealership. He served as an infantry officer in the U.S. Army during WWII in Europe, 1942-1946, and holds the rank of Major in U.S. Army Retired Reserve. He is Past Grand Patron of

Indiana Grand Chapter, Order of the Eastern Star, a member of Cayuga Chapter, O.E.S., and Cayuga Lodge, F.& A.M., a charter member of Cayuga Lions Club, and life member of Post 263 American Legion. As a member of the Cayuga Presbyterian Church, he was S.S. Superintendent for several years and has served on the Session for many years.

Annabelle Gibbs (Fable) was born July 27, 1908 in Cayuga, IN. She graduated from Cayuga High School in 1926. Prior to her marriage she worked in a business office in Danville, IL. Annabelle is a member of the Cayuga Presbyterian Church, the Bethany Class, and the Women's Social Study Club. As a member and Past Matron of Cayuga Chapter of the Order of the Eastern Star, she has served as Grand Representative to the Florida Grand Chapter in Indiana.

Anthony Alan Gibbs was born Feb. 22, 1939, to Marshall and Annabelle Gibbs in Cayuga. He graduated from Cayuga High School (1957) and Indiana State University (B.S. 1961; M.S. 1965). He has been both a public school and college teacher and administrator. He is a member of Cayuga Lodge, F.&A.M. and Scottish Rite, Valley of Terre Haute. He was married to Linda Kay Gibbs (Liehr) in Terre Haute, IN on Dec. 29, 1962. They have resided in Terre Haute since 1965.

Linda Gibbs, born July 3, 1941, in Terre Haute, IN, graduated from Indiana State University (B.S. 1962; M.S. 1966). She is a public school teacher and in 1988 was voted to be Vigo County (Terre Haute) Teacher of the Year. She is listed in Outstanding Young Women of America.

Michele Lynn Gibbs was born to Anthony and Linda Gibbs on Oct. 5, 1968 in Terre Haute, IN. She is a graduate of Terre Haute Schools and is listed in Who's Who of American High School Students. She was a delegate to Indiana Girls State in 1986. As a delegate to the National 4-H Congress in 1986, she was elected Miss Congeniality and was a National 4-H achievement winner. She is a student at Indiana State University where she is a member of Zeta Tau Alpha sorority and a Senator in the Student Government Association. *Submitted by Marshall G. Gibbs*

DAVID GOFF,

was born in Connecticut in 1798. When he was six years old his father immigrated to western New York. When David was 17 he, with two brothers, started west working their way. They were carpenters by vocation. Lumber was cheap and much building was being done. When they reached Carlisle, IN they worked for sometime in a distillery. In 1823 they came up the Wabash River to Perrysville. Here they helped to build the first building. David and Almond each entered 80 acres of land west and north of Perrysville, IN, and spent the rest of their lives here. Each lived to be over 80 years old. Brainard, the other brother left them here and he went on to LaPort, IN where he settled. David Goff married Mary Hughes and they became the parents of six children, two sons and four daughters; namely, the daughters, Elzina, Lucretia, Martha and Mary; the sons, Philander and Squire. David was a very worthy and respected citizen and was a member of the Baptist church for almost 50 years.

PHILANDER GOFF,

son of David and Mary Hughes Goff was born in Highland Township in September 1834 and spent his entire life in this vicinity.

He had a beautiful home two miles northeast of Gessie and lived here more than 40 years.

Mr. Goff was married three times. His first wife was Elizabeth Gouty, she died and left a son, Jeremiah. Jeremiah's children were Oscar, Alma, Basil and Roy. The daughter Alma married Fount Straughn and their son, Earl lives on the homeplace of his grandfather and farms the ground.

Mr. Goff's second wife was Marintha Cossey Gouty. She died and left him a son, William. William Goff was one of the early merchants and implement dealers in Gessie. William Goff's wife was Mary Henderson.

Later Mr. Goff married Anna E. Fox and they had seven children. They were Flora, Lewis, John, Lillian, Stillman, Eva and Bertha.

After Mr. Goff's death, Mrs. Goff made her home with the daughter, Eva (Mrs. Daniel Hicks). Mrs. Eva Hicks' sons, Ray and Carl, live near Perrysville, and Jene lives northeast of Rileysburg.

EDMON R. GOFORTH AND LEILA D. GOFORTH,

Edmon Reid Goforth was born Sept. 15, 1903 in Montezuma, IN, the son of Howard and Ella Reid Goforth. He is the second of four children. His three sisters are Meredith Mikula of Tipp City, OH, Clara Nixon, deceased, and Kathryn Fletcher of Monticello, IN. Edmon lived in Montezuma until he was seven years of age. Then he with his family moved to Vermillion County near Dana where he grew up. He graduated from Helt Township High School in 1921. He then attended Indiana State University from which he graduated. He taught in the Fairview School, Clinton, IN from 1923-1925.

He was married Aug. 14, 1926 to Mariam Bales the only child of Harry and Tott Bales. Her grandfather, Caleb Bales Jr. was a captain in the Civil War and took part in Sherman's march to the Sea. She grew up in the house that Caleb built after he returned from the war. She graduated from Helt Township High School and The University of Illinois, then taught School in Clinton, IN. Following her marriage to Edmon the couple moved to Gary, IN, where they both taught school.

Edmon and Leila Goforth

They became parents of two sons: James Edmon in 1928 and Gene Bales in 1929. They retired from teaching in 1962, returning to their farm near Dana where he was engaged in farming with his sons. James and Barbara live near and are the parents of three children Glenna, Kerry and Douglas.

Gene and wife Frances now live in Tampa, FL but spent their summers on their farm. Both hold doctorate degrees from Indiana University. He was an officer in the Air Force during the Korean Conflict. He is a retired university professor and farmer. Frances is a professor in the University of South Florida. They are the parents of four children. Gene Jr. and wife Tonya, Orlando, FL; Gary and wife Karen and three children - Kelly, Geoffrey and Kristen, West Palm Beach, FL; Steven and wife

Joyce and daughter Ashley, Tampa, FL, and Susan and husband Steve Wegmann, New Orleans, LA.

Following Mariam's death in 1974, Edmon was married to Blanche Botner Saxton who was the daughter of Lucy Hawn and Jake Botner. Blanche died in 1981. Edmon was later married to Leila Church Mack.

Leila was born Aug. 19, 1910 near Clinton, IN the daughter of Alanson and Nettie Curtis Church. She was the youngest of eight children. Alanson was first married to Anna Curtis, their children were Iva, Edna, Ira and Ray. Following Anna's death he then married Nettie, their children were Zula, Willis, Mary and Leila.

Leila grew up on a farm, except for two years when the family lived in Dana. She graduated from St. Bernice High School in 1929 and attended Brown's Business College in Terre Haute. In 1931 she was married to Carleton Mack who was the son of Leila Kerns Mack and Charles Mack.

She married Edmon Goforth in 1981. She enjoys being a homemaker and is the president of the Happy Homemakers Extension Club. Her hobbies are reading and music. She plays the piano and organ. Leila and Edmon attend church at Bono where she is vice president of the United Methodist Women.

Edmon received his 50 year pin in the Masonic Lodge in 1987.

JAMES E. GOFORTH AND BARBARA CRAWLEY GOFORTH,

James E. Goforth was born Jan. 16, 1928 in Gary, IN to Edmon and Mariam Goforth. He is the eldest of two children. James grew up in Gary where he graduated from William A. Wirt High School in 1945. He served one year in the Army Air Force, then graduated from Purdue University in 1951. He then returned to the family farm southeast of Dana, IN which had been in his mother's family (Bales) since 1826.

In 1952 he married Barbara Crawley, daughter of Robert and Lucille Dunkin of Hillsdale, IN. Barbara, her older sister, Mary, and younger brother, Jack, all graduated from Hillsdale High School. Mary lives in Brawley, CA with her husband Ed Church. Jack lives in Indianapolis, IN.

Barbara and James Goforth

Within the next four years a daughter, Glenna, and a son, Kerry, were born. In 1956, they moved to New Mexico where James worked with the Soil Conservation Service for the next 14 years. Another son, Douglas, was born in Alamogordo, NM, and in 1970 the family moved back to Indiana. He joined his father in farming which they are still doing at the present time.

He is a member of the Dana Knights of Pythias Lodge of which his grandfather, Harry Bales, was a charter member in 1890.

Barbara is a computer operator with M.A.B.

Paint Company in Terre Haute. She is also a member of the Dames Club of Dana. They both attend the United Methodist Church of Dana.

Glenna is the Band Director at South Vermillion High School and lives in Clinton, IN with her husband David Gibbs.

Kerry and wife, Cindy, live in Washington D.C. where he works for the National Grain and Feed Association. Douglas works for Corning Ware in Corning, NY.

The family farm has been expanded over the years and now includes several neighboring farms, one of which belonged to Mr. and Mrs. William C. Pyle, parents of Ernie Pule, World War Two Correspondent. The Pyle farm now belongs to his brother Gene and wife Frances. Gene participated in the farming operation from 1974 to 1987.

JAMES EVERETT GRAHAM,

was born at Shepardsville, IN, on Oct. 2, 1922. His parents were James Buchannan Graham and Cecille (Kyger/Sollars) Graham. His father was a coal miner. His parents later moved to Clinton, IN, to live with the grandparents of James E. Graham.

Grandfather John Graham was born at Galston, Ayrshire, Scotland, in May of 1865. He came to America about 1872. He married Christine (Patton/McWherter) Graham who was born at Dundee, Fyfshire, Scotland. They had ten children.

He was raised in Clinton, IN, and attended Clinton schools. James' father was injured in the coal mine in 1934. He and his sister Donna Joann Graham went to live with their mother in Detroit, MI.

Married June 28, 1947, Alice (Belan) and James E. Graham at Detroit, MI, Gethsemane Lutheran Church

He attended school at Gethsemane Lutheran Church/School. He graduated as an honor student and received the American Legion School Award. He participated in baseball, swimming, and boxing. He was also in dramatics, singing mixed chorus. He was also on the local radio stations with the high school plays and pageants. He graduated from the David Mackenzie High School in June, 1941, in Detroit, MI.

At the outbreak of World War II, he enlisted (volunteer) in the U.S. Navy. However, he was destined to become an Army enlisted man. He served in the AntiAircraft Artillery, defending the Northwest Coast of the United States. He served in Europe during World War II earning the Good Conduct Medal, two major battle ribbons, American Defense, European Theater of Operations, Victory medals. He received an honorable discharge on Feb. 26, 1946.

On June 28, 1947, he married Alice Mabel Belan in Detroit, MI, at Gethsemane Lutheran Church. Both were members of this church. From this union five children were born—James Martin, Bonnie Louise, Vicki Lynn, David John, and Benjamin

Robert Frederick. The family lived in the Detroit area and the suburbs of Pontiac, MI, at Walled Lake, MI.

His wife, Alice (Belan) Graham, was born Apr. 8, 1927, at the coal mining town of Galloway, WV. Her father was a coal miner. He died when she was three, and her mother moved to Detroit where she was raised. She had four sisters and one brother.

When World War II was over, James Everett Graham enlisted in the Active Ready Reserve of the Army on Feb. 26, 1946. He served until July 31, 1965. He retired with the rank of Battalion Sergeant Major (M. Sgt.). He received the Armed Forces Reserve Medal.

His civilian life was varied and active. He and his wife, Alice, were busy in the Lutheran Church: Elder, Evangelism, Sunday School, Choir, Missions. He was American Legion, Michigan post, local commander. He was an active leader in Boy Scouts, a scoutmaster and commissioner. He was awarded the Scouter District Award of Merit in 1984. In the Clinton, IN, community, he is president of the Zoning Board of Appeals, and also Hearing Officer for City of Clinton Nuisance Ordinances. He is a Democrat by choice.

His wife, Alice, is a volunteer for the Vermillion County Hospital Guild. She is secretary for her husband in his work as tutor in the Clinton Public Library adult literacy program. Both are active volunteers in the Clinton Senior Center in Clinton. James is a member of the Vermillion County Historical Society. His two sons at home—David and Benjamin—are assistant scoutmasters with Troop 463, in Clinton, IN.

JOHN GRAHAM, was born May 7, 1865 in Galston, Ayrshire, Scotland. He was one of 13 children brought to American circa 1872. He was the son of Archie and Margaret (?) Graham, both of Scotland. They were said to have settled in Boonville, IN, Warrick County. Later the family went to Farmersburg, IN, seeking work or to be near relatives.

About this time John met his wife Christina (McVicar/Patton). She was born in Dundee, Fyfeshire, Scotland. The town was not known by her according to a letter written in 1947 to her grandson, James Everett Graham.

Christina (McVicar/Patton) Graham (1878-1959) and John Graham (1865-1934)

John was a coal miner, sinking mine shafts for some of the coal mines in the Wabash Valley area. John and Christina moved in and out of Terre Haute. Homes in the early years were varied—Rosedale, Bloomington, Lyford, Clinton (circa 1931), Terre Haute (Sixth Avenue, Locust, Maple, 12 points), back to Clinton.

John and Christina had 12 children. Two were lost by miscarriages. Samuel, almost three years old

died from choking on a peanut and is buried in Riverside Cemetery in Clinton. John Evan Graham, died during World War I in France in 1918, and is buried in Riverside Cemetery. Other children were James B., Henry, Andrew, Christina, Barbara, William, Robert, and Elizabeth. All the children were raised in the towns mentioned in Parke and Vigo Counties.

John and his wife lived on Water (First) Street. Later they lived at 325 North Main Street, the north wing of the old Farmers' Institute. Use of the school in Clinton was short lived. It was planned to use it as a United States Army Barracks or Military Academy, but plans never materialized for this use during the Civil War.

Mr. Bogart, a Clinton businessman and owner of the property, separated by the north wing (325 North Main) and the south wing (315 North Main). The center part of the structure was moved about 1901 to Vine and Main Streets. This for many years was Bogart's Opera House. The north wing at 325 North Main became the home of John and Christina and their families. It was used as a rooming house for coal miners. Many Scots lived in the north end of Clinton, many from the same area of Galston, Ayrshire, Scotland. "Pop", as John Graham was called, had many friends who worked the local mines. Most all were members of the United Mine Workers of America.

John Graham died May 21, 1934, at home after two weeks illness. His home at this time was at 136 North Third Street. He is buried in the family plot at Riverside Cemetery in Clinton.

Christina and family, during the depression, lived in various homes in the north end area; also Vine Street, and Fifth and Main. The last home was at 447 Sycamore Street. John Graham's widow was active in the Pocahontas Lodge, Eastern Star, Rebekah's, and the Caldeonian Society of Terre Haute. Christina passed away at age 81 years on Aug. 18, 1959. She is at rest by her husband, John Graham, in Riverside Cemetery in Clinton. *Submitted by James Everett Graham, grandson*

WILLIAM, REBECCA, BILLIE, AND JENNIFER GRAHAM, William (Bill) Graham was born Mar. 16, 1949, in this area, the son of Robert and Christine Graham. He attended school at Sacred Heart and graduated from Clinton High School in 1967. He has an older brother, Robert Graham, who lives in Parke County, and a younger sister, Vickie Graham West of Fairview. (See related story on Bruce and Vickie West).

Billie Graham

Rebecca Reynolds Graham was born Oct. 1, 1952, in Clinton, the daughter of Everett Ott Reynolds and Lenora Reynolds. Her mother's parents were Russ and Evelyn Reynolds and her father's parents were Alex and Blanche Reynolds. Rebecca attended Fairview School and graduated from Clinton High School in 1970.

William and Rebecca were married on Sept. 5, 1970. William is now a security guard at Eli Lilly and Rebecca is an artist. They have two daughters, Billie Suanne Graham, a senior at South Vermillion High School, and Jennifer Rebecca Graham, who is a sophomore at South Vermillion High School. Billie is on the annual staff.

The Grahams have long been involved with athletics. William's father, Bob Graham, has been a boxer, a wrestler, and a semi-pro football player. Bob Graham, William's brother, was a participant in high school football, basketball, and other sports, as was Bill. William is a member of the Clinton Park Board and a softball coach. Billie Suanne has received several awards in high school sports including All Conference in softball; and in basketball All Conference and All-Sectional for 1986-1987 and 1987-1988. She was the Most Valuable Player in basketball in 1987-1988 and leading scorer for the same season. She has also lettered in tennis, and this fall she is doing very well in volleyball. Jennifer Rebecca is a cheerleader and participates in softball and gymnastics. *Submitted by Leo Reposh, Jr.*

PAUL E. AND ESTHER N. (DOWERS) GRUMLEY, One of several famines on Irish soil in the middle 1800's led to a mass exodus of people. Over half of the population (four million) immigrated during 1840-1860. There must have been many O'Gormleys who left their homeland for new hopes, new futures in America. The O'Gormleys were originally part of the O'Neill clan from County Tyrone in the North of Ireland. Speculation suggests that most Grumleys moved West to Pennsylvania where many died in the Johnstown Flood. Grumley immigrants—originally O'Gormley and anglicized to Grumley—included Samuel Grumley who later married Sarah Bryant; one of their children born in the United States in 1852 was John Bryant Grumley. Samuel and Sarah's family survived and ventured into Indiana settling in the central western part along the Wabash River.

Paul and Esther Grumley

Paul Everett Grumley (Nov. 6, 1896) was the son of John Bryant Grumley and Lunda Elmina Barnes. Paul had a brother, Jay Barnes Grumley. Paul served in the Armed Forces in France during World War I and returned home to work at various jobs until he married Esther Nora Dowers on Aug. 6, 1924; they lived in Vermillion County for their married life. PJ "Junior" (Jan. 19, 1926) and Betty Joann (Feb. 6, 1928) were born, raised and educated in Vermillion County. Also in 1924 Paul and his brother Jay bought a general store—the old Charlie Winter's where they worked until the store was sold in 1936. In 1943 Paul and Esther purchased the home of Elizabeth Gilkerson known as "Aunt Lizzy." Esther continued to live in Eugene after the death of her husband Paul in 1954. On Sept. 1, 1963

Esther married Marion Clem Gragg, who was born in Albion, IN on Jan. 1, 1881. "Grandpa Gragg" lived to be 99 years old before his death on June 9, 1980.

Esther has been active in the Democratic party throughout her life. She served as Township Trustee from 1955 to 1979. Before the school district was consolidated Esther oversaw the education in the township schools. Her work as the Township Trustee for 24 years included serving the needs of the hungry and homeless through poor relief, appraiser of property, licensing of dog tags and other local services. During her retirement years she maintains interests in local history, gardening and a special love for her great-grandchildren. She has enjoyed seeing old friends and meeting new acquaintances during Pioneer Days and Harvest Days every Spring and Fall. In 1984 her family honored her with a surprise party at the Community Center in Eugene.

The following is a list of the grandchildren and the great-grandchildren of Paul and Esther beginning with the oldest grandchild:

Paul James is a physician and married to Juliette Ezzell on Aug. 12, 1972; they have four children—James Bryan, Louis Miller, Charlotte Calder and Thomas Hussmann.

Mary Janice is employed in an optometrist's office and married Charles Leland Bell on July 21, 1973; they have one son—James Everett.

Linda Joann is a special education teacher living in Louisville, KY.

Jeffery Everett is a United Methodist minister and married Therese Erickson on Sept. 9, 1983; they have four children—Benjamin Emmanuel, Thomas Erickson, Margaret Elizabeth Erickson and one on the way. They live in Berkeley, CA.

Nora Jane is employed at home and married Jerry Dale Farley on Dec. 2, 1978; they have two sons—Christopher Dale, Russell Walter.

Each year many of the children, grandchildren and great-grandchildren of Paul and Esther return to Eugene to sit on the front porch with "GG" (Grandma Esther) and listen to the chorus of locusts, the evasive mosquitoes, and the occasional train in the distance. The young great grandchildren will play along with "GG" saying "hello—goodbye" to each passing car. Older family members catch up on the year's events occasionally discussing the ever spicey topics of local and national politics.

GRUSE, Joe Gruse (1886-1966) and Johanna Gruss (1889-1970) emigrated from Austria to the United States in 1907. They came to Indiana by way of Pennsylvania and Ohio. Although both came from Austria they did not meet until they were in Ohio. Some years later they renewed their friendship and were married at Sacred Heart Church in Clinton, IN, on Sept. 7, 1918. Joe worked in the coal mines around Clinton. They had three sons, Valentine, Joe, and George.

Joe, Johanna, Valentine, Joe, and George Gruse

When Valentine returned from the service after World War II the family purchased a farm on North Ninth Street Road from a Mr. Herrington. This farm had previously been used as Aimone's dairy. Valentine and George farmed this farm along with their father. After the passing of their parents, Valentine continued to farm until his death in January, 1987.

George married Marysue Tucker, and is 1951 they purchased the Edward White farm just south and west of the family farm. This farm has been in the White family since November, 1831. It was reported to have been the last 200 acres of an original 2400 acre farm.

The only buildings on this farm were a house which was thought to be around 150 years old and a large quonset barn thought to have been built around 1930. The old house was replaced by a modern home. Several other farm buildings were added, all built by George himself. The quonset barn still remains.

George and Marysue have six children. Donna (Smith), Frank, Martha (Sharifzadeh), Monica (Given), Greg and Stephen. The family was active in Sacred Heart Church in Clinton, and all the children attended Sacred Heart School. All graduated from Clinton High School except Stephen who graduated from Cardinal Mooney High School in Sarasota, FL. Donna, Frank and Martha graduated from Indiana State University; Monica graduated from St. Mary of the Woods, while Greg graduated from the University of West Florida in Pensacola, FL. Stephen is currently enrolled in the University of Florida at Gainesville.

Donna is a teacher with the South Vermillion School Corporation, and Martha now lives in California. Although the rest of the family have migrated to Florida, their roots remain firmly in Vermillion County. The farm where the family was raised is still owned by them and George actively participates in its operation.

DONALD PAUL GUILLIAMS AND NANCY LEE ISAACS GUILLIAMS,
Don was born Feb. 28, 1934, one of four children of Oscar and Lily Royce Guilliams. He grew up in Newport, IN. He graduated from Newport High School in May, 1952. He enlisted in the U.S. Air Force and served four years. He married Nancy Lee Isaacs in June, 1954. They live in Perrysville, IN. Nancy Lee Isaacs was born Nov. 14, 1934, one of three children of William and Levona Shelato Isaacs. She grew up in Cayuga and graduated from Cayuga High School in May, 1952.

They are the parents of two children—Gregory Allen Guilliams (Sept. 21, 1957) and Debra Lynn Guilliams (Apr. 7, 1959). Debra died in a car accident in November of 1975. Gregory Allen graduated from North Vermillion High School in 1975 and General Motor Institute of Flint, MI in 1980. He married Deborah Dunn, daughter of James and Barbara Lindsay Dunn of Clinton, IN. Greg and Deborah were married Oct. 2, 1981. They have two daughters, Jamie Lynn Guilliams, born Oct. 2, 1982, and Pamela Diana Guilliams born Apr. 15, 1985. They live in Oakwood, IL.

CHARLES GRANT HALE,
was born in 1866 to Vincent and Elizabeth (Miller) Hale. He was raised in the State Line area in Illinois. Everyone knew him as Charlie. He had many friends in Blanford and Jacksonville.

He married Emma Lowry from the St. Bernice area about 1887. They had two daughters and two

sons: Bertha (Hale) Feaherstone in 1888, Lida Vincent Hale in 1890, Oakland Waren Hale in 1892, and Elgar Sumner Hale in 1904.

Charlie and Emma Hale in their store in Bono about 1913

Charlie started his adult life working in a small coal mine. Then when he started to raise his family he worked for Mallable Foundry in Terre Haute as a grinder. Safety measures then left a lot to be desired and Charlie had bad eyes the rest of his life. A short time later he moved back to Vermillion County and farm work.

Around 1904 Charlie bought Austins store in Bono, now the site of Doyne Conners home. The post office was also in that store. The Government renamed Bono Toronto because there was another Bono in Indiana. Bono never accepted the new name and when the post office was discontinued the name Toronto went too. The store prospered for some time buying produce and goods from area farms and selling them in Clinton via a peddling wagon. Most of his children worked in the store at one time or another.

In 1917 a new coal mine was started two miles west of Bono. After World War I (about 1919) the store went out of business and Charlie went to work in the new mine.

In 1921, their daughter Bertha died and left five children for Charlie and Emma to raise. One child died in 1923. They raised the other four and put them through school.

Around 1924, he moved his family to Dana where he managed a store for Sam Mills. It had a short life, so Charlie went back to the mine at Bono. He kept his home in Dana until the depression hit in 1929. He sold out and invested in a 20 acre farm two miles north of St. Bernice on route 71.

In 1937, he sold that farm and bought another in Kingman.

After World War II, bad health forced retirement for him and Emma. They spent their remaining days with their son and daughter-in-law in Clinton.

Charlie left this world in 1948, and Emma followed her life mate in 1957. *Submitted by Charles G. Hale, son of Oakland W. Hale*

GEORGE S. HAMERSLEY AND SOPHRONIA HARPER HAMERSLEY,
George S. Hamersley was born in 1798 in Pennsylvania and by 1830 had moved to Vigo County. He moved to Helt Township prior to 1840 and on Jan. 26, 1840, he married Sophronia Harper. Sophronia was born Sept. 8, 1814, in Yellow Creek (or Springs), OH. Her family had moved to Vermillion County at about the same time as George.

In November 1840, Sophronia bore her only daughter, Elizabeth. Elizabeth died just five years later and was buried in Helt's Prairie Cemetery. On Nov. 17, 1842, John Wesley was born, followed by Charles on July 11, 1849, and Samuel W. on Nov. 22, 1851.

In 1852, George and Sophronia moved with some of the Harpers to Redfield, IA, where they homesteaded until George's death on May 2, 1860. While they were in Iowa, George Wesley Hamersley was born in 1855.

Ibbie and John W. Hamersley, Hazel Lancaster and Edna Hamersley in front of their Summit Grove home c1914

Sophronia moved her family back to Helt Township after her husband's death. John Wesley Hamersley enlisted in Company D of the 85th Indiana Regiment and Sophronia tended her three younger sons until she died on Sept. 15, 1863. She was buried in the Harper plot in Helt's Prairie Cemetery.

Sophronia's sons were placed in foster homes; Charles went to the Miller home and later married Nancy Jane Miller. Samuel went to the Houghlands and later married Clara Belle Houghland, and George went to live with Martin Harper. George later married Louisa Morgan.

Current Vermillion County descendants of these sons are Nema Dicken Haun, great-granddaughter of Samuel W. Hamersley, and G. Clark Hamersley, Senior and Junior. Clark Hamersley, Sr. is the grandson of George Wesley Hamersley.

John Wesley Hamersley returned from the war in 1865, having fought in Kentucky and Tennessee. He served a term in Libby Prison in Virginia. On Sept. 10, 1865, he married Mary Ann Kiger whose father, James, a native Virginian, had recently moved from Fountain County with his second wife.

During their 35 year marriage, John and Mary Ann had one daughter and five sons. Charles E. Hamersley, known around the county as "Fightin' Charley," was born Sept. 9, 1867. William H. "Harry" Hamersley was born Apr. 13, 1869. Sarah E. Hamersley was born June 3, 1870. She married George Gilmore and they ran the ice house in Clinton for many years.

Sam Hamersley, sometimes referred to as Sam, Jr. to distinguish him from his uncle, was born on June 1, 1872. George Hamersley was born in 1876 and John Wesley Hamersley, Jr. some later date.

John, Jr. died in a sledding accident as a child and was buried in Helt's Prairie Cemetery, as were his brothers George, Harry, and Charley when they died. Sarah was buried in Lake County where she spent her later years and Sam was buried in Vernon, IN, after leaving Helt's Prairie in 1919.

Mary Ann died on May 25, 1901, and John married Ibbie English Lancaster on Dec. 29, 1902. He raised her daughter Hazel and John and Ibbie had a daughter, Edna, in 1904.

John lived in Summit Grove most of his later life. He died on Sept. 14, 1918, just three months before his younger brother Samuel. He is buried next to Mary Ann and John, Jr. in Helt's Prairie Cemetery.

MAURICE HARPER AND VIRGINIA LOHRMANN HARPER,
Maurice Lee Harper was born Feb. 15, 1913, at Hillsdale, IN. He is the second of eight children. He has one brother and six sisters. He is the son of Herman Harper and Minnie (Roeback) Harper.

He grew up on a farm south of Hillsdale, IN, which has been in the Harper Family for many years. He has lived on the farm for 75 years. His great, great-grandfather, James Harper, bought the farm in 1823, from the Land Bank at Vincennes. He bought the farm from his grandmother, Sarah (Miller) Harper, in 1936.

Virginia and Maurice Harper

He attended Summitt Grove School through eighth grade. He graduated from Hillsdale High School in 1932.

Besides farming, he has had various jobs. He worked for Philips Ford Garage for four years, and Dana Implement Company (John Deere) for 23 years, from which he retired in 1976.

On May 8, 1937, he married Virginia Lohrmann, the eldest of 12 children born to James Ernest Lohrmann and Hazel Crane Lohrmann on Dec. 4, 1911. She attended Hillsdale School and graduated in 1929.

They are the parents of two children, a daughter Maurleen, married to Jerry Wright, living on a farm north of Marshall, IN; a son, Marion, married to Susan (Farrington), living on a farm south of Chrisman, IL.

They have four grandchildren - Cynthia Wright Thorpe, Allen Wright, Marla Harper Henson, and Danny Harper. They have two great-grandchildren - Samantha Wright and Amanda Henson.

They are both members of the Salem United Methodist Church.

HEBER,
In Wurtemberg, Germany, John Heber lived his wife, Elizabeth Senger Heber and their two sons, Joseph and Louis.

Joseph, born in 1820, came to the United States in July, 1851. He became a legal citizen on Aug. 22, 1856, at Terre Haute. He began courting a girl by the name of Barbara Wesnitger. They were married Jan. 22, 1860. To this union nine children were born. They were William, Elizabeth, John, James, Andrew, Molinda, Josie and Mary.

John Heber was born Oct. 30, 1865. He married Maude Edwards, May 20, 1891, at Rockville and two sons were born. Lawrence, born in 1892 and Raymond born in 1895. Maude died Apr. 21, 1896, on Raymond's first birthday. Lawrence married Olive Simms in 1909. Children born were Virginia, Herman, and Dorothy. Virginia married and had two daughters; Herman married and had two sons; and Dorothy married and had two sons. Virginia lives in California as does her daughters and grandchildren. Herman married and lived in Indianapolis until his death. His son, Harold Ray, resides in St. Bernice, has one daughter and two grandchildren; James lives in Indianapolis and has two children.

Dorothy is married and lives in Florida, and has grandchildren, also.

Raymond married Ortha Osman in 1914. From this union six children were born, four whom were born and raised in the Center neighborhood; Marzelle, Margaret, Inez, and Raymond, Jr.

Marzelle married Charles Milligan and were parents of three living children. Jan married Jerry Stewart; Carroll married Sandra DeFrietas and she had one daughter; Marvin married Jeanette Kanizer and they have two children.

Margaret married Roy Sturm and had three children. Connie married Verle Meister and have one son. Ronnie married Joy Smith and have two sons. Robert married Robin Conrad and have three living children.

Inez married Ernest Myers and are parents of three living children. Leon married Lois Stafford and have one daughter. Karl Willis married Judy Stewart and have one son. Orthanna married Yale Yager and have two daughters.

Raymond, Jr. married Dorothy Weyhrauch and they have three children. Raelene married Bill McCauley and have two sons. Richard married Patricia Bickel and have two children. Raymond III is married to Anita Faye Reiber Cline and has one son and two step children.

John, Ray, Sr., and Raymond, Jr. all farmed in the Center vicinity. Ray, Sr. was born in the house where he lived all his life until his death in 1975. Ray's children have always lived close by the home place and still do except Marzelle, who passed away in 1986.

WILLIAM AND JUNE HEIDBREDER,
William (Bill) Augusta Heidbreder, grandson of William Heidbreder, a farmer who came to Vermillion County from Prussia in 1854, was born in 1914 to Frederick William (1866-1944) and Nora Switzer. Frederick William was in construction, a builder of many houses in Cayuga.

Bill retired in 1978 from Hyster County in Danville, IL, after 28 years. He is a charter member of Pioneer Days and served two years as president. He is a member of the Cayuga Masons, V.C. Historical Society and trustee of the Eugene Cemetery Association. He is well known for his photography, and belongs to the Photography Society of America.

Bill and June Heidbreder

On June 22, 1942, he married June Roberta Grondyke. Her great great grandfather, John Groenendyke (1756-1824), Revolutionary War Veteran, came from upstate New York (with his family) to Eugene in 1819. One son, James, had the mill on the Big Vermillion River. Another son, Sam (1803-1860), started the pork packing industry in Eugene. Sam Grondyke, Jr. (1836-1907), who shortened the family name, had a general merchandise store. His son, John S. Grondyke (1864-1945), layed out the first lots in Cayuga and was a businessman there for many years. He gave the ground for the Presbyterian Church. He was appointed by the Colletts to serve on the Board of the Collett Home and served for 51 years (1891-1942). He married Elda Stagl (1887-1926). They had three children - Altheda Grondyke (1913-1985), a teacher, June Heidbreder, and John Samuel Grondyke, Indianapolis.

June has been active in the General Federation of Women's Clubs, having served in her club, Cayuga Social Study, and has been County and District President, State Chairman of the Arts, and photographer for the Indiana Federation of Clubs. She is a member of the Eugene United Methodist Church, the Order of Eastern Star, charter member of Pioneer Days, and is secretary-treasurer of the Eugene Cemetery Association.

Bill and June have two children - Treva Newlan, wife of Lewis Newlan, Korean Veteran, owners of Roof-Tech, Inc., Jeffersonville, IN.

Warren Heidbreder, Vietnam Veteran, Vice-President and Corporate Secretary, Bandag, Inc., Muscatine, IA. Warren married Pamela Hietpas, Kimberly, WI.

Both Treva and Warren are graduates of Indiana University and Warren received an MBA from Hofstra University, Long Island, N.Y.

Bill and June have three grandchildren - William, 17, Muscatine, IA; Dale Newlan, 11; and Danna Newlan, nine, Jeffersonville, IN.

MARY SKIDMORE LANGSTON HELT,

the daughter of John Skidmore and his second wife Jane Hopper Skidmore, was born Feb. 8, 1826 in Vermillion County. She grew up in Helt's Prairie helping in a wayside inn that the family maintained. She said sometimes when she went to bed the place was empty, but by morning people would be sleeping everywhere, even on the floor. The horses were fed and cared for, as well as people. The family sewed for the travelers who ordered clothes on one visit and picked them up on the return trip. Mar. 14, 1848, she married John Milton Langston, son of John Langston who was an early settler from South Carolina. Mary and John M. had two children; John Franklin and Sarah Langston Southard. After John Milton died Mary married Hiram Helt, son of Michael Helt, Mar. 18, 1860. They had two children: Alma E. Helt Russell, and Ulysses.

John Franklin Langston was born Feb. 18, 1849. He was married Apr. 14, 1874 to Eliza Jackson. They had two children who both died. Eliza died Feb. 2, 1877. John Franklin then married Sarah V. Taylor Shannon Mar. 15, 1885. Thy had two children; Mable Langston Whisler and Dolly Langston Norris. John Franklin was a mail carrier. He died one day while delivering the mail. The time of his death was determined by the last person to receive mail as the horse faithfully completed the route stopping at each house.

Sarah Jane Langston married Huston Southard Dec. 24, 1870. Three of their children lived to be adults. They were Roy Southard, Emma Southard Fillinger, and Dorothy Southard Hood.

Emma was married to Halbert L. Fillinger and was the only one to have any children. They were Halbert Ernest Fillinger and Norma Fillinger Connell.

Ulysses M. Helt married Flora Hougland and they had two children; Helen Helt Everett and Joe

R. who was born Aug. 25, 1895, and lived in the home place in Helt's Prairie until he died at age 91.

Alma Helt married William Russell and they had two children; Quince and Homer.

Mary Skidmore Langston Helt lived in Helt's Prairie all of her life and was a member of the Salem United Methodist Church. She died Dec. 21, 1910, at the age of 84.

FRANK AND ROSE POTTER HESKETT,

Frank, son of Spicer and Stella Mann Heskett, was born on Sept. 4, 1886, in Summit Grove, in Helt township. Rose Anna Potter Heskett was born Apr. 16, 1885, the daughter of Emmor and Mary Catherine Greathouse (the daughter of James and Nancy Schonover, the great niece of Queen Mary of Scotland). Rose was born in Osceola, MO. Frank and Rose were united in marriage at the Methodist Parsonage, Newport, IN, by Rev. Freeman on Jan. 2, 1908.

Rose Potter Heskett and Frank Heskett

Frank attended Summit Grove School and Rose Anna attended Springhill. Most of their married life, they lived in Summit Grove and were members of the Salem Methodist Church. They were the parents of three sons, Milo, Lloyd, and William, and two daughters, Lillian and Margaret. Frank passed away Jan. 10, 1972, and Rose passed away Jan. 16, 1967. They are buried in the family plot in Helt's Prairie Cemetery.

NELLIE PAINE HESLER,

was born in 1903 and attended Union School in Trego Co., KS, and Central School in Clinton, and graduated from Clinton High School in 1919. She was the daughter of Henry Washburn Paine and Kizzie May Spainhower Paine. She had two sisters, Mary Eleanor Paine Hedges, and Reba Elizabeth Paine Jackson, and three brothers, Robert Burl Paine, James Earl Paine II, and Charle Donald Paine. Reba's picture is with the Galen Brown article.

Nellie Paine Hesler

There is a related article on Charles Donald Paine including a picture of Nellie's parents. Her paternal

grandparents were James Paine and Narcissus Wright Paine, and her great-grandparents were John Paine and Charlotte Bright Paine and John Wright* and Margaret Nichols Wright.

Nellie married George "Red" Hesler whose family originated from Parke County and they had a son, William "Bill" Hesler. Nellie Paine Hesler died at age 42 of cancer. George "Red" Hesler who once ran a gas station at Third and Vine (south east corner) is also deceased. Their son, William "Bill" Hesler, who was a veteran of WW II is deceased as well. He left a wife, Wanetta, and sons, Steve and Matt, and daughters, Dana and Sue Ann. *Submitted by Leo Reposh Jr.*

*see Ulysses Grant Wright article for further family background.

PETE HICKMAN,

From canal boatman to race horse trainer is the story of Pete Hickman, retired farmer, who lives near Bono about five miles south of Dana.

As a boy of 13, Mr. Hickman rode a horse and drove two mules along the towpath of the old Wabash and Erie Canal. Today at 81, Pete has two standardbred trotters, which he works out daily.

The canal article which appeared recently in The Commercial-News stimulated Pete's memory, and he started talking. This is his story:

In 1871 he lived in Montezuma with his parents, who boarded Bill Lyman, the canal boat driver, when he was in town. One night Bill got drunk. When James Mussett, captain of the boat, came to the Hickman home in search of his hostler, he found him in no condition to take the towpath. Mussett offered the job to young Pete, then 13. Naturally, Pete wanted to go and, after much tearful pleading, won parental consent.

The boy spent three or four weeks on the canal, handling the boat's motive power, while his employer handled the tiller at the stern. Pete is not sure just where they went, but thinks the boats went upriver to Lafayette and down to Vincennes.

He says that when he left Montezuma in 1872 there were only two boats left on the Wabash and Erie. These were owned by Colonel Benson, a wealthy riverman who owned a warehouse and slaughterhouse in Montezuma. The Benson Warehouse stood just north of the present Montezuma swimming pool. A basin led back from the canal to the long loading dock and warehouse and the boats were swung from the canal into this basin. Vermillion Co., IN, farmers marketed many hogs by driving them across the frozen Wabash to Benson's slaughterhouse.

Mussett and his wife lived on the boat. In stormy weather, driver, mules, and horses were housed in the 60-foot craft. The boat drew about four feet of water; this left a foot clearance, for the water in the canal averaged about five feet. Boats travelled about three to five miles per hour, as fast as the mules could walk. Excessive speed set of waves which damaged the sides of the canal. Streams like the Raccoon and Sugar Creek were crossed through aqueducts, wooden troughs through which the boat passed, while mules, horse and driver crossed over a bridge in the towpath.

Pete insists that so far as he can remember no canal boats carried passengers regularly. Four steamboats, the Amazon, Romeo, Brazil, and Grondyke, came up the river to Montezuma. Only the smallest of these went on up-river.

Muskrats and railroads brought the canal age to an early close. The former undermined the canal banks; the latter ate i⸻ ⸻usiness and undermined its profits.

In 1872 Pete Hickman c⸻ ⸻ the Bono neighborhood, where he worked at w⸻at he could get. One of his first jobs was as teamster, helping to build the railroad switch at what is now Dana. That was in 1873, the year the town was founded.

Mr. Hickman married Olive Barnhart of Bono. They now live happily on their own small farm. In the pasture back of the house is a third-of-a-mile track.

Drive down there almost any morning, you'll see Pete up behind his colt, Tim Finnegan. And the octogenarian driver, with his two-year-old trotter, will be making considerably more speed than he did on that canal horse in 1871!

An article by Leo Aikman, The Danville Commercial News, Nov. 24, 1940

CARL D. HICKS AND DELORES RICK HICKS,

Carl D. Hicks, the youngest son of Daniel and Evea Goff Hicks was born Feb. 1, 1926. He graduated from the Perrysville High School and served in the Army Air Force during WW II.

In 1947, he married Delores Rick, daughter of Joseph and Esther Lierman Rick of Danville, IL. They reside on their farm west of Perrysville. Besides farming, they operated a farm-related sales operation for many years.

They are the parents of four children: Sherry of Indianapolis, IN, Larry and Randy who are in the family farm operation and other business interests in the community, and Sandy of Farmington Hills, MI.

Carl and Delores have both been active in local politics, both having served many years as Township Trustee as well as other commitments and church obligations.

DANIEL A. HICKS AND EVEA GOFF HICKS,

Daniel A. Hicks was born Sept. 29, 1887, the seventh of ten children born to George R. and Gertrude Riggs Hicks. After spending a few years operating a general store for his uncle in Layafette, CO he returned home to the farm near Perrysville, and in 1918 he married Evea Goff, daughter of Phalander and Elizabeth Fox Goff. They had three sons Jene D., Ray C. and Carl D. all of whom reside in the Perrysville area.

Daniel and Evea spent their entire married life living in the Hicks home, which his grandfather had built. In addition to farming and operating a dairy business they served many civic and church duties.

Daniel served eight years as Highland Township Trustee, an office which at that time was fully responsible for all operations of the public school system as well as other Township responsibilities. He later served as a member of the Vermillion County Council.

His death was in 1966 and Evea in 1969. They are buried in the Hicks Cemetery near Perrysville, IN.

GEORGE R. HICKS AND AMANDA GERTRUDE RIGGS HICKS,

George R. Hicks was born June 10, 1842 to George W. and Mary Curtis Hicks, one of 11 children born in the family home on land entered from the government by his father.

He attended medical school in Poughkeepsie, NY, a profession he did not follow. On Feb. 9, 1871, he married Amanda Gertrude Riggs, the daughter of B. W. and Francis Riggs, who operated the woolen mill in the west edge of Perrysville. To this marriage ten children were born, all of them living to mature age. Their entire married life was lived in the Hicks home where George was born.

His life was spent assisting his father on the farm and in the pork packing business, which at that time was a thriving business on the Wabash. Later he entered the dry goods business in Perrysville.

He was elected to the office of Vermillion County Commissioner for 11 years, during which time many bridges were built including the Wabash bridge at Clinton and Perrysville. He was active in the Masonic Order, serving many years as Master of the Unity Lodge in Perrysville. His wife, Gertrude, died in 1909 and George in 1918. They are buried in the family plot in the Hicks Cemetery.

GEORGE WASHINGTON HICKS AND MARY CURTIS HICKS,

George Washington Hicks was among the very first settlers of the Wabash Valley. He was born Apr. 10, 1795 in Rehoboth, MA, to Nathan and Prudence Rowand Hicks, the son of a former Revolutionary War soldier. George was named in honor of his father's former battlefield commander, General George Washington. On his western journey, he arrived at a Fort near Terre Haute, IN in 1820. He later ventured north about 50 miles up the Wabash River to a place where the river flowed near an ideal landing place on the west bank. There he also found a fertile prairie nearby on the west. It was here that he decided to enter this land from the United States Land office. He was issued a patent land grant, signed by President James Monroe, on Nov. 13, 1822 for 80 acres in Section 33.

He returned to the east to marry Mary Curtis, whom he met while visiting his brother, who had settled in New York.

George W. Hicks and Mary Curtis were married on Sept. 7, 1823 in Allen Hill, Ontario Co., NY.

They moved west to the Wabash Valley area in a covered wagon late in the fall of 1823. They built a log cabin near a natural spring about one mile west of what later became the town of Perrysville, on the land he had entered. As other settlers moved to this area and produced grain and livestock, George built a large flat boat, loaded it with his and other farmers grain and pork and started down the Wabash River to the Ohio, then the Mississippi River to New Orleans, where he sold the grain and pork and also the flat boat. On his return trip, he came north on a steam boat as far as Vincennes, then on foot to Perrysville. He later built a large pork packing plant in the south part of Perrysville near the river and sent many boat loads of pork products to New Orleans. He made his last trip in 1844. In 1830 he began to construct a large brick home on this original land. The brick was made from clay from the farm and all the woodwork was cut from the Walnut trees on the farm. The doors were made from Poplar. The house was finished in 1840. It is still occupied by a great, great, grandson, four generations later. In 1977 it was nominated and passed through five generations and has never been out of the Hicks name. It is now owned by Carl Randall Hicks. George W. died Oct. 1, 1878, and his wife died Feb. 7, 1868. They are buried in the Hicks Cemetery.

JENE D. HICKS,

son of Daniel A. and Evea Goff Hicks was born at the Hicks family homestead at Perrysville, Apr. 24, 1921. He graduated from Perrysville High School and began operating the Hicks' Dairy and farming with his father. He married Pearl L. Prather, daughter of Dewey and Mabel Wilcoxen Prather, May 3, 1942. To them were born four sons and one daughter: Curtis Dene, Dan Merrill, David Jene, Steven Richard, and Jeneil.

Curtis married Lynn Carol Dailey, June 24, 1972 - Children, Dena Lynn and Scott Daniel.

Dan Merrill married Nyanne Jenkins, June 8, 1969 - Children, Douglas Aaron and Bradley Ryan, now live in Blacksburg, VA.

David Jene married Vickie Ann Sare, Jan. 23, 1972 - Children, Joshua David and Catherine Ann.

Jeneil married Darrell Hupfer, Aug. 19, 1973 - Children, Derek Jene, Jeffrey Adam, and Leeann Christine, now live in Westmont, IL.

Steven Richard married Shirley Thompson, Sept. 3, 1977 - Children, Kylie Michelle and Steven Christopher.

Jene and sons Curtis, David, and Steve, farm and operate a cattle-feeding confinement system in northern Highland Township.

Jene has served on the North Vermillion School Board and he and his family are members, officers and teachers in the Perrysville United Methodist Church. They also are active and support several community organizations.

JOHN DORMAN HINES,

(1891-1978), a native of Highland Twp. was the great grandson of a Highland Twp. original land owner. John Hines (1795-1853), who entered land here in 1824, came from Ross Co., OH. He was a peddler and a farmer. He may have traveled as far west as the Sangamon River in Illinois in the 1830's with his well stocked peddler's wagon. He was born in Virginia. He and his wife, Nancy Bowen (1804-1841), had seven children here. Their youngest child, Barnabas B. (1840-1874) married Sarah Ellen Prather (1844-1930). Barnabas and Sarah had seven children. Their first child was James Henry (1862-1909). James Henry married Marie Ellen Cade (1861-1907) and they were the parents of four children, three girls and one boy. Their youngest child was John Dorman Hines.

John Dorman Hines, at work in his blacksmith shop in Gessie. It was located on the south side of the main street through Gessie east of the church. Photo taken 1925.

John Dorman Hines married Mae Frances Keister (1899-1970) and they raised their children in Gessie where John was a blacksmith during the 1920's. He drove a road truck for the county for many years. Later he worked at the C&EI car repair shop in Danville, IL. He retired from that position. Mae was the Postmaster at Gessie for many years and retired when the Gessie Post Office was closed.

John and Mae lost an infant, James Dwight, in 1919. Their other children are Claude Thurl (1920-1981) who married Bernice Palmer (1921-), Gladys Louise (1928-) who married Derald Prather and Norma Earlene (1934-) who married Chris Hughes. Their grandchildren are Mirl Hines, Marlene Hines Goulding, Ronald Hines, Sharon Prather, Norman Hughes, Jon Hughes, and Crystal Hughes Montgomery. Their great grandchildren are Lori Hines, Rick Goulding, Deanna Goulding, Lisa Hines, Ronald Hines, Christopher Hughes, and Zacharia Montgomery.

JAMES F. AND EVELYN WRIGHT HIXON,

James F. Hixon was born Sept. 4, 1935 in Clinton, IN, the son of Phillip W. Hixon and Catherine Lowe Hixon. His stepmother is Sadie Taylor Hixon. He attended Central Elementary School, St. Bernice Grade School, and graduated from St. Bernice High School in 1954. He served in the U.S. Army from August, 1954, until July, 1956, spending one and one-half years of that time in Germany. He has been employed at the Newport Army Ammunition Plant since 1961. (see related article—Phillip W. and Sadie Taylor Hixon)

The Jim Hixon Family: Front: Scott, Brent. Back: Kevin, Evelyn, Jim, Duane.

He had one sister, Mary Evelyn Hixon, and one stepsister, Sarahann Myer. He has another stepsister, June Watson, and two stepbrothers, Floyd Pearman and Harold Pearman. His paternal grandparents were Sam Hixon and Martha Myers Hixon. His maternal grandparents were Roy Lowe and Hattie Plough Lowe. (see related article)

On Aug. 11, 1957, he married Evelyn Wright (Mar. 4, 1936), daughter of Chloral J. Wright and Mildred Reed Wright (see related article). She has one brother, Jerry Wright, of Marshall, IN. Her paternal grandparents were Milton and Retha Hatley Wright (see related article). Her maternal grandparents were Frank and Nellie Jackson Reed (see related article).

She attended St. Bernice Grade School and graduated from St. Bernice High School in 1954. She has her B.S. degree and M.S. degree from Indiana State University. She is employed as a business teacher and librarian at Chrisman (Illinois) High School. She previously taught at Hillsdale High School, St. Bernice High School, Grange Corner Elementary School (Turkey Run School District), and Clinton High School.

They are the parents of four sons—Brent Alan Hixon (July 19, 1959), Duane Eugene Hixon (July 9, 1960), Kevin Lee Hixon (Dec. 20, 1962), Scott Jay Hixon (Mar. 25, 1965).

Kevin married Lori Wetnight (June 6, 1964) from Fontanet, IN. They are residing in Indianapolis. Brent married Belinda Waldridge (Dec. 17, 1964) from Marshall, IN. They are the parents of Chelsea Jo Hixon born July 17, 1988. They reside at R.R.1 (Fairview), Clinton, IN.

Jim and Evelyn reside at R.R.#3, Clinton, IN, along with sons, Duane and Scott. Jim belongs to Asbury Lodge #320 F & AM, Dana, IN, and has been master three times. Evelyn is a member of Zeta Tau Alpha, Delta Kappa Gamma, Sigma Delta Pi,

Chrisman Education Association, Illinois Education Association, and National Education Association.

They are members of Wayside United Methodist Church and formerly were members of Center Methodist Church east of St. Bernice, IN. They are members of the Vermillion County Historical Society and are members of the Terre Haute Antique Classic Auto Club of Terre Haute. They have a 1948 Hudson automobile and enjoy taking it to car shows and driving it on car tours. They also enjoy traveling.

PHILLIP AND SADIE TAYLOR HIXON,

Phillip Wannamaugher Hixon was born Nov. 28, 1907. He was the son of Samuel Hixon and Martha Myers Hixon. He worked on the Chicago, Milwaukee, and St. Paul Railroad out of St. Bernice, the Pennsylvania Railroad out of Terre Haute, and at the Wabash River Ordinance Works at Newport. He was killed Feb. 25, 1972, while working at Inland Steel in Indiana Harbor, IN. He had four brothers—Samuel, James, Basil, and Frank. He had a half-brother and two half-sisters, Lena Hixon Wilson and Myrtle Myers.

His paternal grandfather was William Hixon, Jr. (Aug. 20, 1837-). His great-grandfather was William Hixon, Sr. (Oct. 10, 1801-Nov. 5, 1879). William Hixon, Sr. donated the land for the Hixon Cemetery at Mecca, IN. (see related article—William Hixon, Sr.)

Sadie and Phillip Hixon

The Hixon's came from the north part of England or the south part of Scotland. It seems there was a large family of boys raised in Virginia and they scattered. Two of them settled in Pennsylvania (one in Fulton County and one in Washington County), one settled in Maryland, one settled in Ohio, and Elijah Hixon came to Kentucky. One or more remained in Virginia. Elijah was Phillip Hixon's great-great-grandfather.

Phillip Hixon married Catherine Lowe on Dec. 16, 1933. They were the parents of two children—Mary Evelyn born Aug. 16, 1934 and died Nov. 12, 1934; James Fredrick born Sept. 4, 1935. Catherine was the daughter of Roy and Hattie Lowe. She had one brother, Howard Lowe. (see related article—Roy Lowe and Hattie Plough Lowe)

On May 10, 1947, he married Sadie Taylor Myer Pearman. She had one daughter, Sarahann Myer, and three stepchildren—June Pearman Watson, Floyd Pearman, and Harold Pearman. She was employed for several years at the Vermillion County Home and the Vermillion County Hospital. Sadie's parents were Edward and Sarah Jane Race Taylor. She had five brothers—Edward, Clarence, John, Harry, and Charlie. She had four sisters—Mable Thomas, Lottie Taylor, Fern Braner, and one who died in infancy.

There are four grandchildren—Brent, Duane, Kevin, and Scott and one great-granddaughter—Chelsea Jo, daughter of Brent.

WILLIAM HIXON, SR.,

was born near Crab Orchard, KY, Oct. 15, 1801. He came to Vincennes, IN, in 1806, with his father, Elijah Hixon, and his two sisters, Rachel and Margaret, after their mother died. The mother died at the time of the birth of the youngest daughter. Elijah went west on an expedition and never returned. The children were taken in by the family of an uncle, a brother of their mother, with whom they lived until William was 14 years old. He then was apprenticed to a carpenter, with whom he served until he was 21 years old.

He enjoyed no educational advantages, attending school only four days. He, however, spent all his spare time doing odd jobs of any kind to help educate his sisters. During the Indian troubles of 1811 and 1812, he spent most of his time in Ft. Ellison, near Vincennes, where all the whites were compelled to shut themselves up for safety. He often spoke of a conference which took place under a large tree near the fort between General Harrison and some of the chiefs.

At the age of 21, he came to Terre Haute, IN, bringing his two sisters with him. After two years, he came to Wabash Township, Parke Co., IN.

He first married Sarah Ghormley and they had five sons, James (Aug. 31, 1824-), Samuel (Oct. 20, 1826-), John (Oct. 11, 1829-), Michael (Nov. 4, 1831-), and Joseph (Oct. 1, 1833-). He later married Margaret Levick Bowers and they were the parents of six children—William, Jr. (Aug. 20, 1837-), Aquilla (June 22, 1839-), Margaret, Jr. (Mar. 3, 1841-), Rufus (Feb. 12, 1844-), Sarah (June 20, 1846-), and Alfred (Nov. 11, 1849-).

After his marriage, Mr. Hixon did a mixed business of farming and carpentry until 1830, when he bought the farm on which he spent most of the remainder of his life, farming and teaming. He often made trips to Louisville and Chicago, taking produce and bringing back goods. He also engaged in building flat boats and running them to New Orleans, loaded with produce from the fertile Wabash bottoms. He died peacefully at his home on Nov. 5, 1879, after a long and useful life, honored by all who knew him and loved and respected by his family. Mr. Hixon donated the land for the Hixon Cemetery at Mecca, IN.

The Hixon's came from the north part of England or the south part or Scotland. It seems there was a large family of boys raised in Virginia and they scattered. Two of them settled in Pennsylvania (one in Fulton County and one in Washington County), one settled in Maryland, one settled in Ohio, and Elijah Hixon came to Kentucky. One or more remained in Virginia. Elijah was born in 1760 in Hunterdon Co., NJ, and died in Monroe Co., OH, after 1835. Elijah's father was Timothy Hixon who was born in Scotland between 1730 and 1740 and died at Loudoun Co., VA, either in 1811 or 1812.

HOLLINGSWORTH FAMILY,

Valentine Hollingsworth seems to have been the founder of the Hollingsworth family in America. He was an Englishman, but came to America from Ireland in 1642. He came to America with William Penn (Valentine was a Quaker, too) and settled in Delaware and spent his life there. His descendants then began to spread southward to Virginia and the Carolinas, and the older Hollingsworths who came to Vermillion County in the 1820's gave their birthplace as both Virginia and South Carolina. The younger ones gave Kentucky and Indiana as their birthplace which represents stopping places on their way to Vermillion County.

A book written by J. Adger Stewart published in 1925 shows a Coat of Arms for the Hollingsworth family, printed in color, it shows the shield is blue, a diagonal bar across the shield is silver with green holly leaves and a deer on top of the shield is brown. The motto translates "Learn to endure what must be endured."

Carter Hollingsworth, the son of Valentine, settled in Vermillion Township in the 1820's, and some of his brothers settled in Clinton and Helt Townships. Carter and his wife, Charity, had 13 children, William, Wright, Isaac, James, Hezekiah, Eber, Jesse, Mary Ann, Sarah, Henry, Joseph, Jeanette and Gertrude.

Wright's family is the best known in the Vermillion County area during the period from the 1850's to the 1900's. Wright's son Milton had four children, Oscar, Emmett, Edna and Lena, the youngest daughter, who is the only surviving member of that generation at age 97.

Oscar helped the Hollingsworths hold their own with 11 children as follows: Emory, Howard, Hubert, Clyde, Doyne, Stanley, Maynard, Donald, Lucille, Marion and Paul.

Wright's daughter, Florella, was an unusual person and had a very interesting life. She went to California on her own in the 1880's. After living in Los Angeles for awhile she went to the gold mine camps in Alaska Yukon. She cooked for a mining crew for three years. She was the first woman to shot the 'White Horse Rapids' in the Yukon River in a canoe. She returned to California in 1901 and married. In 1936 she came back to Newport, IN for a visit, her first visit in 56 years. One of the things she wanted to do was "have another drink of the 'sweet' Wabash River water." She couldn't believe that during this period of time the water turned too foul to drink. She returned to California where she lived till her death in 1958 at the age of 101.

Carter's grandson, Milton, the son of Henry Hollingsworth, was sheriff of Vermillion County from 1908 to 1910 and again from 1916 to 1920. His second term was during the early years of Prohibition when there were raids and arrests almost daily.

Down thru the years there has been a Carter Hollingsworth and today is no exception, grandson of Maynard, son of Russell, Carter Hollingsworth of Dana, IN, to carry on the name Carter. *Submitted by Donald E. Hollingsworth.*

A small portion of the Hollingsworth history taken from Newport and Vermillion Township (Vermillion Co., IN) The First 100 Years - 1824-1924. Harold L. O'Donnell.

HOOD FAMILY HISTORY, Thomas L. Hood was the son of Charles Hood of Virginia and North Carolina. Charles was a soldier in the Revolutionary War and the War of 1812. He died in 1830 and is buried in the Hood-Osborne Cemetery southeast of Dana. Thomas was born in 1787 in Virginia and was in the War of 1812. He moved from Knoxville, TN to Honey Creek near Terre Haute in 1821 and to his new farm in Helt Township in 1823. He and his wife, Frances Barnett Hood had two sons; Charles Durham Hood in 1814 and Thomas Simmons Hood Dec. 6, 1815.

Thomas Simmons was married to Rebecca Aye in 1839. She was the daughter of John Aye born in 1818. They had several children; William Barnett Hood, Cornelia Hood Hughes, Cevilla Hood Duncan, Caroline Hood Thompson, Mary Hood Allen, Catharine Hood Fillinger, Isabelle Hood Aldridge, Laura C. Hood Dowdy, and Thomas Corivin Hood. Three boys; Charles, John and James and one girl, Frances died in infancy and are buried in the Hood Cemetery.

Thomas Simmons Hood (1894) and his wife Rebecca (1895) are buried in the Bales Cemetery near Dana.

JOHN M. AND RUTH ENSLEY HOWLETT, a few years following his parent's immigration from England, John (1890-1962) was born and raised on a farm just north of Quaker. During his early years, he farmed. But he spent most of his adult life as a self employed painter and decorator while living in the home where he was born. During World War II, he was employed as a painter at the Wabash River Ordinance Works. John was well known for his honesty and good workmanship.

John and Ruth Howlett

In 1920 he married Ruth Ensley (1901-1984) who was born in Dana, IN and raised on a farm near Humrick, IL. Ruth was a home maker and occasionally helped with her husband's work. Following his death, Ruth lived in Cayuga and later in Rockville near her sister-in-law, May Howlett Hadley. She was involved in several social and service clubs in the communities where she lived.

John and Ruth were both active in the Quaker and Presbyterian churches in their neighborhood. They were especially involved in community music activities. They had two children, Miles E. and Claudia W. Miles married Mary McDowell of Dana. He passed away in 1977 and Mary continues to live in their Danville, IL home. Claudia married Kenneth Wiggins of Newport and they live in Speedway, IN. Their two children, Andrew and Kenna (Mrs. John) Fetherolf also live in Speedway.

CHRIS AND NORMA HUGHES, Chris Martin Hughes, a life resident of Highland Twp., operates the Hoosier Homestead Farm that was established in 1828 by Constantine Hughes. Constantine (1783-1848) and his wife Hannah Gifford (1787-1857) came here from Harrison Co., VA. They were the parents of 14 children, who were all born in Virginia except the youngest, William (1830-1922). William married Cynthia Ann Smith in 1848. William's son John (1851-1930) married Lillie Belle Gouty. Their son Orville (1879-1929) married Estella F. Martin (1886-1986). Their only son Harold M. Hughes (1911-) married Mary M. Gibson (1911-1973). They had four sons; Chris, Kent, Sam and Jim, who are all living in the Gessie community.

Chris and Norma Hughes and daughter, Crystal Montgomery

Chris (1936-) married Norma E. Hines and they have three children living on the family farm, Norman D. (1954-) who married Rachel Howard, Jon M. (1963-), and Crystal S. (1966-) who married Gregory Montgomery. Norman and Jon are members of International Brotherhood of Electrical workers #538 and also work part time on the farm.

Chris and Norma have two grandsons, Christopher Martin Hughes and Zacharia Cade Montgomery, both born in 1987. Chris is interested in antique farm machinery and has several old gas engines and a 1906 threshing machine. Norma is a genealogist who loves collecting and refurbishing antiques. They both love to travel and are members of the Gessie United Methodist Church.

DALE HUGHES FAMILY, Dale Elmond Hughes was born May 15, 1895, the son of Albert and Cassie Hughes of Gessie, IN. He graduated from Perrysville High School in 1912 and Purdue University in 1917. He married Blanche Inez Wait on Nov. 23, 1922. They lived near Gessie, where he farmed, until October 1940. Dale and Inez moved to Perrysville, IN in 1940. Dale served as Postmaster from November 1940 to May 1965. After retirement they moved to Danville, IL, where Dale still resides. Inez died Mar. 29, 1985. They had one son, William Dale Hughes.

WILLIAM DALE HUGHES FAMILY, William Dale Hughes was born July 18, 1923, the son of Dale Elmond and Blanche Inez Wait Hughes. He attended Gessie Grade School and graduated from Perrysville High School in 1942. On Mar. 25, 1944 he married Vivian Marie Marshall. Vivian graduated from Perrysville High School in 1941 and attended Utterback Brown Business College. During World War II, Bill (B.D.) and Vivian lived in Gary, IN, where he worked in the Steel Mills. They moved to Danville, IL, in 1951. Bill worked for Consolidated Products, later known as Kraft Foods, for 36 years. Vivian worked at Hyster Company in Danville for 32 years. After their retirement, they moved to Route #2, Covington, IN. They have one daughter, Marsha Dale Hughes Manley, and two grandchildren, Timothy Dale Manley and Kristen Kaye Manley.

NOAH AND SUSAN HUMPHRIES, Noah Humphries was born in Vermillion Co., IN. He was a farmer. On Nov. 13, 1851 he married Susan and they had seven children. They were, Nancy Jane who married Michael Cheesam; Levi, who married Louisa M.; Newton, who never married but served in the Civil War with Company C 59th Indiana Infantry from Dec. 24, 1864, to July 17, 1865; Mary Ann, who married Benjamin Mayfield, and they had five children - Noah, Levi, Nancy, Benjamin and Mary A.

Levi, Susan, and Lottie Ellen Jackson

Mary A. also had a daughter named Hester; Margaret, who married James Pauley; Susan, who later married Levi Jackson; and Amelia, who married Levi Jackson (born in 1838) on Feb. 8, 1869. They had two daughters Rosetta and Jeanetta. An epidemic swept through their family. Tragically Amelia died on July 24, 1873, at 24 years of age. Rosetta died on July 30, 1873, at two years of age, followed by Noah Humphries (Amelia's father) on Aug. 23, 1873. Then Jeanetta died on Aug. 28, 1873, at age three months. They are all buried at Spangler Cemetery in Centenary, IN.

On Apr. 24, 1875, Levi Jackson married Amelia's sister, Susan, who was born in 1842. They had one child, a daughter. Lottie Ellen Jackson was born June 30, 1878. Lottie Jackson married Decatur "Dick" Robertson on Sept. 24, 1896.

Levi died in 1907 and is buried at Spangler Cemetery.

OLIVER MASON HUNT AND RUTH HAWKINS BERRY HUNT,
Oliver Mason was born Mar. 3, 1879, in Rockcastle, KY, the son of Gabriel Verley Hunt and Orpha Louise Josephine Huston.

He married Ruth Hawkins Berry, daughter of William Clinton Berry and Martha Mildred Hawkins Berry in Dana, IN, Dec. 30, 1903.

Ruth was born in Berry, KY, June 23, 1884. They were both from Kentucky. Ruth came up with her family and Oliver came up to live with his older sister's family to find work in Indiana and Illinois.

Oliver was a farmer or farm hand seeking work wherever he could.

Oliver Mason Hunt Family. Oscar William, Ruth, Mildred Josephine, Oliver Mason, and Wayne Wilbur.

Oliver wrote letters to Ruth and in one of those letters he wrote that he got struck on her as soon as he saw her and thought she was the prettiest girl he ever saw.

To this union were born six children. The first was a son, Oscar William, who married Doris Irene Riley. Oscar was born Jan. 32, 1905, in Dana, IN. Oscar and Doris live in rural Clinton, Vermillion

Co., IN. Children of Oscar and Doris are Annabelle Perrin Hunt who married Robert Cole; William Blaine Hunt who married Gaile Rosalie Wallace; Sharon Kay Hunt who married Roy Pitts; Martha Ann Hunt who married William Peters, and Bradley Keith Hunt who is deceased. Oscar and Doris have 15 grandchildren and 15 great-grandchildren.

The second son of Oliver and Ruth was Wayne Wilber Hunt who married Beulah Taylor. Wayne was born Oct. 9, 1908, in Clinton, IN. They lived in Scottland, IL, until his death, Aug. 25, 1948, of heart failure. They had two children, Jeanne Hunt married David Goodwin; Gary Wayne Hunt married Priscilla Ann Ryan. Gary is also deceased. Beulah has three grandchildren.

Mildred Josephine Hunt was named after both of her grandmothers. Mildred was born in Clinton, IN, Oct. 8, 1911. She married Lester Ranwick Wright, June 19, 1929, and was later divorced. Children of Mildred and Lester are Betty Lou Wright, deceased; Edna Lee Wright married Richard L. Wright; and Ruth Elaine Wright married John Robert Mathes.

Mildred later married Charles Franklin McCauley, who is now deceased. Children of Mildred and Charles are Charles Mason McCauley married to Jeanne Jennings and Donald Eugene McCauley married to Sandra Kay Dunlop.

Mildred has 12 grandchildren and four great-grandchildren. She lives in rural Clinton, Vermillion Co., IN.

Virginia Nell Hunt married Arther Doan. She was born June 26, 1920, in Clinton, IN. Children of Virginia and Arther are Jerry Dale Doan married to Juanita Mullens; Jack Leon Doan married to Carol Jolley; James Max Doan married to Judy Trover; Carolyn Sue Doan married to Jim Newman; John Wayne Doan was married to Hazel York; Ruth Ella Doan married to Dennis Dreher.

Arther and Virginia have 15 grandchildren and nine great-grandchildren.

Oliver and Ruth's last children were twins—Lucy Rae and Warren James—both deceased.

Oliver and Ruth lived on several farms in Vermillion Co., IN. The last farm they lived on belonged to May Whitcom for the house and what they produced. They had a big garden, cows, pigs, chickens, ducks, turkeys, and geese. They lived near the Bicket Two Mine. If you were not a farmer, then you worked in the coal mines. They had a good life, but had to work hard for it. *Submitted by Edna Wright*

THE ANCESTRY OF WILLIAM B. JAMES,
One year after the first Methodist Chapel was built in America, there was a man born that not only would be a physician, but would carry Methodism from Virginia, across Ohio to Vermillion Co., IN, before his death!

William B. James was born in 1769 in Westmoreland Co., VA. He had two brothers and two sisters that is known. His parents had come to America from Wales. After the revolution he emigrated to what is now Hampshire Co., WV, and settled on New Creek. In 1798 he was married to Elizabeth Durling, who was born in 1771. They soon removed to Randolph Co., WV, where they remained 15 years, and six of his 13 children were born. The last of the children born here was Zachariah D. who was born Aug. 30, 1811, and in the fall of 1811, they left Virginia, to go first to Jefferson Co., OH, and then in 1814 settled in Mansfield, OH. The entire trip was made on horseback to Jefferson County, with his mother carrying him all the way.

William B. James Family - about 1890

In 1815 the village of Mansfield consisted of two block-houses built for defense from the Indians in 22 log houses, one of which was built by Dr. William B. James. The Methodists held services there, organizing the first religious organization in Mansfield, a Methodist class, which later erected the first church building built in this county. This church still stands today, having been greatly enlarged and contains a historic library.

In the summer of 1816, Dr. James, with others, laid out the town of Petersburg, now Mifflin, in Ashland County.

As the organizer of the first Methodist society here, Dr. James has a special interest. Dr. James was not a regular pastor. He was a physician, engaged in practicing his profession, but he was a local preacher of the Methodist Episcopal Church. When he received his license to preach is not exactly known. The records of the clerk's office in Romney, WV, show that permission was given January, 1797, to William B. James, minister of the gospel to perform the marriage ceremony according to the form of the Methodist Episcopal Church. He must, therefore, have been at that time an ordained minister.

Dr. James' wife, Elizabeth, died in Mansfield in 1818, the year that Robert S. James was born to them. On Mar. 2, 1820, he married Mary Walton and shortly after he went with his family first to Richmond, IN, and then in October, 1822, he came to Helt's Prairie, Vermillion Co., IN. His religious zeal is shown by the fact that he formed another Methodist class at Helt's Prairie, which like the Mansfield class grew into a church, now known as the Salem United Methodist Church.

Upon arrival to Helt's Prairie, Dr. Rev. James settled at Summit Grove, on the southwest side of the railroad. Six of his sons that came with him were: Edmund, Elijah, Collon D., John B., Thomas and Zachariah. The last son born to them was Samuel R. James, Aug. 2, 1826. That fall Dr. Rev. William B. James left with a boat load of corn for New Orleans, and died on his way back as a result of an attack of cholera, and is buried at Vicksburg.

Dr. Rev. William B. James was tall, straight, and a man of energetic character, and an excellent preacher. His grandson, Prof. Edmund J. James, of the University of Chicago, said of him, "He belongs to the earliest band of pioneer preachers who crossed the mountains into the Ohio valley and wherever he went he carried with him the burning zeal and restless activity of the pioneer Methodist." *Submitted by Patricia Heskett Crum*

JOHNSON - HARVEY - HEGARTY,
Like most early settlers in Vermillion County, the Johnsons arrived via the Wabash River. The earliest known ancestor of the Johnson family was Josiah Johnson who came from Wales and settled in the state of Ohio, on the west bank of the Ohio River at

a spot known as Wee Gee, across from Wheeling, WV and now known as Shadytown on the high bluffs of the Ohio River.

Josiah Johnson married Elizabeth Coleman and to this union were born nine children. He and his sons followed the trade of flat boat builders, but with the introduction of the keel boat and then the steam boat, many of the early settlers turned to the occupation of farming. The third son of Joshah and Elizabeth Coleman, John Coleman, followed this pattern, He was born May 15, 1807 in Belmont Co., OH and married Feb. 22, 1832 to Elizabeth Shaver where their first child, Josiah, was born.

Josephine Johnson Harvey Home; Frank Harvey, Josephine Harvey, Mintie Harvey Sawyer, Helen Sawyer, John Coleman Harvey.

In 1833, John Coleman Johnson set out for the west with the one stipulation from his wife that their home be on a river. The trip brought him down the Ohio, by flat boat, then poling up the Wabash on a keel boat against the current of the river. Finding a spot to his liking (approximately 3/4 mile down the river from the present home of Mary Josephine Harvey Hegarty) he walked to the land office at Crawfordsville and "entered" 78 acres. Then back to Wee Gee, OH to get his wife, young son, and what belongings they possessed. On Apr. 8, 1834 the family landed at the Tilsons Ferry Landing near the site of the small log cabin the husband had built on his first trip. Malaria and high water took its toll. One year, flood forced them out of their home 14 times. Their next three children were born there. After a few years, the family moved up the river about one and one-half miles to a house where all the rest of their ten children with the exception of the youngest, Florence, were born. She was born at a large frame house east of Newport which he built. Although located on a hill high enough to escape flood water from the Wabash, it still was surrounded by water when the river flooded. During all these years, John C. Johnson continued to acquire Wabash river bottom land. After the death of his wife, he bought in 1879, a large two-story brick home on the corner of Market and Elm where he died in 1883. This is at present the home of Mr. and Mrs. Clair VanSant.

The first Josephine born to John C. and Elizabeth Shaver only lived six weeks. However, Josephine was such a favorite name that on Jan. 24, 1842 the fifth child was also named Josephine.

The two counties, Parke and Vermillion, were separated by the Wabash River and the town of Newport and Howard were served by a ferry two miles north of the town which Johnson bought from Daniel Jones in 1856 who in turn had bought it from the Tilson family, who in turn had started it in 1824. This means of transportation between the two counties brings into family history, Nathan Harvey (1834-1871) born in Parke County of Isaac (1784-1851) and Rebekah Kelly (1791-1842) (father Wm.

Harvey, Chester Co., PA). Being the 11th of 12 children, Nathan graduated from the Bloomingdale Academy, a Quaker school, then crossed the Johnson Ferry to Vermillion County to teach school where his future wife, Josephine Johnson was one of his pupils. Prior to the marriage, however, he attended the University of Michigan Law School. Evidently on his return he joined in the practice of law with Wm. Eggleston and married Josephine Johnson. His career was cut short at the age of 37, from typhoid fever, leaving his widow with four children, the youngest of whom died the same year from whooping cough.

The C & E.I. Railroad was under construction at this time and Josephine Harvey fed the construction crew and paid off the mortgage on their home. She then moved to a small house (probably log) two miles north of Newport belonging to her father, John C. Johnson, and the boys, John and Frank, about seven and 11, started farming. Frank, who was large for his age, started by walking behind a one-shovel plow pulled by a blind mule. The mother sold butter and eggs to families in Newport. In 1885, the family moved into a newly built home which cost approximately $2,000.00 and is the present home of Josephine Harvey's granddaughter, Mary Josephine Harvey Hegarty.

See Hegarty Family.

CLEVELAND JONES, was born Nov. 30, 1884, in Jonestown, IN, the oldest son of Alfred C. and Christia (Foncannon) Jones. His grandfather, Matthew Jones, was born in North Carolina and settled in Vermillion County in 1831. They were farmers, originally, but when Cleve was four years old, his parents and two older sisters, Eva and Carrie, moved to Clinton where his father operated a dry goods store. It was located on North Main Street (on the east side, where Lowry's Service Station is now). Two more sons were born in Clinton.

In October, 1891, his father sold the store and the family moved back to Jonestown. Alfred passed away on Dec. 2, 1891. In a few years, Cleve's mother remarried to Ben Jones (maybe a relative of Alfred). He had a son, John, of Danville, IL, who visited friends in Dana. (according to The Old Timers News Column in The Daily Clintonian)

Ben Jones (Cleve Jones' step-father), Christia Jones, Carrie Jones, and Cleve Jones. (taken about 1894 in Jonestown)

Cleve farmed and worked in a coal mine until he was 22 years old. He then started tending store for his cousin, Fred Jones, in Jonestown. He and Sophia Agnes Knopp were married Mar. 6, 1907, at Scottland, IL, by M.C. Gilbra Hutson, Justice of the Peace. Witnesses were Lizzie Davis and Brownie Groves. Cleve worked for Fred six years, then built a new one-room store building there in town which opened in 1913. They now have a son, Kenneth (age three) and a foster son, Frank Ennis, to deliver the

groceries by horse drawn spring wagon. The Milwaukee Railroad terminal had come to West Clinton, about one-half mile south. This increased the population and made business very good. More houses, schools, and business places were built. More land was bought to the south and north and New St. Bernice was established. Cleve bought lots in West Clinton Junction and built a new home and one-room store building next door in 1918. (mud roads at that time) Electric lights and automobiles were coming. The thriving business called for a larger store, so another room was added and stocked with dry goods, such as shoes, boots, hardware, household items, some yard goods, a gasoline pump, plus home killed meats for the grocery department. He raised milk cows, hogs, chickens, and grain on his farm in Jonestown. He had a slaughter house, barn for the horses that he farmed with before tractors, and a small two-room dwelling which he built for his father-in-law Frank Knopp, who came here from Oklahoma, after his wife (Agnes' mother) died. Frank helped with the chores. Frank remarried, therefore, he and his bride were the first to live in the new "Honeymoon House" (as it was called later, as all who have lived there have been newlyweds until later years).

Agnes had a big part in this business—cooking, making head cheese, cottage cheese, etc., for the store, raising chickens and dressing them to sell, as well as numerous chores to be done. One of the chores was transferring the cash to and from the American State Bank in St. Bernice. The payroll at the rail junction was as high as $10,000 every two weeks.

Being the shrewd buyer and businessman that he was, Cleve bought several lots in the area when they were cheap. When the news came the railroad might move to Terre Haute, he bought 11 company houses when they were up for sale, had them moved on his lots and rented some and sold some at a profit. The railroad moved to Terre Haute in 1952. He still operated the store until 1954. His health forced him to give up active participation in the business.

His wife, Agnes, operated the store the next three years. They sold out in 1957 to his cousin, Rex Malone, and Cleve and Agnes retired to their newly remodeled home, formerly the Smith Reed place on the Jonestown Road.

Cleve was a member of the United Brethren Church, Asbury Lodge 320 F&AM at Dana, Independent Order of Odd Fellows 666 at St. Bernice, a Democrat, active in political affairs, and served as a Vermillion County Commissioner.

The couple enjoyed nine more golden years together after retirement—seeing their two granddaughters, Janice Bradley and Nancy Hill, graduate from college, their marriages, and their two great-grandchildren before Cleve's sudden death at home on Aug. 18, 1966, at the age of 81 years.

CRAIG JONES AND BEVERLY E. CURTIS JONES, Craig Jones was born Jan. 28, 1922, in Cayuga, IN. He was the only son of William "Dick" Jones and Ruth Craig Jones. Craig attended Cayuga High School and graduated in 1940. He was called to the service in 1942 and was attached to the 486th Combat Engineers, serving three years in the European Theater during World War II.

He was married to Beverly E. Curtis, the oldest daughter of Norval and Daisy Melton Curtis, on Jan. 9, 1946. Beverly graduated from Cayuga High School in 1943.

The couple moved to the Henderson Chapel area where they were engaged in farming. They operated the Jones Farm Supply Store from 1958-1988.

They became the parents of a daughter, Pamela Sue, in 1948. Pamela married Roger Hazelwood in 1969, and their children are Carrie Sue, Sally Ann, Nathan Craig, and Jason Paul. They live east of Quaker at the old homesite of Earle O. White and the location of the Round Barn.

Craig is a member of the Cayuga Christian Church, American Legion Post #263, VFW #9794, 40&8 Voiture #1264, Vermillion County Fair Association, Collett Home Board, Sheriff's Merit Board, Pioneer Days Association, Chairman of Cayuga Alumni Association, and was awarded Honorary Master of Science in Agriculture from Buckner University by the J.I. Case Co.

PHILLIP JONES,

My great-great-grandfather, Phillip Jones came to Vermillion Co., IN, from Stokes Co., NC, in 1832. He settled about one-half mile south of where Jonestown was built about 30 years later. When Phillip came to Indiana, he had a family of small children and was $45.00 in debt. He sold a pony to pay his indebtedness, and was then left without even a cow or a pig. He and his family were obliged to work very hard to make a living.

Harmon (1847-1927) and Eliza Jones (1850-1914)

Jonestown is in the southwest corner of Helt Township. It was given its name and plotted out by Phillip Jones, who owned part of the land, and Noah Wellman in the year 1862. Noah Wellman was a landowner and a farmer. He was a great-great-grandfather on my mother's side of the family. A log cabin and three or four dwellings were on the site.

Matthew Jones, son of Phillip had a son, Harmon, who married Eliza Jane Reed.

Frederic II known in history as "Frederic the Great" of Germany, had no children, so his sister's son followed him on the throne. Frederic II was born Jan. 24, 1712, and became King of Prussia at the age of 28 in the year 1740. He reigned until 1786. Frederic II married Elizabeth Christina of Brunswick.

Frederic William II, son of Frederic II's sister, took the throne from 1786 and reigned until 1797.

Elizabeth Hohenzollern, daughter of Frederic William II, born Jan. 8, 1753, married a nobleman by the name of Andrew Wray Schmitt. Their daughter, Elizabeth Schmitt, was born Mar. 31, 1793. She married a nobleman by the name of Jacob Reid in 1814. Jacob Reid and his wife sailed for America that same year. Jacob Reid was born June 23, 1789. This is the ages and names of their children: Mary Eliza, July 25, 1816; Michael Franklin, Jan. 8, 1818; Andrew Wray, Oct. 17, 1820; John Washington, Aug. 3, 1822; David Abraham, Sept. 28, 1824; Jacob Lewis, June 15, 1826. Soon

after arriving in America they changed the spelling of Reid to Reed.

Eliza Jane Reed, daughter of David Abraham Reed, married Harmon Jones. They had eight children: Fred, Minnie, Ira, Rose, Ernest, Gus, Gold, and Bessie. Ernest and Bessie died when they were very young, about two or three years old.

Ira was born Feb. 25, 1875, and died Feb. 11, 1961. He married Pearlie Foltz and they were the parents of three children: Harold, Bonnie, and Thelma Grounds. His grandchildren are Walter (deceased), Joyce Cook (deceased), Bonnie Trezise, Barbara Nunn, Betty Sutton, and Ira Jones.

Harmon and Eliza gave the ground that the U. B. Church was built on in 1875. *Submitted by Thelma Jones Grounds*

SOLOMON A. JONES,

one of the first landowners of Highland Township, in the state of Indiana, entered land west of Coal Branch, near the Illinois line in 1834. Born in Tennessee Apr. 3, 1812, he married Margaret Bradburn Nov. 28, 1837. She was born in Virginia ca. 1815. Solomon Jones died Mar. 15, 1887; Margaret died Jan. 22, 1899.

Their oldest son was James Madison "Matt" Jones, born ca. 1846 in Highland Township. James Madison Jones lived in Highland Township all his life, farming 236 acres west of Coal Branch. On Aug. 22, 1867, he married Ellen Skelton in the parsonage of the old Crossroads Church west of Perrysville. Ellen, born Jan. 15, 1848, in Eugene Township, was the daughter of Harvey and Elizabeth Skelton. Matt Jones died Dec. 22, 1926; Ellen died Apr. 6, 1934. They are buried at Atherton Cemetery near Danville, IL.

Matt and Ellen Jones had nine children: Harvey Edward; Ella May; Solomon; Charles; Jennie Leah; Verner Madison; Cortz; Victor H.; and a daughter who died shortly after birth in 1870. Six children survived to adulthood.

Ella May, born May 2, 1870, married Asa Randall Feb. 16, 1902; they lived north of Union Corner in Vermillion Co., IL. Ella died Nov. 10, 1968.

Solomon Jones, born June 2, 1872 practiced as a physician in the Perrysville area and Danville, IL. He married Ella Augusta VanMeter. They had one son, Jerome VanMeter Jones. Solomon died Sept. 25, 1937.

Jennie Leah Jones, born Sept. 20, 1876, married Frank Davidson Houser June 19, 1904. They had one son, Victor Houser. She died in 1972.

Verner Madison Jones, born Feb. 7, 1879, married Myrtle Rogers Oct. 12, 1905. They had two sons, Paul and Harold Jones. Verner died in 1950.

Cortz Jones, born Sept. 24, 1881, married Grace Hines Jan. 4, 1911. She was born Jan. 7, 1872 in Perrysville, the daughter of Thomas and Lillie Volkel Hines. Cortz and Grace lived on a farm west of Perrysville throughout their married life. He was a teacher and a farmer, and served two terms as Highland Township trustee. He was an organizer of the Rural Electric Membership Corporation, serving as a director for 40 years. Cortz died Dec. 24, 1981 and Grace died Feb. 28, 1988. They are buried in Lower Mound Cemetery.

Victor H. Jones was born July 30, 1883 in Highland Township where he was a farmer all his life. He was first married in 1912 to Bessie Bennett, daughter of David and Kate Bennett of Highland Township; she died Aug. 11, 1922. On Apr. 22, 1925, Victor married Anna Louise Murray. She was born June 10, 1900, in Covington, IN, the daughter

of David R. and Mary Elizabeth "Mollie" Martin Murray. Victor died Sept. 7, 1965, and is buried at Atherton Cemetery. Louise Jones continues to live at their family home west of Coal Branch. They had three children; Reva Mae, born Feb. 26, 1926; Doris Lea, born Mar. 19, 1928; and William Murray, born Dec. 30, 1932.

CLYDE W. AND ETTA M. JORDAN,

Clyde W. Jordan was born in St. Bernice in 1924, son of Hazel M. Shuey and the late Wallace O. Jordan. He is the grandson of Vina and Charles Shuey, owner of the blacksmith shop in St. Bernice until 1937. He is one of nine children. Clyde graduated in 1942 from St. Bernice High School. Upon graduation he entered the armed service, where he served for three years in Europe. In December of 1948, he married Etta M. Smith, born in the year 1930. She was one of six children born to the late Marie Griffin and Charles F. Smith of Crompton Hill. Her great grandfather, Solomon Clark Griffin, in the 1800's, owned and operated a steamboat on the Wabash River between Montezuma and Evansville. She graduated from Crompton Hill Grade School in 1944 and Clinton High School in 1948.

The couple resides in Clinton and are the parents of four children: Clyde R. of Rosedale, Deborah of Clinton, Jeffrey of Clinton, and Jenniffier of Clinton. They are also grandparents of ten grandchildren.

Clyde W. and Etta M. were members of the St. Bernice Christian Church. Its door is no longer open. Clyde W. is a member of the American Legion Post 140, Jerusalem Lodge 99, and the National Rifle Association. Etta M. is a member of the AARP and the National Wildlife Federation.

MONTIE AND BETTY COOK KELLER, GEORGIA ANN KELLER,

Montie was born Feb. 13, 1935 in Covington, IN. The son of Cyril and Georgie Smith Keller. He is next to the eldest of four children. A graduate of Covington High School he was employed for 18 years at Harrison Steel in Attica. The last 17 years he's been at Medline Industries in Covington in charge of the warehouse.

Montie and Betty Keller

He is a member of Unity Lodge #344, Order of Eastern Star, White Shrine, and Perrysville Lions.

He has resided in Perrysville, IN since July 6, 1963 when he married Betty Cook.

Betty was born on Nov. 29, 1937 in Perrysville the daughter of Clark and Viola Thomas Cook. She is the eldest of three daughters.

Betty's a graduate of Perrysville High School.

She was employed 20 years at Windbreaker in Danville, IL. The last 12 she 's been Plant Manager at Medline Industries in Covington, IN.

She's a member of the Order of Eastern Star,

Rebekahs, Royal Neighbors of America, and White Shrine.

Montie and Betty are also members of the Christian Union Church.

They have a daughter Georgia Ann Keller born Apr. 19, 1967 in Danville.

She's a graduate of North Vermillion High School.

At the present time she's continuing her education to pursue a career as a dietitian.

Montie also has a daughter Brenda Neeley and two grandsons by a former marriage. They reside in Seely, TX.

DARROL DEAN KUHNS, was born Apr. 8, 1927, to Herman Kuhns and Ruby Pauline Nolan. Darrol married Juanita S. Broady. Darrol was in the Navy from 1945-1950. Darrol graduated from Indiana State Teacher's College in 1950 and went to work for E. I. du Pont. In May, 1957, he was transferred to Pennsville, NJ. Darrol and Juanita had six children, Christine Kuhns on Apr. 10, 1947, Darrol Dean Kuhns, Jr. on Mar. 21, 1948, Steven Bryan Kuhns on Oct. 5, 1952, Timothy Ross Kuhns on Jan. 12, 1958, Anitra Kay Kuhns on Mar. 3, 1959, and Mark Allen Kuhns on Oct. 19, 1965. Darrol and Juanita have four grandchildren.

ERMA KAYWIN KUHNS KELLEY, was born Mar. 30, 1934, to Herman Kuhns and Ruby Pauline Nolan. Erma married Melvin Willard Kelley on May 17, 1953. They had Kathryn Elaine Kelley on May 10, 1962, and Deborah Lynne Kelley on Aug. 8, 1965.

MELVIN WILLARD KELLEY, was born Nov. 3, 1933, to Raymond Willard Kelley and Evelyn Hestella Craft Kelley. Melvin married Erma Kaywin Kuhns on May 17, 1953. Melvin graduated from Indiana University with a B.S. in Chemistry and an M.B.A. on June, 1962. He started working for Eli Lilly and Company on June, 1962, in Indianapolis. In 1970 he was transferred to Roanoke, VA, and was on the team to transfer Elizabeth Arden and Company to Roanoke from New York. When Eli Lilly sold Elizabeth Arden in 1988, Melvin was transferred back to Indianapolis. Melvin and Erma had Kathryn Elaine Kelley on May 10, 1962 and Deborah Lynne Kelley on Aug. 8, 1965.

RAYMOND WILLARD KELLEY, was born Feb. 19, 1913, to Brownie Morgan Kelley and Nellie Jane Shannon. Raymond married Evelyn Hestella Craft. He worked at Beal's Market and Snow Hill Coal Corporation. They had Melvin Willard Kelley on Nov. 3, 1933, Meredith William Kelley on June 30, 1944, and Judith Evelyn Kelley on May 23, 1948. They have four grandchildren and one great-grandchild. Raymond married Bessie White. Raymond died on Aug. 17, 1979.

THE KEMNA FAMILY, Herman Kemna (1848-1925) and his wife Marie (Meinke) (1858-1927), came to the U.S.A. from Germany (as small children) prior to 1865. The descendants say that the voyage took about six weeks and one child of the Meinke family died and was buried at sea.

Herman Kemna worked at the C & E I Railroad Shops and farmed southeast of Danville, IL. The Kemna homestead is still located west of Perrysville on the Indiana-Illinois State line. Herman and Marie had ten children. John and Anna Marie died at two months of age. William, Ernest, Minnie (Martin), Alice (Bowman), Henry, Fred and Herman L. lived to maturity. One daughter Leona, is still living in Danville, IL.

Fred (1895-1980) and William (1883-1951) married sisters, Elsie (1895-1986) and Ethel (1893-1924) Skinner, daughters of Lewis and Rosetta Skinner. They were both farmers and both operated threshing machines.

Fred and Elsie had two children. A son, Richard, lives across the Indiana State line adjoining the Kemna homestead and is a farmer. The daughter, Marietta (Arrasmith) lives east of the Kemna homestead.

William and Ethel's son Lewis, lives west of Perrysville. He is a retired farmer and drove a school bus for many years. He has a step-brother William and a step-sister, Juanita (Wakeley) that live in Danville, IL. Ethel's son, Ray, lives in Virginia.

KILGORE FAMILY, Martin Kilgore, a farmer from Virginia, was born in 1837. May Millison Kilgore was born in Ohio in 1851. My great-grandparents had several children—Nathan, William, Charles, Ann, and Arnet. William, my grandfather, was born Apr. 14, 1865, and died Dec. 14, 1935. He married Nellie Rhodenbaugh, Nov. 29, 1889. She died June 14, 1956. I spent many hours with my grandmother, eating good food and hearing many interesting stories. She also told me that my grandfather was a person who was proud of who he was. Passing this on down to his descendants was always on his mind. He worked on the railroad, in the brick yard, and in later life worked for Sowers Construction Company. This company built the present Vermillion County Court House and the Cayuga Grade School. My grandfather mixed the mortar for laying brick in both. They had several children—Charles, Eva Lena, Mary Etta, Bertha, Annabelle, Arnold, baby, Stella, Carl, Zelma, and Lawrence. Carl Kilgore was my dad, and a very good one, I might add. He married Amelia Snyder on Dec. 24, 1928. My mother was also one to be proud of. She, too, told many interesting stories and was very kind to all. She did lots of sewing, crocheting, and cooking good things to eat. She was a baker supreme. She made yeast biscuits, fried bread, jelly rolls, and pies and cakes fit for a king.

Their children were Bill, Arden, Glenda, and John. My dad worked at gas stations and Fable Motor Company, a Ford dealer in Cayuga. He drove a school bus and worked at Fable's for over 25 years. He later worked for the North Vermillion School Corporation as a janitor for several years. I, too, am proud of who I am and hope to pass this on to others in my family, so that grandfather's words won't be forgotten.

Martin Kilgore, my great-grandfather, had three brothers, who played a big part in the history of Cayuga and Eugene.

Hugh Morgan Kilgore was born Dec. 29, 1839, and died Feb. 1, 1913. He was the first home owner in the town of Springfield, IN, which was near Eugene. He sometimes filled in for the minister at the Eugene Church according to a man named John Wooster, John said he was a very fancy dresser, and he had tried to dress like him when he grew older.

Robert Kilgore, who lived in Georgetown, IL, was born July 4, 1844, and died July 8, 1926. He was a member of the Georgetown Methodist Church and is buried in Georgetown Cemetery.

James Kilgore was born in 1841 and lived in the Brownstown area, near the Illinois and Indiana line. This town no longer exists. He had several children. His first wife was named Rebecca and their children were John, Stephen, Isaac, Alice, Wiley, and Flora. His second wife, Ellen, and he had Lane, Everette, and Willis. Some of James' descendants still live in the Danville, IL, area.

John, Ike, and Wiley became famous for their fights around the Cayuga and Eugene area and on the Illinois side—McKendree, Lickskillet, and Meeks Station area. I heard many stories about these three from Bill Patrick, Bill Hinkle, and my Grandma Kilgore. Wiley wore blue steel guns and could use them. John was a big man, six feet, five inches and weighed 250 pounds. He was said to have broken the handle out of the Cayuga town pump, to defend himself in a fight. Bill Hinkle told me about seeing these three ride on horseback into a saloon called "The Yellow Heaven" and come out drinking mugs of beer, with guns a blazing. My mother also told about her grandfather being in a vigilante group that was in pursuit of Wiley on the Illinois side. Wiley's shots apparently got too close and turned them away.

Robert and Morgan fought in the Civil War in Company K, 97th Indiana. Bill Patrick told me how Robert was shot in the mouth in one of the battles and his older brother, Thomas Patrick, gave him first aid and saved his life.

My grandfather, William, had a younger brother who moved west at an early age. He lived in Wheatland, WY. He had two boys by his first marriage and one by his second marriage. Charles M. Kilgore, was a chiropractor in Wheatland, WY. Just recently, I made contact by phone to Charles C. Kilgore, his son, who is 33 years old and has brothers and sisters who live nearby. He is a chiropractor in Torrington, WY. I plan a vacation in July, and plan to visit Charles and find out more about my cousins in Wyoming.

My grandfather had a brother, Arnet, who was a peddler in Los Angeles in 1926. He stayed with a sister, Anna, who lived in San Pedro, CA. I plan to keep searching for more information about Kilgores who are related to me. I hope to trace our family across the ocean to Scotland or Ireland, which is where I'm told we came from. Any help from anyone who reads this will be greatly appreciated. *Submitted by John L. Kilgore, Sr.*

ROBERT AND BETTY PAYTON KILLEBREW, live in Fairview Park. They have two sons, David, 17, and Robert William (Robby), five. Mrs. Killebrew also has a son, James Muciarelli, 23, who graduated from Indiana State University in 1987.

Robert, born July 16, 1953, is the fourth of seven children belonging to Harold and Helen Hollingsworth Killebrew of Lewis, IN. He graduated from Honey Creek High School in 1971 and moved to Clinton shortly after. He has worked at the U.S. Penitentiary in Terre Haute since 1977 where he is currently a factory manager.

Betty, born Apr. 2, 1945, is the fourth of five children. Her parents were William and Ruth Prulhiere Payton.

William (1910-1979) was a well-known area school teacher with a 40 year career in local schools. He was a lifelong resident of Vermillion County, the 12th child of James and Laura Dugger Payton. James was an early Clinton teamster who worked with his own horses and wagon. Because of his business, in the early 1900's, he was one of the first in his N. Walter St. Clinton neighborhood to have a telephone.

Robert and Betty Killebrew and sons - 1983

Ruth (1914-1973) was the seventh of eight children belonging to Leonard and Emma Metz Prulhiere who moved to Fairview Park from Brazil when she was a small child. Leonard Prulhiere found work in the coal mines.

Betty graduated from Clinton High School in 1963 and attended college at Indiana State for one year. Later, in 1977, she received a Private Secretarial certificate from Indiana Business College. She has been employed as a bookkeeper at the Daily Clintonian newspaper office since 1977.

The couple married in 1973 and have resided at Third and Plum in Fairview Park since 1978.

HERMAN KUHNS, was born Aug. 4, 1901, to William Robert Kuhns and Cora May Beard Kuhns. Herman married Ruby Pauline Nolan Kuhns on June 12, 1926. Herman (Slim) Kuhns worked for Public Service Company and was transferred to Cayuga IN, in 1940. He later worked for E. I. du Pont. Herman was a member of the Masonic Order and a volunteer fireman. Herman and Ruby had Darrol Dean Kuhns on Apr. 8, 1927, Erma Kaywin Kuhns on Mar. 30, 1934, and Carole Kathleen Kuhns on Apr. 22, 1938. Herman and Ruby have 11 grandchildren and eight great-grandchildren. He was a member of the Cayuga Christian Church. Herman died on Feb. 10, 1969.

RUBY PAULINE NOLAN KUHNS, was born Dec. 15, 1902, to Alfred Marion Nolan and Sarah Florence Osmon. Ruby married Herman Kuhns on June 12, 1926. Herman and Ruby had Darrol Dean Kuhns on Apr. 8, 1927, Erma Kaywin Kuhns on Mar. 30, 1934, and Carole Kathleen Kuhns on Apr. 22, 1938. Ruby is a member of the Eastern Star and was a member of the Cayuga Christian Church. She is now a member of the Sellersburg Methodist Church. Herman and Ruby have 11 grandchildren and eight great-grandchildren. After Herman's death in February, 1969, Ruby moved to Sellersburg, IN, where Carole Kuhns Canada lives.

DONALD B. KUYKENDALL AND BARBARA S. DRENGACS KUYKENDALL, Donald was born, Sept. 1, 1935, in New Goshen, IN, to Ruth Daugherty Kuykendall and Bert Kuykendall. Bert died in a mining accident in 1941. Donald has a half-sister, Helen Kuykendall Tevlin. Ruth remarried in 1946; to Joseph Halliwell. Donald grew up in the Fairveiw area. After graduation from Clinton High School, he worked for Scott Oil Co. and White Excavating. He then went to work for Garrard Excavating, but later returned to White Construction, at which time he is presently employed. He has been an Operating Engineer for 30 years.

Barbara was born and raised in Shepardsville, IN, the eldest of two daughters born to James

Drengacs and Lucille I. Bildilli Drengacs. Sandra K. Drengacs Trimble is the youngest daughter of James and Lucille.

Back: Debora Kuykendall, Frank Turchi, Donald B. Kuykendall. Front: Dona K. Kuykendall, Diana L. Turchi, Ashlie L. Turchi, Barbara S. Kuykendall.

On July 14, 1958, Donald B. and Barbara S. were united in marriage. After graduation, Barbara attended Indiana State University in the Business Department. Barbara worked as a Bank Teller for several years, worked at I.S.U. in the Business Office, and also managed the Clinton License Branch. The family has also owned and operated a Tanning Salon for several years.

Donald and Barbara have three daughters, Diana Lynn Turchi, Debora S. Kuykendall, and Dona Kay Kuykendall. Diana is the mother of the only grandchild, Ashlie Lynn Turchi. Diana is a Cosmetologist and a bookkeeper for Shuee & Sons. Debbie is a Math Teacher in Vigo County with a Masters Degree. Dona is a Senior at South Vermillion and will be attending College to pursue a Health Career.

The family is a member of Wayside United Methodist Church. Barbara is a member of the church choir. She is also a member of Jerusalem Chapter #254 Order of Eastern Star. Donald is a member of Jerusalem Lodge F.& A.M., Scottish Rite, Valley of Terre Haute, and Zorah Shrine.

JAMES NEIL LAKE, was born Aug. 9, 1958, in Terre Haute, IN, the son of Madge Thomas Lake (see related biography) and Bernard Neil Lake (see related biography).

He attended Sugar Grove Grade School and Woodrow Wilson Junior High. He graduated from South Vigo High School in Terre Haute in 1976. James graduated in 1981 from Indiana State University with a degree in Radio-TV-Film. He is currently an account executive at WZZQ Radio in Terre Haute.

James moved from Terre Haute to Vermillion County in 1977. *Submitted by Madge Thomas Lake*

MADGE LAVERNA THOMAS LAKE, was born Feb. 4, 1933, in Clinton, IN, the daughter of James L. (see related biography) and Golda Nolan Thomas (see related biography). She has one sister Beulah Thomas Frist. (see related biography)

As a child and through the teen years, she lived on a farm in Helt Township. She attended Hillsdale grade and high school and graduated from there in 1951. After which, she attended Indiana State College for two years.

During the early years of her childhood and until she moved to Terre Haute, she attended Salem Methodist Church.

June 27, 1953, was the date of her marriage to Bernard Neil Lake. One son was born to this union, James Neil Lake (see related biography).

Bernard Neil Lake was born Mar. 14, 1928, in Jasper Co., IL, the son of Hallie and Edna Parker

Lake. He was one of five children. His brothers and sisters include: John (deceased), Guy, James, and Barbara Lake Yates.

His childhood was spent on a farm located in Clay Co., IL. He attended Harmon Grade School near Ingraham, IL, and graduated from Ingraham High School in 1945. He attended a Southern Baptist church in the area.

Upon graduation, he found employment in Urbana, IL. Immediately following their marriage, Bernard and Madge lived in the Chicago, IL, area for a brief period, then moved to Terre haute, IN. The family lived in Terre Haute for 22 years, then in 1977 built a home on a portion of the farm belonging to her parents. From then to the present they have lived in Helt Township in Vermillion Co., IN.

Bernard was associated with Ford Automobile Dealerships for 38 years; including 28 years as parts manager for Jack Thrasher Ford and Doan and Decker Ford in Terre Haute. He was the recipient of several sales management performance awards.

He is currently employed as parts manager for J.R. Rumpza Chevrolet Sales in Clinton, IN.

Madge was employed at Jack Thrasher Ford and Doan and Decker Ford for 20 years.

They are members of the Salem United Methodist Church. *Submitted by Madge Thomas Lake*

LEWIS FAMILY—AARON, GEORGE P., AND CECIL JAMES, Aaron Lewis was born in Ohio in 1820, and died in Parke Co., IN, in 1885. On Sept. 9, 1851, he married Hester Ann Williams. She was born in Ross Co., OH, on Dec. 31, 1833, and died in Parke Co., IN, on May 28, 1908. They were the parents of six children— Aaron married Etta Fulwider; Frank was born Mar. 18, 1870, and married Elizabeth Roberts; Will married Martha ?; Nancy E. married Alfred Nutgrass; Bruce or James married Ida ?; George P. was born July 19, 1852 in Parke Co., IN, and died Sept. 19, 1935 in Clinton, IN.

George P. Lewis married Sarah Elizabeth Pollard. They were the parents of nine children— Florence F., born Oct. 12, 1875; Cecil James, born Dec. 8, 1879; Perley Emmett, born May 12, 1882, died July 4, 1939, married Lena Ponton; Lola Dell, born Mar. 13, 1884, married Homer James; Choeteen, born Nov. 26, 1885, married Samuel James; Grover Cleveland, born Aug. 25, 1888, married Zora Procop; Leta Ann, born Jan. 5, 1891, died Dec. 24, 1949, married James Arnold; Frank George, born Mar. 7, 1894, died Dec. 11, 1894; William Earl, born Mar. 30, 1897, died June 11, 1912.

Cecil James Lewis was born Dec. 8, 1879, at Hillsdale, and died Apr. 7, 1953, at Terre Haute. On Nov. 25, 1904, he married Sarah Elizabeth Van Huss, the daughter of Benjamin Van Huss and Katherine Dugger Van Huss. She was born Feb. 22, 1883, at Hillsdale, and died Aug. 9, 1957, at Mt. Clemens, MI, and was buried in Bono Cemetery. They were the parents of eight children—male, born and died July 24, 1905; Robert Perry, born June 20, 1906, died Feb. 4, 1908; Eleanor Mae, born Nov. 5, 1907, died July 1, 1919; George Arnold, born Oct. 17, 1909; James Orvie, born Oct. 30, 1911, at St. Bernice, died Mar. 26, 1931; Frances Louise Olivene, born Oct. 12, 1913, at St. Bernice, married Forest Turner Downs on Dec. 27, 1935; Henry, born Oct. 9, 1915, at St. Bernice, died Oct. 10, 1915; Doneth Elizabeth, born Mar. 7, 1917, at St. Bernice, married Joe McDonald. (see related article—Benjamin Van Huss)

SARAH "SALLY" CATHERINE (JONES) LEWIS,

was born May 3, 1898, at Dana; the daughter of Wilson Nelson and Millie A. Hollingsworth Jones. She was the granddaughter of Benjamin Jones (b-1816, d-1872), and Sarah Hollingsworth (b-1822, d-?), who were early settlers in the Quaker community. Both her grandparents are buried in Old Hopewell Cemetery at Quaker, IN.

A history of the Hollingsworth family (available at the Indiana State Library) shows Sarah Hollingsworth as the daughter of William (b. Oct. 27-1776, d-1848) and Rebecca Ramsey Hollingsworth.

Sally Lewis and A.J. Lewis

William was the son of Issac (b-1737) and Susannah Wright Hollingsworth (b-Apr. 16, 1755). Both are buried in West Branch Meeting graveyard at Troy, OH. They moved to Ohio from South Carolina in the 1770's. Susannah's parents were John and Rachel Wright. The Hollingsworth's have been traced to Valentine Hollingsworth, Sr. (1632-1711) and wife, Anne Ree (b-1626, d-1671) who immigrated from Ireland.

As a child, Sally attended Newlin School at Quaker. Married at 24, she and her husband, Milton "Whistler" Lewis, lived in the Quaker community. Their two sons, Charles and Robert were born near Tangier. They later moved to Newport where she worked in a number of restaurants. She enjoyed flowers and playing bingo. Sally died May 10, 1987, at Vermillion County Hospital in Clinton, IN.

Milton was born in Putnam County in 1891 and died in Danville, IL, Veteran's Hospital, in 1952. He served in the U.S. Army during W.W.I. His father, William, was born in 1854 in Putnam County, and died in 1918 in Parke County. He is buried in West Union Cemetery near Montezuma. William's parents were Moses and Sarah (Daniels) Lewis. Milton's mother, Caroline, was born July 11, 1855 and died Jan. 15, 1933, Parke County. Her maiden name was Stuart. She was first married to Hiriam Cory. Her parents were James and Ruth (Ages) Stuart. They were from Tennessee.

In addition to Milton (the youngest of the family), William and Caroline were the parents of Nora (Armstrong) (b-1890, d-1966) and Myrtle (McMasters). Half-brothers and sisters from his mother's first marriage include George, Charles, Bright, Maude, and Emmett Cory.

Sally and Milton's oldest son is Charles "Sparky" Lewis of Newport (b. Aug. 29, 1922). He is married to Josephine Hawkins (b. Sept. 3, 1924). They were married June 24, 1943 at Williamsport, IN and are the parents of three sons and a daughter. The sons are: Charles Jr. (b. July 10, 1944) who is married to Patti Porter (b. Apr. 9, 1950). They are the parents of Tricia (b. Mar. 9, 1973) and Stephanie (b. Mar. 13, 1975), both students at Rockville. Jerry

"Crab" Lewis (b. Aug. 26, 1948) married Janet McConnell (b. Mar. 11, 1954). They have a daughter, Jennifer (b. May 7, 1980) and a son, A.J. (b. July 7, 1983). They live in Covington. Larry (b. Dec. 11, 1963) lives in Newport. Their daughter, Lisa (b. July 7, 1966) was married Feb. 14, 1987, to Bret Noggle (b. November, 1966). The couple lives in Georgetown, IL.

Charles Lewis served in the U.S. Army from Oct. 13, 1942, to Dec. 31, 1945. He spent two years in the Philippine Islands with the 202 Anti Aircraft Division. He has retired from Bohn in Danville, IL.

Robert Lewis served in the U.S. Navy from 1943 to 1946. He was on a destroyer escort. He has retired from the county, serving 18 years.

Milton and Sally are buried in Thomas Cemetery near Newport. *Submitted by Janet Lewis*

TRUMAN AND HATTIE LEWIS,

Lee Truman Lewis was born in Mercer Co., KY, on Apr. 10, 1898, to William Leslie and Nancy Gritton Lewis. The family moved to Parke Co., IN, when Truman was about five years old. Truman married Hattie Agnes Jones in 1919 and they lived in the Newport area all of their married lives.

Hattie's great-grandparents, William and Rebecca Hollingsworth, were early land owners in Vermillion Township. They moved here around 1827 and lived in the Edgewood area. Their daughter, Sarah, married Benjamin Jones on July 27, 1840. Benjamin and Sarah's son, Wilson, was born on Jan. 10, 1858, and on Dec. 29, 1887, he married Millie Ann Hollingsworth, daughter of John Riley and Catherine Hollingsworth. Hattie, the daughter of Wilson and Millie, was born on Apr. 2, 1902 near Stumptown.

Truman and Hattie had seven children: Donald Wayne (Mitch), Betty Ann, William Lee (Bill), Herman (Ike), Truman (Sim), Doris Maxine, and Ronald Gene.

Mitch was born on Aug. 17, 1923, and married Jean Lamberth. They had two daughters, Donna Jean Paddish and Carol Diane Farrell. Mitch died in 1974 and is buried in Thomas Cemetery. Jean lives in Newport.

Betty was born on Sept. 19, 1926, and married Milton (Jack) Wilburn, Jr. They have four children: Jackie Gene, Cathy Griffin, Richard (Dick), and Susie. Betty and Jack live in Montezuma.

Bill was born on Dec. 28, 1927, and married Jane Waddy. They have three children: Geri Mock, Tony, and Nick. Bill and Jane live in Newport.

Ike, one of the twins, was born on Mar. 5, 1930. Ike married Darlene and they have four children; Terry, Richard (Rick), Joy, and Sherry. Ike and Darlene have a home in Florida and one in Parke County.

Sim, the other twin, born Mar. 5, 1930, married Betty Miller and they had one daughter, Mickey Lynn Eads. Sim died in 1958 and is buried in Thomas Cemetery.

Doris was born on Aug. 10, 1931, and married Charles Arrasmith. They have two children: Pamela Carroll and David. Doris and Charles live in Eugene.

Ronnie, born Aug. 31, 1939, married Karen Rumple. They have three children: Ronda Jean, James Eric, and Michael Lee. Ronnie and Karen live in Montezuma.

Thurman died Dec. 3, 1970, and Hattie died Sept. 24, 1972. They are buried in the Thomas Cemetery.

ROY AND HATTIE PLOUGH LOWE,

Roy William Lowe was born in Parke Co., IN, Mar.

9, 1895, and died in Clinton, IN, Dec. 21, 1970. He was the son of William H. Lowe (1872-1963) and Pearl Alice Newcomb Lowe (1875-1927). He had one brother Harry and two sisters—Clara Roark and Nora Ann Chaney.

Roy married Harriet (Hattie) Celeste Plough (Oct. 18, 1897-July 12, 1983). They are the parents of two children—Catherine (Katy) Pearl Lowe Hixon born Dec. 12, 1917 and Howard Kenneth Lowe born Feb. 21, 1919 and died Mar. 1, 1977 in Michigan.

Hattie and Roy Lowe

They had two grandchildren, Mary Evelyn Hixon (Aug. 16, 1934-Nov. 12, 1934) and James Fredrick Hixon (Sept. 4, 1935).

They had four great-grandchildren—Brent Hixon (July 19, 1959), Duane Hixon (July 9, 1960), Kevin Hixon (Dec. 20, 1962), and Scott Hixon (Mar. 25, 1965).

Roy's father, William H. Lowe, was a preacher. His parents were Benjamin and Zerelda Farr Lowe. Benjamin was an early preacher in Parke County and a founder of the Sand Creek United Brethren Church. There were ten children in the family, one son drowned in a swine pit when the family lived in Kansas for a short time. Other children were William H., Ira, Elmer, Marion, Grant, Lizzie Miller, Caroline Kirkman, Rosie Haworth, and Lyde Daniels.

Benjamin's parents were John and Caroline Waite Lowe. Caroline's father was a Colonel in the Revolutionary War and later became a General. Ben and Zerelda are buried in Arabia Cemetery north of Mecca.

Hattie was the daughter of Alfred Plough and Sarah Catherine Mann Plough. Her stepfather was Emmor B. Potter. Her half-sisters were Waunita L. Potter Hanks Doyal, Estella M. Potter, Julia Mae Potter Dickerson, and Mary Magdalene Potter. Her half-brothers were Freddie B. Potter and Ora L. Potter. Her stepsisters were Rose Anna Potter Heskett, Bessie Mae Potter Norman, Nancy Fernetta Potter Hinkle, and Mollie Potter. Her stepbrothers were James Potter and Lewis Potter.

Hattie and Roy Lowe are buried in Helt's Prairie Cemetery.

ELI HAYWOOD McDANIEL,

was born in Morgan Co., IN on Sept. 14, 1842, the son of John Randolph and Elizabeth Scotten McDaniel. He was twice married, first to Mary Jane Kimlin in 1868 in Martinsville, IL following over four years service in the Civil War. To this union was born a son, William Kimlin McDaniel. His second marriage was to Alice Cary Updegraff, daughter of George and Nancy Jane Harrison Updegraff in Martinsville, IL where he farmed.

Mrs. Samuel (Mary Updegraff) Todd was Alice McDaniel's sister. When the Eugene Mill burned in 1883, Eli was asked by Samuel Todd and Monroe

Hosford to join their partnership. Eli to provide the money and they the knowledge of the milling business as the Eugene mill was not insured. Eli agreed to join them only if a steam mill was built at Eugene Junction where the Clover Leaf and the C. & E. I. railroads crossed. Agreement was reached and the mill was built in 1884.

Eli Haywood McDaniel

Selling their Martinsville farm they moved to Eugene along with son William and their two daughters, Mary Jane and Florence.

The John Samuel Grondyke family owned the land where a settlement sprang up around the mill. It was eventually named Cayuga for the Grondyke's former home in New York.

The Cayuga Milling Company ground local wheat, corn and oats. Kansas wheat was also ground into flour there in "intransient shipping" over the Clover Leaf. Intransient billing permitted the wheat from Kansas to be stopped intransient, ground into flour, and shipped on east to the coast under one freight charge creating quite a savings in shipping costs. This enabled the mill to operate in slack seasons.

The McDaniel family moved to Cayuga from Eugene early in 1885 following the erection of their home on Division Street just north of the Opera House. It was one of the first homes built and their son Howard was the first baby born in Cayuga.

Ten years later a larger home was built on South Second Street. The family moved there shortly after the birth of their daughter Zoe Hester. A niece, Nellie Updegraff, was raised there by Eli and Alice.

Eli was a dedicated industrious citizen. He served three terms as the only Republican Township Trustee from 1887 to 1893. During this time the brick schoolhouse that sat on the hill on West Curtis Street was built. He was also twice elected County Commissioner by a good round majority.

His businesses include the Cayuga Milling Company, the first lumber yard, and the Wabash Clothing Store.

He quietly helped many of his friends and relatives and was a member of the Masonic Lodge from early manhood.

Eli McDaniel died May 19, 1910 at his home following a stroke and is buried in the Eugene Cemetery beside his wife, Alice, and two of their daughters, Mary Jane and Florence, who died at the ages of 14 and 16, respectively. *Submitted by Mary Zoe (Sager) Brown, daughter of Zoe Hester and Warren R. Sager, and granddaughter of Alice and Eli McDaniel*

THE JOHN McFALL FAMILY, The John McFall family is an example of economic mobility. After the Civil War the Virginia boy's family had very little left. He came to Terre Haute to be an apprentice for a merchant. As part of his pay he was to receive his room and board, but when the proprietor offered him dinner after the family had eaten, this Virginia gentleman struck out for himself. When he had $20.20 in his pocket he became a pack peddler. It didn't take him long to buy a one horse huxter wagon, then a two-horse wagon, then a store in Edgar Co., IL. Soon he built a store in Jonestown. He wasn't satisfied with this, he began buying land, 315 acres by 1888 and dealing in livestock. The family then moved to Dana where he was a merchant and director of the bank.

This man and his wife had six children. The oldest son, Fred, was a land owner in Helt Township as well as past president of Home Packing Co. in Terre Haute. The second son was the student in the family. He studied both music and medicine. Some of his work was done in Germany. He became a medical doctor, but since he was such a perfectionist and patients didn't follow his directions, he went into the teaching of medicine. At the time of his death he was a retired professor of Anatomy at George Washington University.

At least three of the daughters had college degrees. Rose McFall Small began as a teacher in Helt Township, married one of her fellow teachers, Ben Small, who became an eminent lawyer, and ended her teaching career in the English Department at Indiana State University.

The only members of the family who are living at the present time in the county are Mr. and Mrs. Stanley Miller and their families. They own part of the original McFall land and manage the rest for her grandfather, Fred McFall.

This family, who started with practically nothing, produced two professors, one of whom was also a doctor, a company owner, as well as successful homemakers.

DAVID MACK, left Deerfield, MA in 1827, and settled in Toronto, IN. David's son, Spencer Mack, came to the area one-half mile north of Salem Church and had a blacksmith shop at the foot of the hill along the stagecoach trace now known as Indiana State Highway #63. The hill is now known as Mack Hill. He married Permelia James, daughter of Edmund James, one of the early pioneer families of Helt Township. Spencer Mack molded the first steel plow to "scour" in these prairie soils.

Leigh and Barbara Mack

In later years he was postmaster at Summit Grove. His son, Alonzo Mack, was a volunteer in the Union Army, and was with Sherman's army on their march to the sea. He and his wife, Isabel White Mack, lived at the foot of Mack Hill. Their son, Forest Mack, graduated from Purdue University in 1910, with a degree in mechanical engineering, but returned to the home farm for the rest of his life. He married Mae Elliott, a school teacher. They had three sons, Richard, Robert, and Leigh.

Leigh Mack married Barbara Ann Myers in 1947, and they had five children: David, Mariani Michael, Scott, and Fauniel. Leigh and his family live in the brick house built by Samuel Ryerson in 1828. Leigh Mack's great-grandmother, Lydia Hollandbeck, lived in this house as a young girl, and married Enoch White, of another early pioneer family. They were the parents of Isabel Mack, wife of Alonzo.

Barbara Ann Myers Mack was born Oct. 20, 1928, in Helt Township, Vermillion Co., IN and has lived there all of her life. Her parents were Opal Ford Myers and Charles Eaton Myers. Her maternal ancestors were among the earliest settlers on Helt's Prairie, just north of Clinton.

In the spring of 1817, Augustus Ford and his wife Elizabeth Helt Ford, together with their families, came from Delaware Co., OH to settle on Helt's Prairie. Daniel Helt later married Mary Magdalen Ely, and these people became Barbara's ancestor's. Also coming with the Fords and Helts were their friends and neighbors, John and Polly Hopper Skidmore.

John Ford, son of Augustus and Elizabeth, married Jane Skidmore, daughter of John and Polly Skidmore. Their son, Albert, married Eliza Ann Reed of Edgar Co., IL, and to this union was born a son, Birt C. Ford. He married Phoeba Miller, great-granddaughter of Daniel and Mary M. Helt, their daughter Phoeba having married Jacob Miller. Jacob and Phoeba's son, Sylvester, married Sarah Ellen Harris. They were the parents of Phoeba Miller. Birt and Phoeba had four children, one being Opal, mother of Barbara Mack. Barbara's paternal great-grandfather was Samuel Myers. Samuel married Laura Crane, daughter of Stephen and Miriam, and their son, Carl, married Anna Eaton, daughter of Wilbur and Alma Patrick Eaton of Bono, IN. Carl and Anna had two sons, Eaton and Ernest. Carl and his sons were carpenters, doing much building around the area during their lifetimes. The Myers' lived in Center neighborhood where Barbara grew up.

RICHARD ALLEN MACK, was born June 17, 1922, in Montezuma, IN, the eldest son of Forest and Rose Mae Elliott Mack. Richard attended and graduated from Hillsdale High School in 1940. He graduated from Purdue University in 1949. He served in the U.S. Army in World War II, U.S. Army Reserves, and active duty in the Korean Conflict. He taught agriculture classes for returning veterans at Hillsdale High School.

April 22, 1945, he married Mary Ellen Harris of Greenwood, AR. They are the parents of one son, Ronald Allen, and one daughter, Carol Jeannie Mack.

Richard worked for Soil Conservation Service, U.S. Dept. of Agriculture with over 33 years service in Vermillion and Parke Counties, retiring in 1987.

He is still active in agriculture on the home farm.

RONALD ALLEN MACK, was born Oct. 12, 1954, the son of Richard Allen and Mary Ellen Harris Mack of Helt's Prairie.

He attended grade school at Hillsdale, St. Bernice, and Ernie Pyle Elementary. After graduation from South Vermillion in 1972, he attended and graduated from Purdue University in 1976.

November 20, 1976, he married Diana Hartman. They are the parents of two children, Jeremy Lee, born May 21, 1981 and Tiffany Lynn, born June 19, 1985. They reside near Eugene in Vermillion

...nty. Ronald is employed at Lauhoff Milling ...mpany, Danville, IL (since October, 1977).

ANDREW AND LUCILLE MARCINKO FAMILY,
Andrew Marcinko was born in Czechoslovakia, Nov. 11, 1902. His parents, Joe and Mary Marcinko, had eight children of which six are residents of the county. Two are deceased. Besides Andrew in Blanford the others are Mrs. Mike (Julia) Cvengros, Mrs. Tony (Helen) Sengallia, Mrs. Pat (Josephine) Burton, Mrs. Kathryn Fenoglio, and Steve Marcinko. All have homes in the Hazel Bluff area.

At the age of four Andrew and his mother came to America to be reunited with his father. They came to the Indiana coal fields where his father worked in the mines. At the early age of 13, Andrew quit school to work in the mine. He spent 60 years as a miner or owner. He took his 16mm camera below to take movies of the mine in action. A copy of this is now available for viewing at the Little Italy Festival. He has a wealth of coal mining information.

Andrew met and married Lucille Hawkins in 1925, and they have resided in Blanford all of their married life. Lucille is the daughter of Elwood and Ollie Hawkins who was a boss in the coal mines and also lived in the county. Lucille was one of nine children.

Andrew and Lucille have two children, John Andrew and Marjorie Natalie, nine grandchildren and 11 great-grandchildren.

Marjorie is postmistress of the Blanford post office. She was married to Tony Natalie of Centenary, who is deceased. Her children—Tony, James, and Jim live in Blanford, and Kenneth lives in Clinton. Her daughter, Marilyn, is married to a Navy man.

John lives on a farm in Vermillion Township. He and his wife, Betty, retired from CBS in Terre Haute recently but he still does the farming. Two of their four children, Charles and Douglas live in the county, Andrew resides in Parke County, and their daughter, Bonnye, in Vigo County.

Of all the activities, Andrew has been involved in, (politics, etc.) probably the time spent managing the semi-pro team in Blanford was his greatest love. Every Sunday he was over at the baseball field to drag the infield and mark the lines. He would hurry home for Sunday dinner so he could be back in time for the baseball game.

THE VERNON MARSHALL FAMILY,
Edward Vernon Marshall was a farmer in the Upper Coal Branch area in Highland Township. He was born on Dec. 19, 1888, the son of Humphrey Beckett and Cora May Stuttler Marshall. On Jan. 22, 1913, he married Stella Hines, who was born Aug. 15, 1893. Stella died Oct. 11, 1916. Austin Vernon was born May 17, 1914, from this union. Austin was married Feb. 29, 1936, to Inez L. Ping, and died Dec. 1, 1983.

Vernon married Nancy Genevieve Prather on May 14, 1919. Genevieve was born Oct. 14, 1892, the daughter of William Isaac Prather and Hannah Shute. Vernon and Genevieve had three children. Genevieve Eileen was born Oct. 31, 1920, and married Raymond John Rouse on Nov. 16, 1941. Vivian Marie was born Sept. 5, 1923, and married William Dale Hughes on Mar. 25, 1944. Marion Prather was born Aug. 7, 1931, and married Lois Marie Hollowell Sept. 25, 1949.

Vernon died Dec. 21, 1959, and Genevieve died May 15, 1974. They had ten grandchildren.

THE MARTIN FAMILY SINCE 1786,
John Martin was born in Canada in 1786. In 1818 he and his wife Hannah Brown Martin and son James were living in Niagara Co., NY. In the spring of that year he purchased the Martin Homestead, consisting of 160 acres in Vermillion Co., IN.

He purchased this land sight unseen from a man named William Doty, who had been given this land by the U.S. Government for services rendered in Canadian army in the Mexican War with The United States of America.

Christopher Hiddle, an Englishman had purchased 160 acres just south of the Martin land, and he and wife and the Martin family started to Indiana. They reached Fort Harrison in the Fall of 1818 and were advised to stay there until spring because of the severe winter and hostile Indians. While at Fort Harrison another son John J. Martin was born (Dec. 7, 1818).

In the Spring of 1819 the two families settled on their land. The Martin land described as North East Quarter of Section 15, Township 15, Range 10 West.

Six more children were born to the John Martin family. They were—Orin, Mary, Harriet, Hannah, Elizabeth, and George Washington.

George W. Martin the youngest son of John and Hannah Brown Martin was born June 27, 1838, and died Jan. 26, 1899. He became the next owner of the Martin Farm. He was married to Nancy Peyton. They had four children: 1. James Edward Martin (Jan. 4, 1862-Apr. 10, 1939)—married Rhoda Underwood—one child, Howard Scott Martin. 2. Maria Belle Martin (Aug. 7, 1864-Jan. 25, 1899)—married I. M. McGilvery—no children. 3. Winifield Scott Martin (Feb. 17, 1870-Feb. 20, 1925)—married Ethel Ingram—no children. 4. Lucy Grant Martin (May 9, 1871-Apr. 17, 1905)—Married Samuel Elder—no children.

Descendants of Howard Scott Martin and Ollie Mae Martin:

1. Howard Scott Martin, Jr. (Sept. 7, 1923), married Virginia Mae Parsons, 1954. Two children-Scott Allen Martin (May 28, 1956) and Linda Mae Martin (Jan. 14, 1959).

2. LaVaughn Martin (Feb. 3, 1926)—married William R. Phillips 1947. Two children-Elaine Phillips (Aug. 22, 1950) and William R. Phillips (Nov. 6, 1952).

Elaine Phillips married Abbot L. Moffat II—one son Abbot L. Moffat III. Elaine divorced and remarried Bruce Bicknell.

Scott Martin married Deborah H. Winters and they have one daughter Anne H. Martin (Oct. 22, 1982).

James Edward Martin was the third owner of the Martin Farm and at his death it became the property of Howard S. Martin and Ollie Martin the present owners. It is now occupied by Howard S. Martin, Jr. and his family, making six generations to live on the Martin Farm to this date (1988). The present house (built in 1905) is the third one built on the farm.

SAVERIO MASARACHIA AND MARGHUERITA COMIANI MASARACHIA,
Saverio Masarachia was born on Feb. 14, 1873 in Palazzo Adriano near Palermo, Sicily. He came to America in his 20's with an uncle and worked in the sugar cane field in Louisiana, in the silver mines in Colorado and later in the coal mines of Illinois.

Marghuerita Comiani was born on Sept. 10, 1882 also near Palermo and came to this country with her parents, two brothers, and a sister when she was six years old. The family settled in Murphysboro, IL, where her two younger brothers, Nich and Frank, were born.

On a visit to Murphysboro, Saverio met Marghuerita and they were married there on July 7, 1906.

With the urging of his sister, Lena Ferrara, the couple moved to Clinton and Saverio worked in the coal mines in this area.

Saverio died in 1951 - Marghuerita in 1959.

Their family included Josephine, born Apr. 26, 1907; Frank, born Feb. 11, 1909; Carmen, born Apr. 26, 1912; Felicia, born Sept. 8, 1914. All the children attended Columbia, Glendale, and Clinton High schools.

Josephine married Dan Pesavento on Nov. 1, 1931. Frank is married to Ruth Stillwell. Carmen died in 1948. Felicia lives in the family home at 524 North Eighth Street.

MAXWELL FAMILY—JAMES, JOSEPH S., AND JOHN LAFAYETTE BUSH,
James Maxwell was born Jan. 18, 1781, the son of Joseph and Hannah Maxwell. On June 17, 1813, he married Mary Slater, who was born Aug. 3, 1781. They had 13 children—John S., born Apr. 23, 1814; Robert, born Aug. 4, 1815; Martha, born Mar. 17, 1817; William, born Aug. 29, 1818; James, born Nov. 18, 1819; Mary, born June 11, 1821; Margaret, born Nov. 28, 1822; Joseph S., born July 8, 1824, married Hannah Bush and Matilda Jones; Daniel M., born Jan. 5, 1825; George, born Apr. 13, 1826; Thomas, born September, 1827; Andrew, born Mar. 8, 1828; and Nancy B., born July 12, 1833.

Joseph S. Maxwell was born July 8, 1824, and died Oct. 17, 1886. He was the son of James Maxwell and Mary Slater Maxwell. His first marriage was to Hannah Bush and they were the parents of nine children (three sets of twins)—James M., born Apr. 26, 1847, married Susi Hudson; Angeline D., born Apr. 26, 1847; Joseph M., born Aug. 11, 1851, died Feb. 24, 1926; Susan M., born Aug. 11, 1851, married John Jeffers, Dec. 14, 1874; John Lafayette Bush, born July 3, 1854, died Apr. 16 1929, married Hannah Santilla Dark, Apr. 3, 1883; Florinda J., born May 27, 1856, married Frank Winterwood, Oct. 22, 1886; Florilla M., born May 27, 1856, married William McConnell; Laura A., born June 20, 1858; Charles F., born Aug. 20, 1860.

His second marriage was to Matilda Jones in 1866, daughter of William Jones and Sarah Watson Jones. She was born Sept. 5, 1842, in Vermillion Township, and died Oct. 17, 1914, in Vermillion County. They were the parents of four children— Ellen S., born Aug. 15, 1868, died 1945, married Robert Henry Myers on Sept. 18, 1883; Nora M., born Mar. 30, 1874, died Oct. 28, 1875; Kate B., born Oct. 22, 1877, married John H. Wilfong on Dec. 28, 1898; and Malinda Frana, born Oct. 9, 1883, married James Murphy. Matilda had one child from her marriage to Silas Dark—Hannah Santilla Dark born Mar. 29, 1863.

John Lafayette Bush Maxwell was born July 3, 1854, in Vermillion County, the son of Joseph S. and Hannah Bush Maxwell. He died Apr. 16, 1929, in Vermillion County. On Apr. 3, 1883, he married Hannah Santilla Dark, daughter of Silas Dark and Matilda Jones Dark. They were married at Quaker, IN. Hannah was born Mar. 29, 1863, in Vermillion County, and died Jan. 9, 1949, at St. Bernice, and was buried in Hopewell Cemetery. They were the parents of three children—Robert Slater, born May 25, 1883, in Vermillion County, married Tillie Stark in 1902 and Etta Jeist in 1921; Seburn John born Dec. 21, 1885, in Vermillion County; Nancy Ellen born May 25, 1888, in Vermillion County, died Oct. 15, 1957, in Worthington, IN, married Leander Downs on Jan. 19, 1910. (see related article—Leander Downs)

AUSTIN PEARL MAYES, was born Apr. 20, 1898, and died Mar. 3, 1984. He attended Spring Hill School and Hillsdale School through the eighth grade. On Feb. 22, 1923, he married Grace Frances Swinford. Their first home was in the Spring Hill Church building in Helt Township. Mr. Mayes was a farmer all his life. He loved trapping and hunting and earned the nickname "Reddy" because of the many red fox pelts he sold.

Austin and Grace were the parents of three sons, Herman Frances Mayes, born Feb. 18, 1926; Harold Eugene Mayes, born Oct. 23, 1929; and Arthur Edwin Mayes, born Jan. 23, 1933.

Grace Mayes is a 50 year member of the Helt's Prairie Extension Homemakers Club. She is a seamstress and loves doing handwork. She is well known throughout the county for her tatting. Austin and Grace raised chickens and sold eggs for many years in the Clinton area.

The Mayes family have attended Salem United Methodist Church for over 60 years.

Herman Mayes married Betty Lou Frist on Dec. 19, 1948. He graduated from Hillsdale High School in 1944 and served in the U.S. Army during World War II. Herman graduated from Purdue University in 1952 and has worked for the United States department of Agriculture for over 30 years.

Harold Mayes graduated from Hillsdale High School in 1947 and married Carrie Ellen Hancock in 1950. He is a builder and construction contractor. Harold and Carrie are the parents of five children, Linda, Keith, Mark, Lori and Teresa. Harold was remarried in 1969 to Jean Boyer Pearman.

Arthur Mayes was a member of the Hillsdale High School class of 1951. He attended Purdue University, completing the Agriculture Short Course in 1954. He served in the U.S. Army from 1954 through 1957. In 1956 he married Arlene Pascoe. Arthur has been farming since he was discharged from the military service. Arthur and Arlene reside on the property just west of the Helt's Prairie Cemetery. They are the parents of two children, Margaret Ann Mayes Link, born Nov. 14, 1959, and Albert Wayne Mayes, born Nov. 1, 1962.

JAMES MONROE MAYES, was born Mar. 17, 1867 and died in October, 1945. He came to Helt's Prairie in Vermillion Co., IN in 1893 and married Carrie E. Blakesley on March 22 of that year. They resided in Parke County for seven years then returned to Helt's Prairie in 1900 with their two sons, Willard Wesley Mayes, born Jan. 26, 1895, and Austin Pearl Mayes, born Apr. 20, 1898. Monroe Mayes was a farmer. Two more children were born to the family. Orville Merle Mayes was born in 1900 and Mildred Maxine Mayes in 1906.

Carrie E. Blakesley was born Sept. 3, 1870. She was the daughter of John W. and Caroline Kiger Blakesley. John W. was a veteran of the Civil War serving with Company D. 85th Indiana Regiment. He owned several acres of farm land on the Prairie in Sections 9, 10, 15, and 16 of Helt Township.

The Mayes children attended school at Spring Hill. The family attended church at Spring Hill for

about a year. After the Spring Hill Church closed its doors, they became active in the Salem Methodist Church.

Monroe Mayes was also a timber buyer for veneer companies.

Carrie Mayes died in March, 1919, during the flu epidemic of that year. Monroe Mayes was remarried in 1921 to Rose Jones. In 1942 they left Helt's Prairie and moved to Dana, IN.

METZGER, HOWARD AND SHAW FAMILIES, Forty-one acres of fertile land northwest of Perrysville, IN, in Vermillion County, Highland Township, near Interstate #74, was deeded by Mary Metzger (widow of Squire Metzger) to his niece, Ethel Grace (Metzger) Howard on Sept. 10, 1942. It is now being successfully farmed by her grandson, Charles Albert Shaw, Jr., who is the son of her only living child, Mabel. (A son, Cleo, and daughters, Edna and Marie, were killed in a train accident on Nov. 24, 1928). Ethel's husband, Cleve, lived to the amazing age of 102 years and three months (1886-1987). Ethel preceded him to her heavenly home some 22 years before in 1965 (1887-1965).

Metzger, Howard, and Shaw Families

Ethel Grace, who was born in Covington, IN, was married to Grover Cleveland Jackson Howard "Cleve" in 1904. She was a loving, hard-working farmer's wife the major part of her life and a fine Christian lady, as is her daughter, Mabel, who is married to Charles Albert Shaw Sr. of Fountain Co., Covington, IN. Charles and Mabel have enjoyed 60 years of married life thus far and were blessed with three children: Wayne Eugene, Helen Louise and Charles Junior. (All three received their childhood education at Rabb School in Fountain County and Perrysville High School in Vermillion County).

The eldest son, Wayne Eugene, is married to Janet Broz. He is a fine preacher of the gospel, and as well, in his 14th year as the Academic Dean of the Lincoln Christian Seminary, Lincoln, IL. His wife, Janet, also holds a professorship there. They are the parents of four sons: Haydn Stewart, who is married to Laurie Irvine (ministering at Frankfort Square near Chicago, IL); Scott Campbell, doing graduate work at Lincoln Christian Seminary; Barton Charles in undergraduate school at Lincoln Christian College; and Errett Wayne, who died in infancy.

Their daughter, Helen Louise, is married to Charles W. Ridlen, a second generation Gospel preacher. They presently are in their 13th year of ministry with the First Christian Church in Morristown, TN, having served the East Side Christian congregation in Frankfort, IN, for 15 years. Charles also has been serving as Probation Officer for Clinton County for ten years. Though this union was not blessed with children, they've become parents to many foster children.

Charles Jr., the youngest son, was married to Sandra Hewes Tuttle in 1987 and they presently reside in Gessie, IN. (The land on which their home stands was owned countless years before by David and Hannah Metzger, Jr's. great-grandparents). Kent Tuttle, Sandra's son, is with the U.S. Army, stationed in Texas.

In addition to farming the acreage of his Grandmother Ethel's, Chas. Jr. also rents land near it from the original Squire Metzger property on the first road north of Gessie Road (now owned by Bill and Naomi Crane) and also land of Dave Metzger (Ethel's brother), some of which lies across from the 41 acres and some adjoins it. These properties appear to have been owned by Ethel's mother, father, uncle and/or grandmother, Hannah E. (widow of Elias, who had been killed in the Civil War).

Charles Jr. also skillfully farms and cares for 182 acres of his father Charles' family homestead in Wabash Township, Fountain Co., IN. Charles Jr. is the fifth generation of Shaw farmers on this land, his ancestors having come from Lancaster Co., PA. by way of Ohio before purchasing land in Indiana in 1855.

Ethel Grace's husband and children (Cleo, Edna and Marie), her father, grandparents and some of her siblings are buried in Hopewell Cemetery, west of Covington, IN, near Gessie. Her mother and a sister are buried in Bainbridge, IN. *Compiled by Louise Ridlen*

MILLER FAMILY, The Miller Family originally came from Holland. When they came to the States, they lived in Pennsylvania, then moved to Wisconsin, and then to Indiana where they resided most of their lives. David and Isabelle Miller lived on a farm in Summit Grove and had built a large farmhouse there. The house was passed on to their son, Albert. Albert Miller was responsible for bringing bricks across the Wabash River on a ferry, which were used in the construction of Salem Methodist Church in 1878. Albert and Rosetta Miller were married around 1874 or 1875. They were blessed with five children—Morton, Carl, Laura, Bess, and Jesse. Albert Miller passed away in 1927 at age 79, and his wife, Rosetta, passed away in 1939 at age 90.

Carl and Vesta Miller

Their oldest son, Mort Miller, built a machine shop in Summit Grove. It was a very thriving business in the community around 1900 or thereabouts. Mort ran the shop until the time of his death which was in 1968 at age 92 years. He had built steam engines and just about any mechanical thing you could imagine. In the house where he lived in Summit Grove, he had built an elevator to go to the basement and it is still in working condition. The man was a genuis.

His brother, Carl, was a farmer most of his life and lived in Summit Grove in the house which his grandfather, David, had also built. In 1913, Carl married Miss Vesta Tuggle and they were blessed with one boy, Loren, and one girl, Dorothy. Both Carl and Vesta passed away in 1979. He was 92 years old and she was 86 years old. Dorothy Mae Miller married Louise Mussatto in 1946, and they were blessed with three children—Nicholas, Shirley, and David. Louie and Dorothy also lived in Summit Grove most of their lives, and now their son, Nick, and his family live there today.

FRANK AND DAN TUCKER MILLER,
a set of brothers need to be named among the eminent citizens who called Helt Township home. At the turn of the century Frank and Dan Tucker Miller were outstanding young men from the Jonestown area. Frank Miller went to the little Jonestown High School, then to Clinton High School. He taught in some of the surrounding one room schools before studying law. He became a successful lawyer in Terre Haute as well as a teacher of law. He has taught many other men to be lawyers in his school of law. His brother, Dan Tucker Miller, was a doctor in Fowler, IN.

Frank Miller will long be remembered by the people in the area because he has given a lovely piece of land for a park in St. Bernice.

WALTER AND OSA MILLER, Walter
Miller was born Mar. 30, 1907, and died May 10, 1960. Osa Marie Miller was born Mar. 10, 1910 to Thomas and Clara White Collom on a farm near Ridgefarm, IL. She was one of a family of eight children. The family were members of the Friends Church at Humrick, IL.

She moved with them to Cayuga, IN at the age of 13 to a farm her mother heired from her uncle Charlie and Aunt Laura Humrickhouse Brown. On this farm was found gravestones of the descendants of the old Collett family which was located on State Road 234 West of Cayuga and is now owned by the Heirs of the Bill Patrick family.

Her paternal grandparents were Samuel and Sadie Humrickhouse White who went to California to become share croppers and eventually become orange and lemon ranchers there.

Osa attended Humrick, IL and Cayuga schools. She married Walter Miller of Attica, IN in 1929. They had five children, four of whom graduated from Cayuga High School and one from Newport High School.

His parents were Joseph and Bertha Mae Wade Miller. His father was a building contractor in Attica, IN. His paternal grandparents were Frederick and Elizabeth Miller who came to this country by boat from Germany. She attended school with her son Joseph to learn the English language. His maternal grandparents were Aaron and Sarah Wade, owners of the local newspapers in Wingate, Mellott, and Linden, IN. There were copies found of her poems which were edited in the paper.

Osa and her husband, Walter, purchased the old Zell property in west Cayuga, in 1942, from Clarney and Amanda Smith who were buying and selling real estate in Eugene and Cayuga, IN. Walter worked for a year in Hawaii as a refrigeration engineer helping to rebuild the Navy after Pearl Harbor. He was then employed by Du Pont and Company at Newport, IN and followed his trade through the years of changing from one corporation to another. He was employed by Food Machinery and Chemicals at the time of his death in 1960.

The original Zell property consisted of four rooms upstairs and two rooms downstairs. Rooms were added by previous residents. Osa renovated this house and in the process discovered it had cyclone walls and the lath and mortar were as solid as when built.

Osa, at this writing is a retiree, still residing at 203 South 8th St. Cayuga, IN, and is an active member of the Presbyterian Church.

MILLIGAN FAMILY HISTORY, Charles Warren and Verna Milligan moved from Shepherdsville to a farm in the Center neighborhood in 1926. Charles, "Charlie", was born in Kenton, KS, in 1884, to Samuel and Julia Smith Milligan. As a small boy, his parents brought the family to Terre Haute, their hometown. Verna, the daughter of Andrew Jackson and Izora Brewer, was born in 1892, in Centerpoint, IN. After their marriage, they moved to the knoll along the Wabash, east of Shepherdsville. Their ten children, Charles Robert, Julia Florence, Ralph Irl, Reta Alice, Carroll Larence, Paul Eldred, Glen Elmer, Nora Eva, Dora Neva, and Olen Wayne, were born there.

Charlie and Verna were known for their hard work on the farm. Verna raised and dressed chickens, gathered eggs, and made butter to sell in town. As the sons and daughters grew up, they learned to work with their father and mother.

Charles married Marzelle Heber in 1939. He was a tractor mechanic until he built a home in the Center neighborhood where he farmed. They had four children, Larry Lyle, who died in infancy, Carroll Warren, Marvin Lee, and Delores Jan (Stewart). Marzelle died in 1986. Charles celebrated his 80th birthday this year.

Florence married Carl Gibson in 1936, and lived most of her married life in Hammond, IN. They adopted a son, Jewell. Florence died in 1979.

Ralph married a Center neighborhood girl, Edna Ford, in 1935. After farming near Dana, they bought a farm near Bridgeton. They have two daughters, Thelma Ruth (Andrews) and Sarah Lynn (Hartman). Ralph and Edna are retired in Rockville.

Alice married Woodrow Brown in 1940, and moved to Gary, IN. They have twin daughters, Doris (Gilliam) and Lois (Malec). Woodrow died, and Alice is living in Demotte, IN.

Carroll died when he was only two years old.

Paul married Florence Clouse in 1941, and moved to Forest, IN. He is a tractor mechanic and school bus driver. They have a son, David.

Glen spent three years in the Army Air Force during World War II. After returning to the farm, he married Rachel Stratton. While farming near Dana, their three sons, Thomas Allen, John Franklin, and Robert Paul, were born.

Nora and Dora were two years younger than Glen. Dora died when she was three years old. In 1945, Nora married John Ponton, who died two years later when their daughter, Marilyn, was only one year old. Nora has continued to live on her farm southeast of Dana.

Wayne married Norma Jean Higgins, who died in 1964. They had one daughter, Gayle Jean. Later, he married Virginia Waggoner. They have one daughter, Joyce Ann, and live near Shirkiville.

The Milligan's lived near Bono for a few years. Then, they bought and moved to a farm southeast of Dana where Verna died in 1957, and Charles died in 1965.

GLEN AND RACHEL MILLIGAN, met
while they were waiting for the school bus on Stratton corner and began dating seven years later.

Glen was born Mar. 12, 1920, in Shepherdsville, IN. His parents, Charles Warren and Verna Brewer Milligan, moved to the Center neighborhood, Vermillion County, in 1926. Glen attended Shepherdsville Grade School, Frog College, St. Bernice schools and graduated from Dana High School in 1938. He worked with his father on the farm until 1942 when he was drafted into the U.S. Army Air Force. He spent most of the war years in El Paso, TX. Since his discharge in December, 1945, Glen has been farming in the Dana area.

Rachel and Glen Milligan

Rachel, the daughter of Albert and Ruth Westbrook Stratton, was born two miles north of St. Bernice on Stratton corner. She graduated from Dana High School in 1942, and earned her B.S. in Social Studies and English at Indiana State Teacher's College in 1946. In 1965, Rachel earned a M.S. in Guidance at Indiana State University. She began teaching in Jasper Co., IN, but came back to Vermillion County and taught at Newport and Perrysville, Clinton High School, South Vermillion High School, and Fairview and Matthews South Elementary Schools. Rachel retired in 1979, after 25 years in the classroom.

Glen and Rachel were married July 12, 1947, and had three sons, Thomas Allen, John Franklin, and Robert Paul. Tom was born Nov. 6, 1952. He graduated from Clinton High School in 1970, and Purdue University in 1974, with a B.S. in Agricultural Communications. Since that time he has farmed with his father and served in various county, state and national organizations. In 1979, he and Sandra Lindberg, a Registered Nurse from Galesburg, IL, were married. They are the parents of two daughters, Julia Ann and Laura Jean.

John was born Feb. 14, 1955. He graduated from Clinton High School in 1973, and attended Purdue University. John was married and is the father of two daughters, April Lynn and Andrea Marie. He and his daughters live west of Bono and he is employed at Eli Lilly.

Bob, born May 21, 1958, also graduated from Clinton High School in 1976. He graduated from Purdue University with a B.S. in Agricultural Economics. Bob works at Farm Credit Services in Hendricks County as a loan officer. In 1986, he married Jeanne Voida from Beech Grove, who is a family service counselor. They have a son, Matthew Robert, and live in Plainfield, IN.

Glen and Rachel live north of Dana. Glen farms and Rachel belongs to the 49er's Club, Dana United Methodist Church, Vermillion County Retired Teachers, and Estabrook D.A.R. They enjoy their five grandchildren.

HOMER E. AND FLORA MYRTLE
MITCHELL, Homer E. was the son of John and Susan Isabelle Richards Mitchell. He was born on Sept. 15, 1886, in Cass Co., MO. His mother and father were born in Kentucky. Flora was born Aug. 17, 1887, the daughter of John and Emma Hay/ Hayes Hansell. Her father was born Apr. 17, 1854, in Ohio and her mother was born Jan. 26, 1860, in Indiana.

Homer Mitchell

Homer and Flora were united in marriage May 6, 1905. Flora passed away Dec. 1, 1934, and Homer passed away Nov. 6, 1968. They are buried in Shephard's Cemetery south of Clinton, in the family plot, with their infant son, Homer E. Mitchell, Jr. They were the parents of two daughters, Dorothy Mae, born Dec. 12, 1906, who resides in Summit Grove and Wauneta Belle, born Feb. 3, 1913, and is deceased.

Homer was a coal miner for many years and later retired from the Vigo County Schools as a maintenance employee.

THE MITCHELL FAMILY, Robert
Mitchell was born in Londonderry, Ireland before 1700. He married Mary Innis of Edinburgh, Scotland. They had 13 children, but only three are known...Daniel, Robert, James. They immigrated to Pequa, PA in 1735, then to Bedford Co., VA.

Daniel Mitchell was born before 1735 and died 1822. He married Judith Prewitt. Their children were Robert, Andrew, Elizabeth, Daniel and William.

Daniel Mitchell died before 1807. He married Mary Overstreet. Their children were Melinda, Gabriel, James, Lucinda, and Pauline.

James Newton Mitchell

Gabriel Mitchell, born 1800 in Culpepper Co., VA, died 1873 in Neodesha, KS. He married Ruth Van Cleave. They had 12 children, Daniel, John, James Newton, Robert, Sally, Margery, Polly, Melinda, Martha, Amelia, Nancy and Minnie.

James Newton Mitchell was born 1830, died 1908. He married Sarah Harlan in 1850. They had eight children: Basheba, George, John, James

Daniel, Jane, Mary A., Gabriel, and Mary B. Sarah died in 1866 and was buried in Hollandsburg Cemetery near Rockville with two of her babies. In 1866 James Newton moved near Perrysville, IN. In 1867 he married Mary Falls. They had four children: Martha, Sarah, Cassius and Josephine. In 1872 they moved to Vermillion Co., IL.

Mary died in 1894 and James later married Ruth Henthorne. James and Mary are buried in Hicks Cemetery near Perrysville, IN.

When James was 19, he took a contract to make 5,000 rails for 50 cents a hundred.

James Daniel Mitchell, was born 1864 and died 1943. He married Cora May Holdaway in 1886. They had seven children, Ina, Helena Hannah (Lena Sheets), Amelia (Webb), James, Daniel, Elsie (Marshall), and Theodore. He and Cora are buried in Hicks Cemetery. Also buried in Hicks are Amelia, Daniel and Theodore.

Helena Hannah (Lena) was born in 1890 and married Fred Sheets. They had three children, Frank, Merle, June. Lena now lives with her son, Frank, and his wife, Pansy, in Vermillion Co., IN.

Amelia Haley was born 1893 and died 1972. She married Jesse Webb. They had one child, Ruth Cora.

James, born 1895, died in 1954, no children.

Elsie May was born 1901 and died 1979. She married Carl Marshall. They lived in Vermillion County and had one child, Cora May.

Theodore was born 1904 and died 1969. He married Jeanette See and lived in Vermillion Co., IN. They had five children Betty, Robert, Elaine, Jeanne, Carol.

Robert Mitchell, born 1943, married Mary Catharine Reeves. They have one child, Michelle. They reside in Vermillion Co., IN.

Daniel L. Mitchell, born 1898 and died 1966. He married Myrtle Taylor. Their children were James and Dorothy.

James Mitchell married Cathy Houser. They had one child, Amy.

Dorothy Mitchell married Norman L. Skinner in 1972. They have two children, Norman, born 1982, and Nicole, born 1986. They live in Vermillion Co., IN.

ALEXANDER MOREHEAD, came to
Vermillion County from Ohio in 1819. He was the first settler in Vermillion Township. He staked out the land he wanted, had it surveyed, and built a log cabin north of what would later be the location of Newport. Travel in that area in those days was by flatboat since it was too much of a wilderness for travel by land. So, in 1822, when Alexander felt that the homestead was ready for his family, he returned to Ohio by flatboat and brought his family back with him. In the same year he entered his land in Sections 23 and 25 on the First Land Owners' Map.

Alexander was an active figure in the organization of the county and served at one time (1833) as Associate Judge which was an office in the early days.

His son Samuel left the homeplace and is shown on the 1872 map in the Map Section as owning a quarter section in Section 28, just southwest of the covered bridge. Until 1885 when the covered bridge was built there was a ford there called the Morehead Ford and the bridge was known as the Morehead Bridge. There probably was a house there at one time but there is no indication now. When Samuel died in 1896 he was living in Danville, IL.

Alexander's son Joseph's home was well-known as it was torn down only a few years ago and the chimney is still there. It was about a half mile north of the Main Street bridge on old State Road 63 and across the road from Alexander's original log cabin. The owner at that time was the Dwiggins family, grandchildren of Margaret Morehead Harshaw.

Besides the marriages shown in the family diagram, there is one of Margaret Morehead to Nathaniel Washburn in 1831 that seems very likely to belong somewhere in this family although nothing is known in this regard. However, they are both buried in the Johnson Cemetery northeast of Newport where most of the Moreheads are buried and which originally was Morehead land.

Alexander Morehead _____-1844 and Elizabeth _____-1849:

Mary, _____-_____, m. 1833 to Robert Hopkins.

Ferguson, no information except married 1831 to Sarah Benefiel.

Jacob, 1818-1848, m. first to Anna Taylor, m. in 1838. Jacob m. second 1844 to Mrs. Isabel Tincher Glasco.

Samuel, 1819-1896. Samuel m. first 1848 to Rebecca Saxton, 1824-; Samuel A., 1849-, Duanna, no information. Samuel, m. second 1857 to Mrs. Sarah Highfill, 1828-1872; Aquilla, 1858-1885, William, 1861-, Leota, 1862, Joseph A., 1872-.

Joseph A., 1826-1903. Joseph A. m. first 1848 to Sarah Jane Eggleston, 1824-1896. Mary E. 1849-. Alexander, 1850-1897, m. 1886 to Alice Iles, 1860-1952. Iles O., 1887-1955, never married, George C., 1889-1959, never married, Naomi, 1892-1952, m. 1908 to Arthur Holton, 1885-1955. Jewell Aaron, 1908-1961, m. 1937 to Nina Tyler, 1907-. Mary Ruth, 1915-, m. 1945 to Donald L. Collings, 1907-1960. Jean Alexis Cree, 1947-, m. 1971 to Michael Bryan Kelly, 1943-. Melissa Colleen, 1978-, Ina Michael, 1979-. Henrietta, 1854-1898, never married. Horace G., 1857-1912, m. 1896 to Nora Clifton. Retha, 1859-1896, never married. Margaret A. 1862-1930, m. 1882 to Wilson Harshaw, 1855-1885. Joseph E., 1867-1910, never married. Joseph A., m. second 1896 to Anna M. Dunlap, 1848-1917. *Submitted by Harold L. O'Donnell and Jean Collings Kelly*

MOREY-HAIN-GARDNER, Clara
(Swinehart) and William Lee Morey had four children, all born in their home at 453 South Fifth Street, Clinton, IN. First was Lois (1883-1973), married 1909 to Fred Gest Sutphen. They had no children and lived most of their married life in Middletown, OH.

Next was Benjamin Franklin Morey (1886-1945), known by family and friends as "Sanc". He never married, and he practiced veterinarian medicine for a time and farmed the family farm south of Clinton.

Fourth was Lee Bogart Morey (1894-1973). He practiced law in New York City, and he married Elizabeth Ringle King in 1921. They had three daughters.

Third born was Esther Derexa, (1891-1954). She worked for a time in Washington, D.C., then came back to Clinton, IN, where she met and married Dec. 21, 1922, Lee Anthony Hain, (1895-1964). He was born in Cass Co., MI, to Bernice Anthony (1864-1914) and Ulysses Grant Hain (1864-1916). Lee and Esther lived in Marshall, MI, until 1933, when they moved to Clinton and started the Hain Furniture Store. They had two daughters—Sarah

Ann, July 6, 1925, and Elizabeth Morey Aug. 24, 1927. After Mrs. Hain's death, Mr. Hain married Pearl (Glascock) Raney.

"Sally" and "Bubble" Hain both graduated from Clinton High School and Purdue University. Sally acquired a degree in the educational field and met and married Robert L. Sauer, born 1925, in Pennsylvania to Louis E. and Pearle (Miller) Sauer. They currently are residing in Downers Grove, IL, where Mr. Sauer runs his own management consulting firm. They are the parents of: David Robert (Apr. 6, 1951), Roger Hain (Nov. 5, 1952), and Philip Bradley (Nov. 15, 1955). They have one grandson, Neil Alexander Sauer, (Oct. 11, 1982), son of Philip Sauer.

"Bubble" majored in General Agriculture and also met her husband at Purdue—Donald A. Gardner, born 1929, Warren, PA, to Mercedes James, (born 1903), and Donald Dolan Gardner, (1904-1972).

Don and Elizabeth were married 1951 in Norfolk, VA. In 1961, the couple moved from Columbus, OH, with their sons back to the family farm and became the first in the family to actually live on the farm. The sons are: Donald Lee, (May 1, 1952), married to Mary Ann Enyart (daughter of Margaret Ann Dooley and Howard Enyart of Clinton, IN) in 1974, and they have one daughter; Nicole Allison (Feb. 27, 1983); James Morey, (Aug. 6, 1954), married to Carol Beth Shelton (daughter of Julia Pouchain and Cecil Shelton, of Linton, IN) in 1977, and they have one son, James Daniel (Oct. 6, 1982), and one daughter, Julia Elizabeth (Nov. 27, 1987); Matthew Grant, (July 6, 1957), married to Perri Lynn Gummere (daughter of Jack Hanson Gummere, deceased, and Catherine Moreland Gummere Jackson of Terre Haute, IN) in 1982, and they have—Jessica Lynn, (May 11, 1983), Kenneth Grant (Apr. 23, 1986), and Thomas Matthew (Dec. 22, 1987). Mr. and Mrs. Gardner continue to farm, but on a smaller scale and continue to enjoy what they do. *Submitted by Elizabeth (Hain) Gardner, Clinton, IN*

MOREYS AND OTHER EARLY VERMILLION CO., IN, SETTLERS,

Benjamin Franklin Morey (1828-1885) and his wife Sarah Isabel Ferguson (Wishard) Bogart Morey (1821-1909) were married in Clinton, IN, Jan. 28, 1852. Sarah Isabel was the daughter of James Lytle Wishard (1794-1884) and Mary (Glenn) Wishard (1797-1847).

The Wishard family came to Vermillion County from Kentucky (where James and Mary Glenn Wishard were both born) via Johnson Co., IN, where a brother, John Wishard (1792-1878), lived. They came on the urging of another brother, Samuel Wishard (1774-1858), who had land near Dana. James and Mary (Glenn) Wishard bought land near Center Church. They had eight children, of whom seven grew to adulthood. In 1842 Sarah married Henry Bogart, who died in 1846. Their son, John H. (1845-1923), went on to become a doctor in Clinton and married Melissa Nebeker.

B.F. was in Kankakee, IL, before coming to Clinton, IN, in 1848. B.F. probably came because he had two uncles here—Benjamin Raymond Whitcomb (1798-1861) and John Right Whitcomb (1804-1876), both of whom were early businessmen in Clinton.

Benjamin Franklin Morey's mother was Derexa Whitcomb (1802-1877). She was a sister of the two early Whitcomb businessmen in Clinton. Their parents were: Anthony Whitcomb (1766-1806) and Lucy Right (1774-1821) both probably from Vermont.

B.F.'s father was William Morey (1801-1872). He married Derexa Whitcomb in Preble Co., OH, May 6, 1824, and they had 14 children, three of whom died fairly young.

In Clinton, B.F. and Sarah were tavern keepers initially while Mr. Morey practiced his blacksmith trade and then opened a wagon works and subsequently a lumber yard. He also became involved in farming, owning several tracts of land in Clinton Township. They had two children both born in Clinton: William Lee (1854-1928) and Frank, female, (1856-1908).

Frank Morey was married Oct. 25, 1876, to Dr. Charles M. White and had two children: Herbert Franklin White (1883-1919), and Charles Morey White (1891-1970). Charles Morey White married Hazel Kelley, June 16, 1914, and they had three girls: Marynette, Susan, and Martha.

William Lee Morey entered into partnership with his father in the drug store business, and on Oct. 25, 1882, he married Clara Mary Swinehart, daughter of Ann (Palmer) and Reason Harris Swinehart of Clinton.

Ann Palmer was born in Jennings Co., IN, 1833, to Deborah Dickinson (1804-1890), and Lemuel Palmer (1789-1849), who was a contractor on the Erie Canal and the Wabash Canal.

Reason Harris Swinehart (1822-1901) born to Daniel (1799-1873) and Vasta (Hoagland) Swinehart (1809-1849) married Ann Palmer, Apr. 12, 1857, in Terre Haute, where they lived before coming to Clinton in 1871. He opened a tinware and repair shop which later was known as The Swinehart Hardware store. *Submitted by Sally (Hain) Sauer, Downers Grove, IL*

MUSSATTO FAMILY,

originally came over from Northern Italy in 1906. Their first stop being New York, then to Indiana where they resided the rest of their lives. Gioanni (John) Battista Mussatto married around the late 1890's to Domenica Marietti. They were blessed with six children. John (their only child born in Italy), James, Frank, Louis, Charles, and Jennie. John and Domenica Mussatto owned and ran a grocery store at 838 N. 9th Street, Clinton, IN, around the late 1920's or early 1930's. John Mussatto passed away on Dec. 25, 1937, and his wife, Domenica, passed away on Aug. 17, 1951. He was 68 years old and she was 78 years old. Their son, James, lives in Brooksville, FL, and another son, Charles, lives in Cicero, IL. Jennie, John, Frank, and Louis have since passed away.

John and Domenica Mussatto and first son, John

Louis Mussatto and Dorothy Mae Miller were married on Sept. 11, 1946. They were blessed with three children—Nicholas, Shirley, and David. Before they were married Louie had played in an Italian band and later started a band of his own. This musically inclined family was very popular around Clinton, IN, and the surrounding area. Louis played an accordion, his wife, Dorothy, played the clarinet, and their son, David, played the piano and accordion.

Louis Mussatto passed away in 1985. He was 68 years old. They had moved to Brooksville, FL, in 1982 or 1983. Dorothy and their son, David, still live there and still play their music. Their daughter, Shirley, was married in 1971 to Fred Arntz and they were blessed with two children, Amber and Alexander. She has since gotten a divorce and is happily remarried. She married Peter Peterson in 1987, and they also reside in Brooksville, FL. Louie and Dorothy's oldest son, Nick, married Jeannie Ann Wright on Sept. 30, 1972. They were blessed with two children, Korena Ann and Errol Louis. Nick and his family reside in Summit Grove, IN, today.

There are still Mussattos' living in Italy today and other relatives who live around the Chicago area.

CARL MYERS (1876-1971),

The roots of Carl Myers family in Vermillion County can be traced to the early 1800's, when his grandfather, Samuel Myers, and two uncles left Virginia to travel West. Peter settled in Kentucky, George in Ohio, while Samuel chose Newport, IN, as home. Samuel married Livina Trowbridge, and the couple had two sons, Henry and Samuel (1840). When the boys were very young, their father died and Livina married Washington Ingram. The family then moved to a farm in Center Neighborhood (Helt Township).

In 1870 young Samuel married Laura Ann Crane, daughter of Steven Crane. Samuel and Laura Ann had seven sons, George, Carl, Charles, Fred (Happy), Omer, James, and Frank. George died in early childhood, and on consecutive days in December of 1887, both Laura Ann and Charles succumbed to lung fever.

Carl Myers

Because the roads were too bad for the passage of a horse drawn hearse, Jap Frist (the undertaker) and Wilbur Eaton (a neighbor) hauled the corpses in their pickle wagons to Helts Prairie Cemetery for burial. Very soon after that, Samuel's mother, Livina, also died of lung fever. Samuel was left with five boys to raise, the oldest being Carl, age ten, and the youngest being Frank, 18 months. Eliza Ford, a neighbor with a child the same age, kept Frank until he was old enough to re-join his family.

Carl took a job with Wilbur Eaton at a young age, and in 1906 married his daughter, Anna Maria. Carl was a carpenter by trade and the couple made their home in Fairview. They had two sons, Charles

Eaton Myers (1906) and Ernest Elbert Myers (1911). In 1917 Anna contracted influenza and, being in poor health, she died. She was buried in Bono Cemetery. Carl raised his two sons alone with the help of his sister-in-law and friends. In the early 1920's, when the mines closed, the building trade declined and Carl moved his boys back to a farm in Center Neighborhood. There they managed to raise their own food and survive the Depression. They later sold the farm equipment and made their living from odd jobs in the area.

Eaton married Opal Ford. The couple had one child, Barbara Ann, who married Leigh Mack of Helts Prairie. The Macks still reside in Helts Prairie and have five children, David, Marianne, Michael, Scott, and Fauniel.

In 1937 Ernest married Inez Heber, daughter of Raymond W. Heber. Their children, Jon Leon (married Lois Pauline Stafford)—third generation of carpenters in Vermillion County, Karl Willis (married Judith Ann Stewart), and Orthanna Kay (married Yale Yager), all reside in Vermillion County.

Five generations of Ernest and Inez's families attended Center Church in Helt Township. When the church was abandoned, they purchased the building and remodeled it into a home and cabinet shop, where they presently reside. They have four grandchildren, Melanie Beth Yager, Douglas Wayne Myers (son of Willie), Kristy Ann Yager, and Lynell Ortha Myers (daughter of Leon).

PHILIP NAIL'S DESCENDANTS,

Philip Nail first married Anna Heater and had David Nail. Second married Nancy Matthews and had Elizabeth. Third married Elizabeth Smith and had—Marior, Mary Ann, Elrino, Eliza J., Thomas H., John William, Samuel, Elizabeth Ann, Dollie and Phillip M.

David Nail married Lucretia Smith and had John William, Alonzo D., Mary Jane/Carrie Ann (twins), Louiza, Milton, Lillian, Samuel Berton, Martha Pearl, Lena, and Sedona.

John William married Margaret Kester and had Gertrude, Kathryn, John Wm. II, Lettie and Fredrick. Gertrude married John Gill and had Anna Margaret, and Genevieve Elizabeth. John William II married Bertha Marrow and had Patricia Ann, Norma Jean, John William III. Fredrick married Lida Marrow and had Betty Lou-first marriage. Second married Iva Lou Brown.

Alonzo D. married Dollie Nail (Philip's daughter) and had Douglas, David, Louella and Mary. Mary married Roy Loveall.

Louiza Nail married Joseph M. White and had William F., Pearl, Oscar, and Bertha L. William married Ruth and had Ervin, Roy, Helen, Robert and Violet. Oscar married first Hazel Main and second Dorothy Smith and had Norma and Ginny. Bertha married George Sarver and had Lucille, Betty Lorraine, Alfred W., and Maxine.

Changed Nail to Nale: Milton married Emma Niccum and had Edgar, Mable Viola, Florence Irene, Iva Sedona and Russell. Edgar married first Lucille Hinton and second Grace Gordon. Mable married first James Clodfelder and second Russell Huffman. Florence married Orville Brannin and had Harold.

Resides in Vermillion County this date 1988: Iva Sedona married Hollie Dunivan and had Evelyn, Gladys, and Charlotte Ann. Evelyn married George Milde. Gladys Ilene married Russell Bush and had Russell W. and Michael. Charlotte married Richard

Newell and had Kathy Lynn. Russell W. married Mindy Keller and had Tiffany and Ryan. Kathy L. married Duane Hubbard and had Debra Ann, Robert Dean, and William Joe. Debra Ann married Mark Evans. Russell M. married Iona Hershberger and had Rita May and John.

The Nails/Nale families. Top Row: Samuel Nail, I (son of Philip and Elizabeth Nail); Sedona Bishop-holding Robert Everett; Lena Hollingsworth; Joe White-husband of Louiza; Kathryn (Kate Nail)-William John's daughter; William (Bill) White-son of Lou and Joseph White; Robert Bishop-Sedona's son; George Bishop-Seonda's husband; Alice Nail-Sam's wife; Ruth (White)-holding son—Lou and Joe White's daughter; Lillian Everett-Grandma Everett; Glen Everett (Uncle Glen); Margaret Nail-William John's wife; Lou White-holding grandson; Emma Nail-Milton's wife. Second Row: Lucy Nail-Sam's daughter; Pearl and Bertha White-Lou's daughters; Mary Nail-Alonzo's daughter; Alonzo Nail, Vivian Nail-Bert's daughter; Bert Nail; William John Nail; and Milton Nail. Third Row: Clarence Hollingsworth-w/arm on ground; Conrad Hollingsworth; Forest and Thruman Hollingsworth—Lena's boys. Florence Nail-Milton's daughter; John or Fred Nail-William John's boy..probably Fred.

Lillian Nail married Fredrick Everett and had Francis, Mable, and Clarence. They died w/diphtheria in 1900. She then had Ethel, Clifford W., Glen and Robert. Ethel married John Larrew and had Mildred and Inez. Mildred first married Otos Darnell and had Robert, Glenn and Edward. Second married a Hauscher. Inez married John Boyd and had John W. (Jay), Linda, Jimmy and Donnie. Clifford W. married Pearl Huffman and had Russel Gene and Dale Duane. Dale Duane married first Carol Chapman and had Linda. Second, he married Shirley LaBurn and had Joseph and John W. Glen married Roxa Underwood and had Lois. Lois married first James McMahon and had Michael and Patricia Karen. Second, she married Mel Johnson. Robert married first Alice Hester and had Elsie. Second he married Annabelle Beckelhymer.

Resides in Vermillion County to this date 1988: Elsie married William Marshall and had Cheryl, Brent and Bruce. Cheryl married Greg Tolley and had Justin and Charlene. Brent married Linda Rentchler and had Ryan. Bruce married Debbie Foster and had Kyle and Laura.

Berton Nail married Hattie McNeese and had Raymond, Vivian, two twin boys who died within two days, Charles and Delores. Raymond married Beulah Tucker and had Marilyn. Charles married Rita Ryereson and had Charlotte. Delores married a Wagner.

Martha Peral Nail first married Allen Gephart and had Kenneth. Second, she married John Yoho. Kenneth married first Mildred Rhodenbaugh and had Blanchard. Second, he married Mary Florence Cooper and had Dorothy, Verlin G. and Kathryn.

Lena Nail married first Leonard Hollingsworth and had Hazel, Clarence, Denzil, Thurman, Forest and Conrad. Second, she married a Hendricks. Hazel married Richard Joseph and had Stuart. Clarence married first Viola Fouts and had Paul, Myra J. and Jean. Paul married Irene Kavis and had Debra, Dawn and Deanna—first marriage. Second

he married Nancy Muehring and had Jamie Lynn. Jean married John Cekalski and had Larry. Clarence later second married Mary M. Saltzman and had Lenn, Leon and Ladd. Lenn married Ruth DeRuiter and had Ross, Todd and Kipp. Leon married Sandra Wilson and had Michael, Mark, Marilee and Martin. Ladd married Kathy Redpath and had Ladd Justin and Vanessa. Thurman married Francis Beden. Forest married Edna Brown and had Charlotte, Ronald, David and Gerald. Conrad married Adele Langhout and had Sharon and Dan.

Sedona Nail married George Bishop and had Robert. Second she married a William Hollingsworth. *Submitted by Iva Dunivan and Mary Hollingsworth*

PHILIP NAIL/NALE, The Nail that held the family together was Philip Nail, just as steadfast and sure as the nail holding the lumber of their home together in Vermillion County, Highland Township, IN.

Philip Nail was born Sept. 26, 1823, in Bavaria, Germany—a division of Southern Germany. At the age of 14 he left on a ship as a stowaway to come to the land of opportunity—the home of the brave. After arrival in New York he rode from New York in a wagon which was hauling barrels of flour. Not only was his trail a trail of dust but also of flour dust as he ate flour from the knotholes of the barrels until he nearly choked to death on the dry flour. (Survival of the fitness.) Maturing early both physically and mentally we find Philip Nail married to Anna Heater two years later in Fairfield Co., OH. One son was born of this union, David Nail, my Great-Grandfather. Philip Nail applied for his naturalization on Sept. 18, 1840, in Fairfield Co., OH. He could not speak English and was married three or four times.

Philip and Elizabeth Nail

Time marches on, and on West the Nails traveled, settling in Vermillion Co., Highland Twp., IN. Here we find little David lives for a time with the Mosbarger family (Vermillion County Census 1850) and later Philip married Nancy Matthews on Dec. 14, 1857. One child born of this union— Elizabeth Nail.

We assume that the hard winters were too much for the young mother, and she died. We then find Philip Nail and Elizabeth Smith uniting together as husband and wife on Oct. 26, 1852. (Elizabeth Smith was a widow with several children—one of whom was Lucretia Smith, my Great-Grandmother (see census Vermillion County, 1860).

Living in the same household the step-brother and step-sister relationship developed into one of Hearts and Flowers and we find the marriage of David Nail and Lucretia Smith recorded in Vermillion Co., IN. (See also Census Vermillion County 1870.)

The following children were born to Philip Nail

And Elizabeth Smith: Marior Nail, Elizina Nail, Thomas H. Nail, Samuel Nail, Philip M. Nail, Mary Ann Nail, Eliza J. Nail, John William Nail, and Dollie Nail.

David and Lucretia (Smith) Nail's children were: John W. Nail, Louiza Nail, Lillian B. Nail (my Grandmother), Martha Nail, Sedona Nail, Alonzo D. Nail, Milton D. Nail, Samuel Burton Nail, and Magdalene Nail.

The name Nail was changed to Nale—Milton Nail, son of David and Lucretia changed the name for his family. You will find the spelling both ways throughout the years. My Grandmother, Lillian (Nale) Everett has it spelled Nale on her marriage license.

Most of the information was given to me by Iva (Nale) Dunivan, daughter of Milton and Emma (Niccum) Nale, who resides in Perrysville, IN, today. Her Grandchildren attended North Vermillion High School.

Fred and Lillian Everett, Clifford and Ethel

Lillian Nale married Frederick Everett of Danville, IL, and of this union were born six children. Two died of diphtheria and the four remaining were: Ethel, Clifford, Glen and Robert Everett, my father.

Robert Everett farmed and lived at R.#2, Covington, IN, Highland Twp. Vermillion Co., IN for 20 years. Annabelle, his widow is still living there today.

Elsie (Everett) Marshall, daughter, married William D. Marshall in 1957 and they reside now at R.#2, Box 190, Covington, IN, Highland Twp., Vermillion Co., IN.

Cheryl (Marshall) Tolley, Bruce Marshall and Brent Marshall, children of William and Elsie Mashall went to North Vermillion High School.

Cheryl and Greg Tolley live in Cayuga, IN, Vermillion County and their children, Justin and Charlene Tolley attended Newport Grade School, Newport, IN.

Justin and Charlene Tolley

David Nail is buried in the Hicks Cemetery, Highland Twp., Vermillion Co., IN

Philip Nail is buried in the McKendree Cemetery, near Forest Glen—Georgetown, IL.

Alonzo Nail, son of David and Lucretia Nail—and also the Grandson of Philip Nail married Dollie Nail, daughter of Philip Nail and Elizabeth (Smith) Nail.

Farm home of Fred and Lillian (Nale) Everett

Alonzo and Dollie's children would then have been both the grandchildren of Philip and at the same time the great-grandchildren of Philip. Could this be how you get to be—"I'm my own grandpa"? *Submitted by Elsie Marshall, great-great-granddaughter of Philip Nail*

JOHN J. NEWTON AND MARY ELLEN SKIDMORE NEWTON,

lived their married life on a farm two miles north of St. Bernice for over 50 years, first in a log cabin then building a larger home in which nine children were born.

John Jasper, born in 1854, was the son of James and Jemima Thornton Newton who lived in Illinois. James was a school teacher and also a surveyor. He had a knowledge of law of which he did not practice but often gave legal advice to his neighbors.

Mary Ellen, born in 1859, was the daughter of William Skidmore who was the first white child born in Helt Township in 1819. Mary Ellen and John J. were married in 1885 and nine children were born between 1886 and 1905.

The first three were born in the log cabin. They were Madge, Lenora, and Raymond. Madge married Leonard Martin and their daughter is Audrey Martin Gowens of West Clinton. Lenora married William Wallace and their son is Harold Wallace who lives near Scottland, IL. Lenora was a grade school teacher in St. Bernice and Redman, IL. Raymond never married.

John was the fourth child. He was married to Dollie McCauley. Doris and Jean were their children. He later married Elizabeth Peterson and had three more children, Ruth, Carl, and Eddie.

Mary Ellen and John J's next child died in infancy. Nettie was the sixth child. She married Cecil Coleman. Their daughter is Anna Louise. She was married to Lawrence Stultz, and she lives on the homeplace north of St. Bernice.

Dewey never married. Frank was married to Sally North of Alabama.

Mary was the last child. She married Byron Vance. Their three children were Norma, Byron, Jr., and Raymond Stanley. Al is deceased. Norma and Stan live in the Calumet region near Chicago. Mary, their mother, lives in Dana.

Liberty School was built on the Newton property, but was demolished in 1965.

JOSEPH HENRY NICHOLAS,

son of William Nicholas and Mahala Shute Nicholas, was born June 5, 1848, northeast of Gessie, IN. He was the youngest and only boy of a family of six children. He married Sarah Amanda Short Mar. 11, 1883. She was the daughter of Johnathan and

Margaret Haworth Short, and the last of a family of seven children. Joseph H. Nicholas donated the ground for the Hazel Brush (Howard) District Three School. This school was located north of the Hopewell Church on the east side of the road where the present overpass begins. He and his wife had three daughters and they realized the need for their daughters to have a high school education. They bought the farm west of Perrysville, later sold to Mont and Mary Saltsgaver.

Three daughters were born to this union: Etta, Ethel, and Della. Etta and Della were teachers in Highland Township. Ethel taught music. Etta married Charles E. Prather on June 8, 1910. They had one daughter, Coral. Ethel married James E. Snoddy on Aug. 2, 1908. They had one daughter Leah Rae. Della married H. Clyde Hodges on Sept. 4, 1919.

Leah Rae Snoddy married Stanley T. Goff June 8, 1939. They had one daughter Marilyn Rae.

The Nicholas family were very active in the Church, School, and community. *Submitted by Leah Rae Goff and Coral Prather, granddaughters of Joseph and Sarah A. Nichols*

RICHARD E. NICHELS AND BARBARA J. NICKELS,

Richard E. Nickels was born in 1929 to Vera Webb Nickels and Paul E. Nickels. He grew up on his parent's farm along with his sister, Patsy Nickels Harden. He graduated from Newport High School in 1947. Barbara Jean Shaubi Nickels was born in 1932 to Edith Sanquenetti Shaubi and Frank Shaubi who was a coal miner. She graduated from Clinton High School in 1950. She has two sisters; Joann Shaubi Nickels and Rosemary Shaubi Favali.

Richard and Barbara Nickels and grandsons, Chad, Chase, and Cole Contri

In September of 1950, Richard Nickels and Barbara Shaubi were married. They resided on a farm south of Newport until 1966. Daughter Nancy was born in 1952 and daughter Debbie was born in 1957. In 1966, they bought the Charles and Lena Colombo farm in Helt Township. There they built a tri-level home where they have resided ever since. Barbara worked as a glass inspector for 23 years at Midland Glass Company in Terre Haute. Richard works at Hercules Incorporated and operates a farm. He and his father Paul, who lives on a farm nearby, have farmed together for most of their lives.

Daughter Nancy graduated from Clinton High School in 1970 and from Indiana State University in 1973 with a degree in elementary education and library science and completed her M.S. degree in these areas in 1976. She is a second grade teacher at Ernie Pyle School in the South Vermillion School Corporation. In 1976, she married Bob L. Contri. He is the son of the late Aldo and Della Pugh Contri of Clinton. Bob is the guidance director of Riverton

Parke High School. They have three sons: Chad Richard, born in 1980, and twins, Chase Robert and Cole Ryan, born in 1985.

Daughter Debbie graduated from Clinton High School in 1975 and attended Indiana State University. She is an analytical laboratory technician at Eli Lilly and Co. It was there that she met her husband, David A. Greeves, whom she married in 1981. David is a senior instrument technician at Eli Lilly and Company.

Daughter Nancy and her husband Bob built a home on the west side of her parents' farm. Daughter Debbie and her husband Dave built a home to the southeast of the farm.

Richard and Barbara raise draft ponies on their Hillsdale farm. They have been in many local parades throughout the years and have brought home blue ribbons from the Indiana State Fair draft pony show. The whole family gets involved during the summer months when Richard and Barbara travel to several draft pony shows with their wagon hitch.

ELMER NOGGLE AND ROZELLA SYKES NOGGLE,

Elmer (1889-1958) was the son of Mount Vernon (1853-1909) and Martha Ellen Ottinger Noggle (1860-1928). He had a twin brother named Burt and he also had twin sisters. There were 11 children.

Elmer married Rozella Sykes (1894-1982), daughter of George (1865-1919) and Anna Mullins (1874-1903) on Apr. 1, 1910. Rozella had only one brother who died soon after birth. His name was Carmel.

Elmer and Rozella had four daughters and three sons—Evelin Lavon (1911-1983) married Carl Erdmann (1900-1982); Lucille (1912-1921); Forrest married Ruth Downs; Wayne (1915-1915), lived only a few days; Ruth married Herman E. Sprouls; Nellie married Delbert Laughhunn (1909-1972); and Paul married Margaret Benton.

The Noggels spent most of their married life on their farm on State Road 71, about two miles northwest of Newport, IN. After retiring from farming, they sold their farm and moved to Cayuga, IN, where they spent the rest of their years enjoying fishing, traveling, and their grandchildren.

Elmer and Rozella are laid to rest in Thomas Cemetery near Newport, IN.

ALFRED MARION NOLAN,

was born Apr. 10, 1851, the son of Elcain and Sarah Catherine Swan Nolan. He was the grandson of Samuel and Sarah Cellars Nolan and William and Elizabeth Cooper Swan. His grandfather Samuel was owner and operator of several gristmills in the area. He was the nephew of Captain William (Billy) Swan, a barge captain on the Wabash River. Alfred M. Nolan was the great-grandson of James Nolan and Elizabeth Emmerson Nolan.

He was one of four children; his brother and sisters included: George, Amanda Nolan Harper, and Sarah (unmarried).

Sarah Catherine Swan Nolan died at age 26 and Alfred's father married Almyra (Carpenter) Groves. At the age of 11, Alfred was hired out to area families to work. He became a "bond boy"; living first with one family and then another. He earned no money, just his meals and a place to sleep. Thus, he became a self-made man. Through all this, he learned the trade of carpentry.

Alfred M. Nolan had a half-sister Minnie B. Nolan and a half-brother Jesse L. Nolan. (Children of Elcain and Almyra Groves Nolan.)

It was during his employment at the farm of Archibald Osmon, that he met and fell in love with Mr. Osmon's daughter, Sarah Florence Osmon. They were married Jan. 18, 1880, in Vermillion Co., IN,

Eleven children were born to this union. Eight survived, one of which was Golda Lela Nolan Thomas. (see related biography)

He purchased the Gerrish farm located just west of the Ernie Pyle School in Helt Township. He and his wife Sarah lived and raised a family on that farm in the 1880's, 1890's, and early 1900's.

Alfred Marion Nolan died Dec. 6, 1930, and was buried in the Wesley Chapel Cemetery west of Dana, IN. *Submitted by Madge Thomas Lake*

BERTHA MAY NOLAN,

On Jan. 29, 1888 Bertha May Nolan was born in Dana, IN, the third child and third daughter of Alfred Marion and Sarah Florence Osmon Nolan (see related biographies.) She was one of 11 children, eight of whom grew to adulthood. After the Nolan family moved to a farm that would now be just west of the present Ernie Pyle School, she attended Independence School and Frog College.

On May 1, 1909 in Dana, IN, Bertha married a Pentecostal evangelist, Orlie Thomas Collier, eventually moving to Plainfield, IN, where their daughters Doris Marie and Pauline were born on July 18, 1910 and Oct. 29, 1914, respectively (See related biographies.) In November after Pauline's birth Orlie, then a Realtor, disappeared leaving Bertha and children penniless. Returning to the Nolan family farm in Vermillion County for the next two years, Bertha supported her children doing housework for neighbors.

About 1914 Bertha moved into the three room cabin with Permelia Peyton Alberts where she and her two daughters attended Tennessee Valley Church. In the eight years she was Aunt Millie's companion, she saved enough money to buy a home on West A Street, three doors north of the railroad, in Dana. For a year or two she was the cook in Lindley's Restaurant. At its' closing, the regular customers, Verne Standfield, Edgar Green, Uncle Billy Scott, etc. enjoyed her cooking in her home.

Bertha May's goal was an education for her two daughters so, "If they are left stranded as I was, they'll not have to work so hard!" For the next ten years she turned her two bedroom home into a boarding house, renting one room to coal miners, to members of the construction workers who erected the Dana water tower and to those who built route 36. A regular boarder paid $.35 and a drop-in $.50 for a full meal served family style. Bertha was a member of the Rebekah Lodge and the Royal Neighbors and attended the Baptist Church.

In 1936 after both daughters had teaching certificates from Indiana State Teacher's College and Pauline had married a Huntington County farmer, Bertha moved there where she was housekeeper for Dr. Mark Ereharts.

On July 12, 1947 Bertha married Samuel Saunders Pierson and resided south of Huntington until her death Jan. 19, 1976. *Submitted by Pauline C. Shriner*

BESSIE JANE NOLAN,

was born Feb. 19, 1886 north of Dana, Vermillion Co., IN to Alfred Marion and Sarah Florence Osmon Nolan (see related biographies.) On Aug. 9, 1908 she married Fred J. Collins and they settled on a farm NW of Dana where their ten children were born. She, a

member of the Reorganized Church of Jesus Ch[rist] died August, 1968.

CHARLOTTE (LOTTIE) DELOR[IS] NOLAN,

was born Dec. 21, 1881 north of Da[na] Vermillion Co., IN to Alfred Marion and Sa[rah] Florence Osmon Nolan (see related biographies.) On Jan. 31, 1908 at the Methodist Episcopal Church in Dana, IN, Lottie married Wiley Franklin Wagner. They had one son, Samuel, who on Jan. 10, 1939 married Olive Jane Blythe, the daughter of Ray and Iva May Malone Blythe of Dana. Sam was killed in an auto accident Dec. 27, 1971. His mother, Lottie, died Jan. 18, 1963.

JOHN OSMON NOLAN,

was born July 24, 1906 in Helt Township, Vermillion Co., IN to Alfred Marion and Sarah Florence Osmon Nolan (see related biographies.) John attended Indiana State Teachers' College and was a teller in the Clinton Bank. He served as a machinist in the army in World War II. He died single in June 1957.

SAMUEL LEROY NOLAN,

was born June 12, 1900 in Helt Township, Vermillion County to Alfred Marion and Sarah Florence Osmon Nolan (see related biographies.) He served as a Sea Bee in World War II. On Mar. 15, 1945 Sam married Lucille Stickler in Huntington Co., IN, where he died in May, 1957. They have three living children and three Nolan grandsons.

SARAH FLORENCE OSMON NOLAN,

was born Oct. 1, 1861, the daughter of Archibald W. and Charlotte Chestine Tomey Osmon. She was the granddaughter of Phillip W. and Matilda Williams Osmon; also Joseph and Mary Osmon Tomey. A sister and three brothers died in infancy. She had five brothers including: John, William, Fred, Samuel, and Leonard.

Her family lived on a farm located on the prairie, northwest of Dana, IN. Mr. Osmon was in poor health much of the time; thus, she grew up under the influence of a prim, thrifty, and very efficient mother.

Back: Charles Alva Nolan (nephew of Alfred Nolan. Raised from infancy by Alfred and Sarah Nolan) Golda Nolan Thomas, Arch Nolan, Bertha Nolan Collier, Fred Collins, Bessie Nolan Collins, Wiley Wagner, Charlotte Nolan Wagner. Front: John Nolan, Alfred M. Nolan (holding Sam Wagner and Florence Collins Bell), Leroy Samual Nolan, Sarah Osmon Nolan (holding Andrew Collins and Doris Collier Morrow), Ruby Nolan Kuhns.

She attended the first six grades of school. This was accomplished by riding horseback across the prairie for many miles. Her mother taught her all of the basic fundamentals that were necessary for homemakers to know in those very early days.

A young farm laborer arrived to work on her parents' farm. Sarah and the young man, Alfred Marion Nolan (see related biography) fell in love. They were married Jan. 18, 1880.

Sarah Osmon Nolan gave birth to 11 children. [...] of the children survived: Charlotte Nolan [...]ner, Bessie Nolan Collins, Bertha Nolan Col-[...] Golda Nolan Thomas, (see related biography) [...]hibald A. Nolan, Leroy Samuel Nolan, Ruby [...]n Kuhns (see related biography), and John O. Nolan.

Sarah Osmon Nolan died Nov. 16, 1925, and was buried in the Wesley Chapel Cemetery west of Dana, IN.

Sarah Osmon Nolan and her husband, children, and grandchildren posed for this picture in 1910 or 1911. *Submitted by Madge Thomas Lake*

THE OVERPECK'S, as we know them today, had many German spellings of their name—Overbeck, Overback, Oberbeck, and possibly more. They migrated from Hesse-Darmstadt, Germany to Ducks Co., PA in 1745, before finally pushing on to Indiana by wagon, horseback and on foot.

Among the settlers was a lady who started a willow tree by sticking her riding switch in Parke County soil. Perry Overpeck and Susan Ann Pence were married Mar. 14, 1861, and decided to start their family on a hill by the tree northeast of Roseville, now Rosedale, in Parke Co., IN. In November, 1874, the Overpecks and their children—Etta, Ella, Grant, Margarett and Mattie—purchased a Vermillion County farm. The move meant fording the Wabash at a point just south of where Norton Creek empties into the river and settling into a log cabin. Although a new house and barn were built in 1880, only the barn remained after a fire in 1910. The house was replaced with the home that stands beside the original barn on the Overpeck farm today.

Perry's daughters, Ella and Margarett, married brothers Wilbur and Frank Skidmore in the first double-wedding of sisters and brothers in Vermillion County. Mattie Overpeck married David Davis. In 1889, Grant married Rhoda Cowgill, who died in 1895. Their only son, Nicholas, "Knic", was born in 1890 and later married Pearl Ehrmann of Newport. They had no children when he died in 1937.

Grant Overpeck married his second wife, Bertha Weber on Feb. 10, 1904. Bertha died in 1934 and Grant lived until 1943. They had four children—Perry Weber, twin boys who died in infancy, and Donald Grant. Grant bought and sold mules and horses, judged draft horses, and raised livestock. As a member of the Vermillion County Fair Board from 1928 to 1943, he was director of the Draft Horse Department. Bertha's father was the last tollmaster of the Clinton Bridge across the Wabash River.

Perry Weber, known as "Weber", married Helen Clifford of Lawton, OK in 1934. Weber died in 1969, leaving no children.

Donald married Agnes Foster of Clinton on Feb. 10, 1935, which was the anniversary of his parents and his brother Knic and his wife. They have four children, eight grandchildren and two great-grandchildren.

Donald replaced his father on the County Fair Board through the mid-1960's as Director of the Cattle Department. As an active 4-H leader for nine years, he coached winning Livestock Judging Teams to state and international competitions in Chicago. He took his interest for livestock to the Indiana State Fair where he was assistant Superintendent of the Cattle Barns. After nine years, Donald decided to give his full attention to the farm and his family.

As a result, his children and grandchildren have carried on in the family tradition of judging and competition. Donald and Agnes have celebrated their 50th wedding anniversary and are now retired from farming and nursing. They still live in the original Overpeck homestead.

CHARLES DONALD PAINE AND LOUISE ROBERTS PAINE,

Henry Washburn Paine married Kizzie May Spainhower, who had come here from Worthington in Greene County. Kizzie's father, James Spainhower, was a combat veteran of the Civil War and had been held as a prisoner of war by the Confederates. The Paine family resided on a farm near Blanford until 1870. They then moved to the state of Kansas, returning to Clinton in 1884. They again went to Kansas in 1898. On June 30, 1908, Charles Donald Paine was born in Trego Co., KS, the son of Henry and Kizzie Spainhower Paine. Within a day or two a tornado came. Henry ordered the other children, Robert Burl, Reba, Elizabeth, James Earl, Nelle, and Mary Eleanor into the storm cellar while Kizzie and the baby stayed in bed. Henry stayed with the children. The tornado did not harm them. A short time later they moved back to Clinton.

Henry Washburn Paine, Narcissus Wright Paine, Kizzy May Spainhower Paine

After their return, Henry helped with the family grocery store, served as a Clinton City street commissioner, and later as a WPA boss on the Feather Creek Project. He also owned rental property.

Charles Donald Paine attended Central School in Clinton and Clinton High School. He later was employed for some years at Olmstead Dry Cleaners and then for some years at Model Cleaners. He married the former Louise Roberts who has a twin sister Lucille. They are the daughters of Arthur "Pete" Roberts and Ollie Bunger Roberts. Their mother died when they were ten years old. Their father worked in the bank at 141 South Main Street and worked part-time in Horney's Machine Shop.

Louise worked for several years as a bank teller in the Citizen State Bank, Clinton Branch. Don was a Democratic precinct committeeman of Clinton precinct 2A and during the Welsh and Branigan administrations (1961-1968), he was a state highway inspector. From 1957-1959, he was a member of the Clinton School Board.

The Paines' have two children, Michael Henry Paine of New Orleans, who is a geophysicist; and Donna Lou Paine Strain, who lives in Rosedale. She is a mother of three and works at Hercules.

Mr. and Mrs. Paine belong to the Christian Church in Clinton and he is a member of the Masonic Lodge. *Submitted by Leo Reposh, Jr.*

HAROLD AND BERYL COX AND NOBLE PAINE,

Harold Cox is the son of Everett and Alice Cox of Clinton. He is a car salesman at Mace Mercury in Terre Haute and was formerly in the banking business. He is a graduate of Clinton High School.

Beryl Paine Cox is the wife of Harold Cox and the daughter of Thomas Howard Paine (called Howard) and Eola Fern Noble Paine. Her father, Howard is the brother of Frank, Grace, Fred who died at age 15, John R. who was Clinton Mayor in 1926, and Henry Washburn Paine (see related stories on Ethel Reposh and Charles Donald Paine) and the son of James Paine and Narcissus Wright Paine (see related story on Ulysses Grant Wright).

Howard Paine

Beryl is a graduate of Clinton High School and is employed by four doctors at the AP and S Clinic in Terre Haute.

This couple have three children, Linda, Laura, and Jon Scott Cox. Harold and Beryl Cox reside in Fairview Park.

Beryl Paine Cox has three sisters; Clara Grace May, Martha Alice McCarty, and Mary Juanita Horine, and she has three brothers; James Franklin Paine, Daniel Lawrence Paine, and Noble Paine. Noble graduated from Clinton High school in 1939. Former Clinton High School teacher, Glenn Morgan, once commented that Noble was the most intelligent student she had ever taught. He is now a retired bacteriologist and professor from a university in Australia, and he lives in Aimslie, Australia. He visits Vermillion County occasionally. *Submitted by Leo Reposh Jr.*

JOHN R. PAINE, was born in Clinton on Oct. 15, 1869, the son of James and Narcissus Wright Paine. (see related articles on Ethel Reposh, Charles Donald Paine, and Ulysses Grant Wright.) His wife was Ella Scott, daughter of Washington and Anne E. (Bright) Scott. Washington Scott came from Washington Co., IN, where his father was an early settler. John R. and Ella had one daughter, Martha Louise Paine Dick.

Mr. Paine was engaged in the hardware business stocking hardware and farm implements. This was next door to Paine and Son's food store. John R. Paine belonged to the Free and Accepted Masons and the Knights of Pythias, both in Clinton. In 1909, he was elected to the position of Clinton City Councilman-At-Large, his term to expire in 1913.

John R. Paine was elected mayor by the council on Apr. 29, 1924, to serve through 1925, then he was elected to serve for the years 1926 through 1929. *Submitted by Leo Reposh Jr.*

ROSCOE AND HAZEL PARKS, Roscoe Lester Parks was born on Aug. 23, 1891, in Rural Retreat, VA, in Grayson County, to Stuart and Nannie Collins Parks. Roscoe was the oldest of seven children. He moved with his family to Edgar Co., IL, north of Chrisman, in 1902, when Roscoe was 11 years old.

On Oct. 8, 1914, Roscoe married Hazel Olive Vanscoyk in Paris, IL. Hazel was born Apr. 3, 1894, to Issac and Ida Dunn Vanscoyk in Fulton Co., MO. Her mother died before Hazel was two years old. Her father moved Hazel and her brother, James, from Missouri, in a wagon, to Edgar Co., IL, in 1896.

Roscoe and Hazel moved to Vermillion Co., IN on Dec. 1, 1934. They raised three children, all born in Edgar Co., IL.

Carl Eston Parks, born Mar. 19, 1916, married Mary Elizabeth Fahr from Vigo Co., IN. They have two children, both born in Vigo County. Judith Elizabeth was born May 1, 1949 and David Nelson was born July 2, 1952. Carl and Elizabeth reside in Terre Haute, IN.

Raymond Eugene Parks, born Oct. 13, 1921, married Margaret Elizabeth Monninger, from Vigo Co., IN. They have two children, both born in Vigo County. Joanie Kay was born Aug. 27, 1948, and James Steven was born July 22, 1954. Raymond and Margaret reside in rural route, Hillsdale, IN, in Vermillion County.

Doris Louise Parks, born May 21, 1923, married Maurice C. Johnson from Vermillion Co., IN. They have two children, both born in Vermillion Co., IN. Maurice C. (Johnny) Johnson, Jr. was born Feb. 25, 1946, and Linda Jean Johnson was born Dec. 7, 1951. Doris and Maurice reside in Paris, IL.

Roscoe was a farmer and retired in 1959. He was active in politics and served as a County Commissioner for Vermillion County for two decades. He died at the age of 89 on Dec. 31, 1980. His wife, Hazel, died at the age of 84, on July 2, 1978.

Joanie Kay Parks married Warren Neil (Jack) Rumple from the Quaker Community, in Vermillion County. They have three daughters all born in Vigo Co., IN. Jayanne was born July 31, 1967, Susan Rae was born Oct. 9, 1969, and Amy Anne was born Mar. 15, 1973. Joanie and Jack reside near Dana in Helt Township.

James Steven Parks married Rebecca Ann Ornkovich from Madison, WI. They have two sons, Justin William Parks, born in Dane, WI, Aug. 15, 1985, and Perry Alexander Parks, born in Henry Co., IL, Aug. 24, 1987. James and Rebecca reside in Geneseo, IL.

WILLIAM H. PATRICK AND LOUISE BELSER PATRICK,
William Hiram Patrick (1886-1971) was born and lived his entire life in Eugene Township, Vermillion Co., IN.

He was the youngest son of Thomas and Thamer Stewart Patrick. He graduated from Cayuga High School and attended Purdue University. General John Cochran, an ancestor, served in the Revolutionary War.

William and Louise Patrick

His father, Thomas, also served under General Sherman in the Civil War. His Uncle John was also in the Civil War and was killed in the battle of Vicksburg on July 5, 1863. His ancestors came to this county from New York.

In 1915, he married Louise (1897-1984). She was the daughter of Gustav and Katherine Hiberly Belser. Her parents met on a ship when the families were immigrating to America from Germany. She attended schools in Vermillion and Eugene Townships. They are the parents of Mary Ralph, Camarillo, CA, Ruth Dunkerly, Covington, IN, and Viola Howell, Longview, TX. William Jr. is deceased (1934-1953). Mr. Patrick spent a short time on the railroad and later engaged in farming.

He was a County Commissioner from 1927-1930, served on the Vermillion County Hospital Board for eight years, and the Collett Home for Orphans Board for 30 years. He was a life member of Scottish Rite in Danville, IL, 50 year member of Cayuga Masons and Order of Eastern Star, also the Zorah Shriners of Terre Haute, IN, and Royal Arch of Clinton Commandary 48. He was a member of the Cayuga Presbyterian Church.

Louise was also a member of the Cayuga Order of the Eastern Star and a charter member of Cayuga War Mothers.

BILL PEARMAN,
was born on Dec. 11, 1943, in Clinton, the oldest son of Gordon and Ruth Pearman. Bill attended school at Hillsdale and Dana, graduating from Hillsdale High School in 1961.

He served with the U.S. Air Force from 1962-1966 and 1968-1975 in Texas, Okinawa, Italy, South Dakota, and Illinois. During those years he served as an Intelligence Specialist, Recreation Specialist, Administrative Specialist, and Air Force Recruiter.

Bill attended Indiana State University from 1966-1968 and graduated with a B.S. degree in Social Studies Education in 1978, later completing his M.S. degree in education in 1981. He taught school in Terre Haute and Albion, IL, and served as a substitute teacher in South Vermillion and Turkey Run High Schools. Bill has been active in coaching baseball, basketball, softball, football and track—both in the Air Force and in high school.

In 1965, Bill married Margaret Ann McCollum, daughter of Lester and Bernice McCollum, in San Angelo, TX. She was a 1965 graduate of Clinton High School. They have three daughters: Angela Kay Parrish of St. Bernice; Shelley Lynn, a 17-year-old senior at South Vermillion High School; and Stacey Marie, a 14-year-old freshman at South Vermillion High School. They also have one grandson, Timothy Michael Parrish.

Margaret is active in church work and has been a 4-H leader for 13 years. She was named Outstanding 4-H Leader for 1985. Bill is active in coaching Babe Ruth League baseball and is an active member of the Vermillion County Historical Society and the Vermillion County 4-H Council. He also serves as First Sergeant for the 113th Tactical Fighter Squadron of the Indiana Air National Guards and was recently selected as Outstanding NCO of the Quarter. He has also been chosen as his unit's Outstanding NCO of the Year three times. Bill is a part-time free lance writer, specializing in education, and is the President of the Cavalier Foundation for Excellence in Education.

Shelley is active in the high school band and Cadet Corps and has been accepted into Indiana State University in 1989. She was also a Grape Princess for the 1988 Little Italy Festival. Stacey has been active in music and softball and enjoys horseback riding.

EDWARD PEARMAN AND MYRTLE ALLEN PEARMAN,
Edward Pearman was born July 19, 1881, and died Apr. 24, 1942. He married Myrtle Allen, who was born Jan. 5, 1892, and died June, 1963. Nine children were born. They were: Blanche Marie (Mrs. Clyde Brown) born Sept. 5, 1903, and died Aug. 10, 1967. Ralph Edward was born July 27, 1908, and died Sept. 1, 1984. Kathleen Pearl (now Mrs. James Gill of Hillsdale) was born Mar. 3, 1911. John Dee of Hillsdale was born Oct. 9, 1913. Annabelle was born Aug. 19, 1916 (now Mrs. Kenneth Peck of Fairview). Donald Loren was born July 9, 1920, and now lives in Montezuma. Joseph Walter was born Mar. 28, 1923, and Paul Clarence was born Oct. 7, 1925, and died Sept. 22, 1969. Harold Ray was born Nov. 28, 1930. Joseph and Harold also reside in Hillsdale. *Submitted by Shirley Thomas*

JAMES GORDON "BUD" PEARMAN,
a great-great-grandson of Sebert Pearman, was born to Ruie F. Pearman and Iva Boren at Hillsdale on Dec. 20, 1917. Gordon married Ruth Ann Goss, daughter of Rev. and Mrs. V. B. Goss in 1941.

Gordon attended Hillsdale High School and later worked with the Civilian Conservation Corps. In the 1940's and 1950's, he worked for DuPont and Liberty Powder at Newport. During those years he played industrial league softball and basketball and developed a life-long interest in sports which he passed on to his sons. Gordon later worked for the Hillsdale Tile Plant and the Cayuga Brickyard. He is now retired and living in Hillsdale and is an avid South Vermillion sports fan.

Gordon and Ruth have five children: Elnora Thomas of Hillsdale; Phyllis Landrus of Bloomingdale; Barbara Haskell of Terre Haute; Bill Pearman of St. Bernice; and Mike Pearman of Hillsdale. They also have seen grandchildren and three great-grandchildren. Gordon has one brother, Robert, living in Ohio, and one sister, Margaret Amerman of Clinton. He has been a life-long resident of Helt Township.

LEE PEARMAN AND HIS LOVE FOR THE WABASH,
The Wabash River has always been an important part of Vermillion County. It has meant many things to many people. It was there that Lee Pearman supplemented his income to support his family, especially during the depression years.

Lee became very skilled at fishing, both with trotlines and with D-nets. He learned the river like the palm of his hand. He knew where to set the nets and put his lines for the best catches.

Telsa and Lee Pearman

One morning in early 1940's, Lee and his twin

sons, Ora and Lora, and his youngest son, Fern, went out to run a trotline just below the bridge East of Newport, and they caught three flathead catfish that ranged in weight from 38 to 54 lbs. A week later the boys caught another, just one-half inch longer than the 54 pounder, from a line of their own. At that time fish were selling for 40 cents a pound.

Fishing was not the only thing that Lee and the boys did at the river. Many hours were spent "musseling". This is the process of taking mussels from the bottom of the river and cooking them in a large vat. The shells were stacked in a pile to sell and the cooked mussel meat was looked through for pearls. Many valuable pearls were found. The imperfect pieces (slugs) were sold by the ounce. Besides the boys, Lee's wife, Telsa, and their daughters, Madge and Joan, often helped "look for pearls". His daughter, Lois, was much too small to help. At that time the mussel shells sold for $75.00 per ton.

When the different hunting seasons came, Lee brought home various things to eat, he was a "crack shot". There were squirrels, rabbits, ducks, and geese.

Lee was an avid mushroom hunter in the spring. Many times he took a foot-tub full home where his wife washed and soaked them, then fried then to a golden brown. They were delicious eating.

He also helped pick berries which were canned in quart jars for the winter. In the Fall, Lee gathered nuts. He often took home walnuts, hazelnuts, butternuts, hickory nuts, and pecans. All of these things were within walking distance of his home on the banks of the Wabash River.

At dusk, Lee could be heard whistling as he slowly rowed his boat around the North Bend. You could see the miner's lamp on his cap, he was coming in for the night. If you listened, you could hear him lift the fish box lid and one by one drop his catch into the box to keep them alive 'til they were sold.

It took an alert mind and a strong body to make a living on the Wabash. It was long hours and hard work, but Lee enjoyed every minute of it.

Although he had worked on the railroad in Rockville, IN, before moving to Vermillion County, and he worked at the Newport Powder Plant; there was never a job he enjoyed as much as being a fisherman on the Wabash River.

SEBERT PEARMAN, and Sarah Rose Nichols came to Helt Township, Vermillion County, from Hardin Co., KY, in 1830. These pioneers brought with them seven of their soon-to-be 12 children: Malinda (Mrs. Stephen Harrington), John, Jane (Mrs. John White), Benjamin, Samuel, Elizabeth (first wife of William Skidmore), and Sarah (Mrs. John Henderson). Sebert worked the mill at Eugene one year and built mills on the Big Vermillion River and Norton Creek.

Five more children were born to Sebert and Sarah by 1842: Judah (Mrs. Lorenzo Short), William, Elisha, Martha, and David. All 12 children remained in or near Helt Township or Clinton Township. Sebert, Sarah Rose, and several of their children are buried in Mt. Pisgah Cemetery between Bono and Hillsdale.

Sebert served under General Harrison in the War of 1812. Several of his grandchildren fought for the Union in the Civil War while relatives left behind in Kentucky fought for the Confederacy under General Breckenridge.

Family tradition claims Sebert Pearman was a first cousin to Confederate President, Jefferson Davis; however, no records have yet been found to verify that claim.

Sebert's youngest son, David, lived near Dana until his death in 1917. Several of Sebert and Sarah's descendents still reside in Vermillion County including a great-great-grandson, James Gordon Pearman of Hillsdale, and two great-great-great-grandsons, Bill of St. Bernice, and Mike of Hillsdale.

CLAUDE EDGAR PECK AND BESSIE MARGUERITE BARTON PECK, Claude Edgar Peck was born Jan. 12, 1886, at Knightsville, IN to Claude Emerson Peck (birthdate June 5, 1855) and Evaline Turner (birthdate Sept. 7, 1860). Bessie Marguerite Barton was born Sept. 30, 1889, in Clinton to Perry Barton and Margaret Shannon. Claude and Bessie were married July 17, 1906. Children born were Clarence Edgar, born Feb. 5, 1907, in Clinton. Perry Emerson was born Sept. 17, 1909. Kenneth LeRoy was born Aug. 27, 1914, at Fairview. Martha Evalyn Peck (Mrs. Austin Reed) was born Dec. 24, 1918, Bessie Marguerite was born Dec. 24, 1920, and Donald Eugene was born Aug. 20, 1925.

Claude Edward Peck family. Claude Edward Peck, Clarence Edgar, Kenneth LeRoy, Bessie Marguerite holding Bessie, Martha Evalyn, Perry Emerson, Margaret Barton, Perry Barton

Bessie died Oct. 17, 1947. Claude later married Mae Swickard Carty. Claude died Aug. 31, 1962.

Daniel Webster Peck, Claude's grandfather, was born about 1834 and was descended from a Pennsylvania Dutch (German) family by the name of Beck. He told his grandchildren that his grandfather had been named Peter B. Beck and there were several others with the same name in town and they were receiving each others mail. Accordingly, Peter convinced the civil authorities that the spelling of the name should be changed to Peck. *Submitted by Shirley L. Thomas*

CHRIS PESAVENTO AND GISELLA BROTTO PESAVENTO, Chris Pesavento born in Asiago, located in the Alps of northeastern Italy on Oct. 3, 1873, left home at the age of 12 to work as a carpenter in Germany. He came to America when he was 18 with three other friends.

Upon arriving in New York, he and his three friends borrowed $20 apiece from an Italian hotel keeper to buy train tickets to Ironwood, MI where they were to work in the iron mines. The hotel keeper remarked some years later that all four young men repaid him.

He later worked on a canal in Lockport, IL and as a lamplighter in Chicago.

In the early 1900's he moved to the Geneva area to work in the coal mines.

In 1902 he built a saloon on the corner of 7th and Oak streets. The saloon furnished miner supplies, a meeting room where 22 mine locals met and a dance hall which was used for wedding and other celebrations.

One of the Lithuanian wedding customs at the dance hall was to attempt to break plates by throwing money on these plates. The reward was to win a dance with the bride.

Around 1912 a group of people attempted to extort money from some 15 merchants in Clinton. Known as the "Black Hand" they sent letters demanding money or threatening to damage property. Chris received such a letter but refused the threat. Consequently, the house was bombed leaving a gaping hole in the bedroom wall. Miraculously, the parents and infant Irma sleeping in the bedroom escaped injury. Windows in homes one-half block away were shattered from the bomb explosion. Their home was located at 457 N. Eighth Street.

Gisella Brotto Pesavento was born in Valstagna in northeastern Italy on Nov. 6, 1882. She had three brothers. Her brother was a colonel in the Italian Army and had the job of collecting taxes for tobacco grown in that area. Orphaned as young girl, she moved to Asiago to live with an aunt.

On Aug. 29, 1903, on a visit to Italy Chris and Gisella were married in Il Domo in Asiago and returned to make their home in Clinton. Gisella died in 1931, her husband in 1930.

Their family included Chris, born in 1904; Dante, born in 1905; Irma, born 1911, and Walter, born 1916.

Irma graduated from Indiana State Normal School (now Indiana State University). She taught and served as principal at Glendale Elementary School for 42 1/2 years retiring in 1976.

All three brothers graduated from Clinton High School where they played football. Chris attended Indiana University, married Catherine Basso, and owned a tavern in Terre Haute. He died in 1961.

Dan went to Bradley University to study watchmaking. He married Josephine Masarachia in 1931.

Walter graduated from Ball State University where he played football and baseball. He taught school in Pontiac, MI and Michigan City, IN, where he now makes his home with his wife, Shirley. They have two daughters, Sue Ann and Lisa, who are also teachers.

DAN H. PESAVENTON AND JOSEPHINE PESAVENTO, Dan Pesavento, born on Sept. 5, 1905 to Chris and Gisella Brotto Pesavento, attended Columbia, Glendale and Clinton High School where he played football all four years of his high school years. He graduated in 1924 and went to Bradley University to study watchmaking.

Josephine, born Apr. 26, 1907 to Saverio and Marghurita Comiani Masarachia also went to schools in Clinton. She grew up at 524 N. Eighth Street only a half block away from Dan. They were married on Nov. 1, 1931 and have one daughter, Marguerite.

The couple lived in Brazil for a short time and then returned to Clinton to make their home at 457 N. Eighth Street. After working in Terre Haute for 15 years, Dan and Josephine opened a jewelry store at 136 S. Main Street and operated it for five years. In the spring of 1951, they purchased a building at 145 S. Main. After doing some remodeling, the store was opened on Aug. 1, 1951 and they remained in the business until retiring in 1979.

RALPH B. PEVERLY AND CATHRYN H. PEVERLY, were married in 1936 at Pontiac, IL, lived at Decatur, IL, two years, and in 1938

moved to a farm in Highland Township, Vermillion Co., IN, which was owned by her parents, John and Coral Johnson Hughes. The land was originally owned by the Gouty Family dating back to the 1830's. Cathryn's great-grandmother, Catherine Gouty, (who lived to be 90 some years old) passed parts of the land to her heirs. Cathryn Peverly lived on this farm until she was seven, but grew up in Illinois.

Ralph and Cathryn Peverly

Cathryn and Ralph met at the University of Illinois in 1933. Ralph graduated in 1934 and Cathryn in 1936. After moving to Indiana, they farmed for 20 years, raising four children: Patricia Despain is living in Kansas, Martha Berckmueller lives in Ohio, John lives in New York, and the youngest, Jane Brown, lives in Danville, IL.

For economic reasons Cathryn taught school (Home Economics) from 1956-1973. She was at Perrysville High School eight years and at North Vermillion High School for nine years. She earned her masters in Education at Indiana State at Terre Haute, IN, in 1964.

Ralph was raised on a farm near Decatur, IL, attending Decatur High School. He had to quit farming for health reasons. He went back to the University of Illinois to secure a teaching certificate at age 50. He then taught school (Agriculture) at Chrisman High School for two years, followed by 12 years working as a Manual Arts Therapist at the Veterans Administration in Danville, IL.

After retirement, both have concentrated on visiting children and families, and working in activities in the community. These are Farm Bureau, Collett Home Board, Hicks Cemetery Board, and as a volunteer at the green house at the Veterans Administration for Ralph. At home he raises a large garden and truck patch, cares for fruit from apple, cherry, and other fruit trees, plus caring for four acres of poplar, oak, pine, and maple trees which he planted in 1975. He also enjoys taking produce to Farmers' Market in Danville, IL, each summer.

Cathryn has done volunteer work at the former St. Elizabeth Hospital in Danville, completing her 14th year in 1988. Other activities include work with United Methodist Women and as organist of the Perrysville United Methodist Church. She is active on the Vermillion County Library Board, and is the professional teachers' Parke and Vermillion County group of Delta Kappa Gamma.

Both Cathryn and Ralph enjoy babysitting with grandchildren in Ohio and with the one grandson in Danville, IL. They also enjoy the growth and development of all nine grandchildren (seven grandsons and two granddaughters) ages seven thru 25. There are four step-grandchildren: one girl and three boys. Two have graduated from college, two have enrolled in college, and two more have enrolled to start in the fall of 1988.

They are still on the farm that they came to 50 years ago this spring an are hoping for several more years of enjoyment at the same spot in Indiana.

VARDAMAN AND MARIAN PIERCE, On Aug. 17, 1958, Mr. and Mrs. Vardaman (Marion) Pierce and children, Patricia Ann and Vardaman Jr., moved from Danville to 602 W. Curtis, Cayuga, IN, formally the home of the late Mr. and Mrs. Charles Hosford. The home was built in the late 1890's or early 1900's and now Mr. and Mrs. Pierce have completely remodeled the two story house and added a garage.

The Vardaman Pierce Family. Front - Harmonie Pierce, Jessica Pierce, Jennifer Robertson. Middle - Rosemary Pierce, Marian Pierce, Patricia Robertson. Back - Vardaman Pierce, Jr., Vardaman Pierce, Sr., Steve Robertson

Mrs. Pierce served in WWII and worked at General Motors Plant in Danville for 38 years. He has been retired since 1986.

Patricia married Steven Robertson. They were married in her parents house by the same person who married her parents 26 years before in Covington. They have a daughter named Jennifer Irene who is a Sophomore at North Vermillion High School. They reside at 108 Thompson, Cayuga, IN.

Vardaman Jr. married Rosemary Walker. They have two daughters, Jessica Rose and Harmonie Nicole. Jessica, a second grader, and Harmonie, a kindergartener, both attended Cayuga Grade School. Harmonie shares her birthday with her mother, Rosemary, and her grandmother, Marian. It is on the 12th of September. Vardaman and family reside at R.R. 1 Cayuga, IN.

Thirty years ago when the Pierces saw the old horse they fell in love with it and have lived there ever since.

DR. GENE DAVID PHILLIPS, A notable educator is Gene David Phillips who graduated from Dana High School in 1941. After graduation he attended Indiana State University for one year, then Butler University where he received his B.S. degree. He then entered the Navy and taught English, shorthand, and typing. During this time he wrote his first book which was about shorthand. After the war, he came back to Butler University to attain a Master's degree. He was married during his year at Butler and both he and his wife went to England as exchange teachers for one year. During this time David studied at Oxford.

After this he was the youngest man to receive his Doctorate Degree from Indiana University. Since that time he has taught at Arizona State University, Bethany College, and Boston University. At Boston University, he was Chairman of the Philosophy of Education Department and has sponsored students on Around the World trips. After seven years in the university, he received a sabbatical leave to be a Visiting Professor at London University.

He taught at Boston University for 20 years

before coming back to Indiana to become the Head of the Education Department at the Indiana-Purdue University in Fort Wayne.

THOMAS PHILLO PINSON (AUG. 31, 1838-JULY 20, 1926) AND DIREXA SHEW PINSON (OCT. 9, 1846-APRIL 1940), Thomas P. Pinson resided on Section 3, Clinton Township. He was born in Edgar Co., IL, Aug. 31, 1838, a son of Allen (Apr. 4, 1813-Dec. 1845) and Margaret (Noblitt) Pinson (June 14, 1812-Feb. 18, 1893). His parents were born in the state of Virginia, reared in Kentucky and married in Illinois. In 1841 they settled in Vermillion Co., IN. To them were born six children as follows - Sarah E. Bumgardner, Thomas P., Jeremiah, David C., Andrew Jackson and Martha Ann Shew. The father was a liberal, progressive man, and while in moderate circumstances did much toward aiding his children. He was particularly interested in the advancement of the cause of education, and gave a schoolhouse site to his neighborhood. He was a consistent member of the Christian Church. He died in 1845 at the early age of 33 years. Twenty-five years after his death, Mrs. Pinson married J. D. Bozarth. Three sons, Jeremiah, David and Andrew were soldiers in the war of the Rebellion.

Irene Hedges Shew, Direxa Shew Pinson, Permelia Alden Hedges, Edna M. Haskell, Ora Haskell

Thomas P. Pinson was reared to the vocation of a farmer. He was married on Apr. 13, 1862 to Direxa Shew, daughter of the pioneer Henry Shew. They commenced housekeeping on the homestead, and resided there with the exception of 1863-1864 when they lived on the homestead of Mrs. Pinson's parents. They bought out the interest of the other heirs in the Pinson homestead, which consisted of 198 acres of choice land. In connection with farming, Mr. Pinson did a little mercantile trade. Mr. and Mrs. Pinson are the parents of four children - Ora E. Haskell, Henry S., Margaret Irene Elder, and Elva G. Clark. Thomas was a member of the Christian Church and the National Reform Party.

A family picture represents five generations of the Pinson family. The picture includes Direxa Shew Pinson; Direxa's grandmother, Permelia Alden Hedges (Sept. 25, 1804 - June 18, 1889); Direxa's mother, Irene Hedges Shew (Dec. 3. 1823-); and Direxa's granddaughter, Edna M. Haskell (Fitzsimmons). It is interesting that Direxa's ancestors arrived in this country aboard the Mayflower. Her ancestors are John Alden and Priscilla Mullin Alden. *Submitted by Dorothy Elder, source: Vermillion County History - 1888 (in addition to family information)*

PORTER FAMILY OF EUGENE TWSP., are descendants of John R. Porter. He was born in Massachusetts in 1796, graduated from law school and came west in 1819. He settled in Paoli where he practiced law, became postmaster in 1822, and was appointed circuit judge in 1825. As circuit judge he traveled from Lafayette to Paoli by horseback in order to hold court in the various settlements. That same year he married Mary Worth whom he had known in Paoli before she moved to this area with her family.

Porter Homestead

Judge Porter received a land grant from the Government for approximately 1400 acres located west of the Wabash River. He built a log cabin on the hill overlooking the Wabash bottoms near where the Porter Homestead now stands in Portertown. In 1833 the jurisdiction was reduced to a more reasonable limit and in 1837 he was elected judge of Vermillion and Parke County District and remained in that position until his death in 1853.

John R. and Mary Worth Porter raised four children: John W., Isaac, Abigal and Charles Dewey. Orpha Davidson of Henderson Chapel neighborhood is a descendant of Abigal Porter who was married to Dr. David Davidson.

John W. Porter and his wife Hettie Tipton raised seven children. He built the Porter home in 1861. Two of the seven children lived in Eugene Twsp. and their families are listed below.

John C. 1867-1952 m. 1889 to Alice Woodard; Fred 1906-1986 m. 1930 to Mary Dolian; Conrad m. to Marilyn Randolph - El Paso, IL; John - deceased.

Worth W. 1857-1914 m. 1879 to Louisa Campbell;

Jessie 1881-1977 m. to Fred Nelson.

Jennie 1883-1946 m. to Lee Shirk.

Clarence 1886-1944 m. to Inez Falkner.

Kyle 1888-1955 m. to Lucy Morris: 1) Thelma - deceased; 2) James m. to Dorothy Grubbs - Cayuga: Diane Wittenauer - Terre Haute, Phillip Porter - Lafayette; 3) Harry m. to Goldie Brazeal - Cayuga: Sandra Stark - Palm Springs, FL, Carolyn Porter - U.S. Air Force; 4) Betty Parent - deceased: Porter B. Parent - Deceased, Joe Parent - Kokomo.

John 1890-1943 m. to Murrell O'Donnell: Malcolm - Deceased.

Lee 1895-1971 m. to Mabel Porter, m. to Hazel Applegate: 1) Dorothy Green Morgan - El Paso, TX: Randall Green - Shreveport, LA, Pamela Jameson - El Paso, TX; 2) Helen m. to Ottie Dye - Cayuga: Susan Hill - Greencastle, Ottie Joe Dye - Lake Charles, LA; 3) David m. to Virginia Conner - Dana: Russell Porter - Dana, Polly Porter - Dana.

In 1971 Ottie and Helen Dye began a restoration program on the Porter Homestead. The house is framed in black walnut timbers, cut from Walnut Groves located below the hill which were cleared for farming. Today the house stands on the original stone foundation and is still structurally sound after 127 years.

The original land grant acreage has dwindled to the present 150 acre farm. The Dyes were awarded a Hoosier Homestead Award in 1986 in recognition of ownership of the farm remaining in the same family for 100 years.

DEWEY ANA MABEL WILCOXEN PRATHER,

Dewey Prather, the youngest son of Isaac William and Hannah Shute Prather was born Mar. 12, 1898, in Rileysburg where he resided his entire life. He married Mabel Wilcoxen, who lived in the Butternut community, on Sept. 18, 1919. Mabel was born Sept. 18, 1894, the oldest daughter of John and Kate Gibson Wilcoxen of Vermillion Co., IL.

Dewey and Mabel lived in his grandfather's home south of Rileysburg for the first years of their married lives, where their daughter Pearl Prather Hicks was born. They then moved into the village itself across the road from his parents.

It was in this home their second daughter, Irma Lee Prather Crist was born. Dewey and Mabel shared this home the rest of their lives together. The doors to this warm and loving home were always open to their many relatives, friends, and neighbors. As years passed, it was often filled with the sounds of their grandchildren's voices raised in laughter and play.

Dewey was a successful farmer and businessman, opening an implement and farm supply store in Rileysburg in 1924 which he operated for 42 years before selling the business. He was also affiliated with the Rileysburg Grain Company for a number of years.

Mabel used her education from Eastern Illinois University and experience in teaching, at Butternut and other schools, while serving as a member of the Vermillion County Library Board. She was also active in The Rileysburg Ladies Aid and Jessamine Club until they disbanded. She was also a member of the Richard Henry Lee Chapter of the Daughters of The American Revolution.

Dewey and Mabel were active members of The Rileysburg Church, holding offices a number of years.

Dewey had the honor of receiving his 50 year pin from the Unity Masonic Lodge 334, where he had been a Master. He also was a member of the Order of Eastern Star Chapter 302. Other memberships were Zorah Shrine at Terre Haute, Crawfordsville Knight, Templar Commandry 25, Danville Scottish Rite, Crawfordsville Council 40 R&AM and Montgomery Council 34 R&FM. He also was a supportive member of the Perrysville Lions Club.

Mabel was also active in the Order of Eastern Star Chapter 302 where she received her 50 year pin and held several offices, including Worthy Matron.

After Dewey's death Feb. 3, 1970, Mabel continued in most of her activities, maintaining her own home for many years. Her busiest job during this time was staying abreast of their eight grandchildren and 13 great-grandchildren and their many activities.

Soon after her 90th birthday, Mabel made her home with her daughters until she passed away Dec. 13, 1986. She was buried beside Dewey in the Hopewell Cemetery.

FREDERICK PRATHER 1880-1955,

Frederick was born May 9, 1880, in Highland Township, the oldest child of Mahlon A. and Aurelia M. Shute Prather. He attended Rileysburg school through the eighth grade. On Mar. 22, 1905, he married Nellie L. Bennett, born in the township, and daughter of David and Canthey Milum Bennett.

Fred Prather, Nellie Bennett Prather, Aurelia Shute Prather, Mahlon Prather, and Arnold Prather

They set up housekeeping three quarter a mile south and one hale mile west of Rileysburg, just across the state line in Illinois. Their only child was born on Aug. 10, 1906. Arnold married Mary Clawson.

About 1925 the home that Jonathan Prather Jr. started his marriage in was removed, and Fred moved a two-story house that was on the Stutler farm to replace the old house. Fred farmed all his life, on the land three quarter mile south of Rileysburg. For a time he farmed land one mile south of Flatiron. Until his son took over the farming. Fred was a member of Unity Lodge No. 344 F.&A.M. of Perrysville. Fred and Nellie were both members of Chapter #302 Order of the Eastern Star. While on a winter vacation in Florida Nellie became ill and died on Jan. 19, 1948. Fred lived alone at the home place until about 1954. He became ill and moved in with his son Arnold and family. The following year in 1955 he passed from this life.

ISAAC WILLIAM AND HANNAH SHUTE PRATHER,

Isaac William Prather, the son of Jonathan Jr. and Nancy (Martin) Prather, was born on Aug. 7, 1852. On Mar. 4, 1875, he married Hannah Shute, daughter of Ephriam and Elzina (Goff) Shute, who was born Sept. 26, 1855.

Though many homes were located in the Rileysburg Community, Isaac and Hannah built the first house in the village itself. A small three room home was raised within the first months of their married life. The house was altered as necessary to accommodate their growing family of ten children, eight of whom survived to adulthood. A portion of their house is incorporated into the home of granddaughter, Irma Lee (Prather) Crist.

Isaac also built the first store in town, on the east side of the road and north of the railroad tracks. He was also the first station agent for the railroad after the station was promoted from its original flag station status. Isaac became the first postmaster, receiving the first mail in Rileysburg, Apr. 2, 1887.

Hannah was also a native of Highland Township. They were members of the Hopewell Baptist Church and later attended the Rileysburg Church, where Hannah served as a teacher for many years.

Isaac and Hannah had the rare distinction of sharing their 56 years of marriage in one home where they reared their children as youngsters and where some returned during their adult years. Their doors were always open to their children, grandchildren, relatives and friends.

When Hannah passed away Apr. 13, 1931, she was survived by Isaac and eight adult children. The oldest, Charles Edward, born Mar. 18, 1876, first married Agnes Carithers, who died in 1905. He then married Etta Nicholas, June 4, 1910. Their only daughter, Coral Inez, a retired teacher in Danville, survives. Charles died Nov. 23, 1957.

William Edgar, born July 19, 1878, was active in the community, serving as shopkeeper and postmaster. He passed away Apr. 28, 1950.

Nora Elzina was born Mar. 11, 1881. Nora survived both her husbands, Henry Arndt and William Frank Holder, before passing away Aug. 11, 1959. Her step-son Herman Holder survives.

Ephriam Albert, born Dec. 18, 1882, married Della Lewis, Oct. 16, 1909. They moved to California where his descendants, Delbert, Dorothy, Carl and Gladys remain. Albert died Sept. 23, 1959.

Clarence Archie was born June 6, 1887. He served in Co. A, 113 U. S. Engineers in WWI. He died Oct. 20, 1939.

Oral, born Mar. 26, 1889, served in Co. D, 315 Ammunition in Germany WWI. He married Minnie Keller, June 24, 1925. Oral died Feb. 26, 1932. Their daughter Doris survives.

Nancy Genevieve, born Oct. 14, 1892, married Vernon Marshall in May 19, 1918. They raised his son Austin and their children, Eileen, Vivian, and Marion in the Coal Branch area. She died May 15, 1974.

Dewey was born Mar. 12, 1898, and married Mabel Wilcoxen Sept. 18, 1919. Dewey passed away Feb. 3, 1970, and is survived by daughters, Pearl and Irma Lee.

Isaac passed away Aug. 8, 1934, after living his entire life in the Rileysburg area. Most of the family members are buried in Hopewell Cemetery.

JONATHAN PRATHER (1786-1869),

Jonathan Prather was born in Virginia, Mar. 22, 1786; wife Sarah 1784-1851. He was the son of James (1763-1819) and Eleanor (1766-1850). Jonathan came to Illinois from Bath Co., KY, but soon moved to Highland Township, Vermillion Co., IN. He bought 160 acres for $1.25 an acre from the government in 1834, located in Highland Township, east edge of Rileysburg. While he was visiting relatives in Kentucky, cholera was sweeping Vermillion County. Their son James died, and is buried in the family burial grounds east of Rileysburg near the homestead. Jonathan farmed a number of years and was a carpenter. He made the black walnut pews for the church on the Perrysville road. Their children were Mary Ann, James, Jeremiah, Uriah, William, Deborah, and Jonathan, Jr. Jeremiah, Uriah and William chose farm land in the area east of Rossville, Vermillion Co., IL; then only a stopping point in the Hubbard Trail which led to Chicago. Sisters Mary Ann Martin and Deborah Lafferty Rouse married and lived in both states. Jonathan Jr. married Nancy Martin, and purchased farm land near his father, being the only son to stay in Vermillion County.

JONATHAN PRATHER, JR. (1829-1872),

Jonathan Prather Jr. came with his family whose history is also in this book. He was born May 7, 1829, in Kentucky. He was married in Vermillion Co., IL, Mar. 5, 1851, to Nancy Martin - born in Kentucky, Oct. 29, 1824. Nancy's parents were Mahlon and Sarah Martin. Nancy and Jonathan lived three quarters of a mile south of Rileysburg, buying 105 acres in 1857.

Through the years of farming Jonathan bought additional land in Illinois and Indiana.

In their home were two walnut corner cupboards built by Jonathan's father; only one cupboard has survived.

Jonathan and Nancy's children were - Isaac William married Hanna Shute; Sarah Isdore married Frederick S. Gouty; Mahlon Albert married Aurelia Shute; Martha Ann married Jeremich Goff; Salinda Ellen married August Knoth; Joseph Franklin married Malissa Jane Rogers. Jonathan died Jan. 13, 1872; the year the railroad was built through Rileysburg. Nancy lived until May 22, 1907.

Salinda Ellen Prather Knoth, Mable Knoth Carithers, August Knoth. First house south of Rileysburg

Jennie Cunningham, Nancy's cousin, lived with them most of their lives, helping with their family. Jennie was born May 16, 1820, in Kentucky, daughter of James Cunningham. Nancy and Jennie lived together until her death, Mar. 9, 1903.

LAWRENCE AND DONNA PRATHER,

Lawrence (Rodney) Dale Prather was born one-half mile south of Rileysburg, on Jan. 12, 1931. His parents were Arnold and Mary (Clawson) Prather. In 1932, the family moved, one mile south of Flatiron, living there until he married. He attended all 12 years at Perrysville schools, graduating in 1949.

After graduating, he farmed and worked construction at the Newport Plant. In January, 1952, he was drafted into the Army, and after basic training in California, was sent to Germany for 16 months. After being honorably discharged, he went back to farming and a job with Hyster Company in Danville, IL.

In January, 1958, he joined the United States Postal Service in Danville. He transferred to the Perrysville Post Office as rural mail carrier, Apr. 1, 1963, and then in November, 1979, to Covington, IN, rural route two mail carrier, where he is to this day.

He became a member of the Masonic Order #344 in 1952. He is also a member of Gao Grotto, and Perrysville Lions Club. He served on the North Vermillion School Board from 1974 to 1986.

Lawrence married Donna Spezia on Mar. 30, 1957, at Perrysville Methodist Church. They started their marriage in the house where Lawrence was born, and where they are still living.

Donna Louise is the daughter of Camille and Anna (Thompson) Spezia, born Jan. 24, 1937, in Vermillion Co., IL. She lived in Westville, IL, and attended Saint Mary School until 1948. She lived in Highland Township until 1952, and then moved back to Vermillion Co., IL graduating from Bismarck High School in 1955. She worked in Danville until her marriage.

She has been a member of Red Mask Dramatic Players of Danville, Vermillion County Indiana Library Board, President of Perrysville Park Board, and Illiana Genealogial Society. She is now on the Board of the Collett Home for Children. In 1985, she became a volunteer for the Y.W.C.A. Women Shelter in Danville, and since March of 1987, has been employed there with the Sexual Assault Crisis Service.

Both are members of Vermillion County Historical Society, Perrysville Methodist Church, and Chapter #302 Order of the Eastern Star.

Their daughter Lisa Ann, born Apr. 28, 1958, married to Darrell Morgan, and their daughter Elizabeth Jane, born Feb. 22, 1981, all live east of Cayuga. Jonathan Arnold, their son, was born May 22, 1971, and now is a junior at North Vermillion High School.

Lisa and Jonathan are the sixth generation that has lived on the land that Jonathan Jr. bought in 1857.

MAHLON ALBERT PRATHER (1857-1927),

was born in Highland Township, July 15, 1857, son of Jonathan Jr. and Nancy (Martin) Prather. On Nov. 22, 1875, he married Aurelia M. Shute, daughter of Ephrain and Elzina (Goff) Shute, born Feb. 14, 1858, in Highland Township.

New Years Day 1899

Mahlon farmed all his life, building their home three-quarter mile south of Rileysburg. He was a member of Olive Branch Lodge No. 38 F. and A. M., Danville, IL.

Mahlon died while playing horseshoes at his home, Sept. 15, 1927. Aurelia lived in Rileysburg after Mahlon's death and died Mar. 16, 1929.

Their children were: Frederick, married Nellie J. Bennett; Elzina born Apr. 28, 1888, married William Eickleman; Roscoe born Mar. 25, 1896, married Gertrude Tuttle.

Mahlon and Aurelia were born, lived, worked, raised their family, and died in Highland Township, Vermillion County.

WILLIAM EDGAR PRATHER,

son of Isaac William and Hannah Shute Prather was born July 19, 1878 at Rileysburg. He was never married. He died Apr. 28, 1950, and was buried in Hopewell Cemetery.

He operated a general store in Rileysburg from 1900 until his death. He was postmaster and station agent for the C&EI Railroad for many years. He was selected Trustee of Highland Township from 1927 to 1935. He was devoted to improving the schools and enjoyed going to basketball games.

He was a member of the Perrysville Lions Club, Unity Lodge F&AM, Covington Royal Arch Chapter and Council, Crawfordsville Commandery and Knights Templar. He had received the honorary degree of superexcellent master.

JAMES PROCARIONE AND PATRICIA THEISZ PROCARIONE,

Jim was born on June 15, 1925 in Klondyke, IN, the son of Domenick Procarione (1900-1966) and Julia Vargo Procarione (1909-1986). He grew up in this area where he graduated from Clinton High School in 1943.

He served in Europe with the United States Army from August 1943 until January 1946.

Jim and Pat Procarione

On Aug. 30, 1947, he married Patricia Theisz, daughter of Frank Theisz (1896-1970) and Violet Rhoads Theisz (1900-1977).

Pat was born on Feb. 8, 1927 in Clinton and graduated from Clinton High School in 1944.

Pat was employed as a secretary at Quaker Maid from July 1944 until August 1945. She was then employed as a secretary-bookkeeper in the offices of District #11, United Mine Workers of America from September 1945 until October 1962.

Jim was employed by local area businesses during the period from 1946 to 1958.

After attending Terre Haute Business College, he worked as a bookkeeper for Smith-Alsop Paint Co. (now MAB) in Terre Haute from 1959 until 1962. He then began working as a bookkeeper for District #11, United Mine Workers of America in 1962 and retired as an International Representative in 1976 due to ill health.

They are the parents of Jamie Procarione Thompson (Mrs. Cliff) of Indianapolis and Jill Procarione Uselman (Mrs. Phil) of Klondyke. They have one granddaughter, Holly Ann Uselman.

They are members of the United Presbyterian Church of Clinton where Pat now serves as church secretary.

EUGENE MAXWELL RAY AND ETTA WANETA VEARO RAY, Eugene Maxwell Ray was born May 13, 1926, in St. Bernice, IN, the only child of the late Burlin M. Ray and the late Mabel E. Frazier Ray. Eugene grew up in St. Bernice, graduating from St. Bernice High School in 1944. Upon graduation, he went to work for the Milwaukee Railroad Car Repair Shops at West Clinton Shop. On shop closing, he transferred to Terre Haute Milwaukee Shops. Then he went to the C&EI Car Shops at Danville, IL, after marrying Etta Waneta Vearo, May 21, 1954.

Front: Christopher Ray, Jenna Ray, Shannon Ray. Back: David Palmer, Eugene Ray, Etta Waneta Ray

Etta Waneta was the daughter of the late John B. Vearo, born in Italy, and Violet Marie Elliott Vearo of Indianapolis. Etta Waneta was born in the Ver-

million County Hospital and raised in the Hazel Bluff Area in Clinton. She attended Crompton Hill School graduating from Clinton High School in 1953. During school years, Etta Waneta worked for Wilson Insurance Company—Freida Wilson—part time. After graduation, Etta Waneta worked for the Daily Clintonian as a part of the bookkeeping department and still worked part-time evenings for Wilson Insurance.

The couple lived in St. Bernice. After the birth of a son, Eugene Maxwell Ray, Jr., Aug. 22, 1955, Etta Waneta became a homemaker. Then on Mar. 28, 1957, a son, Steven Duane Ray, was born. On Apr. 13, 1965, Keith Allen Ray was born. On Apr. 14, 1965, Keith Allen died. After leaving the Danville Shops, Eugene went to work at the Newport Army Ammunition Plant, Newport, IN. On the Newport Ammunition Site, Eugene has worked for F.M.C., DuPont, Uniroyal, and now Mason Hanger, as Maintenance Mechanic in the I and E Department.

In September, 1965, Etta Waneta worked for Van Duyn School. In January, 1967, she went to work for the Vermillion County Auditor's office. Having worked under three Auditors with State Board of Accounts Schooling, she became a candidate and was elected Auditor in 1980. She again was elected in 1984 and is now completing her second term. Etta Waneta will become Clerk of the Vermillion Circuit Court, Jan. 1, 1989.

They are members of the First Baptist Church, St. Bernice. Eugene is a member of Asbury Lodge F&AM #320; Scottish Rite Valley of Terre Haute; St. Bernice Water Corporation Board; St. Bernice Volunteer Fire Department; Vermillion County Park Board; Half Century Club; Clinton Moose Lodge; Local #157 Pipe Fitters; Clinton Oddfellows Lodge.

Etta Waneta is a member of the Auditor's Association of Indiana counties and also Vice President, Auditor's Association; The Vermillion County Democrat Women's Club; VFW Auxiliary #6653; American Legion Auxiliary, St. Bernice Osborn Post #108; Clinton Moose Lodge; Columbian Rebekah Lodge, St. Bernice #425; Blanford Royal Neighbors. Both Eugene and Etta Waneta are active in community and county affairs.

Eugene M. Ray, Jr., is a graduate of South Vermillion High School, Clinton, IN, and a graduate of Rose Hulman University, Terre Haute. He married Deborah Sanderock, Rosedale, IN. They have two children, Christopher Evan and Shannon Marie. They live at Griffith, IN.

Steven Duane Ray is a graduate of South Vermillion High School, Clinton, IN, and a graduate of Depauw University, Greencastle, IN. He is married to Karen Grossman Palmer of Mount Vernon, IN. They have two children, David Palmer and Jenna Lynn Ray, all living in Terre Haute, IN.

THE WILLIAM DEAN RAY FAMILY, William Dean Ray was born Sept. 28, 1944, the third child of four born to Herman and Lucille Ray. William is a native of Johnson City, IL and married his wife, Hazel Jewel, in Joliet, IL in May 10, 1974. Hazel, the second of three children, was born on Apr. 23, 1942 in Luxora, AR to Homer and Ruby Durham. The Durhams moved to Rosedale, IN in 1967 and were employed by the Glenn Children's Home.

The Clinton Laboratory of Eli Lilly and Company employed William in April, 1979 for their maintenance department; therefore, the Rays moved to the Wabash Valley. William and Hazel

and three of five children have resided in 534 Mulberry, Clinton, IN since July, 1979.

The William D. Ray family. Seated - Becky, Jewel, William. Standing - Cindy, Kathy, Pete, Sherry

Katherine Laquitia Christensen, their eldest daughter, was born in the Vermillion County Hospital on Aug. 19, 1958, and now lives in Coal City, IL with her husband, Dale, and son Joseph Michael. Katherine attends the Joliet Junior College in Joliet, IL. Her education goals are in computer programming and writing.

Sherri Lynn Cox was born in Union Hospital of Terre Haute, IN on May 20, 1961, and now lives in Clinton with her two children, Tiffany Michelle and John Charles Jr. Sherri attends the Indiana Vocational Technical College (IVY Tech) in the Industrial Laboratory Technology program and is a member of the Student Government Association there.

Cynthia Ann Thomas was born in Saint Anthony's Hospital (presently called Regional Hospital) on May 30, 1964. She is a 1982 graduate of South Vermillion High School and in February, 1988, had completed the Licensed Practical Nursing program at IVY Tech and was the secretary-treasurer of her class. Cynthia, her husband Russel, and their daughter Katherine Nicole, reside in West Terre Haute, IN. Cynthia has been employed at the Meadows Manor East Skilled Nursing Facility in Terre Haute, IN since March 1988.

Nelson Eugene Morris, Jr. was born in Vermillion County Hospital on Apr. 29, 1968. Nelson, who is single, resides and is employed in Indianapolis as a baker.

Rebekah Ruth Ray was born in Morris Hospital in Morris, IL on May 1, 1976. She attends Central Elementary School where she is active in cheerleading, basketball, band, and yearly spelling contests. Rebekah is an art student of Rebecca Graham's, also of Clinton.

JACOB REED AND ELIZABETH SCHMITT (SMITH) REED, German descendants, came in 1831-32 to Vermillion Co., IN, from Stokes Co., NC.

They traveled with team, camping wherever night overtook them, cooking by the wayside, and sleeping in their wagons.

They settled in a wilderness tract of government land. (Descendants of this family still have the sheepskin deed signed by President Andrew Jackson). On this land they built a log cabin and log barn, opened up a farm, and spent the remainder of their lives. The log barn was later sold and reconstructed at Fowler Park at Terre Haute, IN.

Their children were Mary Elizabeth Miller (1816-1888); Michael Franklin (1818-1864); Andrew Wray (1820); John Washington (1822-1865); David Abraham (1824-1908); Nancy M. Wishard; and Jacob Lewis Reed (1826).

Descendants of this family still reside in Vermillion Co., IN. *Submitted by Ernestine Crane Brown*

AUSTIN EUGENE REED AND MARTHA PECK REED,

Austin Eugene Reed was born Oct. 1, 1919, in Helt Township, IN, the son of Ernest Edward Reed and Gertrude Patton Reed, the third of six children.

The Reed family are descendants of King Frederick II of Prussia being well documented by entries in an old family Bible dating back to 1753. Briefly, in the spring of 1814, Jacob Reed, who was the son of a Prussian nobleman, married Elizabeth Schmitt, the daughter of Andrew Wray Schmitt and Elizabeth Hohenzollern of the House of Hohenzollern and the daughter of King Frederick William II, who reigned over Prussia from 1786 until 1797. Jacob and Elizabeth Reed came to America in the fall of 1814 and settled in Stokes Co., NC. They moved to the area of what is now St. Bernice, IN, in 1833 with their six children. Their fourth child was John Washington Reed, father of James Smith Reed, Austin's paternal grandfather. Farming was the principal occupation of the new settlers. However, they later opened small business places. The cemetery at Sugar Grove Church west of St. Bernice bears the family name.

Austin graduated from Clinton High School in 1933 after which he engaged in various occupations including mining and trucking. On Nov. 24, 1936, he married Martha Peck, daughter of Claude E. and Bessie Barton Peck and the fourth of six children. Martha was born in Fairview Park, IN, Dec. 24, 1918, and attended school there before moving to Paris IN, in 1932, where she graduated from Paris High School in 1936. She was employed in the law office of J. Lee Sullivan. During World War II she worked at Chicago Title & Trust Co. in Chicago, and was last employed in the Medical Records Department of Vermillion County Hospital. Austin served in the United States Navy during the war years, and upon discharge was employed again in mining until he became engaged in the piping industry from which he retired in 1972.

Austin and Martha are the parents of a son, Richard Allen, born in 1947, and a daughter, Peggy Jean, born in 1954.

They are members of the First United Methodist Church in Clinton. Austin is a member of Jerusalem Lodge #99, Scottish Rite Valley of Terre Haute, Zorah Shrine of Terre Haute, Parke-Vermillion Low-12 Club and the American Legion Post 140 of Clinton.

FRANK AND NELLIE JACKSON REED,

Frank Reed was born Sept. 4, 1886, and died Jan. 7, 1957. He was a coal miner who worked at Binkley Mine southeast of Jacksonville. He also did some farming. He lived in Jacksonville, IN.

His father was William H. Reed, son of Andrew Wray Reed, son of Jacob Reed (Reid), son of John Reid. Jacob Reed didn't like Germany so he changed the spelling of Reid to Reed. Jacob Reed's wife was Elizabeth Schmitt Reed. Her ancestry can be traced back to Frederick II and Frederick William II of Germany. His mother was Mary Farris Reed.

He had five brothers—Jacob, Lewis, Ora, Lawrence (Lon), and William. He had three sisters—Iva Flint, Mae, and Esther Robertson.

He married Nellie Jackson (Dec. 23, 1887 - Dec. 18, 1958) of Jacksonville. Her parents were Thomas Jackson (Jan. 24, 1859 - Jan. 23, 1936) and Emma Roberts Jackson (Nov. 17, 1864 - July 11, 1947). She had one sister, Pauline Holt.

Frank and Nellie Reed

They are the parents of four children. Mildred Wright of Marshall, IN, was born Jan. 8, 1912. Paul Reed was born June 25, 1913 and died June, 1939. Blanche Beard Petker was born Mar. 2, 1915 and lives in Bradenton, FL. Harold Reed was born Nov. 4, 1917 and lives near Clinton, IN.

There are four grandchildren—Evelyn Wright Hixon, of Clinton; Jerry Wright of Marshall, IN; Larry Beard of Indianapolis; and Sandra Reed Gill of Hillsdale, IN.

They are buried at Walnut Grove Cemetery, Clinton, IN.

JOHN HARVEY REED,

was born July 5, 1923 in Easytown, a small community located in southwestern Vermillion County.

His parents were Harry Henry Reed and Fawn Lucy Willis Reed. His father was a private in the army during World War I, and he was wounded in the Argon Woods.

Charley Willis and Lucy Ike Willis were his maternal grandparents who lived west of Clinton on what was known as Willis Hill. Mr. Willis was a farmer.

His paternal grandparents were Austin Reed and Nettie Stafford Reed. His grandfather was a coal miner and claimed heritage with the Plains Indians that were in western Vermillion County.

John H. Reed

John was raised in Bickett Two and Universal (Bunsen). They were mining towns west of Clinton. He was second oldest of five children. His brother Marshall preceeded him in death in an automobile accident when he was only 21. His brother Harry Eugene "Bink" and sister Alice Wilma Cox reside in Parke County. His younger sister lived only a few hours after her birth.

In the mid 1940's he was in business in the City Service Station at 9th and Vine Street which has since been torn down and is the site of Central School.

July 24, 1948, he married Doris Jean Groves Flowers from Vigo County. They lived in Clinton where they raised their four daughters Sue Ann Massa, Virginia Lee "Ginger" Corado, Carol Jean Sanquenetti, Patti Elaine Jakowczyk, and son John Clayton.

He had eight grandsons: Charles DeJon Corado, Michael Scott and Matthew Jon Massa, Leonard II and Clate Sanquenetti. Ryan Justis and Eric Clayton Jakowczyk, and John Clayton Reed II. Also, five granddaughters: Tami Sue Corado, Aimee Lynn Minnett, Bonnie Jean Sanquenetti, Jennifer Leigh, and Brooke Aron Reed.

He was a member of the Clinton First Baptist Church, F & AM 99 Jerusalem Lodge, Scottish Rite Valley of Terre Haute, and was a 30 year member of Local 157 Plumbers and Steamfitters.

He retired in 1983 due to a visual impairment and a heart condition.

He passed away June 14, 1987 and was laid to rest in Walnut Grove Cemetery north of Clinton.

JOSEPH WESLEY REEDER,

was one of the very few Civil War veterans left in Clinton Twp., at the time of his passing at his home in Clinton, Tuesday, Dec. 29, 1931. He was born Aug. 26, 1845, making his age at death 86 years, four months, and three days.

His grandfather, Joseph Reeder, came to this county from Pennsylvania in 1822, and settled on the Reeder homestead abut two miles southwest of Clinton.

Joseph Wesley Reeder

Joseph's father, Nelson, was a native of Ohio, born Jan. 10, 1816. At the time of his death in 1880, he left an estate of 600 acres.

Joseph always lived on the homestead where he was born with the exception of the time spent in the Civil War. He was member of Co. A. 71st Indiana Infantry. He later became a member of the Sixth Indiana Cavalry.

On Nov. 27, 1867, he married Miss Elizabeth Ann Smith, daughter of Joseph Smith, who was born in West Virginia, July 4, 1848, but came to Vermillion County with her parents at the age of seven. Joseph and Elizabeth were the parents of five children: Mrs. Milo Watt, Mrs. Guy II Briggs, Mrs. Dana Wright, Van Valzah and J. Nelson Reeder.

He was a member of the Methodist Church, Odd Fellows Lodge of Clinton, and also a member of the Grand Army of the Republic. He is buried in Riverside Cemetery. *Submitted by Leo Reposh, Jr.*

MYRL C. AND LUELLA REIDELBERGER FAMILY,

Myrl was born on Mar. 18, 1914, in St. Louis, MO, to Henry James and Josephine Reidelberger.

Luella was born on Mar. 6, 1918, to Harry and Doral Phipps Newkirk at Shepardsville, IN. Harry was a coal miner and farmer and was killed in a mine accident in 1920.

In 1937, Luella moved to Decatur, IL, with a Western-Southern Insurance man and his family to help his wife with the care of the home and children. She wore a uniform while working in their home as was customary in those days. She attended Sunday School at the Tabernacle Baptist Church, thereby meeting Myrl. He worked at a roller skating rink and they enjoyed skating together.

They were married on Nov. 6, 1940, at the church and resided in Decatur for awhile. They then moved to the housing project at Illiopolis and Myrl worked at the War Plant as a guard.

Their three oldest daughters, Shirley Esther (Oct. 28, 1941); Lorraine Luella (May 14, 1943); and Mary Alice (Aug. 12, 1946) were all born while they lived in Illinois.

In October, 1946, the family moved to Clinton, IN, on River Road (now known as South Main Street Road) into the house her mother had built after the death of Luella's father.

Myrl worked as a dry cleaner awhile at Model Cleaners in Clinton and later at Compton's Cleaners in Terre Haute from which he retired in 1987.

They had another daughter on May 8, 1950, and named her Lana Louise. The children rode the school bus to Crompton Hill School and then to Clinton High School where they all were graduated.

Shirley was married to Peter Bendza (who died) and then married Jim Simmons. She has two sons and they presently live at Plant City, FL.

Lorraine married John Robinson of Clinton. She has a son and daughter and presently lives at Chesterton, IN.

Mary Alice and her husband, Jerry Anderson, had one son. She and her present husband, Rich Austin, have one son and live at Gary, IN.

Lana married Larry Nusbaumer and they live in Indianapolis with their daughter and son.

Luella and Myrl have both been active in their church, the First Baptist Church, of Clinton, since moving to Clinton more than 40 years ago. Their religious faith is helping them cope with the fact that they both have been diagnosed as having bone cancer.

ROBERT AND DOROTHY REN-NAKER,

Robert Charles Rennaker was born Oct. 31, 1919 in Danville, Vermillion Co., IL, the son of Robert Lee and Mary Hester (Brindley) Rennaker. He was the next to the youngest of seven children. Growing up in Danville, Perrysville and Covington, IN, he graduated from Bismarck High School in 1939. He joined the Navy in the fall of that same year serving six years and two months. During the second World War he served in both the Atlantic and Pacific fleet aboard the U.S.S. Savannah, a light cruiser. During the invasion of Sicily in September, 1943, the ship was hit by a radio controlled aerial bomb, the first such bomb to hit a U.S. War ship. It hit turrett III and the shell went through 18 inches of solid steel, causing severe casualties with 206 dead and 13 wounded. Bob has a fragment of this bomb at his home. After the battle of Salerno, the Savannah was able to proceed to the British Island of Malta for some repairs and then returned to the United States in December of 1943 where Bob was assigned to shore duty.

He was married to Dorothy Lucille Martin, daughter of Earl Grant and Lily Marie (Brown) Martin July 8, 1944, in Danville, IL. She was born Nov. 23, 1925 in Danville. Graduating from Bis-

marck High School in 1943 she became a telephone operator at Illinois Bell. They lived in Newport, RI where Bob was stationed and later transferred to Portland, ME. While in Portland twin sons, Thomas Gene and Richard Karl were born Sept. 4, 1945, just a few days after the war ended. He was medically discharged from the service January, 1946, and they returned to Danville, where he immediately found work at the Veterans Administration Hospital. Another son, Michael Wayne was born to them Oct. 3, 1947. Bob served as a nurses aid, housekeeping supervisor, and later went into management. They moved to Covington, IN where Bob had spent some childhood years along the Wabash river. He was an avid fisherman and taught his children to fish and enjoy the outdoors. They had a daughter, Cindy Marie born Mar. 15, 1962.

Robert and Dorothy Rennaker

After gong into management at the V.A. Bob transferred to Louisville, KY as Laundry Manager in May 1968. He served in this capacity and took part in the consolidation of the Lexington and Louisville laundries there. Returning to their home in Covington and the V.A. in Danville, he retired from there on disability in April of 1975.

Bob was very active with the Boy Scouts for several years, served in P.T.A. work and also served as president of the School board for South Mount Pleasant School in Danville prior to moving to Covington. The family is grown, but Bob and his wife still live in the home they built along the Wabash River in Highland township, Vermillion Co., IN.

THOMAS G. RENNAKER,

was born Sept. 4, 1945, in Portland, ME, the son of Robert C. and Dorothy L. Martin Rennaker. He is the eldest of four children. Tom attended South Mount Pleasant school until the fourth grade and then Vance Lane school in Danville, IL, until 1958. Then he and his family moved to Covington, R#2, along the Wabash River, about three miles northeast of Perrysville.

Tom helped his father build their family's new home. He ran track in high school and broke all the school records for Perrysville. He graduated from Perrysville High School in 1963. That fall he attended Danville Junior College for a year studying botany and zoology.

November, 1965, Tom was employed by Hyster Company in Danville, IL. He also joined the Army National Reserves that month.

November, 1966, he married Sandra J. Hawn, eldest daughter of Forrest W. and Estelle M. Cary Hawn of Dana, IN. Sandra graduated from Newport High School in 1964 and was employed by the General Electric Company in Danville, IL.

February, 1967, Tom was called for active duty by the Reserves and served six months at Fort Knox, KY.

Tom and Sandra resided outside Perrysville until August, 1968, when they purchased a home in Silverwood, IN, and remodeled it.

In 1972, they became parents of a daughter, Molly Corene. October, 1974, they sold the property in Silverwood and some 31 acres they also owned near Dana, and purchased a place three miles north of Perrysville on old Road 63. There they started plans for their new home.

February 13, 1976, they became parents of a son, Wade Ashley.

In 1977, Tom and Sandra started the construction of their new home built of stone and cedar. It was designed and built by them and completed in 1979. From the home you can view Spring Creek.

Tom and Sandra are members of the Church of the Nazarene in Covington. They enjoy hunting Indian artifacts and ornithology. *Submitted by Tom and Sandy Rennaker*

LEO REPOSH, SR. AND ETHEL JACKSON REPOSH,

Leo Reposh, Sr. was born June 30, 1908, in Hohenhausen, West Germany, one of eight children of Frank and Francesca Reposh. The family had originally come from Ljubjana, Slovenia, Yugoslovia. In 1911, the family joined Mrs. Reposh's parents, Martin and Theresa Mohar, who had established residence at 13th Street and Brier Hill, Clinton. Mohars raised grapes, made wine, maintained dairy cattle, operated a small coal mine, and rented out dwellings on their property. Frank Reposh was a coal miner and later a carpenter. Leo Reposh, now retired, worked at the railroad roundhouse at St. Bernice and later for Wabash Valley Asphalt Company, and lives at Route 3, Clinton. He attended school at Sacred Heart School, Glendale School, and Chicago Harrison Tech and is a member of the S.N.P.J. Lodge and the Labor and Hod Carriers Union.

Leo Reposh, Sr. and Ethel Jackson Reposh

Ethel Elnora Jackson Reposh is the wife of Leo Reposh, Sr. and the mother of Leo Reposh, Jr. She was born Mar. 5, 1923, in Clinton, IN, one of four daughters of John H. Jackson and Reba Elizabeth Paine Jackson. (picture of Reba in Galen Brown article) Ethel attended Columbia School, Central School, Glendale School, and Fairview School, and graduated from Clinton High School in 1941. Her great-great-grandfather, David Jackson, was born in Dublin, Ireland, before 1800, and immigrated to North Carolina. The next generation, Samual David Jackson and Martha Alice Albright Jackson moved to Clay Co., IN, and the next, Nathan Robert Jackson and Martha Alice Craig Jackson moved to Parke County where John H. Jackson was born and then to Vermillion County. John H. Jackson was a 32nd degree Mason.

John Paine and John Wright both came to the Clinton area from New York in 1820. John Wright's family has been traced back to the 1400's in Essex County, England, in a book by Esther J. Wright Searcy. (see related article—Ulysses Grant Wright) The family came to America about 1626. In 1839, John Paine married Charlotte Bright, sister-in-law of Benjamin Harrison. (see related article—Madeline Harrison Watson) Her father, John Bright, had come from Germany and had served a long stretch in the Virginia militia in the American Revolution. On Jan. 22, 1845, their son, James Earl Paine was born at Main and Blackman in Clinton. John Wright, who was a farmer and investor, married Margaret Nichol. Among their six children was Narcissus Wright. After Margaret Nichol Wright died, John married Mary Chunn and produced eight more children.

In 1866, James Paine and Narcissus Wright were married. (see Nell Allen article for picture of this couple) Their children were Frank, Grace, Howard (see related article—Beryl Paine Cox), Fred (died at age 15), John R. (became mayor of Clinton in 1926), and Henry Washburn Paine. Henry Washburn Paine married Kizzie May Spainhower (see Charles Donald Paine article for picture of this couple). Henry and Kizzie were the parents of six children—Robert Burl, James Earl II, Nellie, Mary Eleanor, Charles Donald, and Reba Elizabeth (mother of Ethel Reposh).

Ethel is a member of the Parke County Camera Club and the Vermillion County Historical Society. *Submitted by Leo Reposh, Jr.*

LEO REPOSH, JR, was born May 2, 1942, the son of Leo and Ethel E. Jackson Reposh. He graduated from Fairview School in 1957, Clinton High School in 1961 Indiana State University in 1966, and Ivy Tech in 1986.

Leo Reposh, Jr. and Ethel Reposh

He is secretary of the Parke County Camera Club, and a director of the Vermillion County Historical Society, also a member of the Vermillion County Heritage Committee, and the Wabash Valley Archaeological Society. He is an amateur Indian anthropologist and collects Indian Kachina Dolls. He is single, a well-known amateur photographer, and is employed by Futurex Industries. Leo lives at Klondyke Heights (Clinton, R.3). *Submitted by Leo Reposh, Jr.*

RUDOLPH REPOSH, 1219 White Street, Clinton, IN, was born Jan. 30, 1912, in Clinton, IN, one of eight children of Frank and Francesca Reposh and grandson of Martin and Theresa Shuster Mohar who lived at 13th and Brier Hill, Clinton.

Rudolph, who lives at the established Reposh residence on White Street in Clinton, has a sister,

Angeline (Mrs. Ed) Shannon, two doors away, and a sister Mary (Mrs. Tom) O'Rourke of Bridgeview, IL. His three living brothers are Frank of Cicero, IL, Joseph of Lockport, IL, who owned the Mohar property on 13th Street, and Leo (see related story) of Klondyke (R. 3, Clinton). His brothers Louis, who contributed labor to several LIFT construction projects, and Anthony, who was a local janitor are deceased. Rudolph who is single has 21 nieces and nephews and several great nieces and nephews. He has an aunt Eugenia "Tilka" Klancesac Mohar in a local nursing home.

Martin Mohar, Jr., Theresa Mohar, Martin Mohar, Sr., Joe Pucell, and Antonia Mohar Pucell in front of the Mohar residence on the corner of 13th Street and Brier Hill in Clinton. Notice the sticks to support grapes at the top of the hill

His is a retired construction worker and a member of the Labor and Hod Carrier's Union and also a member of the SNPJ Lodge and the Sacred Heart Church. *Submitted by Leo Reposh Jr.*

EMERY RHODES AND MILLIE BILL WRIGHT RHODES, Millie Bill was the third daughter and fifth child of John and Rosa Wright.

Millie Bill Wright

She was born on Nov. 29, 1893, in Vermillion County, rural Clinton, IN. Millie Bill married Emery Rhodes. They had one son. Millie Bill moved to Portland, OR. She died in 1964 and is buried in Oregon. *Submitted by Edna Wright*

RILEY FAMILY, Edward Vance Riley was born on Jan. 10, 1889, in Edgar Co., IL, to John W. and Adeline Ruby Riley. They moved to Syndicate Hill when he was a young boy and he lived at that location until his death on Dec. 18, 1978.

Dora May Phipps Riley was born Aug. 11, 1891, to Reverend John W. and Anna Thomas Phipps southwest of Clinton about three miles. She was one of eight children who survived old enough to attended school. She married Harry Newkirk and had three children: Lowell Morris, deceased; Luella Rosamond (Reidleberger); and Harry Denman Newkirk. Their father, Harry, was killed in a mine accident.

Edward and Dora Riley

She then married an old childhood friend, Edward Vance Riley and they had five children: John William; Herman Virgle; Betty (Shortridge); Herschel Albert; and Mildred Delores (Wallace).

Dora died in her home on Nov. 28, 1988, after being bedfast for 13 years. *Submitted by Luella Reidleberger and Betty Shortridge*

DECATUR "DICK" ROBERTSON (1872-1959), was born Aug. 6, 1872, in Vermillion County, near the Trinity Church. Decatur was a farmer. On Sept. 24, 1896, he married Lottie Ellen Jackson, the only daughter of Levi and Susan Humphries Jackson who was born on June 30, 1878. Lottie and Decatur had five children: Daisy died in 1902 at one year of age, and Levi was born and died in 1903. They are both buried at Spangler. Elsie, (born July 25, 1897), married James Houston, (born Feb. 12, 1887), on July 25, 1917. They had six children, Nora Elizabeth, James Howard, Robert Dale, twins Carolyn Kay and Gloria Gail (who died at childbirth), and Jerry Jack. Elsie died Apr. 19, 1982 and James died Oct. 1, 1956. They are both buried at Helt's Prairie Cemetery.

Decatur "Dick" and Lottie Robertson and Donald and Josephine Robertson

Jessie Robertson married Gilbert B. Jackson Sr. on Sept. 9, 1931. They had one son Gilbert Jackson, Jr. Jessie died July, 1983, and Gilbert Sr. died July, 1982. They are both buried at Three Rivers, MI.

Donald Robertson was born Sept. 9, 1913, in his parents home on Coon Hollow Road, Clinton, IN. He grew up in the Syndicate area where he attended school. Donald was very well known in the Clinton area. During his lifetime he owned and operated a coal mine, Robertson Construction and Robertson Gravel until the time of his death on Apr. 19, 1983. Donald was a member of Local #841, Blanford Sportsman Club, United States Auto Club, where he was an active sponsor of a sprint car, and past president of the Clinton Township Water Board.

In 1934, he married Josephine Isabelle Groves, the only daughter born to William and Cecil Weaver Groves. Josephine had three brothers, Manford, Raymond and Robert. Josephine's father William was born Apr. 15, 1887 and her mother Cecil was born Apr. 2, 1896 in Green County. Cecil had three sisters, Rosie (Weaver) Vestal, Esther (Weaver) Jones, Ida Weaver and three brothers, Ora Weaver, Elza Weaver and Clovis Weaver.

William died June 14, 1954, and Cecil died Nov. 21, 1968. They are all buried at Roselawn. Decatur died Oct. 14, 1959 and Lottie died Mar. 31, 1963.

In 1935, Donald and Josephine became parents to son Donald Ray, who married Karen L. Puckett, and in 1938 to a daughter Geraldine "Jeri", who married Robert Hall.

They have three granddaughters, Tonya Lee Hall-Smith, Twyla Jo Hall-Coletti and Donnetta Rae Robertson-Domeika. They also have four great-granddaughters and two great-grandsons.

DONALD R. AND KAREN L. PUCKETT ROBERTSON,
Donald Ray Robertson was born Jan. 13, 1935, in his grandmother's house on Coon Hollow Road, Clinton, IN, the son of Donald and Josephine Groves Robertson. He is the eldest of two children. Donnie grew up in the St. Bernice area where he attended High School until 1950. His family moved to Clinton in March 1950, where he graduated from Clinton High School in 1953. After high school Donnie served in the U.S. Army from March 1954 - March 1957. He also joined the union Local #841 at 16 years of age. With the help of Donnie, his father Donald formed Robertson Construction in June 1951. In 1967, Robertson Construction was changed to Robertson Gravel with the pit located on Old Highway 63 North. In 1981, most of the gravel at that site was depleted and the company then moved to River Road South of Clinton, where it exists today.

The Donald Robertson Family. Front - Bradley Domeika. Middle - Brandae Domeika, Karen Robertson, Donnie Robertson. Back - Donnetta Domeika, George Domeika, Jr.

On Nov. 1, 1963, he married Karen Lee Puckett, the youngest of two children born to Joseph and Ada Vescove Puckett. Karen was born in Cicero, IL and raised in Clinton, graduating from Clinton High School in 1961. Karen is the bookkeeper for Robertson Gravel.

In 1964, they became parents of a daughter, Donnetta Rae who married George Kenneth Domeika, Jr. George was born Jan. 22, 1962 in Vermillion County Hospital, the son of George K. Sr. and Thelma Plunkett Domeika. He is the third of four children. George Jr. grew up in Universal, where he graduated from South Vermillion High School in 1980. After high school, he attended Ivy Tech with a certificate in welding in 1981. George is employed with his father-in-law, Donnie Robertson, at Robertson Grovel.

In 1981, he married Donnetta Rae Robertson, the only child of Donald Ray and Karen Puckett Robertson. Donnetta graduated from South Vermillion High School and attended St. Mary of the Woods College.

Also in 1981, they had a daughter, Brandae Nikkole Domeika, and in 1983 a son Bradley George Domeika.

George is a member and past secretary of the Blanford Sportsman Club, a member of the Izaak Walton Club and is still an active basketball player.

Donnetta is a member of the Bethlehem U.M. Leader's Class, member and public relations of the Bethlehem Circle and the South Vermillion Covered Bridge Girl Scouts, Assistant Girl Scout Leader, Secretary of Van Duyn P.T.O., and a Sunday School teacher for the Bethlehem U.M. Church where they are all members.

GEORGE ROBERTSON (1846-1905),
was the son of James F. and Mary Ann Sexton Robertson, who were from Virginia. George was born in Vermillion County, one of six children. He was a farmer and coal miner.

George first married Ellen Garber, who was one of three children. Ellen died during childbirth at the age of 27, in a covered wagon. She is buried in Fairfield, IA. George later married Patsy Shorter. They had one child Georgia May Robertson.

George Robertson (1846-1905) - standing from left with his brothers and sisters. Charles "Charley" Robertson, Effie Shew, Oka Anderson, Decatur "Dick" Robertson

George was tragically killed in Parke County near the railroad bridge in January 1905. He is buried at Spangler Cemetery.

The four children of George and Ellen Garber Robertson were: Oka, Effie Laura, Charles D., and Decatur.

Oka Robertson went to Arkansas and married Will Anderson. They had two children, Helen and Katy. After Will died, Oka returned to Indiana and later she remarried.

Effie Laura Robertson was born May 28, 1877 in Clinton, IN. Effie married Eschol Elza Shew (born Oct. 12, 1870) on Nov. 6, 1894. They had four children, Audrey Meies, Merit William, Hazel Ilda and Ray Robertson Shew. Effie taught school and wrote poems. Some of these poems were published. Effie died Feb. 6, 1957, and Eschol died Jan. 29, 1950. They are both buried at Roselawn.

Charles D. Robertson was born January 1880, in Clinton. Charley married Lottie B. Tennis on Mar. 7, 1904. He was a farmer and lived in the East Union Community, southwest of Clinton. They had five children, Ruth (Robertson) Naselroad, Alice (Robertson) Chrisman, Avice (Robertson) Garwood, Mabel (Robertson) Martin, and Anna (Robertson) Pierce. Charley died Sept. 3, 1969 and Lottie died July 28, 1973. They are both buried at Roselawn, and Decatur "Dick" Robertson, was born Aug. 6, 1872, in Vermillion County, near the Trinity Church.

THE RAYMOND J. ROUSE FAMILY,
Raymond John Rouse son of David A. and Ethel Mae Field Rouse, was born June 18, 1916, on a farm

north of Rileysburg, IN. When he was a small boy the family moved to a farm across the state line on Brewer Road, Danville, IL. During World War II, he served in the U.S. Army, European division. He was a carpenter and contractor in the Danville area. On Nov. 16, 1941, he married Genevieve Eileen Marshall. Genevieve Eileen, daughter of Vernon and Genevieve Prather Marshall, was born Oct. 31, 1920. Eileen graduated from Perrysville High School and Lake View School of Nursing. Besides being a wife and mother of two children, Eileen served in various positions as a registered nurse.

Shirley Rae was born July 17, 1943. She graduated from Bismarck High School, Indiana Central College, and Indiana State University. On Aug. 14, 1966, Shirley married Richard Lee Coake. They have two daughters, Debra Sue and Cheryl Lea. They now live in Warren Co., IN. Shirley teaches at North Vermillion High School.

Russell Vern was born Feb. 17, 1945. He attended Bismarck High School, and graduated from Danville High School and Rose Hulman, Terre Haute, IN. On Dec. 20, 1969, he married Shirley June Phillips. They are the parents of three children, Catherine Marie, David Edward and Matthew Philip. They reside in Conyers, GA, where Russell is employed as a Vice President of Engineering with Snapper, Inc.

HESTON AND ELSIE RUMPLE,
Heston Rumple's parents, George and Laura Rumple, were both born in Owen Co., IN, and raised in Clay County. They married, had their ten children, and buried their youngest daughter there before they moved to Edgar Co., IL, in 1924, and then over into Vermillion Co., IN, in 1925. George was born in 1875, and died in Quaker at the home of his son, Hess, in 1950. Laura Belle Burger, his wife, was born in 1876, and died in 1951.

Heston Marco Rumple was born on Oct. 27, 1912, and married Elsie Mae Neild in 1940. She was born on Feb. 7, 1921, in Georgetown, IL, to Robert Leslie Neild, Sr. and Erschel Viva Stark. Robert Neild was born on Apr. 3, 1896, and died on June 25, 1975. Erschel was born on Oct. 20, 1900, and died Feb. 9, 1974. They married in 1920, and spent the first years in the Georgetown and Ridge Farm locality. They purchased a farm in Eugene Township in 1947 and lived there until they retired and moved into Cayuga in 1968. Hess and Elsie Rumple lived their entire married lives in the Quaker Community. They raised five children.

Ronald Ray was born on Aug. 29, 1940, and married Karen Sue Clemenz of Dana and they have two children; Kimma Rae, born Nov. 18, 1962, married David McIntyre and they have a son, Joshua James, born Feb. 25, 1986; Jeffrey Alan was born Aug. 24, 1966. Ronald and Karen live in Dana.

Karen Elaine, born Jan. 15, 1942, married Ronald Gene Lewis of Newport and their children are: Ronda Jean, born Apr. 11, 1962; James Eric, born Dec. 2, 1965; and Michael Lee, born May 9, 1971. Karen and Ronnie live in Montezuma.

George Robert was born Oct. 17, 1943, and married, first, Mary Ann Smith of Vermillion Township. He married, second, Mary June Norman of Ridge Farm. George has two daughters; Gayla Lynn, born Mar. 2, 1966; and Julie Ann, born Apr. 16, 1968. George and Mary June live near Ridge Farm.

James Heston was born Apr. 16, 1945, and married Margaret (Margie) York of New Goshen. They had two daughters: Jamie Lynn was born Nov.

5, 1965, and died Apr. 22, 1983. Jamie is buried in the Bono Cemetery. Their second daughter, Michelle (Shelly) Lee, was born May 29, 1968. Jim and Margie live in Montezuma.

Warren Neil (Jack) Rumple was born Sept. 30, 1946. He married Joanie Parks of Vermillion Township and they have three daughters: Jayanne was born July 31, 1967 Susan Rae was born Oct. 9, 1969; and Amy Anne was born Mar. 15, 1973. Jack and Joanie live near Dana.

Elsie died on Feb. 9, 1974, and Hess died Jan. 18, 1984. They are buried in the Hopewell Friends Cemetery north of Dana.

BROWNIE IVAN RUNYAN,

was born Aug. 25, 1890, in the Blanford-Jacksonville area of Clinton township, Vermillion Co., IN. The son of Jesse Runyan and Laura Jane Bales, he was one of five children; Lena May, Benjamin F. and twins John Elbert and Jesse. Laura Jane was the daughter of Dr. John Bales and Lucinda Jackson also of the Jacksonville area.

The marriage of Brownie Runyan and Hazel Straughn, daughter of William Straughn and Carrie Bishop, took place on Aug. 8, 1912. One child, was born to this union, a son, Hobart, on Sept. 10, 1913. Hobart married Marie Clark on Apr. 16, 1934. Their daughter, Marlene, was born on Jan. 24, 1937, and married Jerry Stateler. Michael Hobart, only son of Jerry and Marlene, was born Jan. 31, 1955, and married Teresa Thomson on Mar. 18, 1978. Brownie's only great-great grandchild, Courtney Marie, was born Feb. 25, 1984.

Brownie Ivan Runyan - 1977

Brownie began his blacksmith career at the age of 12 with a mail order anvil and vise from Sears and Roebuck with which he fashioned his set of blacksmith tools. He soon came to the attention of neighboring farmers who brought their horses to the Runyan farm for shoeing and farm tools for repairs. By the age of 16 he was in the business and in 1913 he opened his own blacksmith shop on the north side of Jacksonville.

He also worked as a coal mine smithy for the Brick-Shirkie Coal Company for 25 years and another five years for Standard Strip Mine. When the mines went out on strike or shut down for the summer Brownie again returned to his shop and took care of the local farmers and townspeople who often paid him in farm produce and other barter. His blacksmith career lasted for 50 years.

Brownie was also a well-known fiddler who performed at local square dances. It was at one of these dances that he met his future wife who was from Parke County. His grandfather, Dr. John Bales, a veterinarian, had purchased a fiddle for Brownie when he was only a small boy and it was still in his possession at the time of his death.

He liked to begin his days with a song and a jig dance on his back porch before going to his work for which he never took a vacation. Young boys came to the blacksmith shop to watch, talk, and joke with the man who enjoyed his work above all and was considered one of the best smithy's in the area.

Brownie shoed his last horse at the age of 65 and for the next 23 years took care of his wife who was bedfast following a stroke.

He passed away on Mar. 23, 1980, and is buried at Roselawn Memorial Park beside his wife. *Submitted by Betty Thomson Edwards*

CHARLES LUTHER RUSSELL, SR.,

was born on a farm in eastern Greene Co., IN on Aug. 12, 1883, the son of William Russell (1834-1914), a Civil War veteran, and Margaret A. Livingston Russell (1858-1937).

He moved to Vermillion County in 1906 and in 1913 married Cora L. Groves in Owen Co., IN. They resided on Water Street in Clinton until their marriage ended in 1920.

On Mar. 30, 1920, he married Blanche Hazel Hobbs. Blanche was born June 15, 1894, in Clinton, to James L. Hobbs (Feb. 7, 1864-Tennessee - Feb. 15, 1937-Clinton) and Annabelle Kitchen Hobbs (May 19, 1867-Henderson, KY - Feb. 5, 1945-Clinton). Blanche's parents came to Vermillion County in 1890 from Kentucky and lived their entire lives in the Clinton area and are buried in the Riverside Cemetery, Clinton.

Luther and Blanche were the parents of 11 children. They were: Infant girl (1921), Infant girl (Dec. 8, 1922), Ednabelle (1923-Mar. 3, 1925), Maudie L. (1925-1971), Charolette R. (1927), Margaret A. (1928-), Gloria J. (1930-), Infant girl (1932), Harold (June 6-June 14, 1934), Charles L. Jr. (1936-), and Nellie E. (1917-1983) by a previous marriage.

Mr. Russell worked for over 50 years in local coal mines, and during the depression and war years, he worked on WPA.

Mrs. Russell died Jan. 8, 1971 in Clinton and was buried in Walnut Grove Cemetery.

Mr. Russell moved to Florida in June, 1971, and it was there that he died Apr. 1, 1974, at the age of 90.

Their surviving children married and raised families of their own in this area: Maudie married Russell P. Wallace in 1945, no children; Margaret married Lawson Shull, Jr. and had four children, one is deceased; Gloria married William Dunlop, had one son; Charles, Jr. married Carol F. Adams. They have six children with one deceased. Nellie married Clyde Searing and they had two daughters. *Submitted by Jeff Russell, grandson*

DR. JOHN A. RUTAN AND MARTHA COLSHER RUTAN,

John Andrew Rutan was born Apr. 5, 1928 in Bartholomew Co., IN, to Cyrus Ray and Bertha Mae (Golden) Rutan. He grew up in Bartholomew County and graduated from Clifford High School in 1945. Later that year he worked in the Engineering Department of Cummins Engine Company in Columbus, IN.

Martha Alta Colsher was born Sept. 19, 1926 in Indianapolis, IN, to Hugh Archibald and Inez Mae (Hockersmith) Colsher. At an early age Martha and her parents moved to Decatur Co., IN. Martha attended schools in Decatur County and graduated from Jackson High School in 1944. Late in 1945 she also worked in the Engineering Department of Cummins Engine Company in Columbus. For a short time John was her supervisor.

John and Martha were married June 12, 1946 in the Mt. Aerie Baptist Church at Letts Corner, IN. They continued to live and work in the Columbus area for nearly ten years. Their first three children were born at the Bartholomew County Hospital. Chester Alan was born Apr. 12, 1947; Linda Carol was born Nov. 30, 1948; and Steven Ray was born Sept. 10, 1951.

In the Fall of 1955 John, Martha and their three young children moved to Bloomington, IN where John attended Indiana University and Martha worked as secretary to the University Architect. John graduated from the Indiana University School of Optometry in 1962.

In August 1962 John, Martha and their family moved to Clinton, IN where John had purchased Owen B. Frye's optometric practice. December 12, 1962 their fourth child Charles Hugh, was born in Vermillion County Hospital.

Before his death Mar. 21, 1987, John was looking forward to celebrating his 25th year as optometrist for Vermillion County and the surrounding area. During those years he had been an active member of the WIOS, IOA and AOA. He was a member of the First United Methodist Church, Clinton Lions Club and local golf and bowling organizations.

Martha and three of their children continue to live in Clinton or nearby. Chester, supervisor at Eli Lilly Company, his wife Freida (Farrington) Rutan and their daughters Amy and Robin, live near Hillsdale. Linda, service representative for State Farm Insurance agent, her husband Robert Spence and their children, Jeremy and Valerie also live near Hillsdale. Dr. Charles and Cherri (Cash) Rutan live in Clinton. Dr. Steven and Vicki (Walker) Rutan and triplet daughters, Stephanie Ann, Catherine Elise, Amberlee Crystal, live in Ft. Wayne, IN.

Following his graduation from Indiana University School of Optometry in May 1987, Dr. Charles H,. Rutan purchased his father's practice and continues to offer optometric care to the Clinton area.

MARY ELEANOR PAINE HEDGES AND LINDA LOU JONES SANDOR,

Mary Eleanor Paine was born in Trego Co., KS, in 1903, the daughter of Henry Washburn Paine and Kizzie May Spainhower Paine. (See article on Ethel Reposh for family background and also article on Charles Donald Paine.) She attended school in Clinton, IN. Her first marriage was to Merl Lindley. Later she was married to Harry Jones who had come from Lyford, and they were the parents of a daughter, Linda Lou Jones. Harry Jones was employed in the steel industry in Gary, IN, and he contracted an occupation related lung disease and died.

Mary Paine Hedges

After Mr. Jones died Mary went to work in Wasserman's Shoe Store on the east side of the middle of the 200 block of South Main Street in Clinton. Wasserman's store was in business many years in that location. The Wassermans were Jewish and Mr. Wasserman had served in the Russian Army in his younger days.

Mary had worked in Gillis's Drug Store across the street from Wasserman's between her marriages to Mr. Lindley and Mr. Jones and she left Wasserman's to again work in Gillis Drugs. She married once more to Mr. Louis Hedges. After Mr. Hedges died she went back to work at Gillis Drugs for the third time for George Walthall and stayed until retirement.

Linda Lou Jones attended school at South in Clinton and graduated from Clinton High School in 1958 having been active in school organizations. She married Ronald Sandor of Clinton who has been a career military man. They have three daughters, Bambi, Darla, and Ronda. Bambi is married and has a little son, Wayne. Ronda is married and has a child, Ashley, born last year (1987) in Hawaii. *Submitted by Leo Reposh Jr.*

HAROLD G. (PETE) SAULTS AND W. SUE CRAIG SAULTS,

Harold G. (Pete) Saults was born July 3, 1937 in Clinton, IN the son of the late Harry B. Saults and Gertrude L. Bryant Saults. Harold (Pete) Saults grew up in Dana, IN, where he attended the Dana school. He worked on the farm for some of the local farmers.

In 1957 he went to work for Ralph Janes at the Dana Feed Mill.

In November 1957, he married W. Sue Craig the youngest of three children born to Mary J. Smith Craig and the late Ira L. Craig. She was born in Scottland, IL and raised in Chrisman, IL where she attended the local schools.

In 1958, they became parents of a son, Harry L. (Butch) Saults.

In 1965, they became parents of a son, Paul K. Saults.

In 1966, Oll Potter, purchased the Dana Feed Mill, Harold (Pete), stayed and worked for him. The mill closed, but they operated the elevator.

In 1973, Cargill, Inc. purchased the elevator, Harold (Pete) stayed to work for them.

Manager for Cargill, Inc. for 11 years was Robert S. Padan, manager now is John W. Handel.

Harry L. (Butch) Saults, married Linda L. Huey, one of four children born August, 1959, to Rev. Phillip Harry Huey and the late Mary Ann Hiebe Huey.

In April 1980, they became parents of a son, David K. Saults, born in Danville, IL at this time they were living in Newport, IN.

Harry L. (Butch) Saults is in the Air Force at the Andrew base in Washington DC and will be on the presidential squad later this year, he is a staff sergeant.

Paul K. Saults is in the Air Force at Lowery AFB, CO. In June he will go to Reese AFB, Texas. He is a buck sergeant.

DR. JONES LINDSEY SAUNDERS AND ELIZABETH SAUNDERS,

Dr. Jones Lindsey Saunders, M.D. conducted his Vermillion County Medical practice from his Newport office and home until his death in 1953. Elizabeth Saunders, R.N. was the second half of the medical team handling emergencies and daily business while "Doc" was on rounds at Clinton hospital or making house calls. Elizabeth also managed their home and the rearing of their daughters, Mary and Margret. In 1927, Josephine Miller came to work for the Saunders family to assist in the domestic duties. She remained for 14 years and became part of the family.

Jones Lindsey Saunders' great-grandparents Martin Patrick (June 27, 1791-Feb. 5, 1871) and Ruth Parent Patrick (Oct. 4, 1805 - Nov. 13, 1858) were married July 15, 1828, and settled in Eugene Township in the early 19th century.

Their daughter, Mary Patrick (Apr. 9, 1834 - Aug. 29, 1914) wed Jones Lindsey (Feb. 21, 1818 - Feb. 1, 1891) on Aug. 19, 1852. They settled on their farm west of Lindsey Chapel. Mary had a brother, Thomas Patrick, who lived west of their farm. Mary and Jones Lindsey lay at rest in Thomas Cemetery.

Their daughter, Margret Lindsey (Apr. 15, 1859 - Dec. 21, 1946), married Joseph A. Saunders (Mar. 17, 1856 - July 7, 1924) on Dec. 3, 1879. Joseph came from Hamilton Co., IN. Joseph and Margret homesteaded a farm directly east of the Quaker Church in Quaker. They had two sons, Jones Lindsey Saunders (Sept. 19, 1881 - Nov. 12, 1953) and Forrest "Faudie" Saunders. Jones Lindsey Saunders became a physician and Faudie became a veterinarian. Faudie was known for his humor and hedonistic lifestyle. He died a young man and was placed to rest next to his parents in the Quaker Cemetery.

Jones Lindsey Saunders became Captain Saunders, field surgeon stationed in France during World War I. After the war, on Sept. 17, 1919, Jones Lindsey Saunders married his second wife, Mary "Elizabeth" Studham (Dec. 13, 1893 - Aug. 24, 1973). She was from Oskaloosa, IA, and had also served in France during World War I.

Elizabeth retired to the Saunders farm in Quaker after the death of her husband in 1953. They had two daughters, Mary Lindsey Saunders (Dec. 27, 1922 - Jan. 4, 1984) and Margret McVey Saunders (July 8, 1924 - May 7, 1973). All are at rest in the family plot in Thomas Cemetery near the Lindsey family.

Mary Lindsey Saunders graduated from Indiana University with a B.S. in chemistry. She accepted a position at E. I. Dupont de Nemours in Wilmington, DE. There she directly assisted in the development of nylon, plastic, plastic wraps, and aerosol sprays. Upon her father's death, she returned to Vermillion County and lived with her mother at the Saunders' farm in Quaker. She continued to work in chemistry at Staleys and as a blood technologist at the Newport Army Ammunition Plant.

Margret McVey Saunders graduated from Indiana University with a B.S. in business. She moved to the Chicago area and became a top model. Margret McVey Saunders wed Thomas J. Loftus (Jan. 26, 1918 - Aug. 23, 1980) on July 26, 1947. They had four children: Michael John Loftus (Mar. 18, 1948), Mary Louise Loftus Craig (Oct. 12, 1949), Joseph Lindsey Loftus (Apr. 28, 1951), and Eileen Theresa Loftus Fitzgibbon (Mar. 8, 1953).

These are the current owners and caretakers of the Lindsey homestead in Eugene Township and the Saunders homestead in Quaker.

These homesteads are being preserved to perpetuate the family tradition in Vermillion County. And with God's blessing, this tradition may be passed to Dr. Jones Lindsey Saunders' great-grandchildren; Kathleen Lindsey Loftus (June 18, 1979), David Thomas Craig (Feb. 28, 1980), Jesse Lindsey Craig (Sept. 6, 1983), Christopher Edwin Fitzgibbon (Oct. 10, 1985), Patrick Thomas Fitzgibbon (Oct. 10, 1985), and Elizabeth Catherine Fitzgibbon (Jan. 16, 1987).

JAMES P. SAVAGE AND DOROTHY G. SAVAGE,

James P. Savage was born Nov. 27, 1915, in Rockport, Spencer Co., IN. He was the fifth of seven children of Louis N. and Teresa Savage. He attended St. Bernard's Catholic elementary school, and after the eighth grade was enrolled in St. Meinrad Seminary at St. Meinrad, IN. In his junior year he returned to Rockport and completed high school, graduating with the Rockport High School class of 1933. He then enrolled in the Jefferson Law School in Louisville, KY. After two years in Louisville he transferred to the Indiana Law School in Indianapolis, where he graduated in 1939. He was admitted to the Indiana bar on Apr. 17, 1939, and was also admitted to practice before the U.S. Supreme Court at the same time.

James P. Savage.

On Nov. 27, 1939, he married Dorothy G. Burdick, the daughter of Joseph E. and Anna K. Burdick of Rockport, IN. Dorothy was born in Rockport on May 6, 1918, and attended the Rockport public schools, graduating from Rockport High School in the Class of 1935. She attended Lockyear's Business College in Evansville, IN, and was employed at Tressler's Variety Store. The Savages took up residence in Rockport, where James P. joined his father's law practice.

In 1942 the Savages moved to Clinton, where James P. became the law partner of Harold H. Wisehart, whose offices were located at 235 1/2 Blackman Street. In 1944 he was commissioned an Ensign in the United States Navy and served as a deck officer on the U.S.S. Suamico (A047), an attack oiler, and participated in 17 invasions in the South Pacific. In the Spring of 1946 he was discharged from active service in the Navy with the rank of Lieutenant. He then returned to Clinton to resume his law practice.

Mr. Savage was a life-long member of the Democratic Party. In 1948 he was the unsuccessful Democratic candidate for Prosecuting Attorney of Vermillion County. He served as County Attorney and advisor to a number of towns in the county. He was an active member of Sacred Heart Catholic Church for 39 years. He was also a founding member of the Runyan Pierce Post 6653 of the Veterans of Foreign Wars, and a member of the American Legion, the Indiana Bar Association, and the U.S. Naval Reserve. He was instrumental in the establishment of the Fairview Park and Universal Water Companies.

Mrs. Savage has been a member of the Sacred Heart Catholic Women's Club, Veterans of Foreign Wars Auxiliary, the Vermillion County Tuberculosis Assn., and the Vermillion County chapter of the American Cancer Society. In 1975 she enrolled in

Indiana State University, and in 1976 was costume co-ordinator for the Clinton Bicentennial Celebration.

The Savage are the parents of two sons, James Louis, born in Evansville, IN, Mar. 11, 1941, and Joseph Paul, born in Clinton, Nov. 17, 1943. They have one grandchild Allison Marie Savage.

James P. Savage died on July 22, 1981, and is buried at Sunset Hill Cemetery, Rockport, IN.

WILLIAM K. SCHWAB AND MONA DUDLEY SCHWAB,

and infant son William D., moved to Cayuga, IN, in 1919, from Clinton, IN. "Bill" had ben the C.&E.I. R.R. station agent there and bid the new job opening in Cayuga. There until his retirement in 1964, he was the manager of the Cayuga Western Union and C.&E.I. day telegraph operator-leverman. The neighbors would remark that their clocks could be set by Bill Schwab going to work from his Curtis Street residence. During World War II he was recruited by the national Civil Defense to log all flying aircrafts because the height of the tower gave good visibility and he worked seven days a week all during the war. He was commended after the war by the United States Government.

Three daughters were born to Bill and Mona in Cayuga. Martha Louise, Helen Ruth, and Charlotte Ann. Only the latter has remained in Cayuga.

Shortly after Bill and Mona's arrival in Cayuga, his parents, George and Rosa Bader Schwab moved from Brazil, IN, and purchased a farm south of Cayuga. They are both German immigrants. He farmed and had a black-smith shop.

William K. Schwab and his parents are deceased.

RUBY AYRES SEATON,

was born Dec. 15, 1930, one and one-half miles northeast of St. Bernice, IN, in the house that her paternal grandparents, William T. Ayres and Lucitta (Nolan) Ayres built circa 1911. William Ayres' family came to Vermillion County in 1876. Lucitta Nolan's paternal grandparents came in 1820. Wayne Ayres, their only surviving son, was born in 1903 just west of Jonestown.

Ilona Seaton, Ruby Ayres Seaton, Wayne Ayres, Beulah Ayres, Gregory Seaton.

Wayne graduated from the first consolidated school in Vermillion County, in Bono. His father died when Wayne was 19 and he took over running the farm.

In 1925, Wayne married Beulah F. Whitesell, the youngest daughter of Joshua Caleb Whitesell and Susan (Kibler) Whitesell of Edgar Co., IL. Beulah graduated from Metcalf, IL, High school. She attended "Normal" college in Charleston, IL, and taught in a one room school near Brocton, IL, for one year before she married Wayne.

The family attended the United Brethren Church

in Jonestown during the time that Ruby was growing up. Beulah was active in church work, teaching in Sunday School, and leading choir. She played the marimba at Graduations, Revival Meetings, and special events at Church.

Wayne Ayres died in 1982. Beulah Ayres died in 1988.

Ruby, Wayne and Beulah's only child, had red hair and freckles. She graduated from St. Bernice High School and was Salutatorian of her class. In 1948, she married William W. Seaton, the oldest son of William Seaton and Marjorie (Cole) Seaton. Information on him is given in his historical sketch.

In 1975, Ruby started working at Liberty Title Company, Ann Arbor, MI. She became a Director of the Company, Title Officer, Commercial Coordinator, Construction Specialist, and Legal Assistant.

Ruby and Bill had two children: Ilona Ayres Seaton, born in 1949, and Gregory Wayne Seaton, born in 1951. Ilona graduated from Dexter High School, Dexter, MI, and was Valedictorian of her class. She attended the University of Michigan, was inducted into Phi Beta Kappa, and graduated Summa Cum Laude. In 1969, she married James Samborn, the oldest son of Al Samborn and Marguerite (McFall) Samborn, Ilona worked at Liberty Title Company, Ann Arbor, MI, becoming a Director of the Company, Office Manager, Treasurer, Title Officer, and Closing Officer. They have one daughter, Alison Claire, born in 1978.

Gregory Seaton graduated from Dexter High School, Dexter, MI. He attended the University of Michigan, graduating with a BSME Degree. Greg went to work at Seaton Engineering in Ann Arbor, MI, and later took a position at Seaton-SSK Engineering as Senior Project Engineer. In 1976, Greg married Deborah Hohenshil, the oldest daughter of Jay Hohenshil and Sue (Kline) Hohenshil. Greg and Debby have two daughters, Lindsey Sarah, born in 1979, and Kara Suzanne, born in 1981. *Submitted by Ruby Ayres Seaton*

WILLIAM WAYNE SEATON,

"Bill" was born Sept. 23, 1929, in Lakeview Hospital, Danville, IL, and lived on the North Fork of the Vermillion River at the foot of Seaton Hill, north of Danville, IL, until 1934. Seaton Hill was named for John Miller Seaton, Bill's grandfather, who had his home, a Dance Hall and a General Store there. The General Store was the typical kind that had a little bit of every-thing, including a cracker barrel, a pickle barrel, and a pot-bellied stove. Friends would stop by to sit around the stove and discuss the problems of the day.

Bill's father, William Seaton, born in 1904, was the youngest child of John Miller Seaton and Nellie Mae Radebaugh Seaton. Nellie Mae died two weeks after William was born. In 1928, William married Marjorie Louise Cole. (youngest daughter of Edward Cole and Dora Estelle Valentine Cole). They lived at the foot of Seaton Hill and William worked on the Milwaukee Railroad at Starr, IL and helped his father in the dance hall.

Bill came to Vermillion County in 1934 when his parents packed up in a Model T car and moved to St. Bernice, where Bill's father went to work for the Milwaukee Railroad at West Clinton as a Section Hand. Bill started school at St. Bernice, attended Dana School fifth thru eighth grades while living on a small farm north of St. Bernice, then returned to St. Bernice High School where he graduated in 1947.

William W. Seaton

By 1943, Bill's father, William, was a Brakeman on the railroad, a job he held until his death in 1958. Bill has a sister, Delores (born 1936), and two brothers, Dennis and Byron (born 1939 and 1944, respectively). Byron died 1968. Bill 's mother, Marjorie Bodle resides in Clinton, IN.

In 1948, Bill married Ruby A. Ayres, the only chid of Wayne Ayres and Beulah Whitesell. Bill and Ruby had two children, Ilona and Gregory. More information is given on them in the historical sketch of their mother, Ruby Ayres Seaton.

In 1950, Bill went to work at General Motors Foundry, Danville, IL. GM sent him to General Motors Institute of Technology, Flint, MI, where he earned a B.S. in Industrial Engineering. In 1958, he joined a Swiss Company, International Automation Corporation, Ann Arbor, MI. In 1973, he formed Seaton Engineering Company as a joint venture with Combustion Engineering. In 1983, Bill sold his Company to CMI International, Inc. The company was then renamed Seaton-SSK Engineering. Bill has had several technical papers published and has lectured at national and international conventions held by the American Foundrymens Society. He has seven U.S. patents and nine foreign patents. Bill and Ruby have travelled extensively in Europe on both business and pleasure.

Bill and Ruby make their home in Dexter, MI, where they raised their children, Ilona and Greg. *Submitted by William Wayne Seaton*

CHARLES EDWARD SHANNON AND ANGELINE SHANNON,

Charles Edward Shannon, 1203 White Street, Clinton IN, normally referred to as Ed, is the husband of Angeline Reposh Shannon. He was born Dec. 28, 1915, in Sandytown (R.R.3, Clinton), and attended Sandytown Grade School. He graduated from Clinton High School in 1935 and then worked for a while as a truck driver. He was inducted into the army in May, 1941, and was in for five and one-half years being stationed in California. Ed and Angeline were married on July 19, 1943. Their son, Michael, was born Sept. 4, 1945, in Clinton. Ed was a mechanic at Clinton Implement and Truck Company an International Harvester Dealership at 558 North 9th Street for several years. His parents were Charles and Bessie Shannon of Sandytown and his grandparents were Rev. Frank and Dollie Wells.

Angeline Reposh Shannon was born Oct. 28, 1915 in Clinton, the daughter of Frank and Francesca Reposh and granddaughter of Martin and Theresa Mohar. She has two brothers in Clinton, Rudolph two doors away (see related story) and Leo of R.R. 3 (see related story). She attended school at Columbia at 8th and Anderson Streets, at Glendale on North 10th, and at Clinton Junior and Senior High Schools.

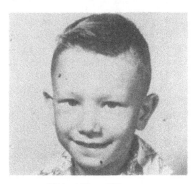

Michael Edward Shannon

Ed and Angeline are members of the Clinton's Presbyterian Church and Ed is a member and has been an officer of the local Lion's Club. Angeline is a member of the local Lioness Club. Ed was director of the 1970 Columbus Day celebration in Clinton. Their son, Michael, mentioned earlier, attended Glendale School, and graduated from Clinton High School in 1963 and Indiana State University in 1967. He is a medical technician at Carle Clinic in Urbana, IL. He has a ten year old son named Eric. They reside in Urbana.

She was employed for some time in the food department of the South Vermillion School Corporation. *Submitted by Leo Reposh Jr.*

CHRISTINA JOHNSON SHANNON, In

the early 1800's my grandparents Andrew Jackson Howe, Sr. and Eliza Howe, left Kentucky and by covered wagon, traveled north into Indiana. They were forced by winter weather to stop over at St. Mary's where their fourth child, my mother, Martha Ann, was born. She was named for one of the sisters who helped them survive that winter.

When spring arrived, they, their sons—Ben and Andrew Jackson, Jr., and daughters—Mary and little Martha, made their way to the Indiana Furnace vicinity. Grandpa got a job as "charcoal burner" at the Furnace.

After the Furnace closed, they moved from the Furnace in Section 27, Range 10, to Range nine which was Section 14 near what is now Geneva, but was in earlier years called Vorhees. It was later changed to "Geneva" after a daughter of the superintendent of one of the early Geneva coal mines.

My mother married John Pierce in 1880. My oldest half-sister, Mary Ann, was born in 1880. Then three years later, Myrtle Pierce was born. In two years, Alonzo Pierce was born, and in 1892, George Pierce was born on December 21. John Pierce died a few days before George was born.

In 1894, my mother met and married my father, a farmer and former "long shoreman" from Sweden. He owned a small farm of a little over 50 acres in Geneva. His name was Mungus Johnson. To this marriage was born two children, Andrew Mungus Johnson and Christina Marie Johnson Shannon. Andy was born Apr. 17, 1894, on my father's birthday. He died Dec. 30, 1976.

I, Christina Marie, was born June 17, 1901, and my father died June 15, 1906, and was buried on my fifth birthday.

When I was born the doctor said I could not possibly live. All my blood would be water because of my parents advanced ages. My dad thought differently. He went to the nearby saloon and bought a gallon of alcohol and a gallon of olive oil. He brought them home and told the hired girl, Hester, just how much water and how much alcohol to put in the wash basin and explained, "Mine, God,

Mine baby is not going to die. What is good in the old country (Sweden), is good in America."

Hester was ordered to bathe me twice a day, once in the olive oil and once in the alcohol solution. My mother said "Well, I don't know if that bathing will do any good but she will surely be the cleanest, if not the greasiest in the county." At any rate, I grew up to be a quite healthy adult.

My brother, Andrew Mungus Johnson, attended school at a small county school which was located at what was then called Vorhees, IN. He and my half-brother, George Pierce, attended this school until it was abandoned. They then walked through the woods to Sandytown School.

Several years after my father's death, my mother married her third husband, Charles W. Willard, who ran a small grocery store near our home. He died in his early 60's.

I married Arthur Ames Shannon, Sr. in 1922. On Dec. 14, 1922, Arthur Ames, Jr. was born. We lived next door to my mother who later made her home with us. Christina Marie Shannon was born Jan. 10, 1925. Ila Mae Shannon arrived Jan. 13, 1927. Betty Jean Shannon was born Apr. 12, 1935, and on Sept. 2, 1943, Carl Wayne Shannon was born.

SHEPARD FAMILY, of Vermillion County has a long and interesting history dating back to colonial Virginia where several were members of the House of Burgess. A land grant from the Commonwealth of Virginia signed by Governor Patrick Henry in 1782 brought them to Kentucky. In 1824, Benjamin Shepard came up from Hawesville, KY, to settle in Newport. He bought 1100 acres near Quaker in 1828, and later built a spacious Victorian home there. 1835 found him married to Eliza Johnson of Ohio, who came from England as a child of five.

To this union were born ten children—Hiram, 1836; Elizabeth, 1838; Lewis, 1839; Harriet, 1844; Caroline, 1847; Selina, 1849; Ellen, 1850; Judson, 1853; Florence, 1857; and Susan, 1860. The three boys elected to stay in Vermillion County. Dr. Hiram Shepard took up practice in Dana; Dr. Lewis Shepard chose Newport, and Judson elected to open a business in Dana. The girls married and moved away.

Still living in Vermillion County are Lucille Betson (Carl), Charlotte Aikman (Herbert), Michael Aikman, Clara Ellen Fortune (Russell), James Fortune, Jay Shepard, Isabel Oye, Laura Ellen Marsh, descendants of Judson; and Martha W. Helt, granddaughter of Dr. Lewis Shepard. All are living in the Dana area. Dale Shepard, Martin Shepard, John Shepard, and Gene Shepard live in Clinton.

E. STANLEY SHEW AND VERA STOOPS SHEW, Edward Stanley Shew was

born Feb. 27, 1928 in Vigo County near Shirkeville, IN, the son of Loren C. Shew and Audrey Viola Hutchinson Shew. He is the eldest of four children. In March 1929 his family moved to Parke Co., IN. He grew up near Bloomingdale, IN and graduated from Bloomingdale High School in 1946. Upon graduation he entered Purdue University and graduated in Agricultural Engineering in August 1950. He was inducted into the United States Army in October 1950 and assigned to the 40th Infantry Division Signal Company at Camp Cooke, CA. The 40th Division was sent to Japan in March 1951 and to Korea in January 1952. He was rotated back to the United States and separated from the service at Camp Carson, CO in October 1952.

Vera and Stanley Shew

After separation from the service, Stanley returned to Clinton, IN where his family had moved in 1949. In May 1953 he married Vera Evelyn Stoops, the youngest of five children born to the late John Walker Stoops and Zula Ellen Price Stoops. Vera was born and raised near Sheridan, IN and graduated from Sheridan High School in 1947. Following graduation she attended Purdue University where she graduated in Home Economics and Spanish in June 1951. She taught Home Economics at Forest High school, Forest, IN for two years.

After Stanley and Vera were married, Vera worked as Vermillion County Home Demonstration Agent for two years and Stanley began farming in partnership with his father and later in partnership with his brother, Ray, which he continues at this time.

They are the parents of four children, Edward Scott, born August 1955; David Brian, born January 1957; Mark Stanley, born January 1959; and Ellen Marie, born July 1961. Ed, a graduate of Clinton High School and Purdue Ag Engineering, lives near Clinton, IN and farms land in Vermillion and Vigo Counties in partnership with his brother, Mark, a graduate of Clinton High School and Purdue Ag Economics. Mark lives in Vigo County near Rosedale, IN. Dave, a graduate of Clinton High School and the University of Cincinnati, is an architect and lives at The Sea Ranch, CA. Ellen, a graduate of South Vermillion High School and Purdue Ag Economics, is an agricultural chemical representative for Dow Chemical and lives in Lafayette, IN.

Vera returned to teaching at Clinton High School in September 1966. She received her Masters Degree in Home Economics and Spanish from Indiana State University in 1971 and she continues to teach Spanish and Home Economics at South Vermillion High School.

They are members of First United Methodist Church in Clinton and the Vermillion County Farm Bureau. Stanley is a former member and president of the South Vermillion School Board and a director of The Clinton State Bank. Vera served as a member of the Vermillion County School Reorganization Committee and is coordinator for student exchange programs. She is also a member of Tri Kappa, Delta Kappa Gamma, American Assoc. of Teachers of Spanish and Portuguese and the American Home Economics Assoc. *Submitted by E. Stanley Shew*

EDWARD S. SHEW AND CAROL A.
BERKES SHEW, Edward Scott Shew was born to E. Stanley and Vera E. Stoops Shew Aug. 15, 1955 in Clinton, IN. He was raised on a farm just west of town near Crompton Hill along with his younger brothers David and Mark, and sister Ellen. Ed attended Crompton Hill and Van Duyn grade schools and graduated from Clinton High School in

1973. During high school he was active in sports, clubs, National Honor Society, and other activities. Ed then went to Purdue University where he majored in Agricultural Engineering, receiving a B.S. degree in May 1977. While at Purdue he was a three year letterman on the Purdue Rowing team, member of Alpha Epsilon Ag. Honorary Society, and involved in dorm government, and intramural sports.

Ed Shew family. Front: Nathan, Jeff. Back: Ed, Carol, John

Ed then moved to DeKalb, IL and began working for DeKalb Ag Research, Inc. as a project engineer in their construction department. During the next two years he traveled throughout the Midwest working on projects at DeKalb's numerous seed processing plants. Leaving DeKalb in the fall of 1979, he returned to W. Lafayette and worked as a carpenter while coaching the Purdue novice women's rowing team. The spring of 1981 found Ed back in Clinton pursuing a lifelong ambition and goal of farming. This opportunity arose thru the rental of 500 acres south of Clinton which is owned by H.L. Cheek. An additional 880 acres in Vigo County was rented in 1986 when his brother Mark joined with him to form the partnership of E&M Farms. Their crops include corn, soybeans, grain sorghum, popcorn, and wheat. Ed is also with his dad's farrow to finish hog operation.

Ed met his wife Carol in 1979 while still working in DeKalb, IL where she was born and raised. She began working there as a registered nurse, later moving to Lafayette and working at Home Hospital prior to their August 1981 marriage. After setting up residence near Clinton, Carol worked in the Coronary Care Unit of Union Hospital in Terra Haute until August 1984. In July 1987 she went back to work at the Vermillion County Hospital in the Emergency Room.

Ed and Carol have three sons for future farm hands; John Edward, born May 1982; Jeff Allen, born October 1984; and Nathan Scott, born January 1987.

Ed and Carol are both active members of Clinton First United Methodist Church. Ed also sings baritone with the Fourumm Gospel Quartet and is a member of the Clinton Optimist Club and Farm Bureau. He has served three years as president of the Vermillion County Extension Board and was a nine year member of 4-H. Carol is a member of Tri Kappa Sorority.

HENRY SHEW (NOV. 14, 1815-) AND IRENE HEDGES SHEW (DEC. 3, 1823-),
Henry Shew resided on Section 36, Clinton Township. He was one of the active and prominent citizens of Vermillion County, and a worthy representative of one of the early pioneer families of the county. He was born in Wilkes Co., NC on Nov. 13, 1815, his parents, Daniel and Eve D. (York) Shew

being natives of the same state, the former of German and the latter of English ancestry. They with their family, then consisting of six children, left their native State and with teams made their journey to Vermillion County in 1826, and settled in the forest on Section 31, Clinton Township. Here the father bought a tract of 62 acres, which he improved and resided upon until his death. He erected a saw-mill on Jennings Creek which he operated about 30 years. They were members of the United Brethern Church. The children born to them were - Philip, Henry, Joel, Eli, Mary M. Shew Moulton, Sarah, Leonard M., Washington, and Matilda Shew Vergen.

Henry Shew was reared to a farm life, but after reaching manhood he learned the cooper's trade which he followed some 15 years. After that, he devoted his time almost exclusively to agricultural pursuits. He was united in marriage on July 2, 1840, to Miss Irene Hedges, a daughter of William Hedges and Permelia Alden Hedges, early settlers of the county. She was born on Dec. 3, 1823 at the pioneer home of her parents. To Henry and Irene Shew were born five children - Lysander, Lura Ann Shew Hay, Levi L., Direxa Shew - wife of Thomas P. Pinson, and Alma C. - wife of James Boatman.

Mr. Shew commenced life with no capital, but strong hands, and a determination to make life a success, and his energy combined with integrity and good business habits, enabled him to obtain a competence for his declining years. When he settled on his homestead in Clinton Township it was covered with a heavy growth of timber. He owned over 400 acres in 1888, the greater part of which was well improved. In politics Mr. Shew was a Republican of Whig antecedents. He served almost three terms as magistrate of Clinton Township, being appointed to the office during the war to fill a vacancy, and elected the two succeeding terms. He was liberal in his religious views, believing in the goodness of God toward all his children. Mr. Shew was widely known throughout the township where he resided, and few local men possessed the confidence and respect of the public to a greater extent than he, being trusted by all who knew him. *Submitted by Dorothy Elder*

Source: Vermillion County History - 1888 (in addition to family information)

LOREN CHARLES SHEW,
was born Apr. 2, 1901 west of Universal into a pioneer family of Southwestern Vermillion County. His great grandparents, Henry and Irene Shew, and grandparents Lysander and Anna Shew lie in Hall's cemetery west of Universal. Loren is the eldest of five children born to Chloral Scott and Faith Ann Barbour Shew. The family moved during his childhood to a farm in the north edge of Vigo County. He attended elementary school there and went to Clinton High School for two years.

Loren Shew

He then attended the newly completed Fayette High School at New Goshen and graduated in 1919. Following graduation he engaged in farming and worked for a time in the nearby Vermillion coal mine. In March 1926 he was married to the late Audrey Viola Hutchinson, one of eight children born to George Lansing and Effie Pugh Hutchinson near Shepherdsville in Vigo County. Audrey attended the local elementary school, Clinton High School for three years and graduated from Fayette High School in 1918. She then attended Indiana State Normal School in Terre Haute and following graduation from there taught at Fayette High School. Their children are E. Stanley and L. Ray of rural Clinton, Martha Parker of Danville, IL and C. Lansing of Milford, MI. There are 12 grandchildren and six great grandchildren.

Loren later married Enid Hay Hutchinson of Muskegon, MI whose childhood was spent in the New Goshen area.

Loren is a member of First United Methodist Church of Clinton and a member of William Penn Lodge F & A M in Bloomingdale, IN from which he received his 50 year membership pin. He also has been an active member and President of the Vermillion County Farm Bureau. *Submitted by E. Stanley Shew*

ROSE JEAN SHEW,
was born June 21, 1952, to Paul James Duchene and Norma Jean Bonomo Duchene. She is the oldest of two children. She was raised in Clinton, attended Sacred Heart Grade School, and graduated from Clinton High School in 1970. After graduation from Indiana Vocational Technical College, she became a licensed Practical Nurse.

Front: Sara Rose Shew. Middle: Bobby Roberts, Rose Jean Shew. Back: Joy Lynn Roberts

She is employed at Union Hospital.

Rose married Howard Edward Shew II in May, 1986. She has three children, Joy Lynn Roberts born Feb. 3, 1973; Bobby John Roberts born Dec. 7, 1976; and Sara Rose Shew born Nov. 10, 1986.

Rose is a member of Daughters of the Nile. She is listed in Who's Who of American Women. She and her husband and children live in Universal, IN.

ISSAC SHORT, SR.,
was born in 1795 in Virginia, the son of John and Mary Short. The family moved to Clermont Co., OH and in 1807, Issac moved his family to Hamilton Co., OH.

On May 20, 1819, Issac married Susanna E. Coombs, born 1798 in Kentucky. They became the parents of 11 children: Issac Jr. (1820-1882), Amassa (1827-1910), Amos (1828), Arthur E. (1829), Richard (1830-1865). The last six children were born in Helt Twp., Vermillion County after Issac Sr. moved his family here in March, 1831. The last born were: Elijah (1832-1918), Lydia A. (1834)

Matilda (1836-1874), Reuban (1840), John (1847), and Susanna (1849).

The Short's resided on a farm in Section 8, Helt Twp. that consisted of 80 acres. Issac and his sons farmed and as the children married off, some were given tracts of land on the farm. Issac Jr., Elijah, Amassa and Richard all lived on the family farm after their marriages.

Issac Jr. married Elizabeth Taylor, Vermillion Co., IL, in 1847. They had a son, John, born 1848. Elizabeth died in 1849 and was buried on the Taylor farm in Illinois. Issac then married Mary Kessler Harmon (Sept. 9, 1829-Dec. 25, 1908) on Dec. 7, 1851. They lived on the farm and their first five children were born here: Sarah E. (1853-1927) her twin, Mary A. (1853-1855); James (1856-1931), Rachel A. (1860-1900), Oliver (1862-1870), the two youngest were born in Parke County, Lydia (1866-1920) and Alexander (1871-1931).

Issac Short Sr. died Sept. 9, 1858, on the family farm and was buried in the family plot on their farm. His wife, Susanna, died Oct. 12, 1872, and was buried in the cemetery on the farm. There were ten burials in the Short Cemetery. The tombstones were removed several years ago. The land was divided and sold after 1880 to cousins of the Short's. *Submitted by Jeff Russell, great-great-great-great-great grandson of Issac Sr. Descended from Issac Jr. and Mary Kesslor Short.*

DANIEL SHUTE, son of Richard Shute was born in 1820, he helped to change this land from a wilderness into well cultivated farms and thriving towns and villages. He owned 250 acres of land north and west of Gessie and south of Rileysburg. He was a farmer and cattle raiser.

He married Jane Gouty, daughter of Henry Gouty. They were parents of seven children namely Henry, David, Elizabeth, Mary, Joseph and Sarah.

When Daniel Shute retired from this farm, he built a home in the southwest corner of Gessie. This house still stands and looks much the same as when he built it.

EPHRIAM SHUTE, son of Richard and Hannah Shute, was born in 1827 and died in 1908, at the age of 81 years.

He came with his parents from Sciota Co., OH, when he was two years old. They settled on the homestead where he lived the rest of his life. He was reared a farmer.

He married Elzina Goff, the eldest daughter of David Goff. They established their home near Hopewell Baptist Church and Hopewell Cemetery. Here they reared eight children, who lived, married and created homes of their own in this vicinity: Martha, Hannah, David, Aurelea, Elias, Squire, Philander and Marentha.

When he died he owned 290 acres of land here and one half section of valuable land in Kansas.

Ephraim Shute was a staunch Republican. He and his wife, Elzina, were received into Hopewell Church, Oct. 14, 1877 by baptism.

RICHARD SHUTE, was born Oct. 16, 1792, at Dover, England. At the age of ten years he came to America with his father, John Shute, and brother, William Shute. They settled in southern Ohio.

He enlisted Sept. 19, 1812, in the War of 1812. He served under Captain Peter Bacus with General William Henry Harrison. They traveled up the Wabash River Valley as far as Tippecanoe. He liked the lay of the land and vowed that he would return later.

He was discharged Mar. 3, 1813. He then went back to Scioto Co., OH. Here he married Hannah McCarty, Mar. 31, 1814.

To them were born 12 children, four were born in Ohio, namely, William, Daniel, John, and Ephraim. This family migrated to this vicinity in October 1829.

They settled on a plot of land near Spring Creek known as Howard Chapel vicinity.

Several more children were born here: Mahala, Sarah Ann, Susan, Jehu, Joseph, Elizabeth, Rebecca, and Harrison.

Rebecca was born in 1837 and died 1839. A burial plot was selected on the farm, and she was the first person buried in what is known as Hopewell Cemetery. This plot of land was donated by Richard Shute as a free public burial ground and church yard. A Predestinarian Baptist Church was built here — size 20 x 30 feet - in 1853.

Richard and Hannah Shute were members of this church.

WALTER "SHORTY" SIECZOWSKI,

Shorty, as Walter Sieczowski was called, came to Perrysville around 1930 and in the more than 40 years he lived there became synonymous with the river in the minds of all who knew him. His tiny frame cabin was located just west of the old bridge, on a dirt lane leading down to the Wabash from Green Street. The turnoff was marked by a town landmark, a concrete watering trough built by Brock Royce in 1907 from local contributions. From the 1940's on, the trough, moss-lined and filled with clear spring water, was known as "Shorty's trough," because he kept it stocked with fish he caught in the Wabash and offered for sale.

Most Perrysville children, and many adults, paid regular visits there, especially to see the immense catfish that lurked, brooding and barbed, in the trough's depths. When customers arrived, the fish would be filleted, wrapped in newspaper, and sent, toothsomely fresh from the Wabash to the dinner table. Shorty's trough was destroyed by the Indiana State Highway Department in 1979, but spring water still flows at the site.

Another source of income for the riverman was freshwater musseling, a seasonal occupation which began after spring thaw and continued through summer and early fall. In addition to Shorty, several Perrysville men regularly used their boats for musseling, among them Leonard Miller, Russell Wilson, Clarence Wilson, Ralph Wilson, Eldon Johnson and Francis Pritchard.

Until the advent of plastics, mussels were used for button manufacture, and could produce up to $40 or $50 a day in income for a hard-working man. In spring when the Wabash ran cold, boats were fitted with "mussel bars," which dragged the river mud for the mollusks. In warmer weather, the fisherman walked the shallows, feeling the mussels with their feet, digging them out and filling their boats. The boats ran south to Cayuga and north to Tree Springs, sometimes becoming dangerously overloaded with the day's haul.

The mussels were boiled on the river bank, at the end of Shorty's land, and the clean shells sold in bulk. Among the local buyers were Dennie Moore's elevator in Perrysville; Don Hall's garage in Perrysville; and Ace Curry, a scrap metal dealer and fishseller in Covington. From these points, the mussel shells were shipped by railroad boxcar and trailer truck to button manufacturing plants.

Walter Sieczowski, "Shorty the Fisherman," was born Apr. 22, 1893, in Poland, the son of Valentine and Elizabeth Sieczowski. He was a veteran of World War I, and a member of Perrysville's Walter Hoyt American Legion Post 350. He died Apr. 3, 1974, in Danville, IL, and was buried in Lower Mound Cemetery. Those who knew him believed his spirit remains on the Wabash River at Perrysville, for nearly half a century his workplace and his home.

THE SILOTTO FAMILY FROM SYNDICATE,

Frank Silotto came to the United States from a small Italian village, Forno Canavese, located in the northern part of Italy. He was a young lad, only 15 years old, when his father and three uncles made plans to travel by a hugh steamship in 1896 to come to the United States to work in the coal mines. He, being the eldest son, was asked to come along. After a year or so, he was here alone as his father returned to Italy since his wife would not join him here. Frank never returned to the homeland so he never saw his parents or family again.

Frank and Lucia Moretto Silotto

In the early 1900's, he married Katy Sanquenetti from Syndicate. To this marriage, six sons—Dom, David, Frank, Charles, Victor, and John—were born. There were also two daughters who died in early infancy.

During World War I, there was a very severe flu epidemic which took the lives of many people. It was at this time that Frank lost his wife. For several years it was a great hardship to him, trying to work and take care of six small boys.

In 1920, he wrote to Lucia Moretto, daughter of friends to their family in Italy, and asked her to come to the United States and become his bride. To this marriage, three more children were born—Rena, Joe, and Pete.

The children attended school at the Syndicate School for the first four grades, and later attended Smith School for the remaining four years. This school house had two rooms, one room for the first through fourth and the other fifth through eighth. Children living in that area attended the first through fourth and children who had attended Syndicate School walked this distance of nearly two miles each day.

Then in 1936, consolidation took place and both schools were closed. All elementary pupils were transported to Universal Grade School by bus.

Up to then very few attended high school, but the bus was available to anyone to go to Clinton High School. Rena graduated from Clinton High School in 1939, and Joe graduated in 1940.

During World War II, three sons served their country, Dom, John, and Joe. John served in the

European Theater and Joe served in the Pacific Theater.

Rena Silotto Riggen is the only survivor left from this large family. She married Robert Riggen who is a native of Dana, IN. They reside in Chrisman, IL, where they moved after Robert served three and one-half years in the Air Force during World War II, and was discharged in February, 1946.

JOHN SKIDMORE, John Skidmore, deceased, was one of the first pioneers of Helt Township, Vermillion County and during his life was an active and enterprising citizen. He was born in Pennsylvania, Aug. 27, 1783, his father, Joshua, being of English descent, and a soldier during the Revolutionary War. His mother was a native of Germany, coming to America when five years of age. Her parents and the rest of her family died of cholera on ship-board while en route for America. Our subject was taken to Kentucky by his parents in his boyhood, his father dying in that state. The family then moved to Columbus Co., OH, where the mother died at the advanced age of 96 years. Mr. Skidmore came to Indiana with a colony. They built a keel boat at Columbus in which they floated down the Scioto to the Ohio River, thence to the mouth of the Wabash River, and from there to Vincennes, where they remained two years or until the year 1818. In the fall of that year they they came to Helt Township, our subject having preceded them in the spring of 1818 and raised a crop. His house was the farthest north in the county, and no house was between his and old Fort Dearborn, now Chicago. Mr. Skidmore was first married May 26, 1807, to Mary Hopper, and of the six children born to this union three are living; Mrs. Catherine Tweedy, Mrs. Jane Ford, and Mrs. Elizabeth Potter. His son William, who is now deceased, was the first white child born in Vermillion County. Mr. Skidmore married for his second wife Jane Hopper, a sister of his deceased wife, Apr. 2, 1822. Of the seven children born to this marriage three are yet living; Mrs. Mary Helt, John, of Douglss Co., IL, and Josiah. On coming to the county Mr. Skidmore entered 160 acres of land on section 22, Helt Township, which he owned until his death. Here he kept a public house for 40 years, which was the traveler's stopping place between Vincennes and Fort Wayne or from Chicago. He served as justice of the peace several years, and was quite a prominent man in the early history of the county. He died Dec. 7, 1863, his widow surviving until Apr. 2, 1870. Both were members of the Methodist Episcopal Church, and were consistent Christians. *Taken from Biographical Sketches published in 1888*

THE SKINNER FAMILY, James John Skinner was the first known ancestor. He was born in Hereford, England, on Jan. 18, 1731, and died on Dec. 27, 1794, in Maryland. He was the first Lieutenant in the Revolutionary War in 7th Maryland Regiment. He was married to Mary Hastings. They had a son Henry.

Henry Skinner was born in 1753 and died in 1827. He was married to Abigail Parney. In 1820, he was in the Gallio Co., OH, census. In 1824, the family and other Skinners moved to Indiana and settled in Vermillion County. Then later some of them moved on to Vermilion Co., IL, and some on to Iowa.

Children of Henry and Abigail were James, Francis, John, Allen and William P. James Skinner operated a tavern on the square in Newport and also furnished the brick for the first court house.

Norman Skinner

William P. Skinner was born in 1795 in Maryland. He died on Oct. 15, 1830, in Vermillion Co., IN. He was buried in Skinner Cemetery near his home, two and one-half miles west of Perrysville. William P. was married to Diana McCloud on Dec. 28, 1815, in Gallio Co., OH. Children were Nancy, William P., Henry, Lewis, Clarissa, Harriet and Norman H.

Norman H. Skinner was born 1816 and died on May 13, 1880, and was buried in Skinner Cemetery. Norman H.'s first wife was Ellen Cossey, 1820 to 1857. Children were William P., Nancy, Harriet, Ellen, Norman, J. and Juliet. Norman H. Skinner's second wife was Martha Hanley; born in 1828 and died in 1882. Children were Lewis, Frank, Martha (Eva). Norman H.'s death was caused by his team running off north of Eugene and throwing him out on May 10, 1880. He died three days later at 64 years of age.

Lewis Skinner was born June 16, 1865, and died Oct. 4, 1941. He was widely known over the county and township, being trustee, commissioner, and road superintendent. He also farmed and operated a sawmill. He was married to Rosetta Wittenmyer in 1892. Children were Ethel (Kemna), Grace (Kinney), Elsie (Kemna), Margaret (Orahood), Elbert, John and Norman Lewis Franklin.

Still living in Vermillion County are Lewis Kemna, son of William and Ethel Kemna; Harlan Kinney, son of Glen and Grace Kinney; Richard Kemna, son of Fred and Elsie Kemna; Marietta (Arrasmith), daughter of Fred and Elsie Kemna; and Rosemary (Kirby), daughter of Lamont and Margaret Orahood, living in Warren County.

Norman L. Skinner was born Dec. 17, 1905, and died Mar. 4, 1978. He was married to Mary E. Cole. Norman, like his father Lewis, farmed and operated a sawmill. Children are Norman L. and Curtis F. Skinner. Children of Norman L. and Dorothy Mitchell Skinner are Norman L. and Nicole Louise. Children of Curtis and Candace Cox Skinner are Cory and Chad Skinner.

PAUL AND SADIE SLAVEN, When Paul Lionel Slaven and Sadie Cecilia Craig married in 1921, their families were neighbors on Clinton's South Sixth Street.

Paul's parents Isaac Slaven and Florence Roberts had moved to Clinton from Staunton about 1918. While there Isaac had worked as a coal miner, and he continued in that labor after they came to Clinton. Isaac died in Clinton in 1936 and Florence in 1940. Both are buried in the Rule Cemetery of their native Clay County.

Sadie's family had been in Vermillion County somewhat longer. Her parents were Ripley Craig and Electa Drake. They were married in Vermillion County in 1889 and had 11 children. Only four of them lived to adulthood: Corintha, Harry, Sadie,

and Bertie. Today, Bertie alone survives. He is a retired army colonel and makes his home in Tacoma, WA. Ripley died in Clinton in 1941 after being hit by an automobile. Electa passed away in Tacoma in 1951.

Paul and Sadie Slaven - 1940

The parents of Ripley Craig were Richard J. Craig and Derexa Dinwiddie. Richard was born in Edgar Co., IL, but, lived all of his adult life in Vermillion County. His parents Eli Crago and Experience Jones were believed captured by Indians about 1839. The "Crago" surname was listed as "Craig" when the children began school, and the error was never corrected. Richard served in the Civil War and died in Clinton in 1908. His wife Derexa Dinwiddie had also been orphaned. Her father William Dinwiddie came to Vermillion County in the 1830's and was said to have been a physician with the regular army. Derexa's sister Mary Southard took her in and completed her upbringing.

Electa Drake's family came to Clinton from Antwerp, OH. Her father John Drake was a Civil War veteran; he died in 1879. Her mother was Corintha Ann Chapman, niece of Johnny "Appleseed" Chapman. Corintha worked at a variety of domestic jobs in the area to provide for her family. While Electa and her brother Len Drake remained in Clinton, Corintha ventured to Greenville, MO, with her son Preston Ellis. She died there during a malaria epidemic in 1902.

Paul and Sadie Slaven were the parents of six children. In 1938 they moved their young family from South Sixth Street to Crompton Hill. In 1942 they moved to Parke County where they spent their remaining years. Sadie died in 1962 and Paul in 1963. Both are buried in the Riverside Cemetery. Four of their children survive: Verna is the wife of Ralph Walton and they reside in Greenfield, IN. Paul Junior is married to the former Phyllis Crowder and they reside in rural Parke County. Alice and husband Richard Robertson live in Rockville. James and wife Patricia Kyle make their home in Lyford.

CLARNEY SMITH (1876-1965) AND AMANDA SCOTT SMITH (1879-1968), married Mar. 31, 1903 at Chester, IL and farming around Neoga, IL, parents of Earl, born Jan. 15, 1904, Esther born Jan. 7, 1909 and Carmie born May 25, 1911, came to Cayuga March 1918 from Strasburg, IL, to the farm they had purchased, located two miles north of Eugene on the east side of the road. They arrived at the Cayuga Depot aboard the Clover Leaf Railroad. They moved household furniture. They brought livestock, two horses which produced two colts; hogs, one cow and one Ford touring car with side curtains. Farming they knew and marveled that grain grew when they were away and out of the field.

Clarney Smith, Esther Smith, Earl Smith, Carmie Smith, Amanda Smith

They attended local churches and schools and the next year being the year of the flu epidemic schools were closed and other community activities discontinued for a time. They survived. Not all did. Neither did they starve.

There was the pasture, the fields of grain; the milk cows, sheep, chickens, turkeys, an orchard filled with apples trees and blossoms in the springtime, bees buzzing in hives on the ground, ripe apples from July first into the fall, cherry trees, 14 of them, three pear trees outside the back door, one with an oriole nest suspended from a limb, a garden with full length grape arbor and three kinds of grapes, peach trees by the side, dewberries down the lane most to the railroad. The front yard was set with five poplar trees tall and spacious and six cedar trees spaced toward the gravel road.

They worked. They went to bed at night and church on Sunday. They farmed 200 acres. They were charter members of Farm Bureau in Vermilion County. The children wee charter members of Vermillion County 4-H Clubs.

Inside the house was cheerfulness, an eight-day clock that chimed the time every hour and half-hour, restful beds, a stove that heated as they gathered around. There was the family Bible, read and announcing wedding and birth dates, Bible stories, singing, a record phonograph, Pathe, classical and religious music and a player piano.

For over 30 years it was home. Before he died they had paid for 600 acres of land and celebrated their golden wedding anniversary in 1953 as had her father and mother in 1925.

Earl graduated from Cayuga high school in 1922. Never married he made his home in El Segunda, CA and died there in 1985.

Esther graduated from Cayuga high school in 1927, worked at the Court House, Farm Bureau office. She married Floyd Wann in 1929. They have one son Arden and one daughter Virginia and are married 59 years.

Carmie graduated from Cayuga high school in 1928 and Utterback's Business college in 1929. She was employed by Civil Service, Washington, D.C., U.S. Treasury for five years. In 1945 she married Leo Fultz, lives north of Eugene. They have four children and 14 grandchildren.

ROBERT H. SMITH, "Scotty, this country has never been the same since you came."

Robert H. Smith was born Apr. 12, 1886 in Glasgow, Scotland. He was the 17th child born to William and Sarah Jane Smith. He lived to see seven generations, had nine children, 14 grandchildren and many great and great-great grandchildren.

His sister, Marie and her husband, Robert Wilson, lived in Illinois and sent Bob money to come to the United States. The money was not spent for the purpose intended. In 1907 they purchased a ticket and sent it to him. On his journey over by boat, he decided to play a joke and not talk, so people thought he could not speak English. After a few days of not eating, he said, "I'm hungry", to which they replied, "you speak English".

Robert H. Smith

Upon arriving in New York, he asked where he might find Robert Wilson's farm and lived with Marie and Robert until his marriage. Robert (Dad) acquired a horse and buggy and soon had a reputation of driving too fast, in his home town of Philo, IL. There was a certain pretty blond, curly headed young girl which refused to ride with him for that reason. He attended her church and one Sunday when she did not attend–the church sent her a flower by way of Robert. That was the beginning of a sweet romance and they were married in 1912. Dad farmed for a number of years and then moved to Cayuga, IN, where he worked at the Dee Brick Plant. He and Katie (Mom) had a two room house with their six children. As their family grew, more rooms were added. Cayuga was their home until they died.

Golden Wedding Anniversary

In Indiana my Dad was called "Scotty", a nickname which followed him until his death. Dad kept his Scottish brogue, and had a beautiful tenor voice. Katie passed away in 1968 and Scotty in 1978, a week before his 92nd birthday.

In Scotland, Robert was a boxer and had his nose broken many times. He taught his children: Anyone who gives up is a loser. We Smith children grew up with two pair of gloves and a punching bag. Dad taught the girls to box with the boys. We learned to punch and we were never allowed to cry.

Back in Scotland

In 1969 Scotty and his daughter, Esther, left for a return visit to Scotland. On November tenth, just 62 years after he landed the first time, he was back in the United States again.

Of his nine children, six are still living. There are five girls and one boy: Mable Henderson, Louise Thatcher, Irene Williams—Cayuga, IN. Esther DeMotte—Ridgefarm, IL. Marie Smith—Indianapolis, IN. William Edward (Mike) Smith—State of Washington. Three of his sons are gone, Herbert, Earl and Glenn.

Scotty was proud of his children. The men he worked with said they liked Monday mornings because Scotty told of his weekend visits from his children who had come by.

Dad didn't get to do big things—but this is about my dad. *Submitted by Marie Smith*

Scotty Smith and family. Back: Esther, Mike, Marie and Glen. Middle: Mabel, Scotty and Katie. Front: Herb, Irene and Louise

THE SPANGLERS,
There were five Spanglers that came to Vermillion County in the early 1800's. They settled in Clinton Township four miles west and northwest of Clinton, IN.

The five were Phillip, died 1825; Cuthbert H. born in Virginia 1793 died 1839; Joseph born ca. 1796; Frederick born in Virginia 1804 died 1853; and Jesse Spangler born in Pennsylvania 1807 died 1884.

Jesse Spangler (June 12, 1807 - Feb. 24, 1884) and Julianne Vaughn Spangler (Sept. 10, 1831 - Oct. 16, 1899)

Cuthbert H. Spangler was the administrator for Phillip Spangler estate in 1826. Four and one half miles west of Clinton on Highway 163 on a hill overlooking Brouillittes Creek is the Spangler Cemetery where many of the Spanglers and their descendants are buried. One-half mile east of the Spangler Cemetery is a county road called the Spangler road. Two miles north on this road, Frederick and his wife Rebecca Spangler donated half an acre of land to the Vermillion County school district 4-14-10 for a school in the year of 1850. Vermillion county built a one-room brick school house which was named for the Spanglers in honor of the ones that donated the land. The Spangler school house was torn down 1931-32.

The Spanglers owned many acres of land in that area. Emily Spangler, born 1807, married May 23, 1827 to Caleb Bales, was born in 1796 in Tennessee; they were married at Cuthbert Spanglers home. Their children were: William F., Catharine (Wellman), Josephine, Martha (Carson) and Caleb.

Caleb Bales died in 1836, age 40. He left his wife Emily with five small children. Caleb, Emily and their children are buried in the Bales Cemetery two miles southeast of Dana. Jesse Spangler and wife Juliann Vaughn (born 1831) lived on their farm at the west edge of Sandytown. In later years the Monkey Mine was built there. Jesse and Juliann Spangler raised five daughters that were born in Vermillion County. Susan Elizabeth Spangler (born 1850), married Benjamin Kelley (born 1849); Caroline Permelia Spangler (born 1853), married Harrison Runyan (born 1843); Harriet Ann Spangler (born 1858), married _____ Jones; Jessie Sophia Spangler (born 1862), married Benjamin Burgess (born 1848); Ruth Esther Spangler (born 1865), married Christopher C. Kelley (born 1865). Benjamin Kelley and Christopher Kelley were brothers. There are many descendants from this line of Spanglers in Vermillion County.

This article is submitted by Josephine Smith. My husband Grover Smith, helped me gather some of the information for this article. I am the daughter of Enos M. and Eliza Shannon Kelley. Enos M. Kelley is the son of Benjamin and Susan Spangler Kelley. *Submitted by Josephine Kelley Smith*

CECIL ERNEST SPELLMAN AND ANNABELLA HAWORTH SPELLMAN,
Cecil E. Spellman (1895-1980) was born southwest of Newport, the only child of Ernest Henry Spellman and Mary Francis Rice Spellman.

As a young man he enlisted in World War I and later graduated from Piano Tuning College in Vincennes, IN.

He married Lorena Davis and had two children, Evelyn Prather and Vernon Cecil Spellman, both living in California.

He later married Annabella Haworth, eldest daughter of Charles E. and Lillie VanCamp Haworth of Newport, IN. To this union were born two daughters, Patricia Ann Hunt and Carol Elaine Knoblett.

Mr. Spellman was a well-respected farmer in Vermillion Township and tuned pianos in this area for over 50 years. In the early 1940's, Mr. and Mrs. Spellman operated a florist shop, namely Spellman's Flowers, and a wartime restaurant called The Bomb Shelter in Newport.

Annabella Spellman (1912-1968) a graduate of Newport High School was active in 4-H work for many years and was a secretary in the Vermillion County Extension Office at Newport.

Patty Spellman Hunt lives at Prairieton, IN, and has three daughters—Mari Sloan, Joy Campbell, and Gail Welch, all graduates of Indiana State University.

Carol Spellman Knoblett lives on the Spellman farm west of Newport. She and her husband Robert have three sons and a daughter—Michael, Kevin, Monte Cecil, and Lisa Gayle Turner. They also have eight grandchildren.

GILBERT ANDREW SPROULS AND DAISY WINTER SPROULS,
Gilbert (1891-1971) was the son of Stephen Andrew (1858-1945) and Mary E. Watson (1861-1931) Sprouls, and grandson of Andrew (1827-1851) and America Pribble (1823-1890) Sprouls, and great-grandson of James and Mary Hathway Sprouls. The James Sprouls family came to Vermillion Co., IN, from Ohio, in 1829.

Gilbert married Daisy Katherine Winter (1893-1986), daughter of Charles Samuel and Loretta Chezem Winter, on Jan. 31, 1915. They spent all of their married life around Cayuga and Perrysville, IN.

They are the parents of three daughters and one son—Helen married Floyd Stuttler, Herman married Ruth Noggle, Mildred married Wilbur Evans, and Mona married Jack Dennis.

Gilbert had three brothers, Alva, Charles, and Clarence; and three sisters, Florence, Bertha, and Ethel.

Daisy had two brothers, Charles and William; and five sisters, Grace, Agnes, Nellie, Mary, and Sarah Bell.

Gilbert and Daisy are buried at the Lower Mound Cemetery near Covington, IN.

HERMAN ELVIN AND RUTH NOGGLE SPROULS,
Herman Elvin Sprouls was born May 7, 1917 in Vermillion Co., IN, the son of Gilbert Andrew (1891-1971) and Daisy Katherine Winter Sprouls (1893-1986). He has three sisters, Helen, Mildred and Mona. Herman has lived his entire life around and in Perrysville, IN. He graduated in 1935 from Perrysville High School, he worked most of his life at Meat Packing Companies in Danville, IL. From 1942 until 1945 he served in the Army of the United States in the 4th Air Depot Group in the Pacific Theater. On Oct. 18, 1946 he married Ruth Noggle daughter of Elmer (1889-1958) and Rozella Sykes Noggle (1894-1982). Ruth had three brothers, Forrest, Wayne (1915-1915) and Paul; also three sisters, Lavon (1911-1983) Lucille (1912-1921) and Nellie. Ruth graduated from Newport High School in 1936, soon after went to work in the Court House in Newport, IN, then when the Army Plant came to Newport and during the war she was secretary for E.I. Dupont.

When they were married they bought a home in Perrysville, IN where they still live. Ruth went to work in 1946 in Danville, IL in the payroll Department for General Electric Company and worked until their daughter Deborah Kay was born Apr. 12, 1955, she took a five year leave and returned and worked until 1977 when she retired.

Their daughter Deborah Kay graduated from North Vermillion High School, in 1973, she has a B.S. degree in Psychological Applications from Indiana State University, a M.S. degree in Vocational Rehabilitation Administration from Southern Illinois University, a M.S. degree in Special Education from Indiana State University and also from Indiana University degree in Occupational

Education with Cognates in Rehabilitation Counseling and Special Education. At the present time she is a Vocational Evaluator for Akron, Ohio Public Schools and part time teacher at Kent State College in Ohio.

Deborah Kay on June 1, 1974, married Dennis A. Nolte from Clinton, IN. Dennis has a B.S. in Mechanical Engineering Technology from Purdue University and a M.B.A. from Indiana State University. Dennis went to work in 1973 at the Newport Army Ammunition Plant and worked there until March, 1987. From there he went to Wadsworth, OH where he is Manager of Production at the Physics International Company at Wadsworth, OH. *Submitted by Ruth Noggle Sprouls*

THE KENNETH G. SPROULS FAMILY,
Kenneth Sprouls was born May 8, 1917, about three miles north of Cayuga. His parents were Alva and Grace Dove Sprouls. He had one sister, Neva, born Sept. 29, 1908 - died Nov. 9, 1978. His brother, Joe Dean Sprouls was born Aug. 30, 1912 - died Aug. 12, 1926. His brother James Eston Sprouls was born Aug. 31, 1923 - died Sept. 20, 1939. His parents and his two brothers are buried in the Eugene Cemetery.

His grandfather was S.A. (Doug) Sprouls. His mother's parents were John C. and Samantha Dove.

His parents and family moved from north of Cayuga to a small farm southeast of Tangier, IN. He went to the first grade at the Sylvania School. The family then moved to Perrysville, IN area where he attended the second grade. The family then purchased the Sprouls dairy from his grandfather and moved there September, 1925. He started to school in the third grade at Cayuga. The trustee of Eugene township was Noah Davis and he was an uncle to the Sprouls children. He graduated in 1935. He continued to work in the family dairy until he went into military service, serving in the Army. He entered the Army in June, 1941 and was discharged with the rank of sergeant. In Nov. 21, 1941 he was married to Helen Samuels, daughter of Joseph B. and Susan Samuels. The Samuels family lived on the Silver Island road, but their children attended Cayuga School. Helen graduated with the class of 1934.

When he was discharged from the Army, he worked at the Dupont powder plant at Newport, IN, for seven months. He then went into business with his father in the Sprouls Dairy and remained there until the dairy was sold out in February, 1954. He worked for almost three years in door to door sales.

He became a Prudential Insurance representative in January, 1957. He and his family moved to Williamsport, IN, where he worked until Jan. 1, 1965 when he transferred with Prudential to Crawfordsville, IN. He worked there until he retired Oct. 1, 1980.

Kenneth and Helen had three sons born to them. Dennis Neil Sprouls was born Mar. 17, 1943. He and his family are living in Lafayette, IN. Gary Lee Sprouls was born Mar. 27, 1945, and he and his family are living in Warsaw, IN. Eric Kent Sprouls was born July 24, 1957. He was killed in a trailer home fire on July 26, 1981. Kenneth and Helen have six grandchildren and two great-grandchildren.

He has had a very special blessing from the Lord in his life. His parents and both sets of grandparents were born again Christians. His heritage is one which will last throughout all eternity. He was privileged to be an elder in the Lord's church for 25 years.

STOKESBERRYS, Peter Stokesberry was born in Ohio and came to Vermillion Co., IN in 1832. He married Vienna Watts in Martin Co., IN. He bought land in Helt Township, Vermillion Co., IN. He was a farmer. They had ten children. Four sons were in the Civil War and one died in the service. One of their children homesteaded in Oklahoma.

Their children were: Richard Ross, Martin Henderson, Alfred Marson, John Washington (all in Civil War - John W. died there), James Madison, Martha Jane, Eliza Emmeline, Mary E. and William H.

Descendants of this family still reside in Vermillion County. *Submitted by Ernestine Brown*

FRED STOUP, In 1967 the Fred Stoup family moved to Highland Township in Vermillion County from neighboring Wabash Township in Fountain County.

Fred was born in Wabash Township in 1929, the youngest child of Frank and Vivian (Stout) Stoup. He attended Whites and Rabb Elementary schools and graduated from Perrysville High School. In 1950 he married Barbara Ann Holycross. Fred is a pattern maker by trade and had worked for Tilton Pattern Works in Tilton, IL, for 33 years.

Fred Stoup Family

Barbara was born in Vermillion Co., IL, in 1929, the youngest child of Mantford and Mayme (Moudy) Holycross. She attended Butternut School until sixth grade when her family moved across the state line to the Upper Coal Branch area. She graduated from Perrysville High School where she excelled in track. In 1946 she established county records in the 50 and 100 yard dashes and in the 440 yard relay that held for several years. Barbara is a homemaker.

The Stoup's have two children, Dwight Duane and Rhonda Kay.

Dwight was born in 1952. He graduated from North Vermillion High School and Purdue University. In 1979 he married Paula Gritton from Tilton, IL. They have two children: Steven Allen Cravens and Eric Duane Stoup. Eric is the only descendant to carry on this branch of the Stoup name. They live in Tilton, IL.

Rhonda was born in 1955 and graduated from North Vermillion High School. Her first marriage to Donald Gill ended when he was killed in an auto accident. They have a son, Donald Wayne Gill, Jr. She later married Mike Hinkle from Cayuga, IN, and they have a daughter, Kayla Michelle. They live in Highland Township.

Fred's ancestors have been traced back to his great-great-grandfather, Andrew Stoup (1794-1878), who was born in Pennsylvania and moved to Warren Co., OH. He married Margaret Bodine (1797-1869), who was born in Virginia and also

lived in Warren Co., OH. They moved from Ohio to a 100 acre farm in Wabash Township, Fountain Co., IN, in 1838. They had eight children: David, John, Mary, Catherine, Caroline, Andrew Jackson, Elizabeth and Rebecca. Andrew and his wife are buried in Oak Grove Cemetery in Covington, IN.

Andrew Jackson Stoup (1830-1912), Fred's great-grandfather, was born in Ohio and married Nancy Drollinger (1827-1900) in 1851. They had seven children: John, Oliver, William, Edward, Ross, Emma, and Monroe. Andrew Jackson and wife are buried in Coal Creek Cemetery.

Ross Stoup (1864-1919), Fred's grandfather, married Lockie Marlatt (1858-1926). They both taught. They had one child, Frank (1895-1965). They lived in Wabash Township until 1906 when they purchased a 240 acre farm and moved to Orange Co., IN.

While in Orange County, Frank married Alna Vivian Stout (1892-1980) in 1916 in Paoli, IN. Frank and Vivian both graduated from Paoli High School and she attended Indiana University. In 1916, Ross sold his Orange County farm and bought the Henry Ramser Farm and both families moved to Wabash Township in 1917. Frank and Vivian had six children: Louise, Charles, John and James (twins), Alice, and Fred. James died at birth. Frank, Vivian, Frank's parents, and James are buried at Mount Hope Cemetery near Covington.

Barbara's grandparents were Ed and Martha Holycross who resided in Highland Township. Her father, Mantford (1873-1961) was one of seven children. Barbara's maternal grandparents were Robert and Sarah Ann (Switzer) Moudy who also resided in Highland Township. Her mother Mayme (1883-1961) was one of five children

Mantford and Mayme married in 1901 and had ten children: Virgie, Kleemon, Mazie, Hattie, Frances, Earl, Harold, Wayne, Mary Mildred, and Barbara.

ALBERT AND RUTH WESTBROOK STRATTON, Stratton corner, two miles north of St. Bernice, was a busy place during the 20's, 30's, and 40's. It was the location of Stratton Farm Meat Market during the winter and the Cottrell Elevator during the summer. It was also the home of Albert and Ruth Stratton and their children, James and Rachel.

Albert, born Mar. 3, 1885, the son of Morris and Francis Houston Stratton, grew up near Logan and Edgar Co., IL. Ruth, born Apr. 10, 1889, in Paris, IL, the daughter of Edward Riley and Mary Belle Watson Westbrook, grew up just down the road from Stratton corner.

Albert attended Jones School and Brown's Business College before farming with his father and brother, Frank. Ruth graduated from Helt Township High School and attended Indiana State Normal. She taught all eight grades in a one-room school in St. Bernice before teaching the lower grades at Frog College.

Albert and Ruth were married Dec. 20, 1911, and lived on his father's farm in Illinois until they moved to the little white house on the corner in 1920. They started custom butchering, killing and dressing hogs and cattle for other farmers. The enterprise grew into a thriving retail and wholesale meat business. During the 20's, they would kill about 25 hogs each day and deliver to Mill's Store in Clinton. They began making sausage, curing hams and bacon, and processing all cuts of beef. Besides selling from the shop, they delivered in all

directions. Stratton Sausage was featured at many fine restaurants. Rationing during World War II killed the small meat markets. Deliveries stopped in 1942.

Cottrell Elevator, located next to the Milwaukee Railroad, was managed by Albert and Ruth. Many horse-drawn loads of wheat and oats were scooped by hand into railroad cars or the large bins that still stand on Stratton land. When farmers started hauling their grain to larger markets in trucks, the scale house was closed and Albert used the bins for his own grain.

The Strattons were parents of two children. James Westbrook Stratton was born in 1913. Rachel Louise Stratton (Milligan) was born in 1924.

Albert and Ruth were members of the Bono Methodist Church. Ruth enjoyed the Dana Home and Health Home Ec Club for many years.

The Stratton family home, the little white house on the corner, burned in 1943. After living in a rented home for a few years, they bought and remodeled the Westbrook home place. They lived there, farmed the land, and raised cattle and hogs until their deaths. Ruth died in August, 1967, at 78 years of age. Albert died in January, 1968, at the age of 81.

JAMES AND EVELYN STRATTON, As a teenager, James "Jimmy" Stratton was known for driving a Model T Ford around corners on two wheels.

James Westbrook Stratton, the son of Albert and Ruth Westbrook Stratton, was born Nov. 12, 1913, near Logan, IL. The family moved to a small farm two miles north of St. Bernice, Stratton corner, in 1920. He attended Helt Township School and Dana High School, and graduated from St. Bernice High School in 1932. After graduation he worked at his father's meat market.

James and Evelyn Stratton

James married Evelyn Juanita Hasty on Nov. 3, 1933. Evelyn, daughter of Forrest and Juanita Williamson Hasty, was born Jan. 1, 1915, in Terre Haute.

James and Evelyn worked together to operate a City Service filling station in St. Bernice and a gasoline tank truck. Then, while James worked on the Milwaukee Railroad for several years, they lived in Crete, IL.

In 1945, they moved to Clinton to manage the Clinton Frozen Food Plant. Then James decided to go back to work on his father's farm in 1954. Evelyn worked in dress shops and retail stores until they moved out to the Westbrook-Stratton homeplace in 1968 after the deaths of his parents.

James and Evelyn have always liked to meet with their many friends. James was a member of the Masonic Lodge in Crete, IL, Zorah Shine and Scottish Rite in Terre Haute, and Low Twelve Club of Vermillion County. Evelyn is a member of Wakofe Club in Clinton, 49er's Club in Dana and Eastern Star. They have both been members of the Vermillion County Country Club, Model A. Club, and the Bono United Methodist Church.

James and Evelyn are the parents of Sharon Elberta and James Forrest. Sharon graduated from Clinton High School and earned her B.S. degree in special education and speech and hearing therapy at Indiana State University. She is married to Charles Tryon and lives in Rolla, MO. Their daughter, Holly, is married to Ed Kuykendall and lives in California. Charles, a hydrologist at the Mark Twain National Forest, and Sharon are professional outdoor writers and lecturers. Their latest accomplishment is publishing their book, *Fly Fishing for Trout in Missouri*, in 1985.

Jim graduated from Clinton High School and earned a B.S. and M.S. in Geology at Indiana State University. Then he earned another M.S. and a PhD in paleontology at Indiana University. He is a professor of geology and paleontology at Eastern Illinois University in Charleston, IL. He is married to Patrice Fanuko, who has B.S. and M.S. degrees in botany from Eastern Illinois University. She is employed at Lakeland College in Mattoon. They have a son, James Arthur.

James never lost his love for old cars. His speed decreased, but his hankering for antique cars grew. At the time of his death in 1985, he owned several vintage automobiles.

Evelyn enjoys living on the Westbrook-Stratton farm in the house that James and she remodeled with walnut wood from the farm.

GEORGE BUCHANON STURM,
was born Mar. 4, 1857, in Eugene Township, Vermillion Co., IN, to George Washington Sturm and Eliza Canaday Sturm. George B. never saw his father, who passed away in September 1856. George B. was raised in the home of John M. Naylor, whom George's widowed Mother married in 1858.

George B. was a grandson of David and Rebecca Moore Sturm, who were among the original land owners of Eugene Township. David, the grandson of German immigrant Jacob Sturm who arrived in America in August 1750, sold his farm on Teverbough Creek in then Harrison Co., VA, in 1833. David moved his family West, settling in Section 31, Eugene Township. David was killed in August 1840 when a log crushed him during a house-raising. Rebecca Sturm continued living in Eugene Township until her death in April 1872. Rebecca is buried in the southwest corner of the Eugene Cemetery.

George B. married Mary Alice Ramsey, daughter of William and Eliza Brown Ramsey. George and Mary had four children: Harry who married Bessie Meeker; Nellie Alice, who married Henry Fred Meeker (brother of Bessie); Nora B. who died at the age of 15 months; and an unnamed infant.

George Buchanon, known as "Buck" to his friends, spent some time after his retirement from the railroad driving the "school wagon", an earlier version of the school bus. George's wife Mary passed away in January, 1900. George died in January, 1929. Both are buried in Eugene Cemetery.

Harry, a railroader and farmer like his father, was transferred to Gessie, Highland Township, and later to Terre Haute. Harry and Bessie had 12 children;

Roy, buried in Eugene Cemetery, Warren (deceased), Eva, Eileen (deceased), Cleatise (deceased), Harrietta, Nellie (deceased), Dorothy (deceased), Evelyn, Ernest, Betty (deceased), and Donald.

Nellie and Fred Meeker remained in Eugene Township their entire adult lives. They had eight children; Virgil, Paul, Wyman, Gerald, Harry, Robert, Mary Jane, and Donald. Fred passed away in September, 1957 and Nellie passed away in March 1976. Both are buried in Eugene Cemetery.

Of Nellie and Fred's eight children, four are deceased, all of whom are buried in the Eugene Cemetery. The surviving children still live in and around Vermillion County.

Virgil died in infancy.

Paul married Wilma Edwards and they have three sons: Darrell, Randy, and Dennis, all of Cayuga. Paul served as Eugene Township Trustee for several years.

Wyman married Iva Howard and they had four children: Phillip, Robert, Charolette, and Billy all living in Illinois. Iva passed away and Wyman married Dorothy Arnett.

Gerald, known as "Pete", married Margaret Jo Fultz and had two children, Sallie Sue and Gaylord, both of Georgetown, IL. They were divorced, Pete then married Mae Price.

Harry died in 1947. He was married to Alice Barclay but had no children.

Robert also died in infancy.

Mary Jane was married to Dillon Newman and they had two daughters: Nita Jo Shields of Cayuga, and Tina Whittington of Kingman. Mary Jane died in March, 1988.

Donald married Lucy White and has two step-daughters: Naomi Butler of Tangier and Leona Keller of Cayuga.

JOHN TAYLOR SR.,
There have been seven generations of Taylor's who have lived and died in Vermillion County. Family tradition has long held that John Taylor Sr. was related to President Zachary Taylor (probably a cousin), but although both men came from Orange Co., VA, this relationship has not yet been proven.

John Taylor Sr. (1790-1867) was born in Orange Co., VA. He moved with his family to Butler Co., OH around 1804. John was quite young when he married Margaret Boyd who died at the birth of their first child. Then John married Joanna Porter. They reared nine children (Margaret Jane, Mary Marie, John Francis, Simeon, Eunice, William, Sarah Ann, David Frazier, Eliza Jane, and Levi Curtis). The family moved to Vermillion County just north of Clinton in the early 1830's. After Joanna's death in 1854, John married Hannah Watson.

Hazel Fairgrief Taylor and Roy Taylor

John Taylor Sr. had three brothers (James, William, and George), and two sisters, Mary who married George Welch, and Anna who married Alexander Simpson.

All five of John Taylor's girls married, Margaret married John Beasley, Mary married Wesley Southard, Eunice married MacFarland Ellis, Sarah married Samuel Ogan, and Eliza Jane married Isaac Hines.

Some of the family settled in Edgar Co., IL, but John and his sons John, David Frazier, Simeon, William and Levi settled near Clinton and practiced their trades of farming and barrel making.

David Frazier Taylor (1825-1890) married Rebecca Jane Cooper and had eight children (Anna Eliza, Rebecca, Sarah Marie, Albert, Martha Jane, James Anderson, Georgia Ann, and Levi Calvin) all born in Vermillion County. David, his son Albert and at least three of the daughters moved around quite a bit, making several trips to Dallas Co., MO and back to Vermillion (around the 1870's) ultimately moving to the northeast corner of Oklahoma. It is said that Rebecca probably spent most of her life in a covered wagon. A granddaughter of Albert is Veda Viola Taylor (Miami, OK) who has actively pursued the Taylor family tree for many years.

Levi Taylor (1833-1866) married Margaret Willman and served in the Civil War.

Simeon Taylor (1818-1870's) married Rebecca Malone and had six children (Sarah Jane married Jefferson Foncannon, Calvin married Myrtle Smith, John was single, Elija, Elizabeth, and Samuel Malone married Jennie Carrell). Samuel Malone was the last surviving child of Simeon.

Samuel Malone Taylor (1865-1930) also made trips to Missouri and Oklahoma around 1895-1900. But he returned and made Clinton his home. For many years he was janitor of the school on South 6th street. Samuel had two sons, Charles Anchrom and Roy, who were both in the heating/plumbing trade. Charles and his son Ray were killed in an auto accident in 1957. Charles' other son Jack lives in Carbondale, IL.

Roy Taylor (1895-1965) served several years in the mounted scouts on the Mexican border chasing Pancho Villa. After that he married Hazel Marie Fairgrief and they raised four sons in Clinton (Samuel Edward, Dale Allen, Bruce Robert and John Gilbert).

Samuel Edward Taylor (1917-) married Vivian Birch, had three children (Jerry, Loretta, and Marinetta) and followed his father in the heating business. Both Samuel and his son Jerry, who married Diane Crooks, still live in Hillsdale. Loretta married William Greenlee, and teaches school in Louisville, KY. Marinetta lives in Clinton.

Bruce Robert Taylor (1923-) joined the Air Force and served through World War II, the Berlin Airlift, the Korean War, and Vietnam, and is retired in California. Bruce married Frieda Eckle and had two children, Mike Allen Taylor and Mary Jean Taylor. Mike married Terri Joy Thompson and they had Krystyl Nancy Roundy Taylor and Suzette Lynn Taylor. Mary Jean Taylor married Michael Duncan. Mary Jean has one girl Jennifer Abrams. Mike and Terri are both avid genealogists and active members of a Baptist Church as were many of their forefathers. Mike, Terri, and Mary Jean are all Computer Analyst/Programmers.

John Gilbert Taylor (1927-) married Kitty Dayon and moved to San Francisco after World

War II. They have two daughters (Linda and Marilyn) and four grandchildren.

Dale Allen Taylor (1919-1982) married Evinale Jones and moved to Michigan City where he had several children including Barbara, Tracy and Terri. *Submitted by Mike Allen Taylor*

CHARLES GENE THOMAS AND SHIRLEY LEE THOMAS,

Charles Gene Thomas was born in Newport on Dec. 16, 1934 to Mirl Thomas and Hazel Marie Harrison Thomas. Mirl Thomas was the middle child of Howard Thomas and Mary Eunice Rohr Thomas. He was born in Montezuma, Mar. 2, 1914. A brother, Ivan, was born in Clinton, Mar. 30, 1910, and a younger sister, Marie (now Mrs. Hubert Hollingsworth, residing in Dana) was born May 23, 1916, in Montezuma.

Hazel Marie Harrison Thomas was the only child born to Leatha Paxton Harrison and Obediah Harrison on Jan. 4, 1910. Mirl and Hazel also had a son, Warren Lee Thomas, born Jan. 8, 1947.

Charles Gene and Shirley Peck Thomas

Shirley Lee Peck Thomas was born Aug. 9, 1936, at Paris, IL, to Kenneth LeRoy Peck and Violet Lorene Davis Peck. Shirley was the only child born to this union. Kenneth was one of six children born to Claude Edgar Peck and Bessie Barton Peck. Kenneth was born Aug. 27, 1914.

Violet Lorene Davis Peck was the only child born to Walter Kenneth Davis and Anna Siverly Davis. She was born July 7, 1918.

Kenneth Peck later married Annabelle Pearman of Hillsdale and Violet Lorene later married Vincent Pollaro of Chicago. Two more children were born to Violet. They are Josephine Maria (now Mrs. Richard Nowarita of Paris, IL) and John Anthony. John moved to Dana in May, 1988, with his wife, the former Peggy Lewsader, and their daughter, Nicole Lorene.

Charles Gene Thomas and Shirley Lee Peck were married Feb. 12, 1955, at the Hillsdale Evangelical United Brethren Church. "C.G." had graduated from Newport High School in 1952 and Shirley graduated from Hillsdale High School in 1954 in a graduating class of nine.

A son, Ronald Gene, was born July 7, 1957. Rhonda Leigh was born Jan. 10, 1961. Ron graduated from South Vermillion High School in 1975 and DePauw University in 1979. Rhonda graduated from South Vermillion High School in 1979, and attended Vincennes University for two years and then Eastern Illinois University, where she met Daniel Stewart Smith, whom she married, May 5, 1984. Their son Bradley Michael Smith was born Mar. 26, 1986. They presently reside in Fairview.

Ron married Lori Lea Rader, Feb. 24, 1985. Their daughter, Keelea Lauron, was born Apr. 13,

1988. They reside at Shawnee Bluffs near Bloomington, IN.

Shirley and "C.G." went to housekeeping in Newport and later moved to HIllsdale. In 1968, they built their present home on highway 63 in Fairview. Both are employed at Eli Lilly and are members of the Wayside United Methodist Church. "C.G." has been very active in different youth baseball programs and officiated basketball for many years. Shirley is a member of the Clinton Tri-Kappa organization and Hillsdale Rebekah Lodge. *Submitted by Shirley L. Thomas*

EVELYN HESTELLA CRAFT KELLEY THOMAS,

was born Sept. 26, 1916, to Pearl Craft and Adelaide Myrtle Steffy. She married Raymond Willard Kelley. They had Melvin Willard Kelley on Nov. 3, 1933, Meredith William Kelley on June 30, 1944, and Judith Evelyn Kelley on May 23, 1948. They have four grandchildren and one great-grandchild. Evelyn married Gerald Thomas on Apr. 17, 1976.

GOLDA NOLAN THOMAS,

was born Oct. 20, 1891, in Helt Township, the daughter of Alfred Marion Nolan (see related biography) and Sarah Osmon Nolan. (see related biography) She was one of 11 children and grew up on the farm just west of the Ernie Pyle School.

As a child she attended Independence School until it was destroyed by fire. For the remainder of that school year the neighborhood children did their reading, writing, and arithmetic in a private home. The Rush Home was large and rambling and two of the rooms were converted into classrooms. The other part of the home was occupied by a young man, his wife, and three children. later she attended school in Dana and then Frog College.

Golda Nolan Thomas and Arch Nolan

Her family raised great amounts of produce. Each summer in the late 1890's and early 1900's, she and her brothers and sisters helped their father "peddle" vegetables and chickens on the streets of Clinton.

In 1915, she married James Leonard Thomas (see related biography) of Clinton. Two daughters were born to this union, Beulah Thomas Frist (see related biography) and Madge Thomas Lake. (see related biography)

The couple lived in Clinton for a short period, but most of their 67 years together were spent on a farm in Helt Township.

She has been a member of the Reorganized Latter Day Saint Church for many years.

She is an avid reader and enjoys writing poetry.

Golda and her brother, Arch Nolan, posed for this picture in the late 1890's. *Submitted by Madge Thomas Lake*

JAMES L. THOMAS,

was born Dec. 15, 1893, in Clinton, IN, the son of John Parker Thomas

(see related biography) and Ruth Alice Green Thomas. (see related biography) He was one of six children. His brothers and sisters included: Charles, William, John, Mattie Thomas Foncannon and Lillian Wiggins Thomas.

He lived in Clinton during his childhood and attended school in the Clinton City School system. He was baptized in the Christian Church by Rev. T.A. Hall on Jan. 8, 1906.

James and Golda Thomas

At the age of eight, he was employed by Mr. Tutwiler at the Tutwiler & Co. grocery store. Additional income was earned by herding cattle from Clinton to graze in the area of what is now the Walnut Grove Cemetery.

In his early teens he was employed at the brick company in Clinton. In 1912, at the age of 19, he began to work in the coal mines. It was a life-long tenure that carried him forward through the years to 1951. It encompassed employment in the area deep mines including: Oak Hill No. 2, Oak Hill No. 1, Crown Hill No. 3, and Crown Hill No. 6. Also, two strip mines: The Vermillion County Coal Co. and Standard Coal Co.

He was an active member of the United Mine Workers of America and served as mine timekeeper during portions of his employment. He also served several terms as president of the Clinton branch of the Local Union of District No. 11.

During the off-periods of coal mining, he did carpentry work; a trade he inherited from his father.

In 1915, he married Golda Lela Nolan. (see related biography) He fathered two daughters, Beulah Thomas Frist (see related biography) and Madge Thomas Lake. (see related biography)

In the late 1920's and early 1930's he purchased portions of the William Harrington farm land located in Helt's Prairie. It was on that land that he built a home; a home which he and his wife shared for half a century.

He passed away in 1982 and was laid to rest in the Helt's Prairie Cemetery.

James Thomas and his wife Golda posed for this photo in preparation for their 60th wedding anniversary celebration in 1975. *Submitted by Madge Thomas Lake*

JOHN PARKER THOMAS,

was born in the Charleston, IL, area Mar. 26, 1855. He was the son of Samuel and Hannah Lamb Thomas; one of eight children. His brothers and sisters included: William, Andrew, Jack, Charles, Assa, Ann Thomas Phipps (wife of Rev. J.W. Phipps) and Sarah. (It is unknown if Sarah was married.)

John Parker Thomas was so-named in honor of a certain Judge Parker from the Charleston, IL, area.

He was an infant when the family moved to Nyesville in Parke Co., IN. The family lost their father at an early age and their mother married a Mr. Peacock.

Building permit issued to John Parker Thomas in 1911 for the purpose of building a carpenter shop on Fifth Street in Clinton, IN

John Parker Thomas eventually settled in the Clinton, IN, area. He was an accomplished carpenter and built many of the homes in Clinton in the early 1900's.

He met and married Ruth Alice Green. (see related biography) Six children were born to this union; Charles, Mattie Thomas Foncannon, William, James L. (see related biography), John and Lillian Thomas Wiggins.

In 1911, he fulfilled a life-long dream when he built a carpenter shop on Fifth Street in Clinton. During the disastrous flood in the spring of 1913, the water level of a nearby creek threatened to wash away the shop. In his attempt to retrieve his tools and supplies, he contracted pneumonia. John Parker Thomas passed away May 1, 1913, and is buried in the Riverside Cemetery in Clinton.

This building permit was issued and gave him permission to build his carpenter shop. *Submitted by Madge Thomas Lake*

L. PAUL THOMAS,

John W. Thomas and wife, Bertha Roach, came to Vermillion County with a young son, L. Paul Thomas, from a log cabin in Parke County circa 1888 or 1889. The Thomas' purchased a pre-Civil War home in Portertown from Isaac Porter. Two more children were born in Portertown, Hazel Ann Thomas and John William Thomas, Jr.

The Thomas family engaged in extensive farming (1,000 acres) at one time (in Illinois and Indiana) and raised thoroughbred show horses, which were shipped all over the U.S. for show, winning many awards. John William Thomas Sr. was killed (at age 55) at the C. & E. I. Railroad crossing in Cayuga - in November, 1920. The home place in Portertown remained in the family until it burned around 1959-60. Bertha Thomas died in 1958. Hazel Ann Thomas died in 1981. John W. (Jack) Thomas returned to the area in his retirement and died in 1978. His widow, Effie Manhart Thomas, lives in their home in Eugene.

L. Paul Thomas

L. Paul Thomas was educated in Cayuga schools, graduating in 1906. He attended Purdue University. He married Gladys Coffin Thomas in 1913. Early married years were spent in Portertown in what was then a tenant house belonging in the Thomas family. In the early 1920's (approximately 1923) Paul and Gladys purchased from the town of Cayuga, the school annex building (built in 1917). A breakfast room, back porch and kitchen, and a sunporch on the southwest were added to the original structure making a ten room residence. This 71 year old family home is still in our immediate family.

Paul was always interested in civic affairs, Eugene Township and Vermillion County. He spent most of his life in this community residing in the family home. He was engaged in farming. He also owned and operated a meat market and blacksmith shop in the early 1920's. He was a Charter member of the Cayuga Lions Club, 50 year member of the Masonic Lodge, and member of the Presbyterian Church. At the time of his death he was County Auditor after eight years as Vermillion County Treasurer. He and his wife, Gladys, celebrated their 50th wedding anniversary in 1963 with an open house in their home. Paul died in 1965 and Gladys died in 1978.

Paul and Gladys had one daughter, Anabeth Thomas Jenkins Lallish, born December, 1920. She resides in the family home in Cayuga. Anabeth, who is the only child of Paul and Gladys, had three children: Janet Lynn Jenkins Martin, Georgetown, IL; William Thomas Jenkins, Danville, IL; and Gregory Joel Jenkins, Indianapolis (Carmel), IN.

There are four great-grandchildren of Paul and Gladys Thomas: Jeffery Scott James, Georgetown, IL; Brian Thomas James, Oakwood, IL; Ryan Scott Jenkins, Danville, IL; and Evan William Jenkins, Danville, IL. *Submitted by Anabeth Thomas Jenkins Lallish*

RUTH ALICE GREEN THOMAS,

was born Feb. 8, 1863, on a farm southeast of Marshall, IL, the daughter of James (of the Greencastle, IN, Greens) and Rebecca Lowe (sister of Judge Lowe of Marshall, IL) Green. She was one of nine children. Her brothers and sisters included: Perry, Joe, Ephram, Ollie, Lou Green Hanson, Em. Green Bartrum, Nan. Green Switzer, and Mattie Green Dugger. The brother, Ephram, served in the Civil War.

Mattie Green Dugger, Ruth Alice Green Thomas with grandson, Robert Thomas

The family lost their father in the mid-1870's and seemed to drift apart. The only child who remained at home with his mother was Ollie; perhaps this was because he was the baby of the family.

Ruth Alice Green and her sister Lou worked in the Grand Hotel in Marshall, IL, for a time. In the year 1879, Ruth Alice and Lou walked from Marshall, IL, to Clinton, IN. Ruth Alice found employment in a restaurant and her sister, Lou, opened a bakery shop in "the Soup Bone Hollow area" of Clinton.

Their mother, Rebecca, brother Ollie, and sister Mattie joined them in Clinton at a later date. The mother, Rebecca was well known in later years as a weaver of rugs and carpets.

While working in the restaurant, Ruth Alice Green met and married John Parker Thomas, a local carpenter. (see related biography) Six children were born to this union, including James L. Thomas. (see related biography)

Ruth Alice Green Thomas died Apr. 1, 1944, and is buried in the Riverside Cemetery in Clinton, IN.

She and her sister and a grandson posed for this picture in the 1920's. *Submitted by Madge Thomas Lake*

NEAL TOMEY,

who graduated from Dana High School in 1931 became well known in Washington, D.C. Since he graduated during the depression he needed to find a career that wasn't expensive. He was fortunate to be one of the few to be accepted by the Navy. During his three and one-half years in the Navy, he applied for an appointment at Annapolis, received it, but couldn't pass the physical. In 1935 after leaving the Naval Service, he entered the Civil Service as a clerical worker. Soon he entered George Washington University as a night and early morning student. He received his Bachelor of Arts and bachelor of Law Degrees from George Washington University as well as doing some undergraduate study at Harvard University. He was licensed to practice in Indiana and the District of Columbia. In 1939 he took his first administrative position in the Civil Service on the National Defense Mediation Board, then he worked on the National War Labor Board.

During World War II he served in the United States Maritime Service. He went in as an Ensign and came out as a Lieutenant Commander. After the war he went into Civilian Service with the Navy Department; from here he went to the Department of the Secretary of Defense, then to the Department of Labor Relations Board. It was here that he became interested in a speciality; administrator of financial management and law.

He was a specialist in government agencies having to do with the law, financial management, and personnel. He has been the director of these agencies: St. Lawrence Seaway Development Association, and the National Labor Relations Board.

In 1965, he was the Director of Administration of the National Capital Transportation Agency. This was an independent agency that reported directly to the President in regards to a transit development program for the National Capital Region.

Neal Tomey died sometime in 1966 and was buried in Arlington Cemetery. This man went a long way after he won the Vermillion County Oratorical Contest for Dana High School in 1931.

HUBERT CLARENCE TURNER,

In 1904 a son was born to Lewis Henry and Martha F. Coleman of Tazewell, TN. They named him Hubert Clarence Turner. Hubert's parents died when he was very young and he was forced to work in the mines at a very young age. At the age of 16, he, his brother Nat and a friend Bill decided to seek employment in Iowa. Heading north, they decided to work, due to the need of funds, for a few months before heading west. They worked on the stretch of road, route 32, between Danville and the Indiana line. During this time, Hubert met and married Laura Jane Snyder, daughter of Robert Henry and Nancy Smith Snyder. She was born in Georgetown, IL. They were married in 1925 and settled on the Plaza farm, in the Coal Branch area, which was owned by Stacey and Van VanValkenburg who were also owners of the Plaza Hotel in Danville, IL. The Plaza at one time was a dairy farm. Leaving the Plaza farm in the mid 1900's, Hubert and Laura settled west of Perryville, IN where Hubert lived for the remainder of his life, passing away Jan. 28, 1983. An infant son preceded him in death.

The Hubert Turner Family

Laura remains on the farm with daughter Arlene. Other children of the marriage are: Clarence Kyle (wife, Barbara Sparks), children: Michael Fletcher - one son and one daughter, and Jeffrey Kyle - one son and one daughter; Lewis Henry (wife, Norma Mast), children: Lewis Stephen and Lonette Louise Loney; Annabeth (Russell) Starks, children: Carol Ann Keller - two sons, Annette Christine Honn - one daughter, and Laura Jean; Max Coleman (wife, Joyce), children: Kelly Lynn - one son and Jessica. Step-children: Gregg - three sons and Jim - one son and one daughter; Sonna Lee (Ronald) Crowder, children: Douglas Lee - two sons and one daughter, Cary Scott - one son, Bart Allen, and Eric Lane; Naomi Jean (Roy) Hershberger, children: Debbie Sue Lowe, Diana Lynn DeSutter - one son, and Lisa Ann; Mary Lou (John) Morris, children: Sheri Lynn Phaneuf - one son and one daughter, Lori Ann Begey - one son and two daughters, and Stacie Jean Terry - two sons.

There are 16 grandchildren and three step grandchildren and 12 great grandchildren and seven step great grandchildren in all.

This brings the family up to the date of July, 1988.

MARGARET MAE HESKETT UMLAND,

was born July 6, 1922, in Parke Co., IN, the daughter of Frank Everett Heskett and Rose Anna Potter Heskett. She is the youngest of five children. Her brothers were Milo, Lloyd, and William. Her sister was Lillian Heskett Fader. Her parents, brothers, and sister are deceased and are buried in the Helt's Prairie Cemetery.

When Margaret was one year old, she moved with her family to Vermillion County, and grew up in Summit Grove. She went for her first grade at the two-room Summit Grove School, and the following 11 at Hillsdale. She won first place in the Dramatic Reading Contests each of her four years in high school and also received the D.A.R. Good Citizenship Award. She graduated as salutatorian of her class in 1940. She attended Asbury College at Wilmore, KY, majoring in elementary education. She was a member of the college chorus and women's glee club. Later she attended Indiana State University. She taught school 11 years in

central Illinois - one year at Long View, three years at Homer, and the last seven years at Farmer City.

She married Herman F. Umland of Farmer City, IL, Aug. 20, 1953. He was the son of Ferdinand Umland and Amelia Gutchnect Umland of Birnamwood, WI. He had seven brothers and four sisters. Herman was the owner of a cheese factory and farm hand. Margaret and Herman became the proud parents of a son, David, Nov. 2, 1957. They lived in Boca Raton, FL, from May, 1961, to November, 1962, and then moved back to Farmer City. Herman died of a heart attack on Nov. 12, 1964.

In June, 1965, Margaret and David moved to Summit Grove. David attended Ernie Pyle Elementary School and then graduated from Clinton High School in 1975. He graduated from Ivy Tech in Auto Body Technology in 1976. He is self-employed and enjoys restoring old cars and trucks. He also enjoys riding motorcycles - street and dirt bikes, as well as three and four wheelers. Playing his drums is his favorite hobby.

Margaret was a Remedial Reading Tutor at the Ernie Pyle Elementary School - 1975-1982 - and was then a substitute teacher prior to her retirement in 1984. She taught Sunday School at the Salem United Methodist Church for several years and is still an active member there. She also belongs to, and is an officer of, the United Methodist Women's Organization.

KENNETH AND MILLICENT URAN,

Kenneth Otis Uran was born in Fort Wayne, IN on June 23, 1908, the first of four children of Otis Walter and Jessie Meisner Uran. During his years at Southside High School he held a variety of jobs. He delivered milk, carried newspapers, sold magazines, was a greeter at a department store, and turned gloves inside out at the glove factory. Kenneth worked his way through Purdue University by waiting tables at dormitories and the Union Building and summer jobs at General Electric and American Smelting Co. He was selected for the chemical engineering academic honorary, Phi Lambda Upsilon. He graduated from Purdue in 1930 as a chemical engineer and moved to Terre Haute to work for Columbian Enameling Co. as Production Control Manager.

While in Terre Haute Kenneth was first a member of the Junior Chamber of Commerce and later the Chamber of Commerce, serving on the transportation committee. He was a member of the Terre Haute Taxpayers Association, American Society of Metals, American Society of Time and Motion Engineers, and treasurer of the Terre Haute Transportation Club. He organized his own company in partnership with Lyman Pendergast called Kenly Co. and worked as a consultant engineer for Terre Haute Advertising and Garwood Products. During World War II Kenneth taught Time and Motion Study at Rose Polytechnic Institute.

Kenneth and Millicent Uran

On Feb. 14, 1929 he married Millicent Marie Gebhart. Millicent was usually called Susie. She was the daughter of Charles and Marie Bauer Gebhart. Susie was born on Oct. 24, 1907 in Fort Wayne, the first of three children. She graduated from Central High School and went to work as a long distance telephone operator for Indiana Bell Telephone Co. For a while she would play the piano while her sister sang for the local radio station. Shortly after Kenneth graduated from college and they moved to Terre Haute, their daughter Jean was born Oct. 29, 1930, followed by their son Kenneth, Jr. on Jan. 8, 1932.

During World War II Susie enrolled in Indiana State Teachers College. She received her bachelor's degree in 1945. In the years that followed she taught Home Economics, Chemistry, or Science at Hillsdale High School, Schulte High School, Concannon Jr. High, Gerstmeyer High School, and Clinton High School. Susie continued her education and received her master's degree from Indiana State University. Susie was interested in politics and once ran for the Legislature. She was chairman of Ways and Means for the Womens Department Club, and a member of Altrusa and the American Association of University Women.

In 1963 Kenly Co. burned and the company relocated to Clinton occupying the old Sands Tool and Die facility. While in Clinton, Kenneth became a member of the Clinton Chamber of Commerce. He organized a Taxpayers Association and served as chairman for several years. With their son Kenneth, Jr. who by this time had graduated from Purdue University as a Mechanical Engineer, they bought and operated the Aragon swimming pool for over 20 years.

Susie died on Apr. 23, 1985 after 56 years together. She was buried in Spangler Cemetery. Kenneth continues to operate Kenly Co. making plastic products daily with his son.

VAN DUYN FAMILY,

An obituary dated 1893 tells the story of young John Van Duyn, Jr. walking on foot through the forest from Hamilton, OH, to the "beautiful, fertile Wabash Valley." The took up a "nice farm" in Helt Township (Center area) in 1826 and later owned and farmed land in both Clinton and Helt Townships.

In 1914: Charles Van Duyn, mother Maria Wright Van Duyn; Wright Van Duyn and wife, Grace Dunkley Van Duyn; Ruth Van Duyn Cluder; Harry Van Duyn and wife, Bertha Dunkley Van Duyn; Bessie Van Duyn. Back: Esther Van Duyn Hayworth.

Both John and his younger brother, Cornelius, had been born in New Jersey to descendents of a family which had come to New Amsterdam (New York) in the mid-1600s. Cornelius settled in northern Vermillion County.

John Van Duyn Jr. was thrice married. Five children were born to his first union to Mary Hepner: James, Elizabeth, Christiane, Mary and John. After Mary's death, he married her sister, Susan, and they had one son, John Wesley. His third marriage was to Sarah Ann Trowbridge in 1847. Their children included Ella W. Van Duyn Hunter, John Henry Van Duyn, Charles Jefferson Van Duyn, Franklin Blair Van Duyn, Marion L. Van Duyn, Samuel Cornelius Van Duyn, Lavine Catherine Van Duyn Hunter, Sarah Belle Van Duyn, and Fred Grant Van Duyn.

John Van Duyn, Jr., led a long and active life as a pioneer in Vermillion County. He was a Republican but also a "great reader of broad and liberal views," according to his obituary report. He served as a justice of the peace for many years and is listed as coroner of the county in 1854. It is said that he traveled to Chicago and by flatboat to New Orleans. At home on his farm, he was a "lover of nature who found great solace and comfort in communion with the flowers, the fields and his domesticated animals."

He was one of the oldest citizens of the county when he died at the home of his son, Frank, on Jan. 18, 1893, just four days before his 90th birthday. Frank had married Maria Wright Van Duyn, the daughter of Vermillion County pioneer John Wright, and they owned several pieces of property in Clinton Township. Their home was located behind the property where Van Duyn School now stands.

Frank and Maria's children included Bessie, who later moved to Clinton; Charles Q., who moved west and prospered in the hotel business in Eugene, OR; Harry E., who eventually took over and expanded his parents' Clinton Township farm; C. Wright, who lived in the family home until 1939, when he purchased a farm in Parke Co., IN; Ruth, a school teacher and Centenary Church leader who married Clinton Township farmer Vernon Cluder; and Esther, who married Leonard Hayworth and moved to Crown Point, IN.

Frank Van Duyn died in 1912; his wife, Maria, lived for another 38 years, and some former Centenary residents can still remember buying butter and eggs from Maria. She died in 1950 at age 91.

HARRY E. VAN DUYN, By the time Harry Van Duyn was born in 1887, his families on both the Van Duyn and Wright sides were well-established Vermillion County farmers.

Harry married Bertha Dunkley in 1911, and they started farming southwest of Centenary with the help of Harry's uncle, U. G. Wright. When they sold this land to a strip mining company, they bought and moved to a farm near Brouillets Creek, west of Hazel Bluff.

Harry E. Van Duyn and Son Stock Farm, East of Centenary, IN - 1950's

Their first-born son, Frank, lived from 1914-1924. A second child, John D., was born in 1919. John helped his father expand his grain, hog, and cattle breeding operation. By the early 1940s, Harry

E. Van Duyn and Son Stock Farm was calving 75 cows, which had to be sold when John entered the Army.

In the 1940s Bertha and Harry refurbished a home on property they had acquired just east of Centenary on State Road 163. From this red and white two-story home they managed their farm with the help of their son and daughter-in-law, Miriam "Gay" Siepman Van Duyn. John and Gay had married while John was in the Army, and their daughter, Candace Van Duyn Conklin, was born in 1944, while John was overseas. They established their home next to John's parents, and three more children were born: Susan Van Duyn Zanandrea in 1948; Thomas Harry in 1950; and Jane Van Duyn (Howell) Minnett in 1951.

During the 1950s the farm grew to include over 1,000 acres, and the Van Duyns were usually raising 200-300 head of feeder cattle, as well as corn, beans and wheat. Harry died in 1961. He had been a charter member of the Vermillion County Farm Bureau, a deputy sheriff, and served as a director of the Collett Children's Home and the Clinton Public Library. He was a member of the Republican Party, the First Methodist Church of Clinton, the Clinton Township Advisory Board, and the Range Riders, a group of horseback riding enthusiasts who used Harry's parents' home place as a club house. Harry was involved in the consolidation of schools in the area, and the family donated the property where Van Duyn School stands to the South Vermillion School Corporation.

Although the large farming operation Harry had started required his son's involvement, it was difficult to keep John down on the farm. He was a race fan who loved fast cars and the Indianapolis 500, operating heavy equipment, traveling and meeting new people, and the company of fellow World War II veterans at Clinton's American Legion Post 140, which he served as Commander.

John and Gay divorced in 1966. John sold the farm to Linda and Mike Lubovich shortly before his death in 1976, ending 150 years of farming by the Van Duyns in Vermillion County. The only member of the family still living in the area is Susan Zanandrea; she and her husband, Jerry, live west of Clinton on a few acres purchased from her father before his death.

BENJAMIN VAN HUSS, was born May 13, 1835, in Carter Co., TN, and died Dec. 25, 1911, in Vermillion Co., IN. In 1867, he married Katherine Dugger, the daughter of Tarleton Dugger. She was born Nov. 10, 1845, in Tennessee, and died Jan. 23, 1905, in Vermillion Co., IN. They were the parents of seven children - James Eli Franklin, born August, 1870, in Indiana, died in 1912, married Rachael Wheeler; Nettie Mae, born July 15, 1873, died May 15, 1962, married George Price; Susie, born Sept. 25, 1875, died Mar. 23, 1963; Willie (Bill) A., born December, 1877, died, 1924; George Benjamin, born April, 1880, died Apr. 24, 1950, married Lee ?; Sarah Elizabeth (Ann), born Feb. 22, 1883, died Aug. 9, 1957, married Cecil James Lewis, Nov. 25, 1904; Orville, born June 18, 1886, died Oct. 4, 1935, married Beulah Wilfong, June 16, 1925. (see related article - Lewis Family)

THE GEORGE VANDEVENDER FAMILY, George David Vandevender was born in Cayuga, Feb. 24, 1936, the third child and first son of William Robert and Gladys May Satterlee Vandevender. A brother, Frank Colva, died at birth,

Aug. 27, 1945. A life resident of Cayuga, he was educated in the public schools, graduating from Cayuga High School in 1954. In March, 1954, he married Iris Eileen Axtell, daughter of George W. and Emma East Axtell of Eugene. Four children were born to them: Keith Alan lives in Montezuma and works at Futurex in Bloomingdale; Cynthia Renee lives in Eugene and works at Steel Grip Safety Apparel in Danville; Mary Ann lives in Attica with her husband, Gary Baldwin, and their three sons, Keith Alan, ten, Kenneth Ray, eight, and Kevin Lee, six; Sandra Eileen joined the Marine Corps in 1981 and is presently completing a tour of duty in Okinawa, Japan. After the death of his wife in January, 1975, he married Clella "Sue" Trammel Pollock, daughter of the late Clell A. and Audrey E. Jones Trammel. Born in Richland Co., IL and raised in Bridgeport, IL, she was educated in the public schools, graduating from Bridgeport High School in 1958. Her daughter, Nancy Jill, resides in Texas with her husband, Bill Anthony, and her three children, Angela Renea, 11, Billy Ray, nine, and Jennifer Nicole, two. He has been employed as an electrician at Tee-Pak, Inc. in Danville, for the past 27 years. Sue has been employed at Tee-Pak, Inc. for 24 years. Both are members of Bethel Baptist Church in Danville. His hobbies include woodworking. He has owned a small business, making picture frames and small wood items, since 1982. Her interests include photography, genealogy, and history.

GIOVANNI B. AND GIOVANNA A. PULLER VESCOVE, Giovanna (Joan) Antonietta Puller was born Aug. 11, 1885, in Asiago, Italy. She was one of many children born to Antionio and Christina Puller, who owned a restaurant in Asiago, Italy.

Joan left Asiago in 1906 and sailed from Italy to Ellis Island on her way to Clinton, IN, to marry Giovanni (John) Baptista Vescove. John was born on Aug. 11, 1882 in Asiago, Italy and he came to Clinton to work in the coal mines.

While her husband worked in the mines, Joan cooked and served meals to people from Chicago and Terre Haute on regular basis, charging current day prices.

Ada (Vescove) Madden, Donnetta (Robertson) Domeika, and Giovanna Vescove

Of this marriage five children were born. Afara "Pat" Vescove, born June, 1907, in Cedar Park, IN. She married Ben Pitman and had a son, Richard. Afara and Ben are both buried at Montezuma.

Adolph "Duke" Vescove was born October 1909 in Cedar Park, IN. Duke married Geraldine Russell and had three children, Marlene, Darwin, and Marshall. Duke was killed Dec. 28, 1968, and is buried at Dayton, OH.

Ardea "Ardy" Vescove was born August, 1912,

in Cedar Park, IN. Ardy married James Wallace Sr. and had three children, James Jr., Sondra and Allen.

Ada Alice Vescove was born December, 1914, in Cedar Park, IN. Ada married Joseph Puckett and had two daughters, Gloria and Karen. Ada died Oct. 13, 1987, and is buried at Roselawn.

Dolores Vescove, born May, 1929, in the Vermillion County Hospital, is newly retired from Public Service Indiana.

John died in 1944, and Joan died Dec. 26, 1970. They are both buried at Roselawn.

DENO AND EDITH CASTAGNA VIGNOCCHI,

Deno and Edith Vignocchi live at 940 Miller Street in Clinton, IN. Deno was born Aug. 22, 1912, and Edith was born July 8, 1915. Their son, David, was born July 17, 1947, and now lives at Schererville, IN; and their daughter, Nancy, was born Nov. 10, 1950, and lives in Chicago.

Deno and Edith both have Italian ancestry as far back as they can remember. Deno's name ending of "gnocchi" means Italian potato dumpling and Edith's maiden name of Castagna means chestnut.

Edith and Deno Vignocchi

Deno's parents, John and Lucia Vignocchi, came from the town of Fannano, Province of Modena, Italy, in 1906. Three of their ten children were born in Italy.

John went to work in the area of South Wilmington, IL, where Deno was born. The family moved to Clinton when Deno was seven years old. After high school and several years of work in Clinton, Deno went to Chicago to seek better employment.

Although they were both from Clinton, Deno and Edith did not meet until they were both in Chicago.

Edith's father, James Castagna, was born in Feletto, Province of Torino, Italy, and came to Clinton in 1913. Here he met and married Mary Markello, who was born in Rich Hill, MO, although both her parents had migrated from northern Italy.

Edith was the oldest of three children all born in Clinton.

A year after she graduated from high school, Edith went to Kalamazoo, MI, and later to Chicago to seek employment. It was in Chicago that she and Deno met, and married in Clinton, Mar. 11, 1944. Deno was discharged from the army in 1945 after having served four and one half years preceding and during World War II.

Deno is retired from Hyster Company in Danville, IL; and Edith retired from South Vermillion School Corporation. She taught sixth grade at Glendale School.

The Vignocchis are members of the Presbyterian Church. Edith is secretary of the Women's Organization, a member of the Hospital Guild, Sigma Delta Pi, and vice-president of the Francis Vigo Italian/American Club. Deno is a member of the Francis Vigo Italian/American Club, American Legion, Clinton Moose Lodge, Clinton Half Century Club, and Clinton Golf Association.

The Vignocchis were honored by being named Re and Regina of the 1988 Little Italy Festival.

DAVID G. WAITE AND MARTHA JENKINS WAITE,

David Glen Waite was born July 9, 1948, in Wabash, IN, the son of Glen Elbridge and Audrey Jane Scott Waite. He is the eldest of seven children. David grew up in Clay City, IN, where he graduated in 1966, from Clay City High School. Upon graduation he moved to Indianapolis, where he worked for Shirley Brothers Mortuaries, and attended Indiana College of Mortuary Science. He graduated from there in 1969.

David G. Waite

After graduation he moved to Brazil, IN, where in November, 1970, he married Martha Joan Jenkins, the oldest of three children born to Evelyn O. Short Jenkins and the late J. Emery Jenkins. Martha was born and raised in Brazil, where she attended local schools and graduated from Brazil High School. Following graduation she attended Indiana State University. In 1967, she graduated from Indiana University Medical Center School of Radiologic Technology, Indianapolis, IN. The couple lived and worked in Brazil for five years before moving to Clinton in October, 1975. David was employed by the Frist Funeral Home, and Martha worked in the Radiology Department of Vermillion County Hospital.

In 1980, they became the parents of a son, Gregory David.

In 1986, David and Martha purchased the Frist Funeral Home. Martha then retired from the position as manager of the Radiology Department of Vermillion County Hospital to work with her husband. They are members of the First United Methodist Church of Clinton. David is a member of the Centennial Lodge F&AM 541, Scottish Rite, Valley of Terre Haute, and Clinton Chamber of Commerce. Martha is a member of ISRT, ASRT, Kappa Delta Phi Sorority, and Valley Pre-School Board of Directors.

TIMOTHY MARK WALLACE AND LOUWANNA MARIE CONARD WALLACE,

Louwanna was born Dec. 26, 1954, at the Vermillion County Hospital, Clinton, IN. She is the daughter of Edward "Gene" and Sally Conard. She attended South Vermillion Schools, graduating in 1972. She graduated from Indiana Central College with an A.D. in Nursing. She works in the ICU Unit at Union Hospital, Terre Haute.

She is a First Class Girl Scout and was active in 4-H four years. She was active in band and choir in school. She is a member of the Dana United Methodist Church.

Louwanna, Tim, and Eric Wallace

Timothy was born in Brazil, IN on June 6, 1957, to Bobby and Betty Wallace. He is the youngest of five children. He graduated from Van Buren High School in Clay County. He spent four years in the Army, spending time in Germany. He has worked in heavy equipment, welding, and printing. He is now employed at the Newport Army Ammunitions Plant. Tim is a Mason and K of P member.

They were married on Nov. 14, 1981 in Knightsville, IN. They lived for a few years in Brazil, IN but are now living in Dana.

They have two sons, Eric Timothy, born on Sept. 23, 1982, in the Clay County Hospital, Brazil, IN. Matthew Scott was born on his mother's birthday, Dec. 26, 1984, at the Clay County Hospital, Brazil, IN.

ALLEN JAY WALTHALL,

1867-1953, spent his life as a farmer in the Quaker neighborhood. His grandfather William B. Walthall came from Dinwiddie Co., VA to Clinton Co., OH in 1830 to get away from slavery. His father, also named William B., from a devout Quaker family as a young man journeyed to Richmond, IN to attend Yearly Meeting. There he met Sarah Haworth. She had traveled across the state with her father, on horseback. They had mutual cousins and became well acquainted. They corresponded after returning home and in 1842 young William decided it was time to strike out for himself and take a wife. He made the nine day horseback ride to Vermillion and William and Sarah were married that year. They settled on a farm near the Hopewell Church and four children were born, namely Martha A., Thomas E., Francis and Levi. Sarah's health failed and she died in 1854. William B. remarried Lydia J. Branson and more children were born, seven living to maturity. They were David B., Sarah, Lydia, Allen J., Almedia, William H. and Smith. Allen attended the Quaker school and then went to the Bloomingdale Friends Academy for a year.

In 1897 Allen married Olive Rees and to them were born two children, Vernon (1898) and Alice (1901). After Olive's death Allen later married Bessie Haworth in 1909. Bessie's mother died when Bessie was very young and she and her sisters lived with their grandparents, Calvin and Malissa Haworth. Malissa Haworth was a well-known Quaker minister for many years. To Allen and Bessie were born five children: Miriam Blanche (1910) died in infancy, Bernice (1911), Elma (1913), William (1914) and George (1924).

Allen Walthall always voted the Prohibition Party and believed in its principles. He was a mainstay in the Hopewell Friends Church where he was an Elder and taught the Young People's Sunday School Class for over 35 years.

WILLIAM A. WALTHALL AND MARY CASTLE WALTHALL,

William Allen Walthall was born Jan. 11, 1914 in the Quaker community northwest of Dana, IN. He is the eldest son of Allen Jay and Bessie Haworth Walthall having a younger brother, George, and two older sisters, Bernice W. Ingram of Winona, MN and Elma W. Smart of Dana. He also has a half-sister Alice W. Majors of Veedersburg and a half-brother, Vernon, is deceased.

William grew up in the Quaker community but attended his last two years of high school at Vermillion Academy, a Quaker school in Vermillion Grove, IL where he graduated. He is a graduate of the Purdue Short Course in Animal Husbandry and later attended William Penn College, Oskaloosa, IA.

William and Mary Walthall

In April 1939 he married Mary Hannah Castle, eldest of seven children born to George and Ruth Fletcher Castle of Ridgefarm, IL. Mary attended local schools and graduated from Ridgefarm High School. Following graduation she attended Eastern Illinois University and Illinois State University. In 1965 she attended Utterback-Brown Business College, Danville, IL and did secretarial work for more than 19 years before retiring.

The couple have always lived in the Quaker community where William was engaged in farming. They have three children. Miriam Jane was born in 1946, graduated from Newport High School and Indiana State University, with a degree in music. She married Lawrence D. Beane in 1969 and they reside in Huntington, MA with their daughters Tricia, Michelle and Stephanie Beane. John David, born in 1951, graduated from North Vermillion High School and Earlham College with a degree in Spanish. In 1985 he married Dianne Skaggs and they reside in Carmel, IN with their son Grant David Walthall. Shirley Ann, born in 1956, graduated from North Vermillion High School and Indiana University with a degree in Consumer Studies. She resides in Denver, CO and works with handicapped children.

William and Mary are members of the Hopewell Friends Church of Quaker, where he is Presiding Clerk and she is organist. William was a charter member of the Vermillion County Soil & Water Conservation Board, served on the School Reorganization Committee, and on the North Vermillion School Board for 14 years. They have both been active in the Parke-Vermillion Gideon Camp, the Vermillion County Historical Society and the Farm Bureau.

HENRY WALTHER FAMILY,

in 1871, Henry, who was born in 1846, and Elizabeth Conrad Walther, who was born in 1847, came with a five-month-old son from Ohio to Clinton.

Henry was a cobbler in Clinton, and made and repaired shoes for many years. He also apprenticed many young men into the trade. After retiring as a cobbler, he moved to a small farm west of Clinton, where he raised many varieties of fruits and vegetables which he delivered house to house in Clinton.

He raised and showed White Wyandotte chickens with some acclaim.

Henry and Elizabeth raised a family of three boys, Frank, who married Emma Rothgeb, Edward who first married Ora Doing, and after her death, married Adena Carlson, and Thomas who married Blanch Cunningham; and three daughters, Zillah who married Frank Fishel, Adah, who married Warren Wright and Hazel, who married Paul Foltz. Another daughter died young.

Henry lived to the age of 89 and Elizabeth lived to the age of 90.

DR. AQUILLA WASHBURN,

Congressman Henry Dana Washburn married Serena Johnson, daughter of Elijah Johnson and Naomi Wright Johnson. Naomi later married Aquilla Nebeker and had daughters Laura Nebeker who married Congressman Washburn's brother John Quincy Washburn, Thirza who married Clinton Mayor (1896-1898) Nelson Crook Anderson, and Maria Nebeker who married Dr. John Henry Bogard, medical doctor.

Home of Dr. Aquilla Washburn and Dr. Henry Washburn. Photo by Leo Reposh, Jr.

Congressman and Mrs. Washburn are the parents of Dr. Aquilla Washburn, medical doctor who lived at 335 South 4th, Clinton. His son is Dr. Henry Evans Washburn who lived at the same address. Dr. Henry Washburn's daughter is Mary Dana Washburn who first married Mark McLane and later Richard Rodriques and had three daughters - Melody McLane, Dana Raquel Rodriques, and Mercedes Victoria Rodriques. *Submitted by Leo Reposh Jr.*

MADELINE M. HARRISON WATSON,

was born Jan. 18, 1911, in Vermillion County, the daughter of George Ackerman and Mary Cooke Harrison who married Aug. 29, 1909. His name is on the Veterans of Vermillion County who served in the World War List at Vermillion County Courthouse in Newport. He was born Sept. 18, 1888, in Vermillion County, the son of Benjamin Fisher and Clara Ackerman Harrison, who married Nov. 10, 1878. Benjamin F. Harrison was born Jan. 8, 1856 in Vermillion County and was a farmer most of his life.

When Claude Matthews was elected Governor and moved to Indianapolis in 1893, Benjamin F. Harrison and family moved into the Governor's House at Hazel Bluff to farm over 500 acres for Mr. Matthews. That farm is now owned by Benjamin's great grandson, Kenneth Ward Farrington.

Harrison Family. George Ackerman Harrison, Benjamin Fisher and Clara Ackerman Harrison and Family, Robert and Elizabeth Fisher Harrison and family.

The attached picture taken about 1894, at the family reunion, shows three generations of Harrisons at the Governors House.

Benjamin F. was the son of Robert Harrison and Elizabeth Brisco Fisher Harrison who married Feb. 6, 1855. Robert H. was born Oct. 11, 1831, in Rockingham Co., VA. He was the son of Benjamin Harrison Sr. and his wife Jane Ann Bright, born Jan. 19, 1806 in Rockingham Co., VA. They were married Jan. 3, 1826, and in 1832 came with their one year old son, Robert, to Vermillion County to make their pioneer home on 500 acres of land on Brouillets Creek. Benjamin Sr. was a well-known farmer and also served as Justice of the Peace, for 38 years, and was called Squire Harrison.

Benjamin and Jane Ann (Bright) were married for 60 years and both are buried in Spangler Cemetery.

Jane Ann Bright (Harrison) was the daughter of John Bright and Jane Ann (Faucett) Bright. John Bright was born Apr. 8, 1753, in Germany. He served as a private in the Virginia Army in the American Revolution, in Captain Rowland Madison's Company, 12th Virginia Regiment Commanded by Colonel James Wood in 1777. He also served in Captain Thomas Bressie's Company, 2nd Virginia State Regiment, Commanded by Colonel Gregory Smith, 1778. In 1779, he enlisted to serve three years in Captain James Moody's Company.

Benjamin Harrison Sr. was the son of William and Molly Harrison of Rockingham Co., VA. William Harrison was a Captain in the War Of 1812. This traces Madeline Harrison's ancestry to both a Revolutionary War Veteran and a War of 1812 Veteran.

Madeline graduated from Clinton High School in 1929, and on Sept. 8, 1945, she married Ralph J. Watson in Indianapolis, Marion Co., IN. They have two children, Robert Ackerman Watson, born Nov. 15, 1946, and Ruth Ann Watson, born Apr. 23, 1952. Both were born in Methodist Hospital, Marion Co., Indianapolis, IN.

Ralph J. Watson, was a mechanic in Indianapolis, starting in 1932, and continued, with four years out for World War II, until his death Mar. 24, 1988.

In World War II, he had five major battle stars, and served in Ireland, England, Scotland, Africa, Sicily, and Italy. Ralph attended Saint Catherine School in Indianapolis.

Their son, Robert, has been employed by the state for 22 years. He married Cindy Gruner and has two daughters. He graduated from Clinton High School. The two children, Candy, graduated from Greencastle High School and works in a state office, Land Acquisition, in Indianapolis; Heather Nicole is a student at Clinton Central School.

Ralph and Madeline's daughter, Ruth Ann, graduated from Clinton High School. She married

James R. Kersey and they have two children, Joshua and Kyle both of whom attend Van Duyn Elementary School. *Submitted by Madeline M. Harrison Watson.*

PAUL EUGENE WATSON, was born July 14, 1924, near Hillsdale, IN, the son of Warren and Marie Crumley Watson. He is the eldest of four children, the others being Darrel, Bill and Pat. He attended Fairview Elementary and Clinton High School. He worked for several companies in this area including DuPont and Allis Chalmers, but the majority of his working years were spent at PSI Wabash Generating Station from where he retired in August, 1986.

Front: Carl Wright, Jill Wright, Dennis Bennett, June Watson, Paul Watson. Middle: Cindy Wright, Janann Bennett, Gail Wright. Back: Dale Wright, Misty Wright.

On Mar. 25, 1944, he married G. June Pearman, who was born May 26, 1925, the daughter of Mervin and Melva Jones Pearman. She was the eldest child, having two brothers, Floyd and Harold. She attended the St. Bernice schools graduating with the class of 1943. She worked at Vermillion County Hospital, DuPont, and CBS, retiring from the latter in November, 1985.

They are the parents of two daughters, Jill Paulette born Sept. 13, 1946, and Janann born July 13, 1948. On Sept. 3, 1965, Jill married Carl D. Wright, son of Roscoe and Mildred Botner Wright and now teaches at Van Duyn School. Janann works as a secretary at Union Hospital. They have five grandchildren, Cindy Joy born Dec. 12, 1966; Gail Gay born Oct. 29, 1968; Misty Dawn born Jan. 19, 1970; and Dale Jene Wright born Sept. 25, 1971; also Dennis Eugene Bennett born Feb. 16, 1974.

They are members of the Tennessee Valley Baptist Church. He is a member of the Half-Century Club and Moose Lodge in Clinton.

ROCK ALAN WEATHERLY AND CINDY RENNAKER WEATHERLY, Rock Alan Weatherly was born Dec. 2, 1960 to Clarence James and Nancy Jo (Johnson) Weatherly in Clinton, IN. He attended Ernie Pyle Elementary and South Vermillion High School. He entered the army as a Combat Engineer in March 1981. He took basic training at Ft. Leonard Wood, MO, and was stationed at Ft. Knox, KY. In February of 1983 he was sent overseas to Heilbronn, Germany and was discharged in March 1984. Rock is still serving in the military as a Sergeant in the Indiana National Guard.

He was married to Cindy Marie Rennaker at the First Baptist Church in Covington, IN, June 5, 1982. She is the daughter of Robert Charles and Dorothy Lucille (Martin) Rennaker. She started kindergarten in Perrysville, but moved, with her parents, to Jeffersonville, IN where she attended Middle Road, Utica, and Riverside Grade schools. Returning to Perrysville, in 1973 she again attended Highland

Elementary and North Vermillion high school, where she graduated in 1980. During high school she worked at the Beef House Restaurant and then Walgreen Disbursing Office, after graduation.

Cindy and Rock lived in Ft. Knox area until he went overseas, when she remained with her parents, and their first child. Zachariah Lee Weatherly, was born Oct. 16, 1983, while there. Lacey Nicole was born June 2, 1988. Zach was six months old, before he met his daddy.

Rock now works for Bumper Works in Danville, IL, in the welding shop. He enjoys hunting, fishing, camping and anything pertaining to the Civil War and WW II. Cindy enjoys all types of crafts, collecting stamps, and cat miniatures. They live in Perrysville and attend the Nazarene Church in Cayuga, IN.

MARCUS WOODRUFF (WOOD) WEATHERMAN, was born in Yadkin Co., NC on Oct. 27, 1872, and came to Dana from Jonesville, VA as a young man. A year later he was joined by brothers Otto Hopkins (Hop) and Messer. In 1899 Wood married Elsie Lenora Carmack, daughter of William Pinckney and Mary E. Asbury Carmack. Their home place was 219 acres in Township 16 North Range 10 West Sections 8, 9, 16, and 17. It was always said to be four miles north of Dana and west to the large frame house. The 1938 plot shows 50 acres more in Township 16 North Range 9 West Sections 6 and 7.

Wood Weatherman Home

They and their six children lived in a Christian God loving home.

Marcus Woodruff (Wood) Weatherman 1872-1936, Elsie Lenora Carmack 1877-1939:

Lowell, 1899-1972, married 1931 to Gladys Todd, 1903-____: 1) Lolleen, 1937-____ married 1963 to Norman Gene Hensley, 1938-____: Mathew Ryan 1969-____; 2) Donald Earl, 1938-____.

Lulu Bell, 1902-1977, married first to Claude Thomas, ____-1930, married second to Charles Mitchell.

Harold E., 1905-1945, married to Ena V. Vandevoir, 1906-1980: 1) Merold Dean, 1932-____, married Mary Mae Lewis: Terry, Tim, Tom. 2) James Woody, 1941-____, married 1961 to Judith Elaine Herrin, 1942-____: Shannon D., 1963-____, Sharril D., 1964-____, married 1984 to Jarold Bradley Burnell, 1962-____: Bradley Scott Burnell 1982-____, Brock Anthony Burnell 1987-____.

*William Walden, 1907-1983, married 1941 to E. Isabel Bubeck, 1912-____: 1) William Edward, 1943-____, married 1964 to Cheryl Louise Endicott, 1942-____: Lisa Dawn, 1967-____, married 1987 to Patrick Douglas Shannon, 1965-____; 2) Elizabeth Lenore (Betty), 1946-____; 3) Mark Steven, 1956-____, married 1984 to Debbi Longman, 1955-____.

James Vernon, 1910-____, married 1940 to Marianna Lundgren, 1915-____: 1) John Wesley, 1942-____; 2) Philip Ross, 1947-____, married 1968 to Carolyn Avis Plummer, 1948-____: Ross Vernon, 1969-____, Krista Avis, 1970-____.

Melvin C., 1912-____, married 1934 to Violet R. Youmans, 1914-____: 1) Linda Lou, 1937-____, married 1956 to Roland Dean Milligan, 1935-____: Shawn M., 1958-____ married 1978 to George Randolph Hayden: Phillip Randolph, 1979-____, Michael Anthony, 1981-____, Mathew Dean, 1983-____; Amy L., 1959-____, married 1983 to Thomas William Kenney: Megan Elizabeth, 1985-____; Robert Patrick, 1965-____; Suzanne Marie, 1969-____. 2) Daniel Lynn, 1947-____.

*William Walden was with the First National Bank of Dana for 42 years where he served as cashier and vice president and as president from 1970 to 1978. He continued his work for the bank as chairman of the board of directors until his death. *Submitted by Isabel B. Weatherman*

THE HAROLD WELLER, JR. FAMILY, Mrs. Harold Weller (Reva Loretta Cole Weller) lives at Rural Route 1, Perrysville, on a part of the farm owned by her Grandfather Smith. Reva was born Apr. 30, 1931, to Bertha Irene Smith Cole and Edgar Allen Cole. She has a brother, Eugene, and a sister, Frieda.

Her great, great, great grandfather, Berryman Smith, son of John Smith, married Elizabeth Martin on Aug. 31, 1785 in Fauquire Co., VA. Patrick Henry was governor of Virginia at the time. (We have a copy of the marriage document from the clerk of Fauquire Co., VA). In 1790, they emigrated to Scott Co., KY; in 1820, to Fayette Co., IN; in 1827, to Fountain County; then to Vermillion County.

Harold Weller, Jr. Family

The linage: Berryman-Rhodes-James-Charles-Bertha Smith Cole-Reva L. Cole Weller. The Smiths were farmers by occupation. The Coles—James came from Essex County, England, born in 1590, emigrated to Hartford, CT in 1635.

The linage: James, Samuel, Samuel, Caleb, Matthew, Milo, Calvin, John Henderson, Edgar Allen, Reva L. Cole Weller. Reva's great grandfather, Milo, came to Vermillion County with his wife's family, the Lacey's, settling near Perrysville.

The Cole history was researched Dr. Ira Cole of Lafayette, IN grandson of Milo Cole.

The Wellers lived in Vermillion Co., IL. Harold and Reva came to Vermillion County, north of Perrysville, to make their home in 1954. They were married in Danville, IL, in February, 1952, and lived in Bismerck until March, 1954. They had four children, Steven Alan of Harvard, IL; Ronald Dean of Ottawa, IL; Kathleen Weller Henney of Monticello, IN; and Mary Ellen of Lafayette, IN.

Steven married Kathleen Knight of Fort Wayne,

IN, in 1982. He and his wife are both landscape architects. Steve graduated from Huntington College of Huntington, IN, in 1975 with a B.S. in Biology. He received a Master's degree in Education in 1980 from IUPU extension in Fort Wayne, and a Master's degree in Landscape Architecture in 1987 from Kansas State University. He works for the McHenry County Parks department in McHenry Co., IL. Steve's wife, Kathy, graduated from Purdue with a B.S. in Landscape Architecture.

Ronald married Kristine Brant of Frankfort, IN, in 1976. They have two daughters, Jessica and Abigail. Ronald graduated from North Manchester College in 1976 with a B.S. in Business Administration. Ronald is Vice President of the First Bank in Ottawa, IL. His wife, Kristine, graduated from North Manchester College with a B.A. in Music.

Kathleen married Fredric Henney in 1978. Kathy graduated from Manchester College in North Manchester, IN, with a B.S. in Elementary Education. Her husband, Fred, has a degree in medicine and is a family practitioner in Monticello, IN. They have two children, Matthew and Margaret.

Mary Ellen graduated from Valparaiso University in 1978 with a B.A. in Geography. She is now attending Purdue working on a B.S. in Landscape Architecture.

Harold served in the Navy from 1945-1946 and the Army from 1950-1952, serving a year in Korea. He was a partner of the Ideal Supply Company, Wholesale Plumbing & Heating, Danville, IL. He worked at Inland Supply for 26 years prior to the opening of Ideal Supply in 1975.

Harold died Feb. 19, 1984, at the age of 56 years. He is buried in Lower Mound Cemetery in Vermillion County, north of Perrysville. Reva is a secretary at the Newport Elementary School in Newport, IN.

BRUCE, VICKI, STARLA, AND REUBEN WEST,
Bruce Wayne West was born May 2, 1951, the first son of Don Lee West and Elizabeth Janet Fisher West. (see related story on Don and Liz). Bruce was quite a fisherman, even as a small boy. He attended school at Crompton Hill and Van Duyn and graduated from Clinton High School in 1970. After high school, he worked part-time for the state of Indiana and attended Indiana College of Business and Technology in Indianapolis for computer programming and systems analyst, graduating in 1971. He later attended Indiana State majoring in business administration.

Vicki and Bruce West

Vicki Graham was born in 1953, the daughter of Robert and Christine Graham of Clinton. She attended Sacred Heart School and graduated from Clinton High School in 1971. After high school, she was a secretary for WAAC radio station in Terre Haute.

In 1971, Bruce and Vicki were married at the First Christian Church in Clinton. By that time Bruce was working for the State Auditor Mary Aikins and Vicki went to work for the State Superintendent of Schools.

Later Bruce took a new job with Weston Paper Company in Terre Haute. In February of 1973, their daughter, Starla Dawn West, was born. The Wests built a new home in Fairview on the site which had previously been the home of John and Neola Davitto, Bruce's grandparents.

Vicki established a school for baton twirling and later for dancing. The studio for the school was built near their home. Her students are girls from tots to mid-teens and each spring they perform in a big review at South Vermillion High School.

In February, 1977, their son Reuben was born. He is an outstanding student at Van Duyn School and a very outgoing, active, and popular kid who takes after his two grandfathers, Don West and Bob Graham.

Starla has always been an honor student. She played basketball and ran track at South Vermillion Middle School as well as being a cheerleader. As a high school freshman, she was a guard on the basketball B-team. She is a 4-H member and participates in the share-the-fun contest. She is one of her mother's best dancing students and she has won several talent contests.

Bruce has two younger brothers, Douglas and Franklin, who are pipefitters. Vicki has two older brothers, Bob of Rosedale, and Bill of Clinton. *Submitted by Leo Reposh, Jr.*

CHARLES WILLIAM WEST,
and Megan Bailey were married Feb. 12, 1949, in Danville, IL. They lived in Indianapolis until moving to Vermillion County in June, 1956. They have two daughters, Dianne Hamand of Eugene, IN, and Judith McClanahan of Pekin, IL.

Charles has done millwright work in several area factories. He now owns and operates Mt. Zion Spring Farm, so named because of Mt. Zion Cumberland Presbyterian Church that was located on the property near a spring that still flows. (See page 139 in Eugene Township *The First 100 Years* by Harold O'Donnell)

DON AND ELIZABETH WEST FAMILY,
Donnie Lee West was born Feb. 4, 1930, the son of Thomas Marion West and Stella Trosper West and grandson of Thomas and Anna West and Jim and Hattie Trosper. He has two brothers, Samuel Marion West and Jack Wayne West, and two sisters, Betty West Van Lieu and Iris May West Vorek. As a boy on Crompton Hill he carried papers and was an outdoorsman and horseman. He attended school at Crompton Hill and Clinton High.

Elizabeth Janet Fisher was born Dec. 4, 1932, in Clinton, the daughter of George Thomas Fisher and Neola Fern Jackson Fisher. Neola is the daughter of John Harrison Jackson and Reba Elizabeth Paine Jackson and granddaughter of Henry Washburn Paine and Kizzie May Spainhower Paine. (See related stories on Ethel Jackson Reposh and Charles Donald Paine.) Neola and her husband, George, separated and while Liz was still small Neola married John Davitto. Liz grew up on a small dairy farm and vineyard in Fairview. She attended school at Fairview and Clinton High.

On July 2, 1950, Donnie Lee West and Elizabeth Janet Fisher were married. On May 2, 1951, their first son, Bruce Wayne, was born. (See related story

on Bruce West) While Bruce was quite small Don and Liz built a new house in the Crompton Hill area and there they still reside.

Elizabeth and Don West

Both Don and Liz are friendly outgoing people. In the early 50's the Young Democrats Club was formed and in 1957 Don became president of the Vermillion County Chapter and in 1958 he went on to became president of the whole Sixth Congressional District Chapter. Since 1951 Don had been precinct committeeman of Crompton Hill and in 1961 he became Vermillion County Chairman of the regular Democratic Party and retained that position until 1982.

During the administrations of Governors Mathew Welsh and Roger Brannigan, Elizabeth served as Director of the Clinton Drivers License Branch and Don served as a state bridge engineer. During this time many state and federal officials visited Vermillion County such as Governor Matt Welsh, Senators Vance Hartke and Birch Bayh, and Congressman Fred Wampler.

In 1968 Liz was appointed to serve as Clinton Township Assessor and was afterward elected to four additional terms. Don became a pipefitter. He was also president of the Clinton Township Water commission and the Isaac Walton League. In 1982 Don sought the office of state senator and was the overwhelming choice of Vermillion County voters, but came up short in the more populous Vigo County thus was not elected. In 1984 Liz was elected Vermillion County Treasurer, served with distinction, and in 1988 has again been nominated for that office.

In addition to their eldest son, Bruce, the West's have two other sons Douglas Albert West born June 16, 1959 and Franklin Lynn West born July 30, 1967. Both are pipe fitters. *Submitted by Leo Reposh Jr.*

WESTBROOK FAMILY HISTORY 1900-1988,
In 1900, Edward "Ned" and Marybelle Watson Westbrook moved to Vermillion County from Paris, IL. They settled on the farm on a knoll two and one-half miles southwest of Bono with their five children, Ruth, Esther, Paul, Marybelle, and Celia. Their sixth child, June, was born that summer.

The children attended Liberty School, a one-room brick school. As soon as Helt Township School (the first consolidated school in Western Indiana, and the second consolidated school in Indiana) was built, Liberty School was closed. In 1908, Ruth and Esther were in the first graduating class of Helt Township High School.

The Westbrook home was the center of much entertainment during those years. All of the young people enjoyed visiting, spending the night, having parties, or just picking blackberries at the

Westbrooks. Mrs. Westbrook was known for her hospitality and wonderful cooking.

Ruth, Esther, Marybelle, and June attended college and taught school until they married. Ruth married Albert Stratton from Edgar Co., IL. Esther married Carl Hathaway from Kansas. Marybelle married O'Clif Winans and moved to his farm in Edgar Co., IL. While June (the only one of the girls who taught high school) was teaching home economics, she met and married William F. King. In 1918, after graduating from high school, Celia contracted tuberculosis and died at age 21.

Paul farmed with his father after graduating from high school. Then, at the age 19, he and a friend went to Montana to homestead. He became a legend to the family as a sheep herder, landowner, gold miner, sheriff, and county commissioner in Virginia City, MT.

The nine Westbrook grandchildren looked forward to every visit to grandma's house. She let them play and taught them how to cook and sew, the art of living, and the love of God.

The family home burned in 1929, and a smaller model was built during the Depression. In 1932, soon after they moved into their new home, Ned died at age 84.

The home place was bought and remodeled by the oldest daughter, Ruth, and her husband, Albert Stratton. They kept improving the farm until their deaths in 1967 and 1968. Their son, James Stratton and wife, Evelyn, moved into the home place. After farming and raising hogs and cattle for over 30 years, James died in 1985 at age 72. Evelyn still keeps the home fires burning in the old Westbrook home place. The land has stayed in the same family for 88 years.

WHITE FAMILY, The White family, as far as Vermillion County is concerned, began in around 1820 when Abram White (June 21, 1762-1853) brought his family up from Bullitt Co., KY, and settled on land that is now a part of the Eli Lilly Company. Abram had entered the Revolutionary Army at the age of 15 from Fayette Co., PA, serving under Colonel McIntosh as part of the Army of Virginia, commanded by General George Rogers Clark. He married Millicent Hopewell (1781-1863). He died in 1853 and was buried in Helts Prairie Cemetery as are all of the Whites. However a genealogist has traced the family back to New Jersey in 1642.

Enoch (1814-1878) was the only son who chose to remain in Vermillion County. In his obituary he is listed as a farmer and grazier. In 1834 he married Lydia Hollenbeck (1817-1876) and built a white columned colonial style house on the same property. They had six children: Phoebe, Isabel, Mary, and Sarah Jane and sons Frank and Samuel.

Round Barn near Quaker

Samuel Ryerson White (1838-1900) left Asbury College...now DePauw University...to join the

Civil War. The History of Company D of the 87th Division from Indiana now in the Indiana State Library was written from his notes and dictation. In 1871 he married Rose Gilmore (1846-1914), daughter of Dr. John Gilmore of Newport. They settled on 800 acres of virgin prairie land just west of Quaker, IN. Their lovely Victorian house still stands. One of his hobbies was planting groves of trees and the maple trees lining the main street of Dana were a gift from him. They had three children: Clifford, Earle, and Milo.

Earle O. White (1877-1959) graduated from Purdue at the age of 19 with a bachelor's degree in Electrical Engineering.

In 1899 he married Grace Shepard (1875-1947), daughter of Dr. Lewis Shepard of Newport and Quaker. After a brief career as Banker he turned to farming. He built the large brick house just east of Quaker on the old Shepard property. He also designed and built the round barn accompanying it...now considered a land mark. His chief interest was in fattening hogs...sometimes handling a couple of thousand a year. In early years, field trips from Purdue called. Four children grew up there...Joe, Mary, Max and Martha.

Martha, widow of Allen H. Helt (another pioneer family) lives in Dana. She was the first president of the Vermillion County Historical Society and served in that capacity for 20 years. She compiled and edited two Vermillion County Pictorial History booklets. The Possum Bottom Covered Bridge was preserved by her persuading the county and state to move it from the destruction of the expanding State Road #63 and locating it on the Ernie Pyle Highway Park. She was co-chairman of the Restoring and Decorating Committee of the Ernie Pyle Home and has been the Vermillion County Historian since 1983.

Two children, Daniel and Mary Elizabeth, as well as four grandchildren, Molly, Kelly, Catharine and Michael, carry on the story.

ROY WHITE, was an eminent son of Dana. He started his career after three years of high school as a telegrapher for the Baltimore and Ohio Railroad in 1900. He climbed up the ladder of success through many phases of railroad work until he became president of the Central Railroad of New Jersey in 1926, then president of the Western Union in 1933, and president of the Baltimore and Ohio Railroad in 1941. In 1943, he was commissioned a colonel in the Transportation Corps and placed in command of the Allegheny region, comprising 25 railroads. He was also associated with the Chase Manhatten Bank at one time. Even though he didn't graduate from high school, he received honorary degrees of Doctor of Law from St. Francis College and Marietta College. He died sometime in the early 1960's.

MAYNARD C. AND ELIZABETH COFFIN WIGGINS, Maynard (1903-1955) was born and raised on a farm near Adrian, MI. He met Elizabeth, who was born and raised in Cayuga, while she was working in Adrian. They were married in 1927. First, they lived in West Unity, OH where he managed Kroger grocery.

They moved to Cayuga. Later they moved to Newport where they made their permanent home. Maynard studied with his father-in-law, Milton Coffin, and with Judge Beeler, while completing a correspondence course through the LaSalle Law School. In 1930 he was admitted to the practice of

law which he pursued until his death. During those years he served as Vermillion County's Prosecuting Attorney and held several offices in the Masonic Lodge, the Lions Club, and the Vermillion County Bar Association. Maynard served on the boards of several organizations including the Collett Home for Orphans, the Thomas Cemetery Association, the Selective Service draft board, and the U.S. Office of Price Administration.

Maynard and Elizabeth Wiggens

During many of those years Elizabeth worked with Maynard and was especially involved in their abstracting and insurance business which she continued until her retirement in 1982. She held many offices in various service and social organizations including the Eastern Star. Elizabeth also served several years as Treasurer for the Thomas Cemetery Association, was a member of the Vermillion County Library Board of Directors and the first woman to be a member of the Collett Home Board.

Maynard and Elizabeth had two children. William lives in suburban Indianapolis, and his daughter lives in California. Kenneth and his wife, the former Claudia Howlett, live in Speedway with their son Andrew. Their daughter, Kenna, and her husband, John Fetherolf, also live in Speedway.

WILCOXEN FAMILY, Progenitors of the Wilcoxens in Vermillion Co., IN, Nathan B. Wilcoxon and his wife, Ruth, came to the Gessie area around 1850, with their children, Parker Kelley; Rebecca Jane; Christina; and Aletha. Nathan B. Wilcoxon was born Dec. 25, 1806, probably in West Virginia, the son of Samuel and Christiana Baker Wilcoxon; his grandfather was John Willcoxon, born 1754 in Prince Georges Co., MD, a Revolutionary soldier. Nothing is known of Ruth Wilcoxon except that her maiden and married names were the same. The death dates of Nathan B. and Ruth Wilcoxon are unknown, but family history states that they were buried near their log cabin in woods west of Gessie.

Parker Kelley Wilcoxen, born Jan. 30, 1835, in Gallia Co., OH, married July 16, 1863, Lucy Ellen Niccum who was born Dec. 14, 1844, in Highland Township, Vermillion Co., IN. Her parents were William and Matilda (Mary) Smith Billings Niccum. Parker and Lucy Wilcoxen moved on to Illinois, but the descendants of one of their sons, John, continued to live in Vermillion Co., IN.

John Nathan Wilcoxen, born Nov. 8, 1869, in Vermilion Co., IL, died Apr. 17, 1953, in Rileysburg, Vermillion Co., IN. He married 1) Kate Gibson, daughter of James and Elizabeth Ogden Gibson, born Apr. 28, 1872, died Mar. 17, 1919, both in Vermilion Co., IL; and 2) Zella Bowen, born 1888, died 1944.

John and Kate Gibson Wilcoxen were parents of 11 children: Lucy Anna Mabel (1894-1986); Elsie Pearl (1896-1910); Tillman Russell (1898-1986);

James Parker (1899-1975); Edith Alice (1902-1954); Lillian Florence (1904-); John Raymond (1906-1923); Irma Elizabeth (1908-); Fred Gibson (1911-1957); Harold Wayne (1915-1933); Clyde Borden (1919-).

Presently living in Highland Township are descendants of Dewey and Mabel Wilcoxen Prather; Russell and Marie Long Wilcoxen; Russell and Edith Wilcoxen Dunham; and Russell and Lillian Wilcoxen Cundiff, who have intermarried with families including those of Hicks, Crist, Spandau, Hughes, Jackson, Price and Lilley. *Submitted by Kate Dunham*

WILCOXEN-LONG, Russell and Marie Long Wilcoxen began farming in Highland Township in 1939, moving to 80 acres north of Gessie formerly owned by the Switzer family.

Tilman Russell Wilcoxen, born Jan. 21, 1898, in Vermilion Co., IL, was the eldest son of John Nathan and Kate Gibson Wilcoxen. He attended the Butternut School, and lived in McKendree Township most of his life until moving to Indiana. He had been employed by Royalty Barber Supply and Alith-Prouty in Danville.

Russell and Marie Long-Wilcoxen

Marie Marguerite Long was born Sept. 30, 1905, in her family's home on the northeast corner of the intersection just north or Rileysburg; This property had formerly been owned by Presley Martin. She attended Rileysburg School. Other members of this Rileysburg family were Marie's parents, John and Sarah Long, and her siblings, Florence, Jessie Minerva, Walter, Ernest, Sophia May, Roscoe, Harry and Russell. John J. Long, an immigrant to this country, was born Johann Joachim Friedrich Lange in his native Germany; he was the son of Johann Christian Lange and Caroline Sophia Stine Lange. Sarah Ann Rouse Long was born in Vermilion Co., IL, the daughter of Edward and Minerva Martin Rouse.

Russell and Marie were married June 24, 1925, at the Congregational Church parsonage in Tilton, IL. They were members of the old Rileysburg Congregational Church. Russell retired from farming in 1963, and died Mar. 22, 1986. He is buried at Hopewell Cemetery. Marie presently lives in Danville, IL.

The Wilcoxens were parents of three sons, Ralph, Raymond and Richard. Ralph Owen Wilcoxen was born Mar. 13, 1926, near Gessie. He married Lois J. Duncan Mar. 17, 1961, and was divorced Dec. 6, 1978. Children: (1) Connie Sue, married Charles Richard Alexander. (2) Janice Kay, married Kenneth Roy Pasco; daughter, Sarah Marie.

Raymond Curtis Wilcoxen was born July 3, 1928, and on Dec. 7, 1946, he married Geraldine Lanham. Children: (1) Velsteana Mae, married

thrice, Charles Hoagland, Richard Smith and Tom McCann; children, Tammy Jo Hoagland (married Terry Miller), Teresa Marie Hoagland (married Shawn Shoaf), and Tabatha Ann Smith. (2) Ray Curtis, married Sherilyn Hendricks; children, Michelle, Paula Kay, Anthony Curtis and Heather Ann. (3) Gladys Marie, married Randy Moore; children, Nicole Renee and Steven Randy. (4) James Carte, married Margaret _____; children, Dana, Brandon and Toni. (5) Elizabeth Ann, married Mark Farner, children, Brooke and Christina Ann.

Richard Lee Wilcoxen was born Oct. 24, 1938. He married Beverly J. Spandau, Nov. 8, 1959. Their children are: (1) Valerie Lynn, married William Brian Jordan. (2) Bruce Alan, married Kelly M. Kilday. (3) Gary Lee. Richard Wilcoxen, a resident of rural Perrysville, continues to farm his parents' land. *Submitted by Marie Wilcoxen*

CHARLES WILSON, immigrated from Sweden and shortened his name to Wilson. He was married to Ada Vestal who died in 1935. They had one child, a son named Clarence.

Charles Wilson

Clarence "Ted" lived in Clinton his entire life and died October, 1970. In his later years, Ted worked as a part-time TV-radio repairman at his home at 115 N. 12th St., where he resided for 27 years.

He married Hazel Kinder of Hymera, IN, and they had three daughters, who survive: Loretta Cohen of State Line, IN; Linda Wildman of Bloomington, IN; and Lois Leach of Edgewater, FL.

TIMOTHY JON WILSON AND DI-ANNA LOUISE WILSON, Timothy Jon Wilson was born Sept. 6, 1956, to Joseph H. and Phyllis J. (Yoho) Wilson at Vermillion County Hospital, Clinton, IN.

Tim graduated from North Vermillion High School in 1975. He is a member of Eugene Methodist Church. He joined Cayuga Volunteer Fire Department in 1979 and was elected as fire chief 1986-1988. He was also voted fireman of the year in 1988.

He was elected to the town board in 1984 and elected President in 1985. He was re-elected in 1988 to run his second term on the board. He was elected as democratic precinct committeeman to serve for the democratic party beginning in 1988.

On Mar. 7, 1987, he married Dianna L. (Huston) Wilson. She is the daughter of James E. and Carolee (Whitaker) Huston. Tim and Dianna had a son Feb. 19, 1988, named Joseph Michael.

In June 1987 Tim moved his auto repair shop at South Division Street, Cayuga where he is the owner of Wilson's Marathon and 24 hour wrecker service.

Tim also has a daughter, Jeanine Marie, born

Apr. 28, 1984, and Dianna has a son, Wes Eugene Vickery, born Oct. 14, 1983.

IGNATIUS WISNESKI AND RU KATHLEEN ALEXANDER WISNES Ruby Kathleen Alexander Wisneski and Ign Paul Wisneski, both Vermillion County reside were married in Clinton, IN in 1932.

Ignatius, "Igg" was born July 22, 1905 in Cl ton, IN, the son of Joseph and Frances Kobe Wisneski. His father and mother immigrated Clinton from Gdánsk, Poland. Joseph worked many area coal mines, and Frances was a midwife in the area, delivering hundreds of babies.

Ruby Alexander and Ignatius Wisneski

Ruby was born Feb. 21, 1912, in Vermillion County, the daughter of Jesse and Myrtle Groves Alexander. Ruby had one brother, Arnold, one sister, Cecile Irene, and one half-brother, Leslie. Arnold married Lesta Foncannon of Clinton, and they had two sons, Arnold Wayne and Warren Lee. They later moved to Three Rivers, MI. Cecile married Wayne Gormong of Terre Haute, and they had four children: JoAnn, Betty Jean, Herbert and James. Cecile also taught elementary school in the Clinton area for several years.

Igg had two brothers, Vincent and John. Vincent died Apr. 25, 1921, at the age of 18. John married the former Cleora Steffey. Igg also had two sisters, Martha and Mary. Martha married Frank Michalski of Clinton, and they had three children: Rose, Sophie and Frank, Jr. "Fromme". Martha later moved to Reno, NV where she lived with her daughter and husband, the Jay Robinsons'. Mary attended "Michael Reese" Hospital School of Nursing in Chicago, IL, and married Walter Bermingham of Willimett, IL. They lived in Evanston, IL, and they had three sons: Twin boys, Joseph and Walter and Thomas.

Ignatius worked in a coal mine during summer vacation for three months and went back to Sacred Heart School when it started in the fall. He quit school to work in the mines, when his brother, Vincent, died to help his dad, Joseph, make a living. He also worked at Ford Motor Co. in Detroit and Buick Motor Co. in Flint, MI, Ford Motor in Chicago, IL and Du Pont. He was a musician and a trap drummer with his band group, the "Melody Boys" which played at dances, parties, election dinners, etc.

Ruby attended Vermillion County schools and was employed in the nursing profession.

Ruby and Ignatius had four daughters, Patricia, Nancy, Janice and Sharon. Patricia married Gilbert Dickey. They live on their farm, "Crystal Springs", near Rosedale, IN, in Parke County. Their children are: Joanie, married to Michael Lunsford, children, Ellen and Evan living in Rosedale; Terri, married to Domenic Nepote, children, Gina and Lisa living in Clinton; Karen, married to Gene Baxter, children,

—lyn and Riley living in Rockville; Annette —ckey, an Indiana State University student, still — g at home with the Dickeys'.

— ncy married Ernest Deplanty, and they had — children, Kathy, Steve, Michael and Curtis. — live in Omaha, NE.

— nice married Jack Gann of Elkland, MO, and — y had four children, Dale, Jock, Brad and Christi.

— haron married John Curtis Hendrix of — dale, IN, and they had four children, Dorenda, — on, Melissa and Curtis Paul. They all reside in — Worth, TX. *Submitted by Patricia Dickey*

JOSEPH WISNESKI AND FRANCES KOBELSKI WISNESKI,

Francis Kobelski Wisneski and Joseph Wisneski, immigrating from their native Gdánsk, Poland, sailed the "Iceland" ship docking at Baltimore, MD in the year 1900. From there, they migrated to Clinton, IN where Joseph worked in many area mines. The couple had previously lived in Dusseldorf, Germany, and Joseph worked in coal mines in Poland and Germany for many years before coming to America. Joseph was born in 1866 and died in 1936.

Frances Wisneski, Joseph Wisneski, Mary Wisneski, Walter Bermingham, Mrs. Bermingham.

Frances, after arriving in America, attended the Polish American College in Chicago, IL where she enrolled in a Midwife Course. She graduated, receiving a college diploma which is still in the children's possession. She worked as a midwife in Cudahay, WI, Everson, PA, Wheeling, WV, and Clinton, IN for many years. Delivering several hundred babies in Clinton area, she kept a large book containing the names of children she delivered in Clinton. She also, assisted Dr. Jury B. Loving of New Goshen, IN, in child birth cases; however, she usually worked alone. She was quite an esteemed lady, held dearly by her patients. Her vocabulary included six languages which enabled her to communicate with the different nationalities in Clinton. As she got older, she retired from midwife delivery. She was born Apr. 4, 1873 and died Oct. 5, 1960 at the age of 87.

Frances and Joseph had five children, Vincent, Ignatius, Martha, Mary and John. The children all attended Sacred Heart School. Vincent died Apr. 25, 1921 at age 18.

Martha married Frank Michalski, and they owned a grocery store on 7th and Sycamore. They had three children, Rose, Sophie and Frank, "Fromme". Frank Sr. was killed in a Peabody coal mine slate fall in Westville, IL. Frank Jr., "Fromme" attended college at Upper Iowa where he played football. He roomed with Coach Spike Kelly family while there. Martha eventually moved to Reno, NV where she lived with her daughter, Rose and Jay Robinson.

Ignatius worked in the coal mines, Ford Motor Co., Buick Motor Co. and Du Pont. He was a musician and a trap drummer with his band group, "Melody Boys". Band musicians were Joe Anderson, Piano; Tom Blower and wife, Piano and Saxophone; Gerald Martin, Violin; Wakefield Jones, Banjo; Andy Daugherty, Saxophone; Beezy Rhodenberry, Piano; Houston, Trumpet. The band's manager was Pete Philips, Greek Candy Kitchen Operator, 1920-1933. Igg married Ruby Alexander, and they had four daughters, Patricia, Nancy, Janice and Sharon. Patricia marred Gilbert Dickey, and they reside on their farm near Rosedale, IN, Parke County. Nancy married Ernest Deplanty. They live in Omaha, NE. Janice married Jack Gann and lives in Tulsa, OK. Sharon married John Hendrix of Rosedale. They reside in Fort Worth, TX.

John worked in the mines, for Ford Motor, as Hoover sweeper salesman, pipefitter, and drummer. He married Cleora Steffey.

Mary attended "Michael Reese" Hospital School of Nursing, Chicago, IL. She graduated in four years with honors. Mary married Walter Bermingham, Willimett, IL, who owned the Bermingham Processing Company and plants. They had three sons, Joseph, Walter and Thomas. *Submitted by Patricia Dickey*

THE WITTENMYER FAMILY,

Wittenmyer is a German name, the family being descended from the Franks, one of the ten German tribes that overran and conquered the Great Roman Empire in 500 AD.

Andreas Wittenmyer was born in 1730 in Alsace Loraine, Switzerland. He married Suzanne Shrove. They sailed to America on the ship "Phoenix" and landed in New York on Aug. 28, 1750. Andreas was a farmer and a cobbler. He worked for three cents a day until he saved nine dollars and purchased land in Snyder Co., PA. Andreas died in 1800 and Susanne on Dec. 4, 1812. Children were Catherine, Susanne, Barbara, Anna, Mary Magdalene, Andrew, Christine, Jacob.

Barbara Wittenmyer and David Wittenmyer

Jacob Wittenmyer, born Jan. 19, 1776, in Pennsylvania, died Mar. 8, 1853, and is buried in Smith Cemetery southwest of Perrysville. Jacob married Mary Magdalene Wittenmyer from the other family that came to America in 1767 (no relation). Children were John, Benjamin, David, George, Jonathon.

David Wittenmyer was born July 6, 1801, at Northumberland Co., PA. He died Jan. 3, 1872, and was buried at Hicks Cemetery west of Perrysville. He married Barbara Cox in 1827, in Butler Co., OH. In 1831 they moved to western Indiana to join his father and two brothers. In 1832 David bought several acres of land in Highland Township and built a log house, 18 x 28, one and one-half story. Besides a farm, David had a slaughter house, a bark mill, a tanyard, and brick kiln. In 1844 David and Barbara built a large two story brick house near the intersection of Indiana State roads 32 and 63. See picture in Highland History section. Children were Mary, James, Adam, George, Catherine, Jacob, Martha Ann, John Riley, Rosanna, Joseph.

George Wittenmyer, was born Sept. 20, 1836, one mile west of Perrysville in log cabin. He died May 30, 1914, at his home four miles west of Perrysville. On Sept. 27, 1867, he married Martha Mandella Morningstar. Children were Rosetta (Skinner), Freeman Otis, Lotta May (Hines), Margaret Ellen (Toby), George William.

Rosetta Wittenmyer married Lewis Skinner on Sept. 25, 1892. Rosetta was born Aug. 21, 1868, and died July 28, 1955. Their children were Ethel (Kemna), Grace (Kinney), Elsie (Kemna), Margaret (Orahood), Elbert, John and Norman Lewis Franklin.

Still living in Vermillion County are Lewis Kemna, son of William and Ethel Kemna, Harlan Kinney, son of Glen and Grace Kenney, Richard Kemna, son of Fred and Elsie Kemna, Marietta (Arrasmith), daughter of Fred and Elsie Kemna, and Rosemary (Kirby), daughter of Lamont and Margaret Orahood, living in Warren County.

Norman Skinner was born Dec. 17, 1905, and died Mar. 4, 1978. He was married to Mary E. Cole. Children are Norman L. and Curtis F. Skinner. Children of Norman L. and Dorothy (Mitchell) Skinner are Norman L. and Nicole Louise. Children of Curtis and Candace (Cox) Skinner are Cory and Chad Skinner.

WILLIAM J. AND AUDREY LINDLEY WOLTER,

William Wolter, son of Frank and Winona Redmond Wolter was born at their farm home one half mile southwest of Gessie, Aug. 24, 1915. This farm was purchased by William's grandparents, William and Louisa Housewalt Wolter, December, 1889.

William Wolter, son of Frank and Winona married Betty Stockard, daughter of Lewis and Pearl Smith Stockard of Marshfield, IN, Nov. 7, 1942. A daughter, Phyllis Ann was born to this union, Nov. 28, 1943. Betty died May 27, 1951, also a day older daughter Pamela Lou.

Wolter and Wilson Families. Front: Audrey Wolter, Cheryl Wilson, Phyllis Wilson, Carol Wilson. Back: William Wolter, Michael Wilson, Kenneth Wilson

Phyllis graduated from Perrysville High school in 1961. She married Kenneth Wilson, son of Lee and Mary Ellis Wilson, Mar. 9, 1963, and they live on a farm one mile south of Perrysville. To this union three children were born. Cheryl Ann born Jan. 23, 1964, is a medical secretary. Carol Lee born May 25, 1965, is a childhood developmental teacher and Michael Leroy born July 28, 1966, farms and is dispatcher jailer.

William Wolter, son of Frank and Winona, married Audrey Lindley, daughter of Samuel and Othelia Gustafson Lindley, Aug. 9, 1952, of Georgetown, IL. Audrey was born Oct. 12, 1917, three miles northeast of Georgetown and graduated from Georgetown High School in 1935, attended Utterback Business College in Danville and was bookkeeper at Modern Machine Shop 1936-1952.

Audrey has one sister, Ruth, born Sept. 28, 1915, and formerly married to Carl Piatt. They had two children. Carolyn Jean born Aug. 24, 1941, is married to Norman Rademacher. They have three sons, Kevin, Kent, and Eric. Samuel Dean Piatt born July 19, 1942, married Jane Walsh. They have two daughters, Lisa and Lori. The Piatts' live near Armstrong, IL, and the Rademachers' near Gifford, IL.

William has one sister, Winona Louise, born Jan. 24, 1918, who is married to Roy Bush. They have two sons. John born Nov. 11, 1948, married Brenda Rogers and they have two children Kristina and Ian. Dan, born Feb. 22, 1952, married Karen Lagler and they have two children, Angela and Andrew.

William has farmed the family farm all his life. His main interests were in the purebred industry; Angus cattle and Hampshire sheep. He participated in several Illinois and Indiana county fairs and also Indiana State Fairs. This farm has been in the Wolter family 99 years.

BROUNA MARION WRIGHT AND ROSELLA ELIZABETH UMMEL WRIGHT,

Brouna was the second son of John and Rosa Wright. He was born May 26, 1888. He married Rosella Elizabeth Ummel on Aug. 30, 1913. Rosella was born Aug. 31, 1890, and died Nov. 9, 1970. Brouna died Jan. 21, 1967.

They had three sons. The first son was Harold Wright who was born Dec. 22, 1914. He married Thelma Bolton, June 17, 1936. Thelma was born June 13, 1911. They have one son who was born Jan. 17, 1937. He married Candice E. Gayheart on Aug. 17, 1974. Candice was born Aug. 1, 1948. They have one son, Aaron. He was born Jan. 6, 1982. Harold Wright died Jan. 30, 1985, of heart failure.

The second son of Brouna and Rosella was Burrel Wright. He was in the Army and was killed in action.

The third son was Logan Wright. He was born May 2, 1922, and died Mar. 31, 1968. He married Martha Robinson on Sept. 19, 1942. They had a daughter, Carolyn, who was born May 27, 1943. She married Dale Bratt on Apr. 13, 1963. They were divorced. They have two children. Michael Allen Bratt was born Dec. 18, 1965, and was killed in a car accident May 24, 1978. Peggy Lynn Bratt was born Nov. 20, 1967.

Uncle Brouna Wright loved to talk politics. Every Saturday night you would find him on any street corner on Main Street in Clinton talking politics.

Uncle Brouna was a coal miner and worked at the Crown Hill No. 5 coal mine near Centenary. *Submitted by Edna Wright*

CHLORAL J. AND MILDRED REED WRIGHT,

Chloral J. Wright was born near Centenary, IN, on Aug. 22, 1909 and died Mar. 19, 1986. He was the son of Milton Wright (Apr. 30, 1876 - Sept. 16, 1962) and Retha Hatley Wright (Apr. 19, 1880 - Jan. 17, 1947). Five brothers—Merle, Emmett, Roscoe, Owen, Harry—are deceased. A brother, Delbert, is living in Florida. Two sisters are deceased—Versa Huffman and Eva Ellen Long. A sister, Nema Merritt, lives at Rosedale, IN.

Mildred and Chloral Wright

His paternal grandparents were Levi Wright (Nov. 8, 1844 - Jan. 17, 1932) and Sarah Foltz Wright (died about 1923). His paternal great-grandparents were Philander Wright (1807 - June 15, 1855) and Catherine Swan Wright. His paternal great-great-grandparents were George Wright (1778 - 1844) and Anna Handy (Nov. 14, 1786 - 1827). His paternal great-great-great-grandfather was Will Wright. Will Wright lived in Gorham, Ontario Co., NY, and then went to Ross Co., OH, where he is said to have died. George Wright was born in Gorham, Ontario Co., NY, and died in Vermillion Co., IN.

He attended Spangler School, Centenary School, and graduated from Clinton High School in 1927.

On May 12, 1934, he married Mildred Evelyn Reed (Jan. 8, 1912) who was born in Jacksonville, IN. She is the daughter of Frank Reed (Sept. 4, 1886 - Jan. 7, 1957) and Nellie Jackson Reed (Dec. 23, 1887-Dec. 28, 1958). She had a brother, Paul, who is deceased and has a brother, Harold, who lives at Clinton, IN. She has one sister—Blanche Beard Petker—of Florida.

Her paternal grandfather was William H. Reed, son of Andrew Wray Reed, son of Jacob Reed (Reid), son of John Reid. Jacob Reed didn't like Germany so he changed the spelling of Reid to Reed. Jacob Reed's wife was Elizabeth Schmitt Reed. Her ancestry can be traced back to Frederick II and Frederick William II of Germany. Her paternal grandmother was Mary Farris Reed.

Her maternal grandparents were Thomas Jackson (Jan. 24, 1859 - Jan. 23, 1936) and Emma Roberts Jackson (Nov. 27, 1864 - July 11, 1947).

She attended Coon Hollow School, Spangler School, and graduated from Clinton High School in 1933.

They are the parents of two children. Evelyn Wright Hixon was born Mar. 4, 1936 and Jerry Wright was born Aug. 16, 1938. Evelyn married James F. Hixon and Jerry married Maurleen Harper.

They have six grandchildren—Cynthia Wright Thorpe (Oct. 23, 1958), Brent Hixon (July 19, 1959), Duane Hixon (July 9, 1960), Allen Wright (May 1, 1961), Kevin Hixon (Dec. 20, 1962), and Scott Hixon (Mar. 25, 1965). Allen married Christine Clodfelter, Kevin married Lori Wetnight, Brent married Belinda Waldridge, and Cynthia married Ron Thorpe.

They have two great-grandchildren—Samantha Jane Wright (Aug. 23, 1984) and Chelsea Jo Hixon (July 17, 1988).

Mr. Wright was a lifelong farmer having spent a short time working in the coal mines. He farmed both in Vermillion County and Parke County.

Mr. Wright was a member of the Federated Church in Marshall, IN, and Mrs. Wright is still a member. They were formerly members of the Center Methodist Church east of St. Bernice, IN. Mr. Wright was a member of the Odd Fellows Lodge and the Royal Knights of Jericho Lodge. Mrs. Wright was a member of the Parke County Choral Club and is a member of the Sugar Creek Home Economics Club and the Federated Women's Club.

CLEATUS GARLAND WRIGHT,

named Jack was born Mar. 19, 1886, in Vermillion Co., IN, and was the son of John and Rosa Wright.

He married Mary Hist. They had two children, Harmon Wright and Mary Wright.

He later married Kate Wilson, and they did not have children.

Jack died in 1951 or 1952 in Veteran's Hospital in Indianapolis, IN. He is buried at Shirley Cemetery in Vermillion Co., IN.

His son, Harmon Wright, married Rosella ?. They lived in California. Harmon was born Aug. 25, 1913, and died May 10, 1986. They have a daughter, who is a school teacher, and lives in Oregon. His wife still lives in California.

His daughter, Mary Wright, married ? Black. They had two children. *Submitted by Edna Wright*

GEORGE FREEMAN WRIGHT,

(Apr. 28, 1882-Jan. 30, 1946) was the great grandson of George Wright who was born in Windsor, CT (1774-1839), a son of David Wright (1742/3 - died before 1811), a veteran of the Revolutionary War. George migrated to Ontario Co., NY. In 1819 he, with his wife, the former Anna Handy (whose parents have not been definitely established), and nine children, went to Vigo Co., IN. In 1820 they moved to Vermillion County where he acquired a tract of 160 acres from Lucius Scott. Life was hard in this pioneer settlement. Bears and other wild animals shared the land. George was a farmer and cooper (barrel maker). Barrels were very important for shipping products down the Wabash River. Anna died at 48 or 50, Nov. 1, 1827. George married on May 28, 1837, Hannah Clover who may have died in 1844. One descendant has in his family Bible a list of 12 children for George and Anna.

Freeman and Philippena Wright

One of his sons, Philander Wright (1807-1855), was the grandfather of George Freeman Wright and was an original land owner in Clinton Township. He married on Oct. 13, 1833, Catherine Swan, who was born in Ohio and died in Vermillion County (May 27, 1816-Apr. 18, 1876). Philander died when he accidently shot himself while cleaning his gun. They were the parents of nine children.

Oliver P. Wright (1837-1907), Philander's oldest son and father of Freeman, built some of the covered bridges in the area. He was a farmer. Oliver married Mar. 14, 1861, Elizabeth Ellen Titus (Dec.

5, 1840-Jan. 7, 1918). She was a daughter of Michael Titus and Mary M. Lambert who died two weeks apart with black or swamp fever, now known as malaria. Oliver and Elizabeth had nine children, all of whom are gone at this writing but quite a few of their descendants live in or near Clinton.

Freeman was a small farmer and made his living raising hogs and hauling coal with a team and wagon to customers in Clinton. He married, Oct. 1, 1905, the beautiful Philippena Emma Ummel, born Mar. 24, 1883, in New Goshen. She was the daughter of William Henry Ummel and Josephine Strole. She died Dec. 27, 1969, in Clinton. They lived and reared their five children on the Range Line Road west of Clinton. Their only son, Virgil Freeman, born Oct. 24, 1908, died at age 14, Feb. 24, 1923. All attended Hazel Bluff School, a two room school with eight grades. Three girls graduated from Clinton High School.

Opal Marie, born July 15, 1906, married Franklin Tully Ralston, a coal miner, and lives in Clinton. Esther Josephine, born Jan. 29, 1912, graduated from Union Hospital School of Nursing. She married William Clarence Searcy, a Terre Haute police officer and later a city councilman. They lived in Terre Haute until they retired to Sarasota, FL. Velma Irene, born June 8, 1914, married Walter Mark Beal, a truck driver of Miamisburg, OH, and they lived there until retiring to Sebring, FL. Lois Hazel married Duane Crowder who served in World War II and was a postal worker. They live in Terre Haute. *Submitted by Esther Josephine Wright Searcy*

JOHN WESLEY WRIGHT AND ROSA A. PROPST WRIGHT,

John W. Wright was born Nov. 24, 1856, the son of Daniel Garland Wright and Mary Adkins Wright of Sullivan, IN. He came to Vermillion Co., IN, and married Rosa A. Propst, daughter of Isaac Propst and Elizabeth Koonce Propst. Rosa was born Apr. 24, 1866.

John Wesley Wright with Harmon Wright, Mary Wright, and Lester Wright

They were married Jan. 20, 1885. He was age 29 and she was age 19. They were married by Justice of the Peace, David H. Bent.

They lived south of Blanford, IN, near Bogle Hill and Furnace Hill Bridge in a log house with a dirt floor. They later put a floor in the house. John worked in the coal mines.

To this union were born several children. The first son was Cleatus Garland, born Mar. 19, 1886. His first wife was Mary Hist and his second wife was Kate Wilson. The second son was Brouna Marion, born May 26, 1888, married to Rosella Elizabeth Ummel. Next was a daughter, Gertrude May, born Oct. 5, 1889, married to Harold William Elliott. Another daughter was Svannah Maude, born Jan. 10, 1890, and married to Charles (Charlie)

Bales. Third daughter and fifth child was Millie Bill, born Nov. 29, 1893, married to Emery Rhodes. Next was another son, Leonard Grant, born Oct. 21, 1895, and never married. Another son, Lloyd Sanford, born Jan. 19, 1898, was married first to Irma Robins and second to Catherine Steenberger. The youngest and the last of John and Rosa's children was my father, Lester Ranwick, born Oct. 27, 1905. He married first my mother, Mildred Josephine Hunt, and later married Elva Castiglione.

All the children of John and Rosa Wright were born in Vermillion County, rural Clinton, IN. *Submitted by Edna Wright*

LEONARD GRANT WRIGHT,

son of John and Rosa Wright, was born Oct. 21, 1895, in Vermillion County, rural Clinton, IN.

Leonard Wright and sister, Millie Bill

He never married. He died in 1913. Leonard Grant was killed in a coal mine accident at age 19. He was pushing a cable car which flipped upside down and threw him and the car into the mine. Leonard Grant is buried in Shirley Cemetery in Vermillion Co., IN. *Submitted by Edna Wright*

LESTER RANWICK WRIGHT AND MILDRED JOSEPHINE HUNT WRIGHT,

Lester Ranwick was the youngest of all the children of John and Rosa Wright. He was born Oct. 27, 1905, in Vermillion County, rural Clinton, IN.

He married Mildred Josephine Hunt on June 19, 1929, in Paris, IL. Mildred Josephine was the daughter of Oliver Mason and Ruth Hawkins Hunt. She was born Oct. 8, 1911, in Clinton, IN.

Lester and Mildred had three daughters, Betty Lucy, Edna Lee, and Ruth Elaine.

Lester Ranwick Wright

Betty Lucy was born Apr. 8, 1930. She died Aug. 14, 1930. Betty Lucy is buried at Shirley Cemetery in Vermillion Co., IN.

Edna Lee was born on Mar. 5, 1933, in Vigo County, Terre Haute, IN. She married Richard L. Wright on July 1, 1951. He is the son of Russell

Sherman and Frances Margie Vaughn Wright. They live in Ridge Farm, IL.

Edna and Richard Wright's children are Jeannie Ann Wright Mussatto; Rita Kay Wright Bendekovich; Peter Douglas Wright; David Timothy Wright; Karen Joy Wright; and Terrie Beth Wright. They have four grandchildren.

The youngest daughter of Lester and Mildred was Ruth Elaine Wright. She was born June 12, 1940, in Universal, IN, Vermillion County. She married John Robert Mathes on July 28, 1962, at State Line Christian Church. Children of Ruth and John Mathes are Dennis Lee Mathes and Melissia Ann Mathes. They live in Urbana, IL.

Lester and Mildred were divorced.

Lester Ranwick worked on the Pennsylvania Railroad in Terre Haute, IN. He was a brakeman until his death. He died of heart failure on Mar. 16, 1959. *Submitted by Edna Wright*

LEVI AND SARAH FOLTZ WRIGHT,

Levi Wright was born Nov. 8, 1844 and died Jan. 17, 1932. He was married June 10, 1866, to Sarah Foltz, who died about 1923. He was mustered into service in the Civil War February, 1860, and served until June, 1865, (Co. 1, Regiment 43). Mr. Wright, a farmer, lived two and one-half miles northeast of Libertyville, IN. He was superintendent of the Sabbath School of the United Brethern Church.

Levi Wright

His father, Philander Wright, was born in 1807 in Gorham, Ontario Co., NY, and came to Vermillion Co., IN, in 1820, with his parents. He was killed accidently, June 15, 1855, while cleaning a gun. He was married Oct. 18, 1833, to Catherine Swan. Both are buried in Chunn's (or Scott) Cemetery near Shephardsville, IN. They had nine children—Mary Ann, Oliver P., Francis M., Mary Jane, Levi, Philander, James F., Thirza, and Laura.

His grandfather, George Wright, was born in 1778, in Gorham, Ontario Co., NY, and died in 1844, in Clinton Township, Vermillion Co., IN. He was married in Gorham about 1800 to Anna Handy, who may have been born Nov. 14, 1786, in Dartmouth, MA, and died in 1827 in Vermillion County. There were nine children—George, Polly, Mary A., Naomi, Philander, William, Handy, John, and Truman. George was later married to Hannah Clover.

His great-grandfather was Will Wright. He apparently lived in Gorham, Ontario Co., NY, later in Pennsylvania, then went to Ross Co., OH, where he is said to have died. He had two known sons, George and Thomas.

Levi and Sarah Wright were the parents of five children—Ada Galeener, Frank, William, Milton and May Martin. (see related article—Milton and Retha Hatley Wright)

They are buried in Riverside Cemetery, Clinton, IN.

LLOYD SANFORD WRIGHT, was the next to the last son to be born to John and Rosa Wright, Jan. 19, 1898, in Vermillion County, rural Clinton, IN. He died Feb. 7, 1973, and was buried in Glasgow, KY.

Lloyd Wright in his buggy with his friends.

Lloyd Sanford first married Irma Robins. They had children, but none lived. His wife died.

He then married Catherine Steeberger, July 12, 1937, at the home of Homer and Mary Bales in Terre Haute, IN.

Lloyd and Catherine raised several children, but had none of their own.

He decided to go into the ministry after his brother was killed in a coal mine accident. Lloyd was a circuit rider "pastored" in the Methodist Church. He had several churches he pastored to.

After 36 years, he was reunited with his sister. She lived in Gaylord, MI. All his parishioners collected trading stamps for his bus ticket. Brother and sister had a happy reunion. *Submitted by Edna Wright*

MILDRED BOTNER WRIGHT,
was born Dec. 5, 1907, east of Center Church. She was the firstborn of Jacob Dawson Botner and Lucy P. Haun Botner. Jacob and Lucy Botner had three other children: Blanche Botner Saxton Goforth, Lester J. Botner, and Dorothy Lucille who died three days following her birth.

Lucy Botner was born in a log cabin northeast of Center Methodist Church on June 17, 1882. She was the daughter of Parret Haun and Elizabeth Heber, who also had three other daughters and one son.

Jake and Lucy Botner

Jacob Botner was born Jan. 12, 1884, near Brocton, IL. They moved to the Center neighborhood around 1890 where they lived west of Center Church. Jacob was the son of Christopher Columbus Botner and Mary Letitia Borders Botner. Jacob had four brothers and four sisters.

Jacob and Lucy were married Thanksgiving Day on Nov. 29, 1906. On Mar. 1, 1908 they rented and moved on the 160 acre farm owned by Mrs. Dyer Harriet Campbell. Mildred was three months old at this time. A few years later they bought this farm,

and it has been farmed and owned by family members since that time.

Mildred, along with her sister and brother, attended school at Frog College and Bono High School. Blanche left home when she married Glen Saxton, but Mildred and Lester remained to help with the farm.

In October, 1940, Mildred married widower C. Roscoe Wright. Roscoe had three daughters— Imogene, Phyllis, and LaDonna. Although Roscoe was born and reared in Clinton township in the large family of Milton and Retha Hatley Wright, he was working at Indiana Steel and Wire Mill in Muncie.

On Jan. 19, 1942 in Ball Hospital in Muncie, Carl Dale was born to Mildred and Roscoe.

Roscoe and Mildred moved back to this area in December, 1943, and bought the farm next to Botner's in 1948. They moved to this farm in January, 1949. After Roscoe's death in March, 1963, Carl continued to farm this land, as well as the Botner farm. The barn on this farm was built in the early 1840's and served as a meeting place for Center Church until the first church was built in 1853.

Carl married Jill Paulette Watson on Sept. 3, 1965. She is the firstborn of Paul Eugene and G. June Pearman Watson, also lifelong Vermillion County residents. Carl and Jill's four daughters are Cindy Joy born Dec. 12, 1966; Gail Gay born Oct. 29, 1968; Misty Dawn born Jan. 19, 1970, and Dale Jene born Sept. 25, 1971. The girls attended Ernie Pyle Elementary School and South Vermillion High School. Three are presently enrolled in Indiana State University.

After graduating from St. Bernice High School in 1960, Carl has continued to farm these two farms where he also lives. Jill attended St. Bernice, but graduated from Clinton in 1964. She has earned B.S. and M.S. degrees from Indiana State University in Elementary Education and teaches in the South Vermillion School Corporation. They, with their family, attend an old church in the county— Tennessee Valley Baptist.

MILTON AND RETHA HATLEY WRIGHT,
Milton Wright was born Apr. 30, 1876, and died Sept. 16, 1962. He was the son of Levi and Sarah Foltz Wright. He had two brothers, Frank and William, and two sisters, Ada Galeener and May Martin. His grandparents were Philander and Catherine Swan Wright. Mr. Wright was a carpenter. (see related article—Levi and Sarah Foltz Wright)

He married Retha Hatley, daughter of Jasper and Adeline Hatley. She was born Apr. 19, 1880, and died Jan. 17, 1947. There were ten children born to this union.

Merle (Mar. 25, 1899-Jan. 12, 1978) married Rose Peer. There were no children.

The Milton Wright Family. Front: Milton, Delbert, Retha. Back: Harry, Emmett, Nema, Merle, Eva Ellen, Chloral, Versa, Owen, Roscoe.

Emmett (Sept. 23, 1901-Mar. 8, 1977) married Martha Chambers. There were six children born to this union—Paul (Apr. 28, 1923-Feb. 15, 1987), David (Sept. 29, 1925), John Earl (Aug. 22, 1927-Mar. 22, 1928), Richard (Feb. 27, 1929), Barbara Sturgeon (July 12, 1932), and Jane Myers (Jan. 20, 1935).

Roscoe (June 6, 1904-Mar. 9, 1963) was married first to Mary Cannon. There were four children born to this union—Imogene Long (Apr. 12, 1930), Phyllis Nesler Edwards (June 5, 1931), La Donna Riggen (Aug. 20, 1932), and an infant son (deceased July 12, 1935). Mary Cannon Wright died in childbirth. He later married Mildred Botner. They had one son, Carl (Jan. 19, 1942).

Owen (Oct. 17, 1906-July 20, 1981) married Elva Huffman. There were six children born to this union—Herbert (Mar. 12, 1929-), Lloyd (Dec. 7, 1930), Francis (Dec. 1, 1931), Velma Wethington (Apr. 10, 1933) Virginia Marie (Sept. 2, 1934-Sept. 26, 1934), and Waunita Reisinger (July 27, 1943).

Versa (Feb. 6, 1908-Oct. 7, 1975) married Leo (Pete) Huffman. There were seven children born to this union—Gladys Nisbet (July 9, 1928), Ray (Feb. 1, 1930), Earl (June 8, 1934), Carolyn (Apr. 23, 1937-May 23, 1937), Cheryl (Oct. 25, 1944), Robert (Sept. 4, 1946), and Wretha Shull (?) (Apr. 19, 1951).

Chloral (Aug. 22, 1909-Mar. 19, 1986) married Mildred Reed. There are two children—Evelyn Hixon (Mar. 4, 1936) and Jerry (Aug. 16, 1938). (see related article—Chloral and Mildred Reed Wright)

Nema (Dec. 12, 1911) lives at Rosedale. She was married to George Merritt. There are four children—Neil (June 9, 1938), Moyne Johnson (Aug. 2, 1941), Tommy (May 12, 1943), and June Harris (Oct. 13, 1944). She has three stepchildren— Donald Merritt, Catherine Merritt, Kenneth Merritt.

Harry (Nov. 19, 1913-Dec. 13, 1980) was married first to Opal Allen. There are four children— Mike (Apr. 10, 1941), Larry (Sept. 12, 1944), Janet Higginbotham (Oct. 20, 1946), and Beverly Higginbotham Fortune (Mar. 18, 1950). He later married Valena Wilson. There are four children— Richard (Mar. 29, 1964), Rosemarie (May 22, 1966), Tammy (July 2, 1967), and Randy (Sept. 2, 1968).

Eva Ellen (Mar. 24, 1916-May 25, 1979) married Jim Long. There are two children—Ronald (June 30, 1946), and Dennis (June 19, 1949).

Delbert (Jan. 14, 1920) lives in Clearwater, FL. He married Virginia Fears. There are three children—Sharon Csikai (Sept. 7, 1941), Gerald (Aug. 27, 1943), and Marvin (Sept. 23, 1947).

RUSSELL SHERMAN WRIGHT AND FRANCES MARGIE VAUGHN WRIGHT,
Russell Sherman was born Apr. 23, 1905, in Vermilion, IL, the son of Sherman Ulysses Wright and Corilla Adaline Bailey Wright. He married Frances Margie Vaughn on Dec. 29, 1928. They were married in Paris, IL, by W.E Anderson.

Frances was born Dec. 29, 1905, near Marshall, IL. She is the daughter of Philip Alexanda Vaughn and Kate McClenthen Vaughn.

They lived in Vermilion, IL, on a farm that belongs to his mother. He was only three months old when his father died.

Russell Sherman's grandparents were from Corydon, IN. Some of the family came up to Illinois and part of them still live in Corydon, IN.

verly Ann Wright, Russell Gene Wright, Richard Lee Wright,
.nd Kenneth Orville Wright.

Russell Sherman and Orville Wright were brothers. Orville Wright lives in Dana, IN.

Orville Wright bought a farm in Indiana, south of Blanford. The Russell Wright family moved from Vermilion, IL, to Indiana to farm this land in 1942.

Children of Russell and Frances were Russell Gene who was age 13, Richard who was age ten, and Beverly who was age seven, when they moved to Indiana. Kenneth Orville was born two years later in 1944.

Russell Sherman died Feb. 13, 1969, at home at rural Clinton. He was buried at Thomas Cemetery near Cayuga, IN.

Russell Gene Wright married Janine Marie Turner, Dec. 7, 1951, in Terre Haute, IN. They now live in Cayuga, IN. Children of Gene and Janine are Michelle Louise who is deceased; Michael Gene who was married to Cheryl Hawn, their children are Laura Michelle and Adrian Nicole; Margie Marie was married to Michael Long, their children are twins, Andrew Albert and Amanda Margie, now married to Tim Faircloth with a daughter, Olivia; Teresa Ann married to Donald Ray Morgan, their children are Brandon Joel and Darren Ray; Susan Lynn married to Matthew Gene Powell, their children are Russell Gene, Shaun Matthew, and Caleb Michael. All of the children of Russell Gene and Janine were born in Vermillion Co., IN, except the oldest who was born in Vigo Co., IN.

Richard Wright married Edna Wright, July 1, 1951, at the State Line Christian Church. They live in Ridge Farm, IL. Children of Richard and Edna are Jeannie Ann married to Nick Mussatto, their children are Korena Ann and Errol Louis, married at State Line Christian Church; Rita Kay married to Anthony Bendekovich, one son, Anthony; Peter Douglas, David Timothy, Karen Joy, Heather Lynn, and Terrie Beth.

Beverly Ann Wright married Ronald Clyde Helms, Aug. 23, 1957, in the Christian Church at Clinton, Vermillion Co., IN. They live in Fort Wayne, IN. Their children are twins, Larry Ronald and Lisa Renee.

Kenneth Orville Wright married Judy Ann Davis, Mar. 28, 1964, at State Line Christian Church. Their children are Robin Lynn, Daniel Joseph, and Amy Nicole. They live at rural Clinton, Vermillion Co., IN. *Submitted by Edna Wright*

MARCO PACIFICO ZANANDREA,

was born in 1904, in Carre, Province Vicenza, Italy. His father, Christoforo, a bricklayer, left Italy because of the pending war. He came to Clinton, IN, because he knew others who had immigrated there. His wife, Giovanna Muraro Zanandrea, immigrated later, arriving in Clinton with children Marco, Cecilia and Domenica (Rena) on Feb. 14, 1914. Daughter Alba was born soon after their arrival.

The family moved west of Clinton to Jacksonville, near Blanford, to be closer to the coal mines. At age 14, Marco falsified his birth date on his grade school diploma so that he could work in the mines to help his parents. "When the mine whistle blew, I worked. When it didn't, I went to school," is how Marco described his education.

Early 1920s' Domenica (Rena) Zanandrea Burton, mother Giovanna Muraro Zanandrea, Marco P. Zanandrea, Alba Zanandrea Burton, Cecilia Zanandrea Giordano, and father Christoforo Zanandrea.

Marco enjoyed telling stories about life in Blanford during the mining boom, when, he said, everyone had a gun in his back pocket. One night he sat in front of Lanzone's store between two men arguing over five dollars. "I'll just give you five dollars," said the man of Marco's left. He proceeded to pull out his gun and shoot the man on Marco's right. Such incidents, he said, were not isolated ones.

Before the Depression, Marco sought work in Chicago. He sent most of his paycheck home and noted that his father was never without a basement stocked with homemade salami and wine. Marco married Rose Vercoglio, the daughter of Genesio and Maria Gorgett Vercoglio, in Crown Point, IN, in 1928. Both were working in Chicago at the time.

The couple bought a home in Jacksonville in 1930. Son Marco C. was born in 1931; daughter Marilyn was born in 1935; and son Jerry was born in 1945. Making a living was difficult, but Marco was ever resourceful and always reliable. Before securing work in the mines, he found small jobs and could always put game on the table for supper.

During his lifetime, Marco worked a total of 24 years in shaft mines and eight years in strip mines. He also farmed, and for seven years he was superintendent with the Vermillion County Highway Department. He was a founding member of the Blanford Sportsman Club and an officer for the Ancient Order of Druids, a society for men of Italian descent.

Rose Zanandrea worked at Central Electronics in Paris, IL, from 1963-1969. She enjoyed her memberships in the Ladies Fish and Game Club and the Little Italy Festival Singers. Marco and Rose considered being selected as Re and Regina of the 1973 Clinton Little Italy Festival a great honor, and they were active ambassadors of the Italian community at many festivals, dancing polkas and waltzes with style and energy.

Rose Zanandrea died in 1985, and Marco died in 1986. Their family remembers them as wise and loving parents who knew the value of hard work, laughter, and good food and music.

Marco and Rose's three children still live in the Clinton area, as do most of their grandchildren: Denise Herrington, Marco W. Zanandrea, Dawn Thomson, Matthew Zanandrea, Kim Stone, Dana Stowe, and Stacy Mills—children of Marco C. Zanandrea; and J.D., Doug and Shawn Wilson—children of Marilyn Zanandrea Wilson.

Group of Range Riders at Columbus Day

Ilia Mae and Jeannette Rowley

West Clinton Junction L. to R.: Tavern, Pool Room, Restaurant/Hotel and Garage. Laura Stevenson and unidentified lady on hotel porch. Roy Rusmisel by car.

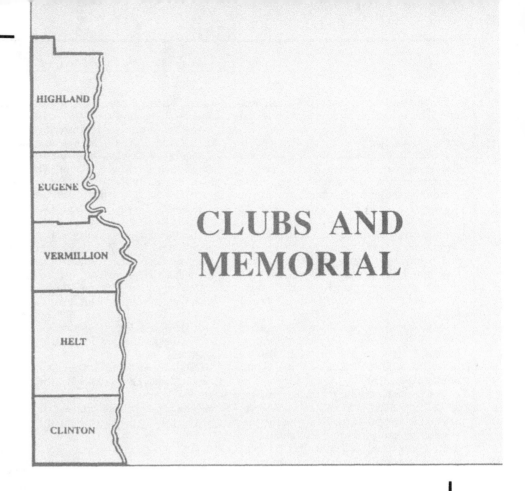

CLUBS AND MEMORIAL

Range Riders at Columbus Day Parade-1949

LITTLE ITALY FESTIVAL TOWN

Twenty-three years ago the small town of Clinton, Indiana, organized "Little Italy Festival Town" (Lift). It was a colorful and unique idea that was to awaken and involve the townspeople, and it did. Nature had given our town a perfect location of natural surroundings—on the banks of the famous Wabash River. The town had always had a large ethnic group due to the surrounding coal mines; but the Italian immigrants outnumbered the others. We were often referred to as the "Melting Pot" and rightly so. Being a mining area, everyone hated the words "Home Go!" The miners would be idle. To many, it meant living from the gardens. Neighbors literally kept each other.

A group of men and women representing the various civic groups met, discussed, and presented the town with the "Lift" that was so badly needed. The group was a non-profit corporation.

We needed something different in which all citizens could help and enjoy. The Jaycees had a dream about a "really real" gondola floating down the Wabash. That dream came true September 1, 1967, when the real gondola arrived straight from Venice, Italy. It was and is a show piece and is taken to many towns to boast of its authenticity. Board members in beautiful costumes of red, white, and green show their friendly Italian heritage by sharing.

One of the most picturesque settings is the Four Season's Fountain — "Quatro Staggioni." The lovely fountain is the focal point of the Festival for both young or old.

North of the Quatro Staggioni is a new stage used for entertainment—children dancing and singing and adults singing in Italian. Listen for the sound of a real Italian accordion!

Various clubs and business people sponsor a girl to represent them before and during the entire festival. Our girls are one of our biggest assets—youth, beauty, and so friendly. They are truly lovely ambassadors! One girl is selected as the Queen previous to the festival.

A highlight of the program is the selection of a Re and Regina. The couple is selected by the Lift Board, and announced at the annual dinner held in August. Luck is with us when the couple are both of Italian heritage. 1988 is a grand year! The long "lost" families come home to Nonna's (grandmother) and Nonno's (grandfather) for it is time to eat Nonna's polenta and spaghetti and sample Nonno's vino!

You may come on Friday (Venerdi) to enjoy an extremely popular parade starting at the railroad tracks on 9th Street and continuing to the Quatro Staggioni overlooking the Wabash. Take time to enjoy the tantalizing odors of the Italian cooking.

Before you start to roam, go to the railroad station that is another part of our heritage. This marvelous collection of mining tools is outstanding.

The 9th Street area is where most of the Italians settled. You'll be welcomed to our famous Wine Garden. Note the one grape vine which is really the roof. This is an unusual growth for a vine. Sit at one of the tables and you'll find music and friends immediately! Dance, sing, and talk. Quite a few will speak the Italian language.

The Pietro Micca Society was a miner's organization. You'll be in one of Clinton's oldest buildings. Inspect the old barrels and winemaking equipment.

Don't miss the Mercato—truly an Italian store with salami and long loaves of bread for sale. Drop in on the little house next door depicting life in the early 1900's—such as using an ice-box, kitchen stove, wash tubs, etc.

Continue north on 9th Street until you see the Immigrant Square. It honors all of the people who migrated to Clinton. Note the black granite fountain and the Bull's Head drinking fountain. This was given to Clinton by Joe Airola (now deceased). It was made for him and it is an exact duplicate of a fountain in Torino, Italy. The flags salute the many countries from which the early settlers migrated.

Our celebration ends with the drawing of a trip to Italy (or money). A burst of fireworks wish all happiness and promise that you'll return. Do hope you stomped some grapes! That's something you'll never forget!

Arrivederce, see you next year.

Sponsored by Lift Board of Directors and the Friendly community of Clinton, Indiana.

It is very difficult to put into words the true meaning of Lift! To most of us it isn't words or entertainment—is is a way of showing our thanks to our courageous and colorful background of people who left their homes and made our homes possible. *Grazie*

Four Seasons Fountain

49'ERS CLUB

For forty years, the 49'ers Club has provided service to Dana and the surrounding communities. This group of twenty women has provided clothing, food, and hospital equipment to those who need it. Poinsettias are given to friends and churches at Christmas. Annual services are the community blood drive, Easter egg hunt, Halloween window painting, and an English Award to a student of each of the Vermillion County high schools. The club also sponsors a jitterbug contest at the Ernie Pyle Firemen's Festival.

Present 49'er members are: Clarabelle Adams*, Shirley Boatman, Pat Cheesewright, Joyce Ellis, Maxine Hendrix, Lois Hess, Doris Hill, Donna Homsley, Dorothy Lewman*, Gayla McMullen, Betty Miller, Rachel Milligan, Margaret Parks*, Marjorie Randall*, Sue Randall, Marilyn Redman, Evelyn Stratton, Sheila Sturm, Jeanne Summerville*, Priscilla. Wimsett.

*Charter members

Dana 49'ers and their husbands as the Dana Firemen honored them for 35 years of service at the Ernie Pyle Fall Festival-1988

Fish and Game Club Valena Taparo, Virginia Gambaiani, Mary Varda, Mrs. Contori, Ginny Ferrari, Mary B. Turchi, Rose Turchi, Virginia Zamberletti, Mrs. Gilleo, Clementina Guerri, Rosaline Natalie, Fene Gambaiani, Angeline Ferro, unknown, Irene Turchi, Mildred Aimone, Maude Brown, Mary Muzzarelli, Elizabeth Guerri, Rose Bonacorsi, Pat Sisson, Linda Uselman, and Hattie Iacoli.

In Memory

In Memory Of

Grandfather Frank Reposh
Great grandparents Martin and Teresa Mohar
Uncle Martin and Aunt Tilka Mohar
Uncle Joe and Aunt Tete Pucell
Uncle Anthony Reposh
Uncle Louis Reposh
Grandfather John H. Jackson
Great Grandparents Henry Washburn and Kizzie May Paine
Great grandmother Martha A. Jackson
Uncle Charles Don Paine
Aunt Nellie Hesler
Cousin Linda Stull who disappeared without a trace in the summer of 1977

In Memory Of

My Grandmother
Frances Reposh
1875-1949
Faithful Member of Sacred Heart Church
40 years

In Memory Of

My Grandmother
Reba Elizabeth Paine Jackson
1893-1980
Mother of
Neola Davitio, Nell Allen, Ethel Reposh,
and Martha Dreher

Tribute To

My Mother
Ethel Elnora Jackson Reposh
who used to look like left above but
now looks like right above
and
My Father
Leo Reposh, Sr.

LR. Jr.

222

IN MEMORY

WEARERS OF THE "C."

Ronald "Candy" Andrews (second from left in middle row).

In Memory of Ronald E. Andrews

He was born Oct. 30, 1895 and died Oct. 20, 1980. His nickname was "Candy". He was the son of Otis and Emma Andrews. Otis and Emma had three children, Zula, Ronald, and Howard. After Emma's death, Otis married Maude Hedges. They had twin girls and a son, Murvin.

The family was originally from the Bono-Tennessee Valley area, then Otis moved to the Bunsen Road where they farmed. After Otis's death, Ronald farmed until Peabody Coal Company mined out the coal on his ground. He then moved to the Vermillion-Vigo county line in Libertyville.

He graduated from Clinton High School Class of 1914 where he played basketball. He was in the U.S. Marine Corps during World War I. He never married, but as my father, his brother Howard, was killed when I was three years old, he was like a father to me. *Submitted by Jo Andrews Jones*

Veterans' Memorial

During the second World War it was the custom for American families who had lost a son in the war to place a star in their windowpane. A gentleman was walking one evening with his small son, who was innocently attracted to and was counting the stars in windows as they walked. "Oh, look, Daddy. There is another house that's given a son in the war,' he would say naively. "And there's one with two stars!"

Finally the father and child came to a gap between roofs. Between the houses could be seen the evening star in the darkening sky. This caught the small boy's breath and he stumbled upon a truth as he said, "Oh, look, Daddy. God must have given His Son, for He's got a star in His window."

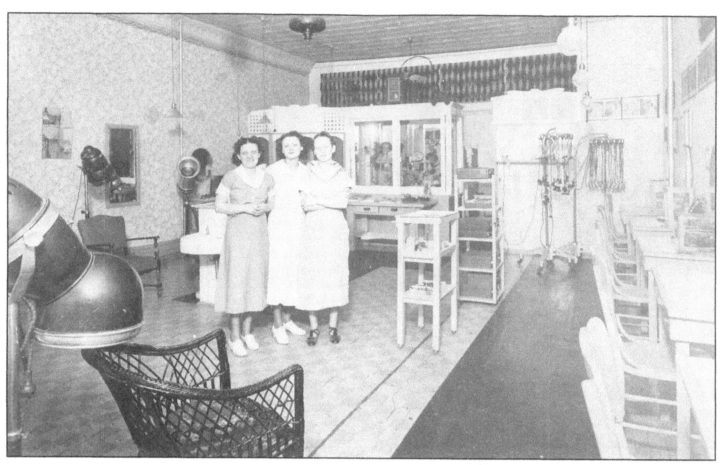

This is the Modern Way Beauty Shop on Main Street in Clinton 1930. The girl on right is Ada Towell and the girl on the left is Jane Nisbet. The highest price permanent was $2.50 and most spiral permanents were $1.00. A shampoo and set was $.50.

Fossi Bakery North Ninth Street Clinton, Indiana. Joe Fossi, Clara Fossi, and Mike Fossi.

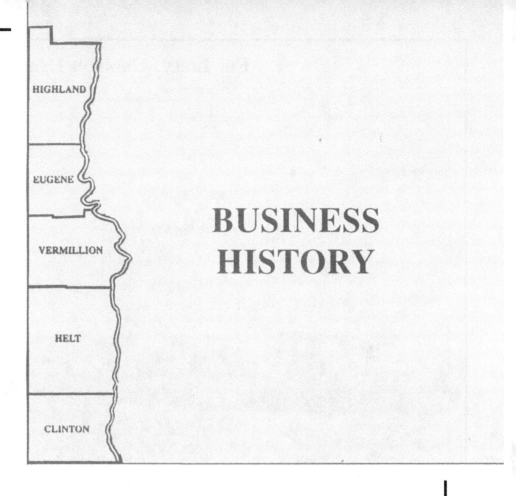

HIGHLAND

EUGENE

VERMILLION

HELT

CLINTON

BUSINESS HISTORY

Sam Rowley's Restaurant

ELI LILLY, CLINTON LABORATORIES

Eli Lilly and Company is a relative newcomer to the Helt's Prairie neighborhood in Vermillion County, Indiana. The corporation's Clinton Laboratories is located off State Road 63 north of Clinton on a 700-acre tract along the Wabash River. Built in 1970, it is among the world's largest, most modern biochemical production facilities.

Clinton Laboratories has grown from a first-year staff of around 300 people to an employer of over 900 associates from around the Wabash Valley. The plant was built by the Indianapolis-based health care products company established in 1876 by Colonel Eli Lilly, a civil war veteran.

Eli Lilly and Company built Clinton Laboratories to manufacture Keflex®, an oral antibiotic which received Food and Drug Administration approval for marketing in 1970. Now employees at the Clinton site help manufacture other products of Lilly research. These include the oral antibiotics Ceclor® and Keflex® and injectable antibiotics Kefzol® and Mandol®, all of which are used by physicians to treat patients suffering from various bacterial infections.

The plant's fermentation, recovery and finishing departments for manufacturing animal health products have also grown over the years. Employees in these areas help produce animal health products which help control certain common diseases afflicting livestock (Tylan®) and poultry (Coban®, Maxiban®, and Monteban®) and increase the feed efficiency of cattle (Rumensin®). The plant is also expected to be the finishing site for Paylean®), a new animal health product designed to help farmers produce leaner swine.

Lilly produces pharmaceuticals at Clinton Laboratories in both intermediate and bulk forms. Then other company manufacturing facilities convert them into final dosage forms, such as tablets and ampoules, sold under the Lilly and Dista labels. The Clinton operation generally makes final forms of animal health products, which are distributed by Elanco Products Company, the agricultural products division of Lilly.

Many associates at Clinton Laboratories network regularly with employees at other Lilly facilities around the world. The company is among the world's ten largest phar-

maceutical companies, and its products are available in 130 countries. During the 1980s Lilly established a Medical Instrument Systems Division which focuses on the production of both cardiovascular products and delivery systems that provide patients with intravenous nutrition and therapy.

At home in Clinton, Eli Lilly and Company strives to be a good neighbor by meeting or exceeding established environmental standards for waste treatment and by striving to be a good citizen by supporting community projects and programs.

Historically, the Lilly corporate culture has emphasized that Lilly employees are the company's most valuable assets. At Clinton Laboratories, a talented group of people have brought a complex, highly technological plant through many changes since 1970.

With the help of some new standardized problem-solving techniques based on shared responsibility teams, they are ready to help usher Lilly into the next decade and next century of manufacturing quality products.

First Funeral Home
Established in 1887

Jasper N. "Jap" Frist was barely past 20 years old when he established Frist Funeral Home in 1887. Like many other funeral homes then, Frist Funeral Home doubled as a furniture store, a common occurrence in America before the turn of the century.

With the assistance of his wife, Etta, his daughter, Enid, and his son Donald, Frist started the business on Main Street. He later relocated to 237-239 Blackman Street, then in 1923, he moved the business to his home at Fifth and Blackman (458 Blackman Street) where it has remained since.

The young entrepreneur soon earned a reputation for being a reliable businessman and a caring friend to the families in the Clinton neighborhood. Notwithstanding, had anyone told him he was building for himself a name that would be remembered more than 100 years later as one of Clinton's most noted pioneers, he probably would never had believed it.

Jap Frist was one of Indiana's first licensed embalmers, and for many years held one of the top three licenses in the state.

Although Frist Funeral Home has weathered the test of time with its myriad of changes, its primary goal has always remained the same: That is, "to relieve the family of the deceased of the many details and burdens involved in the necessary preparations of the funeral service." Its steadfast quality down through the ages is proven by the fact that the century-old facility has been operated by only four owners.

When the founder died in 1934, after operating the business for nearly 50 years, Mrs. Frist was assisted by her Daughter and Son-in-law Louis and Enid Frist Lemstra, in continuing the business. In 1955 Mrs. Frist died, and at that time the Lemstras and Marshall Frist, a nephew of Jap Frist, operated the business until 1965 when the business was purchased from the Frist family by Harold B. Mack an employee of the funeral home since 1929. He operated the business until his retirement in 1974. Mr. Mack died in September of 1980.

The business was purchased in 1975 by Stanley Beatty and Milburn Ruby long-time employees of the funeral home. Mr. Ruby worked until his retirement in 1979, and Mr. Beatty worked until his death in April of 1986.

The current owner, David G. Waite, who joined the firm in 1975, purchased the business from Mrs. Stanley Beatty upon his death in 1986. Milburn Ruby continued to work at the funeral home part-time until his death in March of 1988. Assisting David and his wife Martha are two full-time employees Jeffery A. Bates, licensed embalmer and Director who joined the firm in March of 1985, and Charles "Bob" Howard, Assistant who joined the firm in May of 1987. Also working part-time are John Hayward, Clay Mack, Grandson of Harold B. Mack, and Bill Goodman.

Over the years, several additions have been made to the building. The front porch was enclosed in 1947, a chapel was added during the mid-1950s and just recently, a coffee lounge was installed.

In keeping with the Frist tradition of offering the community the finest in funeral service, facilities and equipment, the funeral home is now being redecorated once again.

Waite says he feels honored to be the proprietor of such a long-standing institution and grateful for the trust that has been bestowed upon him by the residents of the community. "With the dawning of its 101st year, we here at Frist Funeral Home are looking forward to beginning our second century of funeral service."

INLAND CONTAINER CORPORATION

Inland Container Corporation became a resident of Vermillion County with groundbreaking for construction of a new corrugated recycle medium mill on October 23, 1973 located midway between Newport, Indiana and Cayuga, Indiana.a Inland Container was founded by Herman C. Krannert of Indianapolis, Indiana in 1925.

The Vermillion County location was chosen primarily because of the availability of steam which is purchased from Public Service Indiana's Cayuga generating station located immediately north of the mill site. An abundance of groundwater supplies, adjacent rail service, proximity to sources of raw material and midwestern metropolitan centers of population, were also positive assets which were offered by the Vermillion County location. Invaluable assistance was rendered by Mike Rendaci and the Clinton Chamber of Commerce, The Vermillion County Council and Commissioners, and Congressman John Myers.

Construction activity commenced immediately after groundbreaking with Mr. Don Parish being responsible for all phases of the project; he was later named Mill Manager and served in that capacity until 1985. Key department Managers included James W. Ferguson, Production Manager, George Laird, Engineering and Technical Services Manager, Harold Blackwood, Controller,f Charles Welsh, Personnel Manager, and Sam Copeland, Waste Procurement Manager.

Today the Newport Mill employs one-hundred twenty-eight employees with an annual payroll of $4,800,000. The productive capacity of the mill has increased from three-hundred-fifty (350) tons-per-day to six-hundred (600) tons-per-day and production is continuous, twenty-four (24) hours per day, seven (7) days a week; approximately one-hundred and fifty thousand (150,000) miles of paper are manufactured each year.

Inland Container is the fourth largest property taxpayer in Vermillion County.

As we enter the 1990's Newport Mill continues to make significant equipment modifications to increase the speed of the two-hundred and seventy-inch wide paper machine to 2000 feet per minute. In addition, land has been acquired west of the current site for future expansion. Newport Mill is one of the most modern, clean, and efficient recycle operations in the world and is currently headed by William R. Mozley, Mill Manager. Key department managers include: Larry Sholl, Production Manager, Jim Meredith, Manager of Engineering and Technical Services, Harold Blackwood, Controller, Larry Schlomer, Personnel Manager and David Fox, Fiber Procurement Administrator.

Inland Container Corporation has grown from twenty-two (22) box plants and 2 mills in 1973 to thirty-two (32) box plants and seven (7) mills in 1988.

STE-MAR ACE HARDWARE
125 SOUTH MAIN STREET CLINTON, INDIANA

Ste-Mar Ace Hardware is owned and operated by Henry and Betty Shortridge of 145 S. 5th Street, Clinton (the old Hedges house, a Victorian Italianate structure built in 1875). They are assisted in the business by their son, Martin (Marty); Betty Brewer and Dan Wagner. Their two grandchildren, Ryan, 6 years old, and Lindsay, 5 years old, visit the business often, anxious to work there someday, themselves.

Henry (Junior) is the son of the late Martha Collins Shortridge and the late Henry Shortridge of Ashland, Kentucky, and Montezuma, Indiana. Betty's parents are Dora Phipps Newkirk Riley and the late Edward Vance Riley of rural Clinton.

Ste-Mar Ace Hardware originated from the purchase of Harlan Hardware at 356 North 9th Street, Clinton, on Labor Day Weekend, 1960. The Harlan employees, Ernest Harrington and Robert Cox, stayed on with the store for a while after the change in ownership.

It was operated as Shortridge Hardware until February, 1961, when Mrs. Shortridge's brother, Herschel Riley and his wife, Betty, purchased half of the business. It was then moved to 123 S. Main Street into a building which had been occupied by a photography studio and Dr. I.D. White's office. The building at 125 S. Main Street was occupied by Ritchie & Son Barber Shop. At that time, the business was renamed Ste-Mar Hardware; the "STE" for Steven Riley, the Riley's infant son; "MAR" was for Martin Shortridge, the Shortridge's infant son.

The wives ran the store and the men did electrical contracting from the business until the Rileys moved to Florida in October, 1961. Their equity was purchased by the Shortridges and they have remained sole owners since that time.

The building on 9th Street contained 1650 square feet; while the current building has 6600 square feet plus a warehouse.

The business continued to grow so it was expanded back toward the alley in 1979 when the new addition was built.

After the Ritchie Barber Shop moved, that part of the building was occupied by The Lollipop Shop, a children's clothing store owned and operated by Martha Costello and later Fran Evans. When that shop closed, the space was occupied by the Prudential Insurance Company until 1985. At that time, the hardware store expanded into that building known as 125 S. Main Street.

The store joined the Ace Hardware program in June, 1978, and now has the most complete plumbing assortment for miles around. They try to have the newest products as well as keeping a lot of the old-fashioned hard, hardware items.

Henry did plumbing, electrical, heating and air conditioning contracting for many years and has been the only local plumber who worked on and installed boilers in the community for some time.

At present, he is remodeling some of their rentals (apartments and business buildings downtown). When not busy with his remodeling, you can find him in the store assisting the customers with their latest project or at one of the local coffee shops helping "solve" the world's problems.

FOSSI BAKERY

Fossi Bakery, which has been serving the Clinton area for nearly 40 years, was founded by Joe (Boozie) and Clara Fossi in the early fifties. Boozie acquired his baking experience while working under the G.I. Bill at the Home Bakery operated by Mr. and Mrs. Ermete Bonucchi at 443 North 10th Street in Clinton. The Italian bread, pies, and pastries were baked daily in a brick oven fueled by a wood fire.

In 1954, Boozie and Clara assumed ownership of the bakery and continued to operate an ever-growing business at the 10th street location during the next two years. On January 1, 1956, the Fossi's and their three children, Phyllis, Larry, and Ernie, moved their thriving business across the alley to its present location at 456 North 9th Street. The wood-fired brick oven was left behind and replaced by a gas-fired rotating oven and modern baking equipment. Despite this new equipment, the Fossi's Italian bread and breadsticks were still cut and shaped by hand, a practice which continues to this day and results in the special texture and flavor which cannot be duplicated through the use of automated machinery.

In 1955, Clara and daughter Phyllis, attended the Wilton School of Cake Decorating in Chicago and decorated cakes for all

occasions became a specialty of Fossi's Bakery. Business continued to grow and at one time three delivery trucks were required to make daily deliveries of bread and pastries to grocery stores and restaurants in Universal, Centenary, Blanford, Shirkieville, Terre Haute, and other communities.

Over the next three decades, although the bakery remained a family owned and operated business, it also provided employment for many local residents as bakers, sales clerks, and delivery men.

In 1979, after many years of continuous operation and success, Fossi Bakery was closed due to illness. In June, 1981, the bakery was re-opened by Joe and son, Larry. In August, 1981, Boozie passed away and Larry has continued the management of the bakery.

Although the bakery no longer provides decorated cakes or pastries, it continues to supply area residents and restaurants with the same hand-made bread and breadsticks on which it has built its reputation over the past 35 years.

In addition, Fossi Bakery also carries an extensive line of authentic Italian grocery items, such as assorted pastas, canned goods, imported candies and cookies and many other Italian specialty items.

VERMILLION COUNTY FARM BUREAU

Farm Bureau was organized in the State of Indiana in 1919, with 2,000 members and dues of one dollar. Vermillion County Farm Bureau was organized in 1949, with 300 members and today there are over 1,441 with the dues being twenty-five dollars a year! Bill Walthall served as the first president. Roy Stultz served as president from 1952-1964.

From the Farm News of Parke County, August, 1954, the following important article read "Ed White, 90 years of age and having a keen intellect, suggested to his township Farm Bureau president, Wendell Brown, that it would be a great idea to observe Rural Life Sunday in Helt township. Mr. Brown conferred with Mrs. Fern Wright, who carried the idea to Roy Stultz, county president. In turn, he carried it to the county directors of Farm Bureau. The idea developed into a county project.

On August 1,170 people assembled in Hopewell Friends Church, north of Dana to observe Rural Life Sunday.

Loren Shew, the only living charter member today, was president from 1965-1973.

Ann Olmi was elected the first woman county president in November of 1973. She was the first county woman president in the State of Indiana for 13 years, but there are now five other women filling this position in the State of Indiana.

James Chambers has been secretary-treasurer for thirty years; Ralph Peverly completed his thirty years as Vice-President in 1988, and Stanley Shew was elected to replace him. Ralph now serves as Township Chairman for Highland Township. Patti Crum serves as the County Woman Leader. Other Women leaders who have served are: Olean Lamb, Ella Sisson, Doris Beard, Beulah Ayres, Mary Griffin, Viola Hendrix, Louise Naylor, Carol Jackson serves as County Membership Chairman. Other township chairmen are: Clinton, Stanley Shew; Helt, Larry Crum; Vermillion, Tom Milligan.

Township Women Leaders who also are on the county board are: Thelma Wickens, Vermillion; and Vera Shew, Clinton township. District five director is Howard Rippy, District five Fieldman, Tom Carter; and District five Woman Leader is Bobbie Voyles.

Vermillion County Farm Bureau supports 4-H with awards, pins, ribbons, jackets to five year members, round-up trips and many other projects. Every other year, Farm Bureau entertains the Clinton Chamber of Commerce, works closely with extension, and was proud to be a part of 100

years of the Vermillion County Fair in 1986!

Each year, they sponsor a dinner meeting with Superintendents and school board members of both the North and South Vermillion Schools. They also furnish government and school statistical books. They present checks to the 4-H Tenure award recipients as well as the Pet Parade contestants. They helped with the building at the fairgrounds and awards a saving bond to one boy and one girl in Home Ec and Shop in both North and South Vermillion High Schools.

As the Vermillion County Farm Bureau continues to grow, so does agriculture in our county and together we strive to be the best!

VERMILLION COUNTY HOSPITAL

Vermillion County Hospital came into existence in 1924 as a 57 bed facility serving the area's many coal miners and their families. During 1953 an addition to the hospital was completed, and the facility increased capacity to 72 beds. Studies were commissioned in 1973 on the feasibility of renovating the existing facility. The decision was made to build a new modern hospital with reasons cited being that both patient and cost efficiency would be better served. In May of 1978 the new 56 bed Vermillion County Hospital was opened for patient care.

In 1988 the hospital added the Health Center which includes a wellness center providing cardiac rehabilitation services, exercise program and health education classes. the facility also has a child care center for pre-school age children, private physician offices and a pharmacy.

ANCILLARY SERVICES
Radiology (Ultrasound, Mobile CT Scanner)
Nuclear Medicine
Emergency Department
Respiratory Therapy
Cardiac Services
Physical Therapy
Speech Therapy]
Pharmacy
Laboratory

Vermillion County Hospital is a not-for-profit hospital licensed by the Indiana State Board of Health and accredited by the Joint Commission on Accreditation of Hospitals. Other affiliations are: American Hospital Association, Indiana Hospital Association, Affiliated Hospitals of Indiana, Inc., Voluntary Hospital Association, Health Maintenance Organization: Key Health Plan. Preferred Provider Organizations: Blue Cross Blue Shield Preferred Care, Metlife (Methodist Physician Alliance).

COLONIAL BRICK CORPORATION, PLANT AT CAYUGA

In May, 1904, the Acme Brick Works was incorporated and the board of directors consisted of Mahlon, William, Cecil and Leander Boyd. They immediately began building a brick factory on the present site of the Colonial Brick Corporation's plant. It is probable that some of the buildings in use today were built at that time.

The Acme Brick Works produced brick for many years, but finally the Great Depression took its toll and bankruptcy was filed in 1939. The plant was sold to LeRoy and Mary Clark.

In 1946, William Dee, Herbert Miller, and Hubert Nichols purchased the site and began production as Cayuga Brick & Tile Company. The plant operated under this name until 1965 when it was purchased by the Colonial Brick Corporation, owned by Paul Atkinson, Daniel Swartz, and Louis Wasson. It has operated continuously since then and now produces about 12 million brick a year. These brick are generally sold in Indiana and the surrounding states with an occasional load going as far as Florida, Colorado, and Canada.

THE FIRST NATIONAL BANK

The First National Bank of Dana was organized in 1901 with the following officers serving: S.E. Scott, President; S.J. Hall, Vice-President; Charles Wolfe, Cashier and the Directors being S.E. Scott, S.J. Hall, Charles Wolfe, T.H. Catlin, J. Jump, Joel Hollingsworth, S.E. Kaufman, Joseph Jackson and J.H. Fillinger. Present day officers are Lee A. Schroeder, President, Sara P. Scott, Vice-President, Donna L. Homsely, Cashier, Beverly Haga, Assistant Cashier, Mary Susan Armstrong, Assistant Cashier & EDP Manager and our present Directors are Richard J. Lewman, Chairman, Stanley P. Miller, Blaine P. Randolph, Lee A. Schroeder and Sara P. Scott.

The Bank commenced with a capital of $25,000 and now has assets at 12.9 million. The Banks Statement of September 4, 1912 read as follows:

Loans & Discounts	$192,039.71	Capital Stock	$ 40,000.00
Overdrafts	2,382.46	Surplus fund	30,000.00
United States Bonds	25,000.00	Undivided profits	1,630.89
Other Bonds	8,900.00	Natl Bank Notes-out	25,000.00
Furniture & Fixtures	1,908.27	Unpaid dividends	262.00
Cash & Exchange	118,066.96	Deposits	251,404.52

Total Resources $348,297.41   TotalLiabilities $348,297.41

During the Great Depression when the President declared a Bank Holiday the First National Bank of Dana was one of the few Banks allowed to reopen immediately and survived the Depression Era.

FAMILY RECORD

NAME	BIRTH		DEATH	
	Date	Place	Date	Place

FAMILY TREE

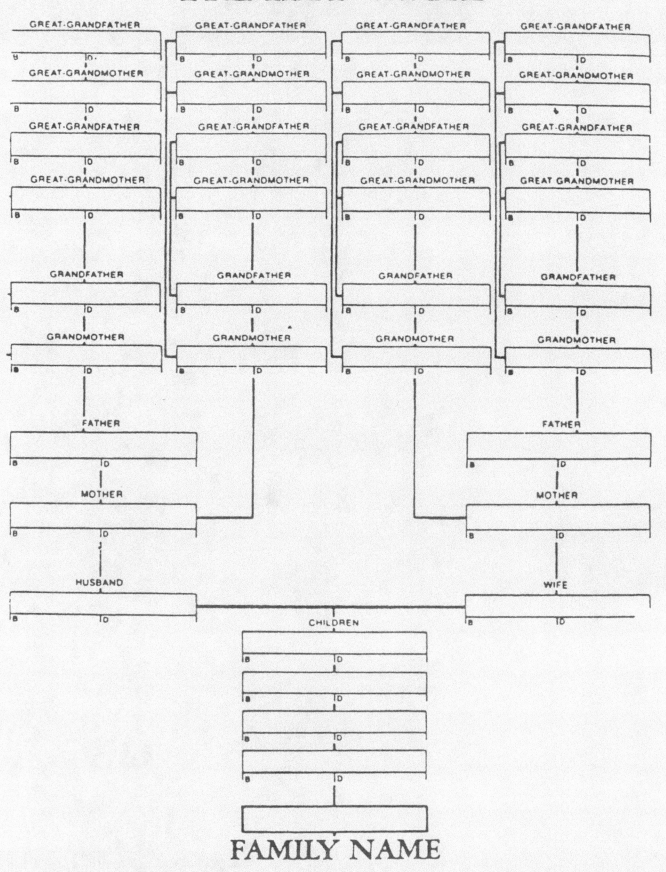

GREAT-GRANDFATHER   GREAT-GRANDFATHER   GREAT-GRANDFATHER   GREAT-GRANDFATHER
B   D   B   D   B   D   B   D

GREAT-GRANDMOTHER   GREAT-GRANDMOTHER   GREAT-GRANDMOTHER   GREAT-GRANDMOTHER
B   D   B   D   B   D   B   D

GREAT-GRANDFATHER   GREAT-GRANDFATHER   GREAT-GRANDFATHER   GREAT-GRANDFATHER
B   D   B   D   B   D   B   D

GREAT-GRANDMOTHER   GREAT-GRANDMOTHER   GREAT-GRANDMOTHER   GREAT GRANDMOTHER
B   D   B   D   B   D   B   D

GRANDFATHER   GRANDFATHER   GRANDFATHER   GRANDFATHER
B   D   B   D   B   D   B   D

GRANDMOTHER   GRANDMOTHER   GRANDMOTHER   GRANDMOTHER
B   D   B   D   B   D   B   D

FATHER   FATHER
B   D   B   D

MOTHER   MOTHER
B   D   B   D

HUSBAND   WIFE
B   D   B   D

CHILDREN
B   D
B   D
B   D
B   D

FAMILY NAME

Printed in the USA
CPSIA information can be obtained
at www.ICGtesting.com
JSHW060051150824
68134JS00032B/2711